The Military History of the Madras Engineers and Pioneers, From 1743 up to the Present Time Volume 2

THE MILITARY HISTORY

OF

THE MADRAS ENGINEERS
AND PIONEERS,

FROM 1743 UP TO THE PRESENT TIME.

COMPILED BY

MAJOR H. M. VIBART,

ROYAL (LATE MADRAS) ENGINEERS.

IN TWO VOLUMES.

VOL. II.

LONDON:

W. H. ALLEN & CO., 13 WATERLOO PLACE, S.W.
PUBLISHERS TO THE INDIA OFFICE.

1883.

INTRODUCTION.

The portrait of General Sir James L. Caldwell, G.C.B., will, it is hoped, be considered a suitable frontispiece for this volume. Previous to giving a record of his services, it will prove of interest to state that, before Major-General Patrick Ross (who was the first Chief Engineer after the Corps had been formed on a purely military footing in 1770) was placed on the retired list, Caldwell had attained the rank of captain ; and, further, that he lived for more than two years after the amalgamation of the Royal and Indian armies, having only died on the 28th June 1863, in his 94th year. He thus not only served under the founder of the Military Corps of Madras Engineers, but was its senior Colonel Commandant when it became a portion of the Royal Engineers, and its extinction as a separate body became a certainty and a mere question of time.

The picture has been reproduced by the Direct-Photo Engraving process from an excellent crayon likeness of the General in the possession of Major General Sir Thomas Pears, K.C.B., who very kindly consented to lend it for that purpose. The General is represented wearing his Ribbon and Star of the Grand Cross of the Bath when he was approaching his 80th year.

The gallant and distinguished officer died in his 94th year at Beachlands, Ryde, Isle of Wight, on Sunday the 28th June 1863. He entered the service of the Honourable East India Company in 1788; was employed in the campaigns against Tippoo in 1791–92; was present when Tippoo's camp at Bangalore was attacked by General Floyd; also in the assault of the Pettah of Bangalore, where Colonel Moorhouse of the Madras Artillery, and many officers and men were killed. He was at the siege of Bangalore, where he was wounded in the trenches. He entered the breach with the storming party, and was near the Killadar when that officer fell, desperately defending the top of the breach. Caldwell was engaged in the battle of Arrikera, where Tippoo's army was defeated by Lord Cornwallis. He served as engineer at the sieges Ryacottah, Raymanghur, and five other forts. He was also at the surprise and capture of the Pettah of Nundidroog, and at the siege of the fort of Nundidroog, which immediately followed. He mounted the breach with the storming party. At the capture of the strong hill-fort of Savandroog, he again mounted the breach. In 1792, he was engaged in the night attack on Tippoo's intrenched camp in front of Seringapatam, and was present at the siege by Lord Cornwallis, when he was wounded in the trenches. He was next engaged in the final campaign against Tippoo in 1799, and was present at the action of Malavelly

under General Harris. At the second siege and capture
of Seringapatam in 1799, he commanded the Brigade of
Engineers, accompanying the storming party, and had
charge of the scaling-ladders. He was twice wounded
during the siege—once in the trenches and a second
time at the top of the breach in rear of the forlorn
hope, when he was shot, and rolled down into the ditch.
He received the medal for Seringapatam, and a pension
for the wound. He was appointed in 1810 Senior
Engineer to the expedition against the Mauritius, under
the command of General Abercrombie. He was thanked
in the public despatch and favourably mentioned in
General Orders : " To Major Caldwell of the Madras
Engineers, who accompanied me from India, I am
indebted for the most able and assiduous exertions.
Since his arrival in these islands, he was indefatigable
in procuring the necessary information in respect to the
defence of this colony, and through his measures I was
put in possession of an accurate plan of the town some
time previous to the disembarkation of the army ; and I
trust your Lordship will permit me to recommend to
your Lordship's protection this valuable and experienced
officer."

Caldwell was on board His Majesty's frigate *Ceylon*
when attacked off and in sight of St. Denis, Bourbon,
by the French frigate *Venus*, of very superior force.
Both vessels were dismasted, and after a night's hard
fighting the *Ceylon* struck to the *Victor*, a second French
ship which came up at the close of the action. It was
recaptured the next morning by Commodore Rowley.

Caldwell was appointed to the charge of the Engineer Department in the Centre Division of the Madras Army in March 1811, and next year was entrusted with the repair of the fortress of Seringapatam. In 1813, he obtained the important post of Special Surveyor of Fortresses. In 1816 he was nominated a commissioner for the restoration of the French settlement on the Coromandel and Malabar coasts, and the same year became Acting Chief Engineer of Madras. He was appointed a Companion of the Order of the Bath in 1815; in 1837 was made a K.C.B., and in 1848 a Grand Cross of that Order.

Besides his military services, he was engaged from time to time in important public works; and in the interval between the two campaigns against Tippoo he served under the orders of Mr. Michael Topping in the Northern Circars, in investigating proposals for the improvement of that part of the country.

He became a Field Officer on 1st January 1806, Major-General on 10th January 1837, and attained the full rank of General the 20th of June 1854.

CONTENTS.

CHAPTER I.

CHAPTER II.

CHAPTER III.

CHAPTER IV.

CHAPTER V.

CHAPTER VI.

CHAPTER VII.

CHAPTER VIII.

CHAPTER IX.

CHAPTER X.

CHAPTER XI.

CHAPTER XII.

CHAPTER XIII.

LIST OF MAPS AND PLANS occurring in Vol. II. of the "Military History of the Madras Engineers and Pioneers."

ADDENDUM.

"Lieut. John Pennecuick served in the Abyssinian Expedition in 1868. He remained at Zulla during the Expedition, and was employed on the Engineering works connected with the landing of stores, &c."

MILITARY HISTORY

OF THE

MADRAS ENGINEERS

AND PIONEERS.

CHAPTER I.

De Havilland's Services.—Report of De Havilland regarding the Engineers and Pioneers.—Reply of the Quartermaster-General.—De Havilland successful in his main object.—Pioneers converted into Sappers and Miners, 1831.—Opposition of the Commander-in-Chief.—His Eulogy of the Pioneers.

In 1821, Major T. F. De Havilland was acting as Chief Engineer at Madras. He had seen a considerable amount of active military service, and had, moreover, distinguished himself as a civil engineer.

He had been present at the siege of Pondicherry in 1793, the year after he entered the service; served in the campaign against Columbo in 1795–96; and as Commanding Engineer, accompanied Lieutenant-Colonel Brown's force (over 4,000 men) which marched from Trichinopoly to assist in the subsidiary operations connected with the campaign against Tippoo in 1799. He accompanied the Indian expeditionary force to Egypt in 1801; and was subsequently captured by the French in January 1804, when returning to India.

As a civil engineer and architect, he distinguished himself in many ways. He constructed the sea-wall or bulwark at Madras, a work of no ordinary difficulty; and he designed and built St. Andrew's church, which is remarkable for its beauty, both as to exterior and interior. While at Seringapatam, he proposed to bridge the Cauvery by five brick arches of 110 feet span, with a rise of only eleven feet.

When we consider that this proposal was made nearly eighty years ago, it cannot be denied that the man who conceived the idea must have possessed great originality and boldness. His proposal having been received with disapproval by the authorities, and, indeed, almost with derision, he determined to show that his proposal was quite feasible, and under his immediate supervision he built an arch in accordance with his design in his garden at Seringapatam, which is to be seen to this day, still standing near some of the officers' old houses inside the fort at Seringapatam.

Sir Thomas Munro thus wrote of De Havilland :—

"I have a high opinion of his talents and of his public services, and have expressed my sense of them on several occasions. In the case of the bulwark in particular, I recommended his claims to the Honourable Court, because I was convinced that he had shown great skill in the plan of the work, and that he had by his extraordinary exertions completed it at a much smaller expense than it could, perhaps, have been done by any other person."

To show further how active-minded this officer was, it may be added that he fixed the mean sea-level at Madras by observations for six months (fully sixty years ago); and although more extended observations have lately shown that his level was not absolutely correct, still almost up to date all levels have been referred to what is known in Madras as " De Havilland's Benchmark," a stone let into the wall of the enceinte of Fort St. George.

As early as 1822, he wrote a report on limestones received from Coimbatore, Madura, Dindigul, Salem, North Arcot, Chingleput, Nellore, and Rajahmundry, and recommended that orders should be sent to Collectors of districts to forward specimens of limestones from their several districts, in order that they should be analysed and experimented on.

The ability, experience, and versatility of talent of this officer has been dwelt on with the object of creating in the minds of readers an enhanced amount of interest in the report which forms the subject-matter of this chapter.

The report was sent in by permission of the Governor, Sir Thomas Munro, on 23rd November 1821 ; De Havilland having succeeded to the acting appointment of Chief Engineer in the previous February.

The paper is an able and interesting one, showing in a very clear manner the status of the Corps at that time, and the difficulties with which the officers had to contend ; as well as bringing out, by the criticism it evoked from the Quartermaster-General of the Army, the jealous feelings with which the Engineers were viewed at that period by the staff of the army. The letter is a very lengthy one, covering as it does 172 pages of closely written manuscript, divided into over 200 paragraphs.

In the first eight paragraphs, he confines himself to the original constitution of the Corps in 1770, and the arrangements previous to that date.

"The duties of the Corps were two-fold :—1st, Military ; 2nd, Civil. Before 1770, persons were selected indiscriminately from military and civil services, to be employed as engineers, and military rank was conferred on those who had not previously possessed it. Many of these men displayed talent, zeal, and valour, but it would appear as if that unsettled system was found defective, and application was made for an officer of Engineers as Lieutenant-Colonel and Chief Engineer to be assisted by one major, three captains, two lieutenants, and two ensigns. It was considered necessary at this time to have a Chief Engineer, on whose opinions with reference to the fortifications of Fort

1 *

St. George the Court could rely, and as a consequence the Engineers were placed immediately under the orders of the Governor, because they were intended to have their head-quarters in the Fort, of which the Governor was Captain and Commander-in-Chief. It is very evident now, however, that the Corps of Engineers is an essential branch of the army."

It is now proposed to give, as concisely as is consistent with lucidity, the tenour of Major De Havilland's observations, commencing at paragraph 9.

9. Major De H. proposed " that in its military capacity the Corps should look to the Commander-in-Chief for its movement and discipline, while the *matériel* would remain in charge of the Military Board, and appointment to civil and general staff duties would continue with the Governor."

10. " By the system now in force, the Corps has been hindered in its gradual advance to perfection observable in the other branches of the services; nor has it kept pace with the rest of the army as regards promotion."

11. "The Commander-in-Chief cannot consult the Chief Engineer, and therefore applies elsewhere for information which the Chief Engineer is best able to give him."

12. " For instance. The Quartermaster-General of the army prepared a memoir on pontoons and military bridges, when the army was about to take the field under Sir T. Hislop, and suggested experiments. This should have come within the province of the Chief Engineer. The Quartermaster-General would not have been taken up with matters foreign to his department, would not have been disappointed in his own means of execution, nor would he have had to recur to the services of an Engineer officer contrary to his intention."

13. "The Chief Engineer may be, and has often been, senior officer in the Fort, but has not been allowed to command. This subjects the Chief Engineer to a mortification equally inconsistent with military principles and the tenour of a military commission "

14. "The Commander in-Chief cannot select officers from the Corps to perform any service."

15. "The Corps of Engineers is a skeleton corps. When Pioneers were first formed, there was no Corps of Engineers; hence they (the Pioneers) were and are still officered by infantry, partly because the Commander-in-Chief cannot appoint Engineer officers without concurrence of the Governor."

16 "Inconvenience of this arrangement is, that on service pioneers are often placed under officers entirely new to them."

17. "The Engineers' department being in itself imperfect and dependent on others, an Engineer officer takes the field under every possible disadvantage. He not only goes soldierless, but he is scarcely allowed assistance of any kind. No preparation seems to be thought necessary for his department."

18. "Component parts of the department should be duly organised and brought together."

19 "Pioneers should at any rate be under Engineers."

20. "They would then be instructed in management of boats and pontoons for military service."

21. "The Quartermaster-General, in his memorandum on pontoons, points out the necessity of a special establishment, states that the Pioneers under their present organisation are disqualified for its management, and that selected pioneers should be obtained from the two battalions for this work, and placed under a qualified officer."

22 "The Quartermaster-General, however, relied for the success of the experiments regarding pontoons entirely on pioneers, to the exclusion of engineers. It ended in his being obliged to ask for the services of an Engineer officer. Lieutenant Grant succeeded in making the pontoons most satisfactorily, although he was thwarted at the very crisis of his labours by the memorable storm of October 1818."

23. "The memoir of Lieutenant-Colonel Blacker, Quartermaster General, speaks volumes to the expediency of putting the Engineer establishment on an efficient and respectable footing with the rest of the army."

24. "The Engineers thus constituted (even the officers) would become better qualified to carry out their work at all times."

25. "This seems a proper time* to form a great road connecting the three Presidencies, and the engineers of the three Presidencies might co-operate."

26. "The system of education and instruction so well carried out at home would be introduced."

27. "The expense of the alteration would be nil."

28. "The Pioneer officer receives double the pay of his rank. This seems in justice to belong to the Engineers."

29. "Many instances have occurred in which pioneers have been employed to the exclusion of engineers. The head of the Engineer department on service has usually been a young officer; thus, in the late campaign (Mahratta war) under the Commander-in-Chief (army 20,000 to 30,000), the Commanding Engineer was a subaltern, although there were then for duty two field officers and all the captains. It was found necessary to raise a small corps of sappers and miners, who had to be organised, trained, and brought into action at the same time by a young officer, aided by a few still younger."

30. "Disparity of rank in heads of departments on service, not conducive to the interests of the army."

31. "It may also occur that an artillery officer of high rank may be present with a Commanding Engineer much his junior; the former will, perhaps, be considered the head of both departments."

32. "During the siege of Asseerghur, under Lieutenant (now Captain) Coventry, it was reported that Major Anbury (Bengal Engineers) was on his way down to perform that service. This shows that even in young officers of Engineers there were found ability and zeal equal to the execution of a duty for which the Governor-General had thought it necessary to detach one of the oldest officers."

33. "If the system proposed was carried out, there would be

* Immediately after the Mahratta war of 1817–19.

no inadequacy of rank; no supersession, no interference or external influence "

34. " The Court of Directors have always done their utmost to uphold the Engineers and render the department efficient."

35. " The Court have always done their best to make their Artillery and Engineer officers undergo a scientific education ; first at Woolwich, then at Addiscombe, and afterwards at Chatham."

36. " The Court's disposition was evinced by the annulment of Mr. Goldingham's appointment as Civil Architect, and again in placing the Surveyor-General under the Chief Engineer. A stronger instance is to be found in the abolition of the Military Institution (formed 1806) for instruction of Officers of Infantry and Cavalry. Its apparent tendency had been to set aside engineers altogether."

37. " The Engineers will be found worthy of the position intended for them, as soon as they have been placed on a permanent footing of efficiency."

38. " The Court of Directors evidently wishes to have a regular Corps of Sappers and Miners at each Presidency."

39. " The men to be given to the Engineers, should form an integral part of the Corps, and not merely be attached to them."

40. " Sappers and miners should bear arms, and be capable of defending themselves."

41. " Best arms probably the fusil and bayonet, with a light pouch, and perhaps a lance and pistol for front-rank men ; they should also have a working dress, dark blue or green."

42. As there does not appear any necessity for both sappers and pioneers, Major de H. says :—" I may be expected to show how the latter can be dispensed with in the Quartermaster-General's Department."

43. " Duties of pioneers are clearing roads on line of march, and ground for encampments."

44. " Gun and store lascars might be provided with light pioneer tools for this purpose. They might have the additional

aid of the tent establishment, and each company of infantry might have one pioneer to precede the Corps in a small body; while the engineers would be available on urgent occasions."

45. "In England there is a Staff Corps attached to the Quartermaster-General's Department."

46. "Taking the pioneers away from the Quartermaster-General would not impede the service, and it would be better to have engineers with the men than merely extend the services of the pioneers as proposed by the Quartermaster General."

47. Having now pointed out how the matter affects the interest of the Honourable Company, Major de H. proceeds to consider how it concerns the officers.

48. "The Corps having no physical strength, their services are seldom required; at least, those of the higher rank. When called for, they have to act under all the disadvantages noticed before, and they are deprived of those means which would enable them to compete in skill and prowess with their brother engineers in the British army, who have lately proved that they are inferior to none in the world."

49. "When they have been employed, it is fair to say that they have bled for their country; and from the recency of the event, I (Major de H.) may be allowed to revert again to the late campaign in the Deccan in their behalf. The engineers employed from the commencement until the surrender of Asseerghur, were four lieutenants and seven ensigns; some of them were, in the course of the service, sent up to replace those who fell *hors de combat*. Of this little corps two were killed, having both been wounded on a former occasion; two of them died of fever while on service; three or four others were wounded, and one was obliged to quit from severe illness. I can, also, with truth aver that some of their operations were arduous in the extreme; that, notwithstanding their youth and inexperience, and the smallness of their numbers (often reduced to a single officer for duty), their services were all performed with cheerfulness and alacrity, as the General Orders of the Commander-in-Chief have testified. But besides this order, highly valuable in itself, this little band thus honourably employed have no prefer-

ment to boast of; no pledge of their services. The heads of
Corps and Departments around, have shared in the Royal favours,
but they have seen themselves left out in consequence of the
senior officers' rank being *too low*; it had not been contemplated
that the Commanding Engineer with an army of this magnitude
would ever be a subaltern."

50. "General officers of Artillery and Engineers are precluded from the General Staff, and they are moreover directed to
be stationed in Fort St. George, so that their rank may not
interfere with officers commanding Divisions. This is an in-
superable bar to any of them rising above the rank of C.B, in
the Most Honourable Military Order of the Bath."

51. "Engineers cannot avail themselves of the order lately
issued, and wear on their banners "Seringapatam, 4th May
1799," like other Corps, as they have no banners. This testimony of their services is, therefore, nugatory in regard to the
Engineers."

52. "Their regimental pay is calculated on the lowest scale
of any in the army."

53. "When an officer of Engineers is called to the field from
being Superintending Engineer, he loses his extra allowances;
obviously placing interests and duty in opposition. They find,
also, that Pioneer officers get better pay than they do."

54. "The Corps not receiving an augmentation with the
other branches of the army, is a source of mortification; as
officers are thereby superseded by their juniors. This ultimately
obliges them to petition, and thus they are placed in the light of
a discontented body of men."

55. "Their being left out of augmentation is chiefly due to
Engineers being a skeleton corps."

56. "In 1819, the Madras Engineers was the only corps
omitted. The Bengal Engineers were increased, because they
had a Corps of Sappers and Miners attached to them."

57. "It is urged that the Engineers is the favoured corps, as
regards comforts and allowances. Their duties are troublesome
and responsible, and the allowances attached are not to be compared with the advantages enjoyed by the Artillery and Cavalry."

58. Major de H. next discusses sufficient and appropriate establishment for the Corps of Engineers. " Officers and men of the Corps, when spoken of collectively, should be known by no other appellation than Engineers, and Engineer soldiers."

59. "Four classes of Engineer soldiers are required, Pontooners, Artificers, Miners, and Pioneers. The whole of them to be enlisted, and to comprise Europeans, men of colour, and natives. The present Corps of Pioneers to be transferred to Engineers."

60. " Corps should be termed Regiment of Engineers, and be composed of two battalions."

Each of the following strength :—

One European Flank Company.

       6 Sergeants.
       6 Corporals.
     20 Pontooners.
     24 Sappers and Miners.
     50 Pioneers.
       2 Drummers.
       1 Bugler.
     ———
    109

Eight Native Companies :—

       8 Sergeants.
       8 Subadars of three classes.
     16 Jemadars   ,,
     32 Naigues   ,,
     32 Havildars   ,,
   160 Pontooners.
   200 Sappers and Miners.
   408 Pioneers.
       8 Buglers.
     16 Drummers and Fifes.
     80 Recruit and Pension boys.
     ———
   968

One Men of Colour Flank Company :—

      6 Sergeants.
      6 Corporals.
     20 Artificers, 1st Class.
     24   ,,   2nd ,,
     50   ,,   3rd ,,
      2 Drums and Fifes.
      1 Bugler.
     20 Apprentices.
     ———
     129

Grand total, 1,206 ; or for two battalions, 2,412.

61. " Regiment should be officered, and have the requisite staff, as follows :—

      1 Colonel.
      3 Lieutenant-Colonels.
      3 Majors.
     12 Captains.
     24 Lieutenants.
     24 Second Lieutenants."

62. " This scale hardly exceeds the rule of the service even in case of Infantry ; but as compared with the Royal Engineers the proposed number falls very short in officers of upper ranks ; the Royal Engineers having eight field officers, and sixteen captains."

63 and 64. Major De H. compares the Artillery and Engineers as to the number of officers. " In the same letter in which the Court mentioned their intention of forming a regular Corps of Engineers in Madras, dated 25th March 1768, they also fixed the strength of the Coast Artillery.

    In 1768. Artillery, 37 ; Engineers, 9.
    ,, 1784.   ,,   58 ;   ,,   19.
 Before 1796.   ,,   54 ;   ,,   24.
    ,, 1796.   ,,   76 ;   ,,   27.
    ,, 1819.   ,,   128 ;   ,,   27.

Proposed strength of Engineers now, 67."

65. "The considerable increase in subalterns proposed is consequent on the establishment of Engineer soldiers, with whom subalterns will be necessary to maintain discipline."

66. "Relative strength of Royal Artillery and Royal Engineers in 1814–15 :—

        Artillery, 580, besides Second Lieutenants.

        Engineers, 208.

"Reduced in 1821 to—

        Artillery, 528.

        Engineers, 162."

67. "Rank of Second Lieutenant should be substituted for Ensigns."

68. "Officers brought in by this increase will be seven Field Officers of the Corps.

The youngest Lieutenant-Colonel, season 1791, 30 years' service.

    „   Major,   „   1795, 26 „   „

And if, in consequence of the late deaths of Colonel Mackenzie and Major Fotheringham, this arrangement should bring in Lieutenant Purton as Junior Captain of season 1811 (10 years' service)—still, he is a distinguished officer, has seen service, and was wounded during the late campaign."

69. "The proposal to employ men of colour is not new. Sir John Malcolm proposed this description of men for employment, and the principle has lately been adopted in the Arsenal by the formation of a Corps of Artificers."

70. "Not necessary now to enter into detail of pontoon train, and siege and field equipments. This will be matter for a subsequent report"

71. "It is necessary to keep up Engineers to full establishment, during peace, especially the *personnel*."

72. "Necessary to have a depôt for this establishment. Vellore, Arcot, or Chingleput suggested, as having rivers near them."

73. "Ultimately horses should be attached to pontoon-trains, as well as to mount the pontooners."

74. "If the establishment be sanctioned, there would be an

insufficiency of officers at first ; but officers from other corps might do duty *ad interim.*"

75. " The officers would be available for courts-martial, but not for mounting guard. The Engineers should have drill and exercising days, as well as practice and working days."

76 to 78. Relates to pay and allowances of non-commissioned and rank and file.

79 to 83. Further remarks about pay of commissioned officers, &c. &c.

84. " Trusts that, to whatever extent an increase of the Corps may be resolved on, such increase will have retrospective effect from 18th September 1818, the day from which the increase to all the other branches of the army has been made to take effect."

85. Major De H. " does not dwell on the utility derived from the sappers and miners raised in the last campaign, because, he is convinced, those members of the Military Board who were present with the army will readily attest it, and give their testimony to the services of that little corps, and of the Engineers on that occasion."

86. Major De H. now proceeds to the second part of the subject—the employment of this Corps in time of peace.

87. "The duties of the Engineers are the erection, repair, and demolition of works and buildings, civil, military, and irrigation, surveying and levelling connected with them, and the construction of roads, bridges, &c. Although the principles on which these are carried on have varied from time to time, and have now arrived in many respects at a salutary result, they are in the main point still defective ; that is, in the executive duties not being separated from those of projection, superintendence, and report."

88. " This principle has been adopted, to a limited extent, in Bengal."

89. " At present, the Superintending Engineer plans and estimates the work, which he is afterwards to execute, and committees are appointed to inspect it once or twice during its execution, and

after completion. Inspection of these committees generally a matter of form."

90. "The Chief Engineer individually would be a fit man to exercise the check at the Presidency; but not as a member of the Board."

91. Major De H. says, he is "aware of the difficulties there are to combat from the first view of the extent of territory for which inspection as well as execution must be provided."

92. "The only objection to this principle is a supposed interference which might be apprehended from an officer acting under distinct authorities; but it will only require that those officers should possess common zeal, and common method, to enable them to carry into effect the wishes of their superiors to the advantage of the service."

93. "Executive officer at Presidency has long been subjected to various authorities, and no inconvenience has flowed from the practice."

94. "Another possible objection is confusion of accounts; but this will be no objection to the system proposed."

95. Major De H. now proceeds to explain how the Inspecting and Executive Departments will be distinct from each other.

96. He proposes that both Departments should be appointed to Divisions, and that Chief Engineer should be head of Inspecting branch, and called Inspector-General of Works.

97. "Each principal Division to have an Inspector, and an Executive Officer. Inspectors should have Assistants where the service may require it."

98. "These officers selected from Engineers should be considered Staff Officers."

99. "The Inspecting Department would embrace many useful objects, all more or less connected together; while it would effectually meet the views of Government in the primary consideration of establishing a perfect check over the Executive branches of the building department."

100. "The system will, as far as concerns the Tank Department, operate to effect the wishes of the Court to preserve and improve means of irrigation judiciously and economically."

101. "The additional number of officers which the proposed system would afford for the Tank Department, would much improve that branch. The following moderate establishment was proposed:—

Inspecting Department.

1 Inspector-General.
1 Deputy Inspector-General.
4 Inspectors of Divisions.
4 Assistants-in-charge.
4 Assistant Inspectors.
4 Sub-Assistant-Inspectors.

18

Executive Department.

1 Principal Executive Officer.
4 Executives.
4 Deputy Executives.
2 Assistant   ,,

11

---

102 to 105. "The Deputy Inspector-General may ultimately be required. The Inspector-General would have a seat at the Board. If called to the field would then assume the character and title of Commanding Engineer."

106. "In time of peace the whole Corps would be distributed thus:—

With the two battalions—

1 Major.
4 Captains.
9 Lieutenants.
12 Second Lieutenants.

26

---

1 Lieutenant at the Depôt ...	...	1
Inspector's Department ...	...	18
Executive ,,	...	11
On foreign service ...	...	3
Absentees, leave, &c. ...	...	8
Total ...	...	67

107. " The regiment would not only be employed on making roads, and reducing passes, but also in repair or demolition of fortifications."

108. " Government have not yet determined which forts should be preserved, so some which should be kept in good order have been allowed to fall into a state of decay, while others not required still exist."

109 " One of the first dùties of the Inspector-General, with the assistance of the Inspectors, would be to make a military tour, and report upon the condition of, and desirability of retaining or otherwise, the forts in the country."

110. " Wherever there are European infantry soldiers in garrison, an officer of Engineers with a small party of the European companies might be stationed, so that the infantry soldiers might be employed on works, and thus obtain habits of labour in this country."

111 to 113.—Details connected with the above proposal.

114 to 116.—Relate to allowances of officers.

117 to 144.—Several establishments of subordinate persons required for each department, such as surveyors, draughtsmen, writers, &c.

145. " Proposes now to review the various systems which have been followed for a series of years past, up to the present day (1821) in executing works."

146. " In 1754, a Committee of Works was formed, composed of Members of Council and the Chief Engineer, to whom the

management and superintendence of buildings and repairs at Fort St. George were assigned.

This Committee merged into the Military Board."

147. "The first few years' proceedings were governed by no defined method. It was a sort of agency to disburse what might be called for without previous plans and estimates."

148. "After a time they abandoned this desultory method, and came to the resolution of having the works executed by contract. In 1769, Black Town wall was undertaken by Mr. Benfield at 2 fanams * 62¼ cash per cubic foot of masonry. In 1773, when the great reform of Fort St. George was resolved on, a double contract was entered on—one for supplying bricks at 90 to 105 pagodas † per lac, and chunam ‡ at 9 to 11 parahs § per pagoda; and the other for executing work with those materials at 2 fanams 27½ cash on land face, and 2–65 on sea face. At these rates in ten or eleven years 14,00,000 to 15,00,000 pagodas were expended. These contractors had the monopoly for workmen as well as material."

149. "A third contract was entered into about the same time for buildings and repairs, in which charge for plain brick and chunam stood as high as 3 fanams 40 cash.‖ In 1777, rate was reduced to 3 fanams; the term was for three years, but Mr. Garrow held it for ten. During the last five or six years he was not strictly bound to any condition, and some of his charges were very heavy. Among these may be quoted the burying-ground wall on the island, for which, in 1787–88, he was paid 13,190 pagodas.¶ Besides this he laid claim to and received allowances for loss during the war."

150. "In 1779, a civil architect was appointed from home. He sometimes planned and reported on works; at others he

---

* About 3½ annas.
† 80 cash   1 fanam.
    45 fanams = 1 star pagoda (3½ rupees).
‡ Burnt lime.
§ A measure containing 4,000 cubic inches.
‖ About 4⅜ annas.
¶ More than 46,000 rupees.

also executed them.   In 1781, Mr. Plumer contracted to level
Hog Hill for 34,000 pagodas, which was at a rate of seven cubic
yards per pagoda.   This would now (1821) not be charged at
less than thirty to forty yards per pagoda."

151. "Individuals were sometimes allowed to repair their
quarters themselves, but this was found inconvenient and pro-
hibited in 1785."

152. "In 1785 regulations were framed on more expedient
principles, and the Engineers were declared 'the proper officers
to direct, superintend and execute all public works by contract
or otherwise.'"

153. "In 1787 the double contract was again advertised.
Six competitors came forward for one, and seven for the other.
Messrs. Garrow and Torin obtained that for bricks and chunam
at 100 pagodas per lac, and 8½ to 9½ parahs per pagoda. Messrs.
Wolfe and Shaw that for buildings and repairs; brick in
chunam 2 fanams 40 cash per cubic foot.

"In 1791, Messrs. Roebuck and Abbott obtained contract for
buildings and repairs, finding their own materials, plain masonry
2 fanams 20 cash."

"This contract expired in 1795–96, and was the last."

154. "By the regulations of 1796–97 the Engineers were
directed to execute the works upon trust to a certain extent, on
a moderate commission of 8 per cent. to field officers and
captains, and 5 per cent. to subalterns."

155. "In 1800 this system was superseded at the Presidency
by an order of Government to the Military Board, passing a
most severe censure on the Corps of Engineers at large, and
appointing Mr. J. Goldingham temporary agent of Government
at Presidency, Mount, and Poonamalee, allowing him 15 per
cent. on all his bills on honour. The officer he relieved had
only received 5 per cent. Mr. Goldingham was also to prepare
a plan for the introduction of a better system. The Chief
Engineer having made it clearly appear, in his appeal to the
Court of Directors, that the failures alluded to in the letter from
Government had occurred during the contract of Roebuck and

Abbott, and that none had obtained since the Engineers had executed the works on trust, the regulations of 1797 were again put in force in 1802, and a Superintending Engineer was reappointed, although the sentiments of the Court of Directors were not communicated to the Military Board or to the Chief Engineer."

156. "In 1808, Sir George Barlow attempted to introduce contracts, but the attempt failed."

157. "Salaries were substituted for the per-centage in 1810–11."

158. "It was suggested that the Commissariat should supply materials for buildings, &c. in order to put an end to competition for the provision of supply of timber required for the public service. The Chief Engineer dissented from this arrangement, but the Governor concurred in the opinion of the Board, and the system of Commissariat supplies was established in 1813. Major De H. will have the honour to show that the grounds of the Chief Engineer's dissent were by no means erroneous."

159 and 160. "The Court of Directors desired that the appointment of Superintending Engineer at Presidency should be discontinued, and practice in use in Bengal established. It was, however, found too expensive, and the Government accordingly resolved that the general system then in force, should continue."

161. Major De H. here offers "his opinion, which a knowledge of the previous circumstances had induced him to form, of the present state of things in Department of Works."

162. "It occurs readily as a fact, without seeking the causes, that, in the remotest period referred to, the prices were highest, and the rates were gradually lowered in contrary ratio of prices of materials and labour, which have since that time been increasing. The present rates are (although the price of labour, &c. has since that date been enhanced) nearly the same as in Roebuck and Abbott's contract in 1795–96."

"The present rates are established on fair and true data, and Major De H. has no hesitation in declaring that no public

2 *

works under any British Government are erected at a more moderate rate than by the Engineers of the Presidency under the existing regulations."

He then quotes the following instances :—

" 1st. St. Andrew's Bridge, built independently of Commissariat.

" 2nd. The Company's astronomer's house, built with the agency of Commissariat."

" In the first, the arches and casing of piers of cut stone brought eight or ten miles cost 13,000 pagodas, and the second less than 8,500. This, contrasted with 13,190 pagodas, besides contingencies, for burying-ground wall built on island thirty-five years ago (1786), will convince the Government that great improvement has taken place since that time."

163. " All that has been adduced serves to justify Major De H.'s opinion that general contracts are not desirable, and that if any prejudice still exists against the Engineers executing the works on trust, it must be the remaining impressions of former times when the Engineers, without any sufficient grounds for the same, were but too closely identified in the public mind with the contractors who made immense fortunes at the expense of the Company."

164 and 165. " The conclusions Major De H. draws from the above, are that the Engineers would generally, if not always, perform the whole below the ostensible prices; the contractors never."

166. " The Commissary-General frequently declared that the system by which his department supplied the Department of Works with materials was troublesome to his department, and wished that it might be relieved, but stated that he could not accede to the measure being adopted under any impression of inefficiency or want of despatch in his department "

167. " The Board have already reported that the system has not answered the expectation entertained, and Major De H. can corroborate this fact "

168. " On the score of actual charge, it would be better for

Engineers to get their own materials. Again, as to expedition
and despatch, it is evident that the mode and form of the present
system militate against this principle, but in point of means and
resources I may venture to say that the Engineers, when reasonably supported, have never failed. Witness St. Andrew's Bridge,
whose arches were completed within five months of foundation-
stone being laid. Major De H.'s report on the Bulwark, now
nearly finished, will corroborate all that he urges on the expediency of having only one department concerned in the execution
of public works."

169. "The present system involves a great deal of delay."

170. "The Commissariat servants stand thus much in the
light of a contractor, that provided he obtains the Engineer's
receipt for his superiors, be the material good or bad, his part is
performed ; and though it may be readily admitted that the
Commissariat officers have no direct interest in supplying what
may not be of the best, the servants *may*."

171 to 175. Contain other objections to the present system
of the Commissariat supplying materials to Works Department.

176. "There are only two ways likely to effect the desired
reform, either to leave the supply of his own materials to the
Executive Engineer, or to supply him in wholesale on general
indents, as other departments are supplied."

177. "If either of these expedients be adopted, the establishment proposed for Engineers will suffice; otherwise not."

178. "Major De H. will submit a draft of regulations when
the Government have decided, but meantime wishes to suggest
a few leading rules for the previous consideration of Government
which appear of importance :—

No officer of Engineers in charge of Corps allowed to employ
persons in aid of the men under his command.

No officer of Engineers to be employed on any staff duty
till he has served two years with the regiment.

Executive Engineers should take an oath only on their appointment, and not on every individual bill.

Executive Engineers not to be kept in arrears.   When a

work has been previously sanctioned on estimate by Government, the officers' bills to be adjusted without further reference.

The Inspector-General not to be charged with the especial supervision of any contract."

179 to 183. Major De H. makes certain suggestions regarding rules for the proposed department.

184. " As in a former part Major De H. pointed out cases of interference with the duties of Engineers in their military character, so he now begs to show how the department has, in its civil capacity, been visited by intrusions of a similar nature. Engineers prejudiced, amongst other things, by what occurred on the part of the Pioneer officers in demolishing fortifications of Pondicherry in 1793–94 ; the filling-up of the ditches in Seringapatam in 1801–2 ; the clearing of the ditch and the repairing fortification at Vellore in 1807–8."

185. "Major De H. points out that he does not object to the labours of any body of men being employed for the good of the public, but he conceives that their services would be of greater utility if directed by professional men under established rules.'

186. " Other persons have also been employed contrary to established rules, to the exclusion of the Engineers. These measures have a tendency to lower the officers of Engineers in the opinion of their employers, and of the world."

187. "Except in cases where the Company reap an obvious and decided benefit from it, the practice does not appear consistent with the usage of the service at large."

188. "If it be in order to employ old materials, or to adopt a more temporary or less expensive style, the Engineer can do it with as good effect, at least, if so ordered, although his judgment may have induced him, in the first instance, to recommend something of a more permanent nature. No man should be better qualified to vary the modes of execution."

189. "If it be on the score of efficiency, and of a proper adaptation of the edifice to the object in view, I would propose that the professional officer should be put in communication with the department to which the building belongs."

190. "Another advantage of employing a professional officer is that he is subject to certain rules of check."

191. "Finally, the public edifices are in less danger of suffering under the Engineers' hands than under those to which neither professional character nor personal responsibility attaches. The truth of this is evinced by the following instance :—

"The Land Custom House is composed of a set of buildings valued at a lac of rupees. The collector, who had been making extensive alterations in them, apparently at discretion, had enlarged the lower story of the main edifice by building up the verandahs, and he had actually removed the lintels of the doors and windows in the principal walls of the main edifice in order to open large arcades in them, not adverting to their having to support an upper story and about 300 tons weight of stationery, boxes, racks, &c. ; when, on my calling in on other business, he had the opportunity of consulting me, and he was induced, at my representation, to desist from his scheme and to replace the lintels."

192 to 198. Certain other objections to the present system.

199. "Before quitting the subject of officers not professional being employed in the construction of works, Major de H. brings to notice a small bridge at Buffalo, near Cannanore, lately erected by the Pioneers. It consists of four arches of masonry, two of them 11 feet, and the others 10 feet span, 4 feet thick at key, supported by two abutments of 12 feet, and three piers of 16 feet. If the officer who conducted that work had possessed science and experience, he would have adopted very different dimensions. Here, then, is an aggregate thickness of masonry just equal to the aggregate breadth of water-way, *and it is not possible* to imagine circumstances under which a construction similar to this could be advisable. The masonry in this bridge, properly disposed, would have been sufficient for a bridge of same width over a river two and a half times the breadth of the nullah in question ; and that such a river would have passed more freely under such a bridge, and with less danger to the edifice than the stream now referred to, under the present erection, is certain."

200. "The actual cost of this building is not known to the Military Board. The Quartermaster-General may probably be able to give the information; but at any rate your Honour will observe that this is a desultory mode of executing public works."

201. "The Government are at present ignorant of the extent of work which the Pioneers execute in the course of the year, either collectively or in detail."

202. "None of these proceedings could take place under the system suggested by me."

203. "Until the Corps of Engineers arrives at its proposed strength, assistants in the Inspecting Department could be furnished from other sources."

205. "The result of this proposition reduces itself to these few heads :—

1st. Raising the Corps of Engineers to an efficient and honourable estate.

2nd. Giving them equivalent rank with their contemporaries in the army.

3rd. Increasing the physical strength of that army by 400 Europeans and 1,600 natives, armed and well instructed men, in the place of 1,440 unarmed pioneers.

4th. Restoring sixteen officers for the duty of the line; adding to the Corps a sufficient number to replace them and to complete the Regiment of Engineers.

5th. Obtaining means of having at all times, pontoon, siege, and field establishments duly organised; as well in the *personnel* as in the *matériel.*

6th. Placing forts, which it is intended to retain, in a proper state of defence, and razing the rest.

7th. Construction of high roads.

8th. Applying the labours of the Engineer men to the best advantage, and keeping Europeans of the Line in health and out of idleness.

9th. Establishing a perfect system of inspection and execution for every kind of public works.

10th. Establishing a Corps of Surveyors and Draughtsmen.

11th. Eventually comprehending the charge of the Survey Department in the Inspector-General's Office.

12th. Providing for the gradual improvement of the territorial revenue, and of the inland trade of the country, by judicious works of irrigation and inland navigation."

206. "Major De H. asks, in conclusion, that the decision of the Court of Directors on the representation, which the Chief Engineer made on behalf of the Corps on the appointment of Mr. J. Goldingham in 1800 to be Civil Engineer at the Presidency, may be communicated for record in the Chief Engineer's Office. As the Superintending Engineer was re-appointed to the Presidency in 1802, Major De H. assumes the decision to have been favourable."

This letter is dated November 23rd, 1821, and on the 22nd of December the Quartermaster-General wrote a Minute in reply, which it will, I think, be interesting and amusing to give in some detail.

The Quartermaster-General was Colonel R. B. Otto. The Quartermaster-General, "without attempting systematically to follow the thread of this very elaborate performance," proposes to show "that the services of the Pioneers are essential to the Quartermaster-General, and that they consequently cannot be separated from his Department; then to reply to certain remarks on the present constitution, and mode of conducting the above Corps; and third, to advert to some other propositions, the adoption of which would materially interfere with the duties of the Quartermaster-General; and finally, to make some cursory remarks on the remaining objects of the papers, it being strictly fair that where such a freedom of comment had been indulged in, regarding a branch of the department under my actual superintendence, it should be returned by such observations as may occur to me on the projected reform of the Corps, of which Major De H. is merely in temporary charge."

Major De H. replies to this Minute on 27th December 1821, by explanatory notes opposite to each paragraph of the Minute.

The Quartermaster-General says : "The very groundwork of the Acting Chief Engineer's proposals being to wrest from the Department to which I belong the services of a Corps the direction of whose labours has been consigned to it for more than fifteen years, it is necessary I should show, from the most approved military authority, that the Quartermaster-General cannot perform his duties in the field without pioneers."

He accordingly cites extracts "from the most celebrated book* on tactics of the last century."

Major De H. in reply to this says · "He has no objection to the Quartermaster-General having a Corps of Pioneers at his disposal if Government authorise the expense; but merely wishes to get men for the Corps of Engineers, to give them physical strength and the means of performing their duties."

The Quartermaster-General then proceeds to give extracts from the "excellent Guibert in his admirable *Essay of Tactics*," in support of his view that pioneers are absolutely essential for the Quartermaster-General's department.

The Chief Engineer remarks that "Guibert means not so much a 'Corps of Pioneers' as a 'working party.'" He also says "the necessity of reconnoitring a route is not denied, and likewise that it is a part of the duty of the Quartermaster-General"; but that Guibert simply says "this work is to be done by workmen at the head of the column." De Havilland stated that until the Quartermaster-General lent him his copy of Guibert's work, he was quite ignorant of the author; "but if not, he would not have referred to him—first, because he considers a work written in 1770 quite obsolete in point of practice; secondly, because it does not appear that the Engineers came within the scope of his work; and, thirdly, because I should

* M. Guibert's.

have doubted his being a good authority. He was, it seems, a mere military stripling, twenty-five or twenty-six years of age, and what he wrote was, therefore, scarcely the result of his own experience ; but he was modest and did not put his name on the title page."

" He was not, at the same time, an officer of rank or renown ; he rose to the rank of colonel in Corsica ; but as he left the profession to become a dramatic writer, it is possible that his work proceeded more from a sort of *cacoethes scribendi* than from his own knowledge of the military profession and practice."

The Quartermaster-General points out that "if the authority of a celebrated military writer be considered a mere speculation on the practice of modern Europe, and inapplicable to this country, it will be in vain to urge such objections to the sentiments of the present Governor-General in India, who prescribed the following regulations for the Quartermaster-General's department."

The regulations are that the Pioneers are to be at the disposal of Quartermaster-General, &c. &c.

The Chief Engineer in reply "regrets to see the orders of the present Governor-General quoted only secondarily to this author in corroboration"; and adds " that there is a Corps of Pioneers in the Bengal Army, and they are, of course, the workmen to be employed as directed in the order."

The Quartermaster-General urges that the Assistant Chief Engineer is fully aware of the necessity of the Quartermaster-General having workpeople at his disposal, by his "impracticable expedient" of providing substitutes for the Pioneers in paragraphs 43 and 44.

The Chief Engineer maintains that "what the Quartermaster-General considers 'impracticable,' can readily be carried out. The one pioneer from each company would, of course, be at the disposal of the Quartermaster-General for the march, to use in a body or otherwise as circumstances might require."

The Quartermaster-General writes: "The Chief Engineer may still maintain that the Pioneer officers are deficient in skill, or, to use his own expression, that 'they may neither have studied the profession of engineering, nor have any pretensions to it.' Both these cases are certainly very possible, but even admitting both, it does not appear to me (the Quartermaster-General) to follow as a necessary consequence, that such unscientific officers are at all unequal to the work of the Pioneers." He goes on to say that "it is almost farcical to talk of science, when speaking of the construction of roads or opening of passes. Every work of that description must necessarily be of the most simple kind; and it is a fact that the best road-maker now in England is a *ci-devant* purser of a ship."

Major De H. replies: "I cannot admit that road-making which comprehends bridge-building and the directing of waters, needs neither skill nor science. How far the operations of the Pioneers in that line may have proved *farcical,* the Quartermaster-General is better able to judge than I am. Nor can I admit that Mr. McAdam having been the purser of a ship, establishes that road-making is so simple an art. We have lately had a Governor at a sister Presidency, who, it is understood was also a purser, and before he came out to this country he had long been employed in a high situation under the British Government. We must often err if we judge of men by their out-set in life, and thereupon contemn their merits or subsequent acquirements. Lord Erskine was once an ensign in a marching regiment."

The Quartermaster-General turns to that part of the Assistant Chief Engineer's letter where "his evident object is that the Corps to which he belongs should be employed in those duties which have of late years been considered as belonging to the department of the Quartermaster-General."

Major De H. retorts that he "does not wish the Corps to be employed otherwise than as the Court of Directors have ordered from time to time, and on such grounds I may surely be permitted to set forth the pretensions of the Corps without offending the Quartermaster-General."

The Quartermaster-General cites certain passages from the report of the Assistant Chief Engineer, and then adds, "My object in citing the above passages was to show the extent of the Chief Engineer's proposal, which is, evidently, that the Corps to which he belongs should engross every duty and service, which can be construed to be of a scientific nature. These lofty pretensions of the Corps of Engineers are nothing new, nothing unprecedented; and when they assumed in the French service the proud title of the Corps of Genius, they showed pretty evidently the extent to which they were inclined to push their exclusive claims to all scientific requirements. On the subject of this title, Guibert thus expresses himself:—' From the above it results that tacticians ought to be acquainted with the art of fortifications, and an engineer with that of tactics. The first of this truth is admitted by the military, the second does not seem to be acknowledged by the Engineers; for in general they are ignorant of the manner in which troops manœuvre, or how they should be conducted. They even object to that knowledge; considering their own as the first of all arts, they look down with disdain on every other branch of the military service. If this prejudice is kept alive amongst them by the fine name of Genius, with which their corps and the science which it cultivates have been honoured, I beg leave to inform them that this pompous designation is of a new creation; that in the time of Vauban they were called simply the Corps of Engineers, and that the word Engineer is derived, both in conformity with the origin of the profession and the spirit of all the languages of Europe, not from Genius, but from the word Engine, because the Engineers were originally the constructors and directors of all warlike machines, particularly those used in sieges.' "

Major De H. rejoins: "I must beg here again to set the

Quartermaster-General right in regard to his favourite author M. Guibert. He does not say exactly that the French engineers 'assumed' the proud title of 'Corps of Genius'; but that they and the sciences they cultivate have been 'honoured' with the appellation."

"The derivation of the term Ingénieur is well understood, but the new title of Corps du Génie is not so well rendered by Corps of Genius. M. Guibert seems to have been a little *wrath* when he wrote that chapter, and therefore he must not be taken 'à la lettre' when he says that the Engineers know nothing of tactics. The fact of their having armed men placed under their command, both in England and in France, and that those men are kept in good discipline, upsets this unfounded position; and the standing orders by Colonel Pasley for the Royal Engineer Department show that no less attention is paid to tactics so called than to the other studies of that Corps."

The Quartermaster-General then asserts:—"The fact is that the officers of the Engineers, although most useful and meritorious in their own immediate line, are not particularly qualified by the habits of their service for the duties of the Staff. They are not accustomed to the troops; they never, except by accident, exercise any military command; they have no professional acquaintance with military manœuvres; and although an Engineer officer may, like any other man of talents, acquire a theoretical knowledge of tactics, it is evident that such knowledge is not a necessary part of his profession. Still, however, supposing, for the sake of argument, that an Engineer officer should be completely qualified for the Staff, it still remains to be proved why he should be selected for these duties, when he has already sufficient in his own department to engage his attention; or why, when officers of the Line can be found completely qualified to assist the Quartermaster-General in his duties, he should be obliged to have recourse to another department."

Major De H. replies :—" The more general opinion, I believe, is that officers of Engineers and Artillery should necessarily be the best qualified for commands and General Staff duties. Captain Young, in his considerations on the Indian Artillery and Engineer Corps, is very clear upon this point, and both he and General Trapaud, on a late occasion, have quoted numerous instances of command in the British and foreign services, and in the Indian service also, in evidence of the practice. To these lists may be added Colonel Johnson, Quartermaster-General; Colonel Couper, Commissary-General; Colonel Brooke, Adjutant-General, all three of the Bombay Engineers ; Colonel Mackenzie, Surveyor-General, Madras Engineers ; Colonel Aubury, of Bengal Engineers, Commissary of Stores ; indeed, the very term implies that all the duties of the General and of the General Staff extend over and to every branch of the army.''

Professor Vernon says :—" Among all the officers of the État Major who have written and directed Generals in that important part of the art of war, the military *coup d'œil*, General Bourcet, de l'Arme du Génie, must be distinguished as the person who has surpassed every other in military topography, and the science of position and marches.''

After this discussion, which was submitted to the Governor in Council, Major De Havilland expressed a wish to proceed to Europe by an early opportunity. The Adjutant-General thought that " his absence at this moment, when so many important works are on hand and in contemplation, may be productive of inconvenience to the public service.''

The Quartermaster-General, however, differed from the Adjutant-General, and conceived that " Major Cleghorne has sufficient rank and experience to render him eligible for the performance of the duties which will then devolve on him.''

Major De Havilland does not appear, however, to have left for England till January 1824.

These papers were forwarded to the Court of Directors, and

the result was that, in 1823, they issued orders for the reduction of one of the battalions of Pioneers, and directed that the remaining battalion should be officered from the Corps of Engineers.

"The following extract from their letter shows clearly enough that Major De Havilland to a considerable degree succeeded in his main object.

"It is obvious that the utmost advantage cannot be derived from the labours of the Pioneers unless it is scientifically directed, and consequently that it would be for the interest of the service that the whole of the Pioneers should be put under the command and direction of officers of Engineers, regularly instructed in the art of sapping and mining, making pontoons and bridges, roads and surveys, fortifications and other buildings. We have for many years. with equal care and success, and at a great expense, educated young men for these purposes at Addiscombe (since 1809–10), and it seems to be high time that we should reap the benefits derivable and expected from that institution. We therefore direct that the Pioneers be transferred to the Engineers, and the officers of the Line at present attached to them returned to their respective corps."

"One battalion of Pioneers will, in our opinion be sufficient under this arrangement, and we therefore direct that our former orders for disbanding the 2nd battalion be carried into effect."

When these orders were received, the Corps of Engineers was too weak to spare officers for the Pioneers without detriment to the public service; so Sir Thomas Munro, who was then Governor, advocated the maintenance of both battalions on the existing footing for the time being; but as he anticipated the most beneficial results from eventually converting one battalion into "Sappers and Miners" he recommended that a party of non-commissioned officers, duly instructed at Chatham, under Colonel Pasley, R.E. (afterwards Sir Charles Pasley), should be procured from England.

The Court agreed to this, but their orders were not carried out till 1831, in which year one sergeant, one second corporal, and eight privates arrived from Chatham. About this time the services of several officers of Engineers became available owing to the discontinuance of the forces in the Dooab and in Travancore, and the subject of the reorganisation of the Pioneers was again taken into consideration by Government.

It seems strange that so obvious an improvement should have been postponed because the Corps of Engineers was too weak. The way to remedy that would have been to add to the strength of the Engineer Corps. Even in 1831 the opposition to the change was very great. Sir George Walker, G.C B., then Commander-in-Chief, opposed the change in a Minute, 7th February 1831, on the grounds that the Corps of Engineers could not supply officers in sufficient numbers to preserve interior economy and discipline, and because he assumed that the Corps, as newly constituted, would cease to be under the immediate control of the Commander-in-Chief.

The Government, however, did not agree with the Commander-in-Chief, and on 19th April 1831 it was resolved that the 1st battalion should be converted into a Corps of Sappers and Miners, and officered from the Corps of Engineers, and that the men should be regularly instructed in mining, sapping, pontooning, &c.

The order was issued on 24th May 1831.

The following establishment was fixed :—

         1 Captain commanding.
         8 Subalterns.
         1 Assistant Surgeon.
         1 Adjutant.
         1 Sergeant-Major.
         1 Quartermaster-Sergeant.
         8 Sergeants.
         8 Jemadars.

1 Havildar Major.
24 Havildars.
24 Naigues.
640 Privates
48 Recruit Boys.
8 Puckalies.
8 Pay Havildars.
1 Assistant Apothecary.
1 Second Dresser.
2 Totees.
1 Vakeel.
Besides 5 Bazar servants and 17 artificers.
Grand total, 809.

Captain Lawe, of Engineers, was appointed to command the Corps, and Lieutenant Lawford adjutant.

The following subalterns were posted to the Corps:—

First Lieutenant Stafford Vardon.
,,   Jasper Higgenson Bell.
,,   Frederick Ditmas.
Second Lieutenant, John Clark Shaw.
,,   Henry Watts.
,,   John Parry Power.
,,   Thomas Smythe.

Sir George Walker, in objecting to the arrangement proposed, wrote in the very highest terms of the Pioneers:—

"They have now been in existence as distinct and separate battalions for a great numbers of years; and during that period they have shared in every active service that has gone forward. In the Ava War they may be said to have essentially contributed to the success of our arms. The constitution of the Corps, as it at present stands, I consider to be hardly capable of improvement. . . . ."

"The experience of the last twenty-five years will best vindicate the constitution and establishment of the Pioneer

Corps. They have ever been mentioned in terms of the highest
commendation, and in Ava particularly their conduct was beyond
praise."

The Sappers and Miners were placed under the immediate
control of the Chief Engineer, who was to communicate direct
with Government on all subjects connected with its employment ;
the discipline and economy of the Corps was to be directed by
H.E. the Commander-in-Chief.

In June 1833 a despatch was received from the Court ordering
the reduction of the establishment of Sappers and Miners or of
Pioneers, whichever they might be called, to one battalion, and
in conformity with this the remaining battalion of Pioneers was
absorbed in the Corps of Sappers and Miners from 1st February
1834, and on that date the eight companies of Sappers and
Miners were thus distributed :—

          Head-quarters, Bangalore . . 3 companies.
          Detachment, Neilgherries . . 2   ,,
               ,,   Madras . . . 1   ,,
               ,,   Hydrabad Road. 2   ,,
                                        ——
                              Total   8   ,,

CHAPTER II.

ALTHOUGH the British Government had given the Burmese
no cause for offence, it was treated with great haughtiness and
injustice. In 1794, some robbers from Arracan took refuge in
Chittagong. The Burman Prince marched a body of 5,000
men into the Company's territories, and had 20,000 on the
border. He then sent a letter to the British judge, and said he

would not withdraw until the delinquents were given up. The result was the robbers were surrendered. This concession was neither dignified nor wise. A mission to Ava under Colonel Symes followed, but this in no way assisted the British.

In Chittagong there were a number of refugees from Arracan, these made occasional sallies into the Burmese territory for the purpose of plunder, &c. In 1811 a more formidable movement was made by these men; they were defeated and returned to British territory. Another mission was sent to Ava, under Captain Canning. He was unable to proceed beyond Rangoon, and after being exposed to much insult and danger, returned.

The refusal to give up the parties who had been engaged in these attacks was regarded as an unpardonable offence. In May 1816 the depredations of these bands on the Burmese territory were finally suppressed by the surrender of the chief Kyngjang. Two years, however, after, the surrender of these persons was demanded by the Rajah of Ramree, in a letter to the Magistrate of Chittagong. This was again refused. The Burmese Government did not reply. A few months afterwards, towards the close of the Mahratta war, a second letter was received from the Rajah of Ramree, demanding the cession of Ramoo, Chittagong, Moorshedabad, and Dacca, on the ground of their being ancient dependencies of Arracan, and threatening hostilities in case of refusal. The Governor-General returned for answer that he supposed the Rajah of Ramree had for some unworthy purpose of his own assumed this tone of insolence and menace; but if it was written by order of the King, he repeated that persons unable to form a just opinion of the British power in India had imposed on his judgment. No reply was sent to the Governor-General. Assam had been conquered by the Burmese for a chief of their own nation, and the Burmese frontier was thus advanced to that of the British. In 1821 and 1822 they seized and carried off elephant-hunters in the Company's employ, under the pretext that they were within

Burmese territories. An outrage on a boat with rice entering a nullah on British side of the River Nauf, led to more vigorous measures of resistance. The military guard was increased, and a few men were placed on an island called Shapooree. An agent of the Viceroy of Arracan required that these should be withdrawn, as the island belonged to the Burmese. The requisition was accompanied by a threat of war. This took place in January 1823, when the Marquis of Hastings left India.

On 24th September, 1,000 Burmese landed on the island, killed three sepoys, wounded four, and drove off remainder, six in number, the whole guard consisting of 13.

The Rajah of Arracan was so proud of this, that he reported it himself to the British Government, and said if the island was resumed he would take Dacca and Moorshedabad.

Shapooree is little more than a sand-bank. The records showed it belonged to the British, and it lay on the British side of the main channel of the river Nauf, the acknowledged boundary of the two states, and it is only separated from the mainland of Chittagong by a narrow and shallow channel, fordable at low water. The island was again occupied by us.

Munipoor was another recent acquisition of the Burmese. The Rajah of Munipore fled to Cachar, where his brothers were. They received him well at first, but afterwards quarrelled, and the defeated one fled to the Company's territory. The disordered state of Cachar invited the aggression of the Burmese; the brothers sought British assistance, which was not withheld.

A force was advanced from Dacca to Sylhet, divisions of which were posted at various places in advance of Sylhet. In January 1824, 4,000 Burmese advanced from Assam into Cachar, and took up a fortified position. Another force entered from Munipore and defeated Gunber Singh, the youngest of the three brothers. A third force advanced by a different route.

Major Newton commanding at Sylhet, marched on 17th

January 1824, and attacked the party from Assam. One attack was made on the village, another on a stockade. The troops in the village fled; those in the stockade made a vigorous resistance, but at last yielded. Major Newton withdrew his troops from Cachar, and the Burmese advanced to Jatripore, where they effected a junction with the force from Munipoor, and erected stockades on both sides of the river Goorma, and pushed on to within 1,000 yards of the British at Budderpore, when, being attacked by Captain Johnston, they were driven from their unfinished works at the point of the bayonet.

The Assam division fell back on Bhurteeba pass, and the other stockaded itself at Doodpaltoo. The enemy were dislodged, with some difficulty, from the Pass, by Lieutenant-Colonel Bowen, but the force at Doodpaltoo was attacked unsuccessfully. They afterwards withdrew into Munipore.

Two officers were now deputed to meet agents of the Burmese Government. They met, when the right of the Burmese to the island was asserted, but they afterwards said they would be satisfied if it was considered neutral ground. The Governor-General replied to this, " that worthless as the place might be to either of them, the Governor-General might have been willing to listen to the proposal, if it had been brought forward at an earlier stage, but that the assault on the post and the slaughter of British sepoys precluded any compromise."

When the British troops were withdrawn from Shapooree, a pilot schooner, the *Sophia*, was stationed off the north-east point of the island.

On 20th January 1824, some armed Burmese pulled alongside and asked a number of questions of a very suspicious character. In the afternoon, a second boat approached, and invited the commander to go the following morning to Mungdoo to meet some officers of high rank who had arrived. The commander, Mr. Chew, was at the time absent, but on his return he accepted the invitation. He was accompanied by an officer and **eight** lascars, the whole of whom were seized and carried into the interior, where they were detained till 13th February. They were then released without apology or explanation.

The deputies at Mungdoo proceeded to the island with four large boats of armed men, planted the Burmese flag and burnt a hut; having done this, they returned.

The two Governments were now to become avowedly at war, a state in which they had actually been for some time past. The British Government explained its motives to the Government of Ava on the 24th February, and in a public Proclamation of 5th March. Soon after, the Government received from the Governor of Pegu an exposition of the views of the enemy, couched in terms of singular arrogance.

In acting on the declaration of war, it was determined that on the frontier operations should in a great measure be defensive, but not so exclusively as to preclude the expulsion of the Burmese from Assam, &c. where they had recently established themselves by usurpation. A force was accordingly assembled at Goolpur, under the command of Brigadier-General McMornie. Seven companies of Native Infantry, some local corps, Irregular Horse, and Artillery, with a gun-boat flotilla, on the Brama-pooter. This force moved on 13th March along both banks of the river, through thick jungles and long grass, with vast labour. No enemy was seen till the 17th. Next day the force arrived at Gowhati. Here were some stockades, but found abandoned.

The main blow was intended for the maritime possessions of the Burmese. A part of the force was provided in Bengal, but the larger portion came from Madras.

From Bengal, the 13th and 38th Regiments, 2nd battalion 20th Native Infantry, two companies European Artillery. Total, 2,175 men. They had four 18-pounders, four 5½-inch howitzers, four 8-inch mortars, and four 6-pounders. Attached to the expedition were twenty gun-brigs and schooners, each manned by fifteen lascars and commanded by an European, armed with two 12-pounders, carronades, and four swivels; twenty row-boats carrying an 18-pounder each; two King's sloops, the *Lorne,* Captain Marryat (author of *Midshipman Easy*), and the *Sophia,* Captain Ryves; several Companies' cruisers, and the *Diana* steamboat, the first ever employed in war.

The force from Madras was in two Divisions, and consisted of Her Majesty's 41st and 89th, Madras European Regiment, seven Regiments of Native Infantry, and four companies of Artillery, 1st battalion of Madras Pioneers, besides Golundauze and gun lascars; altogether 9,300 fighting men. The total force engaged in the expedition was thus 11,475 men, of whom nearly 5,000 were Europeans.

Major-General Sir Archibald Campbell, K.C.B., commanded the whole force; while Brigadier-General McBean had charge of the Madras troops, and Captain Canning accompanied the Expedition as Political Agent and joint Commissioner with the Commander-in-Chief.

The Bengal expedition sailed from Saugor Island in the middle of April 1824, and reached the rendezvous, Port Cornwallis in the Andamans, before the end of the month. The first division of the Madras troops sailed on the 16th April, and joined the Bengal force at Port Cornwallis.

On the 5th May the armament commenced its progress towards Rangoon. The 2nd Madras Division left on 23rd May, and joined at Rangoon in June and July. Further additions to the force were received from time to time, and by the end of the year the whole force engaged in the first campaign was nearly 13,000 men. From Port Cornwallis two detachments were sent against Cheduba and Negrais. The main force arrived off the mouth of the Rangoon river on the 9th, and stood in on the 10th morning. Captain J. Mackintosh accompanied the Madras Division as Commanding Engineer, while Lieutenants G. A. Underwood, E. Lake, and A. T. Cotton (now General Sir

Arthur Cotton, K.C.S.I.), were his subaltern officers; Lieutenant E. Lake being adjutant of Engineers.

The 1st battalion of Madras Pioneers, 552 strong, accompanied the force, commanded by Captain Milne. The meritorious conduct of the Pioneers was brought to the notice of the Governor-General by Sir Thomas Munro, in a letter dated 22nd May 1824. "We have got the Pioneers, whom I did not expect so soon; they have been able to join only by very extraordinary exertion. A detachment of them, from the neighbourhood of Hydrabad, has marched at the rate of twenty-five miles daily for fifteen days without a halt, at the hottest time of the year. Our sepoy battalions have embarked without a man being absent. Their conduct has been highly meritorious; no European could have evinced more readiness to go on foreign service than they have done."

Very little opposition was met with in taking possession of Rangoon.

Rangoon was on the north bank of a main branch of the Irrawaddy; twenty-eight miles from the sea, 900 yards along the river, and 600 or 700 yards wide in its broadest part.

The town was an irregular parallelogram, having one gate in each of three faces, and two in that of the north. At the river-gate there was a landing-place, where the chief battery was placed. The whole place was defended by a palisade, ten or twelve feet high, strengthened with earth.

A fire was opened on the fleet, which was soon silenced. Meantime three detachments were landed: one above the town, one below it, and the third was to attack the river-gate. The Burmese fled from the advance of the troops, and in less than twenty minutes the town was in our possession.

Rangoon was found entirely deserted. The absence of the population was productive of serious inconvenience to the expedition, and disconcerted the expectations which had been formed of its immediate results. The capture of Rangoon resulted in the liberation of twelve prisoners, seven of whom were British, and two American missionaries.

Immediately after the capture of Rangoon all the troops were landed and posted in the town, in the great pagoda of Shoe-da-gon, about two miles and a half from the town, or on the two roads which, leading from the two northern gates, gradually converge till they join near the pagoda. Parties of seamen were employed in scouring the river.

In one of these excursions, a stockade having been observed under construction at Kemendine, four miles from the town, it was attacked by the grenadier company of H.M.'s 38th, and the boats of the *Liffey*, stormed with great intrepidity, and carried with some loss. Lieutenant Kerr, of 38th, and one man were killed, nine men wounded ; Lieutenant Wilkinson and five seamen wounded.

Detachments were also sent into the interior, to endeavour to bring back the population, but without success. On these occasions skirmishes ensued. Lieutenant Cotton, of the Engineers, was employed on these services in jungle fighting.

Cover was now provided for the troops with as little delay as possible. They were cantoned along the two roads, in the pagodas and other buildings, while the staff and departments were placed in the town, and the terrace of the Great Pagoda was occupied by part of the 89th and the Madras Artillery. This pagoda formed the key of the position. The Shoe-da-gon Pagoda stands on a mound (ascended by 80 or 100 stone steps), the summit of which is 800 yards square. It very soon was seen that there was no chance of quitting this position before the end of the rainy season, as the disappearance of the inhabitants rendered it impossible to provide and equip a flotilla, and the force was entirely dependent on Madras and Bengal for supplies, &c.

This had not been foreseen, and no preparations had been made to meet this difficulty. Negrais had been found uninhabited, and Major Wahab, who commanded the detachment, having destroyed a stockade which he observed on the opposite mainland, re-embarked his men and sailed for Rangoon.

The capture of Cheduba by the force under Brigadier McCreagh was more vigorously contested.

On 14th May, boats containing 200 of H.M.'s 13th, and 100 of the 20th Native Infantry, proceeded a mile up the river, where they discovered the enemy. The troops landed, and compelled them to retreat and retire to a strong stockade. The guns from the ships were landed, and a battery was opened on the gateway by the 18th; this weakened the defences, and an entrance was forced into the stockade without much difficulty.

On the 19th the Rajah of Cheduba was taken prisoner, and sent, shortly after, to Calcutta. Brigadier McCreagh, leaving Lieutenant-Colonel Hampton with a detachment of the 20th Native Infantry as garrison, together with the sloop *Slaney*, proceeded to Rangoon, where he arrived on the 11th June. Between the attack of the Kemendine stockade and this date, several engagements had taken place with the Burmans, who had been for some days closing on the British lines, and entrenching themselves.

On 28th May Sir A. Campbell marched out. He passed and destroyed three unfinished stockades; the artillerymen being exhausted, the guns were sent back, and Sir Archibald advanced with the Europeans. After a most fatiguing march of eight or ten miles through rice-fields, the enemy was discovered in great numbers at Joagong, defended in front by two stockades. These were carried at the point of the bayonet. The Burmese then fell back. Our loss was severe: Lieutenant Howard, of the 13th, killed, and Lieutenants Mitchell and O'Halloran each lost a leg.

The next day the enemy were driven from a stockade in the jungle, not far from the Great Pagoda, and on the same day a detachment under Colonel Godwin was sent against Siriam, which

fort was found, on the opposite side of the Pegu river, abandoned.
Lieutenant Cotton accompanied this detachment. The strongest
position occupied by the Burmese at this time was at Kemendine
on the river. They had one main stockade of unusual strength,
and several other smaller ones in the vicinity.

On the 3rd June two columns marched from the Great Pagoda
by land, while Sir Archibald Campbell proceeded up the river.
Troops were landed from the vessels, and burnt the village. The
land columns had a very harassing march ; by some mistake
they were fired on, being taken for Burmese. This occasioned
some loss, and disconcerted the troops, so that they could not
afterwards be led to the attack, and the object of the expedition
had to be abandoned.

On the 10th June, a strong force was sent once more against
Kemendine and the stockades inland between it and the pagoda.
The force was nearly 3,000 strong, with four 18-pounders, and
four mortars, and moved out under the Commander-in-Chief ;
whilst two divisions of vessels proceeded up the river. The land
columns came upon a strong stockade, about two miles from the
town. It was invested on three sides, and a breach being made
by two 18-pounders, the troops made good their entrance. The
enemy fled, but left 150 dead. Several of the British officers
and soldiers distinguished themselves by their personal prowess
on this and similar occasions, being repeatedly engaged in single
combat. Before the Burmans learnt to appreciate the valour of
their enemies, these conflicts were sanguinary, as they neither
gave nor expected to receive quarter. After carrying the post,
the force moved forward to the river, and invested the chief
stockade. The left of the line communicated with the flotilla,
but the right could not be sufficiently extended to do the same.

Notwithstanding heavy rain, batteries were erected during the
night, and opened at daylight on the 11th. After a cannonade
of two hours, a party advanced to observe the breach, and found
that the enemy had evacuated the stockade, carrying with them

their dead and wounded. It was occupied by a small European force, and a battalion of Native Infantry. The Burmese, after this, retired for a time from near the British lines, and continued to concentrate at Donabew. Before any advance could be attempted, it was necessary to annihilate the force immediately opposing the British. This was far from easy. The Burmese were very dexterous in throwing up entrenchments. Moreover, the vicinity of Rangoon was covered with swamps or jungle, and sickness began to thin the ranks of the invaders. Fever and dysentery were the principal maladies, but scurvy and hospital gangrene were also prevalent. Although the force was considerably reduced from these causes, sufficient troops still remained to effect offensive operations, and to repel the assaults of the Burmese.

During June several minor affairs occurred, and on the 1st July the first general action took place. Thakia Woongyee had been despatched to collect as large a force as possible, and to surround and capture the British.

On 1st July, the Burmese were observed in motion. The main body drew up in front of Kemendine stockade and Shoe-da-gon Pagoda. Three columns of about 1,000 each moved to the right of the line, and were met by the picquets of the 7th and 22nd Native Infantry. The enemy then penetrated between the picquets, and occupied a hill, but they were speedily dislodged. The sepoys were ordered to charge, and the enemy broke and fled to the jungle. The main body also fell back, owing to this failure.

This check did not alter their plans. It became necessary to repel them to a greater distance, and on the 8th July a column 1,200 strong, under Brigadier-General McBean, moved out to operate by land; while General Campbell, with 800 men, proceeded by water. The boats advanced to Pagoda Point, where they found the enemy strongly posted. The land force proceeded about a mile, when the road narrowed so much that the artillery had to be sent back. Four miles further on, the enemy were discovered. At this point a bridge had been destroyed by the enemy; but in a short time the Madras Pioneers made another. About 300 yards beyond the bridge, two stockades were seen on the right. The halt was sounded to wait till the pioneers with the ladders came up. Brigadier McCreagh ordered an Engineer officer, Lieutenant G. A. Underwood, to reconnoitre. He returned in a short time, and reported that there were two stockades on our right, and one on our left. The first stockade was stormed in the most gallant manner by H. M.'s 13th and 38th, and the Burmese fled with precipitation. The 13th and 38th were reinforced by the grenadier company of the 89th, and then proceeded to storm the second large stockade. The Madras Pioneers advanced most gallantly to place the ladders, without even waiting for a covering party. Very great resistance was made, but our men were soon masters of it. Another stockade was found inside it, and as there were no scaling-ladders, the men assisted one another over, on their shoulders. Here the slaughter was tremendous. Major Sale* of the 13th Light Infantry engaged the Burmese Commander-in-Chief, and cut him in two. Two other stockades were now taken right and left in the same gallant style, as well as two others which were abandoned. Seven stockades had now fallen into our hands, all being taken by escalading, without the help of artillery, in half-an-hour.

The enemy lost 1,000 killed, besides their Commander-in-Chief. Our loss was trifling, only thirty men killed and wounded, owing to the suddenness of the attack.

The river force was also successful; the troops landed and stormed two stockades, and a third was abandoned by the enemy.

The inundated state of the country now precluded the pos-

---

* Afterwards Sir Robert Sale of Jellalabad.

sibility of undertaking any movements of importance, but the time was not allowed to pass unimproved.

Sir A. Campbell having heard of the assemblage of a force at Kykloo, a column of 1,200 men was despatched by land on 19th July, while the Commander-in-Chief, with 600, went up the Puzendown creek. The land column was unable to make good its advance, so both detachments returned to head-quarters.

The head-man of Siriam, near the junction of the Pegu and Rangoon rivers, having collected a considerable force, and being engaged in constructing works to command the entrance into the river, the Commander-in-Chief embarked on the 4th August with 600 men. As the troops advanced to storm they were received by a brisk fire, but the enemy had not resolution to await an escalade. They fled to a pagoda, but were pursued, when they abandoned the post.

On the 8th August, a force of 400 men was despatched up the Dalla creek; about two miles from the mouth, they came on two stockades, one on each bank of the river. The troops had great difficulty in getting through the mud, but as soon as the escalade was attempted the entrenchments were carried, and the Burmese fled into the jungles.

In the beginning of August, Major Canning, Political Agent, became ill, and returned to Bengal for his health. He died shortly after. Captain Mackintosh, Commanding Engineer, also suffered in health, and returned to Madras on the 11th August. On arrival there, he obtained six months sick leave, and went to Port Louis in the Isle of France; he died, however, at that place on the 22nd October.

From August to December, the senior Madras Engineer with the force was Lieutenant G. A. Underwood.

On the 21st December 1824, Captain Grant was appointed Commanding Engineer with the Madras Division.

As it was impossible in August to engage in any active opera·tions in the direction of Ava, it was deemed advisable to reduce

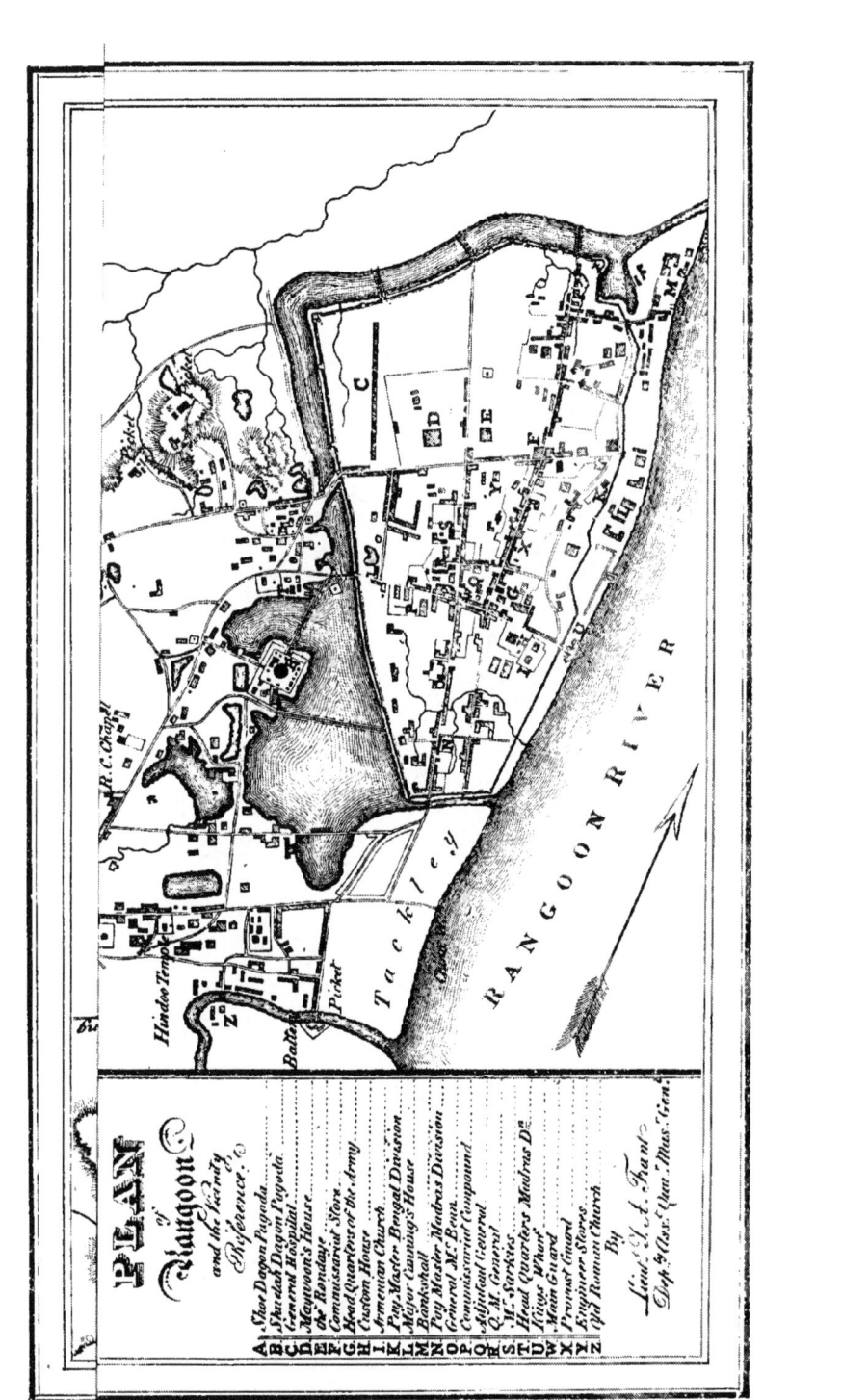

PLAN
of
Rangoon
and the Vicinity

Reference.

A. Shoe Dagon Pagoda ....
B. Shuelah Dagon Pagoda ....
C. General Hospital ....
D. Maywoon's House ....
E. O' Rendayt ....
F. Commissariat Store ....
G. Head Quarters of the Army ....
H. Custom House ....
I. Armenian Church ....
K. Pay Master Bengal Division .....
L. Major Canning's House ....
M. Bankstoll ....
N. Pay Master Madras Division .....
O. General Mc.Bean ....
P. Commissariat Compound ....
Q. Adjutant General ....
R. Q.M. General ....
S. Mc.Sarkies ....
T. Head Quarters Madras Dn. ....
U. King's Wharf ....
V. Main Guard ....
W. Provost Guard ....
X. Engineer Stores ....
N. Old Roman Church ....

By
Lieut. A. Frant
Dep.y Ass.t Qua.r Mas.r Gen.l

R.C. Chapel

Hindoo Temple

Z

Batta

Picket

Tackley

Puca Point

Picket

RANGOON RIVER

C

D

E

E

F

G

H

Tenasserim. An expedition was accordingly detached against Tavoy and Mergui, consisting of the 89th, and 7th Native Infantry with several cruisers and gun-brigs, under Lieutenant-Colonel Miles. Lieutenant A. T. Cotton accompanied this expedition.

They sailed from Rangoon on the 20th August, and reached the mouth of the Tavoy river on the 1st September. Owing to difficulties in the river, the vessels did not arrive off the town till the 8th.

A conspiracy in the garrison facilitated the capture, and the town was occupied without opposition.

The force then went on to Mergui, where it arrived on the 6th October A heavy fire was opened from the batteries of the town, but it was silenced by the fleet in about an hour. The troops then landed, escaladed the stockade in the most gallant manner, and the enemy fled.

After leaving a garrison of native troops, and part of the flotilla, Colonel Miles returned to Rangoon in November, in time to take part in the more important operations about to take place.

In the end of August and throughout September, nothing of any importance took place near Rangoon. The Burmese continued in force about Pagoda Point and Dalla. They engaged in perpetual night-attacks on the picquets, and on two occasions a large number of chosen men called the "Invulnerables" made attacks on the picquet of the Shoe-da-gon Pagoda, but were repulsed with heavy loss.

The beginning of October was marked by a failure of some magnitude at Kykloo, fourteen miles from Rangoon.

Colonel Smith was detached against this place on the 5th October with 800 Madras Native Infantry, two howitzers, and forty pioneers under Captain Milne.

They carried a stockade at Tadajee, but hearing Kykloo was very strong, Colonel Smith applied for reinforcements, especially for Europeans. Three hundred Madras Native Infantry were sent with two howitzers, but no Europeans.

On the 8th October they arrived near the stockades, and carried a succession of breastworks thrown across the road, which delayed their approach to the main position, an entrenchment resting on an eminence on its right crowned by a fortified pagoda.

As the storming party advanced to escalade, a round of cannon was fired from the pagoda, and when the assailants were fifty or sixty yards from the stockade, volleys of grape and musketry were poured down. Major Wahab and the leading officers and men were knocked down, and the rest so panic-struck that they lay down. As the evening was far advanced, Colonel Smith ordered a retreat.

The loss on this occasion was twenty-one killed and seventy-four wounded, amongst these two officers killed and five wounded. Among the latter were Captain Moncrieff and Lieutenant Campbell of the Pioneers.

The force retreated to Tadajee, which it reached at 11 P.M.

Colonel Smith, in his despatch, says :—" The wounded were immediately collected, and through the indefatigable exertions of the medical officers of the 3rd, 34th, and 28th Regiments, and the zealous aid of Captain Milne of the Madras Pioneers in procuring the means of carriage for such men as could not be provided with doolies, I was enabled to move again at 2 A.M."

Again he says :—" I cannot too highly appreciate the services of Major Ogilvie and Captain Milne, whose judgment, bravery, and steadiness I had frequent opportunities of witnessing."

Complete success attended an expedition directed at the same time (8th October) against Thantabain at the junction of Lyne river. Major Evans of H.M.'s 38th commanded this detachment. He reported :—" I cannot close my report without mentioning the very meritorious services of Brevet Captain Wheeler, and the detachment of Pioneers that accompanied me,

Their prompt and ready zeal in situations of difficulty and danger was not less conspicuous than their indefatigable exertions in performing other parts of their laborious duty, and the very gallant style in which they repeatedly dashed forward with scaling-ladders was as honourable to themselves as it was a gratifying mark of faith and confidence in the troops employed."

Nor were the Burmese allowed to imagine that the Kykloo stockades were impregnable, for the same day that Colonel Smith's detachment returned to head-quarters Brigadier McCreagh was sent with Europeans and natives to attack the post.

He arrived on the 11th, but the enemy had deserted the stockades and fallen back on stronger entrenchments. The Brigadier followed, and came up with them ; but they again fled and dispersed, after setting the village and stockade on fire. The detachment further destroyed the works, and then returned to Kykloo and thence to Rangoon.

The Brigadier reported that during his "march a considerable portion of the road presented to us the horrid spectacle of the sepoys and pioneers (twenty-eight bodies were counted) who had been lost in the unsuccessful attack of the 7th, fastened to the trunks of trees on the roadside, mangled and mutilated in every manner that savage cruelty could devise."

The Brigadier thus winds up his despatch :—" The manner in which the Bengal Artillery was forced over the most unfavourable ground, and various difficult obstacles, reflects high credit on Lieutenant Lawrence and his detachment, and the effective exertions of the Madras Pioneers under Captain Milne attracted the notice of everyone."

During the rest of October and November the troops enjoyed a state of comparative repose, and the force gathered vigour for the renewal of active operations.

By the end of November, an intercepted despatch from the

4 *

Bundoola to the Governor of Martaban, announced the departure of the former from Prome at the head of a formidable army.

The Burmese force was estimated at 60,000 men, of whom half were armed with muskets, the rest with swords and spears; a considerable number of jingals carrying balls from six to twelve ounces, and 700 Cassay Horse, were with the army, while a numerous flotilla of war-boats and fire-rafts proceeded along the stream.

This army formed a regular investment of the British lines, extending in a semicircle from Dalla, opposite Rangoon, round by Kemendine and the Great Pagoda to Puzendown, on the creek communicating with the Pegu branch of the river, their extreme right being opposite to the town on one side, and their extreme left approaching it on the other.

The enemy commenced on the 1st December by attacking the post at Kemendine. They were repulsed. In the afternoon a reconnoissance was made of the enemy's left; the detachment broke through their entrenchments.

Several other minor attacks were made, but beyond this, and the reply to the enemy's fire by the artillery, nothing was attempted for a few days, in order to encourage the Burmese generals to trust themselves completely within the reach of the British Army.

On the 5th December, a division of the flotilla and gun-boats, under Captain Chads, was ordered up the Puzendown creek, to cannonade the enemy in flank.

Two columns of attack were formed to advance from the Rangoon side; one, 800 strong, under Major Sale, and the other, 500, under Major Walker Lieutenant A. T. Cotton was with the latter force.

The columns advanced at 7. That under Major Walker first came in contact with the enemy, and the entrenchment was carried at the point of the bayonet. The other column was equally successful, and the whole of the left of the Burmese army was driven from the field, leaving numbers dead on the ground, and their guns and military and working stores in our hands.

Our loss was small, but Major Walker was shot while gallantly leading his men.

The Bundoola made no attempt to recover the position, but carried on his approaches to the Great Pagoda.

On the 7th, Sir A. Campbell ordered an attack to be made by four columns. The advance of the columns was preceded by a heavy cannonade. The left column, under Colonel Mallet, advanced against the right of the enemy, and that under Colonel Brodie on their left, whilst the other two marched directly from the pagoda on their centre. They were met by a heavy fire, but, in spite of it, they advanced to the entrenchments and quickly put the defenders to the rout.

The Burmese main force was completely dispersed, and their loss is supposed to have been 5,000 men. 240 pieces of ordnance were taken, as well as a large number of muskets.

The right division at Dalla was expelled from its entrench-ment on the 8th December, when we took ten guns. A party of pioneers accompanied this force.

Our loss in these affairs was less than fifty killed, but more than 300 wounded. The Pioneers had one havildar and four men wounded.

The Commander-in-Chief thus noticed the conduct of the Engineers and Pioneers:—"To Captain Cheape (the late General Sir John Cheape, Bengal Engineers), Commanding Engineer, and every individual of the department, the greatest credit is due, and the conduct of Captain Wheeler and the Madras Pioneers is justly a theme of praise to every officer under whose command they are placed."

Maha Bundoola speedily reorganised his troops at no great distance, relinquishing the command to an officer of rank and celebrity, Maha Thilwa.

The Burmese were soon stockaded at Kokien, a place about

half-way between the Lyne and Pegu rivers—four miles north of Shoe-da-gon Pagoda.

On the night of the 14th December a great part of Rangoon was in flames, and more than half the town was burnt. The troops were at their posts to repel any attack that might be made, while parties of seamen and soldiers subdued the flames. The fire was got under in about two hours. As this fire was the work of incendiaries, it was deemed essential to drive the enemy at once from Kokien. Accordingly, on the morning of the 15th, Brigadier-General Campbell moved out against them in two columns; the right, of 540 men, with sixty of the Governor-General's Body-guard, under Brigadier-General Cotton—the left, of 800 men with 100 of the Body-guard, under General Campbell; the former to take the work in the rear, while the latter attacked the enemy in front.

The works were found to be of great strength, consisting of two large stockades on either flank, connected by a central entrenchment, the whole occupied by 20,000 men.

The right column gained the rear and attacked the centre, while the left, dividing into two parts, stormed the flank stockades. In a quarter of an hour the whole of the works were in our possession.

The loss of the enemy was severe. Our loss was eighteen killed and 114 wounded, of whom twelve killed and forty-nine wounded belonged to the 13th, commanded by Major Sale. Four officers were killed and six wounded; amongst the latter was Major Sale.

During these operations the boats of the flotilla, with the assistance of the steamer *Diana* succeeded in capturing thirty gunboats and destroying several rafts.

The Commander-in-Chief made the following remarks in his despatch :—

" When it is known that 1,300 British infantry stormed and carried by assault the most formidable entrenched and stockaded works I ever saw, defended by upwards of 20,000 men, I trust it is unnecessary for me to say more in praise of men performing such a prodigy. The exertions of Major Montgomerie, commanding the artillery in the field, together with those of Captain Cheape and Lieutenant Underwood of the Engineers, were most conspicuous."

The 1st battalion of the Madras Pioneers had three officers and one man wounded—Brevet Captain F. Wheeler (favourably noticed in Order issued to the army by Governor-General in Council on 24th December), Lieutenant J. Macartney, and Lieutenant J. A. Campbell.

These actions changed entirely the character of the war. The Burmese after this restricted themselves to the defence of their positions along the river, and did not attempt offensive operations.

As neither Madras Engineers nor Pioneers were engaged in the expedition against Assam, Cachar, or Arracan, these campaigns will not be referred to.

The capture of the stockades at Kokien resulted in the complete dispersion of the Burmese army. Maha Bundoola retreated to Donabew, where he concentrated a respectable force, which he strongly entrenched.

The Commander-in-Chief now determined on an advance upon Prome, and, in order to leave no obstruction in his rear, he sent Colonel Elrington against the old Portuguese fort and pagoda of Siriam.

When the force came before the fort and bridge over the nullah leading to it, the landing-place was found broken down. Much labour and delay was occasioned in repairing it, and a smart and well-directed fire was kept up by the enemy on the head of the column, and some loss caused to us; but as soon as the troops could cross, they rushed on and carried the place by storm. The force then went on to the pagoda, which was abandoned as soon as the enemy saw the troops advance to the assault.

Our loss was one officer killed and three wounded, and one man killed and thirty-one wounded. The Pioneers had Ensign McLeod and four men wounded.

Before breaking up cantonments at Rangoon, the Commander-in-Chief considered it expedient to dislodge an advanced division of the Burmese at Thantabain on the Lyne river, and Colonel Godwin was despatched for this purpose with detachments of H.M.'s 41st, 30th, and 43rd Native Infantry, with various vessels and gunboats under Captain Chads, R.N.

The stockade was carried with little difficulty, but the enemy suffered severely.

There were no Engineers or Pioneers with the force.

The Commander-in-Chief formed his force for the advance into two columns. One, 2,400 strong, was to move by land under his own orders; while the second, 1,169 strong, under Brigadier-General Cotton, was to proceed by water to Tharawa (where the land column was to reach the banks of the Irrawaddy), carrying the entrenched posts of Paulang and Donabew. The flotilla consisted of sixty-two boats, carrying each one or two guns, and the boats of all the ships of war off Rangoon, under the commander of Captain Alexander, R.N.

A third division of 780 was sent to the district of Bassein, under Major Sale, who was to occupy Bassein; thence to proceed across country to Hengada on the Irrawaddy, and form a junction with the main army.

Four thousand men were left in Rangoon, under Brigadier McCreagh, to form a reserve column, to follow the Commander-in-Chief as soon as transport could be collected.

The Commander-in-Chief began his march on 13th February 1825. The water column moved on the 16th, and the detachment for Bassein sailed on the 17th.

Two hundred and fifty-seven Pioneers were attached to Sir Archibald Campbell's force.

The land column proceeded along a narrow and difficult path

on left bank of the Lyne river. On the 17th it arrived at Mophi, where it halted till the 19th, when it moved on to Lyne, arriving on the 23rd. Next day the march was resumed, and on the 26th the force halted for two days at Soomza. On the 1st March the column forded the Lyne river at Thabon, and on the 2nd came to Tharawa on the Irrawaddy.

The water-column reached Teesit on the 17th, and destroyed three unoccupied stockades. On the 19th they reached Paulang, where the Burmese were strongly stockaded. These stockades were taken, and General Cotton advanced to Yangen-chena, where the Rangoon river branches off from the Irrawaddy. He arrived on the 23rd February, and on the 27th the whole of the flotilla entered the main stream, and next day the advance came in sight of Donabew, where Maha Bundoola was posted with 15,000 men.

The post consisted of a series of formidable stockades, extending a mile along the bank, commencing at the Pagoda of Donabew, and continuing to increase in strength till completed by the main work, situated on a commanding height, and surrounded by a deep abbatis, with all the usual defences.

On the 6th March, General Cotton sent a summons to surrender, which was refused. The next day an attack was made. The first stockade was taken with the loss of twenty killed and wounded. The enemy fled to the next defence, leaving 280 prisoners. An attack was then made on the second defence ; but this failed, and entailed a severe loss. In consequence of this, General Cotton deemed it advisable to abstain from any further attempt till joined by Sir A. Campbell, and he accordingly dropped down to Young-yoon, to await the result of his communication with the Commander-in-Chief.

When the latter heard of the failure he was at Nangurh, twenty-six miles above Tharawa, and immediately determined to retrace his steps, and attack the post with all his strength.

On the 25th the army came before Donabew. On the 27th

communication was opened with the flotilla, and both divisions then co-operated in the reduction of the place. Batteries armed with heavy artillery were constructed without delay.

Spirited sorties were frequently made by the Burmese to intercept their progress, and on one occasion the Bundoola ordered out his elephants, seventeen in number, each carrying a complement of men, and supported by infantry. They were gallantly charged by the Body-guard, Horse Artillery, and Rocket Troop. The elephant-drivers were killed, and the elephants made off for the jungle, while the troops rapidly retreated.

The mortar and enfilading batteries opened on the 1st April, and the breaching batteries commenced their fire on the 2nd, shortly after which the enemy were discovered in full retreat. The entrenchments were taken possession of, and large stores of grain and ammunition, as well as a great number of guns, were captured.

The sudden retreat was occasioned by the death of their General, Maha Bundoola, who was killed on the 1st by the bursting of a shell.

In his despatch reporting the capture of Donabew, Sir Archibald Campbell says :—

"The unremitting zeal and activity of Lieutenant-Colonel Hopkinson and Captain Grant, commanding officers of Artillery and Engineers, during a most trying period, merit my peculiar notice, and their skill and attention in carrying on the approaches before this place, reflect on them the highest credit."

After the capture of Donabew, Sir A. Campbell at once resumed the forward march, and again reached Tharawa, on the 10th April, where he was joined by reinforcements. From thence he pushed on to Prome, the Prince of Tharawidi, the King's brother, falling back as the British advanced.

The force reached Prome on the 25th April, and occupied the place without opposition. Immediately after, the Commander-in-

Chief despatched Colonel Godwin with 800 infantry, a troop of the Body-guard, two field-pieces, with Pioneers, to the east towards Tonghoo, to ascertain the strength of the enemy, &c. This force left on the 5th May and marched north-east till the 11th. They there came on a mountainous and difficult country beyond which were forests. They then moved west to Meaday, sixty miles above Prome, on the Irrawaddy. This place was found deserted, and they returned to Prome on the 24th.

Captain Alexander Grant,* Commanding Engineer, who had particularly distinguished himself at Donabew, died at Prome on the 20th May. The exposure and privations he suffered during the advance of the army from Rangoon, brought on an attack of liver, which terminated fatally.

He was succeeded as Commanding Engineer by Lieutenant G. A. Underwood, Madras Engineers.

June, July, and August were necessarily spent in inactivity, owing to the setting in of the rains, and the prevalence of the inundations. The Pioneers suffered greatly from sickness at this time—out of 542, 133 were in hospital, $24\frac{1}{2}$ per cent.

The Burmese made great exertions to collect a force, and as it was formed it was advanced to Pagahm, Melloon, Patangoh, and, finally, to Meaday, where the troops arrived at the beginning of August, to the amount of 20,000 men. The whole force was estimated at 40,000 in movement, besides 12,000 at Tonghoo. To oppose these, Sir Archibald Campbell had 3,000, and had ordered 2,000 more to join him. Negotiations were at this time entered on regarding peace. An armistice was proposed and accepted, and hostilities were suspended till the 17th October.

On the 3rd October, Major-General Sir A. Campbell, Commo-

---

* This officer greatly distinguished himself, under General Pritzler, in the Southern Mahratta country. Received thanks and high approbation of the Commander-in-Chief, the 8th May 1818, for his zealous and valuable services at the siege of Badami.

dore Sir J. Brisbane, Brigadier-Generals Cotton and McCreagh, and three other officers, met six or seven Burmese chiefs on the part of the Government of Ava, to discuss formally the terms of peace. From this discussion it did not appear that the Court of Ava was prepared to make any sacrifice, either territorial or pecuniary, for the restoration of peace. The Burmese Commissioners, however, requested a prolongation of the armistice till the 2nd November, and this request was granted. It was soon seen that nothing remained but a further appeal to arms.

On the 30th November, Sir A. Campbell took measures for making a general attack upon every accessible part of the Burmese line, extending, on the east bank, from a commanding ridge of hills on the river to the villages of Simbike and Sembeh on the left, distant from Prome eleven miles northeast. The enemy's army was divided into three corps. The left was stockaded in jungles at Simbike and Hyalay, upon the Nawine river ; 15,000 men, of whom 700 were cavalry. The centre was entrenched on the hills of Napadee, inaccessible, except on one side by a narrow pathway commanded by seven pieces of artillery, and on the river side the navigation was commanded by several heavy batteries. This corps consisted of 30,000 men, and the space between left and centre (a thick forest) was merely occupied by a line of posts. The enemy's right, occupying the west bank of the Irrawaddy, was strongly stockaded and defended by artillery.

On the 1st December, the British marched upon Simbike. On reaching the Nawine river, at the village of Ze-ouke, the force was divided into two columns ; the right, under General Cotton, advanced along the left bank of the river, while General Campbell crossed at the ford of Ze-ouke, and advanced upon Simbike and Lombek in a direction parallel to General Cotton's route. This brought him in front of the stockaded position at Simbike, which he at once assaulted, the other column being a mile and a half distant to his left and rear. General Campbell detached a force to guard the ford at Ze-ouke, while he pushed on towards Sagee, in hopes of falling on the enemy retiring on Wattygoon. General Cotton and his gallant division did not allow him time. In less than ten minutes every stockade was carried, and the enemy routed. The attack on Simbike was led by Lieutenant-Colonel Godwin. The enemy left 300 dead upon the ground, including their old Commander, Maha-Nemion, seventy-five years of age. The whole of the enemy's Commissariat and other stores, guns, 400 to 500 muskets, and more than a hundred Cassay horses, fell into our hands. The enemy's left corps was thus disposed of, and General Campbell resolved to march back to Ze-ouke, to attack the centre of the enemy next morning. Our loss at Simbike was two officers and fifteen N.C.O. and men killed, and two officers and forty-one N.C.O. and men wounded. The Madras Pioneers had Lieutenant J. Smith dangerously wounded, as well as four rank and file.

At 6 P.M. on the 1st, the whole force was again at Ze-ouke, where it bivouacked, after a harassing march of twenty miles.

At daylight on the 2nd they were again in motion. Early in the morning, Brigadier Cotton was detached, to push round to the right, and to gain the enemy's flank, but after great exertion the effort was abandoned. Our artillery opened with great effect, while Sir James Brisbane cannonaded the heights from the river. Brigadier Elrington was ordered to follow through the jungle to the right, where he was opposed with great gallantry and resolution. On the Brigadier's left six companies of the 87th drove in the enemy's posts to the bottom of the ridge. The enemy was driven from all his defences in the valley, retreating to his principal works on the hills. These works were very formidable, the hills could only be ascended by a narrow road, commanded by artillery, and defended by numerous stockades and breastworks. As soon as the artillery and rockets had made an impression on the enemy's works, the troops were ordered to the assault. The 1st Bengal Brigade was ordered to advance by the breach and storm the heights in front, and the six companies of the 87th to advance through the jungle to the right, and drive everything before them. H.M.'s 38th, which led first, entered the enemy's entrenchments on the heights, driving him from hill to hill, until the whole of the formidable position, nearly three miles in extent, was in our possession. The Commander-in-Chief, in his despatch, says:—"Lieutenants Underwood, Commanding Engineer, and Abbott, Bengal Engineers, who had closely reconnoitred the enemy's position, both volunteered to lead the columns, and were, I am sorry to say, both wounded on that service." Lieutenant Underwood was shot through the neck, severely. Our loss was one officer and nine men killed, and six officers and eighty-two men wounded. The Madras Pioneers had two men wounded. The defeat of the enemy was most complete, with the loss of all his artillery, and great quantities of ammunition and stores.

On the 4th, a detachment under Brigadier-General Cotton proceeded across the river to dislodge the enemy, situated in stockades on the right bank of the river. He had 780 men of the Royal Regiment, the 41st and 89th, the light company of the 28th Madras Native Infantry, and 100 Pioneers. The operation was completely successful.

The enemy retired from their stockades on the river, owing to the severe artillery-fire ; but another stockade being observed half a mile in the interior, fully manned, it was at once stormed. 300 of the enemy were left dead, and the remainder dispersed in every direction. In this affair our loss was trifling, being only one killed and four wounded.

As General Campbell knew that the enemy had fortified the positions along the river from Meaday to Paloh, he determined to move on them circuitously with one division, so as to turn them at Bollay, while another division proceeded along the river. General Campbell commanded the 1st Division, General Cotton

the 2nd, and Commodore Brisbane the flotilla, with which there
was a military force under Brigadier Armstrong.

The 1st Division marched to Wallygoon on the 9th December.
The column was detained on the 11th by a heavy fall of rain,
which continued for thirty hours, and the troops did not reach
Bollay till the 16th.

The enemy abandoned Meaday, and General Campbell pushed
on to Tabloo, whence he detached the Body-guard in pursuit.
They came up with the Burmese five miles from Meaday, and
made some prisoners. General Campbell fixed his head-quarters
at Meaday on the 19th December.

General Cotton's column arrived at Meiong, on the Irrawaddy,
on the 14th, and marched on the 16th to Bollay, but it was
obliged to encamp three miles to the south, at Seimbow, in consequence of encountering an impassable nullah. The column
halted at this place on the 17th, while the Pioneers and strong
working-parties under the directions of the Engineer officer,
were employed in constructing a bridge. The bridge was
finished on the 18th, and the force then moved to the Ing-gown,
a few miles south of Meaday.

On the 26th December General Campbell was met by a flag
of truce with a letter from the Burman commanders expressing
a desire to conclude a peace. Officers were deputed to ascertain
what arrangements were contemplated; meantime the army
advanced to Patanagoh, opposite the Burmese entrenchments at
Melloon. It arrived at Mungeom on the 28th, when a letter was
received postponing the meeting till the 24th January. This
delay was declared inadmissible, and a definite reply was
required before sunset of the 29th, when the army encamped at
Patanagoh.

The result of this was that a first conference took place on
the 30th December, in a boat fitted up by the Burmese, on the
Irrawaddy between Patanagoh and Melloon—Sir Archibald
Campbell, Mr. Robertson, and Commodore Brisbane on the side

of the British, and two Wongyees on the part of the Burmese. At this meeting the terms were stated generally, and their further discussion postponed till next day.

The following day the Burman Commissioners acceded to the terms, but the pecuniary demand was reduced to one crore of rupees.

A third meeting took place on the 2nd January, when the Burmese strove to evade the money payment. They were also reluctant to concede Arracan. Finding the British Commissioners could not be induced to deviate from the conditions stipulated, they finally yielded.

The English copy of the treaty was signed on the 2nd, and the Burmese on the 3rd, and an armistice agreed on till the 18th, by which date it was supposed the treaty would be ratified by the King.

On the 17th January five Burmese chiefs came to the British camp to apologise for the non-ratification of the treaty. At the same time they offered to pay five lacs of rupees as instalment of the crore, and to deliver hostages for the safe return of the British prisoners at Ava. They solicited, in return, the retreat of the British army to Prome, or, at least, a further suspension of hostilities. This, of course, could not be complied with, and hostilities commenced again on the 19th.

General Campbell ordered " the construction of batteries and the landing of heavy ordnance from the flotilla to commence immediately after midnight, and every requisite arrangement made for an early attack on Melloon."

" His Lordship in Council will be enabled to appreciate the zeal and exertion with which my orders were carried into effect, under the direction of Lieutenant-Colonel Hodgkinson, commanding the Artillery, and Lieutenant Underwood, the Chief Engineer (aided by that indefatigable Corps, the 1st battalion of the Madras Pioneers, under the command of Captain Crowe), when I state that by 10 the next morning I had twenty-eight pieces of ordnance in battery. on points presenting a front of more than one mile, on east bank of the Irrawaddy, which corresponded with the enemy's line of defence on the opposite shore.   At 11 A.M. on the 19th the batteries and rockets opened fire on the enemy's position.   It was warmly kept up with great precision."

While this was going on, the troops intended for the assault were embarking in the boats.   About 1 P.M., everything being ready, the brigade under Lieutenant-Colonel Sale, consisting of H M.'s 13th and 38th Regiments, was directed to drop down the river and assault the main face of the enemy's position, near its south-east angle; while Brigadier-General Cotton with the flank companies of H.M.'s 47th, 87th, and 89th, the 41st, 28th, and 18th Madras Native Infantry, and flank company of the 43rd Madras Native Infantry, was to cross above Melloon, and after carrying some earthworks, to attack the north face of the principal work.

Although the whole of the boats pushed off together from the left bank, the current and a strong breeze from the north carried Lieutenant-Colonel Sale's brigade to the point of attack before the other columns could reach the opposite shore.   The brigade landed (Lieutenant-Colonel Sale was wounded in the boats), rushed to the assault, and were in a short time complete masters of the work.

When Brigadier-General Cotton saw that the works were carried, he ordered a brigade under Lieutenant-Colonel Hunter Blair to cut in on the enemy's line of retreat, which was accordingly done with much effect.

The enemy's loss in killed and wounded was very severe, as also in captured ordnance, stores, arms, and ammunition.   A large sum of money was also found in Melloon.   Our loss was small, and consisted of three officers wounded, thirteen men killed, and forty-five wounded.   Lieutenant W. Dixon, Bengal Engineers, was amongst the wounded.

II.   5

The original treaty was found in the lines of Melloon. At first sight it appeared that the Burman Commissioners had sought only to protract the war by their negotiations; but it was ascertained subsequently that a copy of the treaty had really been sent to Ava. The original treaty was returned to the Burmese with a letter stating that as they had left behind a valuable paper, it was forwarded to them. This was done to show that the Commander in-Chief was aware that the treaty had not been sent to Ava. The Burmese were in no way abashed, but replied, thanking the Chief for his courtesy, and mentioning that, as a large sum of money had also been left behind in their hurry, perhaps the Commander in-Chief would be good enough to forward that also.*

The capture of Melloon created great consternation at Ava, and Mr. Price, a member of the American Mission to Ava, and Mr. Sandford, Surgeon of the Royals, both prisoners, were sent down to treat. They reached head-quarters on the 31st January, 1826, and after conferring with the Commissioners, returned to Ava on the following day. The terms proposed at Melloon were still open to the acceptance of the Court, and the army would retire to Rangoon on payment of twenty-five lacs, and evacuate Burman territory on the discharge of a similar instalment.

The army still continued to advance towards Pagahm-mew. It left Patanagoh on the 25th January, and reached Yaysay on the 8th February. The enemy were discovered five miles in advance on the road to Pagahm-mew.

On the morning of the 9th, the army proceeded to the encounter. The Burmese for the first time abandoned their system of combatting behind barriers, and prepared to dispute the day in the open field in front of their position at Logoh-nundah Pagoda. They numbered 16,000 men.

* The reason the Burmese had for not forwarding the signed treaty was that they had exceeded their power in signing it.

Our army advanced in two columns. The attacks were quite successful, and the Burmese soon broke and fled Part retreated to a field-work, from which they were soon dislodged by the bayonet with great slaughter. They then made an attempt to rally within the walls, and about the Pagoda of Pagahm-mew. They were followed with great activity, and in the course of five hours this last hope of the Kingdom of Ava was annihilated.

Our loss was trifling—one officer wounded, two men killed, and fifteen wounded.

While these operations were taking place on the Irrawaddy, the province of Pegu was the scene of some military transactions. Lieutenant-Colonel Conry made an attack on a stockade at Sittang on the 7th January. His force was inadequate, and he was repulsed with the loss of two officers, one native officer, and nine men killed, and two officers and eighteen men wounded. Among the latter was Lieutenant-Colonel Conry.

Colonel Pepper, on hearing of the repulse, moved with reinforcements, and reached Sittang on the 11th. The force advanced to the attack in three columns. A simultaneous advance was ordered, on which the creek was forded, and the stockade carried in twenty minutes.

The advance was made under a heavy fire, and our loss was severe. Two captains were killed, and a major and two lieutenants wounded; fourteen men were killed, and fifty-three wounded.

The Pioneers lost one man killed and four wounded. The enemy was computed at 3,000 or 4,000, and their loss was 500 or 600.

The whole of the defences were destroyed on the 13th. The efforts of the enemy were not, however, relaxed. In the month of February they made a vigorous attack on the British post at Meckroo, between Pegu and Shoe-geen They were repulsed by Ensign Clark, who held the post with a small detachment of the 3rd Madras Native Infantry. A reinforcement of 100 men of the 13th, and twenty Pioneers, was sent, under Captain Leggett, as well as 100 men from Pegu, and the post was secured.

The establishment of peace suspended further operations in Pegu. After halting two or three days at Pagahm-mew, General Campbell resumed his march. The King and his Ministers now had no hesitation in acceding to the terms of peace. General Campbell declined to suspend his march till the ratification of the treaty was received, and had advanced to Yandaboo, within four days' march of Ava, before Mr. Price and the Burman Commissioners made their appearance with the ratified treaty, and twenty-five lacs in gold and silver bullion.

The treaty was concluded on the 24th February 1826. The Burmese Government engaged to abstain from all interference with the affairs of Assam, Cachar, and Jyntra, to receive a British Resident at Ava, and depute a Burman Resident to Calcutta; to concur in a commercial treaty, and to cede four provinces of Arracan, as well as Yeh, Tavoy, Mergui, and Tenasserim.

The Pioneers in the campaign had three men killed, and seven officers, one havildar, and thirty-five men wounded. The Pioneer officers were Captain Moncrieffe, Brevet-Captain Wheeler, Lieutenant and Adjutant Campbell, Lieutenant J. Macartney, Lieutenant J. A. Campbell, Lieutenant J Smith, and Ensign Macleod.

The following order was published by Government :—

" To mark the high sense which the Government entertain of the indefatigable exertions of the Corps of Pioneers throughout the war in Ava, the Honourable the Governor-in-Council is pleased to resolve, as a special case, that Jemadar Andoo, of that Corps, whose gallant conduct has been particularly brought to notice, shall be promoted to the rank of Subadar, that he be presented with a palankeen, and an allowance of seventy rupees monthly for the support of that equipage, and that a pension of half-pay be granted to his nearest heir after his decease."

This was dated the 15th May 1827, No. 94.

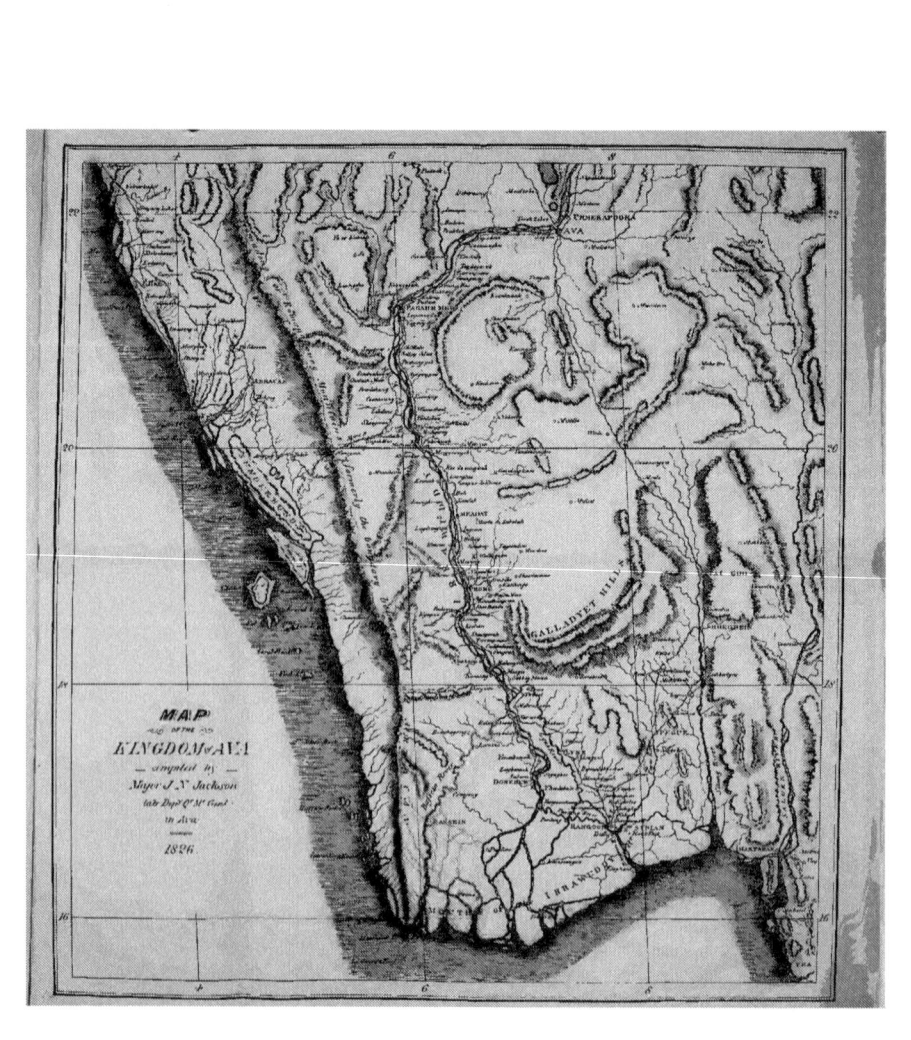

MAP
OF THE
KINGDOM OF AVA
compiled by
Major J. N. Jackson
late Depy. Qr. Mr. Genl.
in Ava
1826.

Two Engineer officers died from disease brought on by exposure—Captain Mackintosh and Captain Grant, Madras Engineers ; and three were wounded, Lieutenant Underwood, Madras Engineers, and Lieutenants Abbott and Dixon, Bengal Engineers.

Total casualties, fifty-one, of which twelve were officers.

The Pioneers suffered much from sickness in the campaign, owing, doubtless, to their laborious duties and constant exposure —at one time nearly one-fourth were in hospital.

On the 5th March the troops commenced their return, the greater part proceeding by water to Rangoon. In the general orders by the Governor-General in Council, the Pioneers are spoken of in the highest terms :—

" The Governor-General in Council acknowledges with peculiar approbation the gallant and indefatigable exertions of that valuable corps the Madras Pioneers, under Captain Crowe."

Strange to say, in this general order no mention is made of the Engineers, although they were frequently mentioned with great approbation by the officers in command, and in spite of the fact that two officers died, and three were wounded. Lieutenant Underwood, finding that the services of the Engineers had been omitted, wrote an address to the Governor-General regarding the omission. He received the following reply :—

" Adverting to the repeated mention by Major-General Sir Archibald Campbell of the zealous and gallant conduct displayed by the Engineer Department, under Captain Cheape, of the Bengal Establishment, and Lieutenant Underwood, of that of Fort St. George, and to the acknowledgment of those services in the general orders of the Governor-General in Council of the 24th December 1824, there can be no doubt that the merits of the Engineer Department were duly appreciated by the Government of that period. The Governor-General in Council is satisfied, indeed, that the omission of the mention of the Engineer Department in the general orders of the 11th April 1826, was purely accidental. Under these circumstances, and at this distant period of time, the Governor-General in Council feels himself precluded from making the services of the Engineer Department in Ava the subject of a special general order; but he is happy to avail himself of this opportunity of declaring his sense of the zeal, gallantry, and professional talents of that arm of the service, as repeatedly brought to the notice of the Supreme Government in the despatches of Major-General Sir Archibald Campbell, and as warmly acknowledged by the Supreme Government in the general orders of the 24th December 1824. The Government of Fort St. George is accordingly requested to convey the above assurances to Lieutenant Underwood, in reply to his letter on the subject."

Captain Cheape was mentioned three times in despatches, as also Lieutenant Underwood. Captain Grant, Lieutenants Lake, Abbott, and Cotton were each mentioned once. The Pioneer officers mentioned were—Captain Milne, twice; Brevet-Captain Wheeler, three times; Captain Crowe and Lieutenant Macartney, both once.

In the year 1824, the town of Kittoor, twenty-eight miles south of Belgaum, was the scene of an insurrection. Mr. Thackeray, the Civil Officer, seems to have treated the Chief of Kittoor in a somewhat harsh manner, and attempted to coerce him with very inadequate means. It ended in his repulse and death, as well as the loss of Captain Black and Lieutenants Sewell and Dighton, and several men. This act and a considerable show of resistance, brought a large force against Kittoor under Colonel Deacon.

The force consisted of 4th and 8th Madras Light Cavalry, H.M.'s 46th, with the 6th and 14th Madras Native Infantry, 1st Bombay Europeans, 3rd and 6th Bombay Native Infantry, 23rd Light Infantry, Madras and Bombay Horse and Foot Artillery, Madras and Bombay Engineers (Captain Pouget of Bombay Engineers to command), detachment of 2nd battalion of Madras Pioneers, under Lieutenant Clendon; Lieutenant Alexander Lawe (Madras Engineers) was also with the force.

The troops arrived at Kittoor on the 2nd December 1824. Messrs. Stevenson and Elliot, who had previously been taken prisoners by the insurgents, were surrendered; but the enemy seemed determined not to deliver up the fort. Twenty-four hours were allowed to the insurgents to reconsider the matter; but as they decidedly refused, some guns were advanced to a point fronting the enemy's fortified post, Kummuruntly, to attract their attention, while a party of infantry advanced to storm the enemy's position on their left. The guns directed by Major Palmer opened about half-past 5 with shell. The enemy's post was soon taken, and they fled to the upper fort, 1,000 yards distant. We sustained no loss, but Mr. Munro of the Commissioners' party, was wounded. The remainder of the night was occupied in strengthening the post, and by daylight next morning an excellent battery had been prepared for 18-pounders, which commenced about 9 A.M. to effect a breach in the wall of the upper fort. The fire was so effective that at half-past 3, a person came out to Mr. Chaplin, the Commissioner, to ask permission to send a vakeel. He was told to return, and say that if they were disposed to surrender, and deliver over certain persons as prisoners, they should hoist a white flag. The flag was soon visible, and all hostilities ceased. Some delay occurred in rendering up the fort, and preparations were made for renewing the attack; but at 8 A.M. on the 5th, the fort was surrendered.

Colonel Deacon reported that the spirit and determination of the troops was excellent throughout. "The useful and indefatigable Corps of Pioneers, under Lieutenant Clendon, were most actively employed throughout." "In the operations of reconnoitring," Colonel Deacon reported that he "was most ably assisted by the abilities of Captain Pouget of the Bombay Engineers, and his decided exertion and operation, as well as those of Lieutenants Lawe and Outram of the same branch, were of the greatest use to me, and I am convinced that Captain Pouget would have been entirely successful in filling up the ditch of the upper fort by the dispositions he was making for the same."

Our loss was only three killed and twenty-five wounded. The Pioneers had only one wounded. Thirty-six guns were captured, as well as a large number of matchlocks, swords, and a quantity of powder and shot, &c. The upper fort was very strong, nowhere commanded, and the surrounding country being highly cultivated, was ill-adapted for carrying on approaches, so that a resolute body of men might have defended it for a long time.

This insurrection led to an expedition against Kolapore.

Bava Sahib,* the Raja of Kolapore (60 miles north of Belgaum), was oppressive and profligate, and was very anxious to shake off the protectory influence of the English. The events at Kittoor, and the rumours regarding a great disaster which was supposed to have occurred in Burmah, announced to the Raja that the time for action had arrived. He suddenly left his capital with 5,000 infantry, 1,000 cavalry, and seven guns. He attacked and captured the fort and Jaghire of Koongul, and then marched to the frontier of Sattara.

Towards the close of 1825 a British force† marched into Kolapore, and compelled the Raja to sign a treaty binding himself to attend to the advice of the British Government, to reduce his force, and never to grant an asylum to rebels. The Raja, however, paid no attention to the treaty, and behaved in a manner showing himself hardly to be of sane mind.

A British force had again, in 1827, to be sent against Kolapore.

On 5th March our troops, leaving Belgaum, Kaludghee, and Sholapore, formed a junction at Kotabangee on the Gutpurba, thirty-two miles north of Belgaum, on the 15th.

The Raja of Kolapore, though at the head of 12,000 men,

---

* From Colonel Malleson's *Native States of India.*

† Lieutenant Lawe accompanied this force as Commanding Engineer.

retreated immediately, by forced marches, to Kolapore, and our force marched back again to their original positions.

On 7th September our whole force was again in motion, and marched again to Kotabangee,* the Raja being again troublesome, and having collected an army of 20,000 men. Our force consisted of 250 Artillery with twenty field-pieces, 1,000 Native cavalry, 1,300 European infantry, and 2,500 Native infantry; 260 Pioneers, of whom 160 were of the Madras Establishment, under Lieutenant G. Burn.† Colonel Welsh commanded the troops, and Captain J. J. Underwood accompanied it as Commanding Engineer.

On 24th September, a party was ordered to proceed to Yenklemurradee, a post about twelve miles south-west. Although very strong, the enemy evacuated it, and we took possession of it without opposition.

On the 10th October, a strong reinforcement joined us from Poona, and the whole force encamped within six miles of Kolapore. It was formed into five brigades amounting to 6,200 men, besides 500 Native horse, with a train of ten heavy guns, twenty 6-pounders, seven mortars, and four howitzers. The Raja, however, declined to fight, and surrendered on 13th October. Again a treaty was forced on the Raja. He bound himself to reduce his army to 400 cavalry and 800 infantry. Kolapore and Panallagurh to be garrisoned by British troops at the expense of the Raja. He had, besides, to restore villages he had resumed, to pay Rs 150,000 for damage done by him, and to accept a minister appointed by the British Government and irremoveable by him.

Ever since the Mutiny of 1857, the construction of a place

---

* A ford on the Gutpurba.

† This officer served with the 2nd battalion Pioneers from 1825 to 1833. He served at Kittoor in 1824, Kolapore in 1827, in Goomsoor in 1836, and in the first China War; from 1859 to 1861 he commanded, as Brigadier, the troops at Singapore.

of refuge at Bangalore has been contemplated, and numerous reports have been sent in with various proposals. In the year 1874, a committee sat to report. They agreed that the present old fort was quite useless, and even dangerous, and should be removed, an entirely new one being built north of the railway near Shevanhully. Nothing has since been done to remedy the evil complained of, and the arsenal and powder magazines are still in the old fort. In examining the Madras military records, I happened to light upon a report, which confirms in a very considerable degree the decided opinions of the committee of 1874 above mentioned. In the year 1827, Captain J. Purton,* Madras Engineers, was directed to report on the fort and the alteration which would be desirable. He completed his report in the following words :—

" It will appear evident from what has been already said, that the first step towards any reform would be the removal of a great proportion, if not the entire demolition, of the existing work. Thus no advantages would accrue from the present building, but the accumulation of material and the excavation of the ditch, which last, indeed, is questionable, as no doubt many parts would require to be filled up. But objections of a still more important nature exist against a general reform. Independently of the artificial cover afforded by the pettah and other villages, the banks of tanks, and its outworks to the very edge of the ditch, the position of the fort may, with very little labour, be safely approached under cover of some small hills and nullahs in the south-west to within three or four hundred of the glacis. Further, a considerable portion of the rampart on the east and west faces is exposed to a reverse and enfilading fire from positions in or adjoining the pettah."

" To conclude. I can recommend no further repairs to the fort than such as are absolutely necessary to stop the progress of decay into which it is rapidly falling, and not even to this

* John Purton entered the service in 1812, and retired as Major and C.B. in 1838, having highly distinguished himself in the Mahratta campaign of 1817-19.

extent unless measures are taken to clear away the numerous avenues by which even the most contemptible enemy might be encouraged to make an attack, which he would never attempt over an open esplanade."

The* ex-Panghooloo of Nanning, generally known as Dool Syed, was installed in 1802, by Colonel Taylor, the British Resident at Malacca, and it was agreed that he should remain in possession of the same rights and privileges as those which had been enjoyed by his predecessor under the Dutch, provided he substituted the English seal for that of the Netherlands Government.

In 1828, the Panghooloo of Nanning, who had latterly shown symptoms of turbulence and dissatisfaction, was summoned to Malacca, but positively refused to obey the requisition. In consequence of this refusal, the Government despatched a Commissioner. The mission was totally unsuccessful, as the Panghooloo rejected each stipulation. Mr. Fullarton, the Governor of the Straits, resolved to enforce by the sword the adoption of those measures which negotiation had failed to effect. An expedition was equipped, but it was shortly afterwards countermanded by Mr. Fullarton. His reason for this was his desire to obtain the sanction of the Supreme Government. The Supreme Government referred the matter home, and it was not till June 1831 that the decision of the Court of Directors was received.

Early in August the expedition was ready to start. It consisted of 150 men of 29th Madras Native Infantry, and 24 Artillery, the whole force being less than 200. The detachment was commanded by Captain Wyllie. This small force was considered far too large, and the expedition was looked upon as a mere picnic. Some hinted at the sufficiency of a havildar's guard, while others more roundly asserted that a red jacket amongst the bushes would scare every Malay out of the

* Chiefly abbreviated from Begbie's *Malayan Peninsula.*

country. The expedition met, however, with much more opposition than was anticipated, and before the end of the month of August was compelled to retreat to Malacca with the loss of its guns. The retreat left the whole country at the mercy of Dool Syed, and he speedily began to make incursions into Malacca proper.

Meanwhile, the British Government was exerting itself to break the existing league, in the interim, between Dool Syed, and the chiefs of Rumbow; and the latter agreed to meet the British authorities at Linggy. A treaty was made with the chief of Rumbow, and the British party returned to Malacca. A day or two after their return, the reinforcements from Madras began to arrive.

The force now consisted of the 5th M.N.I., five companies of 29th M.N.I., two companies of Sappers, and some European and Native artillery.

This was the first expedition undertaken by the Pioneers after they had been formed into a corps of Sappers and Miners, and placed under the direct command of officers of the Madras Engineers.

> Lieutenant-Colonel Herbert commanded;
>
> Captain Wyllie, Brigade Major;
>
> Lieutenant J. H. Bell, M.E., Commanding Engineer, with Second Lieutenants Watts and Smythe as his Subalterns.
>
> Captain Bond, commanding Artillery;
>
> Lieutenant Milnes, commissariat; and
>
> Major Farquharson, commanding 5th M N.I.

By the end of January 1832, nearly the whole had arrived, and preparations were at once made for an advance into the interior.

On 7th February, the light companies of the 5th and 29th Native Infantry, with one company of Sappers under Lieutenant Bell, and 100 Malay Contingent, marched for Roombiyah.

On the 9th, the grenadier company of the 5th moved on to occupy Ching, half-way between Malacca and Roombiyah, to support the party in advance. Lieutenant Watts at this time joined the advanced party.

On the 16th, intelligence was received at Malacca that the chiefs who had been wavering had actually joined Dool Syed, and resistance was now a matter of certainty.

On the 9th, the second company of Sappers arrived

It may be necessary to premise that the whole of the second expedition was carried on by detachments; that is, that parties of various strength went out daily as covering parties to the sappers, and consequently the operations of the day were carried on by the senior officer with such covering party.

On the 25th, a brigade of 6-pounders, under Lieutenant Begbie, and another company of Sappers, under Second Lieutenant Smythe, M.E., marched for Roombiyah.

On 2nd March, Colonel Herbert joined the force in advance. At Roombiyah a stockade was found, and the Sappers were busily employed in cutting through the felled trees, and hewing down the lofty forests of Roombiyah, to a distance of eighty yards on each side of the road.

On 7th March, three of the sappers were severely hurt by the falling trees, and on the 9th and 10th four more men were hurt.

On the 13th, Colonel Herbert with his staff and Lieutenant Bell, Commanding Engineer, started to reconnoitre Soongiepathye.

On the 17th, a gallant and successful affair took place. Captain Burgess was commanding Reserve, and Captain Justice the supports and covering party to the sappers who were employed in clearing the jungle under Lieutenant Smythe.

The Malays occupied stockades in the vicinity of Soongiepathye, and were attacked between 4 and 5 P.M., Captain Justice taking his right subdivison of the light company of 5th

M.N.I. across rice-fields to attack the left flank of the stockade, whilst Lieutenant Poole with the left sub-division attacked the right. This party was somewhat amazed by the ranzows, which the enemy had planted in thousands.

Captain Justice carried the left of the stockade at the charge without firing, and Lieutenant Poole the right.

The fire of jingals and musketry became general, but the five defences fell one after another. All five were demolished and fired, and a party sent to destroy a sixth which flanked the road. This having been done by 7 P.M., the whole party returned to Roombiyah.

The success was complete, and every officer and man engaged behaved excellently. Only one man was wounded by the fire, and eight or ten by the ranzows.

On the 25th, Colonel Herbert marched for Soongiepathye. At 7 A.M. a detachment from that post, under Captain Poulton, carried five stockades at Kalama; another, under Captain Justice, carried two others in a different direction. The Engineer officers with these detachments were Lieutenants Bell and Watts.

On the 27th, a small force, with which was Lieutenant Bell, crossed the Malacca river and burnt five stockades at Malacca Pinda.

On the 29th, another very strong stockade at Ayer Mangis (the Mangoe stream) was taken. Lieutenant Herding was killed on this occasion. The very last man that issued from the stockade unexpectedly confronted Lieutenant Harding. Before Harding could draw his pistol, the man fired from his hip The ball passed through Harding's throat and injured the spine, down which it passed. After several ineffectual efforts, Harding was removed. He lingered till next day and then died. He was much liked by his brother officers, and universally regretted. In person he was remarkably fine, being six feet four inches, and stout in proportion.

On the same day, the E. company 5th Native Infantry, under Ensign Wright, accompanied by Lieutenants Bell and Smythe of the Engineers, formed the covering party to the cutters. There was heavy "sniping" carried on all day, and the two engineers volunteered to head different sections.

The Sappers and Miners were now employed in cutting down the jungle in advance towards Taboo, and constant skirmishing took place daily.

On 3rd May, the Malays made a grand attack on the camp, but were repulsed with loss. After this, the usual daily exchange of shots was carried on, while the enemy were busy building stockades, in the hope of hemming in the camp, and the duties became very harassing.

By the evening of the 24th, the road to Priggito-Datus was sufficiently cleared, and the cut jungle burnt. Colonel Herbert now determined to take possession of Bookit-si-Boorsoo, and on the morning of the 25th he detached Captain Poulton and Ensign Stoddart with the grenadier company 5th Native Infantry, Captain Wallace and Lieutenant Stevenson, F. company 46th, and Lieutenants Begbie and Lawford with a small detail of artillery; Lieutenant Bell and thirty sappers, with a large body of convicts.

The first shot was fired at a little before 7 A.M., and the works were gained at half-past 9, two hours of which time were passed in active conflict.

Our casualties were Captain Poulton wounded by a ranzow, eighteen rank and file wounded; eight by musketry and ten by ranzows; three of Artillery in addition were wounded. The Sappers lost one man.

On the 27th, three stockades which were one mile in advance at Bukit-pur Ling, were ascertained to be unoccupied. A small force was sent forward, and they were taken possession of.

By this success, there was every prospect that the troops would soon be in possession of Taboo.

On 4th June, the Panghooloo made his appearance to meet Mr. Westerhout, who was to negotiate on the part of the Government.

An exchange of upper garments took place as a mutual assurance that no treachery was meditated ; and the metamorphosis of either party was most grotesque. On the one side stood the athletic and portly Dutchman with his body confined in the linen badjoo of the Malay : on the other was the half-starved and miserable Panghooloo sinking under the weight of the huge coat, which well-nigh concealed him altogether from view. He furnished Mr. Westerhout with the terms on which he would surrender, and an armistice was agreed on till a reply should be received to those terms.

During the night, in defiance of the armistice, the enemy attacked Pur-Sing, but were driven back.

On 6th June, the reply of our Government was received, which stated that the Panghooloo must appear at Malacca, and bring the guns with him, in which case his life would be spared, and he be permitted to live in Nanning as a private individual.

On the 8th, news was received that Dool Syed did not intend closing with the offer, and next day the head-quarters of the force moved on from Bell's stockade to Tangong-pur-Ling

On the 14th, our troops arrived in front of the works at Taboo.

The Engineers next day commenced throwing up a log battery for the artillery, the enemy meanwhile keeping up a constant fire.

At half-past 12 the battery was completed and opened fire, while a force under Captains Simcock and Justice moved off to the left to get to the rear of the stockades, and in a short time the defences of Taboo were in our hands. We had only five men wounded.

The Taboo defences would not have fallen so easily had not the rapidity of the attack prevented the junction of the Sebang people.

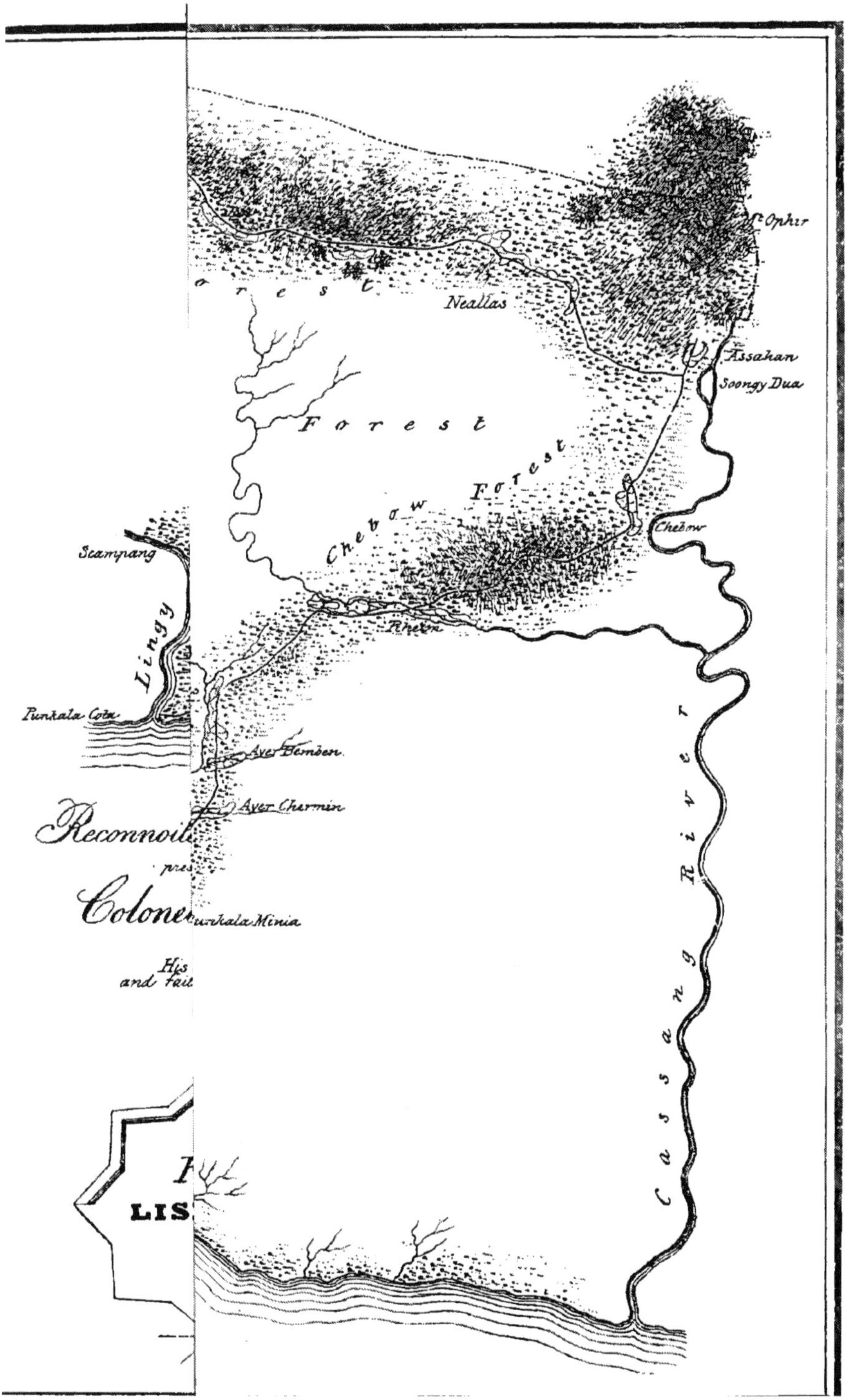

Mt. Ophir

Neallas

Assahan

Soongy Dua

F o r e s t

Chebow Forest

Chebow

Scampang

Lingy

River

Punkala Cota

Aver Bembon

Aver Chermin

Reconnoit

pres

Colone

Punkala Minia

His
and Fait

LIS

Cassang River

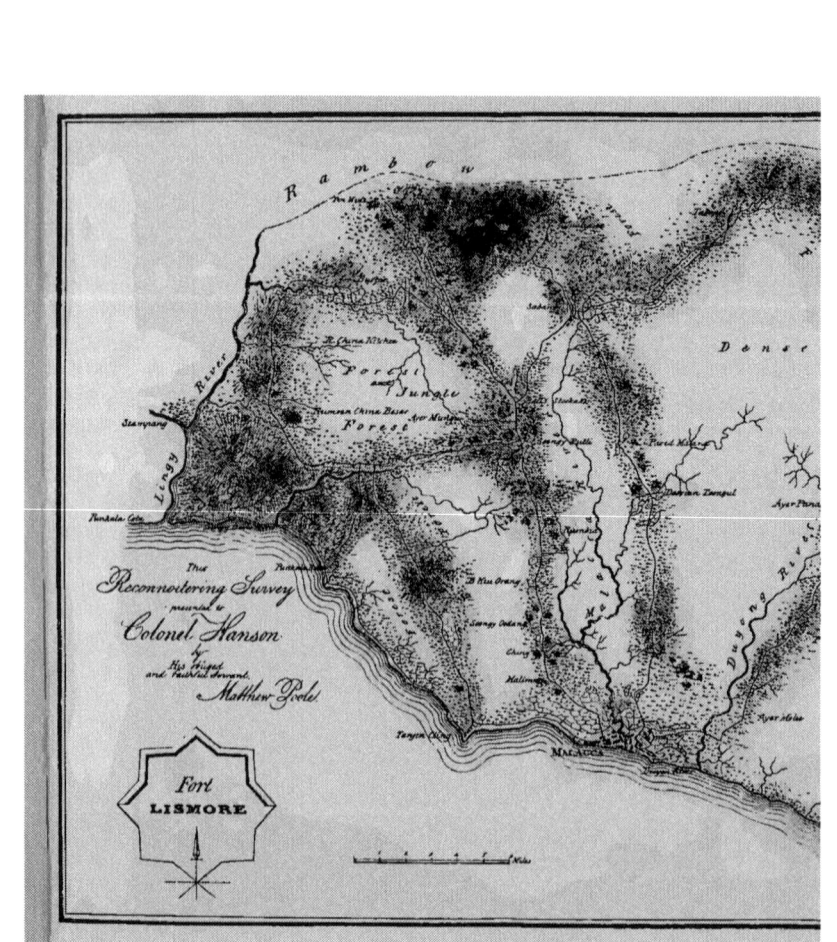

This
Reconnoitering Survey
presented to
Colonel Hanson
by
His Wright
and faithful Servant.
Matthew Poole

Fort
LISMORE

The principal line of the work measured 284 yards, inclusive of its angles, while the straight line from flank to flank was 180 yards.

On the 10th, the British standard was hoisted.

Captain Lawe and Lieutenants Lawford, Ditmas, and Horsley, with 328 N.C.O. and men of Sappers and Miners, proceeded to Malacca in July 1832, but were too late to take part in the operations, and returned at the end of August to Fort St. George.

Lieutenant Bell, Commanding Engineer with the force, remained some time longer in the country, doubtless to give his advice to Colonel Herbert regarding points to be occupied and strengthened.

Colonel Herbert and Lieutenant Bell did not arrive at Cuddalore till 3rd December 1832.

Edward Lake was the eldest son of Admiral Sir Willoughby Lake, K.C.B. (younger brother of Sir James W. Lake, Bart., the father of Sir H. Atwell Lake, K.C.B.), and in 1829 was Military Secretary and Aide-de-Camp to the Governor of Penang. He embarked towards the end of that year in the ship *Guildford*, accompanied by his wife and three infant children. The ship was, it is believed, at the time, rumoured to be unsound. It foundered at sea, and was never heard of again.

Lake* highly distinguished himself in the Mahratta war. He was stated to "be distinguished for professional skill and gallantry on several occasions; his conduct at Talneir was honourably recorded in G. O. 28th February 1818, and General McDowell repeatedly published his high approbation of his conduct." He was Adjutant of Engineers in the First Burmese War.

In the year 1834, a force was employed, under General Taylor, in a portion of the Ganjam district which had been disturbed

* He was the author of *Sieges of the Madras Army*.

II.   **6**

The force consisted, of 41st Regiment, detachment of 8th, detachment Golundauze, three companies of 49th, two companies of 21st with head-quarters, 3rd Punjab Light Infantry, and a detachment of Sappers and Miners under Lieutenant Power, M.E.

"The Governor in Council observed with high approbation the exemplary conduct of all the troops employed in this arduous and harassing service, their patient endurance of extraordinary fatigue and privations, and the gallant and resolute spirit with which they were led by their officers, whose activity and energy have been conspicuous."

A gratuity of one month's pay and allowances was granted to European officers, and one month's pay to native officers and men of all ranks employed.

Lieutenant John P. Power died at Kimedy on 5th April, and was succeeded in command of the detachment of Sappers and Miners by Lieutenant Macaulay, an infantry officer.

As soon as the country was quieted most of the troops were withdrawn, but the 21st were retained, as well as the detachment of Sappers and Miners.

In 1836-37, a force under the command of General Taylor was again employed in the northern districts against Goomsoor.

It appears that Dhunagi Bunje had just succeeded his father as Raja in Goomsoor. For a long time he and his father had been giving great trouble and causing great disorder in Goomsoor. First the father had been removed, and his son placed in his stead. Matters continued just as bad, and the father was allowed to return. This failed to improve matters, and he was deposed, being again succeeded by his son. This change was again fruitful of the greatest disorder, and he finally revolted and defied our Government. It was then that the force under General Taylor* was sent against him.

* This officer had served previously, and was wounded, in Goomsoor in 1801-2 (having entered the service in 1799). He was present at the battles of

On 7th October 1836, Lieutenant Smythe, M.E., was ordered to take charge of the detachment of Sappers and Miners proceeding from Hydrabad to Goomsoor, and Second-Lieutenant Armstrong, M.E., was directed to proceed to join the Field force with the European Sappers he had under him.

The operations in this campaign did not come to an end till March 1837, and " they would have lasted much longer had it not been for the treachery of some of the Rajah's adherents. The Khond leaders were surrendered by the tribes who, unable to continue the contest, sued for peace by delivering them up. The Raja was hunted from place to place, and finally died in a small mountain fortress. Dora Bissye, the foremost supporter o the Raja, escaped to Ungool, but was subsequently given up, and became a state prisoner at Gooty."

" The campaign was of unexampled severity. We had no knowledge of the country, were frequently cut off from supplies, and suffered fearfully from the pestilential nature of the climate. Hardship, privation, and peril were the lot of all who took part in the campaign."

" The casualties from the bows and arrows of the Khonds were not very great, but on one or two occasions they came in force on weak detachments, and hacked them to pieces. Two European officers (Lieutenant R. B——, Madras Artillery, and Ensign Charles J. Gibbon, 14th Native Infantry), with thirty men, were on one occasion surrounded by the Khonds in the Pass of Oodiagherry, and slaughtered to a man."

After the close of the campaign, the force received the thanks of the Government " for this trying and arduous service."

Lieutenant Smythe served in command of the detachment of Sappers till 26th December 1836, when he was ordered to

Assaye and Argaum, and at the siege of Gawilghur. At Assaye he was wounded twice. In 1807, he served with the Hydrabad Subsidiary Force, and up to May 1817 with the field forces under Doveton, Close, and Rumley. He was appointed a C.B., and eventually advanced to the Grand Cross of that Order. He died in 1875, having attained the great age of ninety-two.

return to his duties at the Presidency, and the command devolved on Lieutenant Armstrong, M.E.

On 13th March 1837, " His Majesty was graciously pleased to nominate Major-General J. L. Caldwell a Knight Commander of the Order of the Bath," and about the same time Major Purton was appointed a Companion.

Purton entered the service in 1812, and served with distinction in the Mahratta campaign. He was with General Doveton in Berar in 1815 ; at Adoni with General Pritzler ; and in Kandeish under Colonels Macdowell and Huskinson. He was present at Dharwar, and the battle of Mehidpore, in 1817, and in 1818 at Talneir, Rajdeir, Trimbuck, Malligaum, and Amulnair. In 1819 he was at the siege of Asseerghur. He was wounded at Malligaum, and frequently mentioned in despatches.

On 3rd February 1837, the Establishment of Sappers and Miners was revised as follows:—

1 Captain-Commandant.	24 Naiques.
8 Subalterns.	640 Privates.
1 Assistant-Surgeon.	16 Artificers.
8 Jemadars.	24 Recruit Boys.
1 Conductor.	24 Pension Boys.
1 Sergeant-Major.	8 Puckallies.
1 Quartermaster-Sergeant.	1 Assistant Apothecary.
12 Sergeants.	1 Dresser.
12 1st Corporals.	1 Chowdry.
12 2nd „	2 Peons.
24 Havildars.	2 Toties.

In the beginning of 1831, there were two battalions of Pioneers, but, as has been already stated, the 1st battalion was converted into a corps of Sappers and Miners in May of that year. The 2nd battalion was, however, retained as a Pioneer body, until it was also incorporated with the Sappers in 1837. Whilst the Sappers were employed in Malacca, the Pioneer Corps was employed on the Koondah Ghaut, in the Neilgherries.

Captain William Murray at this time commanded them, and Lieutenant Le Hardy served with them.

On 10th December 1831 (a half-century ago), Captain Murray wrote as follows :—

" Lieutenant Le Hardy and I endeavoured to descend the pass on 21st November (never used except by smugglers), descended three miles, and then returned to avoid being benighted. I sent on a havildar, with pioneers and guides, with orders to reach Mungaree, not far from Beypore river. They took three days doing it, having had to cut their way through many parts of the jungle."

On 9th June 1832, the final report of the Koondah Ghaut was sent in. It was stated by Captain Murray : —

" This report will show the Governor what the Pioneers have done, and are capable of doing. It will be an appropriate supplement to his own (the Governor's) general order, and will manifest to all India what the Madras Pioneers have been able to execute.

" Since the period of the Governor's visit to the Koondahs, six miles of mountain road have been completed and every impediment surmounted, being a progress, I imagine, rarely equalled by any body of men of equal strength.

" This stupendous work, in which there were vast forest trees to be felled, deep chasms to be built up, causeways over every river and mountain-torrent to be constructed, and rocks to be removed, was begun on 10th January and finished 31st May 1832."

Although the above can in no way be considered a military work, I think it is worthy of record as showing what an extremely valuable body the Madras Pioneers were in times of peace as in war. It is further noteworthy as being a very important work (of a similar character to those which the Pioneers might have had to carry out during hostile operations), and forms a fitting close to the record of this gallant and distinguished Corps, which merged shortly after in the Madras Sappers and Miners.

CHAPTER III.

Expedition against Coorg.—East column.—North column.—Repulse at stockade of Buck.—West column.—West auxiliary column repulsed.—Raja surrenders.—Expedition against Kurnool.—Action of Zorapore.—Services of William Farquhar.—Services of Colin Mackenzie.—Services of William Monteith.

THE origin of the expedition against Coorg was the frightful tyranny of C. Vera Raja, who reigned from 1820 to 1834. He stopped at no enormity; he killed, mutilated, starved to death, and imprisoned whom he pleased.*

In January 1833, the Governor of Madras wrote to him, giving him a lecture on good government, and demanded in future compliance with the Government order of 1827; to report all capital punishments in Coorg. Mr. Casamajor was sent, at the same time, to have a personal conference with the Raja. The Resident warned him to abstain in future from cruelties, and advised him to relax the rigour with which he had shut up his people in the country. The Raja said Coorg was an independent country, and that he would do as he pleased.

The Resident replied that Coorg was now subject to the Company, as it was in former years to Tippoo. The conference was fruitless, and the Resident returned to Mysore.

The Raja continued to behave as bad as ever. Mr. Graeme,

* Chiefly extracted from the *Manual of Coorg.*

the Resident at Nagpore, who happened to be at Bangalore, was then sent to the Raja; but the latter was unwilling to meet an English Envoy, and seized and kept in confinement two of Mr. Graeme's native agents, Daraset and Kulputty Karmhara. Menoon. The former was allowed to return to Tellicherry, but the latter he refused to give up until the Raja's relatives, Channa Basava, a Coorg, and his wife, Devammaji, sister to the Raja of Coorg (who had fled to the Residency of Mysore in September 1832, to save their honour and lives, and implored the protection of the British Government), were given up to him by the Government.

He addressed most insolent letters to the Governor of Madras, and to the Governor-General, and, having an extraordinary idea of his power, and strength of his country, resolved on war.

A British force was accordingly organised, and marched towards Coorg to depose the Raja. Coorg itself, at this time, was covered with forest. Near Sommiarpett, in the north of Coorg, the hills are gently rounded, alternating with sloping glades interspersed with forest trees.

Near Mercara the hills are more abrupt, and the ravines deeper and more wild. Towards Fraserpett the country is more like the Mysore plateau with scattered hills. South of Mercara the country is open. The eastern frontier between the Cauvery and the Lakshmana Urthee river, had an impervious forest when the expedition was undertaken against Coorg. The roads were in a primitive state—quite impracticable for wheeled traffic, and scarcely less so for bullocks; it having been the policy of the Rajas to make their country as little accessible as possible.

For this reason, it was considered necessary to break up the invading force into several columns, owing to the difficulty of conveying supplies and ammunition, &c., and it was arranged that the several forces, from different sides, should converge on Mercara.

The force was 6,000 strong, divided into four columns.

Eastern column, under Colonel Lindsay :—

    1 company Foot Artillery ;
    3 Light Howitzers ;
    2 Heavy   ,,
    2 Mortars ;
    1 6-pounder ;
    400 men of H.M.'s 39th ;

and 4th, 35th, 36th, and 48th Regiments Madras Native Infantry, with the rifle company of 5th Native Infantry, and 300 Sappers and Miners.

This column marched on 2nd April from Bettadapura upon Sula-cotta, and reached the Cauvery opposite Hebbaul, where a barrier had been thrown up on the Coorg side, consisting of a wall of mud and stone, loop-holed. Colonel Fraser, who was Political Agent, attempted to cross with a white handkerchief in his hand but was fired upon. Two howitzers then oper l with grape, and under cover of this the advanced-guard cro. d and the enemy gave way, retiring towards Ramasammy Ka .wé. The strong position at the fortified pagoda, near Ramasa..my Kanawé, was carried in about a quarter of an hour. A breast-work and barrier near Haringe, six or seven miles west of Ramasammy Kanawé, was also taken, at the sacrifice of a few men wounded.

On the 4th April the force only advanced five miles on account of the difficulty of the road, obstructed as it was by large felled trees. A flag of truce, sent by the Raja, now came into our camp at 4 P.M.

On the 6th the troops entered the fort of Mercara, and the British colours were hoisted under a salute of twenty-one guns.

The Engineers with the division were Captain G. Underwood, Commanding Engineer, Lieutenant Stafford, adjutant, and Second-Lieutenant Horsley.

A sub-division of the eastern column under Colonel Stewart, advanced on 2nd April from Periapatam towards the Cauvery opposite Rungasamoodrum. The enemy, after being plied with a few cannon-shot, left their entrenched position. Colonel Stewart crossed the Cauvery at Kondagherry, and proceeded to Virarajendrapett, to co-operate with the western column. Captain C. J. Green was the engineer with this force.

The northern column, under Colonel Waugh, composed of 1st brigade 6-pounder guns, 300 of H.M 's 55th, 9th, and 31st Light Infantry, and the rifle company of the 24th Native Infantry, with 200 Sappers under Lieutenant Ditmas and Second-Lieutenant Orr, marched on 1st April from Hosacotta to Shanivarsante.

On passing the Hemavutty, the enemy's advanced posts retreated. Our force moved into Codlipet, where 200 men occupied an entrenched high ground. Their flanks were turned, and they fell back. The English advanced guard had another skirmish at Mudravalli.

The next day they had hardly gone a few hundred yards when they found the road blocked with trees. As the column approached a village in a wood near the bottom of the pass, fire was opened on them. This stockade was known as the stockade of Buck, and was remarkably strong. Outside, it was protected by thick bamboos and trees, and surrounded by a deep ditch ; inside was a mud wall, faced with stone, and loop-holed. Colonel Waugh attempted to carry it by assault, and the troops under Major Bird, of 31st Light Infantry, attacked it for four hours and a half, during which they were exposed to a severe fire ; but all was in vain After this a double flank movement was attempted by Colonel Mill, with the 55th ; but the two parties, instead of meeting in the rear of the obstruction, by some error, met in front of it. Colonel Mill was shot dead ; also Ensigns Robertson, 9th Native Infantry, and Babington, 31st Light Infantry. Major Bird now withdrew the column, and with little additional loss brought it under cover, and retreated several miles. In this affair forty-eight were killed and 118 wounded, including three officers killed. The Sappers lost seventeen men.

The western column marched from Cannanore on 31st March, under Colonel Foulis. It consisted of half a company of Golundauze with four 6-pounders, 300 of H.M.'s 48th, and 200 Sappers under Lieutenant Bell and Second-Lieutenant Rundall. It was ordered to force the Heggala Ghaut and occupy Virara-jendrapett.

On the 2nd of April the light company of the 48th and the grenadier company of the 20th Native Infantry proceeded beyond Stony river into Coorg. Their progress was checked, and Lieutenant Erskine of the 48th was killed. At 6 the following morning the main body advanced, and had to fight its way up the pass. There were three regular stockades, as well as breastworks and felled trees at every 100 yards. The first stockade was taken with small loss; but after that, till 4 P.M., a series of hard conflicts took place in carrying the successive barriers. The last stockade was taken by attacking it in reverse, as well as in flank.

On the 4th of April a flag of truce appeared, with a proposal for a suspension of arms. Colonel Foulis replied that if the Coorgs did not fire, his troops would also abstain; but that his orders were to go up the Ghaut, and up he intended to go. He effected his march without opposition, and at 2 P.M. passed through the guard-house at Heggala, where he halted, and was supplied with grain by the Coorgs. In these skirmishes we lost twelve killed and thirty-six wounded; of these six were sappers.

On the 13th of April, a detachment marched, without opposition to Nalkanaad, and took possession of the palace, which was about ten or twelve miles north-west of Heggala, and fifteen miles south by west of Mercara. A detachment was left at Virarajendrapett, five miles north-east of Heggala, under Colonel Brock, while the main body of Colonel Foulis' column marched towards Mercara, and encamped seven miles south of it near the Muddaramudy river.

Colonel Stewart's force (part of the east column) had joined the west column at Virarajendrapett, and proceeded to open the Siddapur Pass into Mysore.

The west auxiliary column, under Lieutenant-Colonel Jackson, consisted of 150 of H.M.'s 48th, and 400 men of the 40th Native Infantry, without guns or sappers. This small force was intended to occupy the lower talooks of the Coorg dominions. If possible it was to take up its position at the ruined fort of Sulya, at the foot of the Ghaut, but the force was to be kept together. Sulya is twenty-five miles west by north of Mercara. Colonel Jackson advanced from Kumbla, on the coast, about twenty miles south of Mangalore.

On the 29th of March, at 3 P.M., nine miles to the east, his advanced-guard fell in with the enemy's picquets half a mile in advance of their stockade. The Coorgs would not quit the stockade, so it was assaulted and taken without difficulty.

Next day the column marched to Uppanangulla, on the 31st to a pagoda near Belhur, and the following day to Ishvaramanagala Pagoda. Here Colonel Jackson learnt that there was a strong stockade on a hill in the midst of a thick jungle near Mahur and Bollary. A reconnoitring party, consisting of four officers, forty Europeans, and eighty natives was sent to ascertain its locality. This party was attacked on 3rd April when it had received orders to retire, and it reached camp with the loss of two officers and more than half of the men, the greater proportion being killed. Colonel Jackson fell back upon Kumbla, but hearing his retreat would be cut off, turned across country to Kasergode, eight or ten miles south of Kumbla, and reached it on 6th April. His retreat was greatly harrassed by skirmishers, and the sick and wounded were massacred by the enemy with the most horrible barbarity. Part of the ammunition and stores fell into the hands of the Coorgs, and several of the officers' horses were shot. Our total casualties amounted to two officers and thirty men killed, and thirty-six wounded.

The failure of this column was due to the inadequacy of the force for the task imposed on it, and not in any degree to the conduct of the commander or troops, who behaved well on all occasions.

The success of the war had already been decided by the occupation of Mercara by the eastern column.

On 10th April, the Raja, accompanied by his unarmed attendants and his women, gave himself up at Mercara.

The object of the campaign having been attained, the Coorg Field Force was broken up, and only a small body of troops was kept in Mercara for an emergency.

Brigadier Lindsay, C.B., received the entire approbation of the Governor-General, and the Commander-in-Chief, " for the manner in which the military operations against the Raja of Coorg had been brought to a speedy and successful termination."

Brigadier Lindsay was nominated a Knight Commander of the Royal Hanoverian Guelphic Order.

The total loss in the Corps of Madras Sappers was twenty-three killed and wounded.

The whole loss sustained by the force was as follows:—

    Eastern Column—a few wounded.

    Northern Column—3 officers and 45 men killed, and 118 wounded.

    Western Column—1 officer and 12 men killed, and 36 wounded.

    Auxiliary Western Column—2 officers and 30 men killed, and 36 wounded.

    Total—6 officers and 87 men killed, and about 2(0 wounded.

Havildar Chokalingum, of the Sappers and Miners, distinguished himself for eminent bravery in the advance of the column under Colonel Foulis; and the Governor-General, as a mark of the high sense he entertained " of the distinguished conduct of

30°

2°

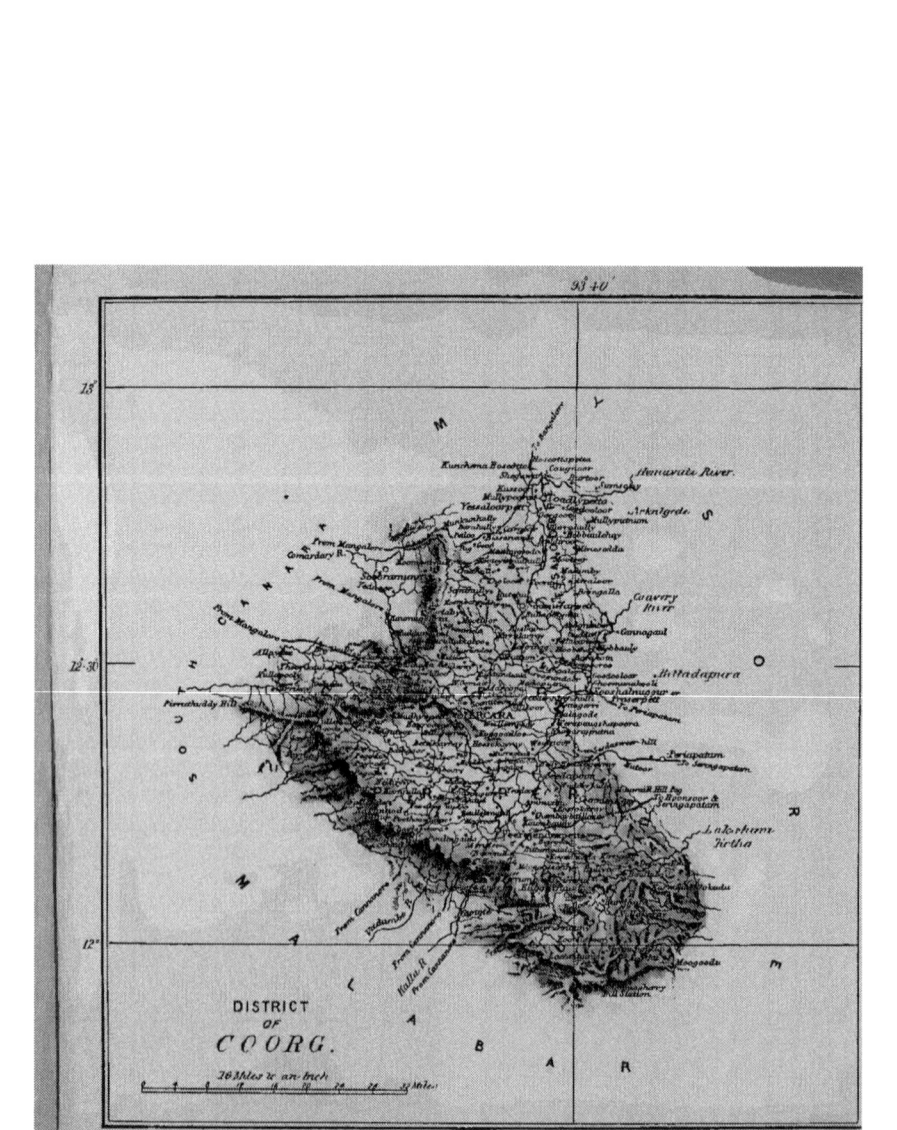

DISTRICT
OF
COORG.

that N.C.O., conferred upon him an honorary medal, and an increase for life of one-third of his present pay."

At the close of the campaign, Captain C. Le Hardy (who had joined the Pioneers in 1826, and had been Adjutant), was appointed the first Superintendent of Coorg. This officer distinguished himself greatly in 1837, during the insurrection in Canara. There was a panic at Mangalore—Captain Le Hardy, with a few hundred Coorg Volunteers, descended into the plains and quelled the disturbance by shooting a few score of the rebels. The Government, in recognition of this service, presented him with 5,000 rupees, and afterwards gave him the post of Superintendent at Nuggur, in Mysore Province. He retired from the service in 1849, as a Brevet-Major, and died in April 1882, in his eighty-first year.

In the year 1839, an expedition was resolved upon against the Nawab of Kurnool, who was accused of having collected large quantities of warlike stores, which was contrary to stipulation of treaties.

At this time it would appear as if a fanatical spirit had been excited among the Mussalman chiefs and people of India. Emissaries were sent (apparently from Scinde) to induce the chiefs to engage in a holy war against the English.

One of these had frequent interviews with the Nawab of Kurnool. The Nawab was called upon for an explanation, which he refused to give, and a British force was accordingly moved towards Kurnool, attended by two Government Commissioners.

Captain Pears, Madras Engineers, was at this time engaged in road-making near Closepett, and was informed that he would have to proceed with his Sappers to Gooty. He at once marched into Bangalore, a distance of thirty two miles, in one day, and on the 13th August left Bangalore with the 34th Light Infantry.

The movements ordered were as follows:—F. troop Native Horse Artillery, wing 13th Light Dragoons, Sappers and

Miners, and 34th Light Infantry from Bangalore. H.M.'s 39th, one company Foot Artillery, 39th Native Infantry, and 7th Native Cavalry, with heavy guns, from Bellary; one company European Artillery, 3rd and 51st Native Infantry, with mortars from Hyderabad; all to assemble at Adoni. The force amounted to some 6,000 fighting men.

Captain Pears was appointed Commanding Engineer of the force, and had command of the Sappers as well. Lieutenant Dobbie, 29th Native Infantry, and Lieutenant J. W. Rundall were attached to the Sappers, and four other Engineer officers were sent, Lawford, Ouchterlony, Tombs, and Fast.

On the 25th August, the Sappers and 34th Light Infantry reached Anantapur, on the 29th they were at Gooty, and on the 2nd September they arrived at Adoni; the force from Bellary being still two marches off.

The Sappers were now ordered to Madaneram on the banks of the Toomboodra, to assist in the crossing of this force; and on the 4th they reached that place.

The Sappers now had very severe work in making arrangements for the passage of the troops over the river, and it was not till the 21st that this was effected.

On the 24th the force was at Kopatoal, thirty-five to forty miles from Kurnool. The Sappers were now left behind to prepare materials for the intended siege, assisted by a company of the 29th, and one of the 16th Native Infantry, the main force being encamped about six miles ahead.

On the 29th September, Pears submitted a project for the attack on Kurnool, but this, as will be seen, was not required.

After remaining at Kopatoal for about a fortnight, the Sappers were ordered to the front, a couple of miles in advance of the main camp. The main camp was on the right bank of the river, while the Artillery and Engineer parks, and Ordnance stores, were on the left.

On the 10th the Sappers received orders to march to Kurnool, and next day they moved off. The detachment consisted of the 34th Light Infantry, two companies of the 39th, two 6-pounders, with half a troop of Horse Artillery, and two howitzers, with European company of artillery, a squadron of the 13th Light Dragoons, one of Native cavalry, and the Sappers, under the command of Colonel Dyce.

On the 12th they reached Kurnool, and camped two miles off, while the Sappers marched into the fort, and were placed under the orders of Colonel James.

Colonel James, with the 51st Native Infantry, two companies of the 39th, and a small party of Sappers, had taken possession of the fort some days before. All this time the main force had been left at Codamoor, about twenty miles south-west of Kurnool.

" From the 12th to the 18th they were employed in the fort, searching for the Nawab's concealed guns. This searching was attended at first with much amusement. Houses, courts, and storehouses were so completely built up, that we walked round and round them without being aware of their existence. The great number and height of the walls rendered it most bewildering. By degrees all the places and stores came to light, assisted as we were by some of the Nawab's own servants and spies, and even by his own brother. The latter, however, only made a fair show, and both he and Waunder Khan the Vizier, held up their hands in amazement at the various and enormous quantities of stores found. In carrying on the search, many were the tricks resorted to for the purpose of evading it. The most common was to vow that the zenana of the Nawab or some noble was within. The first time this was done was while the Commissioners, Colonel Steele and Mr. Blane, were observing the progress of some of the sappers knocking a hole through the wall. On a sudden, up jumped a couple of old women from within, and popping their heads over the wall, scolded and cried, and declared the world was turned upside down, when men dared to break into a zenana full of ladies. Colonel Steele's gallantry was immediately aroused, and he declared that 'British officers were all the ladies could wish, gentle and polite,' &c., and they retired. However, they returned next day to the work, re-assured, by some intelligence received in the meantime, and in they went, and found the zenana full of shot, shell, and guns of all sorts and sizes. The whole amount of stores discovered may be taken at 600 guns nearly; shell, shot, and bullets almost unaccountable; swords, matchlocks, suits of chain armour, double-barrelled guns and pistols (both English), enormous quantities of saltpetre, sulphur, copper, lead, and five or six hundred thousand pounds of powder. In one place was found a room full of reams of paper for cartridges. Of the guns, forty or fifty light field-pieces, from 2-pounders to 6-pounders, were found, with carriages complete, ready for the field. The guns were nearly all his own casting, and very fairly made. The carriages were not so good, but sufficiently so to have done us mischief in the field if well handled; three or four hundred guns were found laid in regular order in a court-yard, and overgrown with grass; these were mostly small. The large guns (except a few on the ramparts) were all buried, and very amusing work it was turning them out — guns, howitzers, mortars, laid as thick as they could be crammed in a court-yard and under the adjacent sheds. Behind a wall which acted as a screen, we found a "Malabar" gun, ten feet long, on a huge carriage, wheels ten feet high, and the trail extending about twenty-four feet. It had a calibre of about a foot, and would carry an iron shot of 240 lbs.: although screened by a wall, it was so placed as to look right down the main street upon the great gate. Fancy it loaded to the muzzle with grape! Another monster was a howitzer cast by the Nawab, and found in a garden, nine feet long, twenty seven-inch bore, and nine inches of metal at the muzzle. A shell, if it could be propelled from such an article, would look like a balloon. His shot and shells were a most curious assortment, and of astonishing variety, very large and very small, mostly made of pewter. Shells of two feet in diameter, and things like shells, of half-inch bar-shot, chain-shot, chain-bullets, and many fanciful absurdities. The treasure, which was pointed out by the ladies in the zenana (Oh, inconstant woman !), has not yet been counted ; it will not be above eight or ten lacs. There can be no doubt that had we come six months or a year later we should have found, as the Nawab's brother said, plenty of men and grain ; and if those men had been Arabs and Rohillas, we should have had a most ' glorious ' siege. He had now only 800 or 1,000 men, and perhaps the state of his powder led him to reflect that one shell would blow them all into the river. He, therefore, tried to put off our ' civilities ' by dissimulation, buried his guns, blocked up his stores, and said, ' Walk in, gentlemen, and see, I am only stuffed with straw ' Hence arose the report of the two first officers who went in, and who said he had but seven or eight old guns, and shot that would not fit them.

" The Commissioners had so little left to their own judgment, that some delay took place after the discovery of these things, and meanwhile the Nawab with his troops remained in the enclosure (near his father's tomb) to which they had retired. The fort was still called his, and he had liberty to send things in and out as he pleased ; of this he took advantage, and got out some money and jewels, but, it is believed, not very much."

All this time the Nawab with his followers had occupied a durgah and choultry with enclosure near the village of Zorapore.

On the 17th October, Colonel Dyce received instructions as to how he was to deal with the Nawab.

Two days before, some of our officers paid the Nawab an impromptu visit, which is thus described by Captain Pears, who was the senior :—

" On the 15th, six or seven of us, unarmed and in white jackets, rode to the place, and seeing a small gap in the enclosure wall, turned our horses into it. I at first thought it wrong, not unsafe, for I placed great reliance on the rude but soldier-like good faith of these fellows; but it certainly was imprudent and improper, considering the doubtful position in which he stood towards the Government. However, when we got in the midst of them, I jumped off my horse, and said, 'Is the Nawab here?' 'Yes,' was the reply; 'come and see him.' We pushed on, guided by one, among the old tombs and through the crowd of fine independent-looking fellows assembled, every one armed to the teeth. The Nawab came out from the Durgah a few yards to meet us. His followers pressed round us, but without rudeness. With one exception (an officer of Dragoons) all our party were slight men, whereas the Nawab's people were mostly tall men, with broad and deep chests, and very ' able-looking' limbs; we were very fair, shaved, and smooth-faced; they, with large mustachios and thick black beards. The Rohillas had an immense quantity of very black hair flowing over their shoulders. We were dressed in white open jackets, and nothing beyond a stick or a riding-whip in our hands Among them, every man was well-armed, with sword, dagger, and often pistols. The Nawab was a very tall dark man, very ill-dressed, with a pair of loose drawers, a short angribra or shirt, a small dirty skull-cap, from underneath which his black hair hung in great abundance and beauty nearly to his waist. He could not have been less than six feet two, with a high forehead, prominent well-marked nose, finely formed head and face, and commanding figure and gait; but his eye was as wild as Bedlam itself—it made him look like a demon It was quite 'glaring' as he offered his hand to each of us in succession He led us to an elevated platform in front of the Durgah, and I was requested to do speaker, and began talking to him about trifles, apologising for our intrusion, &c. Suddenly he began on his case, talked of our attack on him, and our accusations, declared he was a warm friend to the British, and that his views were greatly misunder-

stood. I gave him a soft answer, told him we were humble
individuals, servants of the Sircar, who only had to do as we
were ordered, and, in accordance with Eastern etiquette, then
begged his leave to retire. He called out for baskets of fruit as
presents, which I firmly declined, but to no purpose, for our
villainous horsekeepers, as we rode home, came trotting after
us, every man with a basket full of fruit on his head. So ended
our visit."

On the 18th morning, arrangements were made for surrounding the Nawab and his adherents, as it was intended to insist on
the personal surrender of the Nawab.

Captain Pears and Lieutenant Ouchterlony only heard of this
early in the morning, and at once mounted their horses, and
galloped over about a mile to the village of Zorapore, between
which and the Nawab's enclosure our troops were already in
position.

" On the right were at intervals small bodies of our dragoons
and native cavalry ; on the high and open ground, at some
little distance to the left, were the artillery, placed in a field some
300 yards from the Nawab's palace, which it was clear would
soon be rendered, by the two howitzers and two 6-pounders, too
hot to hold them. To the left of the artillery, and right in front
of the burial-ground, was the 34th Light Infantry extended
across a cholum-field to the road, while across the road stood a
handful (eighty men) of H.M.'s 39th—the *real* fellows.

" When Captain Pears reached this point, he found Colonel
Dyce parleying with some of the leaders, who had met him half-
way. Most of them were disposed to come in to the terms,
which were most reasonable—' To give up the Nawab, and all
to receive full arrears of pay, and a safe-guard to enable them
to go with their arms in their hands to their own country.' They
went backwards and forwards with idle excuses and requests.

" A little ugly Persian Moonshee was employed when these
fruitless personal conferences were given up. He said the

7 *

Nawab was evidently anxious to give himself up, but that some, especially Wullee Khan, would not allow him to do so. This latter had displayed something of his insolence to Dyce. When the Colonel first went down to see the chiefs, he said, ' Where is Wullee Khan ; will he not come and speak to me ? ' ' No,' they said, ' he says he will have nothing to say to it.' ' Well,' said Dyce, ' tell him that if he will not come to me, I will go to him. See, I have nothing but my walking-stick ; but I will trust his honour.' Hearing this, Wullee Khan came stalking down the road. A very tall man, covered (arms, legs, and breast) with superb armour, and an enormous broadsword which he held over his left shoulder He would not even make salaam to Dyce, much less shake hands with him as the others had done, but stood looking scorn, daggers, and pistols, stroking his long black beard. He said many most insolent things to Dyce, and when the paper containing the terms was put into his hands, he cast it from him on the ground, saying, ' I believe none of you ; you, your Government, and your papers, are all equally full of deceit.' Dyce, who (even alongside Wullee) was an imposing representative of the British, being a finely made man of six feet six, turned round calmly, and said, pointing to the men of the 39th, ' You see those fellows, if I once let them go I cannot very easily stop them.' ' Hah ! ' said Wullee, ' you are afraid of us.' After this the little Moonshee went and came three or four times On one occasion Wullee said to him, ' If you come here any more I will cram your papers down your throat.' And when the last message was taken and received with defiance, it was matter for a month's laughter to see the little squinting Moonshee with his awkward slippers come shuffling back, as if in momentary expectation of a tickler *a posteriori.*

" The Patans, &c., in the meantime, threw themselves out in front of our left, leaving the enclosure, which they foresaw would be touched up by the artillery from the other side. After having waited four hours (one more than he had been directed to do),

Dyce got the 39th men across the road, and ordered the buglers
to sound the ' Fire.'

" The Nawab, with thirty or forty of his followers, took shelter
in the Durgah, but the rest moved out in our front, some to show
fight, others to get away, if possible, to the river.

" The Rohillas and Patans in our front kept up a heavy fire for
ten minutes, and we lost a few men. Ouchterlony had a shot
through his cap.

" The conduct of the Europeans was admirable ; they evinced
the most extraordinary and entertaining coolness and compo-
sure. In a game of cricket they would have been more excited,
at morning drill they could not have been less so. I saw one
man take a step to the rear, and, placing his musket on a branch
of the milk hedge, take a very deliberate aim through, fire, and
walk on as he reloaded, without making any sign or uttering one
word of what he had accomplished. One man who was shot
through the thigh, was attended to by a surgeon, who put him in
a dooly, and said the bone was uninjured, upon which, the moment
his back was turned, the man got out, coolly rejoined his com·
rades, and got shot though the other thigh."

" All this time the fellows were getting on our flank, and Captain
Pears was sent to bring some dragoons. When he reached the
river's bank, he found they had plenty of work, for hundreds of
the enemy were trying to get round them, by getting into the
river, while the dragoons were trotting about trying to get at
them. Some of the 34th Light Infantry were then sent down to
the river, and shot a good many of the poor fellows in the
river and on the various sand-banks. The artillery were now
ordered to cease fire, and the 39th to advance up the road The
moment the Europeans began to advance, the 34th moving on
at the same time, five Rohillas (Wullee Khan, his brother, and
three others), came out on the right flank, sword in hand ;
they moved on with desperate daring to attack these British.
Powerful, bold, and skilful as they were, they were immediately

bayoneted, without injuring a man. ' Where they fought there they fell.'

"The Europeans now got into the Durgah, the verandah of which was still full of the enemy. Captain Pears arrived by this time, and went in to save the Nawab; Major Armstrong was, however, before him, and had that moment seized him, and Captain Pears met him, Nawab in hand, pushing his way out. Three of his own men were hanging on to him, when Captain Pears shook them off, and then helped to get rid of a European soldier, who had his hand twisted into the Nawab's long hair, swore he had killed his officer, Lieutenant White, who had just fallen, and was much disposed to take summary vengeance. Just then a man rushed out and killed young Yates of the 34th. Another, equally desperate, made a dash to the front and stabbed Colonel Wright. Both assailants were instantly killed.

"The affair was now over, and a few dropping shots were alone to be heard.

"Captain Pears was ordered by Colonel Dyce to report the capture of the Nawab to the Commissioners, which he at once did, and returned with orders regarding the disposal of the Nawab.

"Our party engaged consisted of 350 to 400 Native Infantry, eighty Europeans, 150 dragoons, 150 Native cavalry, and our guns. The enemy had 900 men, but no artillery.

"We had two officers killed, two wounded; five or six Europeans killed, a few wounded; one native killed, and twelve or fourteen wounded.

"Lieutenant Ouchterlony was among the wounded. He was with the Dragoons, and was proceeding to help a sepoy engaged in personal conflict with a Rohilla, when he was himself suddenly attacked by a man on foot, who repeated his blows in the most determined blacksmith-like manner. He gave him three cuts, one of which was a very severe one, in the left elbow joint. Some sepoys coming up, delivered him from his troublesome acquaintance, and Ouchterlony (bad as his wound was) swam his horse half through the river afterwards.

"Two hundred prisoners were taken, and fully 150 were killed.

"The most famous of the chiefs were killed, and the rest made prisoners.

"Shaikh Said, the brave Arab chief, was the man who killed Lieutenant White of the 39th.

"Wullee Khan (who was chiefly the cause of the fight) had been in the service of the Nizam or his brother at Hyderabad, and had long been the terror of that city. Through our influence he had been turned out, and from thence came to Kurnool.

"A guard of Europeans and Natives was left at the Durgah to secure the money found there (about 25,000 rupees).

"Some very young children were found placed high on the trees to be out of harm's way. It was pleasant and amusing to see the care and kindness which the European soldiers showed towards them. Most of these had lost their fathers in the affair, but they all found new ones Major Armstrong of the 34th got one poor little girl, a pretty child, shot through the thigh, but not severely hurt. Lawford returned to Bellary with two, carried by a Cowry cooly, a man who with a bamboo over his shoulder, carries a load swinging from each end thereof, before and behind."

"Captain Pears with the Sappers remained for some little time at Kurnool.

"The Nawab was imprisoned in a tent within the enclosure that surrounds his father's tomb outside the. fort. He asked permission to have his family with him, so they said he might have three wives, but he demanded his whole houseful, about 250 ladies, and as this was considered too great a blessing for a man in disgrace, it was denied, and he sulked and would see none of them.

"On the 5th December the whole force still at Kurnool was paraded, when the gallant Subadar-Major of the Sappers (Coomarasawmy) was invested with the insignia of the first class of the Order of British India, with the title of Sirdar Bahadoor."

"It appears certain that at the time of the expedition to Kurnool an insurrection was in preparation throughout Southern India. The principal points to which our foes directed their attention were Hyderabad, Sattara, Kurnool, Cuddapah, Oodigherry, and Madras. The serious plots in Southern India which afterwards came to light were ripe and ready for execution ; but when about to explode, all was checked and postponed by the un-expected march of our force into Afghanistan—a march ordered, it is believed, without any knowledge of these intrigues in the south. They recovered from their alarm, and again fixed a day for the rise (1st of the Mohurrum), when the discoveries were made at Oodigherry, which led to their laying open the whole affair. The Rajah of Sattara, Nawab of Kurnool, and tributary Prince of Oodigherry, and a well-known cha-racter, Moobary-o-Dowlah, brother of the Nizam, were the most prominent characters, the last-named a bigoted Wahabee."

"The correspondence lay principally between Moobary-o-Dowlah and him of Oodigherry. Oodigherry lies between Nellore and Cuddapah ; the latter is a rugged hilly country, and the town of Cuddapah, in the heart of this district, is full of Patans, descendants of the Afghan invaders of India. Nellore is a large town with a treasury, &c., eighty miles from Madras, Cuddapah being about 160."

"In the correspondence was found most minute instructions. The Rajah of Sattara would bring 30,000 men ; 13,000 good troops (Rohillas and Arabs) would come in small detachments (so as to be unobserved) out of Hyderabad and would assemble at Kurnool. This latter place was the depôt of arms and military stores. The Oodigherry Prince was to collect two years provisions in the fort."

" Their first proceeding was to be, to occupy Oodigherry and Cuddapah, then Nellore was to be captured. An insurrection in Madras was arranged for, with the sacking of Black Town, and the murder of as many principal Europeans as possible. This being accomplished, and their forces concentrated, Moohary-o-Dowlah was to be Subadar of the Deccan, and the others rewarded with extension of territory."

" The first thing that checked the conspirators was the news that the Ameers of Scinde had yielded to us, and permitted our troops to pass through Scinde. Then came our successes against Dost Mahomed, who had been looked to by these people for assistance. After this, our march to Kurnool and the death of Wullee Khan. Much interest attaches to our doings at Zorapore, as Wullee Khan was constantly alluded to in the papers as the hero, the champion, the defender of the faith. The Oodigherry Rajah was now upset. The Bombay Government looked after the Rajah of Sattara, while General Fraser at Hyderabad caused Moobary-o-Dowlah to be arrested, and these three with the Nawab of Kurnool became State prisoners."

" There appears to be no doubt that the Mahomedans were in earnest, and doubtless every native power wished them good luck. One thing is very gratifying : they failed, by their own confession, in their attempts to corrupt the native army."

Before proceeding any further with the records of the regular campaigns in which the Madras Engineers and Pioneers have been engaged, it may prove of interest to allude to the services of a certain officer of the Engineers who was enabled to serve the Government in a detached situation of a semi-military character.

William Farquhar, having obtained a commission as ensign of the Madras Engineers on 22nd July 1791, served throughout the campaigns against Tippoo in 1791–92 ; was present at the capture of Pondicherry in 1793, and at the taking of Malacca in 1795. He was appointed to the expedition against Manilla in 1797, but was recalled to Madras, owing to the abandonment of the expedition, and returned to Malacca on 25th April 1798. On 12th July 1803 he succeeded Lieutenant-Colonel Taylor as the Chief Civil and Military Authority at Malacca. In 1811 he was appointed to the expedition against Java, and was placed by the Commander-in-Chief, Sir Samuel Auchmuty, in charge of the Department of Intelligence and Guides.* He returned to Malacca towards the end of October 1811. In July 1818 he was employed in a political mission to the Eastern Malay States of Pontiana, Lingen Rehio, and Siak, for the purpose of forming commercial treaties. Subsequently he officiated as British Commissioner in restoring Malacca to the King of the Netherlands, which was effected on 21st September 1818. On 23rd December 1818 he finally quitted Malacca for Penang, where he soon received an order from the Supreme Government, appointing him to take charge of such new establishment as might be formed east of Malacca. On 19th January 1819 he sailed from Penang with a detachment of troops under his command. He visited the Carimon Islands and Singapore on the 29th January, and proceeded thence to Rehio, returning to Singapore on 4th February, immediately after which arrangements were made with Sir T. S. Raffles for founding the new establishment.

The British flag was hoisted at Singapore on 6th February 1819, and from that date Lieutenant-Colonel Farquhar assumed the civil and military charge of the new factory. On 20th January 1824 he quitted Singapore for Calcutta.

* He landed at Chillingcling, near Batavia on 4th August; was present on the 10th, under Gillespie, at the action of Weltervreden. He assisted in constructing the batteries against the enemy's works of Cornelis, and was engaged in their storm and capture on the 26th. He commanded a division of British troops at surrender of Gressei, Sourabaya, Fort Ludowyck, on 22nd September. He was offered by Lord Minto (Governor-General) the situation of British Resident at the Court of Djoejocarta, which he declined in order to return to his former command of Malacca.

In an affray with the Malays at Singapore on 11th March 1823, he, at the head of part of his own guard—whilst endeavouring to apprehend a chief who had run "amokh"—received a dangerous wound from a cris, in his left breast, which penetrated his lungs. On this occasion His Excellency, the Commander-in-Chief in India, was pleased to mark his sense of the good conduct of the havildar and naique of the guard, who accompanied the Colonel, and were instrumental in preserving his life, by promoting the first to the rank of jemadar, and the latter to that of havildar. It is presumed that this wound was the cause of his leaving Singapore, for we find that early in 1824 he went on furlough to Europe. Previous to his quitting Singapore he received the following addresses, from all classes of inhabitants ; and the European community requested his acceptance of a piece of plate as a testimony of their high regard and esteem.

One address was from the European merchants, to mark their sense of his private worth and uniform kindness and hospitality during his residence at Singapore, and to request his acceptance of a piece of plate to the value of 3,000 Sicca rupees.

A second was from the Kling merchants of Singapore, which was signed by 128 of the principal Hindoo and Mahomedan merchants.

A third was from H. H. Areng Belaiva (the Captain of the Burgis), and the Burgis inhabitants of Singapore. While the fourth was from the Chinese merchants, which was signed by forty-nine seafaring men, fourteen Canton merchants, and forty-one Fokin merchants.*

Major General Farquhar died at Early Bank, near Perth, on 13th May 1839.

Colin Mackenzie was another officer who, by his eminently scientific character, in addition to his excellent military service,

---

* The addresses are entered as an Appendix.

was enabled to benefit the Honourable East India Company,
and science in general, by the most active and indefatigable
researches into the history and antiquities of India.   He
obtained his commission on 17th May 1783 ; served throughout
the campaigns of 1790, 1791–92 against Tippoo ; at the siege
of Pondicherry in 1793 ; at Columbo, as Commanding Engineer,
in 1795–96; in campaign against Tippoo in 1799 ; as Chief
Engineer of the expedition to Java in 1811, and he remained in
that island till March 1815   He was appointed Surveyor-
General of Madras in October 1810,* and on the extension of
the Order of the Bath, in June 1815, to the officers of the
Company's service, he was appointed a Companion of the Order.
The first thirteen years of his life in India, from 1783 to 1796,
may be considered as of little moment to the objects pursued
latterly in collecting observations and notices of Hindoo
manners, geography, and history.   After his return from the
expedition to Ceylon in 1796, accident rather than design threw
in his way means that he unceasingly pursued of penetrating
beyond the common surface of the antiquities, the history, and
the institutions of the South of India.

After the close of the war in Mysore in 1792, he was engaged
in the first attempts made to methodize and embody the geography
of the Deccan.

The voyage and campaign in Ceylon may be noticed as intro-
ductory to part of what followed on his return to resume the
geography of the Deccan in 1797.

Mackenzie was present in the campaign of the Nizam against
the Mahrattas in 1795, when the Nizam was utterly defeated by
the Mahrattas at the battle of Kurdla.   The British officers present at this battle had removed from the camps of the Nizam
and the Peishwa, and were mere spectators of the event.

In 1796 a general map of the Nizam's dominions was sub-

---

* On his return from Java in 1815 he was appointed Surveyor-General of
India.

mitted to Government for the first time.   In 1798 measures were proposed, and in part methodized, for describing the whole Deccan.   This was interrupted, in 1799, by the campaign against Tippoo.   After that campaign Mackenzie was appointed to survey Mysore.*   This work was completed in 1809, and considerable materials were acquired illustrative of statistics and of the history of that country.

In 1810 Mackenzie was appointed Surveyor-General.   In March 1811, however, his services were required in Java.   After the capture of Java he remained in that island till 31st March 1815, and was employed in collecting and arranging the topographical and military reports and survey of the former Government, in investigating the history and antiquities of the island, and in ascertaining the state of the landed tenure and the general condition of the inhabitants.

On his returning to the Presidency he found the office of Surveyor-General at Madras abolished; but he was at once appointed Surveyor-General of India on a new system.

The Court of Directors had a high opinion of the scientific and literary labours of Colonel Mackenzie; and on the 9th February 1810 addressed a letter to the Government of Fort St. George, reviewing the services of Colonel Mackenzie in the survey of Mysore and certain provinces adjacent to it.   In this they state :—

" We feel it to be due to Lieutenant-Colonel Mackenzie, and it is great pleasure to us, to bestow our unqualified and warm commendation upon his long-continued, indefatigable, and zealous exertions in the arduous pursuits in which he was employed, and upon the works which those exertions have produced.   He has not confined his labours to the leading object of his original appointment—in itself a very difficult one—the obtaining of an

* This included all the dominions of the late sovereignty of Mysore, as it existed a few years before, in the plenitude of its power and territory, and amounted to some 70,000 square miles.

accurate geographical knowledge of the extensive territories
which came under the dominion or protection of the Company
in consequence of the fall of Tippoo Sultaun in 1799, but has
carried his researches into two other very important branches—
the statistics and the history of those countries—and in all
of them he has succeeded to an extent which could not have
been contemplated at the commencement of his undertaking.
The actual survey, upon geometrical principles, of a region containing above 40,000 square miles (maps for 30,000 square miles
more were sent home shortly after), generally of an extremely
difficult surface, full of hills and wildernesses, presenting few
facilities or accommodations for such a work, and never before
explored by European science, in a climate very insalubrious, is
itself no common performance, and the minute divisions and
details of places of every description given in the memoirs of
the survey, with the masterly execution, upon a large scale, of
the general map, and its striking discrimination of objects, rarely
equalled by anything of the same nature that has come under
our observation, form altogether an achievement of extraordinary
merit, adding most materially to the stores of Indian geography,
and of information useful for military, financial, and commercial
purposes. . . . On a full review of these labours, and of others
which were not so immediately within the scope of Lieutenant-
Colonel Mackenzie's commission, we must admit that his merits
have not been merely confined to the duties of a geographical
surveyor . . . We direct that you present him with the sum of
9,000 pagodas (36,000 rupees), as full remuneration for his past
labours, and as a mark of our approbation of his work."

  " We next proceed to notice his statistical researches . . .
though they were adverted to in the original instructions given
to Lieutenant-Colonel Mackenzie ; the ample and successful
manner in which he has pursued them, in the midst of other
arduous labours, proves the zeal by which he has been actuated
and adds to the value of his services and his discoveries."

" This observation applies with at least equal propriety to his
superadded inquiries into the history, religion, and antiquities
of the country; objects pointed out, indeed, in our general
instructions to India, but to which, if he had not been prompted
by his own public spirit, his other fatiguing avocations might
have been pleaded as an excuse for not attending. . . . Lieutenant-Colonel Mackenzie has certainly taken the most effectual
way, though one of excessive labour, to explore any evidence
which may yet exist of remote eras and events by recurring to
remaining monuments, inscriptions, and grants preserved either
on metals or on paper; and his success in this way is far beyond
what could have been expected."

" The numerous collections of materials * he has made under
the different heads above noted must be highly interesting and
curious, and the specimens he has adduced in the manuscript
volumes he has sent us abundantly answer this character. . . .
It must be allowed that this effort promises the fairest way of
any which has yet been made to bring from obscurity any
scattered fragments which exist of true history, and undoubtedly
encourages the expectation of obtaining at length both considerable insight into the state of the country and its governments
in more modern periods, and some satisfactory indications of its
original institutions and earlier revolutions. We are, therefore,
very desirous that Lieutenant-Colonel Mackenzie should himself
digest and improve the materials he has collected. After he
has accomplished it, the original materials are to be transmitted
to us to be deposited in our Oriental Museum."

The *Asiatic Journal* for 1822 contains " A Brief View of the
Collection of Notes, Observations, and Journals of Thirty-four
Years, and of Collections of MSS., Inscriptions, Drawings, &c.
for the last Nineteen Years, made by Colonel Mackenzie in

---

* This collection was afterwards augmented in a quadruple proportion both
in the Peninsula and Hindostan, and ultimately extended to a new field—the
Oriental islands, seas, and coasts of Asia.

India ; exclusive of a considerable Collection of Native MSS. in all languages" To give some slight idea of the labours of Colonel Mackenzie in collecting these MSS., it may be stated that in a *Catalogue Raisonnée of Oriental MSS.*, by the Rev. William Taylor, Mackenzie's collection takes up no less than 570 pages.

The great interest which Mackenzie always exhibited in connection with the history of the East appears to have been originally put in motion before he went to India, when he was quite a young man. It appears that Mackenzie was known to Francis Lord Napier as a youth of considerable mathematical attainments. Lord Napier was anxious to publish a memoir of his celebrated ancestor, the inventor of logarithms, and he employed Mackenzie to search different works in India to ascertain what amount of knowledge the Hindoos possessed of mathematics.

Lord Napier subsequently procured for him an appointment to the East India Company's Engineers, and he proceeded to Madras in 1782.

In 1817 Mackenzie addressed a letter to Hon Sir Alexander Johnstone, Chief Justice of Ceylon, which contained an epitome of his life. This high official naturally took a deep interest in Mackenzie, as he was the grandson of Lord Napier, who had originally employed Mackenzie, and had known him personally as a young man.

On Sir Alexander Johnstone returning to England he explained to Mr. Grant (a former Chairman of the Court of Directors) the great advantage it would secure for Oriental history and literature were Colonel Mackenzie to be allowed to come to England, on leave, to arrange his valuable collection of materials. Mr. Grant accordingly determined to propose to the Court of Directors to give Colonel Mackenzie leave, with full pay and allowances, for three years.

No steps were, however, taken in this matter because, in the meantime, accounts were received of Mackenzie's death at Calcutta in 1821.

The Mackenzie collection was purchased by the Governor-General, Lord Hastings, from his widow, for £10,000.

The services of William Monteith will prove interesting, as showing, further, how varied have been the positions in which officers of the Corps have been utilized.

Whilst Sir John Malcolm was at Tabreez, in July 1810, he permitted (at the request of Abbas Meerza*) Lieutenants McDonald and Monteith to reconnoitre the Russian posts on the banks of the Arras near Megeri. These officers, finding that no attention was paid to their advice, shortly after returned to Tabreez. Four days after their departure the Russians surprised the Persians, who fled across the Arras, and were only saved from entire destruction owing to the Russian commandant being severely wounded.

McDonald (afterwards Sir J. McDonald Kinnear) returned with Malcolm's mission to India, but Monteith remained in Persia.

At the end of August the Prince Royal's army assembled at Nackshiwan and that of the Turks at Kars.

There was but little prospect of much co-operation between the two armies, but even this was destroyed by an accident. According to custom, on the arrival of a great personage there was a display of horsemanship, &c.; and the Seraskier appears to have become excited as the play proceeded, and to have joined in the exhibition. By some accident his pistol, which had before missed fire, went off as he was handing it to one of his guards, and the Turkish Pasha was wounded in the head.

Abbas Meerza sent his English surgeon (Dr. Campbell) with condolences and offers of assistance, which were refused in no very courteous manner, and the Turkish army retired. Among the Persians the accident caused more merriment than regret.

* The Prince Royal of Persia.

Abbas Meerza now moved to Erivan, and prevented the Russians from taking advantage of the confusion in the Turkish camp ; and he then ordered Hussain Khan, the Sirdar of Erivan, to proceed to Akhiska, and co-operate with the Pasha of that province. Lieutenant Monteith accompanied Hussain Khan on this expedition into Georgia.

The Persians were almost invariably unsuccessful in this campaign, and on one occasion they lost their tents and baggage. They were successful in an attack they made on Hummamaloo. A marriage was taking place in the village, so that a number of Russians were in church at the time of attack. Forty Russians and many of the peasants were killed, and the women, including the bride, were carried off.

On the advice of Sir Harford Jones (British Envoy), Abbas Meerza now began to pay serious attention to the condition of his army. Lieutenant Lindsay (afterwards Sir H. Bethune) brought the artillery to a condition of great efficiency, fourteen pieces being well horsed and equipped. The other troops received new arms, and their equipment was greatly improved. A battalion of the infantry of Agerdbyan was placed under Lieutenant Christie. An arsenal and gun-carriage factory was started under English supervision. The army was well clothed, and nothing was wanting but an efficient commander-in-chief.

The fortifications of Khoi were rapidly progressing, and Abbasabad had been rendered capable of defence according to the plan traced out by Captain Lamie, a French officer.

By this the Persians obtained a strong position for the support of Erivan. Several field-works were constructed close to the most exposed roads ; and when, in July 1811, the Persian army was assembled at Nakshivan, Persia was in a better state of defence than she had ever been since the commencement of the war.

In September 1811 the Persian troops were at Nackshiwan, and a brigade under Captain Christie, with the horse artillery, was detached to Erivan, as it was supposed the Russians meditated an expedition.

In October the Russians advanced with 2,500 men and twelve guns, and destroyed many villages; but although the Persians had two favourable opportunities, they did not attack them, and shortly after the Persians, leaving a garrison at Erivan, returned to Tabreez, and dispersed as usual for the winter.

Early in 1812 the troops were ordered to the plains of Mogan. They marched for five days over high mountains covered with deep snow, and, having crossed the river, advanced on the Russian post of Sultanboot. The Russians were compelled to surrender, and the Persians destroyed the post, and brought away 2,000 families of Ibyects, nearly depopulating the region of the Karabaug. As a set-off to this, the Russians surprised the fortress of Akhalkalak, north of Gumri.

In August 1812 the Persians again took the field, and a division was detached to drive the Russians out of Talisch, situated on the Caspian, which afforded (from the position of the Isle of Sari) the best station for the Russian fleet.

The Russians fled from Lunkesan to Sari, and the chief of the district, Mustapha Khan, retired to the peninsula of Gameshiwan.

Ameer Khan (uncle of Abbas Meerza) refused to attack the works, although strongly urged to do so by the English officers.

A strong field-work was constructed at Laberun, and a garrison of 3,000 or 4,000 men, with four 12-pounders, being left to defend it, the British officers returned to the Persian camp at Aslandoose.

Meantime, owing to Napoleon's invasion of Russia, the policy of England was entirely changed, and our Ambassador was now as anxious for peace as he had before been to push on the war.

The English officers were withdrawn from the Persian army, and it was only at the earnest entreaty of Abbas Meerza that

8 *

Captains Christie and Lindsay were permitted to remain in the camp, and Lieutenant Monteith with the Erivan force.

Orders were given to the English officers to quit the Persian camp if any forward movement took place; but Abbas Meerza assured the British Ambassador he had no intention of advancing, and it was improbable that the Russians would attack the Persian army, as it was five times as numerous, supported by a superior artillery, and defended in front by a deep and rapid river.

The Persians were lulled into such perfect security that they did not plant picquets along the river, and even withdrew those posted by Major Christie.

On 27th October 1812 the Russians marched to the banks of the Arras, over a perfectly open country. They experienced great difficulty in crossing the river, and lost one of their guns with the horses harnessed to it, but they finally succeeded, and at 9 A.M. on 30th October, their troops were within a mile and a half of the Persians, the latter having no suspicion of their vicinity. The Persians were so totally unprepared, that Captain Lindsay had been ordered to employ his limber-boxes to receive treasure, and to proceed himself with all the mounted men to attend a hunting party beyond the Arras. He (Captain Lindsay) had just reached the point indicated, when he perceived a large body of men issuing from the brushwood in the bed of the river. He galloped back to camp, and arrived there just as the head of the Russian column entered it. The guns were withdrawn with great difficulty, but they were without ammunition; nearly all the arsenal and baggage having fallen into the hands of the enemy. The brigade under Major Christie had already been withdrawn by him. Abbas Meerza was distracted, and lost his head. Captain Lindsay could not fire his guns, having no ammunition. He offered to try to save some if Abbas Meerza's Body-guard would volunteer for the service; as only two volunteered, he turned to his own men, told off thirty of them, and provided each with a bag; and then was performed a feat of daring not to be surpassed in any army, and attended with a success quite unparalleled. This small body actually contrived to reach the artillery park, fill their bags with ammunition, and quit the camp on their return before the suspicions of the Russians were aroused. Two companies of Russian Yayas were sent to intercept them, but Major Christie with some light infantry advanced to their succour, and they regained the Persian camp without the loss of a man, bringing with them some musket cartridges and 300 rounds of 6-pound shot.

It was now proposed to attack the Russians. The Persians were at first very successful, and the Russians turned and fled towards their main body. Abbas Meerza, thinking that the Russians would retreat, resolved to remain on the ground near the hill of Timour. About midnight General Kutlerousky, the Russian commander, descended the Karsoo, marched round the Persian position, and attacked them from the side of Mogan. The Persians massed round the hill of Aslandoose began to fire, in the darkness and confusion, at one another. The attack was so sudden that the English officers had no alternative but to fight on the side of the Persians. Major Christie was shot in the neck, and more than half the battalion he had raised and disciplined fell in the attempt to bring him off. Their attempt was, however, unsuccessful, but afforded a noble proof of their attachment and devotion. Christie was discovered in the morning by the Russians, who offered assistance, but he had determined never to be taken alive. A report was sent to General Kutlerousky that there was a wounded English officer who refused to surrender. Orders were sent to disarm, and to secure him at all hazard. Christie, however, made a most desperate resistance, and is said to have killed six men before he was shot by a Cossack. His body was found by Dr. Cormick, and buried near the spot where he fell. Twelve out of fourteen English guns were taken, but Captain Lindsay rejoined the

Prince Royal in the pass, where he had recommended the troops should reassemble after the surprise of the camp.

The Russians' next object was to drive the Persians out of the post at Lunkesan, and reinstate Mustapha Khan in his Government of Talisch; and they advanced through Mogan in December. On reaching Lunkesan, they cannonaded the entrenchments; but finding their artillery inferior to that of the Persians, they resolved on an assault on the 12th January 1813. Their first attack was repulsed with heavy loss, but they made a second, Kutlerousky leading the assault himself. The place was carried, and many of the Persians killed. Kutlerousky was shot through the head, and though by a miracle he survived for many years, he never was fit for service again. Half of the Russian force was killed or disabled.

The Persian loss amounted to 3,000 men. About half of the Persian army were either disabled or taken prisoners. The ranks were, however, quickly filled up, and by the spring the army was as numerous as ever, while arms arrived from India, and guns were provided by the foundry at Tabreez to double those that had been lost; but the *morale* of the army was entirely changed.

In March and April 1813 the Russians made an irruption into the Erivan territory to collect provisions. They laid waste sixty villages, and carried off 500 carts of grain and 30,000 sheep.

The Persian troops were commanded by Hussain Khan, brother of the Sirdar, a most incompetent chief, who allowed two favourable opportunities of attacking the enemy to pass, and harassed his troops until they were quite exhausted. Lieutenant Monteith was in command of a battery of six guns, and some cavalry, at the ford of the Arras. Hussain Khan sent him orders to retire, but he refused to obey, as while he remained the Russians could not cross without being under fire. Hussain Khan then directed the gunners to bring away the guns, but they replied they only received orders from their own officers. The other troops, however, fell back, and Monteith thought it advisable to retire sufficiently to feed and rest his horses. Orders to change ground were sent him twice in the night, but he disregarded the orders, and thereby saved the men a march of twenty miles, as Hussain Khan actually came with his own troops to the place where Monteith was.

Hussain Khan's brother soon arrived, and determined to attack the heavily laden convoy. As the Russians were able to take up a covered position for their carts, the Persians were repulsed, after an action of three hours, and the Russians succeeded in carrying off the provisions, though with a loss of 250 men.

During the winter and spring, negotiations were carried on through the British ambassador. An armistice was agreed upon, and the preliminary treaty of Gulistan was contracted in October 1813, by which both parties were to retain the positions they then occupied.

During the years 1810 to 1813 there were four active campaigns, and during this time Lieutenant Monteith commanded a frontier force and the garrison of Erivan. He was engaged in many skirmishes, and was wounded in one at a place called Kulky Tippa.

In 1814 Mr. H. Ellis, in conjunction with Mr. Morier, was deputed to negotiate a finally definitive treaty between Great Britain and Persia. Lieutenant Monteith was secretary to Mr. Ellis. The treaty known as the Treaty of Teheran was signed on November 25th 1814, and continued in force till the war between England and Persia in 1856–57.

In 1819 it was found necessary to send an expedition against the El Jawasmi pirates of the Persian Gulf, who had become Wahabees, and were most desperate and audacious.

In 1816 Ibrahim Pasha took the field against the Wahabees, and in 1818, after a long siege, he captured Ed-Dir-'Iyyah, their capital, and sent their chief Abdallah in chains to Constantinople, where he was barbarously put to death.

The depredations of the Wahabee pirates did not cease with the fall of Ed-Dir-'Iyyah, and at length it became necessary to send another (the first was sent in 1810 under Colonel, afterwards Sir Lionel, Smith) English expedition against them. A small squadron under Captain Collier, and a force of 3,000 men commanded by General Sir William Grant Keir sailed from India in November 1819.

Captain William Monteith, who was at this time in Persia, accompanied the expedition as aide-de-camp to Sir William Grant Keir.

The piratical stronghold of Ras El Khima was besieged. The Arabs displayed extraordinary bravery and military skill, both at sea and on shore, but the place was captured by the English; 2,000 boats were burnt, and many Indians were released from slavery. A garrison of native troops was left ' there, which was afterwards removed to El Kishim. The hill-fort of Fyah, defended by a veteran Wahabee, was also captured after a gallant defence.

After the treaty of peace between Russia and Turkey, Lieutenant Monteith was appointed Commissioner to ascertain the limits of the respective countries, and Captains Lindsay and Hunt were allowed to remain in charge of the infantry and artillery, under condition that they should not be employed against any country at peace with England.

In 1821 war broke out between Persia and Turkey, arising out of insults offered to Persian pilgrims going to Mecca.

Muhammed Ali Meerza invaded the Baghdad Pashalik, and was on the point of taking Baghdad when he was carried off by cholera. His brother, Abbas Meerza, then invaded Turkish territory, and took Bayazid. The Turkish army advanced to Toprakala, but were severely defeated, and fled in confusion,

pursued by the Persian cavalry. Two thousand five hundred
Turks were killed, and all their camp equipage and baggage fell
into the hands of the victors.

Cholera then appeared, and put an end to the war. The long
threatened storm from the North was now about to burst over
Persia. The unsettled boundary question afforded a pretext for
constant disputes, and the Governor-General of Georgia took
every opportunity of exasperating the Persians. Believing that
war was inevitable, Abbas Meerza took the initiative and commenced hostilities in the summer of 1826. Abbas Meerza
crossed the Arras, occupied Talisch, and at first met with
success ; but on September 14th, 1826, he was defeated near the
river Jain, about four miles from Elizabethpol, and in November
was obliged to retreat across the Arras.

In the spring of 1827 General Yermaloff was superseded by
General Paskiewitch. In April the Russians captured Outchkelisea. Abbas Meerza and the Sirdar of Erivan advanced
to relieve Abbasabad which was invested by the Russians.

Paskiewitch crossed the Arras (by hides forming air-bladders)
and found the Persians posted in a very strong position. The
Russians forced their centre, and the Persians broke and fled,
leaving 5,000 men on the field. This was the battle of Jewan-
bulak, fought on 18th July 1827, and Abbasabad surrendered on
31st July. Abbas Meerza then tried to retake Outchkelisea.
A very bloody battle was fought at Abbasan on 29th August.
The Persians fought gallantly, and, though defeated, inflicted a
very severe loss on their enemies. One thousand two hundred
Russians were killed. Paskiewitch then advanced against the
Persians, forced Abbas Meerza to retreat across the Arras, and
laid siege to Erivan, which surrendered on 13th October. Abbas
Meerza retreated to Khoi, and on 10th October Tabreez was
surrendered to the Russians without a show of resistance. On
9th November the Persian Government submitted to the terms
of the conqueror, and hard conditions were wrung from it.

Negotiations were carried on at Tarkananchai; the British Envoy, ¡Sir John McDonald, acting as mediator. The treaty was signed on 21st February 1828. Erivan and Nakshivan were ceded to Russia, including Outchkelisea. Persia was forced to pay an indemnity of £4,000,000 for the expenses of the war, and was not to be allowed to have any armed vessels on the Caspian. Captain Monteith was appointed Commissioner for paying the indemnity, and part of the treasure was actually conveyed to the Russian camp by Captain Monteith. He states that much of the gold was Indian coin, spoil brought from Delhi by Nadir Shah. During the payment of the contribution levied on Persia, Captain Monteith had a great deal of communication with Prince Paskiewitch, having access to him at all hours when any difficulty arose about the payment, an annoyance that was constantly taking place from the caprice or insolence of the inferior agents. It was thus Monteith's acquaintance with Prince Paskiewitch began, and he was afterwards on terms of considerable intimacy with him, which led to Monteith accompanying the Russian army to Tiflis, and being an eye-witness of part of the operations against the Turks.

The whole Russian army assembled within thirty miles of Kars, and on 26th June 1828 it crossed the Arpachai, or Turkish frontier. The next day the Russian camp was at Tickniss, and on the 28th at Mecho, about twenty miles from Kars. The siege of Kars was undertaken, and it fell towards the end of July. Twenty-two mortars and 129 cannon with ammunition were found in the place, and 6,000 sacks of grain in the magazine.

The Russians lost thirteen officers and 400 men killed and wounded, while the Turks had 2,000 killed and wounded, and 1,361 prisoners. The whole garrison had amounted to 11,000 men; but 8,000 had either retired or been disarmed before the fortress surrendered.

Kousa Mahomed Pasha, Seraskier of Erzeroum, had assembled

50,000 men on the mountains of Soganlook. He made a forced march to relieve the place, but was just too late; and he was obliged to retreat as quickly as he had advanced, in the direction of Ardahan and Akhiska. The plague now made its appearance in the Russian army. General Paskiewitch acted with decision and good sense The different divisions were separated into distinct camps, and quarantines and fumigating chambers established in each; as soon as any decided case of plague showed itself, the patient was carried to the quarantine, and all articles capable of being washed were conveyed to the river, while others were fumigated and exposed to the air. Such articles as could not be subjected to either of these operations were burnt, but a recompense for their loss was made to the owners. The men by whom these duties were performed had wax-cloth coverings, and their hands and arms covered with oil and pitch. The whole army was obliged to bathe daily in the river; all military movements were suspended; and in twenty days the terrible pestilence was at an end in the army. Five hundred and thirty cases had been sent to the plague hospital, but only 267 died. The great secret in dealing with this fearful enemy appears to have been separating the men, especially the sick, as much as possible.

The fortress of Kars was now strengthened, some of the useless works destroyed, and the great tower at the south-east angle united to the citadel by a stone wall. A hundred of the Turkish guns were placed on the ramparts, and a garrison, under General Berymann, with ten field-pieces, was left in the place. On 17th July General Paskiewitch made a demonstration on the Erzeroum road, when the Seraskier retreated with great precipitation to the pass of the Soganlook, and the Russian army countermarched. It was now considered indispensable to call up the reserves, which could be most quickly accomplished by the Akhalkalak and Hertweis route, from whence the army could either advance on Akhiska, or place itself between that city and the Turkish army. By this means the Russian army would be covered by the Tchildar Lake. General Paskiewitch joined his park on the 18th July at Kembel. The passage of the baggage was here attended with great difficulty, for the descent to the Klaimchie was very rapid, and the great chain of the Tchildar on the opposite side offered still greater obstacles. The summit of Gouk Dang was gained on 21st, and on the 23rd the army encamped on the Gen-derra-soo, from which the white towers of Akhalkalak were visible.

General Paskiewitch sent a summons to surrender, but it was rejected with disdain.

The castle is 300 yards long, 60 or 80 broad, and stands at the angle formed by two small streams. It was defended by fourteen guns, and 1,000 men. A battery of eight guns and two mortars was established on the opposite side of the Gen-derra-soo (one of the small streams), and on another point, nearer to the place, a battalion had two guns and six cohorns.

The works were finished by dawn. Half-an-hour after the batteries opened, the enemy's batteries were silenced, and the principal tower began to crumble. General Paskiewitch sent another summons, which was a second time rejected. Another battery of four guns was now added, at a distance of 300 yards. The situation of the defenders now became desperate, and they were falling fast. Some attempted to escape, but were intercepted, and the besiegers made use of the ropes the defenders had used to escape to ascend the walls. The Russian flag was soon hoisted on the principal tower, and the troops entered on all sides. 600 of the garrison perished.

It was now necessary to take the fort of Hertweis, commanding the road to Akhiska. This is built on the summit of a high rock near the junction of the Kur and Akhakyck rivers; it was defended by fourteen guns and 200 men. Although apparently impregnable, it was taken by cavalry, who were dismounted for the purpose. Poto was also taken at this time by General

Hesse, after a siege of seven days. Direct communication with Georgia by two routes was now secured, and General Paskiewitch was quickly joined by Prince Bebutoff with 2,500 men of the reserve, and operations were immediately commenced against Akhiska, though Kousa Mahomed Pasha still occupied the Soganlook, with the intention of recovering Kars.

On the 30th July, General Mouravieff was ordered to advance from Hertweis in direction of Ispindza. General Paskiewitch now learnt that the Seraskier had at last moved from the Soganlook, and was advancing with 35,000 men and fifteen guns to cover Akhiska. He determined to advance, attack the Seraskier before he reached Akhiska, and drive him back to Soganlook. The route lay over a continued succession of rapid ascents and descents. They advanced forty miles in three days, and on the 3rd August the advanced guard took up a position on the right bank of the Kar. The whole of the Turkish army was encamped at the junction of the Kar and Akhiska, four miles from the town General Paskiewitch had not received all his expected reinforcements, for those under General Popoff had been detained in the pass of Bordgain.

However, on the 5th August the army forded the Kar, and formed in order of battle. The enemy made little opposition to the Russian advance Sixteen position guns of the Russians advanced at a trot, opened a heavy fire on the Turks, and dispersed them. The Russian cavalry was despatched in pursuit, and gained the height of Tanchan Pasha, which Prince Paskiewitch had been anxious to prevent the Seraskier from occupying, the ground being naturally strong and commanding the west side of the town. The Seraskier and Mustapha Pasha had brought 10,000 infantry and 15,000 cavalry, with some militia, amounting to 30,000, who formed four camps outside the town, the principal one being the Sookelisia (water church). The Russian army occupied a formidable position for attacking both the town and the Turks. Prince Paskiewitch felt the great

difficulty there would be in capturing a town containing a garrison nearly equal to his own army, and protected by a covering
army three times as large as the force he could bring against
them.

On 7th August he was reinforced by General Popoff with 1,800
men. The Russians attempted to surprise the Turks in their
principal camp. The rear-guard lost its way, and it was found
necessary to halt two miles from the enemy. The day broke,
and the Turks discovered them. A desperate contest took place,
which was for some time uncertain ; but the Russians ultimately
secured the victory, and the Turks, pressed on every side, abandoned their camp, and were pursued to the palisades of the town,
leaving four guns, standards, and 1,000 men dead on the
field.

The capture of this important point decided the battle ; the
remainder of the Turkish army, scattered over an extent of
seven miles, were cut off from the fortress, and the southern
heights were strongly occupied by the Russians, who now
threatened to take in flank the other positions of the Turks.

The Russian cavalry fell upon them suddenly. The Turks
fled in confusion to their remaining camps, and Kousa Mahomed
Pasha, though wounded in the thigh, made a vain attempt to
rally this confused mass ; when, finding a Cossack regiment
marching on his right to cut off his retreat, he hastened to enter
Akhiska with 5,000 infantry. The remainder of the Turkish
army sought their other camps in detached bodies, pursued by
the Cossacks and other irregular horse with much spirit.

The Turks had 1,200 men killed, and fled towards the Algura
mountains, the pursuit being continued all night. This battle
had been obstinately contested on some points. The Russians
took four entrenched camps, ten standards, and a quantity of
carts, provisions, and ammunition ; they lost 1 general, 7 officers,
and 73 men killed ; and 2 generals, 22 officers, and 377 men
wounded. Total casualties, 482.

The wreck of the Seraskier's army retired by Ardahan, hoping to be able to unite with the troops of the Pasha of Moush, then advancing.

General Berymann had been sent by Prince Paskiewitch to Ardahan to intercept the fugitives, and Prince Tcherkaskoi surprised the rear of the Pasha's army, dispersed his troops, and recovered a number of Christians he was carrying into slavery.

The Turkish army being dispersed, the siege of Akhiska could be undertaken without interruption.

The Turkish entrenchments which had been taken were turned against the enemy, and at daylight a large battery was finished in front of bastion No. 3 of outer line of defences of Akhiska, at a distance of 400 yards from the palisaded entrenchment, and 1,000 yards from the citadel. This battery had four mortars, four 24-pounders, two howitzers, twelve 16-pounders. six field-pieces, eight light guns, and eight Turkish guns. Akhiska was now summoned, but the only answer returned was that the men of Akhiska were determined to bury themselves under the ruins of their town. The troops in the town were 15,000, and the entrenched line mounted seventy pieces of artillery.

The Russian guns all opened fire at the same time ; the suburbs took fire in several places, and the shot did great execution. Other batteries were made by the Russians, and the Turks made several sorties, which were repulsed. On the night of the 12th the place was completely invested.

A second summons was sent by General Paskiewitch to the garrison, but it was rejected with contempt.

On the 13th and 14th breaching batteries were erected.

The 15th August was selected for the assault, the hour being 4 P.M., at a time when the Turks generally retired to their quarters to sleep and refresh themselves ; and this being the hour when the Russians were accustomed to relieve their guards and working-parties, the assembly of the storming-parties occasioned no alarm. The principal attack was made on bastion No. 3, and two other false attacks were made on other points.

The Turks being completely surprised the bastion was carried in a few minutes; but, roused by the news, the garrison and inhabitants flocked to oppose the Russians. Desperate fighting took place, and it was not till 7 p.m. that the attack was decided. At that hour the howitzer shells set fire to some of the buildings, and the General determined to try to burn down the town. The town was set on fire in several places, but the houses had still to be carried by storm, as those barricaded refused to surrender. The fire extended with great rapidity, so that the garrison was forced to retreat to the citadel. The tower of Kia Daiy was now attacked; this was abandoned by the Turks, and five guns fell into the hands of the Russians, which were at once turned on the Turks. The garrison was now entirely withdrawn from the north and west faces, but the besieged still occupied No. 1 and No. 2 batteries of the old palisades. These were attacked in flank. The Turks in No. 2 battery surrendered, with two guns and five standards, while Commandant Simonwitch carried No. 1. The Russians were now masters of all the palisaded line, and five-sixths of the place, and the flames quickly forced the Turks to evacuate the remainder, so that at 3 a.m. the firing had entirely ceased.

A deputation from the garrison now waited on the General, and demanded a five days' truce. This was, of course, refused, and they were told that the Russian artillery would be directed against the citadel. The garrison must soon have been compelled to surrender at discretion, but it was preferred to allow the few that remained to depart with their baggage and arms. At 8 p.m the Russian standard was hoisted on the citadel. In this obstinately-contested assault the garrison lost 5,000 men; of 400 Artillery only fifty remained—of 100 Janissaries the chief alone, the rest died to a man; of 1,800 Lazi, 1,300, and of the inhabitants 3,000, were killed. Several women in male attire were found among the slain. The Russians lost 2 generals, 8 other officers, and 118 men killed ; and 1 general, 51 officers, and 437 men wounded. Total, 617.

A force was now sent against Abskur, which surrendered at the first summons. Another force was sent against Ardagan, situated at the junction of the Kars and Erzeroum roads, a force being at the same time directed to advance from Kars. This place also surrendered. Many districts of Akhiska still refusing to submit, General Paskiewitch marched to Ardagan, and the report of this movement spread such terror to the gates of Erzeroum, that part of the Turkish forces which had begun to reassemble, retired or dispersed. All the chiefs of Akhiska sent in their submission, and the authority of the Russians was finally established The province of Bayazid was occupied by Prince Tcherfechlwadza, a Georgian nobleman, and Major-General in the Russian service.

The campaign was now ended, and the troops took up their winter quarters.

In this campaign of 1828, which only lasted five months, the Pashaliks of Kars, Akhiska, and Bayazid had been conquered, three fortresses, three castles, 313 cannon, 195 standards, eleven howitzers, and 8,000 prisoners had been captured.

The Russian army consisted of only 18,000, and their total loss had been 3,200.

Lieutenant-Colonel Monteith was present with the Russian main army throughout this campaign, and at its close he was ordered by Colonel McDonald, Envoy to the Court of Persia, to remain in Persia till the frontier between Russia and Persia had been settled. He was not able to leave Persia till October 1829.

He does not, however, appear to have hurried home, for we next find him as a volunteer at the French capture of Algiers in June 1830.

The French effected a landing on the peninsula of Lidz-el-

Ferruck, five leagues west of Algiers, on 14th June, and converted it into an entrenched camp. The enemy occupied Staweli and constructed some redoubts.

The French force was 21,000, while that of the Algerians was estimated at 35,000 to 60,000.

On the 17th the battle of Staweli commenced. It lasted from 4 A.M. to 7 P.M., when the enemy were driven back with great slaughter, and Staweli was occupied by the French.

On the 24th the Algerians attacked the French, but were repulsed.

Next day there was a great deal of hard fighting, the enemy having planted some batteries on hills in front of Mount Bougareah.

Before investing Algiers itself, the Emperor's fort had to be taken. On the 28th the French were within five miles of this position.

At 2 A.M. on the 29th the French surprised the Algerians, and drove them out, and at 2 P.M. the French General found himself on the top of Bougareah.

At daybreak on 4th July the French batteries opened fire on the Emperor's fort with tremendous effect. The General in command of the fort was ordered by the Dey to retire to Kassambah, and leave three negroes to blow up the fort. One of them was killed by a cannon ball; the other two, in revenge, fired a cannon three times; a shot took off the leg of one of them, when the last retired to the tower with two flags. The breach was now almost practicable, when a terrible explosion took place, and the fort was blown to pieces.

In half an hour the French sappers were repairing the ruins, and their engineers had broken ground within 700 yards of Kassambah.

At 2 P.M. a flag of truce was announced, and at 12 noon on the 5th, the French General and staff entered Kassambah, and all the other forts were taken possession of.

In a few days the Dey of Algiers embarked for Naples, and the French became possessors of Algiers.

Lieutenant-Colonel Monteith, K.L.S., did not return to India till 6th July 1832, when he was appointed to act as Chief Engineer of Madras.

In January 1834 Lieutenant-Colonel Garrard returned from England, and, being senior to Monteith by ten years, was appointed Chief Engineer, while Monteith took up the post of Superintending Engineer at the Presidency.

On 2nd September 1836 Colonel Garrard died at Ootacamund, and on the 9th Lieutenant-Colonel Monteith became Chief Engineer, which post he retained till 18th July 1842. He became Major-General on 23rd November 1841, and retired from the service on 10th December 1847.

9 *

CHAPTER IV.

THE FIRST CHINESE WAR.*

First Chinese War.—Tinghae occupied.—Captain Anstruther kidnapped.—Mrs Noble.—Hostilities recommenced, January 1841.—Preliminaries for peace. —Hong Kong occupied.—Hostilities resumed.—Capture of Bogue Forts.— Hostilities again suspended.—Arrival of Sir Hugh Gough.—Anstruther released.—Rundall wounded.—Terms of Peace.—British troops attacked.— Gallant conduct of Hadfield and 37th Madras Native Infantry.—Amoy entered.—Attack on Chin-hae.—Ningpo occupied.—Attack of Chinese on Ningpo, and on Ching-hae.—We attack Tsekee.—Changki Pass.—Capture of Chapoo.—Repulse from a Joss house.—Fleet proceed to Woosung.—March on Shanghae.—Shanghae occupied.—And evacuated.—Ching Keangfoo.—Its capture.—Heroic conduct of General Hàiling, the Tartar general.—Advance on Nanking.—Treaty of Nanking signed.

"This war was not very popular in England, as it was supposed by many that it was undertaken to enforce upon the Chinese the opium traffic, and it was considered a domineering and disgraceful attempt to compel the importation of an article strictly forbidden by their own laws."

"The opium question should be regarded merely as a spark blown into a mine, which during the past half century the vindictiveness and arrogance of the Chinese Government had been gradually charging; and it can be no more considered the

* This account is chiefly abbreviated from *The Chinese War*, by Lieutenant John Ouchterlony, F.G.S., Madras Engineers. Published by Saunders and Ottley in 1844.

primary cause of the war than can the match which ignites the train be styled the cause of the breach made by the explosion. The quarrel was on our part just and unavoidable, and that the demands of our Government were reasonable, and based upon the principle of reciprocity in commercial intercourse, must be allowed after a dispassionate consideration of all the circumstances of the case."

Singapore was the rendezvous of the force, forming what was called the "Eastern expedition." The ships of war assembled at Singapore in May 1840 were—the *Wellesley*, 74; *Conway*, 28; *Alligator*, 28; *Cruiser*, 18; *Larne*, 20; *Algerine*, 10; *Rattlesnake*, 6, troop-ship; *Atalanta* and *Madagascar*, Indian service steamers; and twenty-six transports. These had on board H.M.'s 18th, 26th, and 49th; a battalion of Bengal native troops, two companies of Royal Artillery, with 9-pounder field-pieces and 12-pounder howitzers, and two companies* of Madras Sappers and Miners, with a large Engineer establishment from Madras, under the command of Captain Pears (now Major-General Sir T. T. Pears, K.C.B.).

Colonel Burrell of the 18th Regiment commanded the force.

After being detained three weeks at Singapore, the expedition arrived off the Ladrones, near Macao, on the 21st June. The Commander, Sir Gordon Bremer, ran into Macao Roads with the *Wellesley*, to communicate with Captain Elliot, R.N., who was the Chief Superintendent of British trade in China.

The river and port of Canton were blockaded on the 28th June.

On the 24th the fleet outside the Ladrones was ordered to sail for the most southern island of the Chusan Archipelago. The whole fleet anchored to leeward of Buffalo island.

---

* A. and B. companies were at Kurnool. Being ordered to Madras for service, they left that place and proceeded by forced marches to Madras. They marched *vid* Cuddapah and Circumbaddy, and reached this last place in sixteen days.

The Commodore reconnoitered the Chusan northern harbour, and found the Chinese quite unprepared for a hostile visit. The *Wellesley* and several of the other ships entered the harbour of Ting-hae.

A deputation from the capital, consisting of the two principal Chinese functionaries with retinue, came on board the *Wellesley*, and finally left with the understanding that, if before 2 P.M. next day no pacific overtures were made, the town would be attacked.

On the morning of the 5th July all the transport succeeded in entering the harbour, and the troops were prepared for landing. At 2 P.M., no overtures for a peaceable occupation of the town having been received, a shotted gun was fired from the *Wellesley* at a round tower. It was immediately returned from the junk of the Chinese admiral, and the fire shortly became general. In a short time the fire of the enemy had generally ceased.

The troops were now directed to land, and the grenadiers of the 18th and a detachment of Royal Marines were formed on the landing-place in a few minutes, and commenced the ascent of Joss-house Hill. These were the first European troops who had ever landed on the shores of China as conquering invaders. A joss-house was taken possession of, and some guns of the Madras Artillery, with a detachment of Madras Sappers and the regiment of Cameronians, defiled through the narrow streets, and pushed forward till within 400 or 500 yards of the ramparts, and placing four field-pieces and howitzers in position, threw shot and shells into the enemy's works, while the Sappers loop-holed and strengthened some farmhouses for occupation as an advanced post.

Colonel Burrell did not think it prudent to precipitate his attack, and the troops were ordered to prepare for action early in the morning.

During the night the approaches to the city gates were

reconnoitered on two points by Captain Pears and a party of Engineers. The reconnoitering party were fired on.

When the morning dawned, Colonel Burrell advanced to reconnoitre the main gate. It was then discovered that the enemy had abandoned the place during the night. Two or three officers got over the wall, and, removing the bags of grain with which the gates were blocked up, opened an entrance for the leading column.

It was the 5th July that Ting-hae was occupied by our troops. Colonel Burrell was appointed Military Commandant and Civil Commissioner.

A squadron, consisting of the *Wellesley*, 74, the *Blonde*, 42, the *Modeste*, 20, the *Pylades*, 20, the *Madagascar* steamer, and two or three transports, was now prepared to proceed to the Pei-ho ; but before starting, the Admiral sent a messenger in a steamer to Chin-hae, at the mouth of the Ning-po, with a letter from Lord Palmerston to the Emperor's chief advisers. The letter was received by a mandarin, detained long enough to admit of its contents being transcribed, and then returned with an intimation that its style and subject were such as they could not venture to expose to the glance of the Imperial eye.

A similar letter was sent to Amoy in the *Blonde*. The mandarins not only refused to receive the letter, but fired on an unarmed boat ; and the frigate thereupon opened her broadside on the fort and town walls, and continued to do so till all resistance had ceased.

On the 30th July the Admiral and Captain Elliot set sail for the Bay of Petcheelee, having previously proclaimed the blockade of the Ning-po river, and of the line of coast north as far as the Yang-tse-kiang.

While our troops occupied Chusan they suffered very heavily from fever and dysentery. From the 13th July to the 31st December 1840 the total deaths in the European regiments alone was 448.

Madras Artillery ...	...	16
H.M.'s 18th Regiment	...	52
H.M.'s 26th Regiment	...	238
H.M.'s 49th Regiment	...	142
Total ...		448

The expedition to Petcheelee proceeded north, and, passing Shang-ting on the 5th August, anchored off the mouth of the Pei-ho on the 9th.

On the 10th Captain Elliot approached the shore, got safely over the bar, and anchored off one of the low forts which guarded the approach to Ta-koo. Immediately the steamer anchored she was boarded by a messenger, who informed Mr. Morrison (Captain Elliot's presence not being made known) that Keeshen, a member of the Imperial Cabinet, had arrived near Ta-koo to receive letters, &c.

On the 13th a mandarin came out with supplies.

On the 15th an aide-de-camp of the Governor, a mandarin named Showpei Pih came off. (He got the nickname of "Captain White," Pih signifying white.) He was charged to receive the letter from Lord Palmerston, and was instructed to state that it would be sent to Pekin, and a suitable answer returned in ten days.

This was at once acceded to, and during that time the vessels of the squadron cruised about in various directions, picking up information both geographical and with reference to supplies.

On the 27th the fleet again assembled, but there was no sign of an Imperial messenger, so it was determined to make a hostile demonstration; and on the 28th morning the light squadron was to run in as close as possible to the Ta-koo forts.

A mandarin hastened out to meet them, and said that an answer had been received from Pekin earlier than usual, and a communication from Keeshen had been sent out to the anchorage of the flag-ship on the 24th and 25th, but finding the British vessels still absent, the despatch of Keeshen had been taken to Ta-koo. It was now produced, and contained a proposal from the Minister to Captain Elliot for a conference on shore.

Captain Elliot at once consented, and it took place on the 30th. The result of the interview was a further reference to Pekin, and additional delay.

On the 8th September the final reply of the Imperial Cabinet was received, which was to the effect that the matter could be better discussed at Canton, where the difficulties had arisen, and that the Emperor had deputed Keeshen to proceed thither, and requested the British plenipotentiaries to meet him there. This was agreed to, and the fleet left the anchorage on the 15th September.

On the day after the arrival of the squadron at Chusan, the Admiral issued an official notification of the truce which had been agreed upon.

Inquiry was now made into the cause of the great sickness, and active measures were taken to fortify and protect the British position in the island. The Chief Engineer, Captain Pears, proceeded to scarp the slopes of Joss-house Hill, and to excavate the foundations of a retaining wall to form enceinte of a small fort to crown its summit. The batteries were marked out and commenced, but it was soon found that, to give the work its proper strength, it would be necessary to remove a mass of earth which had at first been considered a part of the hill, but which proved to be a vast accumulation of coffins built upon tiers, with earth and stones, so as to form a mound. This had to be cut away at once, and in the course of a few days hundreds of coffins were to be seen tumbling over the cliffs, or rolled down into the fields at the foot of the hill. The sappers engaged in building the fort were directed to collect the remains and burn them to ashes with the fuel furnished by the coffins.

During August and September the Chinese spies, and others in the pay of mandarins, commenced the practice of kidnapping, which was at a subsequent period carried to a serious extent. Amongst others they seized Captain Anstruther, of the Madras Artillery.

About this time, also, a transport brig, the *Kite*, was wrecked on a sand-bank between Chapoo and the mouth of the Yang-tse-kiang, and all on board were seized by the Chinese.

Mrs. Noble, the wife of the commander of the brig, was on board, and was subjected to much cruel treatment and indignity. She was confined in a cage three feet and a half in length for thirty-six consecutive hours, and exposed in the market-places of several towns to the gaze of the populace, and to the jeers and hooting of a canaille who consider any woman who quits her home to appear abroad, save in the seclusion of a sedan-chair, to have lost all claims to the consideration due to her sex.

During all this time surveys were made of the passages up the Yang-tse-kiang. The chart constructed showed that up to thirty miles west of Tsung-ming Island, there was a passage free from danger of any magnitude, and navigable for vessels of considerable tonnage.

An elaborate survey was at the same time proceeding at Chusan of the archipelago and adjacent main line of coast.

The plenipotentiaries quitted Chusan on the 15th November, and arrived at Macao on the 20th.

The Admiral sent the *Queen*, on the 21st, to the Bogue to announce the arrival of the plenipotentiaries, and to deliver a despatch for the High Commissioner. The *Queen* carried a white flag at her mainmast head, and on approaching Chuenpee she sent a boat with a white flag towards the Chinese position. A gun was discharged at the boat from the batteries, the shot from which struck the water so near her bows as to throw a sheet of spray over her crew. The boat was at once recalled, and the *Queen* stood in towards the fort. The steamer threw several shells and shot into the Chinese lines, and then returned to Macao. Shortly after, an apology was sent by the Chinese authorities for the untoward mistake made by the Commandant of Chuenpee.

On the 26th November, Keeshen made his public entry into Canton.

On the 20th it was announced that Rear-Admiral the Hon. George Elliot had resigned the command of the fleet into the hands of Commodore Sir Gordon Bremer.

Until the latter end of December negotiations proceeded between Captain Elliot and Keeshen in a satisfactory manner; but, unfortunately, political intrigue was at that time too powerful in Pekin. The state of the public mind in Canton, the tone adopted in edicts which began to make their appearance, the activity displayed by the Chinese military authorities at the Bogue, and Chuenpee, and the delay and procrastination which marked the conduct of Keeshen, all tended to create a belief that hostilities were about to recommence.

Captain Elliot, in the *Wellesley*, remained at Lintin, near the forts of Chuenpee and the Bogue, supported by a formidable fleet. Day after day wore on, bringing no indication of peace. The patience of Captain Elliot began at last to give way, and he determined on active hostilities.

On the 7th January 1841 the troops destined for the land attack on the fort of Chuenpee were landed about two miles south of the point of attack, while the steamers stood in, anchored abreast of the Chinese batteries, and commenced the action. The Chinese opened a smart fire as the heads of the columns came within range, but upon the ships of war ceasing their firing as the troops neared its line, the fort was carried at a rush.

Many of the enemy were killed, while the British had only thirty eight men wounded.

While this was going on, a squadron under Captain Scott, R.N., proceeded towards the fort of Tycocktow on the opposite side of the river, bombarded it for an hour, landed some marines, &c., and drove the enemy from the works.

At the same time, the *Nemesis*, a small iron vessel of light draught, ran in among the junks in Anson's Bay, and burnt no less than eleven of them. In the meantime the 74-gun ships went higher up the river to prepare for the attack on the defences of the Bogue.

The 7th and 8th January were employed in dismantling the captured works and disabling the guns, ninety-seven in number. The troops were then all re-embarked, and the signal made for the leading ships to weigh. As the fleet was gradually closing on the great Anunghoy battery, a mean-looking boat appeared, rowed by an old woman, and carrying a white flag. The envoy on board (a quack-doctor of low degree) bore a request from the Chinese Commander-in-Chief, Admiral Kwan, on the part of Keeshen, to suspend hostilities, pending a further discussion of terms for a treaty. The signal to annul action was at once hoisted on board the *Wellesley*, much to the disappointment of the fleet.

On the 20th Captain Elliot announced that he had concluded preliminary arrangements with the Imperial Commissioners, involving the following conditions :—

1st. The cession of Hong Kong in perpetuity.

2nd. Indemnity of six millions of dollars.

3rd. Direct official intercourse between the two countries on an equal footing.

4th. Trade of Canton to be opened.

Hong Kong was taken possession of on the 26th January 1841, and the British flag, for the first time, hoisted on it.

On the 23rd the *Columbine*, one of the fastest sailers in the fleet, left with instructions to the authorities in Chusan to evacuate the island without delay, and proceed at once to Hong Kong.

On the 27th January the plenipotentiary proceeded up the

river in the *Nemesis* to near Whampoa, to hold a conference with Keeshen.

On the 13th February Captain Elliot had another interview with Keeshen, but no direct result affecting the opening of the trade accrued therefrom, and it became manifest that another appeal to arms was inevitable. The *Nemesis* was despatched to demand a written ratification of the Chuenpee Treaty. The *Nemesis* returned with an unfavourable report. Captain Elliot once more reluctantly ordered the resumption of hostilities.

On the 20th February Sir Gordon Bremer proceeded with the fleet to the vicinity of Anunghoy, and on the 25th the fleet intended for the reduction of the Bogue forts was assembled near the island of South Wangtung, and a close reconnoissance made of the defences of the enemy. The ordinary passage into the Canton river was between the islands of North and South Wangtung and the Peak of Anunghoy; but there was also a safe channel to the west of the Wangtung Islands, and two batteries had been built to render the latter difficult, one on the west end of North Wangtung, of forty-five guns, and the other on the opposite, or right bank of the river, of fifty guns. From Anunghoy a strong chain had been carried right across the eastern passage to a rocky point near a formidable battery on North Wangtung. South of the North Wangtung island, about point-blank distance, is situated another island, affording an admirable position for the establishment of a battery to enfilade those on the east and west points of North Wangtung.

Accordingly, on the evening of the 25th, Captain Birdwood,* with the Engineer officers, marked out and erected a sand-bag battery on a saddle in the middle of South Wangtung, and before daylight on the 26th three howitzers were in position. The working-party suffered no loss, although the enemy's batteries fired heavily during the night. The howitzers opened

* Captain W. J. Birdwood was in command of the A Company: he served throughout the whole campaign, and returned with the Sappers in January 1843.

at daybreak, and threw shells into the two low batteries on North Wangtung with great effect. Owing to a calm, it was not till 11 A.M. that the leading ships were able to move into the positions assigned to them.

The naval arrangements were now carried out in an admirable manner. The *Wellesley*, 74, the *Druid*, 44, and the *Modeste*, 18, entered the western channel, and anchored abreast of the battery at the south end of North Wangtung, which they engaged with their starboard batteries; while shells and shot were thrown from their larboard 68-pounders at the battery on the opposite bank. Meanwhile, the advance squadron, *Calliope, Herald, Samarang, Alligator*, &c., passed on to the north of the Chinese defences. The firing now became general on both sides. After the cannonade had lasted about an hour, Sir Le F. Senhouse landed under Anunghoy with 300 seamen and marines, and carried the works with but little resistance. North Wangtung was carried in the same manner by the detachment of all arms under Major Pratt.

The whole line of the defences of the Bogue having now been carried, except the fort on the west side of the river, the *Nemesis* was sent, with some boats of the *Wellesley* in tow, to expel the Chinese troops. Directly the marines landed, the fort and encampment were abandoned by the Chinese. The British loss was small, while of the Chinese fully 500 fell, including their brave chief, Admiral Kwan, whose body was found near the gate of Anunghoy.

The day after the action a party of Chinese came with a coffin to remove it, and as the procession moved away minute-guns were fired from the *Blenheim*, and the Chinese ensign was hoisted half staff high.

Large parties of seamen were employed, under Lieutenant Johnston, of the Madras Engineers,* in destroying the long

* Lieutenant Rundall was also appointed to this work, but was subsequently ordered to join a portion of the force higher up the river.

line of batteries at Anunghoy, and in a very short time the imposing granite fortifications which had so long been the pride and boast of the Southern provinces were crumbled into ruins. The three formidable batteries were blown up. Their revetments, with their parapets, were formed with large blocks of granite, varying from forty to eighty feet; the intervening spaces were filled up with stones, brick, and clay, while the upper surface of the ramparts was covered with large slabs of granite

The north Anunghoy fort was 462 feet long, with a rampart twenty-four feet thick, mounting forty guns. The south Anunghoy long fort was 771 feet in length, and its rampart nearly thirty feet thick; it mounted sixty-four guns. The total length of the rampart of the south Anunghoy circular fort was 742 feet, its width nearly thirty feet, and it mounted forty guns.

The majority of the guns were spiked, had their trunnions knocked off, and balls wrapped in wet canvas rammed tightly into them. Six of the largest were burst by loading them with a charge of thirty-two pounds of powder, and then tamping them well up to the muzzle with small bags of sand. A smaller charge than thirty-two pounds was found to be useless, as it merely blew out the sand tamping. A hundred and seventy-two guns were found in the forts. The forts were destroyed by Chinese powder, which was found in considerable quantities in the magazines of each fort. Between 9,000 and 10,000 pounds of powder were required for the destruction of the forts.

A garrison was placed in North Wangtung. While the 74-gun ships and transports remained at the Bogue for the demolition of the forts, the advanced squadron, under Captain Herbert, proceeded up the river to attack a strong position at Second Bar, where a strong raft had been constructed from bank to bank, flanked on one side by the guns of a large entrenchment, and on the other by the battery of the *Cambridge*, the ship purchased by the Chinese for warlike purposes before the arrival of the expedition.

The attack took place on the 27th, and was successful; the enemy were driven from their entrenchments, the raft was cut through and destroyed, and the *Cambridge* was boarded, taken, and set on fire, when she blew up with a very loud report, "which must have been heard at Canton," to use the words of the despatch.

Captain Herbert's squadron anchored at Whampoa Reach, and on the 2nd March the *Sulphur*, with boats, had an engagement with a masked battery on the north-east end of Whampoa Island, which was carried.

Howqua's fort, or folly, was next occupied, and four vessels came to anchor in the stream between the fort and Napier's Island.

On the 3rd March there was another suspension of hostilities. About this time Major-General Sir Hugh Gough, K.C.B., arrived from Madras to assume command of the land forces.

On the 7th March Captain Elliot announced that he had again been deceived, and that, the armistice having expired, Napier's Fort and some works in advance had been occupied. All the enemy's works on the banks of the river, as far as the factories of Canton, were seized, as well as those of the great branch called the Macao Passage.

On the 20th His Excellency announced that another suspension of hostilities had been agreed upon between the Imperial Commissioner Yang and himself. About this time Yihshan was appointed Generalissimo and "rebel-queller," and Yang to be Assistant Minister in the room of Keeshen, who was degraded and recalled to Pekin. Before this suspension of hostilities, the *Nemesis* conducted a series of successful operations in the passage of the Broadway. This Broadway forms a back, or western communication between Macao and Whampoa. Through this, the *Nemesis*, with a small flotilla of boats, made its way on the

12th and 13th, in spite of the shallowness of the channel. At every favourable point well-constructed batteries were found to dispute her passage, and in the many other gallant dashes made to carry them, no fewer than 105 pieces of cannon were taken between Macao and the posts of defence nearest to Whampoa, and nine junks were seized and burnt. The Broadway had never before this been entered by a British vessel. It had, indeed, been considered inaccessible, except by vessels of the lightest draught.

During the early part of this month the fleet and late garrison of Chusan arrived in two divisions, bringing the prisoners from Ningpo. These prisoners were only just released in good time, as a few days after their release, an edict arrived from Pekin directing Eleepso on no account to surrender them, but to take summary vengeance on several of them, especially marking Captain Anstruther (Madras Artillery) as an object of peculiar detestation to his Imperial Majesty.

After the arrangement of the armistice at Canton, the fleet, with the exception of a few light craft left to watch the factories, dropped down the river and returned to Hong-Kong, where Sir Hugh Gough lost no time in re-organising the small force. Early in April an edict was received from Pekin conveying the sentiments of the Emperor upon the capture and destruction of the Bogue forts, breathing the direst vengeance against the English, and declaring that both Powers could not stand under the same heaven, and that one of the two must forthwith perish. Keeshen, as we have seen, was degraded. He was commanded to repair, without delay, to Pekin, there to be handed over to the Board of Punishments to be tried for the traitorous offences he had committed against his enlightened employer!

At this time, a ruthless outrage was perpetrated on Captain Stead of the *Pestonjee* transport, which had come direct from London to China. Thinking that it was still in possession of the British, he landed on Kittow Point for supplies; he was murdered by villagers, instigated by soldiers. This cowardly murder caused a deep feeling of indignation and excitement among the British, and Captain Elliot despatched the *Columbine* to the Government of the Kiang province demanding instant redress. All intercourse with the brig was refused at Chusan, and she returned to Hong-Kong.

On 11th April Captain Elliot paid a visit to Canton, and had an interview with the Kwang-chow-foo, and was satisfied that it had now become his duty to put forth the whole of his strength, in order to bring the quarrel to an early conclusion. The whole of the force accordingly passed the Bogue on the 20th.

On the 21st Sir Le F. Senhouse took the *Blenheim* up the Macao passage, and on the 22nd the whole fleet had assembled there, and the next morning the two chiefs of the combined forces proceeded to Canton to reconnoitre. On the night of the 21st a number of fire-rafts were sent adrift upon the cutter *Louisa*, and schooner *Aurora*. The *Modeste*, *Pylades*, and *Algerine* engaged the batteries with as good effect as the uncertain light would permit, while the boats towed the fire-rafts clear of danger to the ships. Meantime the *Nemesis* was carrying on a contest with the Shaming battery, and after a time succeeded in almost silencing it, in spite of the darkness. In the morning the funnel and paddle-boxes of the *Nemesis* were found to be riddled with balls, but the casualties among the crew were trifling. The Shaming battery being deserted, the *Nemesis* pushed up the river and destroyed a flotilla of thirty-nine war-junks and boats. The Chinese mob, meantime, finding the factories deserted, began a work of destruction and plunder. After the mob had been in possession for two hours, they were dislodged by a detachment of Chinese troops, who completed the work of plunder. The mask being now fairly thrown off, the general and the commodore lost no time in bringing the whole of their forces to bear upon the point most favourable for a decisive blow at the city.

On the 24th May the troops, having been put into boats,

started for the creek towed by the *Nemesis*. The force was divided into two columns; the right, under Major Pratt of the 26th Regiment, was to land and occupy the factories; the left, landed at Tsinghae, under Major-General Burrell, and marched on the morning of the 25th in the direction of the heights selected as the first point of attack. There were four forts on these heights which formed, collectively, a formidable position. Some guns, &c. having, through most extraordinary exertions on the part of the artillery, been brought up and placed in position 300 or 400 yards from the forts, a heavy fire was opened upon them at 8 A.M., which was returned with spirit for an hour, when the columns of attack having been formed, the advance was sounded, and the whole of the forts were carried at the point of the bayonet. As soon as the forts had fallen, the Chinese garrison opened upon them along the whole northern face of the city, and the fire was so well directed and steadily sustained that the British forces suffered greater losses than they had in the operations by which the forts had been carried. The fire on both sides slackened towards evening, leaving the British in possession of the whole chain of heights which commanded the city on the north-east face, and masters of a formidable entrenched camp a short distance to the eastward, which had been carried in the morning by the 18th and 49th Regiments, though not without considerable loss of men and officers, including a brave and zealous officer of the Madras Engineers (Lieutenant J. W. Rundall) who received a dangerous grape-shot wound in the right knee. The want of ammunition prevented Sir Hugh Gough from undertaking any serious operation against the place next day, which was employed in bringing up cartridges and shot, as well as additional guns, and the artillery exerted themselves so greatly, that before night fifteen pieces were in position before the walls, with a plentiful supply of ammunition. The mode of attack was obvious, as opposite the fort on the left of our position was a hill (within

10 *

the city walls) of a commanding position, which, once possessed
by the British, would place the city at their mercy. Arrangements were made to escalade near a high building close to the
walls, while a second party was ordered to blow in the north
gate, and the parties were to unite in a general advance upon
the hill. When the attack was on the point of being made, a
messenger arrived from the Plenipotentiary, acquainting the
commanders that hostilities were again suspended, the Commissioner and Governor of Canton having proposed terms which
had been accepted.

The terms were :—

1st. The Imperial Commissioners and troops to quit the
city within six days, and proceed to a distance of
sixty miles.

2nd. Six millions of dollars to be paid ; one million to be
paid before sunset of the 27th.

3rd. The British troops to remain in position. If the sum
agreed upon be not paid within seven days, to be
increased to seven millions. If not within fourteen
days, to eight millions, and if not within twenty
days, to nine millions. When the whole was paid,
the British forces were to return, without the Bocca
Tigris.

4th. Losses sustained by destruction of factories, and of
the Spanish brig *Bilbaino*, to be paid within a week.

5th. The Kwang-chow-foo to produce full power to conclude these arrangements.

The troops remained in position whilst the ransom-money
was being delivered ; after four days, Captain Elliot having
notified that five millions had been paid, and the remainder
accounted for, the force was re-embarked and dropped down to
the Bogue, where the garrison of North Wangtung was received
on board and conveyed to the rendezvous at Hong-Kong.
Before, however, the British troops had evacuated the position

on the heights, they were attacked by the inhabitants of the surrounding villages. These were soon dispersed, and the British troops having destroyed a village in which the enemy had taken post, were about to retire, when a body of 5,000 or 6,000 strong was seen descending the opposite heights and advancing in a determined manner.

The weather was fearfully oppressive, but it soon changed, and was followed by a heavy thunderstorm. Some rockets were thrown among the advancing masses, but as they were not checked by this, a general charge of the whole British line was ordered, and the enemy were soon put to flight. Torrents of rain now came down, and a retreat was ordered towards the heights occupied by the main body of the army. The muskets of the troops were furnished with flint locks, and by this time were utterly useless, and as the various detachments withdrew the Chinese harassed them in a most spirited manner, closing and engaging with the troops hand to hand.

The rain still continued, and, owing to the dense mist, a company of the 37th Madras Native Infantry, fifty or sixty strong, became separated from the main body, and found themselves in front of a formidable body of Chinese. The company was commanded by Lieutenant Hadfield, supported by two subalterns, Devereux and Berkeley. The sepoys never wavered for a moment, and succeeded in making their way towards the heights as far as the village. Darkness having now set in, and Ensign Berkeley and many men having been cut down, Lieutenant Hadfield ordered his men to form square. Thus the Chinese were kept at bay for an hour. The enemy then brought forward a gun. A change of position now became unavoidable, and Lieutenant Hadfield was about to direct the movement, when well known shouts were heard in the distance, and in a few minutes two companies of Royal Marines were distinguished advancing.

The Marines formed and soon swept away the Chinese, and

the value of the then new percussion musket, with which the Marines were armed, was at once seen.

Sir Hugh Gough sent a messenger into the city to say that if any more hostile movements were made on his position he would attack the town itself. The Kwang-chow-foo of Canton arrived on the field, and assured the Commander-in-Chief that the assemblage had not been sanctioned by the authorities, and he finally succeeded in dispersing the force.

The total loss of the British was about 130, while that of the Chinese was very great.

The conduct of the A and B Companies of the Madras Sappers employed at Canton, received the warm approval of the Commander-in-Chief, Sir Hugh Gough, in a letter dated the 6th June.

Lieutenant F. Cotton was promised a brevet-majority for his services on this occasion, and Lieutenant Hadfield obtained a similar promise.

At this time Sir Le F. Senhouse died of fever. His remains were taken to Macao, and interred there.

Captain Elliot was now recalled by the British Ministry, and Sir Henry Pottinger was appointed in his place.

On the 3rd August, Sir H. Pottinger and Sir William Parker (the Naval Commander in-Chief) arrived at Macao.

By the 20th, the whole fleet, including twenty-one transports, was ready to put to sea.

The military force consisted of the 18th Royal Irish, four companies of the 26th Cameronians, the 49th and 55th Regiments, detachments of Royal and Madras Artillery, two companies of the Madras Sappers and Miners,* and a rifle company of the 37th Madras Native Infantry; altogether about 2,700

---

* On the 13th April 1841 the native sappers were allowed working pay—Subadars, five annas; jemedars, four annas; havildars, two annas; naiks, one anna and a half; private, first class, one anna; private, second class, ten pies. An addition to the Corps was also made of one drill havildar, one drill naik, one bugle major, together with a reduction of fifteen men per company.

fighting men, with light field artillery and a rocket brigade. Amoy was their destination.*

A small garrison was left at Hong-Kong, under the command of General Burrell, consisting of the head-quarters and five companies of the 26th Regiment, a small number of the 18th, two companies of Bengal Volunteers, and the remains of the 37th Madras Native Infantry, with small detachments of Madras Artillery and Sappers and Miners.

A fort was constructed on Kellett's island, and two batteries for heavy pieces were erected at either end of its southern coast.

The fleet anchored outside Amoy on the 24th August.

It was found that the batteries along the shore contiguous to the island, had been strengthened; and on Ko-long-soo, an island near the east opening of the bay, some strong works had been thrown up. A number of war-junks and gun-boats had been moored, so as to cover the entrance to the harbour, and the whole line of defence bristled with cannon.

The two seventy-fours were laid alongside the great shore batteries, and the *Druid*, *Blonde*, and light-draught vessels engaged the batteries of Ko-long-soo, while the steamers were employed in landing the troops and destroying the war-junks.

The Sappers assisted in disembarking the guns.

The fire of the seventy-fours had very little effect on the batteries.

After the bombardment the troops were landed at various points, and the enemy driven out of their works. Our troops bivouacked on some heights near the city of Amoy.

The next morning the city was entered without opposition, the enemy having abandoned it.

* On the 10th July 1841, Captain Pears was in orders to take charge of a detachment of artillery proceeding to China in H.M.'s troopship *Jupiter*. After the first capture of Chusan, Captain Pears returned to Madras, Brevet-Captain Cotton being left in command; Captain Pears was not, in consequence, present at the capture of Canton and Amoy.

Amoy being too extensive to be occupied, a garrison was left in Ko-long-soo, consisting of four companies of the Cameronians, and the left wing of the 18th Regiment, with a small detachment of artillery, and a few sappers.

The *Druid, Pylades,* and *Algerine* were left to blockade the place.

The fleet sailed for the Chusan Archipelago; but owing to baffling winds and fogs, many of the vessels separated, and did not re-unite near Chusan till the close of the month (September).

The fort on Joss-house Hill, which flanked the opening of the valley of Ting-hae, had been strengthened. On the seafront a battery of eighteen guns had been completed, and from the inner epaulement of this battery along the wharf of the suburbs, and across the entire mouth of the valley, an immense line of earthen battery had been thrown up, mounting 150 to 200 guns, which commanded every spot in the inner harbour on which a vessel could float, and bring her fire to bear against the defences; while on the right was encamped a strong body of troops partially covered by entrenchments. The Chinese had, however, overlooked the necessity of protecting the flanks from being turned.

The hills on the right of the valley formed the key of the position. This point was accordingly selected for the attack, while the attention of the enemy in Joss-house Hill fort, and near the suburb, was to be distracted by the fire of a howitzer-battery, which Captain Birdwood constructed on a small island called Trumball, on the eastern side of the inner harbour.

On the 1st October, the 55th, 49th, 26th, and 18th Regiments, with the Rifles, Artillery, and Sappers, were landed under the brow of the hill, which the enemy had occupied in force to his right. Several men-of-war anchored so as to bring their guns to bear upon the right flank of the long battery, and shortly after dawn the firing became general.

The 55th, as soon as they had formed, advanced in column to gain the heights in their front. This duty was gallantly performed, and the enemy were soon in full flight across the low ground which separated the position from the artillery, leaving a large number of dead and wounded, and the whole of their guns, stores, &c.

Our force was now divided into two columns; one, under Colonel Tomlinson of the 18th Regiment, was directed to advance through the long battery, and drive the enemy before them till they reached the foot of Joss-house Hill, and then to carry by escalade the fort on its summit; while the other, with the General, moved forward towards the city walls in pursuit of the enemy. The latter column performed their duty without any check, the ladders having been planted against the southern face of the ramparts without any loss, and their summit gained by Captain Pears with an advanced party in a dashing manner.

On the right there was more opposition, and the 18th Regiment and Royal Marines suffered in sharp encounters with bodies of troops, who rallied from time to time in the long battery before the Joss-house Hill fort was gained.

The total loss of the Chinese was very considerable, but ours was trifling.

Sir Hugh Gough was struck by a spent ball.

Preparations were now made for a movement against Chin-hae, at the mouth of the Ningpo river, distant about fifty miles from Chusan.

A small garrison was left to occupy Ting-hae and the Joss-house forts, and the remainder of the force moved from Chusan to the anchorage of "Just-in-the-way," so called from a rock which rises above the water in mid-channel of the entrance to the Ningpo river.

On the 9th October a close reconnoissance was made of the enemy's position. The heights on either side of the river were crowded with troops, and bristling with batteries and entrenchments, while the entrance to the river was impeded by a double row of piles, and by a line of junks and gun-boats moored behind this barrier. The citadel, on the top of a sharp and craggy hill to the right of the river's mouth, had been strengthened, and at every suitable point earthen batteries had been thrown up.

Early on the morning of the 10th October a strong column of infantry and artillery was landed on a sandy beach, far to the east of the Chinese position, and made a circuit round the base of the hills on which the main body of the enemy were posted, so as to get in their rear, while another column was landed near the mouth of the river to divert their attention, and the men-of-war were anchored as close in as possible to demolish the defences of the citadel. A small detachment of Sappers and Miners, under Captain Cotton, of the Madras Engineers, having been attached to Sir William Parker's column, the naval portion of the force was assigned the duty of carrying all the enemy's works on the west bank of the river; and accordingly, after a brisk and effective cannonade of the citadel, the boats of the squadron pushed in shore, the men scaled the rocky heights, entered by a gate partially ruined by the fire of the *Wellesley*, and speedily made themselves masters of the position, while the Chinese fled. The scaling-ladders were then planted against the ramparts of the city, and the naval column was soon in possession of the place.

Sir Hugh Gough thus mentioned the Sappers in his despatch: " The scaling-ladders had been brought up on most difficult and rugged heights, by the great exertions of the Madras Sappers, and were now gallantly planted under the direction of Captain Pears, who was the first to ascend."

Meanwhile, a dreadful scene of slaughter was enacting on the right bank of the river. The Chinese troops had been retiring before the advance of the centre column, under Sir Hugh Gough, in hopes of retreating by a bridge of boats. They came sud-

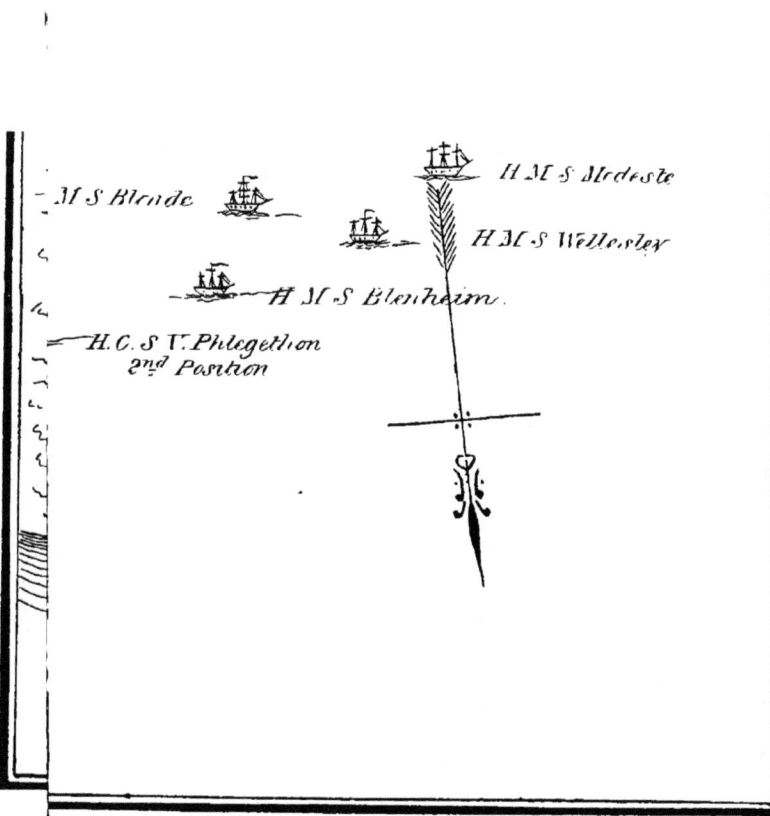

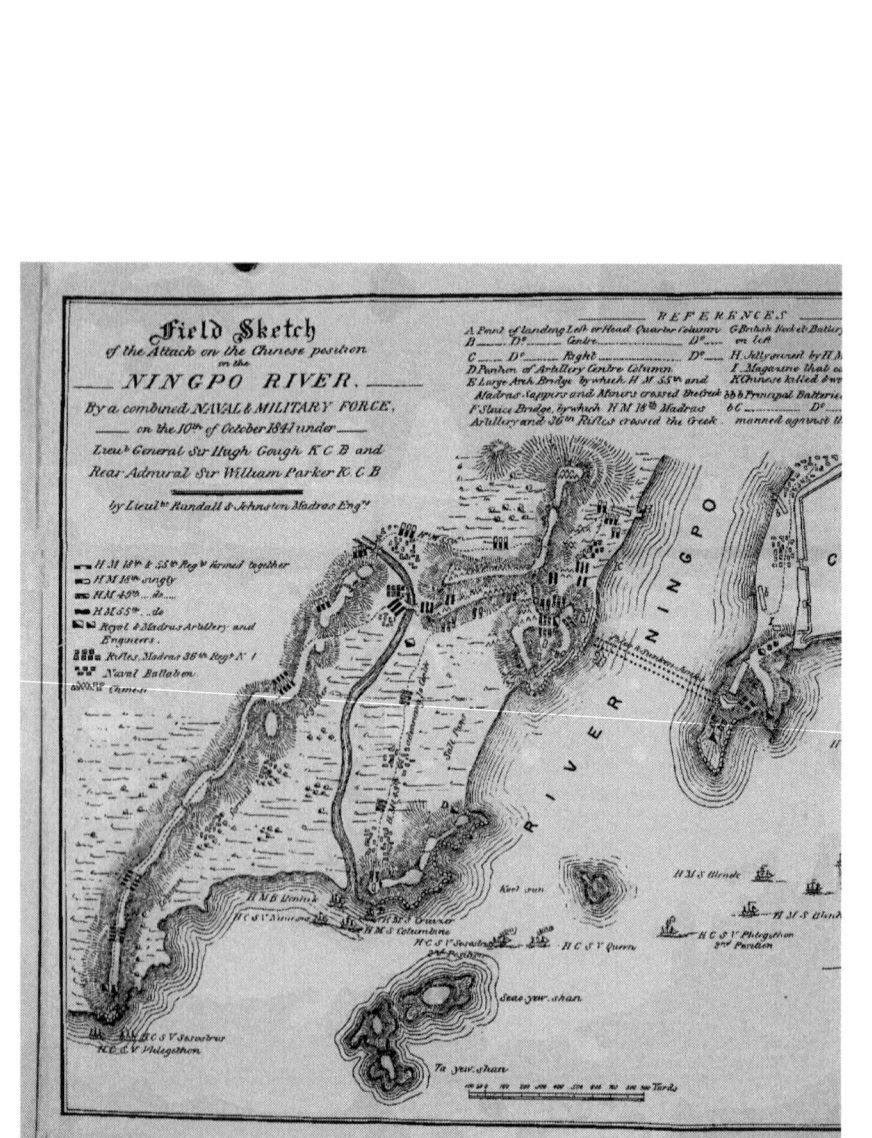

Field Sketch
of the Attack on the Chinese position
on the
NINGPO RIVER.

By a combined NAVAL & MILITARY FORCE,
on the 10th of October 1841 under

Lieut. General Sir Hugh Gough K.C.B. and

Rear Admiral Sir William Parker K.C.B.

by Lieut. Randall & Johnston Madras Eng.rs

REFERENCES

A Point of landing Left or Head Quarter column G British Rock et Batte
B   D.°   Centre   D.°   on left
C   D.°   Right   D.°   H. Jellygourd by H. M
D Position of Artillery Centre Column   K Chinese killed by
E Large Arch Bridge by which H.M.S.S.th and   Magazine that cc
Madras Sappers and Miners crossed the Creek bbb Principal Batterie
F Sluice Bridge, by which H.M. 18th Madras   bc   D.°
Artillery and 36th Rifles crossed the Creek manned against th

RIVER NINGPO

HMS Blonde

HMS Blonde

HCSV Phlegethon
2nd Partition

Keet sun

HMB Unite
HCSV Nemesis
HMS Columbine
HCSV Sesostris
HCSV Queen
HCSV Pylades
HCSV Phlegethon

Seao yew shan

HCSV Sesostris
HCSV Phlegethon

Ta yew shan

denly upon the head of the left column, which, having overcome all opposition in its course, had completed the circuit of the hills, and was debouching on the banks of the river so as to intercept the retreat towards the bridge. Hemmed in on all sides, and overwhelmed by the fire of a complete semi circle of musketry, the Chinese rushed by hundreds into the water. The loss of the Chinese was terrible, and "cease firing" had to be long and often sounded before the fury of our men could be restrained.

The 55th Regiment and Madras Rifles, having observed a large body of the enemy escaping from the citadel and the batteries which the Naval Brigade had stormed, crossed the bridge of boats, cut the retreating column in two, and shot down a great number, while many were driven into the water and drowned. The loss of the Chinese was immense, and a vast number of prisoners were taken, besides many cannon, and a large quantity of camp-equipage, ammunition, arms, stores, &c. Many of the prisoners were deprived of their tails by the soldiers and sailors. Sir Hugh Gough, hearing of this, sent an officer to put a stop to it. The officer arrived when the last was about to be operated on by a tar. The officer hailed him to cease his proceedings, when he hastily drew his knife across the victimised tail, saying, "It was a pity that the fellow should have the laugh against the others."

The British loss was small.

The citadel was converted into a strong post, and a garrison, consisting of the 55th Regiment, with detachments of Artillery and Sappers, was left to occupy it, under Colonel Schoedde.

On the 13th a light squadron advanced up the river to Ning-po. The city was found to have been evacuated by the enemy, so the troops were landed on a floating bridge which connected the city with the suburbs on the right bank; the walls were scaled, possession taken of the ramparts, and the city gates thrown open. Major Anstruther, who at this time marched in at the head of the Madras Artillery, found in the prison the cage in which he had been tortured, still standing in the yard, and the marks of his pencil still on the wall.

Shortly after the occupation of the town, steamers were sent up the river to reconnoitre. The reports brought down were favourable, and it seemed as if the Chinese did not intend any aggressive operations against Ning-po. The chiefs of the expedition intended no further hostilities along the coast, and the troops employed themselves in making their quarters comfortable.

All this time the small force at Hong-Kong had not been inactive. Towards the end of September it was brought to the notice of Captain Nias, of H.M.S. *Herald,* that preparations were being made on the banks of the two principal channels of the Canton river (the Macao passage and Junk river) to form barriers. Captain Nias signified his intention to proceed up the river with the squadron to carry out the orders of the Plenipotentiary—that was, to destroy defences, &c., and, if necessary, to occupy Wangtung.

General Burrell, thinking 200 men would be required, declined to detach a garrison for its occupation. An Engineer officer, with a party of Sappers and Miners, was attached to the squadron. They were conveyed to the Bogue, and in the course of a few days utterly destroyed the formidable and well-built works which covered it. Captain Nias burnt and sunk a number of store junks, fired some houses, shot a few persons implicated in the treacherous proceedings of the Mandarins, and then withdrew his squadron.

At the close of 1841 peace was still far distant.* The commencement of 1842 found the British in quiet possession of Ning-po, and the inhabitants friendly. The winter had set in with great rigour, the snow lying thick on the ground. At this

* In January 1842 Lieutenants Shaw and Hitchins went on service to China, with F Company of the Madras Sappers.

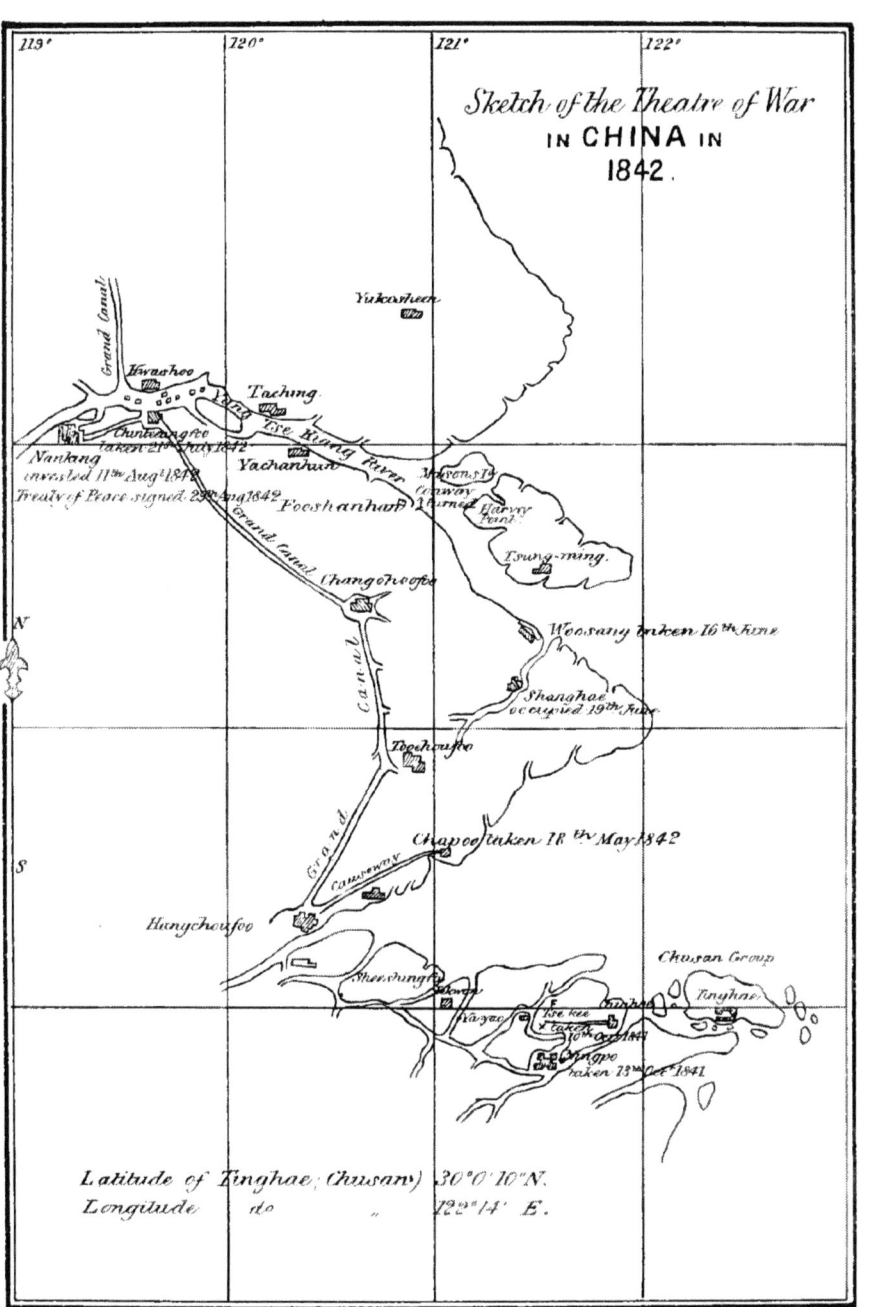

Sketch of the Theatre of War
IN CHINA IN
1842.

period the only natives with the force at head-quarters were the
Madras Sappers and the rifle company of the 36th Regiment.
It is worthy of record that, although accustomed to such a
climate as that of Southern and Central India, the men of these
corps not only bore the severity of the winter of Ning-po without
any constitutional injury, but appeared to improve in strength
and condition under its unwonted influence.

At Chinhae the force consisted of the 55th Regiment, and a
strong detachment of Artillery and Sappers. At Chusan, detachments of the 55th and 18th Regiments, Artillery, and Sappers.
At Amoy, two companies of the 18th Regiment, with some
Sappers. On the island of Hong Kong, at the beginning of this
year (1842), the force consisted of the 26th Cameronians, the
37th Regiments Madras Native Infantry, two companies of the
1st Regiment Bengal Volunteers, and detachments of the 18th
and 49th Regiments, Artillery, and Sappers. The 26th Cameronians were withdrawn, and sent to Ning-po. The 37th Madras
Native Infantry—which had suffered so severely through the
shipwreck of the *Golconda*, in 1840, with their ill-fated head-
quarters and flank companies on board, as well as through fever
and dysentery—on their return to Hong Kong were sent back to
India.

At Ning-po, kidnapping was carried on by the Chinese. Our
soldiers were enticed by offers of samshoo or other indulgence
into houses frequented by the kidnappers, and, being dosed till
their senses were overpowered, they were bound hand and foot
and carried away on a pole by two coolies, disguised like a bale
of goods, or were put into the hold of the small vegetable boats
which plied on the canal, and carried through the water gates
adjoining the south-western entrances.

During January and February 1842 two small expeditions
were despatched, the one to find out the practicability of the
approach of the fleet to Hang-chow-foo; and the other to
examine the navigation of a river which flows into the sea near

Peikwan, forty or fifty miles from Ning-po. Both were unsuccessful.

Towards the end of February the Rev. Mr. Gutzlaff heard that an attack on the city might be expected on the 9th, but the warning was disregarded, and considered merely as a cry of " Wolf."

The night of the 8th March, and the whole of the following day, brought no indication of the approach of an enemy. Midnight passed away without the appearance of a foe; but about 4 A.M. the sentry on the ramparts over the west gate saw a Chinaman advancing along the road leading to the outer entrance into the square bastion in which the double gateways are situated. He called out to him to go. The man continued to approach. and said he would not go. The sentry fired, and the man fell.

This was the signal for a general onslaught. The troops turned out at once. The suburbs appeared alive with enemies, who poured down upon the gates in enormous numbers. At the west gate (which had a guard-house well calculated for defence) all their efforts to effect an entrance proved fruitless. The guard, commanded by Lieutenant Armstrong, of the 18th Regiment, poured a steady fire into the dense mass of men below, while large heavy bricks and blocks of granite, of which the parapets are composed, were thrown over the ramparts on the heads of the assailants.

In spite of all this, they persevered for a long time in their desperate attempt. One man (a powerful and courageous one) actually gained the summit of the walls by means of a rude sort of ladder, at a point clear of the fire of the guard. As he issued from an embrasure he was encountered by Michael Cushion, who had just been liberated from the solitary cell. Cushion wrested the Chinaman's matchlock from him, brought the butt down upon his head, and felled him to the ground. Cushion then lifted him up, and threw him through the embrasure upon the bodies of his comrades who lay crushed and mangled below.

Success, however, attended the efforts of the enemy at the south gate, where the guard-house was situated below the rampart; and the Chinese having penetrated by the water-gate, the officer commanding the guard retreated along the rampart towards the bridge-gate, which post he reached without loss. From the south gate the enemy proceeded towards the market-place in the centre of the town, and thought that Ning-po was again their own. But their advance was suddenly arrested by a Company of the 49th Regiment, which had been sent to reinforce the guard at the south gate. The officer in command at once formed his men across the street, and opened fire at pistol-shot distance. It was returned for a short time, but the Chinese commenced a retrograde movement, which was soon converted into a flight, until they were driven out again through the south gate into the suburbs, when the victorious band took possession once more of the bastion, and closed the gates.

When morning had fully dawned, Colonel Montgomerie, of the Madras Artillery, conceiving that the obstinacy of the attack on the west gate was favourable for a sortie, brought a couple of howitzers along the rampart, and running one of them through the gateway (while the other was sent round to the south gate), ordered the outer gates to be thrown open, and the sortie to be made.

A short time before this the enemy had begun to draw off, and a few artillerymen under Lieutenant Molesworth pushed forward into the suburb, and opened a smart fire of musketry, which was returned by the Chinese. Captain Moore's howitzers now came up, and being run to the front, opened upon the living wall before them with case-shot at a distance of twenty or thirty yards. The effect was terrific, and soon a mound of dead and dying barricaded the street. The howitzer only discontinued its fire from the impossibility of directing its shot on a living foe, clear of the writhing and shrieking mass which it had already piled up. The infantry now resumed their platoon firing, and advanced over a closely-packed heap of dead and dying for fully fifteen yards.

A company of the 18th, and one of the 49th, now coming up, the pursuit was continued along the banks of the west canal for six miles. The repulse of this bold attack was now complete.

On our side not a single man was killed, and only a few wounded; while of the enemy upwards of 400 had fallen, consisting of their bravest and best.

Much credit was given by the Commander-in-Chief to Colonel Montgomerie, for his conduct during the assault.

Simultaneously with the attack on Ning-po, an attempt was made to surprise the gates of Chin-hae. The enemy was received with a heavy and destructive fire, so they drew off at once, and were soon beyond the reach of pursuit.

It was now ascertained that a force of 5,000 or 6,000, commanded by a Tartar general, was near Tungwa, intending to move on Ning-po, in concert with the renowned chief Yang, who had for some time been forming a camp near Tse-kee.

Sir Hugh Gough quitted Ning-po on the morning of the 13th, with a force of 900 men of all arms, and moved rapidly on Tung-wa. Information was, however, soon received that the enemy, who had two days before advanced within seven miles of Ning-po, had on the 12th retreated over a high range of hills in a south-westerly direction. The troops countermarched to Ning-po, and there awaited the steamers which were to take them to Tse-kee.

On the morn of the 15th the troops were embarked, and proceeded up the river in a north-easterly direction to a point four miles from Tse-kee, where they disembarked, and pushed on to a range of hills on which there was a large encampment. After an hour's march, the head of the column came within long range of the town, and the troops halted in the fields before the city, and awaited the order for attack.

Sir Hugh Gough and Sir William Parker now reconnoitred the town and the extensive position taken up by the enemy. The troops were directed to enter the city at various points, pass through it to the gate opening on the plain enclosed between the ramparts and the heights of Segaon, on which the enemy were posted, and there dividing into three columns, the ascent of the slopes to be made on the right, centre, and left, so timed that the right column should be able to crown the left of the enemy's position, and thence enfilade the centre and right encampments, and direct their march so as to intercept the retreat of the enemy.

This judicious plan was not persevered in, for the 49th in the centre, and the seamen and marines on the left, soon gained the summit, and drove the enemy from their entrenchments at the point of the bayonet with great slaughter. The 49th were the first to gain the enemy's position. The regiment was directed to move down the heights on the opposite side, and throw two companies into the rear of a strong body of the enemy observed to be marching to the right of their position to support the entrenchment threatened by the Royal Marines and seamen.

The manœuvre was perfectly successful, as the defenders of the hill recoiled from the Marines on the crest of the ridge, the supporting body was thrown into confusion, halted, and opened a feeble fire, then broke and fled down the hill, at the bottom of which the 49th were awaiting them with loaded firelocks.

The Naval Brigade now came pouring down the heights, while the 49th pressed on the rear and flanks of the enemy. Few out of the whole body escaped unhurt, and the field was strewn far and wide with their slain.

On the right column completing their laborious march and ascent of the left extremity of the heights, they found no enemy to oppose them, and perceived the plain below covered with fugitives. They accordingly descended, and moved in the direction of the Chang-ki Pass. The 26th Regiment also pushed out and joined in the pursuit, which was kept up for a considerable distance along the road to Yu-yao.

The 18th succeeded in turning a great part of the enemy from the Chang-ki Pass, and inflicted severe loss upon them.

The loss of the British was trifling, while that of the Chinese was large, 400 to 500 killed and wounded being left on the field, while many more were slain and drowned in the pursuit.

On 16th March Sir Hugh Gough moved towards the. Chang-ki Pass, seven miles from Tse-kee; but the position recently occupied by the enemy was found abandoned. The General accordingly retired again to Tse-kee. The British troops remained there during the night of the 16th, and next morning marched back to the steamers, with the exception of a small detachment sent, under the Chief Engineer, Captain Pears, upon the route to Chin-hae, to ascertain the nature of the communications, and to break up any post of refuge which the enemy might have formed.

The General reached Ning-po on the 17th, and the men returned to their quarters.

It was now resolved that Chapoo, about thirty-five miles from Hang-chow, should be attacked. The troops were withdrawn from Ning-po, and dropped down the river to Chin-hae, where they were embarked on 6th May 1842. Although the distance was only sixty miles, the voyage took nine days.

On the 16th the fleet arrived off Chapoo; the next day a reconnoissance was made, and on the 18th the whole of the troops, supported by seamen and marines, landed and formed in two columns. The right was to turn the left of the position taken up by the enemy, and to march by their rear in the direction of the town, so as to intercept the retreat of the main body posted on the hills, while the left column advanced up the

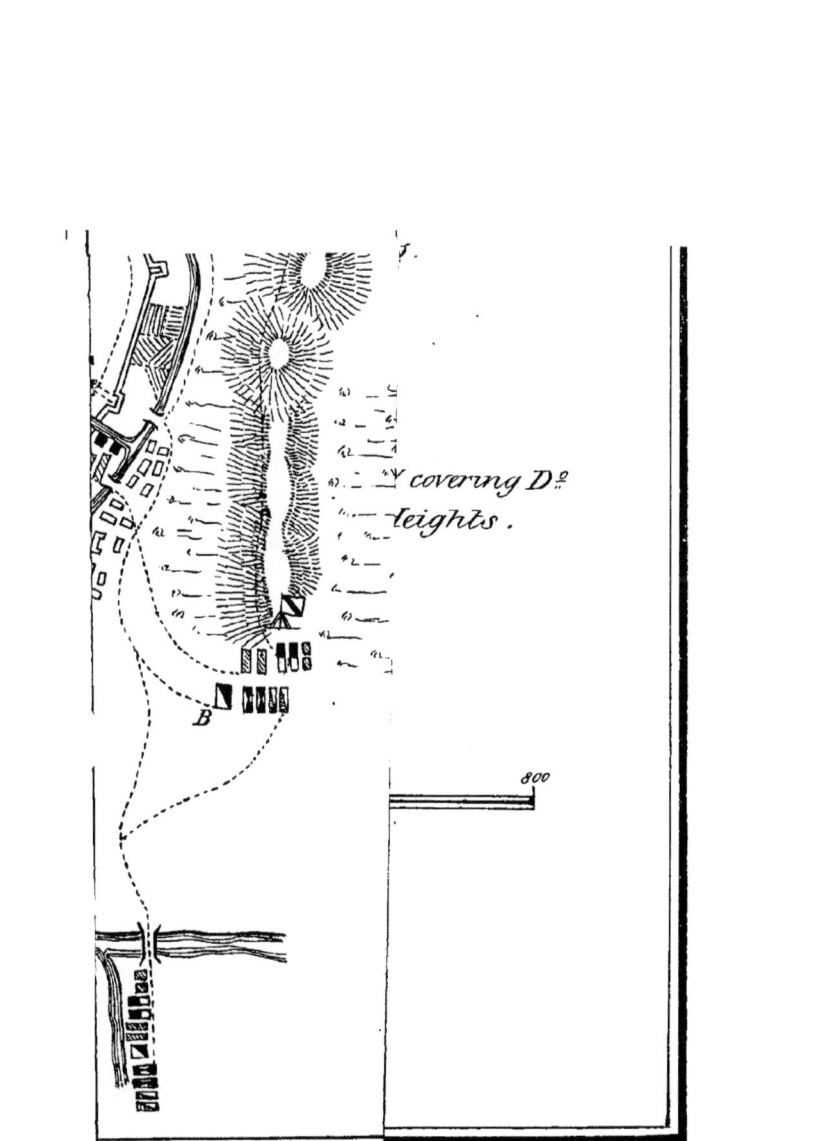

covering D.º teights.

B

800

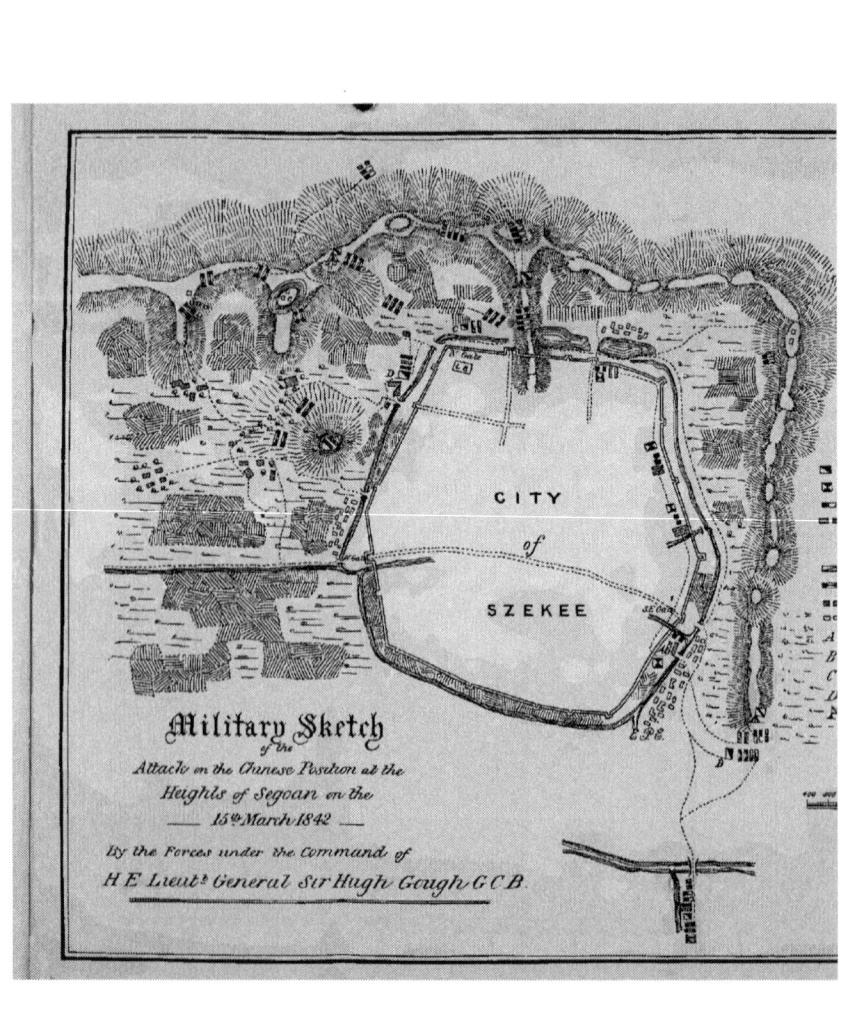

CITY

of

SZEKEE

Military Sketch

of the

Attack on the Chinese Position at the

Heights of Segoan on the

15ᵗʰ March 1842

By the Forces under the Command of

H. E. Lieutᵗ General Sir Hugh Gough G.C.B.

heights to take the Chinese entrenchments in flank, and drive them into the plain.   Upon the extreme left of their line the enemy defended themselves with resolution for some time, but finally broke and ran, descending the slopes of the heights in the direction of the city, scattering themselves over the fields, where their numbers were soon increased by the fugitives from the redoubts, and from the centre of the enemy's position, driven thence by the advance of the left column after a pretty stout resistance.   The mass of the fugitives was encountered by the right column at the foot of the hill, and suffered considerable loss.   Meanwhile the left column, having cleared the heights of the enemy, pursued their march along the road leading towards the city, which was entered by escalade at the north-east angle without opposition, the troops parading the ramparts as victors, with all the pomp of unfurled colours and the music of their bands.

While this was going on, a desperate struggle was taking place in the very heart of the enemy's recent position.   The extreme right of the Chinese line had been occupied by 300 or 400 Tartar troops, who, on observing the rout of their left and centre, retreated in good order towards the town.   After descending the hill, they discovered that their retreat was cut off by the advance of the right column, while the direction taken by the Naval Brigade, which had landed on the rocky point near the suburbs, showed them that escape towards the south was also impracticable.   They threw themselves into a large joss-house, situated at the bottom of a valley formed by the slopes of the right extremity of the Chinese Heights, and of a small range of hills between it and the city.   So secluded was the position, that the main body of the British left column, inclining to the right before they reached the head of the valley, had skirted the base of the lower range of hills, and passed on without being aware of the body they had left in their rear.   This was the case also with the Naval Brigade.

11 *

It happened, however, that a small body of men who had detached themselves from the left column inclined to the left, came suddenly upon the joss-house, and received a volley from the matchlocks of a party drawn up in its front. The detachment, which consisted of no more than thirty men of the 18th, 49th, and Sappers, with a few seamen and gunners, closed upon the building and opened a fire on its entrance, which was briskly returned by the Tartars. Meantime Captain Pears, the Chief Engineer, who happened to be present, sent messengers with intelligence of what was happening. A company of the 18th was intercepted in its advance. It proceeded to the valley, and, uniting itself with the small force blockading the joss-house, formed a body considered strong enough to carry the building at the point of the bayonet. The Tartar soldiers silently awaited the attack of our detachment, and as soon as the leading files and officers had passed through the entrance, opened a heavy fire on them, killing and wounding most of those who had passed the barrier, amongst others, Lieutenant-Colonel Tomlinson, who was shot through the neck and expired at once. A retreat was unavoidable, and the detachment was withdrawn. Soon after this a party of artillery came up with some rockets, and a few were thrown into the building without any visible effect upon the resolution of the Tartars.

After some further delay, it was resolved to make a breach in the outer wall near one of the angles, and after a few round shot had been thrown into it, a 50-lb. bag of powder was placed at the foot of the wall by Captain Pears, and its explosion opened a wide entrance for an assaulting party. But the Tartars still remained cool and undismayed; received the storming party with a heavy fire, and the assailants were once more compelled to retreat with loss. Upwards of three hours had now elapsed since the first shot had been fired, but the Tartars exhibited no token of submission, or disposition to surrender. Small parties of two or three now and then sallied out and

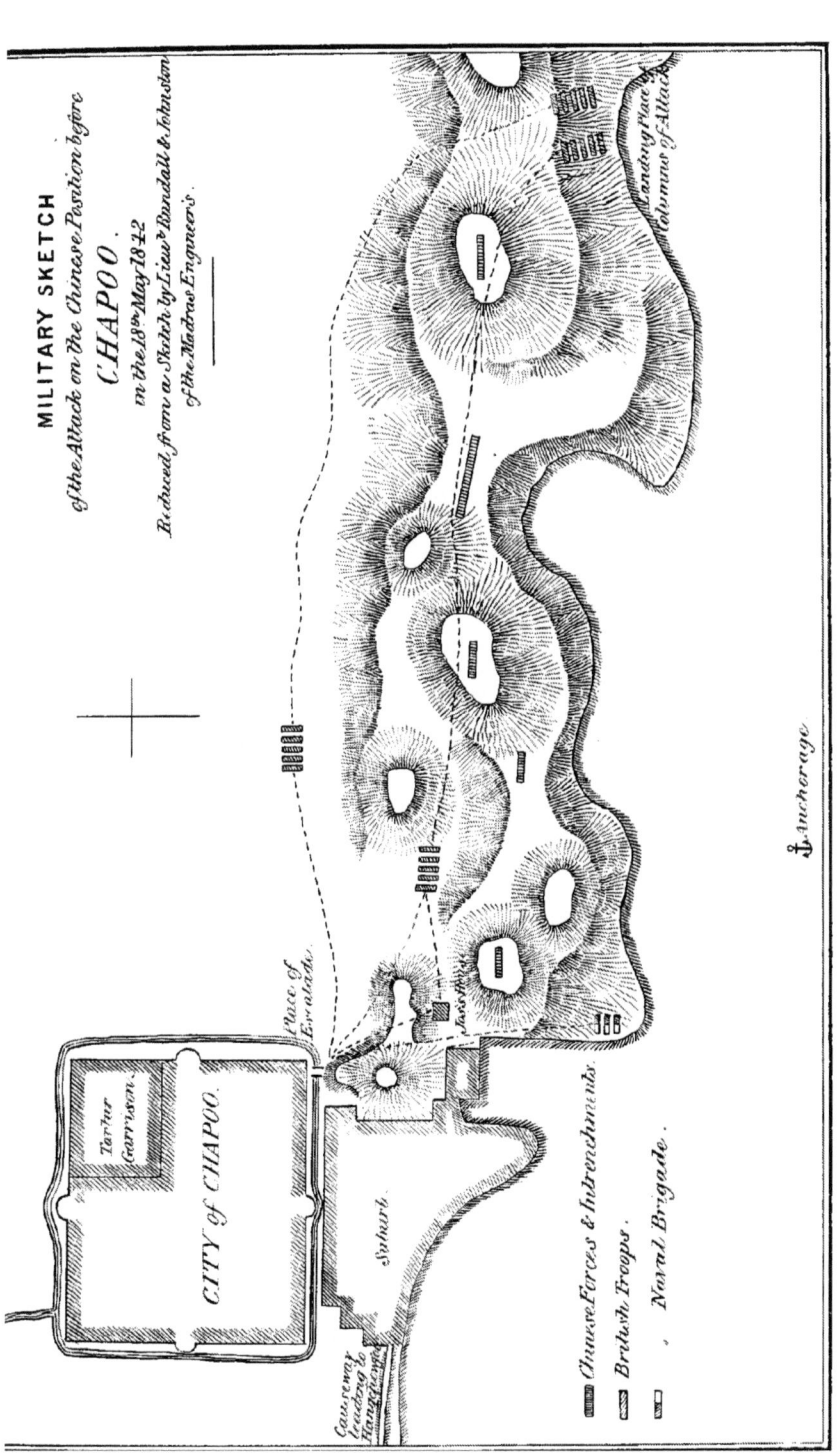

MILITARY SKETCH
of the Attack on the Chinese Position before
CHAPOO.
on the 18th May 1842

Reduced from a Sketch by Lieut Rundall & Johnston
of the Madras Engineers.

CITY of CHAPOO.

Tartar Garrison.

Causeway leading to Hangchow

Suburb.

Place of Execution.

Joss house.

Joss house.

Landing Place
Columns of Attack.

⬛ Anchorage

▦ Chinese Forces & Intrenchments.

▦ British Troops.

▦ Naval Brigade.

attempted to escape down the valley towards the harbour, but few of these managed to get away.

A second breach was now blown in the opposite side, and wood being collected, a fire was kindled, and in a short time the house was a ruin. Our troops, at last, were able to enter, and the action came to an end. Of the whole body of Tartars, only sixty were made prisoners, many of them wounded; all the rest having been either shot, bayoneted, or burnt.

This affair had the effect of exalting the Tartar troops in no slight degree in the estimation of the British, who could not but think with respect of men who could maintain, to the last, such steady coolness and indomitable valour.

In the capture of Chapoo two British officers were killed and six wounded; amongst the latter, Lieutenant J. G. Johnston of the Madras Engineers. Of N.C.O. and men, eight were killed and forty-four wounded.

A body of troops, under command of Major-General Schoedde, was sent out to reconnoitre the road to Hang-chow-foo, the capital of the richest province of the Empire, about sixty miles west of Chapoo. The Commander-in-Chief decided that a movement on the city would interfere with our ultimate operations on the Yang-tse-kiang; accordingly the troops re-embarked on 28th May, and all stores of gunpowder and arms, together with a few public buildings, were destroyed. The same day the fleet made sail for the mouth of the Yang-tse-kiang; its destination being Woosung, about 100 miles from Chapoo.

The fleet anchored off "Rugged Islands" on the 29th; remained there till the 5th June, then moved on towards the river. Anchored again, on the 7th, at "Dangerous Rocks"; sailed again on the 11th, and finally anchored off Woosung on 13th June.

About twelve miles up the Woosung river is situated Shanghai. This place it was resolved to attack. Before entering the river it was necessary to get possession of the line of defences which on either side covered the approach to its mouth. The 14th and 15th were devoted to reconnoitring and taking soundings, as also buoying off a line of anchorage for the ships.

On the 16th the squadron anchored as near the works as possible, leaving the transports about four miles out in the stream. The cannonade was kept up for two hours, the Chinese batteries replying at intervals. The boats' crews and marines were landed, who, entering the enemy's works at various points, soon put to flight the troops left in them, except on the extreme left at Powsham, where the Chinese manned the parapet, and received them with so resolute a fire, that they were compelled to retreat. Shortly after the troops were landed, and all opposition soon ceased.

On 16th June H.M.'s ship *Dido* anchored off Woosung, convoying transports containing 2,500 reinforcements from India. It was not thought necessary to employ the whole of the newly-arrived force, so only 2nd Madras Native Infantry, and detachments of Artillery and Sappers were disembarked.

Sir Hugh Gough formed the force into two divisions; one under Colonel Montgomerie, C.B. (Madras Artillery), to march on Shanghai by the left bank; while the other, under Major-General Schoedde (55th), proceeded by the river.

Colonel Montgomerie's column advanced without encountering any obstacles which the Sappers and Miners were not able speedily to overcome. The inhabitants of the villages passed *en route*, were astonished at the field-pieces, drawn by horses, so much larger than their own, but did not show any fear of our troops, with whom they found the strictest discipline to prevail; and before the column had advanced a couple of miles, the heavy scaling-ladders had been transferred by the Sappers to the shoulders of willing, or at least not dissentient natives, and the drag-ropes of the guns, whenever it was necessary to unyoke the horses, were manned by Chinese labourers, mingled with our gunners.

Meantime the left column proceeded up the river, and arrived within half a mile of the town, having passed, about midway, a battery pierced for twenty guns, which had opened fire the previous day on a reconnoitring steamer, but which was now found deserted and the guns withdrawn. Just below the town was another battery for eighteen guns; this was silenced and the gunners put to flight by a few broadsides and shells. The left column had forgotten that the right column might reasonably be expected to have reached the town, and Colonel Montgomerie's division heard on a sudden the report of guns close at hand, and found round-shot hurtling over their heads. As they moved on, they saw a body of 500 or 600 Chinese troops hurrying from the batteries with which the squadron was engaged, but they were too far off for pursuit.

On the approach of the 18th to the north gate of Shanghai, a few matchlocks were discharged at them from the hills, but on pushing forward the place was found evacuated and the column marched in and took possession.

On the 20th the *Nemesis* was sent up sixty miles, until finding the water regularly shoaling, and no indications of a town, it returned. It was afterwards ascertained that the smoke of the steamer had been seen from the walls of Soo-chow-foo.

The failure of this attempt to find a passage to Soo-chow-foo determined the abandonment of the project for an expedition in that direction, and arrangements were made for withdrawing the troops from Shanghai, and dropping down the river again after a few days had been spent in the town.

Lieutenant Ouchterlony, the author of the *Chinese War*, from which this account is taken, was one of the Engineers with this expedition, and in his history he gives a ludicrous description of the sale of plunder at Shanghai. The sellers (our troops) being on the ramparts, while the buyers (the Chinese) were at the foot of the ramparts.

The heat was found more oppressive than in any other town occupied by our troops in 1842.

A large store of ice was found in the city, and this was freely used by our troops for iced drinks. The Chinese only make use of ice for the sake of preserving fish in the summer season.

On 23rd June Shanghai was evacuated, one division embarking on board the steamers, while another proceeded by land with the guns to Woosung.

The whole of the force destined for the campaign of the Yangtse-kiang mustered 9,000 bayonets, exclusive of Marines and sailors.

The whole land force was divided into three brigades :

> 1st, under Major-General Lord Saltoun, K.C H.
> 2nd, under Major-General Schoedde, C.B.
> 3rd, under Major-General Bartley.

The 1st Brigade consisted of—

> 26th and 98th Regiments.
> Battalion of Bengal Volunteers.
> Flank companies of 41st Madras Native Infantry.

The 2nd Brigade—

> 55th Regiment.
> Madras Rifles.
> 2nd and 6th Madras Native Infantry.

The 3rd Brigade—

> 18th and 49th Regiments.
> 14th Madras Native Infantry.

The Royal Artillery and Madras Artillery formed a separate brigade, under Colonel Montgomerie, C.B.—

> 1 troop of Horse Artillery.
> $4\frac{1}{2}$ companies of Fort Artillery.
> 4 companies of gun lascars.

The Engineer department and three companies of Madras Sappers (A B and F) formed also a distinct command under Captain Pears, Madras Engineers, the Chief Engineer.

To each brigade a detachment of Artillery and one of Sappers, with an officer of Engineers, was attached when they moved against the enemy.

On 29th June the Admiral despatched two surveying vessels up the river to ascertain soundings, &c., and on the 30th the Admiral's ship, the *Cornwallis*, was towed out into the stream, where she anchored till the 6th July.

The fleet consisted of ten men-of-war, five armed troopships, two armed surveying vessels, five steam frigates, five iron steamers, and fully forty transports.

On the 19th the fleet anchored safely abreast of the town of Chin-keang-foo. The place at that time appeared to be entirely deserted, not a creature was to be seen on the walls, and no flags were flying.

After anchoring off Golden Island on the 20th, the first symptom of hostilities was the appearance of a large raft of wood in flames. This was towed clear of the anchorage. It was succeeded by another, and shortly after by two at once, but no accidents were caused by them.

Meantime a reconnoissance was made by the General from some hills which overlooked the city. The city seemed deserted, but on a low range of hills to the south two large entrenched camps were observed.

The 2nd Brigade was directed to land under cover of the town, and take post within gun-shot range of the walls, making a feint to attack them if any troops appeared on them.

The 3rd Brigade was to land to the right of the town, and to act as circumstances might demand.

The 1st Brigade, destined to attack the entrenched camps, was to land to the right, opposite Golden Island, and await orders at place of disembarkation.

As soon as the 1st Brigade had landed, Sir Hugh Gough ascended heights to the west of the city to reconnoitre.

Orders were then sent to Lord Saltoun to advance on the Chinese position, while the 3rd Brigade was moved across the heights in the direction of the city walls, throwing its right forward to be in readiness to co-operate with the 1st Brigade, and to prevent the enemy, when driven from their camp, retreating in direction of the town.

The movements commenced at 8 A.M. The column commanded by Lord Saltoun passed out, and after a march of three or four miles came in sight of the encampments. The whole of the enemy's tents had been struck, and the Chinese had united their forces and drawn them up behind an entrenchment on a gently sloping hill.

The Chinese took no notice of our approach till the light company of the 98th and a party of Madras Sappers gained the top of a gently swelling ridge forming one boundary of the low valley which separated them from the Chinese position. They then opened fire with round shot and grape, while at the same time a large body of troops appeared upon the brow of a range of hills on our right, and descended a short distance to threaten an attack on our flank.

Our force was formed into two columns; one to move by the right to turn the left of the enemy's position, another to press on their right, so as to cut off their retreat.

Major Anstruther was instructed to open fire on the entrenchments with his field-pieces, while two companies Bengal Volunteers were to take post in some gardens, &c., for the purpose of keeping in check the troops on the ridge to our right, while the attention of the enemy was diverted by the sharp fire kept up by our guns.

The 98th, Sappers, and 41st Native Infantry on the right, and the Volunteers' Regiment on the left, were pressing forward to close.

But long before our men could gain the crest of the hill on which they stood, the whole gave way and fled over the hill. The light company of the 98th and the Sappers were after them without loss of time, but few were overtaken. The entrenched camp was found almost stripped, and the only trophies of the day were some arms, ammunition, tents, and camp furniture.

We threw out some light troops to occupy a commanding hill in advance, while the remainder was formed near the place recently evacuated by the enemy, and piled arms awaiting further orders.

The 2nd Brigade landed to the east of the city, and created as serious a diversion in favour of the attack of the 3rd Brigade as was practicable.

This brigade had scaling ladders as also 18-pounder and 32-pounder rockets, in addition to field-pieces.

General Schoedde* was suffered to occupy a commanding slope within 300 yards of the walls without opposition ; but as soon as the artillery and rocket-tubes had been planted on the top of the eastern heights, the Chinese commenced a smart fire of round and grape shot.

The *Auckland* opened a well-directed fire from her 68-pounder with 10-inch shells, while the Royal Artillery threw rockets over the ramparts.

From the hill on which General Schoedde had taken his stand, he had a very extensive view of the country south and east of the city, and the whole of the movements of Lord Saltoun's Brigade were distinctly visible.

About the time of Lord Saltoun's successful advance, the attack of the 3rd Brigade was commenced. Perceiving the importance of gaining the ramparts and gateways on the east, General Schoedde adopted the resolution of carrying the place by escalade.

* Johnston with seventy Madras Sappers was with this brigade.

The grenadiers of the 55th, under Captain McLean, were told off as a storming party to precede the main column, while the Madras Rifles were to extend along the walls and pick off men who might show themselves while the ladders were being placed against the face of a square bastion.

The Rifles did such excellent work that the party of Madras Sappers who carried the ladders, and had to cross an open space exposed to the full fire of a face and flank of the works, gained the foot of the walls without a single casualty.

Captain Simpson was shot in the head, and a havildar who attempted to remove him had a shot sent through his cap.

The ladders were fixed, and a considerable number of our troops had ascended the ramparts, and formed on the terreplein before scarcely a shot was fired at them, the attention of the enemy being completely engrossed by the covering party. The terreplein was bounded by a rear-wall of brick running parallel to the parapet twelve to sixteen feet distant, and having low walls at intervals intersecting it at right angles in the form of traverses.

Lieutenants Cuddy, 55th, and Johnston, of the Engineers, were the first two on the walls, and could not at first see an opponent.

The Tartars appear to have been utterly unprepared for the mode of attack adopted, and had suffered the ladders to be carried to the foot of the walls and planted without detaching a man to watch the movements of the Sappers, who, under the direction of Lieutenant Johnston, performed their duty in a skilful and resolute manner.

Bodies of troops, however, soon came along the ramparts to the point of danger, and maintained a heavy fire on the assailants, who, now divided into two bodies, strove to win their way along either face of the work. Their advance received a check, especially on the left, where Captain Reid,* 6th Madras Native

* Afterwards Quartermaster-General of the Madras Army.

Infantry, who commanded after the death of his Colonel (Drever), was not able to bring his column round the re-entering angle until after a desperate struggle, and had to fight his way almost inch by inch to the nearest gateway, which General Schoedde had opened to admit the 2nd Native Infantry.

The Tartar troops for a long time clung to the guard-house above the gateway, and defended the wickets which led into the work in the most resolute manner. At length, a gate leading from a ramp in the inner gateway having been forced, Captain Reid charged through it and bayoneted the defenders. The gates were then thrown open, and the 2nd Native Infantry entered, united themselves with the 6th, and the column went along the rampart to the west gate.

Meantime the advance of the right column was made good, though obstinately contested.

The Tartars retired slowly before their assailants, and made a determined stand at a small two-storied guard-house at a re-entering angle of the works. However, this house was finally carried at the point of the bayonet.

As soon as the head of the column tried to push forward round the angle of the curtain, the enemy charged desperately down and bore the advanced files back. Several savage hand-to-hand conflicts took place. Major Warren maintained his reputation as a swordsman by vanquishing in single fight two powerful Tartars who assailed him, killing one and disabling the other. Shortly after, this gallant officer received a severe wound from a matchlock ball.

The check was not of long duration, and Captain McLean's grenadiers once more charged into the guard-house, and the survivors of those defending it retreated along the curtain to the salient angle.

Here another determined stand was made by the Tartars, but they were at last driven with great slaughter from the ground they had so gallantly maintained, and they now sought refuge in the buildings and gardens of the town.

The advance of the 55th was now continued as far as the west gate without opposition of any consequence.

The 3rd Brigade was still kept at bay on the west.

It was now near noon, and the determination of the Tartars may be estimated from the fact that, although the ladders were planted at 8 A.M on the east side, the west gate was not gained till fully three hours afterwards, although the distance was only a mile and a quarter.

General Schoedde, seeing that the enemy were still in possession of the large square bastion which covered the entrance to the inner gateway, and that the outer entrance had not yet been forced, directed a party to push into the bastion, clear it, and throw open the gates.

The inner gates were seized by the 55th, and a barricade of grain and sand-bags having been removed, Lieutenants Heriott and Johnston (Engineers), with some men of the 55th and Sappers, ran across the bastion, through the fire of the enemy from the walls, gained the cover of the archway of the outer gate, and began dragging away the sand-bags piled against the gates.

Finding the task too laborious, and imagining from a cessation of firing that the 3rd Brigade had withdrawn and were effecting an entrance elsewhere, the two officers withdrew their men. It was as well they did so, for they had no sooner retired than an explosion took place which shook down the walls of the houses and guard-houses in the inner space of the bastion. The gates had been blown in, and the cessation of firing must have been caused by the advance of the party to fix the powder-bags.

The 18th and 49th Regiments rushed in, and encountered, instead of the Tartars, the 55th drawn up along the main street.

The 3rd Brigade, after the advance of Lord Saltoun, had moved forward towards the town, and halted outside the suburb which commanded a view of the ground over which the 1st Brigade had to advance, as well as that occupied by the enemy in their front.

As soon as Lord Saltoun routed the Chinese, and the firing of the 2nd Brigade commenced, Sir H. Gough moved the 18th and 49th through the suburbs to the west gate, occupied the houses at the water's edge, and opened a heavy fire of musketry on the parapets; while Colonel Montgomerie threw shot and shell among the Tartar troops.

At this time a detachment of Artillery, with four field-pieces and howitzers, in two boats of the *Blonde*, proceeded to the mouth of the Grand Canal and pulled along its course towards the walls, hoping to find a spot in the outer bank where they could conveniently land the guns. Suddenly, shooting past the cover of some high buildings, they found themselves unexpectedly close under the ramparts, with the bridge leading to the west gate directly in front. A heavy fire was at once opened on them, disabling the greater part of the detachment. They could not pull back, so the leading boat made for the stone bridge, in hopes of finding shelter under the arch, while the other was run ashore not a pistol-shot distance from the city, and the boat, with guns, ammunition and arms, left at the disposal of the garrison after the wounded were removed.

The crew and detachment retreated through the suburb to the river, while the party under the bridge, finding their place of refuge too "hot" to hold them, also abandoned their boat and retreated along the inner bank of the canal, the enemy keeping up a brisk fire on them till they got under cover of the houses; but they made no attempt to sally out.

In fact, they had so effectually barricaded their gates, that they were unable to do so, except after considerable labour and loss of time.

As soon as the Admiral heard of this, he sent a strong party of Marines to recover the boats. The boats were found uninjured, except by the enemy's bullets, and were again taken possession of, and a gunner whom it had been found impossible to remove, owing to a bad fracture of his leg, was found lying, in other respects unhurt, at the bottom of one of the boats.

Meantime the attack of the 3rd Brigade was concentrating on the west gate.

Captain Pears, the Chief Engineer, had closely reconnoitred the approaches to the bastion, and his report and recommendation, and the appearance of the outer pair of gates, decided the Commander-in-Chief to effect an entrance by blowing the latter open and escalading the inner wall, should obstacles still be found.

It was near noon when Captain Pears and Lieutenant and Adjutant J. Rundall, with Conductor Almond, of the Sappers and Miners, heading the party of sappers, who carried three powder-bags (containing fifty-eight pounds each), pushed across the stone bridge under cover of a rapid discharge of musketry from the 18th and 49th, and, gaining the gateway without any casualty, planted the powder-bags against the great gates.

The result of the explosion was most successful, and the storming-party, though advancing through a cloud of dust and smoke, found their footing sure and free from hindrance

The outer gateway was a long arched passage seventy feet long, twelve feet wide, and twelve feet and a half high. The gate consisted of two massive folding-doors fixed six feet within the archway, thus affording perfect shelter to persons fixing the bags. The doors were ten feet seven inches by six feet each and five feet thick, well constructed and fitted, their outer surface being neatly and closely covered with iron plates.

After the explosion the arch remained perfect, and did not appear shaken, while the two massive doors were blown completely out of their places without being broken, and lay, one flat in the middle of the passage, and the other against the side wall at a distance of nineteen feet from its original position.

Some beams placed as props were shattered and cast beyond the bags of earth behind the door, and some appear to have been thrust entirely away, and the rest pressed down so as to offer no impediment to the men even in the dark.

About the time that the 3rd Brigade rushed through the west gate, the party of Marines, Artillery, and seamen, who had come up in the boats of the *Cornwallis*, having landed with one scaling-ladder close under the right flank of the bastion, escaladed near a small postern, and although the first man was shot through the head, and others were wounded, they soon made good their lodgment on the ramparts; and the gallant remnant of the enemy, refusing to surrender or accept quarter, perished by ball or bayonet.

The contest being now terminated, the 2nd and 3rd Brigades were directed to take post at the various gates.

The heat had now become intense, and many veteran soldiers could bear up no longer against its effects. Sir Hugh Gough, although equal to almost any degree of fatigue and exposure, after entering the town, was compelled to seek the shelter of a house and lie down.

All now appeared at rest within the walls, when the attention of all was arrested by the report of a heavy volley, followed by sharp, steady, rolling fire, which seemed to proceed from a considerable body of men in conflict. It was the last rally of the devoted garrison of Ching-keang-foo.

It appears that the 18th and 49th were, in accordance with orders, making a partial circuit of the ramparts before occupying their quarters. On a sudden, a few shots were discharged at them from some houses, and immediately afterwards a strong column of soldiers, with two Mandarins, emerged from a neighbouring street, and poured in on the British regiments so fierce a fire that at the first volley two officers and many men fell killed and wounded. Our men halted, exchanged a few volleys and then charged down the slope of the rampart, and getting among them in the open ground below, a savage conflict ensued, but the issue was never for a moment doubtful.

The grenadiers of the 18th, rendered furious by the loss of a favourite officer (Captain Collinson), pressed hotly on the Tartars, and made great havoc among them, but ignorance of the localities put an early stop to the pursuit.

Evening was now closing in, and guards having been placed at most of the gates, the victorious troops got into quarters.

The night proved one of incessant alarms, as attempts which were made from time to time by small parties to escape from the city, caused a rattle of musketry. Several desperate rushes were made on sentries and guards by Tartar soldiers who had secreted themselves in houses, and a great many men were killed during the night by the Cameronians, who were frequently roused.

Shortly after day-break, parties were sent out to patrol the Tartar quarter, and to destroy arsenals and depôts of stores; while fatigue detachments of Sappers and Miners were employed in collecting and burying the dead.

General Hailing, who had so nobly conducted the defence of Ching-keang-foo, was one of the Mandarins who had commanded the Tartar troops in their desperate attack on the 18th and 49th Regiments. After the failure of this attack, it appears he returned to his house, and calling for his secretary, desired him to bring his official papers into a small room. He then deliberately seated himself, and causing the papers and some wood to be piled up around him, he dismissed his secretary, set fire to the funeral pile, and perished in the flames.

Hostilities had now entirely ceased within the city walls, and their immediate vicinity; but partial attacks were made on the outposts of Lord Saltoun's brigade, which was quartered some miles from the city.

Preparations were shortly made for an advance upon Nanking, and the *Plover* was sent to reconnoitre.

A force, consisting of the 55th Regiment, 2nd and 6th Native

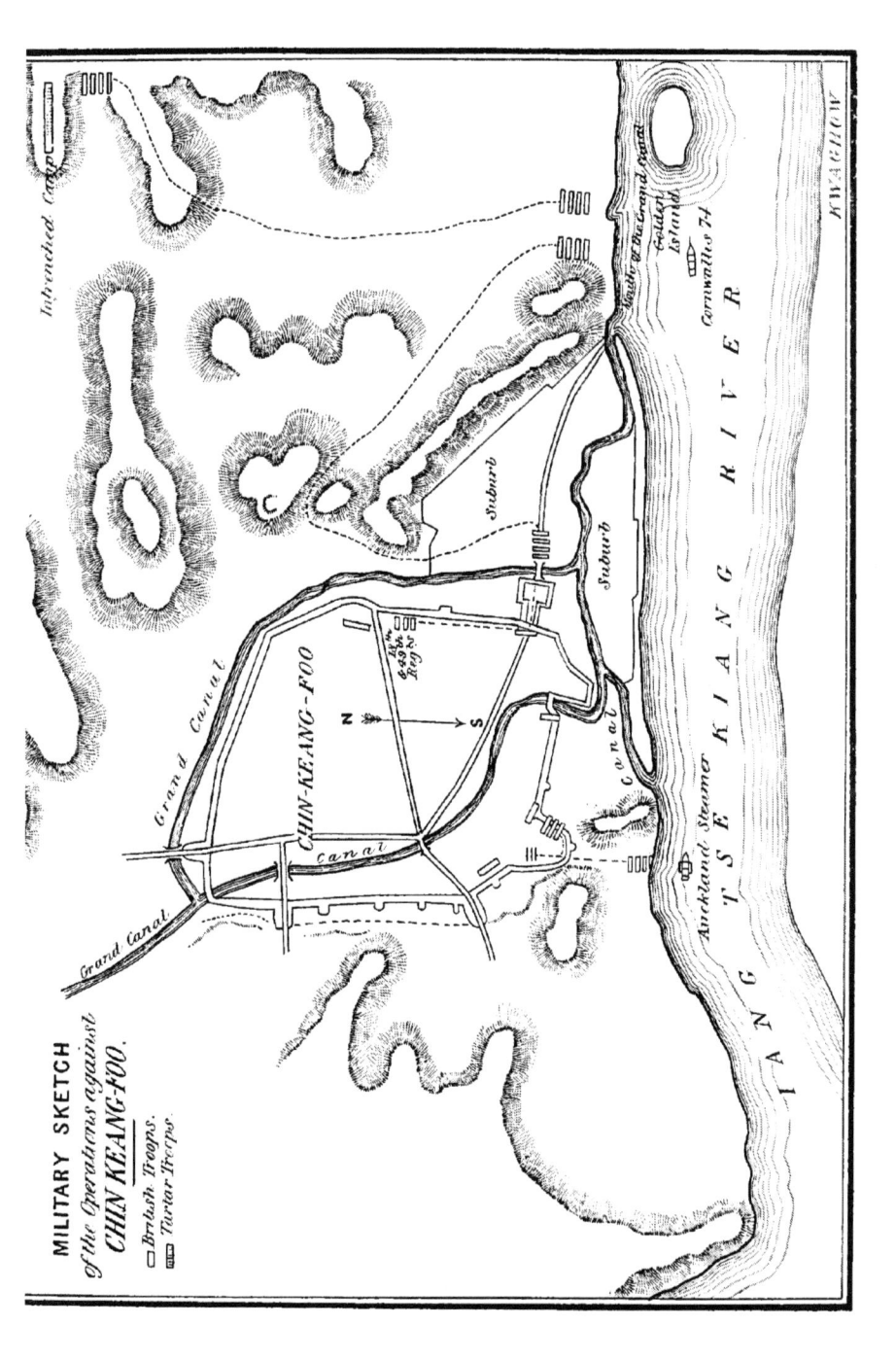

MILITARY SKETCH
of the Operations against
CHIN KEANG-FOO.

British Troops.
Tartar Troops.

Intrenched Camp

Mouth of the Grand Canal
Golden Island
Cornwallis 74

Suburb

Suburb

Suburb

CHIN-KEANG-FOO

Grand Canal

Grand Canal

Canal

Canal

55th & 69th Regts

N

S

Auckland Steamer

Y A N G   T S E   K I A N G   R I V E R

KWACHOW

Infantry, with strong detachments of Artillery and Sappers, was left at Ching-keang-foo, under command of Major-General Schoedde.

Before withdrawing the remainder of the troops, the Engineers were ordered to form an extended and practicable breach in the rampart which faced General Schoedde's position, and four mines having been made in the revetment, they were charged, successfully sprung, and a breach thirty yards wide produced. The parapets for several hundred yards along the east face were also dismantled, to prevent the enemy from forming under their shelter to resist our entrance.

The *Cornwallis*, and several men-of-war, left Ching-keang-foo on the 1st and 2nd August, and arrived off the northern angle of the walls of Nanking on the 5th.

The fleet of transports followed, but were not able to reach the anchorage till the 8th, although the distance was only about forty miles.

A large white flag waved from the walls of Nanking over a battery near which the *Cornwallis* lay at anchor. Some Mandarins came off to the flagship immediately on her arrival, to beg that no hostilities might commence, for Eleepoo was close at hand with full powers to treat. They were informed that operations should be delayed for a short time, and meantime a reconnoissance of the defences was made.

On 9th August the promised communication from Eleepoo was received, and found by the Plenipotentiary to be altogether insufficient to warrant any further delay. The envoys of Eleepoo were dismissed with the assurance that the next day Nanking would be attacked.

The *Cornwallis* moved into a position from which the northern angle of the walls could be battered, and the *Blonde* was towed down the creek till her guns bore on the point which the Admiral had selected for breaching and enfilading the battery which covered it.

12 *

Meantime, Lord Saltoun's brigade was placed on board steamers, and towed on the evening of the 10th to the lower extremity of the creek, where they were disembarked.

To assist in making the breach proposed to be made by the *Cornwallis*, Colonel Montgomerie landed four howitzers, to be placed in a battery near the mouth of the creek, and General Bartley's brigade was detached to form the storming column, supported by marines and seamen, to carry the breach on the following morning, and then to proceed by the ramparts to the Tai-ping Gate (on which Lord Saltoun's brigade was to make a feint), throw it open for their admittance, and the forces being united, to proceed against the Tartar citadel.

Captain Pears, however, having landed under the walls on the 10th evening, to mark out the site of the proposed battery, made his way to the foot of the escarp. He there discovered that between the bank of the river and the ramparts there was a wide and deep ditch, which it would have been impossible to cross, except by boats or a flying bridge. The project was therefore abandoned, and on the 11th Sir Hugh Gough and Lord Saltoun* landed with an escort to mature a new plan of attack.

Meantime Lord Saltoun's brigade moved in a southerly direction by the paved road from the village near the creek, and halted about three miles from the gate.

During the 11th and 12th the artillery were engaged in getting some 9-pounders and howitzers on shore, and by the 13th evening a formidable park had been formed at Lord Saltoun's head-quarters.

A Mandarin of high rank was now sent to intercede for delay, which was refused. The Mandarin seemed forcibly struck with the determination of the reply.

On 18th August Sir Hugh Gough received a letter from the Plenipotentiary, Sir Henry Pottinger, to the effect that negotia-

---

* Accompanied by Captain Pears, who reconnoitred the Tai-ping Gate closely.

tions had reached such a stage that hostilities must be considered suspended.

On 29th August the Treaty of Nanking was signed.

China was to pay 21,000,000 dollars in four years.

Canton, Amoy, Foo-chow-foo, Ningpo, and Shanghai were to be thrown open to British merchants.

All prisoners (British subjects) to be unconditionally released.

Island of Hong Kong to be ceded to the British.

Correspondence to be conducted on terms of perfect equality among officers of Governments.

On the Emperor's assent being received, and the first payment of 6,000,000 dollars, British forces to retire from Nanking and Grand Canal, also from Chin-hae; but Kolangsoo and Chusan to be held till money payments and arrangements for opening the ports were completed.

This brought the war to a close.

On 20th September almost all the transports started in divisions for Chusan, and on 12th and 14th October the fleet of transports got under weigh in two divisions, and proceeded with the Commander-in-Chief to Hong Kong, the Admiral remaining with the *Cornwallis*, and a squadron of men-of-war and steamers, after having despatched four vessels to England with the 6,000,000 dollars, which had been paid in.

Lord Saltoun was left in command of the forces in China (head-quarters Hong Kong), consisting of remains of the 98th, left wing 55th, right wing 41st Madras Native Infantry, company of Royal Artillery, one of Gun Lascars, and one of Madras Sappers and Miners, altogether 1,250 men; and, on 20th December 1842, the rest of the force took its final departure from China.

Lieutenant Ouchterlony, Madras Engineers, remained at Hong Kong as garrison engineer, and Lieutenant Hitchins in command of the F Company, Madras Sappers.

The following is the complimentary order of Sir Hugh

Gough regarding the services of the Artillery and Sappers, dated Singapore, 1st January 1843 :—

" The Artillery and Sappers and Miners deserve more particular mention, as they joined me in the Canton river in March 1841, and have borne a gallant part on every occasion when the enemy was in the field throughout the whole war.   In mentioning to the Governor-General of India the respective commanding officers, I have specially noticed Lieutenant-Colonel Montgomerie and Captain Pears, from whom, in their capacities as Brigadier of Artillery and Commanding Engineer, I uniformly received the most zealous and efficient assistance."

The Governor-General in Council wrote :—" On that occasion (capture of Ching-keang-foo), as on all others, the Madras Artillery and Madras Sappers and Miners maintained the high reputation which has always been attached to their respective corps in the Madras army."

Captain Pears for his services received a brevet-majority on 23rd December 1842, and was nominated a Companion of the Order of the Bath.

Brevet-Captain F. Cotton was promised a majority as soon as he obtained his captaincy, for his services at Canton when Captain Pears was absent. He was promoted to captain on 10th December 1847, and got his brevet-majority next day.

Lieutenant J. Rundall, who was severely and dangerously wounded at Canton, was, on the 27th August 1844, appointed to command the Madras Sappers and Miners.

On 22nd September 1843 an order was issued by the Governor-General in Council granting honorary distinctions to certain corps of the Madras Army for service in China, and the A, B, and F companies of Madras Sappers then received permission to wear on their appointments a golden dragon bearing an imperial crown, and also the word " China."

Subadar-Major Comarasammy, Madras Sappers, Native A.D.C. to Sir Hugh Gough, particularly distinguished himself, and was brought to the notice of the Governor-General. He had distinguished himself in campaigns previous to this. He served in the Mahratta Campaign of 1817–19, was wounded in the leg at Nagpore, and was recommended by General McDowell. In the First Burmese War he served at Rangoon, Kemendine, Pegu, Donabew, Prome, and Maloun, and was wounded in the thigh at Donabew. He was again recommended by Sir Archibald Campbell in 1825.

On the institution of the Order of British India on 25th May 1838,* he was admitted into the Second Class of that Order as a Bahadoor, and for his services in China he was promoted to the First Class as a Sirdar Bahadoor.

Lieutenant Ouchterlony remained as Garrison Engineer at Hong Kong till September 1843, when he was relieved by Major Aldrick of the Royal Engineers; but the F Company of Sappers, under Lieutenant Hitchins, did not leave the colony till October 1846.

Before they left, the officer commanding the forces in China, Major-General the Hon. D'Aguilar, C.B., wrote the following :— " The Madras Sappers, under Lieutenant Hitchins, have rendered important services in carrying on the military works of this colony, and the cheerful and soldier-like manner in which they have invariably performed their arduous duties, especially merit the Major-General's commendation. The Major-General will not fail to make known the sentiments contained in this order to his Lordship the Commander-in-Chief at Madras.''

Lieutenant Doria and Ensign Clerk, both of the Native Infantry, accompanied the F Company to China in 1842, and probably one of them remained at Hong Kong with the com-

---

* On 25th May 1838 thirty-four Native officers were selected from various regiments for admission into the 1st Class Order of British India, one of whom was Subadar Chokalingum of the Madras Sappers, who had highly distinguished himself in Coorg. At the same time thirty-three Native officers were admitted into the 2nd Class, and Subadar-Major Comarasammy was selected from the Sappers for this distinction.

pany.   Assistant-Surgeon Jackson was in medical charge of the company.

All officers and men who on 21st August 1841 formed part of the expeditionary force intended to act against the north coast of China, and served with that force from the date of its leaving Hong Kong until 29th August 1842, the date of the treaty of peace, received a donation of twelve months' batta, but it was not given to those who joined subsequent to 21st August 1841. The A and B Companies must have received this batta, but as the F Company did not join until 1842 they could not have enjoyed it.

CHAPTER V.

C Company to Scinde, Kutchee, and Beloochistan.—Detachment to Cabul.—War
in Scinde.—March across desert to Imaumghur.—Imaumghur destroyed.—
Outram to Hydrabad.—Outram defends the Residency.—Battle of Meannee.
—Six Ameers surrender.—Hydrabad occupied.—Battle of Hydrabad.—
Meerpore taken.—Oomercote taken.—War at an end.—Napier's eulogy of
Madras Sappers.—Madras Sappers at Aden.—Establishment of Engineers
and Sappers.

WHILE the A, B, and F Companies were employed in China, the
C Company was experiencing severe service in Kelat, Afghanistan, and Scinde.

The company quitted Belgaum on the 9th November 1840,
arrived at Vingorla on the 13th, and embarked for Kurrachee on
the 27th, which place they reached on the 4th December, and
having been employed in facilitating the landing operations for
a couple of weeks, they proceeded to join Major-General Brook's
force. They marched through Lower and Upper Scinde to Bagh
in Kutchee.

In February 1841 they marched from Bagh, and thence
proceeded to Kugguck, where they were employed in destroying
the fort, after it had been evacuated by the enemy.

Next month they returned to Dadur and proceeded thence
through the Bolan Pass with only forty-six muskets, the smallest
body of British troops that ever passed through this defile

(sixty miles long) by deliberate marches. Only one-third of the company was armed, the rest of the men carrying working tools.

Shortly after its arrival at Quetta, the company was sent to Thobee, Moosbung, Turee, &c., to make the road in the direction of Kelat practicable for artillery. On this duty it was employed till June, and in July it returned to Quetta.

At this time Lieutenant Outlaw, 26th Native Infantry, commanded the company, and Lieutenants Orr and Boileau, of the Madras Engineers, were attached to it.

In May and June 1841 a detachment under Lieutenant Orr accompanied a force to Nooshky.

In October 1841 the company returned to the plains by the Bolan Pass with the head-quarters of the force, with the exception of a jemadar (Ramen) and twenty-two men, who accompanied a battery of European artillery and two companies of the 41st Regiment to explore the country in the direct line from Quetta to the seaport of Soameanee, and thence to that of Kurrachee.

It was at this time that Captain Henderson assumed command of the company.

The head-quarters of the company continued with the field force at Sibi and Dadur, while its detachments extended all over the country from Sibi to Kurrachee, employed in various public works.

Meanwhile the insurrection at Cabul broke out, and in April 1842 the company proceeded above the Bolan Pass a second time, still leaving detachments in Kutchee and Scinde.

The head-quarters of the company remained at Quetta till September 1842, employed in repairing the fort of Quetta, and constructing other defences.

On 26th April a detachment consisting of one havildar (Amaraputty), one naique, and twenty-eight privates, left Quetta with General England's force, and was present at the second affair of Hykulzie on 29th April, when the enemy were driven

from the heights which they had occupied. It then proceeded
on to the Kojuck mountains, where the force was again opposed,
to Kandahar, and joined General Nott's army.

From Kandahar the party accompanied the force that relieved
Kelat-i-Ghilzai (a brigade under Colonel Wymer), and after
destroying the fort and buildings erected by the British, returned
to Kandahar.

From the 18th to the 29th June the detachment was
employed in destroying several posts of the enemy in the surrounding country, and on the 10th August marched with the
force towards Cabul.*

The party was present in the general action with Shumshoodeen, near the source of the Turnuck,† on 30th August.

On 1st September, General Nott resumed his march, and
found himself before Ghuznee on 5th September.

The day was spent in desultory fighting, and the detachment of
Sappers having been engaged in the action, were employed
during the night in preparing mines to breach the walls, which
although got ready, were not required, as the post was found to
be evacuated in the morning.‡

The engineer had proposed to establish a battery on ridge of
hills north of the town, in advance of Bullal, and 350 yards from
the walls. This battery was to open the flank wall connecting the
citadel on the west with the town wall. The defences of the citadel
could be swept from the same point by light artillery, and
there was a thick dam of earth across the ditch opposite the
point marked for the breach.

Principal assault was to be supported by an attempt to blow
in water-gate (both the others being built up and causeways
cut through) ; another to escalade a weak point near Cabul gate.

---

* Major Edward Sanders, Bengal Engineers, with the force.

† Thirty-eight miles south-west of Ghuznee.

‡ Three hundred and twenty-seven sepoys of 17th Native Infantry were here
released from slavery

At dusk a working-party of Sappers and 160 men from regiments on the hill, commenced work; by 4 A.M. cover had been secured, and so much progress had been made as to lead to reasonable expectation that four 18-pounders and two 24-pounder howitzers would be ready to open during the day.

Towards morning it was believed that the fort had been evacuated, and this was ascertained to be the case at daylight by Lieutenant North of Engineers.

The party was afterwards employed for two days in ruining the defences, and it then marched with the army, arriving at Cabul on the 17th September, having destroyed a fort on the road.

On the 14th and 15th September, Shumshoodeen, Sultan Jan, and other chiefs, occupied with 62,000 men a succession of strong mountains, intercepting the march on Beenee, Badan, and Mydan. Our troops gallantly dislodged them.

At Cabul the Sappers were variously employed, but chiefly in opening up a channel to supply the camp with water, which had been cut off by the enemy.

On 12th October the whole army quitted Cabul, and was daily engaged with the enemy till its arrival at Jellalabad on 25th October.

The party of Sappers reached Ferozepore on the Sutlej on 23rd December with Nott's force, and quitted that place for Sukkur on 5th January 1843, in order to open the road for Leslie's troop of Horse Artillery.

From Sukkur the detachment came down the Indus in boats to Hydrabad, rejoining head-quarters on 24th March 1843, just in time for the battle of Hydrabad.

Lieutenant-Colonel Leslie, C.B., wrote the following regarding the assistance he had received from the detachment:—

"I do hereby certify that Jemadar Amaraputty of the 3rd (C) Company Madras Sappers and Miners, in charge of a party of thirty men of the above company serving in Afghanistan, was for a long time attached to the troops under my command, and marched with his party at the head of the troops through the whole of that difficult country. I have considered it a point of duty to give the jemadar (who was only then a havildar) this certificate as a record of my high opinion of his services and zeal. I have never met a more willing or efficient man. He and his sturdy and hardworking comrades were ever ready and always successful in making a road for the guns over the most difficult ground ; and having their tools always in their hands, their work was never delayed. In short, I am anxious to bear testimony to the unwearied zeal of the whole party, and wish them success with all my heart."

The head-quarters of the C Company remained above the Bolan Pass till September 1842, and then returned to the plains of Kutchee with General England's retiring force.

This movement was effected in three columns, which followed each other after three or four days' intervals, and the company was accordingly divided into three detachments.

The company (with the exception of that part with General Nott's force) assembled at Sukkur and crossed the Indus to Roree with the force under Major-General Sir Charles Napier.

The following officers served with the company in Scinde :—

Brevet Captain Henderson, Madras Engineers.
Lieutenant T. F. V. Outlaw, 26th Madras Native Infantry.
First Lieutenant C. A. Orr, Madras Engineers.
Second Lieutenant A. J. M. Boileau, Madras Engineers.
Assistant Surgeon Carlow, Medical Department.

As early as the 20th December, Sir Charles Napier had informed Lord Ellenborough, the Governor-General, that the desert was the place to strike at the strength of the Ameers of Scinde.

In the deserts to the east of the Indus, the Ameers had two forts, Imaumghur and Shahghur, about twenty miles apart, and distant in a south-easterly direction from Roree about eighty or ninety miles.

Sir Charles Napier said that if he advanced south against the Ameers and defeated them, they would proceed to Imaumghur and rally in a place where it would be almost impossible to follow them. If he attempted it, the Ameers from Hydrabad would march against his rear, while if he continued his march to Hydrabad, the force which had rallied at Imaumghur would follow him and intercept his communications with Roree and and Sukkur. He accordingly conceived an enterprise as hardy as any of which military records tell. He resolved to attack Imaumghur, which was accounted impregnable as a fortress, and inaccessible from its situation.

It was in the very heart of the waste, eight long marches, while its exact position was unknown.

The General pushed on to Digee-ka-Kote, which he reached about 4th January 1843, and where he was joined by Outram.

The native agent sent to explore the route to Imaumghur came back with a tale of arid sand and dried-up pits, so that Napier resigned all hope of effecting his march with his whole army. He accordingly selected 350 men of the 22nd, two 24-pounder howitzers, Captain Whitler's camel battery, 200 Scinde Irregular Horse, and thirty Madras Sappers; officers and men being all mounted on camels. Besides these, there were ten camels with provisions and eighty with water.

At 2 A.M. on 6th January the detachment started and marched twenty-two miles and a half.

No forage could be obtained for the horses, so 150 of the Scinde Horse were sent back.

On the 7th the reduced force marched ten miles to Doomb. On the 8th, eleven miles to Tuggul. On the 9th they went twelve miles to Luk. On the 10th to Muttree, eleven miles, crossing a succession of steep heavy sand-hills, over which the howitzers were dragged with great difficulty.

On the 11th they marched eight miles and a half, being employed for two hours in making a road up one sand-hill.

The next day, the road being of much the same character, they marched six miles and three-quarters, and arrived at Imanmghur.

The entrance to the fort was through a gate on the east side of an outer enclosure mud wall twelve feet high, which was in the form of a rectangle. In the enclosure was a good well, a few stable huts, and two small powder magazines. From this enclosure the entrance was through a strong well-flanked gate, in a redoubt attached to the fort, which served to cover another gate situated about midway on the eastern side. These gates were of good material, well bound with iron, and commanded by lines of fire from loop-holes in every direction. There was a tower at each angle of the fort, and one mid-way on the west side. Three guns and numerous wall-pieces, &c., were found mounted on the walls. The fort was built of brick masonry. The walls and towers were forty feet high, and the large tower on the south-east corner fifty feet.

Napier found that Mahomed Khan, although he had a strong fortress, well provided, and garrisoned by a force six times as numerous as the band coming to assail him, had fled with his treasure two days before. Taking a southerly direction, he regained the Indus, leaving all his grain and powder behind.

The Engineers present on this expedition were—

Major Waddington, Bombay Engineers, Commanding Engineer.

Brevet-Captain Henderson, Madras Engineers, Field Engineer.

First Lieutenant Brown, Bengal Engineers.

Second Lieutenant Boileau, Madras Engineers.

On 13th January the Sappers went down and formed seven mines under the exterior wall of the northern curtain Some shafts were also commenced in the galleries and towers by a working party of the 22nd.   The powder was also removed from the fort.

In the afternoon of the same day two 24-pounder howitzers played into the fort.

On 14th January the shafts commenced the day before were carried down eight or nine feet, and chambers made.   The howitzers were again practised with good effect   In the afternoon they commenced to charge and explode the mines.

There were altogether twenty-four of these mines, and the destruction of the fort was effected on the 15th January by Major Waddington, all the other Engineer officers being present. Matches of all having been lighted, the Assistant Engineer took refuge behind some cover.   He perceived his chief bending over the train of one mine, and called out, "The other mines are going to burst!"   Waddington replied, "That may be, but this mine must burst also," and then, having arranged the match, he walked away, holding up his hands to guard his head from the huge fragments which the bursting mines sent into the air to fall in showers.

Orders were now given for the destruction of the rest of the powder which had been found in the fort; accordingly 7,000 lbs. were placed in a room inside the fort and fired.

The result was a magnificent explosion ; not a vestige of the house was to be seen ; the adjoining well was filled up, and bits of walls which had remained standing were shaken down.

Four thousand pounds of powder were then collected just inside the gate of the outer enclosure.   This was fired by Lieutenant Brown, and the explosion surpassed in appearance the last one.

After the destruction of Imaumghur, Napier intended at first to go on to Shahghur, but hearing that the tribes were gathering head at Dingee, he resolved to move back as rapidly as possible to the Indus to rejoin his army.

The Duke of Wellington, on hearing of this expedition, said :

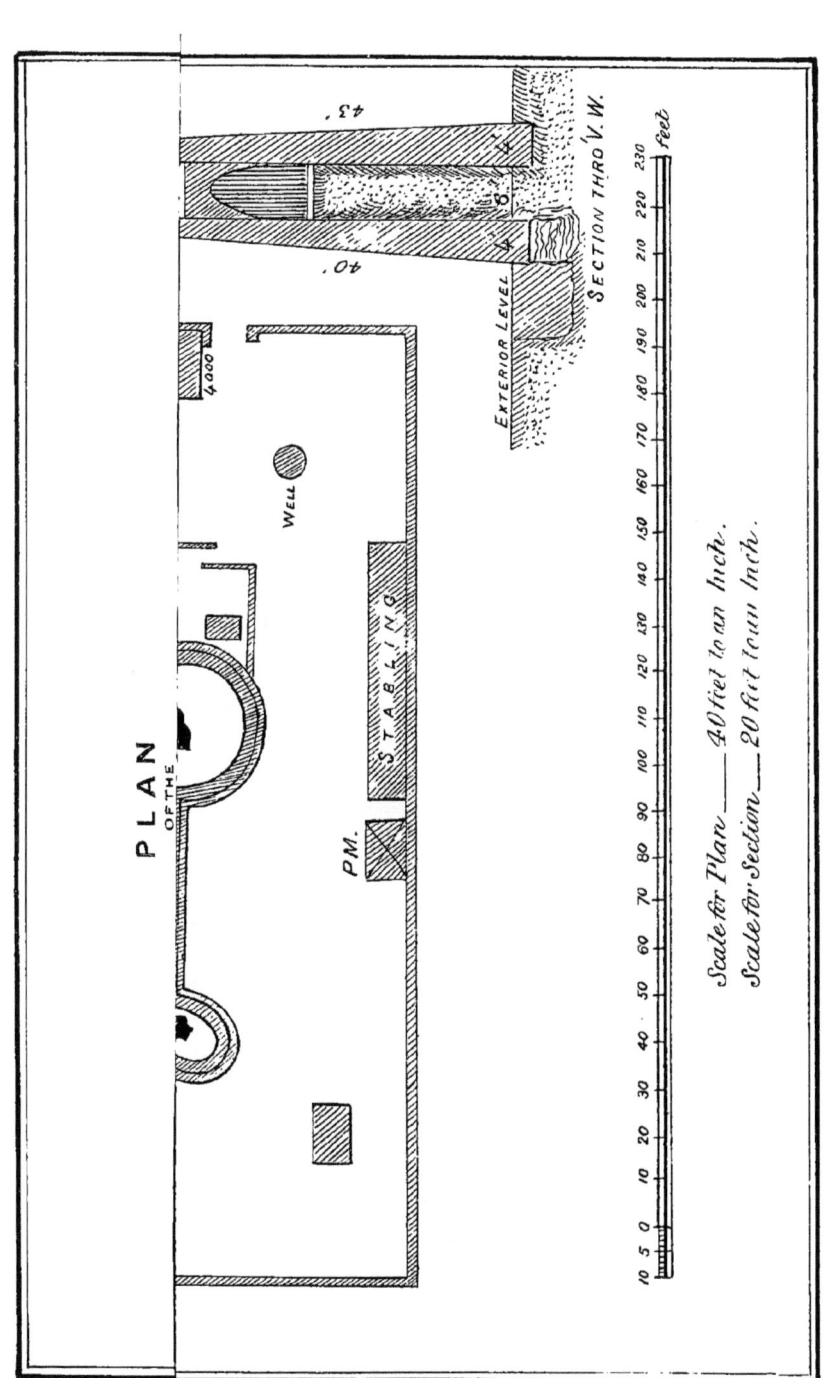

PLAN OF THE

4000

WELL

PM.

STABLING

43.

40.

6.

EXTERIOR LEVEL

SECTION THRO' V. W.

Scale for Plan ____ 40 feet to an Inch.
Scale for Section ____ 20 feet to an Inch.

10 5 0   10   20   30   40   50   60   70   80   90   100   110   120   130   140   150   160   170   180   190   200   210   220   230   Feet

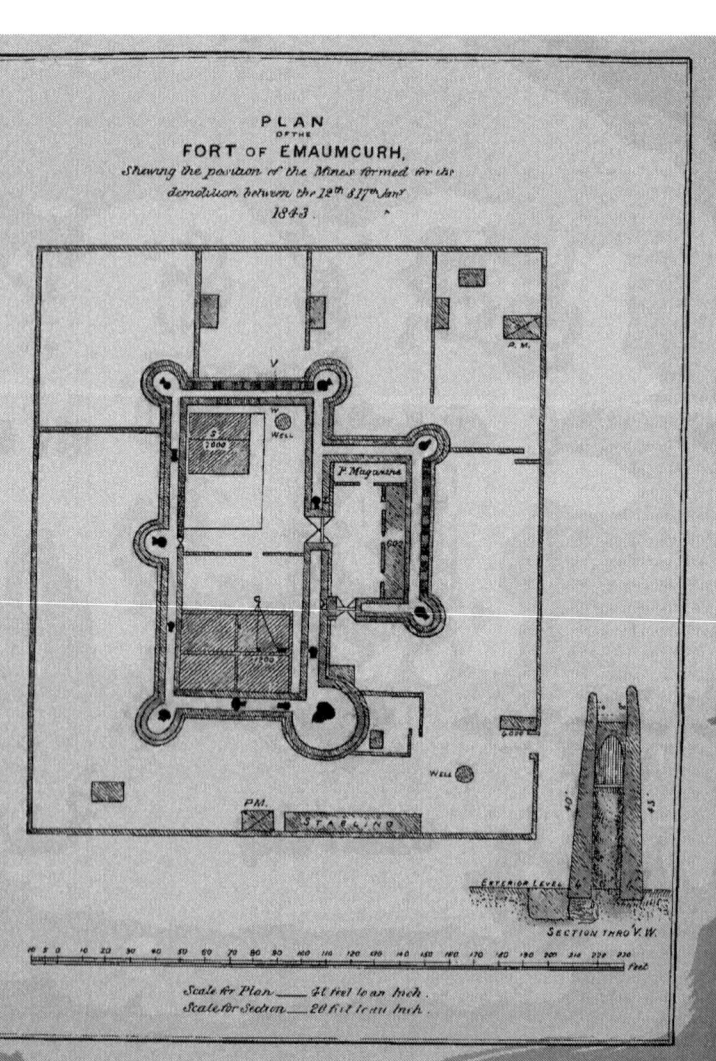

PLAN
OF THE
FORT OF EMAUMCURH,
Shewing the position of the Mines formed for the
demolition, between the 12th & 17th Jan'y
1843.

Scale for Plan ____ 4t feet to an Inch.
Scale for Section ____ 20 feet to an Inch.

" Sir Charles Napier's march on Imaumghur is one of the most
curious military feats which I have ever known to be performed,
or have ever perused an account of in my life. He moved his
troops through the desert against hostile forces. He had his
guns transported under circumstances of extreme difficulty, and
in a manner the most extraordinary, and he cut off a retreat of
the enemy which rendered it impossible for them ever to regain
their positions."

Napier chose a new route for his return, more to the south,
leaving Imaumghur on the 15th.

On the second day he reached Tuggul, and then directed his
main body of troops to descend the left bank of the Indus from
Degee-ka-Kote, and meet him at Peer-Abu-Bekr.

The first three days of his march were very trying. On the
fourth he found water and forage. On the eighth day (23rd
January) he reached Peer-Abu-Bekr.

Eighteen days in the waste, he came back triumphant, without a check, without the loss of a man, without any sick, having
dispersed the Ameers' army and baffled their plan of campaign.

From Peer-Abu-Bekr, Napier marched south, and on the 31st
reached Nowshera.

Here he halted five days, while Outram proceeded to Hydrabad as a negotiator, and the light company of the 22nd was sent
with him as a guard.

On 8th February Outram reached Hydrabad with thirty
sepoys, under Captain Wells. The company of the 22nd arrived
three days after.

The Ameers, it is believed, now made up their minds to
murder the Commissioner and his officers, destroy his escort,
and then give battle with 60,000 against our force of 3,000, of
whom only 500 were Europeans.

On the 12th, Outram and his officers were invited to a durbar.
General Napier had meantime reached Sukkerunda, sixty miles
from Hydrabad, and halted.

In hopes of entrapping the General, the Ameers suffered Outram and his officers to leave unhurt, and countermanded the attack on the Residency.

Our army was on the left bank of the Indus, and drew all its supplies from Roree and Sukkur, by the Indus. On its left was the desert, and on a line drawn east from Hydrabad, perpendicular to the Indus, were Meerpore and Oomercote, the first at the edge of the desert forty miles from Hydrabad, the second sixty miles from Meerpore, right in the heart of it.

The Belouchees of Lower Scinde, 30,000 strong, were then assembled on the plains of Meannee. The Princes of Upper Scinde had 7,000 men at Khonhera. The Chandians, 10,000 strong, had crossed the Indus in rear of the British camp; 10,000 men were at Meerpore; Oomercote was garrisoned, and thousands of the hill tribes were coming down to the Indus.

On the 14th the Ameers commanded Outram to depart, but of this Outram took no notice. Outram had to resist the assault of 8,000 men and six guns, with two armed steamers, a stone house, and 100 men who had only forty rounds of ammunition apiece.

He had with him Captain Conway, Lieutenant Hardinge, and Ensign Pennefather of the 22nd, and Captains Grant and Wells of the East India Company's service.

Captain Brown, Bengal Engineers, went on board the steamer and directed the guns.

The Residency was gallantly defended by its small garrison for three hours, when Outram retreated to the steamers, the *Satellite* and the *Planet*.

The two steamers then proceeded up the river, assailed on both banks. At Muttaree, one march north of Meannee, they found the army, and joined it.

Our army reached Muttaree on the 16th morning, the troops of the Ameers being at Meannee, ten miles off, in a position formed by the dry bed of the Fullailee. The English army was reduced to 2,600, of whom 200 were detached, under Outram, to drop down the river again and to burn the shikargahs on the bank.

On the night of the 16th the army marched, and at 8 A.M. on the 17th the advanced guard discovered the Ameers' camp. The Ameers' forces consisted of 30,000 to 40,000 Beloochees, with fifteen guns. Five thousand of the force were cavalry. Their front extended 1,200 yards, and lined the dry bed of the Fullailee. In front of this, their guns were massed in two places, covering their flanks. Their wings rested on large, dense, shikargahs. That on the Beloochees right was intersected by minor nullahs, very deep, running at right angles to the Fullailee, and that great nullah took a sudden bend to the rear behind the shikargah, forming a deep loop, in which was the Ameers' camp and cavalry. All the nullahs were carefully scarped. The shikargah on the left was very extensive, enclosed towards the plains by a high wall, having one not very wide opening about midway between the two armies. Five or six thousand troops were in it.

The position of the Beloochees could not be turned, so it was necessary to make a direct attack. The British army was only 2,400 strong; the Poona Horse and four companies of infantry were left as a guard to the baggage, so that order of battle was formed with less than 2,000, of which 1,780 were bayonets and sabres.

On our right we had twelve guns, under Major Floyd, flanked by fifty Madras Sappers, under Captain Henderson, Madras Engineers. On the left of the artillery was the 22nd Regiment, 500 strong, under Captain Pennefather. Further on was the 25th Native Infantry, under Major Teesdale; then the 12th, under Major Reid, and the 1st Grenadiers, under Major Clibborne, while on the extreme left was the 9th Bengal Cavalry, under Colonel Pattle.

In front of the right were some infantry skirmishers, while

13 *

the Scinde Irregular Cavalry, under Captain Jacob, covered the left.

A plain extended between the two armies for about 1,000 yards; the first 700 yards of this was covered with low jungle, but the other 300 had been cleared by the Beloochees. The line now advanced.

The right of the Ameers' was found to be much strengthened by the village of Kathree, but the general detected a flaw on their left in the shikargah. The wall had not been loop-holed, neither had any arrangements been made for firing over the top. The grenadiers of the 22nd, under Captain Tew, were placed in the opening before mentioned, to block up the entrance, and they received orders never to give way, but to die there if necessary.

This opening was gallantly and successfully defended, but, unfortunately, Captain Tew was killed.

The British right passed securely under the wall of the shikargah. When the 22nd had got within 100 yards of the Fullailee the column opened line to their left. This formation was still incomplete, when the General ordered a charge. The English guns were run forward into position, the infantry closed on the Fullailee at a run, and rushed up the sloping bank. When they reached the top of the bank they found crowds of Beloochees in their front, but the 22nd dashed on. During this time the small band of Madras Sappers on the right fought gallantly and protected that flank of the artillery, which from its position swept diagonally along the bed of the Fullailee, tearing the masses with a horrible carnage. The sepoys now came into action. The Beloochees fought with desperate courage, never more than three yards apart, and often intermixed. The English were several times violently forced back. Pennefather fell wounded. Major Teesdale was killed. Major Jackson, of the 12th, also killed, fighting splendidly.

Many of the European officers were either killed or wounded.

The sepoys now began slowly to recede, but the General was there, and brought them up again. On one occasion Sir Charles Napier was assailed by a chief, but Lieutenant Marston of the 23rd slew the sirdar.

For three and a half hours this fierce fight continued. During all this time the grenadiers of the 22nd maintained their post at the opening from the shikargah. Major Clibborne should have stormed Kathree, but instead of doing so kept his sepoy grenadiers in a position where they were but slightly engaged.

The General perceived this, and sent orders to Colonel Pattle, second in command, to charge with all the Bengal and Scinde cavalry on the right. This order was at once carried out. Major Storey led the Bengal troopers on the enemy's infantry to the left, while the Scinde Horse fell on the Ameer's camp and cavalry. Now the Beloochees began to waver. The 22nd leapt forward, pushed them into the ravine, and closed in combat again; the Madras Sappers did the like, the Sepoys followed, and at the same time those in the shikargah abandoned that cover and joined the left, where the conflict was renewed. The battle was, however, lost, and the Beloochees began to retreat slowly, but with no marks of fear. The victors followed closely. Two or three thousand Beloochees kept their position on the extreme left, but the British guns were turned on them, and they at last went off also.

The General now halted his army, recalled his cavalry, and formed a large square, placing baggage and camp-followers in the centre. During the battle it is recorded that in every quarter astonishing feats of personal bravery were performed.

Twenty officers, including four field officers, went down in battle, six being killed; 250 sergeants and privates, of whom sixty were killed. The loss of the Beloochees was enormous; carefully computed to be 6,000. A thousand bodies were heaped in the Fullailee alone. In four hours 2,000 men struck down 6,000, three to each man. The General, at break of day, sent word to the Ameers that he would storm Hydrabad if they did not surrender.   Soon after noon six Ameers entered his camp and offered themselves as prisoners.

On the 19th the army took possession of the city of Hydrabad, and next day the fortress was occupied.

Fifty-five officers were mentioned in the General's despatches as having distinguished themselves at the battle of Meaunee. Amongst them were Major Waddington, Bombay Engineers; Captain Henderson, Madras Engineers; Lieutenant Brown, Bengal Engineers; Boileau, Madras Engineers; and Lieutenant Outlaw, commanding the company of Madras Sappers and Miners.

In a letter, Sir Charles Napier made honourable mention of Subadar Tondroyen, of the Sappers, as follows:—

" At the battle of Meannee, Subadar Tondroyen led his company most gallantly down into the bed of the Fullailee.   He followed Major Henderson, his commanding officer, who for that gallant action received the Companionship of the Bath. At this time the part where these two brave men led was about the most dangerous part of the field.   I saw with admiration the boldness of the behaviour of the company and its commander, and the Subadar was at his side on all occasions.   This old warrior's courage, energy, and great bodily exertions excited my admiration, and Major Henderson can confirm my opinion of him.   If I am entitled to the Red Ribbon of the Bath, he is to the Order of Merit."

Captain Henderson captured one of the enemy's standards, which he presented to the head-quarters of the Corps.

In his despatch after the battle of Meannee, dated 18th February 1843, Sir Charles Napier thus notices the Engineers and Sappers:—

" Captain Henderson, of the Madras Engineers, took a standard, and did good service with his excellent little band of Sappers and Miners, not only in this engagement, but through the campaign. His Lieutenants, Boileau and Outlaw, have also distinguished themselves."

Captain Henderson received a brevet-majority and a C.B.

After the battle of Meannee, the General sent to Kurrachee for reinforcements and supplies of ammunition. Colonel Roberts, who was at Sukkur, despatched a supply of ammunition down the river, knowing how important this matter was.

Lord Ellenborough caused three regiments from the Sutlej to be warned for service in Scinde, also 350 of Chamberlain's Horse and a camel battery, and sent the whole to Sukkur. Shortly after, Captains Leslie's and Blood's batteries of Horse Artillery and 3rd Bombay Cavalry were despatched.

The small band of Madras Sappers who had accompanied Nott's force to Cabul came down with Leslie's battery, and arrived in time to take part in the battle of Hydrabad.

Sir Charles Napier now formed an entrenched camp on the left bank of the Indus, as well as a post on the opposite side of the river, and placed his hospital and stores in the camp.

Ameer Shere Mahomed (or the " Lion," as he was called) was still at the head of 25,000 to 40,000 men.

He advanced his main body to within ten miles of Hydrabad, and the whole country became disturbed.

The Ameers who had surrendered, and were imprisoned in a garden near Hydrabad, continued to intrigue, so Napier thought it advisable to put them on board the steamers.

On 18th March the " Lion " sent Vakeels to Napier, saying, " Quit this land, and your life will be spared, provided you restore all you have taken." As they delivered the message the evening-gun fired, and Napier replied, " You hear that sound ? It is my answer to your chief. Begone ! "

The " Lion " now advanced in force to Alika Tanda, ten miles from Hydrabad, and thence detached 8,000 men to Dubba on his right, and 5,000 to Kooseree on his left, while he retained 12,000 at Alika Tanda.

His army thus occupied a triangle, his left wing to assail our camp, his right to attack Hydrabad, while his centre gave battle to our troops advancing from the camp.

Before the 10th the British army had received six months' provisions, recruits, money, and ammunition. The camp was strongly entrenched, and Hydrabad Fort had been repaired and strengthened.

The 21st Native Infantry arrived from Sukkur, and on the 19th 800 sepoys under Major Stack, 300 cavalry, and Leslie's battery of Horse Artillery, with a small party of Madras Sappers, moving down, were within two or three marches.

On the 21st Stack reached Muttaree, and received orders to push on, as information had been obtained that the Lion intended to attack him.

Napier concluded he would do so at Loonar, two miles from Dubba ; so he sent McMurdo with 250 Poona Horse to push on to Muttaree and reinforce Stack.

McMurdo found Stack on the 22nd morning, and on the same day the General ordered Jacob, with the Scinde Horse, along the same road, and moved himself afterwards with the Bengal Cavalry and some guns, followed by the whole infantry.

Stack marched from Muttaree at 11 A.M. on the 22nd, and passed the Fullailee. He marched with his guns, infantry, and cavalry in advance, followed by his baggage, so that when the guns had passed the small nullah at Loonar, the rear of the baggage had only just crossed the Fullailee at Meannee.

As the baggage approached this nullah, the Belooch match-lock men crossed the Fullailee from a shikargah, and opened fire. Captain McMurdo charged with a few of the Poona Horse, and sent to Major Stack for a troop.

McMurdo, meantime, was attacked. He sustained their fire for three-quarters of an hour, and saved the baggage. The troops at last came up, when he charged and drove the enemy across the Fullailee. McMurdo then, leaving Lieutenant Moore in charge, galloped after Stack, took back two guns, and, placing them in a flanking position, raked the enemy's troops.

Stack, sensible of his error, now halted and formed up. Jacob's Cavalry came in sight, the baggage was closed up, and the movement conducted properly ; but the column did not reach our camp till midnight.

Further reinforcements arrived from Sukkur and Kurrachee on the 23rd The recruits were thrown into Hydrabad, and the veteran troops which occupied it joined the army.

At day-break on the 24th 5,000 fighting-men were under arms in front of our camp, 1,100 cavalry, and nineteen guns, five of them being horse artillery.

Two pieces were left in the camp, and seventeen went with the army.

The army marched in the direction of Kooseree.

On the 22nd a part of the company of Madras Sappers was employed in forming an easy descent for the artillery into the Fullailee ; and on the evening of the 23rd they formed part of a force, consisting of two regiments of native infantry and a battery of two 8-inch howitzers, sent forward to take possession of the bank of the river where these preparations had been made.

Early on the morning of the 24th they crossed the river, and formed on the opposite side, and Sir Charles Napier appeared at the head of the main body and the reserve which had marched from Hydrabad.

The whole now advanced in order of battle, the company of Madras Sappers being at the head of the advanced guard. They had proceeded about three miles when the General discovered the enemy were in position, and moved towards them with the Scinde Horse.

Shortly after this the enemy opened their artillery-fire. This continued during the advance, and the British line took up its first position 1,200 yards from the enemy.   Here a bold reconnoissance was undertaken by Major Waddington, Commanding Engineer, who rode along their whole front at a distance of 300 yards.

During the advance Captain Henderson received orders to make a slight detour in order to make a nullah passable for the heavy battery, and, finally, the Sappers remained attached to these guns. The company was formed into sub-divisions, one to each gun, and assisted also in limbering and unlimbering in action.

Our artillery opened fire at 1,200 yards, but as it was not sufficiently effective, the line advanced a further distance of 500 yards. From the second line a heavy cannonade was opened from each of our batteries, which continued for about an hour.

Several of the enemy's tumbrils exploded.

Shortly after this there was an evident commotion amongst the enemy, and a movement towards their right. Our infantry was now ordered to advance.

The 22nd was the first to close with the enemy, who were found to occupy a double canal running along their front, each being thirty to forty feet wide at top, and provided with an embankment on each side, forming a front of two ditches and four parapets; from ditch to top of rampart twenty-five feet high. Besides this there were other canals running in their rear and on their left; while their right rested on the village of Dubba, the walls of which were pierced with loop-holes; and in the vicinity there were several breastworks.

The 22nd advanced in the most steady and determined manner. The regiment suffered a good deal, but reserved their fire till within forty paces, when they poured in a volley, ascended the first embankment, and continued their fire till they were enabled to surmount the obstacles opposed to them, and then wheeling to the left, drove the enemy before them.

Meanwhile the 21st and 25th Native Infantry advanced in a similar manner, formed on the right of the 22nd, and the three regiments working together, drove the enemy back into the village, where they were exposed to a heavy fire from the Horse Artillery, whose guns were now on the top of the first embankment.

At last the enemy were obliged to quit the village, when they were pursued by the cavalry, which completed the rout of the right of the enemy's line. While this was going on on our left, the right of our line was also actively engaged.

When the commotion and movement of the enemy, previously noticed, took place towards their right, it was discovered that some of the enemy had taken flight towards their left. The Bombay Cavalry and Scinde Horse immediately charged, and slew many of the fugitives.

The other three regiments of Native Infantry (1st, 8th and 12th) continued their advance and crossed the canals; but our cavalry being amongst the enemy in their front, they had to cease firing. Opposition now soon ceased. The field was ours, and the whole of our force formed line along the bank of the Fullailee, east of Dubba.

With regard to the company of Sappers: after the infantry were ordered to advance the artillery could no longer use their guns, and the men were formed up and left under command of Lieutenant Outlaw, with the artillery. Captain Henderson proceeded on and crossed the canals; Lieutenants Outlaw and Boileau soon followed with the company, as it was found that the artillery were not to advance over the canals.

But by this time the enemy began to take to flight, and as the artillery were ordered to form line on the bank of the Fullailee, the Sappers returned to assist the heavy battery over difficult ground. Captain Henderson, in his report, mentions the great assistance he received from Lieutenants Outlaw and Boileau, and the excellent conduct of Jemadar Tondroyen and the whole company.

Corporal McDonough, of the Sappers, received a matchlock-ball in his foot.

The Bengal Cavalry and Poona Horse pursued the retreating masses on the right. The Scinde Horse followed further to the right, and actually got sight of the "Lion's" elephant and camel, and would have been able to secure him, when Colonel Pattle, second in command, put a stop to the pursuit, and the "Lion" escaped.

We lost 270 men and officers, of which number 147 belonged to the 22nd Regiment. The Beloochees lost 5,000 men; 800 bodies were lying in the nullahs and at Dubba, and all the villages and lanes beyond were filled with the dead and dying.

Seventeen standards and fifteen guns were captured. Eleven of the guns were taken on the field, and four next day. There were thirteen wounded prisoners; this was a slight improvement on the day of Meanee, when there were only three.

The General ascertained that the retreat of the enemy was chiefly in the direction of Meerpore, and he again put his troops in motion. The thermometer on the day of battle had stood at 110°; the troops had marched twelve miles, and fought for three or four hours, when they rested for eight hours. In spite of this fatigue they marched twenty miles further, and passed through two entrenched positions which the "Lion" had prepared to fall back upon.

Next day the Poona Horse reached Meerpore, forty miles distant from the field of battle.

The "Lion" fled to Ooomercote, while Meerpore was taken possession of by our forces. It was found strongly fortified and full of stores.

Napier sent on the Scinde Horse under Jacob, and a camel battery, with Captain Whitlie; he supported them with the 25th Native Infantry, under Major Woodburne. The company of Madras Sappers also formed part of the force. To assist in the capture of Oomercote, where opposition was expected, the General ordered the troops in Cutch to march on that place also. When Captain Whitlie was within twenty miles of Oomercote, he received orders to retreat, " as the river was rising before its time, and with unusual rapidity."

At this time Captain Whitlie heard that Oomercote had been abandoned, so he halted while Lieutenant Brown (Bengal Engineers) rode to Meerpore to get fresh instructions. Brown rode to Meerpore, forty miles, without stopping, and returned as rapidly as possible with instructions for Whitlie to push on.

On the 4th April, Oomercote opened its gates, the garrison retiring into the small interior fort. Major Woodburne, with the 25th Native Infantry, arrived by forced marches, placed guns in position, when the garrison, after a short parley, came out and laid down down their arms. Nine guns were found in the fort. The British flag was now hoisted on the highest tower. A small garrison was left in the place, while the remainder returned to Hydrabad by the 11th April. Oomercote was thus taken only ten days after the battle, although 100 miles distant, and situate in the heart of the desert.

The " Lion " now fled northward, and our army was concentrated at Meerpore.

It should here be noted that, after the battle of Hydrabad, some men of the 22nd concealed their wounds, in order to get on with the force, expecting another fight.

Their names were—

John Durr
John Muldowny
Robert Young
Henry Lines
Patrick Gill
James Andrews

} Wounds not severe.

Sergeant Haney, wound rather severe.

Thomas Middleton
James Mulvey

} Severely wounded in the legs.

Silvester Day ; a ball in the foot !

The march of troops from Cutch was now countermanded, and Napier with his army marched back to Hydrabad.*

On 8th April Sir Charles Napier was in the Palace of the Ameers, having in sixteen days, with 5,000 men, defeated more than 25,000, captured two great fortresses, and marched 200 miles.

The "Lion" still had an army, and attempted to get reinforcements from the other side of the river, but he was foiled by the General's vigilance. Steamers were sent up the river to destroy boats, and on one occasion 100 sepoys were sent up to drive away the Chief, which was effectually done. In the north-west Ali Moorad and Chamberlain were placed to intercept the "Lion." Roberts† was ordered to march from Sukkur down to Sehwan, with 1,500 men and a battery.

On the evening of the 7th Colonel Roberts heard that Shah Mahomed, the "Lion's" brother, was at Peer-arres near the Lukka Hills, fourteen miles from Sehwan Roberts marched in the night, surprised and defeated him, and took the Chief prisoner. Roberts then crossed the river.

Jacob was now at Meerpore, and troops were ordered from Deesa.

When this had all been arranged, the troops all marched on Koomhera. Roberts from Sehwan, south-east; Ali Moorad and Chamberlain from the north; Napier from Hydrabad, and Jacob from Meerpore, up the margin of the desert.

The "Lion" tried to break through Jacob's force, but was defeated, and fled with ten followers across the Indus. These operations terminated without the loss of a single man in action, but more than sixty officers and men died from the effects of the extreme heat.

Thus the war terminated in Upper Scinde ; and the General, turning his attention to the Delta, quickly tranquillized it by

---

* A plan of Oomercote was taken by Captain Henderson, M.E.

† Afterwards Sir H. Roberts, K.C.B.

means of his native police.   After the conclusion of the war the company of the Madras Sappers remained in Scinde for about a year.   Detachments from the Company were sent to all the principal stations in Lower Scinde, and were employed in various public works, such as building forts, erecting barracks for European and native troops, constructing a stone pier in Kurrachee harbour, &c. ; with the exception of a short period when a naique's party of Sappers accompanied a force under Major General Simpson, second in command, in an expedition, on which the General, in a note to Lieutenant Outlaw, expressed his high appreciation of the naique and his party.   The company embarked at Kurrachee for Bombay, on board the steamer *Nemesis*, on 25th March 1844, having been on foreign service for nearly three years and a half.

On the company quitting Scinde, the following General Order was issued by His Excellency Sir Charles Napier, G.C.B., Governor of Scinde :—

" Captain Henderson, and officers, N.C O., and privates of the Madras Sappers and Miners, you have earned laurels in Scinde ; no troops have more honourably conducted themselves. Associated in all the glories of the Bombay Army, you leave this country regretted by your companions.   You have served under my immediate command for a year and a half.   Your labours during our march into the desert were greater than those of any other troops, and were undergone with spirit.   You did your duty bravely in the battles of Meannee and Hydrabad.   In the former of these two actions you were conspicuously placed and nobly acquitted yourselves.   I regret to lose you, but justice to you after your hard service has made me send you to your own homes, where an honourable reception awaits you.   Go where you will, you will be attended by my sincere regards, and my heartfelt respect.   To my friend Captain Henderson, I have given a letter for the Commander-in-Chief of the Madras Army, that his lordship may be aware of your worth."

Just as the C Company left Scinde, the Government ordered Madras Sappers to serve at Aden. This they continued to do till 1854.

D Company from April 1844 to April 1847.
E   ,,   November 1845 to November 1848.
A   ,,   February 1847 to February 1850.
C   ,,   September 1848 to December 1851.
B   ,,   January 1850 to April 1852.
F   ,,   September 1851 to December 1854.

From November 1845 to April 1852, there were always two companies at Aden at the same time, and occasionally, for periods of two or three months, there were three companies, or one-third of the whole corps, which consisted at that time of nine companies. Up to the end of 1846 the F Company had been engaged in China, and it was only after the China War of 1842 that the Corps had been increased from six to nine companies.

All this, in addition to the brevity of those campaigns, will possibly account for the fact that the Corps was not called upon to furnish a detachment for service in the Sikh Wars of 1845–46, and 1848–49.

Several Madras Engineers served at Aden.

Lieutenant E. Hemery served as Assistant Field Engineer, from 17th March 1846 to 17th May 1847.

Lieutenant J. C. Anderson was Assistant Field Engineer, as well as Second and First Assistant Executive Engineer and Assistant under the Commanding Engineer, from 17th March 1846 to 20th October 1849.

Lieutenant G. V. Winscom was at Aden as Assistant Executive Engineer from August 1848 to the close of 1851.

In August 1846, the Arabs made an attack on Aden. The D and E Companies of Madras Sappers were present, as also Lieutenants Hemery and J. C. Anderson of the Madras Engineers.

On the 3rd August information was received that the tribes were collecting beyond Lahig, thirty miles north-west of Aden (for a religious war against the British) under Syed Ismael Ibn Hussain-al Hussainee.

On the 7th, the troops at the Turkish wall were reinforced.

Between 1 and 2 A.M. on the 17th, the Arabs attempted a surprise. The defences consisted of a mere breastwork with a shallow ditch, and three small field-works covering the flanks ; the centre was strengthened by a double redan with two flêches, right and left. Sentries were posted at every ten yards.

A heavy fire of round shot, shrapnel and canister, speedily made them retreat.

The heavy ordnance at Dhumal Hosh also fired on them.

The Arabs lost twenty killed and wounded, including a chief.

On the 25th they again appeared, as also on the 27th, but a few doses of shrapnel was too much for them.

On the 19th May 1829, the establishment of Engineers at Madras had been fixed at forty-six officers :—

> 2 Colonels.
> 2 Lieutenant-Colonels.
> 2 Majors.
> 16 Captains.
> 16 First Lieutenants.
> 8 Second Lieutenants.

A memorial was sent in by certain officers of Engineers regarding their unprecedented supersession by the other branches of the army. This was sent home on 10th June 1844, and a reply to it was received, dated 27th November 1844.

The concessions due to this were very meagre, for the only alterations granted were to increase the first lieutenants to twenty and the second lieutenants to ten.

By this [increase four second lieutenants were promoted to

II.   14

first lieutenants, but the addition of six officers to the junior ranks of the Corps, without increasing the number of the higher ranks, tended to make promotion still slower, and in no way met the grievance of the petitioners.

Previous to the First China War, the establishment of Madras Sappers and Miners consisted of six companies. On that service they were found of so much value that they were increased to nine companies.

In November 1857 the establishment was still further augmented to twelve companies, and shortly afterwards the allowances of the Commandant were raised from 400 rupees to 600 rupees per mensem to equalise the pay with that of an Executive Engineer First Grade in the Department of Public Works.

Early in 1862 the number of companies was fixed at ten in place of twelve, and the two junior companies (L and M) were accordingly reduced, and up to date the Corps has remained at that strength.

CHAPTER VI.

Second Burmese War.—Martaban taken.—Rangoon taken.—Expedition to Bassein.—The General returns to Rangoon.—First expedition to Pegu.—Prome occupied temporarily.—Lord Dalhousie at Rangoon.—British Army of Ava. —Great Pagoda fortified.—Advance on Prome.—Pegu captured.—Pegu besieged.—Reinforcements arrive.—Pegu relieved.—Action near Pegu.— Night attack on Prome by Burmese.—Annexation of Pegu proclaimed.— Expedition to Martaban.—Advance thence to Tonghoo.—Burmese Chiefs set out for Ava.—Tonghoo occupied.—Disaster near Donabew.—Expedition under Sir John Cheape to retrieve it.—Myat-toon entirely defeated—but escapes.—Cheape returns to Donabew.—British frontier fixed.—Second visit of Governor-General to Rangoon.—Assault of Nattom.—Captain Geils wounded.—Boundary fixed by Major Allan

THE Treaty of 1826 with Burmah guaranteed the safety of our merchants and commerce. The King of Ava had also agreed to receive a Resident at Ava, but two or three of them were so badly treated that the British Government resolved to refrain from sending any more. Our merchants were subjected to great oppression and exaction.

This oppression culminated in the Governor of Rangoon placing a British ship-captain in the stocks on the false complaint of a Burmese pilot, and fining him (the captain) 900 rupees.

The Governor-General demanded the removal of the Governor of Rangoon, the payment of £900, and the admission of an agent at Rangoon or Ava.

14 *

The Court of Ava at first seemed disposed to agree, and sent a new governor to Rangoon, but he turned out more arrogant than the former one; and, finally, a deputation sent to wait on the Viceroy by our Commodore, consisting of a number of British naval officers, was grossly insulted, and, as a consequence, all British merchants and residents of Rangoon were requested to repair on board the flag-ship.

All the British subjects embarked by 8 P.M. on 6th January 1852, and by midnight the whole of the ships were removed by the steamers off the town. The men-of-war, also, moved; and the King of Ava's ship, then lying in the harbour, was seized, and taken some five miles down the river.

Next day all ships were ordered to prepare for departure out of the Rangoon waters.

On the 9th the Burmese ship was towed down by the *Hermes*. As she passed the stockade, fire was opened on her, which fire was immediately returned. The cannonade was continued for two hours, and did great damage to the works. About 300 of the enemy were killed and 300 wounded.

The action of the Commodore was entirely approved of by the Governor-General, and a written apology was demanded by the Governor-General from the Rangoon Governor.

This, it was soon found, the Governor had no intention of giving, and on the 10th or 12th February it was decided to send an expedition to Burmah.

On 2nd April the Bengal Division arrived off the mouth of the Rangoon river, in four steamers and four transports, under General Godwin. The next day it left for Moulmein, and on the 5th the force appeared in front of Martaban, and opened fire against its defences.

A storming-party was formed, which attacked the chief position under a heavy fire, and in a few minutes Martaban fell.

Two companies of Madras Sappers were present under Lieutenant Ford.

On the afternoon of the 8th the force was again at the mouth of the Rangoon river.

On the 11th the force from Madras arrived. It consisted of H.M.'s 51st, the 5th, 9th, and 35th Native Infantry, three companies of Artillery, and two more of Madras Sappers.

The Sappers were under the command of Brevet-Captain J. W. Rundall, M.E. Lieutenants Dennison, Blagrave, and Mayne, M.E., and Conductor Almond, Sappers and Miners, were with these two companies.

There were now four companies of Madras Sappers in Burmah, A, B, C, and E.

The following officers served with the Sappers during the war :—

> Madras Engineers—
> > Captain Rundall, commanding.
> > Lieutenant Carpendale.
> > > ,,　　　　Oakes.
> > > ,,　　　　Rogers.
> > > ,,　　　　Ryves.
> > > ,,　　　　Dennison.
> > > ,,　　　　Vaughan.
> > > ,,　　　　Mullins.
> > > ,,　　　　Mayne.
> > > ,,　　　　Gahagan.
>
> Madras Infantry—
> > Lieutenant Mackintosh.
> > > ,,　　　　Ford.
> > > ,,　　　　Carter.
> > > ,,　　　　Wilson.
> > > ,,　　　　Shortland.
> > > ,,　　　　Farquhar.
> > > ,,　　　　Harris.
> > > ,,　　　　Allan.
> > > ,,　　　　Furlong.
> > > ,,　　　　Daniel.

On the morning of the 12th April the troops landed under cover of a heavy fire from the steamers.

The right column consisted of the 18th Royal Irish on the right, H.M.'s 51st on the left, and the 40th Bengal Native Infantry in the centre. The Madras Sappers were drawn up with their ladders in rear of the left flank. The Artillery formed in rear of the brigade.

The left column consisted of a wing of the 80th in the centre, 9th Madras Native Infantry on the right, and 35th on the left.

The Artillery opened with spherical case at 800 yards.* Shortly after the artillery ceased firing, a storming-party was formed from H.M.'s 51st and Madras Sappers. The Engineers were Major Fraser, B.E., Chief Engineer, with the Madras Sappers under Captain Rundall.

The third division of ladders was in rear under Lieutenant Ford

While passing on to join the leading division, the enemy opened a heavy fire on them, when the Sappers had to ground their ladders and open fire. They silenced the enemy and marched on to the front. At this time they passed Lieutenant Donaldson, B.E. (formerly Madras), mortally wounded.

On reaching the White House stockade they found ladders reared against it. Four ladders were planted. Closely following the gallant Major Fraser came Captain Rundall. The storming-party immediately carried the stockade, but with considerable loss on our side.

The companies of Sappers suffered severely, and their bravery was everywhere conspicuous. Three of them alone reared a ladder, four more having been shot down beside it. Lieutenant Trevor, B.E., was here wounded, and Lieutenant Williams, B.E., had a narrow escape for his life.

The Burmese fled precipitately. The artillery were now

---

* At this time Major Oakes, M.A., got a sunstroke.

instructed not to advance till further orders, and after a good deal of sharp skirmishing a general cessation of operations took place.

The 13th April was employed in disembarking and taking into camp four 8-inch howitzers, required for the advance on the Great Pagoda.

Wednesday morning, the 14th, saw the force moving on. H.M.'s 80th, with four guns of Major Montgomerie's battery. formed the advance, covered by skirmishers.

About 7 A.M. the sound of musketry was heard, and at 10 the heavy howitzer battery was brought into position and opened fire. This continued for about an hour and a half. At this time (11.30) Captain Latter, the interpreter, proposed an attack on the east entrance of the Great Pagoda. This was agreed to.

The storming-party was formed of a wing of H.M.'s 80th, two companies 18th Royal Irish, and two companies of 40th Bengal Native Infantry.

The troops crossed over to the Pagoda in the most steady manner under a heavy fire. At length they reached the gate, which was at once pushed open. A grand rush was made up the long flight of steps they had discovered. The storming-party suffered severely, but they gained the upper terrace, while the Burmese fled in all directions, and the Shoé-Dagon fell for a second time into our hands.

The same morning, at about 11 A M., Conductor Almond came from the front, where he was with the clearing-party, to get some more tools. The A Company of Sappers were all, at the time, sitting down under cover. Lieutenant Ford, who commanded the company, called out for volunteers. Corporal Brooks and Bugler McNerny started up to go, but Lieutenant Ford told them to let the natives go. Naique Moonien (who afterwards died at Prome) and Private Ramasammy stepped out, went for the tools, and brought back Bengal Lascars carrying them. They had to cross a large plain exposed to a heavy fire, and this, of course, they did twice. The Committee who were afterwards assembled to decide on their claims to the Order of Merit, stated that the naique and private " evinced conspicuous and undoubted gallantry in voluntarily facing great danger in a matter of duty," and considered that they were worthy of the third class of the Order of Merit.

On this day both Captain Rundall and Lieutenant Ford were wounded, and the former received the thanks of the Governor-General, under date the 28th April.

The following account of the stockade at Rangoon is taken from Laurie's *Second Burmese War* :—

" Conceive a row of upright timbers extending for miles, as they do round the entire place, except in parts of the north and east sides, each timber fit to be the mainmast of a ship; these timbers three deep, and so close to each other that a walking-stick could not be passed between; behind these upright timbers is a row of horizontal ones, laid one above another, and behind all is a bank of earth twenty-four feet broad on the top, and forty-five feet at the base. The height of the top of the uprights from the bottom of the ditch, in which they are deeply planted, is generally fourteen feet. The upper part of the ditch, and that nearest the stockade, is filled with a most formidable abattis, in the shape of the pointed branches of trees, stuck firmly into the earth, and pointing outwards. Beyond this is the deep part of the ditch, which in the rains is, of course, filled with water. The upright timbers are strengthened with connecting planks, the ends of which are inserted on their tops, and secured by strong wooden pins in the bank inside. They are of such enormous, massive thickness, that firing at the face of a stockade would be throwing away powder."

On 17th May General Godwin proceeded to take Bassein. The detachment consisted of 400 Europeans, 300 Native Infantry, 67 Madras Sappers, and a party of Marines. The vessels which carried the force were the *Sesostris, Moozuffer, Tenas-*

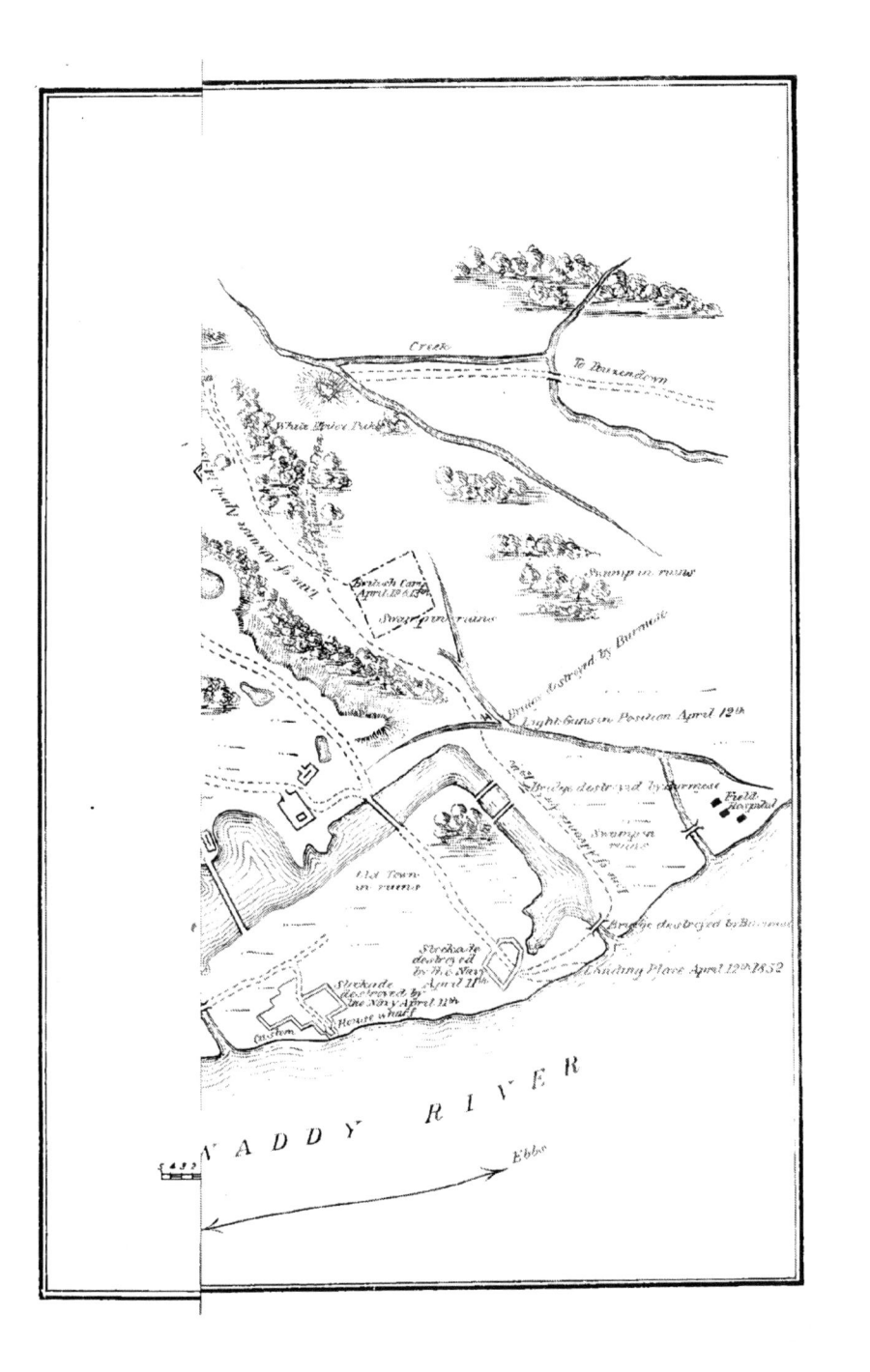

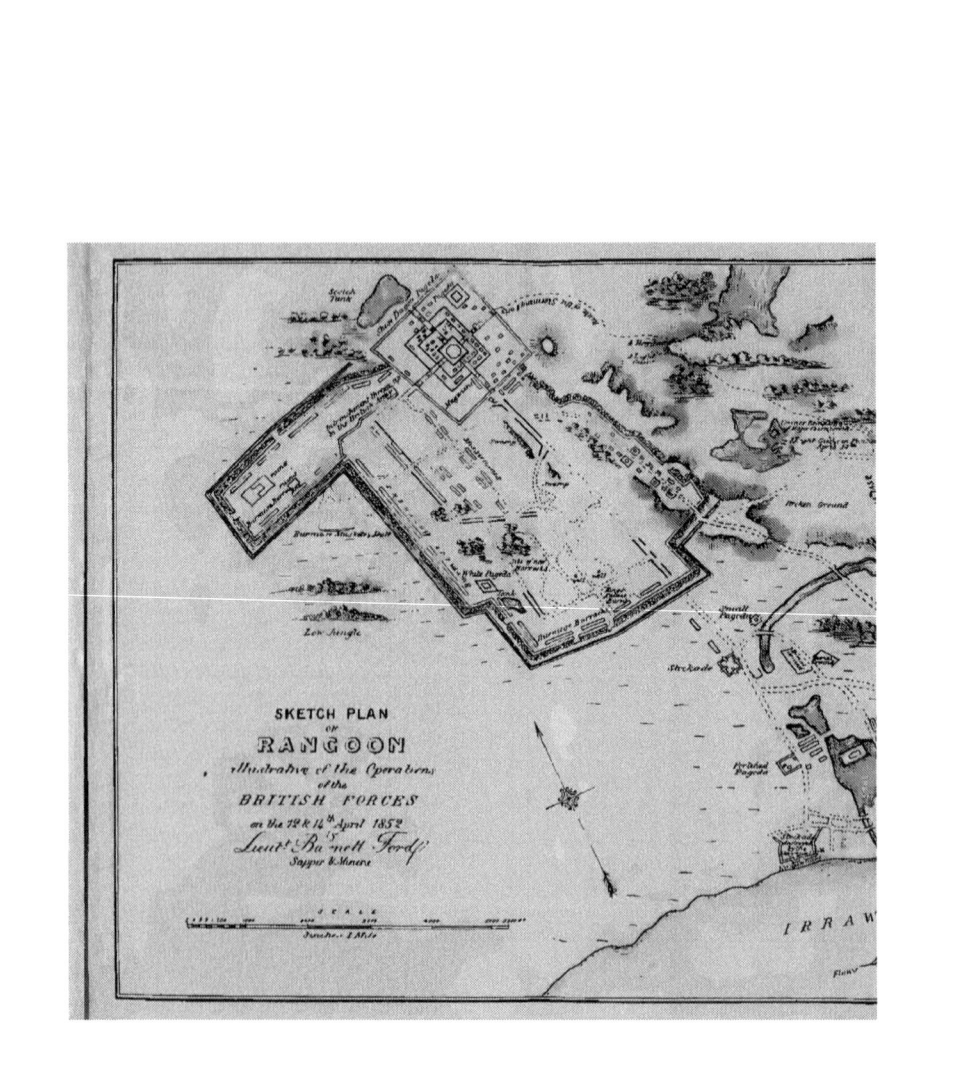

SKETCH PLAN
OF
RANGOON
Illustrative of the Operations
of the
BRITISH FORCES
on the 12 & 14th April 1852
Lieut. Barnett Ford
Sapper & Miners

serim, and the *Pluto,* under the command of Commodore Lambert. They had to make for Negrais, and then proceed up the Bassein river. Bassein, about sixty miles above Negrais, was reached on the 19th.

At half-past 4, a signal was made for the troops to land. The whole had not landed when the enemy opened fire. Our troops at once advanced, the stockade was surmounted, the pagoda gained, and the enemy driven in every direction within fifty minutes.

A fortified position to the south of the town had still to be taken. A company of H.M.'s 51st, two of Madras Native Infantry, a few seamen and marines, a party of Madras Sappers with ladders, under Lieutenant Ford, and a sub-division of 9th Native Infantry were selected for this work.

A route was taken which brought us in rear of the stockade. A small party was detached to attack the north-east side. Our progress was impeded by water and thick jungle; this obliged us to take another direction, which brought the party out on a brick-road leading straight to the north-east angle of the work. When within fifteen yards of the position a severe fire was opened upon us, and several officers were here shot down. Lieutenant Anstey, of the 9th Native Infantry, and Lieutenant Ford, mounted the parapet in the most gallant manner, the former being wounded in the hand.

The enemy now gave way in every direction, and were followed by the troops. After we got inside this battery, and were pursuing the enemy across it, Naique Mootooveerapen, of the Sappers, was in advance. The Burmese, unable to retreat, faced us, and the naique charged, shot one, and bayoneted two others. Lieutenant Ford particularly noticed his gallantry, and he obtained the distinction of the third class of the Order of Merit.

Our loss was two men killed, and five officers and eighteen men wounded.

Lieutenant Craster, of the Bengal Engineers, and Lieutenant

Ford received the thanks of the Governor-General in Council, and the Governor-General noticed with approbation "the gallantry and good conduct of officers, N.C.O., and men of H.M.'s 51st, 9th Madras Native Infantry, and Madras Sappers and Miners."

On 23rd May the General returned to Rangoon.

Early in May the Peguese had risen against the Burmese, and turned them out of the town; but at the end of the month the case was reversed, and Pegu was again in the hands of the Burmese.

On 3rd June a small expedition left Rangoon for Pegu, consisting of one company H.M.'s 80th, rifle company of 67th Bengal Native Infantry, and a detachment of Madras Sappers, under Lieutenant Mackintosh, with Lieutenant Mayne as Field Engineer, the whole force being commanded by Brevet-Major Cotton, of 67th Native Infantry.

On the 4th the troops stormed the pagoda at Pegu, after some heavy skirmishing, with the loss of one killed and six wounded, and after destroying the fortifications returned to Rangoon on the 5th.

After our troops left Pegu, the Burmese came down, 3,000 or 4,000 strong, and again drove out the Peguese.

Prome was temporarily occupied on the 9th July by Commodore Tarleton. Twenty-two guns were taken from the enemy by the steam flotilla. The flotilla was attacked on the 7th by a strong force of the enemy at Konougee. The enemy's fire was silenced in an hour, and the steamers proceeded.

On the 10th they fell in with the rear of General Bundoola's army (he was son of Bundoola of first war), and after an exchange of shots the enemy fled in great confusion.

On 27th July the Governor-General of India, Lord Dalhousie, arrived at Rangoon, and left again on 1st August, after publishing an order "offering the combined force his most cordial acknowledgment of the valuable and distinguished ser-

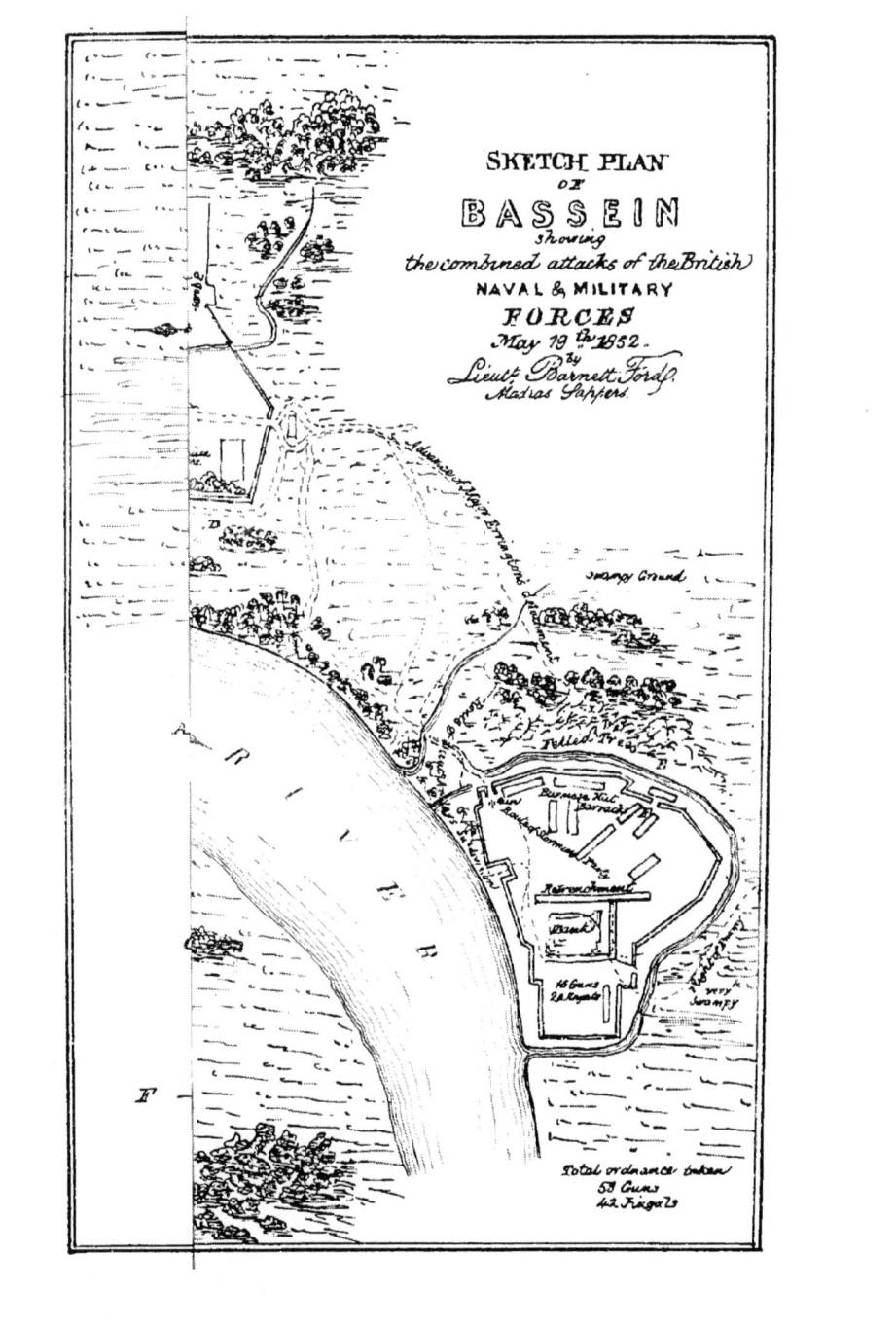

SKETCH PLAN
OF
BASSEIN
showing
the combined attacks of the British
NAVAL & MILITARY
FORCES
May 19th 1852.
By
Lieut. Barnett Fords.
Madras Sappers.

Total ordnance taken
58 Guns
42 Jingals

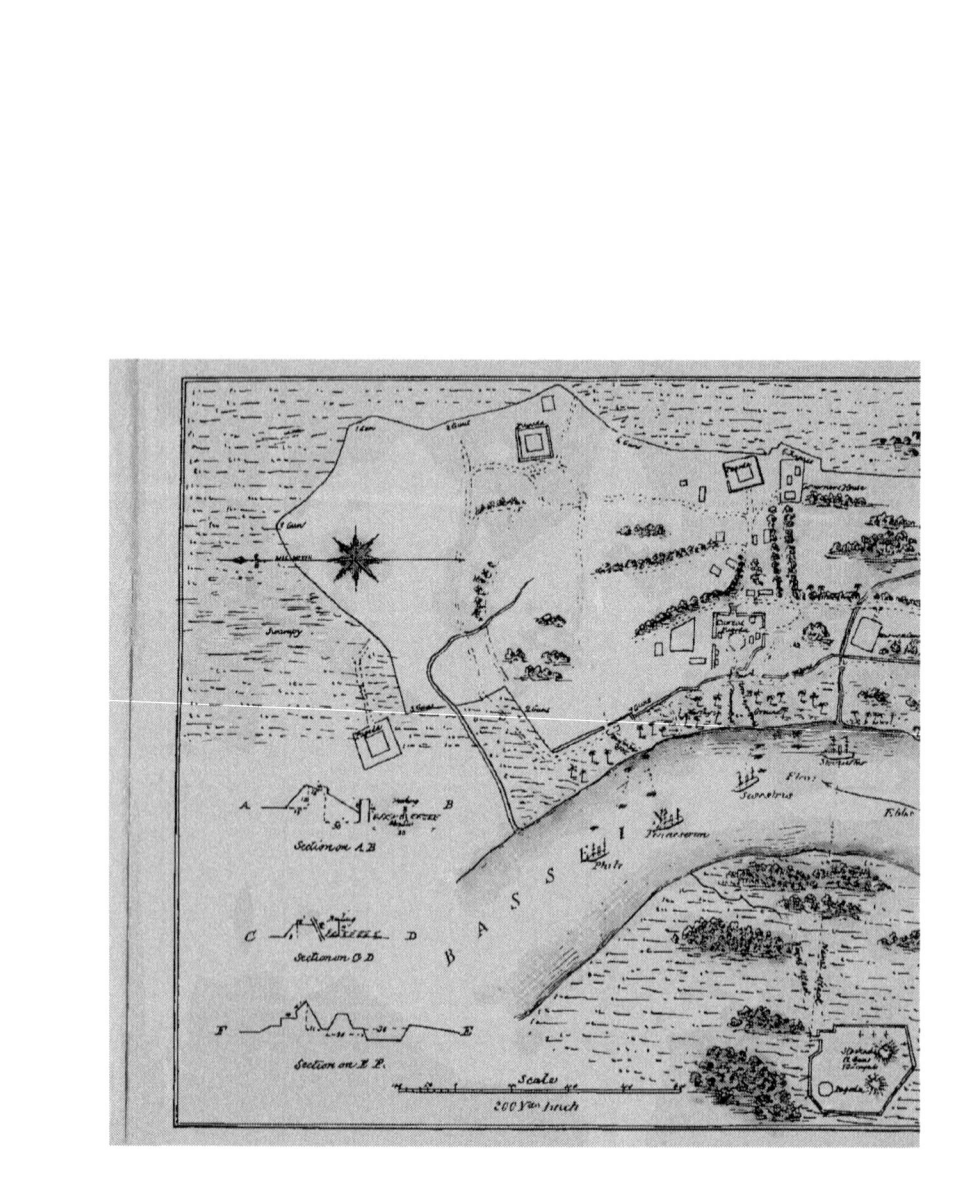

Section on A B

Section on C D

Section on E F

Scale

200 Yds Inch

vices they have rendered here." Rangoon, Martaban, and Bassein were in our possession, giving us complete control over the Irrawaddy.

Still the King of Ava seemed indisposed to give way; accordingly, after the departure of the Governor-General from Rangoon, measures were taken to forward reinforcements from Bengal and Madras.

The army of Ava was composed of two divisions, each of three brigades.

Brigadier-General Sir John Cheape, K.C.B. (Bengal Engineers), commanded the Bengal Division, while Brigadier-General S. W. Steel, C B., commanded the Madras one.

The whole force consisted of six regiments European, and twelve of Native Infantry, with a full complement of Artillery, together with Sappers and Miners; in all some 18,000 or 20,000 men.

The Madras Sappers were attached to the Madras Division, and consisted of head-quarters, and A, B, C, and E companies, under the command of Captain Rundall, M.E , Field Engineer.

On the 6th September it was announced that active operations would begin on the 18th.

During the month of August the Engineers and Sappers were engaged in fortifying the upper and second terraces of the Great Pagoda, preparatory to our advance on Prome.

By the 27th September the whole of the 1st Division had left Rangoon, and Brigadier Steel remained in command at that place.

On the 26th the *Medusa* had left for Prome, carrying Major Fraser, B.E., and his officers, together with Captain Rundall, M.E., and his Sappers.

On the way up the river two steamers grounded, and detained all the other steamers for three days.

Admiral Austin was taken ill on 5th October, and died on the

7th, near the Island of Shouk-Shay-Khune, ten miles distant from Prome.

On the 9th the expedition left the island at daybreak, and in two hours was under the fortifications of Prome. The enemy opened fire on the steamers, which was steadily returned. During the day the steamers were employed in bombarding the place, to cover the disembarkation of the troops.

By 5 P.M. H.M. 80th, the Sappers and Miners* and Artillery, had landed with two guns, and rested during the night.

The next morning (10th October), with H.M.'s 18th and 35th Madras Native Infantry, they proceeded to the Pagoda, which was found deserted, and was at once taken possession of.

General Godwin ascertained that ten miles east of Prome the Burmese had a large force, on which the garrison of Prome retired when we advanced.

On 13th October General Godwin returned to Rangoon, leaving Sir John Cheape in command at Prome, and Major Fraser, B.E., and Major Allan, Deputy Quartermaster-General, were entrusted with the arrangements for the housing of the troops.

During the month of October, Bundoola delivered himself up to Sir John Cheape, and was placed as a prisoner on board the *Sesostris*. He had been ordered to appear before the King in the dress of a woman, as a disgrace for losing his army in July, which order he very naturally refused to obey.

Nothing of any great consequence occurred at Prome during the month of November. There were a few trifling attacks made on our outposts, without much result, and the Sappers lost several of their men from cholera. In one of the small affairs near Prome, Carpendale of the Engineers got a blow in the back from a splinter of a jingal he was trying to burst; and on 29th November a party of Burmans fired at Mackintosh, of the

---

* One hundred and nineteen men, under Lieutenant Allen.

SKETCH PLAN

OF

PROME.

SHEWING THE BURMESE POSITION
AND CAPTURE BY THE BRITISH;
on the 9th & 10th October 1853.
BY
LIEUT B. FORD.
d.d Sappers

Sepr 1853.

Nawring O

Schooner

Enterprise

Schooner

Mahan

Sand Bank
in dry season.

NB ⊢ Burmese Guns

⊢ Jingals

ds to 1 inch.

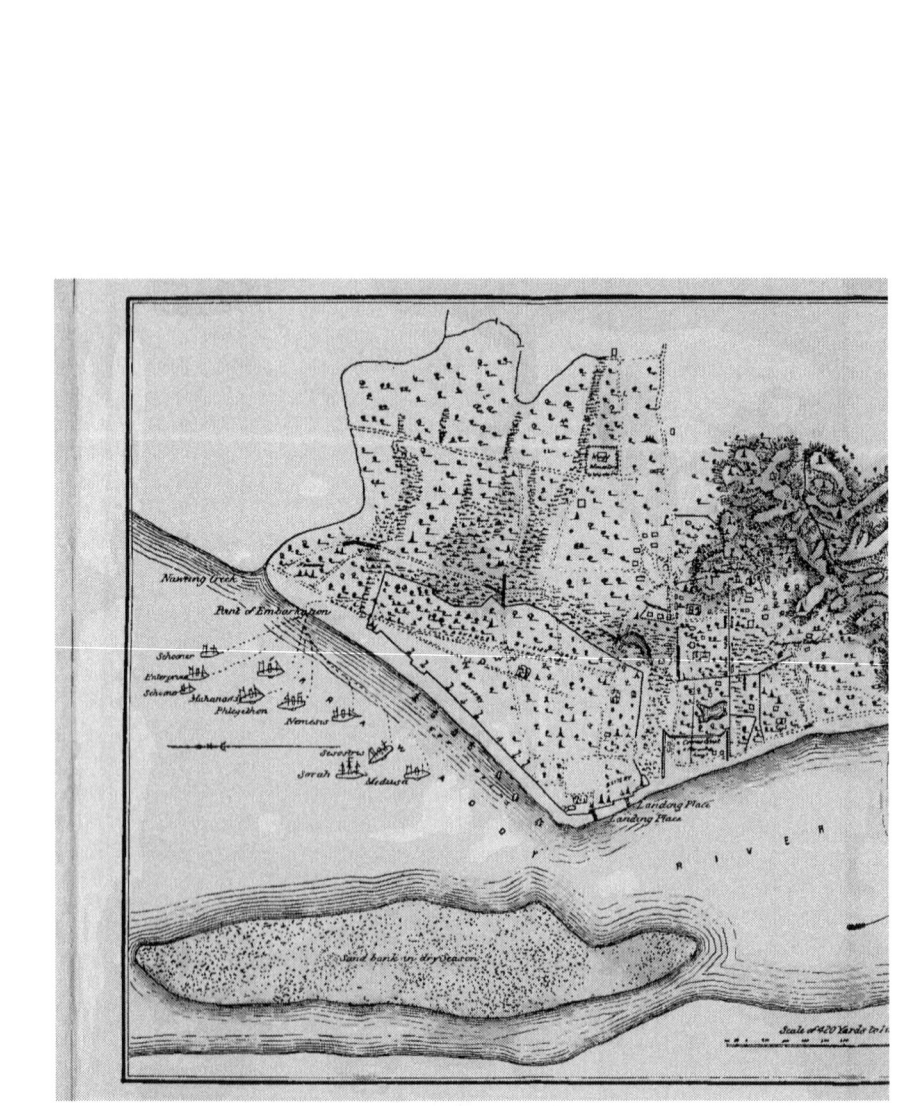

Sappers, while he was out road-making. The ball struck a dah close to him, and then grazed a coolie's leg.

Captain Rundall,* of the Madras Engineers, died at Prome on the 12th November. He was an excellent officer, and served with distinction in the China War, as also at Rangoon. He was succeeded in the command of the Madras Sappers by Lieutenant John Carpendale, M.E.

In the middle of November a force was sent, under Brigadier McNeill, to Pegu. It consisted of 300 Bengal Fusiliers, 300 Madras Fusiliers, 400 of 5th Native Infantry, with Artillery, Sappers, and two guns. The Sappers were under Lieutenants Shortland and Harris. They embarked on 19th November, and anchored at sunset on the 20th a little below Pegu. The force landed on the morning of the 21st, at 4 A.M. It was first intended to advance between the river and the wall, but the severity of the fire proved that the enemy were in a strong position there, and a flank movement was commenced parallel to the south wall, through high grass and dense jungle. Before the movement commenced, a working party was sent forward to clear a track. They did their work well, the whole force following as well as they could. The guns and Sappers were sent to the front. This took four and a half hours. The sun was very hot, and the fatigue great. By the time General Godwin arrived opposite the gateway which was to be stormed, it was found that most of the force were dead beat, and that some time must elapse before anything like proper columns could be formed. At last the best part of the Bengal Fusiliers were got together, as well as about half of the Madras Fusiliers, and allowed breathing time, the Rifles forming a line of skirmishers in their front.

General Godwin harangued them, and they were then let loose on the gate. The storming parties drove the Burmese before them, and then, returning, made for the Pagoda, about a mile

---

* " He was a zealous soldier of high talent and of the most exemplary character. He died in the prime of life, beloved and regretted by all."

distant. A few volleys were exchanged, and Pegu was in our possession.

Our loss was three officers wounded—one, Lieutenant Cook, mortally—and thirty-five to forty men killed and wounded A few officers were disabled by the sun, amongst them the Brigadier McNeill. He died on 8th December, never having recovered from the fatigue and exposure attending the capture of Pegu. The fighting had lasted from 7 A.M. to 1 P.M.

By the 24th the General, with most of his troops, had returned to Rangoon.

On 9th December news arrived that Pegu was besieged. The small garrison which had been left in Pegu, consisted of 215 Madras Fusiliers, 220 5th M. N. I., and two guns, with 30 Bengal Artillery, and 40 Madras Sappers, the last under Lieutenant Harris. Lieutenant J. D. Campbell, B.E., was the only Engineer officer.

On the 24th November the enemy made an attack upon our gunboats, and on the 27th they commenced a most daring attack on all sides of the Pagoda, but they were vigorously repelled.

On the 4th December the enemy again attacked the garrison.

On the morning of the 6th the enemy surrounded the Pagoda and attacked us in great force.

From the 7th to the 13th the enemy were firing jingals and musketry day and night.

On the 11th two gun-boats had arrived from Rangoon with stores and ammunition. In trying to relieve Pegu they were driven back with heavy loss.* Major Hill commanded the garrison, and was doing his utmost in hope of a speedy reinforcement, but his position was very critical.

A termination to the affair was brought about by the arrival of reinforcements under General Godwin on the 14th.

---

* The gun-boats were under the command of Commander Shadwell, of the *Sphinx*, and contained 133 officers and seamen, besides Captain Mallock, B.A., and twelve artillerymen. They lost four killed and twenty-eight wounded.

From the 5th to the 14th the garrison of Pegu lost forty-five killed and wounded. Amongst these the Sappers had one N.C O. and one man wounded. Major Hill, in his report, wrote: " Little that I can say with respect to the practical knowledge of Lieutenant J. D. Campbell, B.E., which he has already gained on field service, could add to his reputation as a good service officer, but his unremitting zeal in planning and carrying out his suggestions has mainly contributed to the small loss sustained by the troops. Lieutenant James, B.A., the only artillery officer, has performed his arduous duties much to my satisfaction. Lieutenant Harris, Madras Sappers, has proved himself to be a most efficient Sapper officer."

On the night of 11th December 1,200 men embarked at Rangoon in two steamers and a number of boats, and disembarked six miles below Pegu on the 14th, and the whole were ready to move off the ground by sunrise. The General resolved to enter the Pagoda by the east gate. Only a large body of skirmishers were met, who were gallantly repulsed by the Bengal and Madras Fusiliers and Sikhs, and Pegu was relieved after a most fatiguing day's work.

It was now the intention of the General to advance into the country and free Pegu from the near position of the Burmese Army. It was understood that the Burmese were entrenched at Kaleebal, four miles north of the Pagoda.

On 17th December at 7 A.M., a force, composed as follows, left the Pagoda.

> 570 Bengal Fusiliers ;
> 150 Madras Fusiliers ;
> 182 10th Bengal Native Infantry ;
> 330 Sikhs;
> 30 Madras Sappers ;
>
> ———
> Total 1,262 men.
> ———

They passed through a very dense jungle for about two miles,

and then debouched into a large plain, where they found the
enemy admirably posted behind an entrenchment with abattis,
about a mile long, filled with masses of men.   Our force
advanced on the enemy, inclining to their own right, to threaten
the enemy's left, which was open.   The Burmese fired a gun
occasionally as we advanced.   When within 400 yards of
their position 200 men of the Bengal Fusiliers were detached to
drive in outposts on their right.   The outposts retired on their
main position.

Columns of attack were now formed, and the General was
confident that he would get in amongst them, but the Burmese
considered flight their only safety.

After the action the troops rested for an hour, and then proceeded to Lephangoon, ten miles, which they reached at half-
past 4 P.M., but again the enemy retired on our approach.

On the 18th the force marched to Montsangoosoo, ten miles,
arriving at noon.   About 3 P.M. the General was informed that
some of the enemy were about, and he accordingly advanced in
two columns, but the enemy again retreated for two miles to a
long range of barracks.

Two advanced columns were now thrown out for attack, but
the enemy once more retired, leaving the barracks in our possession.   The barracks were then burnt, and our troops returned to
their bivouac three miles distant.

On the 19th, the state of the commissariat being deficient, it
was necessary to return to Pegu.

The General now proposed to detach Brigadier-General Steel
to Moulmein, to proceed to Belung, Shoe-Syen, and Sitang,
while he himself embarked on the 20th, and returned to Rangoon
on the 22nd.*

---

* "About a week after the second defence of Pegu commenced, lasting till declaration of peace, some ten days later. During this defence we were in no great
anxiety, as we had plenty of food and ammunition. and our defences were stronger
than before. We had, besides, 100 more Europeans, and a fair supply of artillery
and rockets. We lost one officer and twelve men killed, and several wounded."

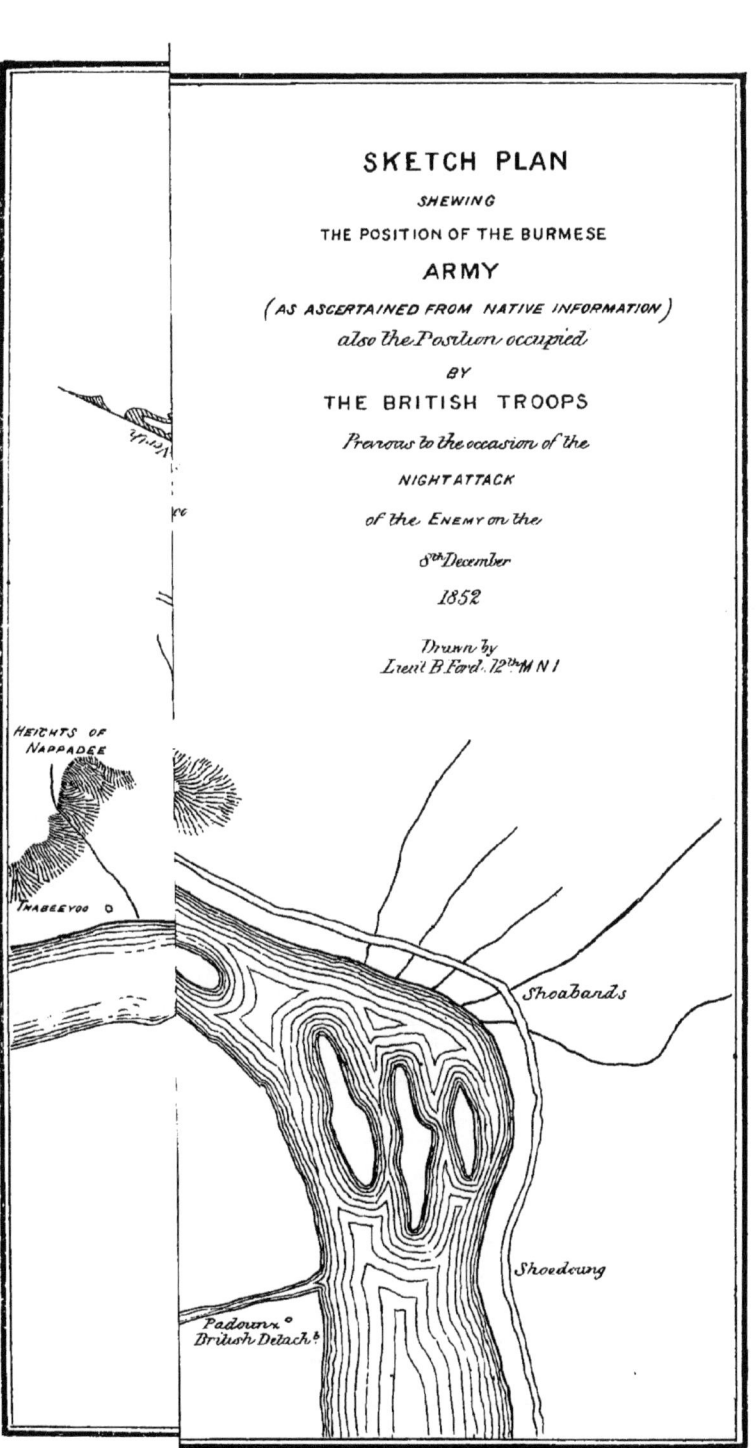

SKETCH PLAN

SHEWING

THE POSITION OF THE BURMESE

ARMY

(AS ASCERTAINED FROM NATIVE INFORMATION)

also the Position occupied

BY

THE BRITISH TROOPS

Previous to the occasion of the

NIGHT ATTACK

of the Enemy on the

8th December

1852

Drawn by
Lieut B.Ford. 12th M N I

HEIGHTS OF
NAPPADEE

THABEEYOO ○

Shoabands

Shoedoung

Padoun ○
British Detach.t

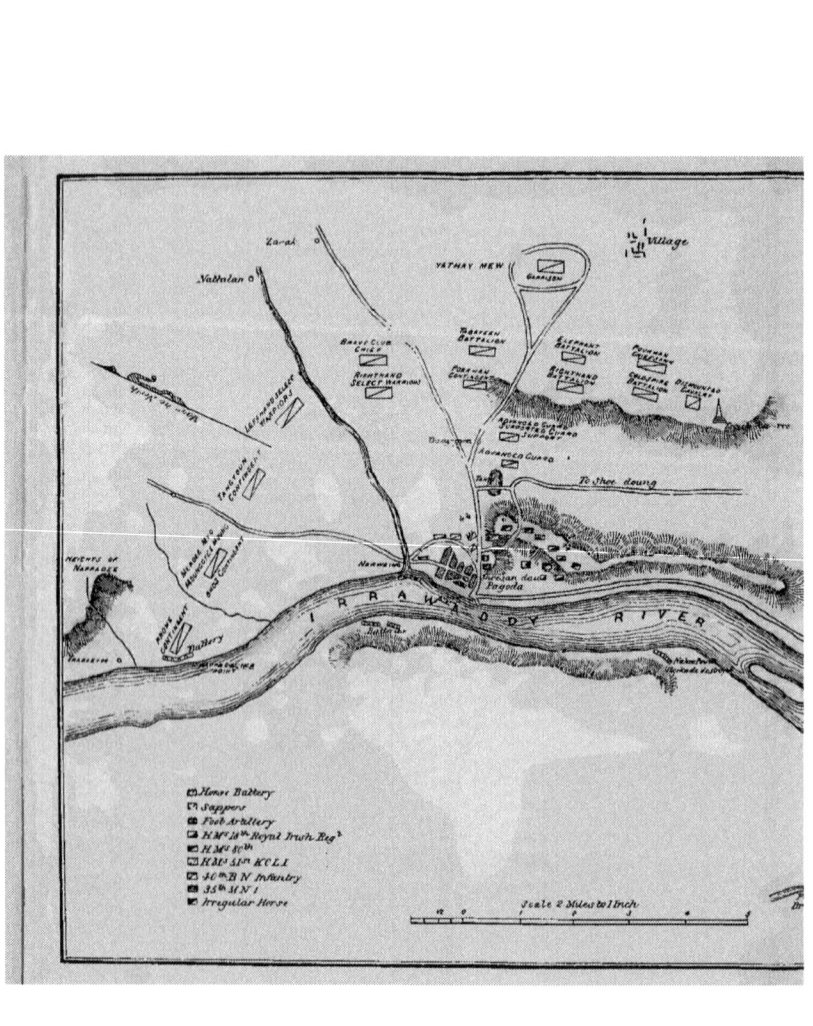

The General in his despatch says :—"To Majors Garrard and Seaton, of Bengal Fusiliers, Captain Renaud, of Madras Fusiliers . . . and Lieutenant Harris, of the Sappers, who rendered important assistance, I am much indebted."

On the night of the 8th December the Burmese made a most daring attack on Prome. About midnight three signal-guns were fired from the enemy's advanced post. This, of course, at once roused our troops. The fire of musketry and jingals soon announced that our picquets had been attacked. The attack was rapid, but our picquets were soon reinforced, and every point occupied. A detachment of the 35th Native Infantry held Narwing, to the north of Prome, supported by picquets of H.M.'s 18th and 51st. The Madras Sappers, with double picquets, supported the 40th Bengal Native Infantry and 18th Royal Irish on the heights on our right, south of the town.

The enemy made repeated attacks, but they were as often driven back. These attacks were continued till dawn of day ; the enemy, finding all their efforts vain, drew off at daylight, but appeared again shortly after, on observing a body of Sappers going out to work, and they drew up in regular order across a plain.

A covering party of Europeans was then sent forward, and the Burmese retired on Gattray Mew.

In the afternoon Sir John Cheape moved out with a small force close to the advanced post of the enemy, but finding it too late to attack, returned, having made a close reconnoissance of the position.

Here may be introduced a few remarks, regarding the Madras Sappers, made by Lieutenant Laurie, M.A., in his narrative of the Burmese War, from which the above account is extracted.

"We cannot omit in this chapter to bring to general notice the admirable conduct and untiring exertions of a small body of the native army—men who, although they had been broken

II.   **15**

down by disease, had rendered the most valuable service previous to the above night attack, in the construction of breastwork, battery, abattis, parapet, bridge, and road—the small body of Madras Sappers worked with the right spirit of soldiers."

At Rangoon on the morning of the 20th December 1852, the annexation of Pegu was proclaimed on board H.M.'s ship *Fox*, and next day it was published to the army, and a grand parade was ordered.

On 29th December, a field force was ordered to embark for Martaban, &c., under the command of Brigadier-General Steel, C.B., consisting of one battery Madras Artillery, one company of Madras Sappers, 450 Bengal Fusiliers, 150 Madras Fusiliers, wings of 10th Bengal Native Infantry and 5th Madras Native Infantry, and a detachment of Ramghur Irregular Cavalry. Fraser of the Bengal Engineers was to accompany the force.

On 4th January 1853, General Steel embarked, and next day all the troops were anchored off their destination.

It was not till the 14th January that the column marched out of Martaban by the Beling Gate to advance on Tonghoo.

It consisted of about 2,100 men besides followers. The artillery, consisting of four 24-pounder howitzers and four $5\frac{1}{2}$-inch mortars, was under Colonel Anstruther, C.B. The Madras Sappers, about seventy strong, were under Lieutenant Vincent Shortland.

On the first day a small affair took place at Kyouk-ye-dwing, about four miles from Martaban.

On the 18th the force left that place for Gongoh, where another skirmish took place.

On the 21st, the column moved on to Ouchbada, and on the 23rd to Yew-gyike A passage for the troops had to be cut through dense jungle, the work being performed by the Sappers.

On the 24th they marched to Zenghyen, when it was necessary to cross a creek of considerable width. The Field Engineer (Lieutenant Fraser) and Lieutenants Shortland and

Farquhar, with their Sappers, constructed a bridge of Burmese canoes.

On the 25th the force arrived at Thaboung.

On the 26th it reached Kyoke-ko, and next day encamped near Beling Creek.

On the 28th they crossed over to Beling, the depth of the creek being only three feet at low water.

From Beling the force marched by Kokado, Kyi-ketho, Kysek-ka-tha, to Sittang, which place it reached on the 3rd of February.

On the 2nd, Imuug-Goung, the Governor of Sittang, came into camp.

The force had now marched over 100 miles, and was upon the banks of the Sittang river, 700 yards in width.

On 5th February the column left Sittang and marched by Toung-Zayat to Nyoun-ky-dowk, which was three miles north from Meekyo and thirty-one miles from Pegu.

At Meekyo were found 180 carts with provisions, sent from Pegu by Major Hill, escorted by some Fusiliers, 9th Native Infantry, and Sappers.

A halt of two days was now made to land stores and to send away the sick, 130 in number.

On the 10th the force marched again, and reached Shoe-Gyen the next day.

The stockade had been evacuated by the enemy, so we encamped beyond the town to the right of the road leading up to the Hill Pagoda and stockade.

Lieutenant Fraser at once commenced the alterations necessary to convert the stockade into a strong post.

A light division was now selected for an advance on Tonghoo. It did not exceed 900 men, 400 being Europeans.

> 200 Fusiliers (Bengal).
> 170   ,,   (Madras).
> 60 European Madras Artillery.

15 *

50 Madras Sappers.

Detachments of 10th Bengal Native Infantry and 5th Madras Native Infantry, and Ramghur Cavalry.

Two 24-pounder howitzers and two 5½-inch mortars.

The artillery under Captain and Lieutenant-Colonel Anstruther, and the Sappers under Lieutenant Shortland.

The force left on the 15th, the route taken being—

Yong-Danig, 15th	...	...	...	...	7 miles.
Bogatha, 16th	...	...	...	...	14 ,,
Kyouk-ghee, 17th	...	...	...	...	15 ,,
Kyoum-bea, 18th	...	...	...	...	12 ,,
Moung-goa, 19th	...	...	...	...	12 ,,
Langlangoh, 20th	...	...	...	..	10 ,,
Thandobain, on left bank of the Sittang river, 21st	...	...	...	...	18 ,,
					88 ,,

The heat was very great, and some of the marching was very difficult and tedious, over uneven ground and through rough dense jungle. Nine iron guns and eleven jingals were captured at and near Kyouk-ghee.

On our first approach to the river-side near Thandobain, we saw a Burmese chief on the other side. The Assistant Quartermaster-General rode down to hear what he had to say. He wanted to know the cause of our appearance, and said he would not fire on us if we would not fire on him. He was told he might come across and see the General, but he declined, and rode off to Tonghoo.

It afterwards appeared that on his arrival the Governors of Tonghoo, Martaban, Shoe-gyen, and all the chiefs, set out with great haste towards Ava.

On the 22nd our whole force crossed the Sittang river, mostly on elephants, and then marched on Tonghoo. The principal men of the city came out and surrendered the place.

The complete expulsion of the Burmese troops from all the country, from Martaban to thirty miles north of Tonghoo, was thus effected on 22nd February 1853.

The Irregular Cavalry, with a few volunteers, pursued the fugitive chiefs for more than twenty miles, and only halted when their horses were exhausted, and they learnt that the chiefs were still many miles ahead.

Although unsuccessful, this attempt to overtake the chiefs was a gallant one, as only thirty horsemen were employed to follow up the fugitives.

This march from Martaban to Tonghoo was a severe and difficult one, chiefly through forest. The actual distance was 240 miles, and took thirty-nine days.

The Brigadier in his despatch spoke highly of the services of the force employed, and with regard to the Engineers and Sappers, said:—

" Lieutenant A. Fraser, B.E., Assistant Field Engineer, has been indefatigable in his exertions, both in the higher professional duties of an Engineer and at the head of the company of Madras Sappers and Miners, who have maintained their well-earned name in overcoming the many difficulties of the route of march."

At Tonghoo we captured eleven brass guns, thirteen iron ones, and 121 jingals.

We now come to the disaster near Donabew. A robber chieftain, Nya-Myat-toon, had captured our boats in their progress up and down the river, and he was so successful in his dacoities that it was resolved to send a force against him.

This party left Rangoon early in February, under command of Captain Loch, R.N., C.B.

It consisted of 185 seaman, sixty-two Marines, and 300 of 67th Bengal Native Infantry, with twenty-five officers and two 3-pounder guns.

They advanced from Donabew, and proceeded a long distance

without observing any signs of an enemy, when they arrived on the banks of a small nullah. The road was very narrow, and, owing to the thick brushwood and bamboo spikes in the ground, it was impossible to deploy.

As soon as the leading files appeared, they were assailed by a heavy fire from a masked stockade. All men in front were at once struck down. Captain Loch himself was struck by a bullet, which smashed his watch and passed through his body. Lieutenant Kennedy, R.N., was killed, and Captain Price, 67th, mortally wounded.

A retreat was resolved on; and this was carried out in a cool, able, and gallant manner, under most trying circumstances.

Out of 225 Europeans who advanced to the attack, six were killed and fifty-three wounded. The Bengal Regiment lost five killed and eighteen wounded. Altogether eleven killed and seventy-one wounded. The guns had to be abandoned and were spiked.

Captain Loch died of his wounds on 6th February.

Shortly after, a force of about 1,500 men with two guns was sent under Sir John Cheape to retrieve this defeat.

The Brigadier-General left Prome to proceed against Myattoon. He had with him—

> 200 of H.M.'s 18th Royal Irish.
> 200 of H.M.'s 51st.
> Rifle company of 67th Bengal Native Infantry.
> 200 4th Sikh Locals.
> Seventy Madras Sappers under Lieutenants Mullins, M.E., and Trevor, B.E.
> Two guns—one 24-pounder howitzer and a 9-pounder field-gun—with some rocket tubes served by the Madras Horse Artillery.

Sir John Cheape landed and collected his forces at Henzadah, about thirty-five miles north of Donabew.

The force left Henzadah on the 22nd, expecting to reach

Myat-toon's position in three or four days, and only took seven or eight days provisions.

On the 26th the General found himself still a long way from the stronghold ; so, fearing a failure of provisions, Sir John made a flank movement to Zooloom, where he arrived on the 28th, after a very harassing march.

The General now waited at Donabew for reinforcements expected from Rangoon, as well as to make every preparation.

On 7th March, every arrangement having been made for an advance on Myat-toon's position at Kyou kazeem, the force left at 2 P.M., the Sappers marching immediately in rear of the advanced guard.

The party now consisted of 500 Europeans, 500 Natives, two light guns, three rocket tubes, two mortars, and seventy Sappers, with a detachment of Irregular Horse.

"On reaching Akyoo at 5 P.M., they found a broad nullah 130 yards wide. Rafts had been made at Donabew by the Sappers, and brought up in carts. These carts having arrived, and a favourable site having been selected, the Sappers, though under a considerable fire of musketry and jingals, formed a raft for the passage of the guns and troops in about two hours. By two hours after daybreak on the 8th, the second raft was completed, and the Brigadier directed the passage to be commenced. The two rafts, filled with troops, were rowed across by the Sappers, a rope being carried across by each raft and fastened to trees on the opposite bank, in order to work the rafts backwards and forwards. By midnight the whole of the troops had been carried across.

"On the 9th the troops marched at 9 A.M. Up to that hour the fog had not cleared. The Sappers proceeded as before with the advanced guard, and felled a few trees *en route*. On reaching Kyon-tanau in the evening, they commenced constructing the rafts for crossing the nullah at that place, but the Brigadier-General considering some cover requisite for the safety of the picquets, which had been sent across in boats, they threw up a small breast work for this purpose.

"On the 10th, at daybreak, the nullah was bridged by means of the two rafts, some planks, and old canvas, the nullah being some fifty yards wide. The troops and light baggage having crossed, the bridge was broken up, and the guns transported on the detached rafts, the whole being carried over by half-past 4."

"On the 11th the force started at the usual hour. The Burmese had obstructed the track by cutting down trees; consequently the Sappers were hard at work from 11 A.M. till dusk removing the trees and clearing jungle."

"On the 12th the force retraced its steps to Kyon-tanau, as the way could not be found and provisions were failing again. Having returned, the Sappers were employed in putting together one of the rafts, after which thirty of them, under Lieutenant Trevor, B.E., started with the detachment proceeding to Donabew for provisions, and the rest were employed in bringing up materials for hutting the troops."

Meanwhile the troops were put upon half rations.

The force remained at Kyon-tanau till the 16th, when Colonel Sturt, who commanded the force sent to Donabew for provisions, returned. Cholera had meantime attacked the force, and there were thirteen deaths in one day.

"During the halt at Kyon-tanau the Sappers were employed in constructing a breastwork and stockade for the protection of the detachment which the Brigadier-General had ordered to remain for the purpose of forming a depôt for the commissariat stores."

"At 2 P.M. on the 17th the right wing under Major Wigston, 18th Royal Irish, was sent on the old road, the Sappers accompanying him for the purpose of clearing the road for the advance of the main column."

"On the following morning the road was found to be entirely blocked up with felled trees. These, however, the Sappers, after great exertions, succeeded in clearing away as far as the lake stockade, which was stormed a few minutes before sunset, with the loss of one officer and five men wounded."

"On the 18th, at daybreak, the rest of the force started, leaving the sick and provisions in a small stockade at Kyon tanau. They joined the right wing at the breastwork, and the sick and wounded of Major Wigston's party were sent back to Kyon-tanau."

"The columns continued their march, the left wing under Colonel Sturt in front, till they came to the second stockade about 4 P.M."

"The Sappers were again occupied from early morning till nearly sunset in cutting a road and removing obstacles (part of the time, at the second stockade, being under a heavy fire) to enable the guns to come into action."

This second stockade was gallantly carried by H.M.'s 51st Kings Own Light Infantry, and 67th Bengal Native Infantry. Our loss was Lieutenant Boileau and one sepoy of 67th killed, and one ensign 51st and six sepoys 67th wounded.

At 5 P.M. the force was encamped a mile further on.

Cholera was raging in camp.

At 7 A.M. on the 19th the General was advancing with his troops, the right wing in front. Having gone out a mile, the enemy were found in a breastwork or stockade on the opposite side of the nullah (third stockade).

"During the whole of this day the Sappers were hard at work as before, and for three-quarters of an hour under very heavy fire in front of third stockade they were occupied in rendering the road practicable for the advance of the artillery."

"The Sappers worked admirably, and the guns were shortly got into position and opened a well-directed fire, which gradually became heavy on both sides."

"The third stockade was an extremely strong position. Its length was some 1,200 yards, its left flank was protected by a morass, and along the whole front there was a nullah with a good deal of water and soft mud at the bottom.

The ground near the right flank was nearly dry, and was covered by an abattis which was penetrable by individuals with extreme difficulty and some danger, even after the capture of the stockade, and was altogether impracticable to troops under fire. The only entrance to the stockade was a narrow path, across which, at intervals, pits had been dug, and this path was commanded by the two guns captured from the previous expedition, and by several jingals."

The fire of the enemy on the path leading up to the stockade was so heavy, that the advanced party did not succeed in carrying it. Our troops sustained a heavy loss in the attempt to make good their way. A 24-pounder howitzer was at last brought up (the men of the 51st assisting to drag it along), and opened an effectual fire on the enemy at a range of about twenty-five yards. Major Reid, B.A., who brought up the gun, was immediately wounded, but the fire was still kept up by Lieutenant Ashe.

The right wing was now reinforced from the left, and the troops advanced in a manner that nothing could check, and the stockade was carried. Many of the enemy fled in confusion, but some stood to be shot or bayoneted.

Myat-toon was now entirely defeated.

Our loss was severe, eleven bodies were buried on the spot, and nine officers and seventy-five men were wounded in this well-fought action, which lasted about two hours.

"Lieutenant Trevor* was slightly wounded on this occasion, as also several Sappers. Trevor, with Corporal Livingstone and Private Preston, H.M.'s 51st, were the first to enter the enemy's breastwork. The two guns lost by the former expedition were now recaptured. The enemy had used them with great effect. In attempting to carry off one of them twelve of the enemy were killed by a discharge from our 9-pounders. The enemy suffered heavily, but the chief Myat-toon, with a few followers, managed to escape."

* Now Colonel Trevor, V.C.

Sir John Cheape says : " His whole force and means were con-centrated in this position, and I imagine he must have had 4,000 men in these breastworks, which extended 1,200 yards."

Lieutenant Mullins brought to the " notice of the Brigadier-General that Lieutenant Trevor, B.E., was the first to enter the stockade on the 19th, and that I received most valuable assist-ance from him during the whole of the advance on Kyou-kazeem. Sub-Conductor Vernal likewise merits great praise for his zeal and intelligence, especially in the formation of the rafts at the various nullahs. The Sappers, throughout the expedition, worked in front of the column under the protection of the advanced guard, which practically consisted of skirmishers, there being no room for any formation until the Sappers had cut a road through the jungle. Piling and unpiling arms perpetually was found to be very troublesome, and carrying arms in addition to tools a great fatigue ; consequently the arms of the Sappers were placed in a cart, and the men on more than one occasion entered stockades with the storming-party armed only with felling-axes and dhars (a Burmese weapon, a sort of sword with a handle about the same length as the blade, and very useful for felling small trees).

" On the 19th March the men had to cut a road all along the front of the stockade, and at a distance of from thirty-five to fifty yards only from its face, under a fire of great severity, which did not cease for a moment till the stockade was stormed. Their work throughout was most laborious, for, in addition to clearing the way, which involved cutting through and removing large trees, levelling the ground, &c., from morning until night, or constructing rafts and bridges for crossing the nullahs, they were called upon to provide for the safety of the picquets and outposts, and sometimes their work was not over until some hours after sunset. No men could have done better, or have been more cool and steady under fire, and the circumstances of the expedition made their services invaluable."

Sir John Cheape, in his despatch, thus mentions the services of the Engineers and Madras Sappers:—

"To Lieutenant Mullins and the detachment of the Madras Sappers and Miners the greatest praise is due ; the work executed by the men was most laborious, and the zeal and talent with which their energies were directed by Lieutenant Mullins are most creditable to him. He was ably seconded by Lieutenant Trevor, and I am mainly indebted to these officers and the men under them for enabling the troops to reach the enemy's position."

Our losses in the expedition were heavy, considering the smallness of the force : 2 European officers killed, Lieutenant Taylor, 9th Madras Native Infantry, and Ensign Boileau, 67th Bengal Native Infantry; also 1 Native officer and 18 warrant officers, N.C.O.'s and men, and 1 lascar; total, 22. Twelve European officers wounded, Lieutenant Cockburn mortally, 7 severely, and 4 slightly ; also 1 Native officer, 93 warrant officers N.C.O.'s and men, and 2 lascars ; total, 108. Grand total, 130 killed and wounded.

After the action a party was sent out to Myat-toon's own village, but not a person was to be seen, either at Kyou-kazeem or in another village passed on the road to it. These villages, situated on the Pautanar Creek, were three-quarters of a mile apart. Colonel Sturt, with the Commissariat, remained in the first village, while the rest of the force proceeded to Kyou-kazeem.

On the 20th, Captain Tarleton, R.N., arrived with some gun-boats, having cut through obstructions in the creek for some fifteen miles. Some 900 boats, crowded with people who had been kept in subjection by Myat-toon, passed down the creek.

On the 22nd the force was ordered to return ; 4 P.M. was the hour fixed for departure, but at 2 P.M. the village of Kyou-kazeem caught fire. Sir John Cheape was able to cross, but with difficulty, and even then not without being scorched. The fire spread with great rapidity. The sick, guns, and ammunition

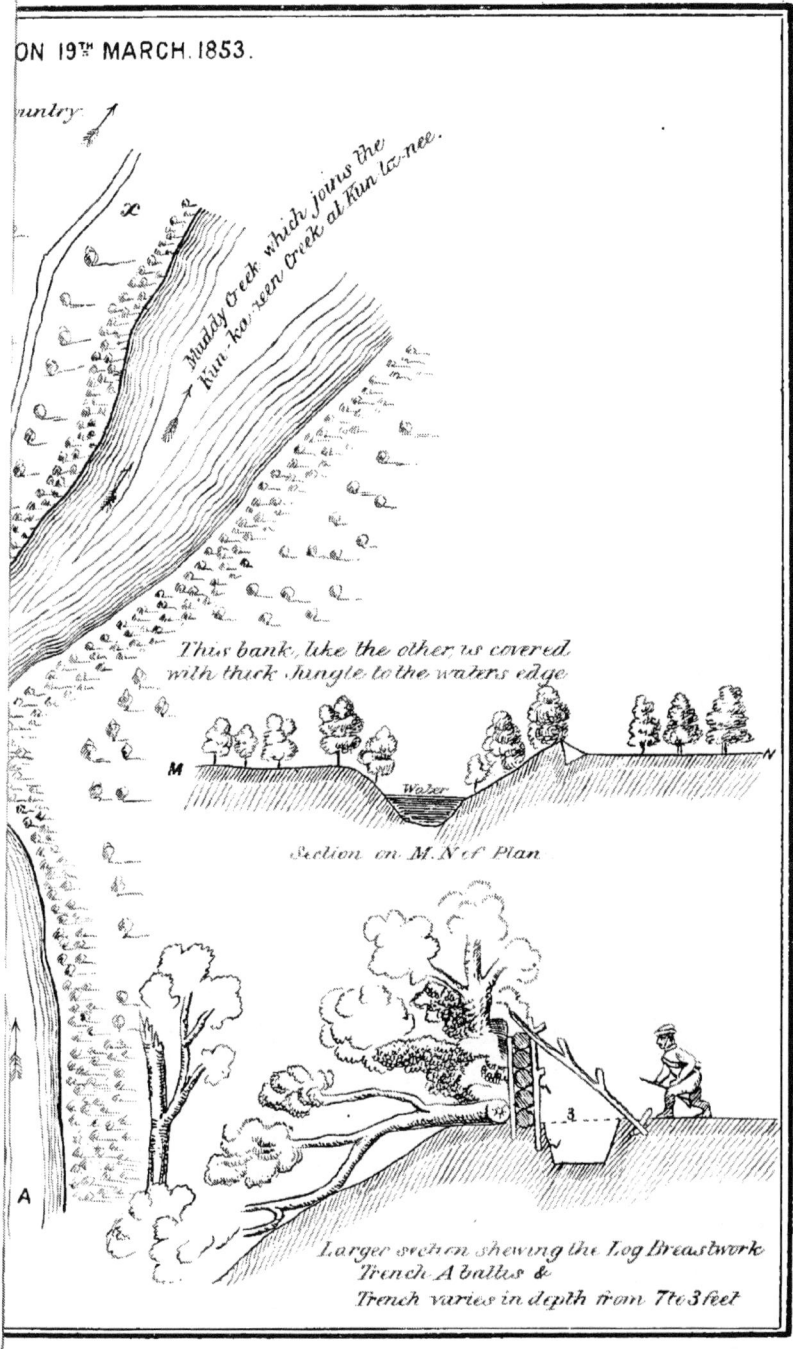

untry

x

Muddy Creek which joins the
Kun-ka-seen Creek at Kun-la-nee.

This bank, like the other, is covered
with thick Jungle to the waters edge

M

Water

N

Section on M.N of Plan

A

Larger section shewing the Log Breastwork
Trench Abattis &
Trench varies in depth from 7 to 3 feet

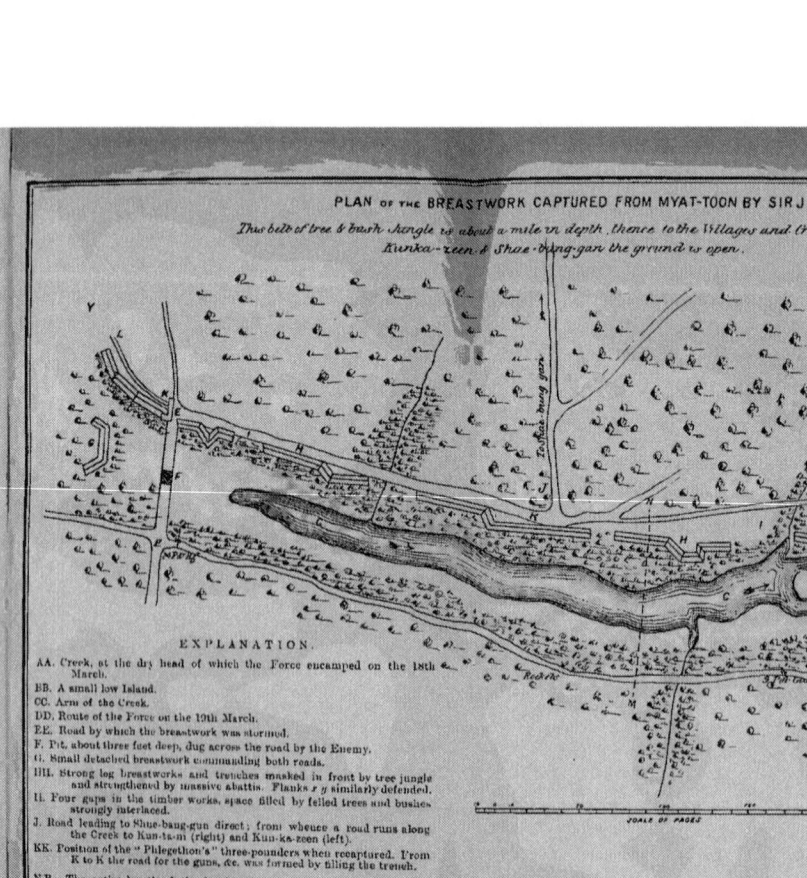

PLAN OF THE BREASTWORK CAPTURED FROM MYAT-TOON BY SIR J C

This belt of tree & bush Jungle is about a mile in depth, thence to the Villages and tree
Kunka-zeen & Shue-bung-gan the ground is open.

EXPLANATION.

AA. Creek, at the dry head of which the Force encamped on the 18th
    March.

BB. A small low Island.

CC. Arm of the Creek.

DD. Route of the Force on the 19th March.

EE. Road by which the breastwork was stormed.

F. Pit, about three feet deep, dug across the road by the Enemy.

G. Small detached breastwork commanding both roads.

HH. Strong log breastworks and trenches masked in front by tree jungle
    and strengthened by massive abattis. Flanks x y similarly defended.

II. Four gaps in the timber works, space filled by felled trees and bushes
    strongly interlaced.

J. Road leading to Shue-bung-gun direct; from whence a road runs along
    the Creek to Kun-ts-ni (right) and Kun-ka-zeen (left).

KK. Position of the "Phlegethon's" three-pounders when recaptured. From
    K to K the road for the guns, &c. was formed by filling the trench.

N.B.—The entire length of the log breastwork (from L to L) inclusive of
    Gaps II, and exclusive of flank abattis x and y, was 500 good paces,
    or between 450 and 480 yards.

SCALE OF PACES

had luckily already been sent off. Great confusion reigned for some time, but eventually all were collected in Colonel Sturt's camp, and the force marched to Kyou-banao the same evening.

On the 23rd a nullah was crossed to Akyoo, and next day Donabew was reached.

Our total casualties amounted to nearly 250, as upwards of 100 died of cholera.

On 31st March the Burmese Commissioners arrived at Prome, and their formal meeting with the British Commissioners took place on the 4th April.

Negotiations lasted for a month, but no treaty could be signed, as the new King would not cede any of his territory. The Governor-General refused to give up one place we had taken, and said that any attempt to disturb our new possessions would meet with severe retribution.

The frontier of the British territories was finally fixed to the northward of Meeaday and Tonghoo.

On 30th June 1853 the Governor-General notified that " the army of Ava will no longer be maintained on a war establishment, but at the same time a force will be permanently retained in Pegu, amply adequate for its defence, and fully prepared for the event of war." A donation of six months' batta was granted to all naval and military forces that had been employed during the war.

On 3rd August General Godwin left Rangoon for Calcutta, but did not long survive the campaign, as he died at Simla on 26th October. A monument was erected, by the army, to his memory, in Rangoon.

Naique Mootoo Veerapen and Private Ramasammy, of the Sappers, were admitted to the Third Class of the Order of Merit, for conspicuous gallantry during the campaign.

On 14th December the Governor-General made a second visit to Rangoon. He left Rangoon for Prome three days after, and on the 26th went to Meeaday, six miles further to the north.

A pillar of demarkation was built and saluted, when he returned to Mecaday. The Governor-General returned to Rangoon from Prome on 6th January 1854, and left for Bassein on the 9th, whence he proceeded to Calcutta.

On 21st January 1854, Major Allan, D.Q.M.G., arrived at Tonghoo from Prome as a Special Commissoner, accompanied by a detachment of Sikhs and a small party of Madras Sappers. They accomplished the distance, 140 miles, in sixteen days ; the sappers vastly improving the road as they went along.

A force was now organised to accompany Major Allan, to fix the boundary. One company Madras Fusiliers, a detachment of 5th Madras Native Infantry, another of Madras Sappers, and a few Rampoor Irregular Horse ; all under the command of Captain Geils. The force left Tonghoo on 24th January. At Kaleen, seventeen miles distant, they had a skirmish, and a second one took place at Tewah, nine miles further on.

On the 30th, as no further news arrived from Major Allan, it was resolved to send out reinforcements under Colonel Poole. A detachment of Madras Fusiliers, a strong force of Sikhs, and another party of Madras Sappers, under Lieutenant Shortland, together with a party of Madras Artillery, with two 24-pounder howitzers and a rocket-tube. This party reached Yagay, and were about to start for Kaleen, when a messenger arrived from Major Allan. The letter was dated Myeehau-Yoah, forty-two miles north of Tonghoo. The force had met with stong opposition, and breastworks, &c. had been brought into play to oppose our progress. Captain Geils was severely wounded while leading on his men at the assault of Nat-toon, four miles from Myo Khla, and the affair became a somewhat serious one. The Burmese had to be repelled at the point of the bayonet, and we had eight or ten men wounded.

The 5th Native Infantry and Madras Sappers highly distinguished themselves. Lieutenant P. A. Brown succeeded Captain Geils in command, and accompanied Major Allan to the boundary point opposite Mahaw, six miles beyond Myo-Khla, having crossed and re-crossed the Sittang river.

The boundary-line was marked forty-eight miles from Tonghoo, in a line with one six miles north of Meeaday.

On 2nd February Colonel Poole's force arrived at Myo-Khla, but could not find Major Allan. The next day news arrived that he was returning to Tonghoo, and on the 7th the whole force arrived there.

On the 10th a small force of Engineers, Fusiliers, and Madras Native Infantry, with two howitzers, under command of Captain Tulloch, left for Yagay to protect the surrounding country, and a temporary military post was formed there by Lieutenant A. S. Moberly, of the Madras Engineers.

CHAPTER VII.

THIS memorable defence must form a part of the history of the Madras Engineers, as the Engineer who planned the works, and who was one of the principal men engaged in the defence belonged to that Corps—Henry Atwell Lake, at that time a major.

In August 1854, Colonel Williams, C.B., had been appointed British Commissioner in Asia Minor. He found the Turkish army in a most demoralised state, and every difficulty was thrown in his way when he strove to amend matters.

Before the end of the year General Williams applied for three officers to assist him. One of Artillery, one of Engineers, and one a Rifle officer. The following were appointed—Captain William Olpherts, Bengal Artillery; Lieutenant Henry Langhorne Thompson, 68th Bengal Native Infantry; and Brevet-Major H. Atwell Lake, Madras Engineers.

Towards the end of March 1855, Olpherts and Thompson

arrived at Kars; and Teesdale (General Williams' A.D.C.) then rejoined the General at Erzeroum.

All the officers engaged in this work obtained a step of local rank.

On 31st March, Lieutenant-Colonel Lake assumed charge of the post at Kars which had just been vacated by Teesdale.

Kars is 7,000 feet above the sea, 40° 15′ north latitude, 43° 16′ east longitude, with an extensive plain in front, and high mountains in rear. It is built in a kind of semicircle, formed by the Kars Tchac, where the river enters the narrow gorge of the mountains.

The fortress is an irregular polygon, built of stone, with a double enceinte of walls, and four towers.

The citadel is at the north-west angle, very strong in itself, but commanded by the hills in the rear.

The inner wall of the fortress is flanked by numerous small towers, and the outer wall forms a circuit of a mile and a half.

The mountain of Karadagh, east of, and commanding the fortress, was, in 1828, fortified by a battery of earthwork, and well furnished with cannon. There was also a tower called the Castle of Temir Pasha, on the opposite bank of the river, west of the fortress.

In 1828 Kars was captured by Prince Paskiewitch in a few days. General Monteith, Madras Engineers (then a Lieutenant-Colonel), was present at this capture, and accompanied the Prince during a considerable part of the campaign. The fortress in 1855 was in much the same state as it was in 1828.

It was not till the middle of April 1855 that Lieutenant-Colonel Lake was enabled to make a proper inspection of the fortifications, as, up to that time, the snow had not sufficiently disappeared. In order to prevent the enemy from coming too near the fortress, it had been deemed necessary to surround the place with an entrenched line, extending from the foot of the Karadagh to the river on the west. This line had to be carried to a considerable distance, owing to the ground rising from the town to the plain, and then falling immediately. The position was thus, unfortunately, too extensive for a limited garrison. This breast-work was in a very damaged state. In several places there was a great hiatus, and it afforded no cover for the men, while flanking fire seemed to be a thing unknown. At the east end of the south line, three sides of a large rectangular redoubt, called Hafiz Pasha Tabia (battery), had been built, but it was entirely open at the gorge, had insufficient parapets, and had no magazines. At the other end was a small battery, Kauli Tabia, also a useless work as it then stood. Between these two batteries two small lunettes, Zeni and Feyzi Bey Tabias, had been thrown up. On the west line part of the breastwork had been strengthened, and salients thrown out to form an open battery for guns *en barbette*. Nearly at the foot of the Karadagh, on a badly chosen site, was a small battery, called Koltuk Tabia, to com-mand the Gumri road. These works, with dilapidated remains of a wall, which originally enclosed the principal suburb, and two round batteries at the angles, Chicbeck and Yusuf Pasha Tabias, constituted the whole of the lower defences. The Karadagh was fortified by long straggling open works, with one small redoubt on the highest point. To the north of Karadagh was a very large redoubt called Arab Tabia, on a hill very little lower than the Karadagh. It was, however, incomplete, and unprotected at the gorge.

The defences on the north side of the river consisted of a few works quite unfitted for purposes of defence, with the exception of one small lunette on the edge of a precipice overhanging the river, planned and constructed by Major Teesdale in 1854.

The most commanding spot of all was north-west of the fortress, and on it had been constructed an unmeaning work, called Veli Pasha Tabia. To the right of this battery, along a ridge running parallel to the river, were three small works, lunettes open at the gorge; one noticed, as being constructed by Major Teesdale, the other two badly placed. There was one work called Tehim Tabia, favourably placed on rising ground commanding the river, west of the town.

These were all the works in April 1855.

Lieutenant-Colonel Lake had gone to Kars with full powers from General Williams, and the Mushir commanding the army, to remodel the fortifications and construct such new works as he might consider necessary.

As a preliminary step, eighty men were told off under Captain Hadji Agha to form a band of Sappers, to be taught how to make gabions, fascines, &c., and to set up profiles.

About the middle of April 500 men were at work on the entrenched line, under Major-General Hafiz Pasha. The engineer stores were very inadequate; but in spite of this, an entirely new line of breastwork was marked out in some places, and the whole was put into a thorough state of repair. The necessary openings were adequately protected, and the batteries bearing on the several roads passing through the lines were strengthened, added to, and altered where necessary. All were closed at the gorges, and provided with magazines. Chevaux de frise were put up in each battery, and at every opening. Many small works were constructed for the purpose of flanking fire, and shortly the lower works assumed a defensive appearance.

Koltuk Tabia was demolished, and a new battery, larger and on a different plan, was built higher up the slope of the Karadagh. Where Tehim Tabia stood, a large enclosed redoubt, called Vassif Pasha Tabia, was made, with command not only of the river, but also of a great part of the town, and permanent stone bridges. Two large magazines were made under the traverses. In nearly all the batteries the body of the parapet was composed of loose stone, packed with great neatness and dexterity, thickly covered with earth, well beaten down and turfed, so that the strength of the work was enormous.

On site of Veli Pasha a large and very formidable redoubt was

16 *

built, capable of containing a garrison of 2,000 to 3,000 men. Magazines were made, and a very large strong wooden block-house, loop-holed all round, revetted with earth, and turfed over, so as to render it completely shot-proof, was constructed at the gorge. The block-house was large enough to hold 300 men, and was fitted up with sleeping places. This redoubt received from the Turks the name of Fort Lake. The two lunettes on the heights were strengthened and closed at the gorges, and the same thing was done with the work on the edge of the river. They were named Zohrab, Thompson, and Teesdale Tabias, and the whole formed the " Ingliz " batteries.

The fortifications on the Karadagh were much strengthened. Arab Tabia was put in a state of defence; and as it was considered too large, and that there was no time to reduce its dimensions, a redoubt was built in the centre commanding the whole work.

The bulk of the ammunition had hitherto been kept in the citadel in a most insecure place. One of the existing buildings was altered and converted into a secure magazine. Two temporary bridges were thrown across the river, to afford easy communication between the lower works and those on the heights. They were constructed of wooden pontoons, which had been used for the same purpose the previous year, of a very clumsy description, and not even well adapted for stationary work, still less for service should the army take the field.

During all the time these works were being carried on, the officers had other various duties—procuring information regarding the plans of the enemy, examining deserters, and supervising the drill of the garrison; the infantry under Captain Thompson, and the artillery under Major Olpherts, Bengal Artillery, who was afterwards sent by General Williams to join Veli Pasha's army near Erzeroum.

The garrison at this time consisted of 10,000 infantry, 1,500 artillery, and 1,500 cavalry. The last were very badly equipped, had wretched old horses, and the men could neither ride nor manœuvre. The artillery was good, as also some of the infantry.

During the time Lieutenant-Colonel Lake was engaged at Kars, General Williams and his aides-de-camp were incessantly employed in fortifying Erzeroum.

Towards the latter end of May it was ascertained that a large Russian force had crossed the Arpa, a boundary river.

A new Mushir, or Commander-in-Chief, was sent up from Constantinople to command the army in Asia Minor, and had arrived at Kars in April.

Early in May the whole of the Kars garrison was paraded before the Mushir. By this time the garrison had been considerably increased.

In May commences the great fast called the Ramazan, and it lasts forty days, during which time Mussalmans are enjoined to abstain wholly from water or food during the day.

A few days before the beginning of the fast, Lieutenant-Colonel Lake waited on the Mushir, and pointed out the disastrous consequences likely if this custom was observed. It necessarily followed that they must cook and eat at night, and, consequently, could get no proper rest; they would be prevented from working with energy on the fortifications, and their strength would be reduced in an encounter with the Russians, who were likely for that very reason to attack.

The Mushir hesitated to issue any order, and Colonel Lake applied to General Williams to interfere. General Williams accordingly wrote to the Mushir, but meantime the Mushir relented, and issued an order to the garrison to consider the Ramazan for the present a dead letter.

On 7th June, General Williams and his personal staff arrived at Kars.

Two days afterwards the enemy advanced and encamped near Zami-Keni, eight miles from Kars on the Kars Tchac.

The Turkish cavalry outposts had been thrown out on heights overlooking the village.

Lieutenant-Colonel Lake and Dr. Sandwith visited the outposts on the 14th. He found that the outposts had been thrown too far forward, and when day broke a regiment of Russian cavalry was observed approaching.

The patrols were called in, and the whole outposts, 250 badly mounted and worse armed cavalry, with fifty Bashi-Bazouks, were retired.

At first the Turks retreated in good order, but the Bashi-Bazouks, finding the enemy coming on at a gallop, took fright and fled, when the rest of the detachment, headed by many of their own officers, put spurs to their horses, and the flight became general. They were closely pursued by the enemy, but they managed to get within reach of the guns of the fortress with trifling loss.

By this affair it was fully proved that very little confidence could be placed in the cavalry of the Kars garrison.

The 16th of June was the great day of the Beiram. Orders were issued that all ceremonies should be dispensed with, as the enemy was much too near.

This precaution was most fortunate, as about 10 A.M. the Russian army was seen drawn up in line of battle on top of the first hill beyond the town.

A trifling engagement took place between the cavalry, the Turks retreating to the protection of their guns, when the guns of the Karadagh opened fire, as also those of Hafiz Pasha Tabia. This checked the Russians and they finally retreated.

The general opinion in camp was that the affair was an attempt of the enemy to get into the lines by a *coup de main*, hoping to find the garrison indulging in the pleasures of the Beiram.

The Russians now retired, and encamped at Zemi-Keni.

Captain Thompson had charge of the Karadagh and adjacent works.

Lieutenant-Colonel Lake patrolled the lower works from mid-night till 3 A.M., at which hour General Williams visited all the most important posts.

Major Teesdale had supervision of all works near Fort Lake.

The duty was now most severe. Torrents of rain fell incessantly, and in some parts of the camp the water stood a foot deep.

Picquets were placed round the entire works, 200 paces in front, and in advance of them mounted sentries, under the superintendence of Colonel Baron Schwartzenburg, formerly of the Austrian service.

General Williams with Lieutenant-Colonel Lake daily visited the works, and many additions were made to strengthen the defences.

The provisions and ammunition were now found to be very limited, and the men's rations were accordingly gradually reduced.

On the 18th the Russian army advanced from Zemi-Keni towards Kars. The garrison stood to their arms.

Towards the afternoon the enemy arrived in front of Kars, but far out of reach of the batteries. Before sunset they halted at Magharadjik, three miles and a half south of the town, and pitched their camp.

The army appeared to be 35,000 or 40,000 men of all arms, with a large field-train, but no heavy siege guns. It was commanded by General Mouravieff.

The Russians were now able to cut off all communication between Kars and Erzeroum, by the direct route, and the only road which was now open was by Pennek.

The defences having now been completed to a certain extent, it was deemed advisable to carry them still further, by fortifying the heights of Tachmash, which commanded Fort Lake on the

west at a distance of 1,900 yards   The first intention was to
construct open works to protect the approaches to the hills with
light field-pieces, which at the same time would prove useless to
the assailants should the Turks be compelled to retire.   A
similar work called Laz Tabia, was also built between Tachmash and Fort Lake.   The batteries of Karadagh and Arab
Tabia were connected by a breastwork to protect the valley
between these two hills from a sudden attack.   A breastwork
was also constructed to unite the English batteries with each
other and with Fort Lake, and a semi-circular battery called
Churchill battery was erected on a rising ground, capable of
holding three light guns.

The staff of the Turkish army was not efficient.   An Hungarian officer serving under the Turkish Government (General
Collman), under the title of Fezzi Pasha, was at the head, but he
laboured under many disadvantages, the chief of which was want
of an able assistant.   Twelve foreign officers served under him,
but nearly the whole were utterly useless.   Fezzi Pasha was a
man of energy and talent, and nothing but his indefatigable
attention could have kept matters straight.

The Commissariat was under a council of Turkish officers
directed by Mr. Churchill, General Williams' private secretary.

Soon after the beginning of the blockade it was ascertained
that the accounts of provisions in store were totally false.   It
was found that large blocks of stone had been mixed with the
flour to make it appear a greater quantity.

The storekeeper was confined in irons, and died before the
surrender of the place.

On 26th June the Russians made a reconnoissance in force,
advancing on Hafiz Pasha and Kanli Tabias.   They halted
within long range of the guns, and after remaining more than
an hour, retired to their encampment.

This reconnoissance apparently convinced General Mouravieff
that the position could not be carried without great loss,

and determined him to decide on blockade, so that he might have his army intact to oppose the force which might reasonably be expected to be sent to the relief of Kars.

On the 28th the whole of the Russian army was discovered to be on the move, and they pitched their camp a league further south, where they took up a position on a ledge of rocks, which rendered all approach nearly impossible.

There were left about 5,000 infantry with artillery and cavalry, while all the rest marched south to Chiplakli, and thence to Zemi-Keni, where they destroyed the magazines.

On the 6th July the Russians returned and encamped near Komanroor, north of Azad Keni, leaving a garrison at the latter place.

On 13th July they made another reconnoissance in front of Tachmash, and after remaining several hours retired.

On 1st August a very large force of all arms left the Russian lines under General Mouravieff in person, and took the road towards the Soghanli Dagh.

It was supposed he intended to attack Erzeroum, but after a fortnight the force returned to camp.

Had the Russians attacked Veli Pasha at the Devi Boynon Pass, there is every reason to suppose that, in spite of the position having been well fortified by General Williams, owing to the pusillanimity of the Turkish military authorities, the result would have been fatal, and Erzeroum could then have offered only a feeble resistance.

The Russian force was only 8,000 to 12,000 men, while the Turks had 25,000 in an entrenched position, so they ought to have felt secure.

Luckily, however, after a halt of a few days, the Russians retired towards Kars.

The British Consul, Mr. Brant, in his despatch of 7th August 1855, dated Erzeroum, says with regard to the Pashas :—

"I have not spoken with sufficient severity of the imbecile

and cowardly conduct of the Pashas. They would undoubtedly have run away if they had been attacked, although, with the number of guns they had, their position could not have been forced by treble the number of Russians."

Early on the morning of the 7th August a force of about 8,000 men of all arms was seen advancing towards Kanli Tabia. The garrison was instantly under arms, and batteries, &c. manned as soon as the Russians came within range. The Turkish guns on the south line opened fire with great effect, and after two hours the whole Russian force retired to its encampment. It was supposed that the intention of the Russian commander was to entice the Turks from the works. In this he failed, and paid very dearly for his temerity in coming so close to the batteries, as they lost a general and several superior officers, besides a total loss of killed and wounded very considerable. Not a single Turk was touched.

A few days after another grand reconnoissance was made by nearly the whole of the Russian army in front of the Tachmash heights. On this occasion they did not approach within range of the Turkish guns, and after a few hours they again retired.

As it was now considered probable that the next serious attack would be on this side, the line of breastwork was extended to the south. At the point where the two lines formed an angle, an enclosed redoubt was built, and at the southern extremity a small return was made with two salient angles for guns, *en barbette*, to sweep the road running in front of the position. About 1,000 yards to the north of these works a small redoubt was constructed, which afterwards played a conspicuous part in the defence of Tachmash. To the south of this work a small open battery was built on a lower level, called Yarmi Ali Tabia, and to the north a long line, consisting of battery and breastwork, called Shishanagee Lines, was built on a range of hills commanding the valley, leading to the front of the English batteries, and intended to prevent the Tachmash works being taken in flank.

A very important position opposite the village Telukmak, and commanding the road leading from the valley to Fort Lake, was also fortified by an open battery, called Tetch Tabia. All these works were engaged on the great day of assault, so the precautionary measures taken were by no means thrown away. A rough stone bridge was thrown across the Kars river (with a wooden platform), where its width was fifty feet, and its depth considerable. This was to facilitate the communications between the Arab Tabia and the English batteries on the other side of the river, a zigzag road being formed on both sides down to the river. A battery, named Williams Tabia, was formed on dead ground lying in rear of the English batteries, close to precipice overhanging the river, and intended as a refuge in case the garrison was driven from the line in front. Six thousand men were encamped on the heights under Major-General Ismail Pasha (General Kmety), a Hungarian officer of great ability. His services were brought especially to the notice of Lord Stratford de Redcliffe by General Williams, who stated that he showed great personal bravery at the battle of Infe-Derah, and that since that battle he had been the eye of the army. General Williams requested that he might receive the pay of his rank (Ferik), and have a decoration for personal gallantry. He also stated, "He is one of those men who abstain from complaints or intrigue, and I make this appeal in his favour without a request on his part." Major Teesdale was directed to afford his assistance to this officer.

Hussein Pasha, a Circassian, also held a command at Tachmash.

On the plain below it was thought desirable to form an inner line of defence, and a breastwork was built to connect the fortress wall with the burial ground, and carried on till it joined Chicheck Tabia. The fortifications uniting this battery with Yusuf Pasha Tabia were improved, and Telek Tabia was made to the right of Yusuf Pasha Tabia, a breastwork connecting the two batteries, as well as a second carried from the other flank to the steep precipice in the rear, above the river.

Three rows of *trous de loups*, three to four feet in diameter, were excavated in front of nearly all the batteries and breastworks. All these works were formed under great disadvantages: no Engineer establishment; the ground to be fortified comprised a circle of nearly ten miles; the difficulty, and in many places the impossibility, of digging a ditch, owing to the rocky nature of the soil; and, lastly, want of time. A work was decided on, at once marked out, and profiles immediately set up; working parties were told off, and, as the Russians afterwards remarked, batteries appeared to rise by magic.

The able supervision of Major Teesdale and Captain Thompson, the cheerfulness and dexterity of the men, and the quantity of loose stone in every direction, tended very considerably to counterbalance the disadvantages under which Lieutenant-Colonel Lake laboured, and enabled him to complete the fortifications to such an extent as to render the place defensible.

Towards the end of August the enemy formed a camp of cavalry, with eight guns, at Borkali, four miles north-west of Tachmash; and other camps at Chalgour and Ainalli, north of the position; and Kars was thus completely invested.

The men's rations were again reduced, and desertion began to take place, and gave signs of rapidly increasing. The Mushir, on General Williams' earnest remonstrances, issued an order that in future the punishment for desertion would be instant death. A case very shortly after occurred, and the man was tried, condemned, and at once shot. This example had a good effect on the troops, but desertion, of course, was not completely stopped.

A Turkish force, commanded by Veli Pasha, was stationed near the Bayazid line at Euch Kelisea, to keep in check the

Erivan Brigade of the Russian army, about 6,000 men. He had orders, in the event of the Russians advancing, to retire gradually on Erzeroum, and early in the month of August, in obedience to his orders, he retired on the Devi-Boynon Pass, lately fortified by General Williams.

It now was apparent that spying took place in Kars to a great extent, and it was found necessary to put this down with a very heavy hand. A short time after an inhabitant was convicted of conveying intelligence to the enemy's camp. He was sentenced to death, and hanged the same afternoon in the middle of the town.

On the 21st August a convoy was seen approaching the Russian camp, and it was reported that two siege-guns and a large mortar accompanied it. It was, therefore, considered necessary to strengthen the Kanli Tabia, the south-west angle of the lower works. Three of the barbettes were at once raised four feet; additional height was given to the parapet; embrasures were constructed; and at midnight two heavy siege-guns were brought there and masked with gabions.

Hitherto the garrison had been unusually healthy, but it was now attacked by cholera. In spite of the praiseworthy efforts of Dr. Sandwith, it committed great havoc, and carried off 1,500 of the garrison, exclusive of some of the inhabitants.

On the 23rd September, Arslan Agha, a Chief of Bashi Bazouks, forced his way through the enemy's outposts into Kars with six followers, and brought in the welcome news that the south part of Sebastopol had fallen, and the Mushir received a letter from Omar Pasha. A salute was fired at noon and another at sunset, and the order of the day was read to the paraded troops. Omar Pasha said that in twenty days he would come to the assistance of Kars.

Day after day and week after week had passed without signs of succour; the weather was becoming every day colder, the soldiers on duty suffered most severely, and the hospitals were getting more crowded. The enemy remained perfectly quiet. The garrison was not lulled into a feeling of security, and no relaxation of discipline was permitted.

At 4 A.M. on 29th September, it was reported to General Kmety by the officer in charge of outposts, that he fancied he heard a rumbling noise in the direction of the enemy's main camp. The troops were under arms, the guns manned, and every officer at his post a few minutes after the alarm had been given.

Information was at once sent to General Williams. Lieutenant-Colonel Lake had, as usual, been patrolling round the lower works, and Major Teesdale round the English batteries; the latter had just reached his tent and was in the act of dismounting, when he was startled by a gun flashing through the darkness directly in front. He at once galloped off to the battery, and heard that the Russians were advancing. It was now half-past 4. The guns continued to fire steadily from the Tachmash works.

The Russians were now close to the works, the guns loaded entirely with case-shot, assisted by the rolling fire of musketry, swept the enemy completely from the front. The column thus split, swerving to each side of Yuksuk Tabia, overwhelmed the small open battery called Yarim-ai Tabia, and on the right forced its way round and got among the tents in rear. Teesdale was in Yuksuk Tabia; and the fire of two guns, besides musketry, was concentrated on the interior of the work, which soon cleared it, and the Russians took refuge on the reverse slope of the parapet, and kept up a galling fire on Yuksuk Tabia.

While this was going on, a part of the Russian column which had re-formed rushed upon an almost undefended point in its rear, and so sudden was the assault, that the Russians swarmed up the parapet, and many of them actually got inside the work. The Turks wavered ; the moment was most critical for Yuksuk Tabia. Major Teesdale rushed up into the salient already occupied by the enemy. This probably saved the battery. The column of attack, although checked, still came rushing up, and another body was seen approaching to their support.

Teesdale left the Turks fighting well, and went to try to bring a gun from the front. He found one limbered up, and with the help of four gunners, ran the piece up into the salient, when the gun was brought into action. It was loaded only with grape. Six times the iron shower tore through the Russian ranks; the column then broke, and fled past the redoubt down the hill.

Day had now dawned. The force disposed of was the centre one of the three which attacked together. On the left Tachmash Tabia, with its flanking line of breastwork turned, seemed a mass of smoke and fire. On the left eight battalions had rushed on the Remison lines. Here General Kmety commanded. The Turks lined two faces of a re-entering angle, into which the Russians penetrated.

Leaving the guns, which protected their flank, to do their work, until the enemy was close upon them, the Turks then opened a converging fire on the head of the column. Though many fell, the rest still moved up, but they could not stand the deadly fire. The Russians were at last brought to a standstill by a mound of dead bodies. The Turks, then led on by Kmety, leapt over the breastwork, and completed with the bayonet the utter rout of the enemy. This column left 850 corpses in a space of about an acre.

While the heights of Tachmash were being attacked, a force of all arms appeared advancing against Kanli Tabia. Lieutenant-Colonel Lake at once went to this battery, and finding that although the enemy opened fire they remained stationary, it became evident that the attack was only a feint. Lieutenant-Colonel Lake leaving strict orders with the Turkish officers in command not to fire at the enemy till he came well within range, proceeded to Vasif Pasha Tabia.

General Williams, with the Mushir, and Fezzi Pasha, the Chief of the Staff, were at Telek Tabia.

From Vasif Pasha and Telek Tabias a continuous fire was opened with heavy guns against the enemy's artillery, drawn up on the left flank of the Tachmash line of works. The Russians suffered much from this fire, and attempted to return it, but without much effect.

All this time the enemy persevered in their attempts to take Tachmash and Yuksuk Tabia.

Day had now broken, and the Russians having turned the left of Tachmash, had got up sixteen guns and placed them in position, the fire from which fell heavily upon Yuksuk Tabia without that garrison being able, from the confusion at Tachmash, to reply to it. This artillery-fire was reduced to silence by the Turkish artillery at Vasif Pasha and Telek Tabias.

General Kmety now came up from the Remison lines with four companies of chasseurs, dashed into Yarmi-ai Tabia, drove the Russians out, re-formed, and went on in the highest spirits to Tachmash.

Major Teesdale had remained in Yuksuk Tabia, and had directed the fire of the guns on the column opposed to his right, which was endeavouring to come up a second time. This column made several attempts, but was received with such a heavy and precise fire that it was compelled to retire, and was seen no more.

While this was going on, another column was suddenly observed advancing against the line of works called English Tabias. This column consisted of eight battalions of infantry, two batteries of artillery, and a division of cavalry. The English Tabias, as has already been stated, were defective in site. In addition to this, they were unavoidably under-manned. Fort Lake was fairly well garrisoned, but the other batteries contained only 300 men each, while the intermediate breastworks were partially lined by the Lazi Irregular Riflemen and the Town Bashi Bazouks.

The attack on these works commenced at a quarter to 7. The

enemy fired three rounds at the work from their artillery when they reached the rising ground in front of the batteries, and then charged the breastwork. They immediately effected an entrance; the Turks retiring to Williams Pasha Tabia. The Russians now made a breach in the entrenched line, and brought in their artillery and began to fire on the town; but little damage was done. Several guns were directed at Fort Lake.

The position taken up by the Russians was commanded by one spot in the Karadagh, and Captain Thompson, taking advantage of this, moved a heavy gun to this place, and opened fire on the enemy.

At the same time two large guns were run up on the east side of Fort Lake, and commenced a well-directed cannonade.

Teesdale Tabia had by this time fallen into the hands of the enemy, and the heaviest of its guns were turned on Arab Tabia, but they were soon silenced by the heavy artillery of that redoubt under Lieutenant Koch, a Prussian officer.

As soon as the capture of the English batteries was known, Lieutenant-Colonel Lake, who had been in Vasif Pasha Tabia, proceeded to Fort Lake, and assumed superintendence of the operations in that quarter.

General Williams at once ordered reinforcements to be sent.

Four companies of Chasseurs crossed the river by one of the permanent stone bridges, and, climbing up the hill, entered Williams Pasha Tabia by the rear, without the knowledge of the enemy.

At the same time (8.30 A.M.) a battalion of infantry was sent from Fort Lake, and 1,100 men by Captain Thompson from Arab Tabia, across the bridge lately thrown over the river.

The Russians were now trying to carry Williams Pasha Tabia and to engage the fire of Fort Lake, but the guns of this latter work swept the front of Williams Pasha Tabia; and the three reinforcements, arriving simultaneously, gallantly charged the enemy, and drove them out at the point of the bayonet, the

II. 17

Russian artillery having been about a quarter of an hour previously forced to retire from the position they had taken up, by the murderous cross-fire, which they had withstood for one hour and three quarters, in spite of their great loss of men and horses.

The enemy in their retreat took five Turkish guns with them, two of which were afterwards regained, having been left at a short distance from the works; the other guns which were left behind were spiked by the Russians.

During the retreat a regiment of Dragoons made a most gallant and unprecedented charge against the breastwork, but were received with a tremendous fire, and the confusion which ensued from the horses falling into the triple line of *trous de loup*, baffles description.

The cavalry covered the retreating column, and the whole retired in excellent order.

The loss of the Turks was considerable, but the slaughter among the enemy was fearful, and in Thompson and Zohrab Tabias the number of dead bodies (more than 200) showed how obstinately the Russians endeavoured to retain the advantage they had gained.

Most unaccountably, not a shot was fired from the citadel when the enemy were in possession of the English batteries, although two large guns were available.

The officer in command of the citadel failed to give any excuse, and was disgraced after the battle.

The battle on Tachmash heights was meantime carried on with persevering courage.

The expulsion of the Russians from the English batteries was of the greatest importance. Had the Russians succeeded in capturing Fort Lake, it would have been impossible for the Turks to hold Tachmash Tabia, as their rear would have been under the guns of Fort Lake, and the town of Kars would have been entirely at the mercy of the Russians.

At the moment the Russians were driven out of the English batteries, a battalion of the enemy debouched from the right flank of the Tachmash breastwork, with intent to repeat the manœuvre which had so nearly succeeded at Yuksek Tabia, but the Turks opened such a heavy fire of grape on them from Yuksek Tabia, that the Russians again took refuge inside the line. Here they were met by some reserves, which cut off their retreat to the left. They, therefore, took the direction of the small work called Telck Tabia, which commanded the village of Tachmash, and contained two guns. This work was a mile north-west of Fort Lake. A fearful cross-fire opened on them from Yuksek Tabia and Fort Lake, but they effected their retreat in good order, although with a loss, afterwards acknowledged, of 250 men.

Colonel Kauffman for this gallant act was decorated with the Cross of St. George.

In spite of success on every other point, the fight stiil continued to rage round Tachmash Tabia.

General Kmety had taken up three companies and Major Teesdale had sent three more with a gun, but these reinforcements hardly made up their losses, and their ammunition was expended.

The last hour of the battle was carried on with the ammunition of the Russian dead.

Sallies were made for the express-purpose of obtaining the needful supply, and at one time part of the garrison were engaged in stripping off the pouches of the fallen on one side of the redoubt and throwing them to their comrades, who were thus able to repulse the enemy on the other.

At last, out of the whole Russian infantry, there remained but two battalions that had not been engaged.

The Russian General gave the order to retire, but it was too late. General Williams had already sent a reinforcement from below, and Colonel Lake had sent a battalion from Fort Lake.

17 *

These met as they were ascending the hill to the scene of action, and immediately charged the enemy and drove him from the interior lines.

Major Teesdale now led a charge against the enemy's chasseurs and stragglers. On reaching the exterior of Tachmash Tabia they found themselves in the presence of a regiment of the enemy firing heavily along their front. The brave garrison of Tachmash Tabia, under Hussein Pasha, rushed furiously out to share in the combat, and the Russian regiment seemed to melt before them, and the ground was at once covered with the killed and wounded, a small remnant flying in utter confusion.

The Turks could not be stopped till they got to the bottom of the hill, but the affair was then over.

The Russian infantry straggled away from the scene of action, and only rallied in some sort of order when far out on the plain to the left of the hills which faced the Tachmash position.

The Turks, having no cavalry worthy the name, were unable to pursue the repulsed enemy, and were compelled to remain in the lines whence they had so triumphantly driven the Russians.

General Kmety, Hussein Pasha (a Circassian), and Major Teesdale, particularly distinguished themselves by their coolness and daring.

Captain Thompson, who was in command of Karadagh and Arab Tabias, contributed largely to the happy termination of the attack on the English batteries.

Colonel Yamib, Mustapha Bey, General Kerim Pasha, the Reis or second in command, and Colonel Kadri Bey, greatly distinguished themselves.

The Reis received a contusion, and had two horses shot under him.

Mr. Churchill, General Williams' secretary, directed the fire of a battery throughout the action.

Mr. Zohrab, Colonel Lake's interpreter, remained with him

during the battle, and was constantly employed in conveying
orders and instructions.

Mr. Remison, Major Teesdale's interpreter, was in the whole
of the action, during which his clothes were shot through ; he
did also excellent service.

Many Turkish officers performed most valuable services
during the battle. Those mentioned by Colonel Lake were :—

> Colonel Zachariah Bey.
>   ,,   Kurd Ali Bey.
> Lieutenant-Colonel Temoa Bey.
> Major Omar Effendi.
>   ,,   Mehemet Effendi.
>   ,,   Hussain Agha.
> Captain Halil Bey.
>   ,,   Aarif Agha.
>   ,,   Ibrahim Agha.
>   ,,   Mehemet Effendi.
>   ,,   Bekir Agha.
>   ,,   Hussain Agha.
> Lieutenant Koch (formerly in the Prussian army).
> Lieutenant Gratoffsky (a Pole who was wounded).
> Musa Agha.

General Hussain Bey received a contusion, while Major
Teesdale got a bruise on the leg from a case-shot. Major Selim
Agha, Aide-de-Camp to General Kmety, received a ball in the
arm.

Too much cannot be said in praise of the Turkish soldiers.
The practice of the artillery was perfect, nor were the infantry
at all behindhand in this respect. The number of Turkish
troops employed did not exceed 10,000 fighting men, while the
attacking force was between 30,000 and 35,000.

It must, therefore, be allowed that the defence is worthy of
record in the annals of military history, particularly when it is
considered that the garrison had been living for several months

on less than half rations.   But while we praise the garrison, we must not forget the firmness of the enemy, who for more than seven hours fought exposed to such a heavy fire of musketry and artillery.

The loss of the Turks in killed and wounded was 1,092, besides 101 townspeople, and a number of Bashi Bazouks.

The losses of the Russians were enormous, 10,000 to 12,000 killed and wounded, 250 to 300 officers being among them.

On 3rd October (four days after the battle) Captain Thompson wrote : " Up to this morning we have buried 6,250 bodies, and more still remain."

Four wounded Russian officers and 150 soldiers were taken prisoners.

General Williams in his first letter to Lord Clarendon, wrote of the " gallant conduct of Lieutenant-Colonel Lake, Major Teesdale, and Captain Thompson." He also named Mr. Churchill and Messrs. Zohrab and Remison, as well as Dr. Sandwith.

Cholera, which had for a short time ceased, now again broke out. and seventy or eighty men died daily.

The supply of meat entirely ceased, and the men had to subsist on farinaceous food.

The nights were piercingly cold.

It now seemed as if the great excitement of the battle had been too much after such protracted anxiety, and a gloom appeared to be spread over the place from the moment the last shot was fired.   It was supposed that the victory, together with the arrival of Omar Pasha on the coast, would remove the blockade.

Days passed by, but no succour appeared, neither did the Russians move from their position.

Omar Pasha, though he landed ostensib'y to create a diversion in favour of the garrison, never gave them any intimation of what his movements had been or were to be.   He only wrote twice; his first letter contained advice regarding fortifications and provisions, which was superfluous; his second a mere formal acknowledgment of General Williams' letter, conveying intelligence of the victory of the 29th September.

On the 17th October a large meeting of officers took place in the tent of the Mushir. This was held for the purpose of distributing the Order of the Medjidie to the various officers for their distinguished services on the day of the battle.

General Williams received the First Class of the Order, also Lieutenant-General Kerim Pasha, the second in command under the Mushir. Major-Generals Kmety and Hussain Pasha received the Second Class, and Colonels Fezzi (General Kollman) and Baron Schwartzenburg the Third Class.

Lieutenant Colonel Lake of the Madras Engineers received the Second Class, while Major Teesdale, Captain Thompson, Mr. Churchill, and Dr. Sandwith, obtained the Third Class.

On Messrs. Zohrab and Remison were bestowed the Fourth Class. Several Turkish officers of inferior rank were invested at the same time.

Colonel Lake was named at the same time a General of Brigade in the Turkish army, Major Teesdale a Lieutenant-Colonel, and Captain Thompson a Major in that army.

In a despatch dated 2nd November 1855, Lord Clarendon wrote as follows :—

"It is my agreeable duty to convey to you, and to the British officers under your command, the cordial approbation of the Queen, and of Her Majesty's Government, for the energy, the perseverance, and the valour with which for many months, and under circumstances of extraordinary difficulty, you have laboured with Lieutenant-Colonel Lake, Major Teesdale, and Captain Thompson, together with Mr. Churchill and Dr. Sandwith, to sustain the spirit and discipline of the Turkish troops, and to place the defences of Kars in a state to resist successfully the attack of the Russian army. I shall not fail to recommend these officers to the Queen for the rewards due to their gallantry."

Provisions were now running so short that it was easy to calculate how many days or weeks the place could hold out if not succoured from without.

Since the day of the battle there had been no animal food. A great change in the appearance of the Turks became daily more and more visible ; their step was less firm, and their eyes less bright, but scarcely a murmur of discontent was heard.

It was difficult to imagine, even at this late period, that the garrison would be utterly forsaken, and the hope of relief still kept the devoted garrison from succumbing.

It had become very difficult to send a post to Erzeroum through the enemy's picquets, as after the battle they had been doubled, but General Williams having arranged a cypher with the Consul at Erzeroum before he came to Kars, he made known the wretched plight of the garrison by sending triplicate copies on short despatches, rolled and inserted in quills. Usually one of the three reached its destination.

Several attempts were made by the people to leave Kars, but they were nearly always captured and driven back by the Russians into the place.

Cholera, which up to this time had committed fearful ravages, now began to disappear, but famine soon supplied its place. It was no rare thing to find soldiers dead on the roads, while others were scarce able to walk.

Aftes the battle the men were again employed in adding to the fortifications, but they no longer worked with the same energy. Nevertheless, several new works were completed.

A small star fort was thrown up on the left extremity of the Tachmash lines, the battle having sufficiently shown that a closed work was required to prevent this flank being turned.

A similar star fort was built midway between and in rear of Thompson and Zohrab Tabias to strengthen the English batteries, and an open battery was thrown up for three heavy guns and a mortar to protect Arab Tabia and to sweep the ground between it and the Karadagh, behind the breastwork connecting these two batteties. It was constructed so that if it fell into the hands of the enemy it would be useless, being commanded in rear by the citadel and Teli Tabia, at the north-east angle of the fortress.

As the garrison was much reduced, it was thought desirable to raise the heights of the parapet along the whole south line between Hafiz Pasha and Kanli Tabias.

Deserters were now principally among the sentries in front of the works at night; the sentries were therefore kept entirely behind the breastworks, having a numbers of officers patrolling along the lines from sunset to sunrise.

On the heights of Tachmash it was found utterly impossible to keep the men on sentry within the lines from deserting, and a number of officers were induced, by promise of promotion, to shoulder the musket and do the duty of common soldiers at night.

On 31st October letters were received by the Mushir from Selim Pasha, announcing his arrival at Erzeroum at the head of a fine army, cavalry, artillery, and infantry, all in the highest spirits.

It was now supposed that the Russians must raise the blockade. High time it was done. Men were now daily seen digging small roots from the ground, which they eagerly devoured, their hunger not even allowing them to wait while they washed off the earth which adhered.

The quarters of the English officers were besieged by the inhabitants for food. As much as could be spared was given to them every day, but this was, of course, quite insufficient.

General Williams ordered horses to be killed near his quarters during the night, and the flesh was sent up to hospital to make soup for the sick. This soup had become a luxury. It was administered with great effect upon men who had dropped at their posts.

Towards the middle of November snow began to fall, and General Mouravieff began to construct pyramids of stone to mark the road to Alexandropol.

At this time Lieutenant-Colonel Lake and Major Teesdale used to take it in turn to remain out all night, so as to be able to send a report to General Williams the moment anything occurred in camp.

The stock of wood now came to an end, and the deserted houses had to be destroyed to get some, as it was absolutely necessary to have fire. It is to be remembered that the town is three miles from the extreme positions.

The apathy induced by great exhaustion made many men neglect to provide themselves with firewood, and numbers were, as a result, found daily in the tents quite inanimate.

All the sugar, coffee, and tobacco which could be found had been bought up by General Williams, and this was carefully distributed to the several regiments at stated periods.

Every possible contrivance was resorted to to make the stores last till the expected succour should arrive.

Day after day elapsed, no symptom of Selim Pasha's army appeared, and the garrison again began to get disheartened.

The enemy seemed to be making preparations for remaining some time in their positions; and it became evident that whatever Omar Pasha's or Selim Pasha's movements might be, they did not frighten General Mouravieff.

Much of the duty had to be done on foot. Almost all the Turkish officers were dismounted, and the stud of General Williams and his staff had to be greatly reduced.

Captain Thompson's health had been failing for a long time, but he had kept steadily at his post. The cold and exposure now quite unfitted him for exertion, so he at last came into the town, and was put under the care of Dr. Sandwith.

In order to divert the men's minds, Lieutenant-Colonel Lake was directed by General Williams to construct a barrack in rear of the fortifications of the principal suburb. The work progressed but slowly, as it was found very difficult to induce the half-starved soldiers to work, and consequently the barrack was only just completed when the place was surrendered.

It will now be necessary to explain how it was that, Selim Pasha being so close, Kars was not succoured.

Major Stuart was the principal English officer at Erzeroum, under whom was Captain Cameron.

Major Olpherts, B.A., had on the 9th September been transferred, at his own request, to the Turkish Contingent.

On 3rd October reports reached Erzeroum of a terrible struggle at Kars, ending in the defeat and almost total annihilation of the Russian army.

Major Stuart waited on Veli Pasha, the Turkish Commander at Erzeroum. The consultation ended by Veli Pasha engaging to advance from Devé-Boynon with 4,000 infantry, 500 cavalry, 500 Bashi-Bazouks, and thirty field-guns.

Despatches were received from General Williams and the Mushir on the 4th October, and next morning Major Stuart again waited on Veli Pasha, accompanied by Major Peel and the other British officers, when, to their surprise, they found the Pasha's views had undergone a total change, and he made all sorts of excuses for inaction.

However, on the matter being referred to General Williams, he stated that, in the present condition of Veli Pasha's army, it would be objectionable to advance further than Ku-pri-kui, and that as long as the Russian detachment of Byazid existed it would be dangerous for Veli Pasha to move on Kars.

Selim Pasha arrived at Trebizonde on 11th October with 1,100 men, the first instalment of the promised succour, and on the 21st he set out for his command. Great things were expected from Selim Pasha, as he had a reputation for energy and courage.

New life seemed to be suddenly infused into Veli Pasha, and an immediate advance on Kars was resolved upon.

On the 22nd the force commenced its forward movement.

Majors Stuart and Peel accompanied Veli Pasha, while Captain Cameron remained behind to look after the defences of Erzeroum.

The first day's march was across the plain of Passainwar to Korusjuk, a march of two hours.   Here the force encamped for several days, Veli Pasha stating that he could not advance without orders from Selim Pasha, who was daily expected at Erzeroum.

On the 25th Selim Pasha arrived, and next day Veli Pasha pushed on to Hassan Kallah.   Here occurred another tedious halt.

On the 29th October it was reported that the Russians, who were said to have fallen back some days before from Deli-baba, had again advanced.

On the 30th Veli Pasha moved to Aloara, south of Hassan Kallah, one hour's distance.

The order for this retrograde movement came from Selim Pasha, and Major Stuart at once rode to Erzeroum to ascertain the cause.

Selim Pasha said that with such inefficient troops he was afraid to push forward, but that as soon as his own reinforcements from Trebizonde came up he would take immediate steps.

On 1st November, a report having been received that a party of Russians had made their appearance in the plain towards Ku-pri-kui, the Turkish army fell back to the foot of Devi-Boynon, near the village of Taber, where they remained till the approach of winter closed the campaign and obliged them to return to Erzeroum.

Selim Pasha had been preceded by flattering reports of courage and energy.   It was thought his delay at Trebizonde of ten days was unavoidable, also that his taking nine days from

Trebizonde to Erzeroum was because it was considered undigni-
fied to travel in haste.   Every allowance was made for him; but
the confidence of the people began to give way when it was
found he allowed eleven days to elapse before he visited his
troops, distant only a few hours' ride.   When this was hinted
to him, he said his time was fully occupied in correcting the
vicious administration of his predecessors.

There was some truth in this, and it soon became notorious
that in carrying out beneficial measures Selim Pasha incurred
the ill-will of some whose duty it was to give him every support.
It was but too evident that there were two distinct parties in the
Divan.

On 5th November Selim Pasha for the first time proceeded to
Taber, and inspected his troops.

Major Stuart asked for a " parade state," but it was refused.
The troops on the ground he estimated at 9,000.

On 5th November despatches arrived from General Williams,
dated 31st October.   In this General Williams congratulated
Selim Pasha on his arrival, and said that the Kars army was
inspired by Selim Pasha's letter with increased courage.   He
trusted that not a moment would be lost in directing the
succouring army on Kars.

Selim Pasha's letter, to which General Williams alluded, was
the one he wrote from Baiburt on 22nd October, giving a most
exaggerated account of the means at his disposal for the relief of
Kars.

Major Stuart at once proceeded to the Serai, accompanied by
Mr. Brant, H.B.M.'s Consul, and the English officers then in
Erzeroum.

Selim Pasha had evidently been much disturbed by General
Williams' letter.   To all the questions put to him he replied
vaguely, dwelling on the difficulties he apprehended from the
Russians at Deli-baba.

The Pasha was urged to advance to Ku-pri-kui to develop the

real intentions of this Russian force. But all was in vain: all he would promise was that he would attack the Russians at Deli-baba as soon as 2,000 Bashi Bazouks were collected in their rear to cut off their retreat.

This was neither more nor less than a grave mockery, as the greater part would have to be collected in the surrounding country, a work of some weeks at least, but more probably of months, if it could be accomplished at all. It was subsequently learnt that an order to this effect was given, which resulted in 250 being assembled at Erzeroum in the following January.

Day after day the English officers waited on Selim Pasha, and on 9th November they extracted from him a promise to advance. The 14th was the day named, but the 14th passed and nothing was done.

On the 15th he stated he was expecting more reinforcements. A second instalment of 1,000 men had arrived at Erzeroum, and and a third of the same strength, coming at the rate of three hours' march a day.

There were now at Taber and Erzeroum 11,000 men, to be increased in a few days by 1,000 more. In addition to these there were six field-batteries, well horsed. With such a force a general of ordinary skill and courage ought to have at least attempted something for the relief of Kars; but it became more and more apparent every day that Selim Pasha had not come to Erzeroum with intent to fight. He constantly evaded Major Stuart's applications for a state of the army.

On 21st November Major Stuart addressed the Pasha, demanding a return of the force, and saying he had already asked for it six times, now did so for a seventh. Major Stuart also asked him his intentions, and pointed out that on the 9th he had said he would advance on the 13th or 14th.

The next day Major Stuart obtained the return. The total force was set down at 6,900 men and 816 horses.

Selim Pasha gave as a reason for inaction the weakness of

his force; but it was well known to the English officers at Erzeroum that in the returns furnished to the Porte the numbers were set down at upwards of 14,000, and as regards horses the difference was still greater.

Mr. Consul Brant, who was at Erzeroum, saw clearly that nothing was to be expected from Selim Pasha. Accordingly, on 19th November 1855, he addressed a letter to H.M.'s Ambassador at Constantinople, pointing out that " Selim Pasha was neither active, nor energetic, nor brave," and that " he has a new excuse for delay every day; to-day it was that he must wait a change of weather. It is much finer than we had any reason to expect at this season—beautifully clear, though a little cold at night; and I can only say that, as finer weather cannot be expected before next summer, it is evident His Excellency will not leave Erzeroum." He urged the Ambassador to see that a general of character was at once sent up, with positive orders to arrive at Erzeroum in twenty or twenty-five days. Omar Pasha was too slow in his movements to hope anything from him.

Mr. Brant winds up his letter thus: " I ask your Excellency, Is the Kars army to be allowed to perish? I now fear it must surrender, and to confer honours on its gallant defenders, while they be left to perish, is a cruel mockery, and an indelible disgrace to the Turkish Government, as well as to those of the Allied Powers."

Affairs at Kars were now as bad as they well could be. Unless some very unexpected good news arrived, it was evident that the garrison must abandon the position they had so long and gallantly defended.

The possibility of a retreat was now discussed. The plan was confided only to the Mushir, Chief of the Staff, and General Kmety. General Williams still continued to send messengers from Kars every night.

On 23rd November a despatch in cypher, dated the 19th, reached the British Consul at Erzeroum in the following terms:

" Tell Lords Clarendon and Redcliffe that the Russian army is hutted, and takes no notice of either Omar or Selim Pashas. They cannot have acted as they ought to have done. We divide our bread with the starving townspeople. No animal food for seven weeks. I kill horses in my stables secretly, and send the meat to the hospital, which is now very crowded.

(Signed)   " W. F. WILLIAMS."

On 24th November Mr. Brant wrote to Lord Clarendon :

" That, after so gallant a defence, Kars should fall into the hands of a thrice-beaten enemy, on account of the apathy of the Porte, and the cowardice and imbecility of Selim Pasha, is intolerably distressing ; but the consolatory feeling remains that the brave garrison, and the immutable director of its energies and operations, will to the last maintain a character for valour, skill, and foresight, and every soldierly virtue ; and that while noble deeds are appreciated, the defence of Kars will stand prominent among the achievements of a war unsurpassed by any other in acts of daring and gallantry."

" I fear there is nothing to be done to help this neglected army ; a retreat without cavalry or artillery, in face of an enemy who commands a large number of both, seems inevitable, and I tremble for the result."

" The garrison has nothing to depend on but its own bravery, and the unflinching resolution, the consummate prudence and skill, of its gallant commander and his heroic band of European officers."

Retreat having been determined on, Major Teesdale and General Kmety were ordered to prepare a proposition for the best line of march.

It was decided that the garrison should have marched to Tachmash by the road leading past Fort Lake, and have continued on the road to Chalgour. They were then to have made straight for a small camp of Russian Irregulars that occupied the southern corner of the plateau. The retreating army having

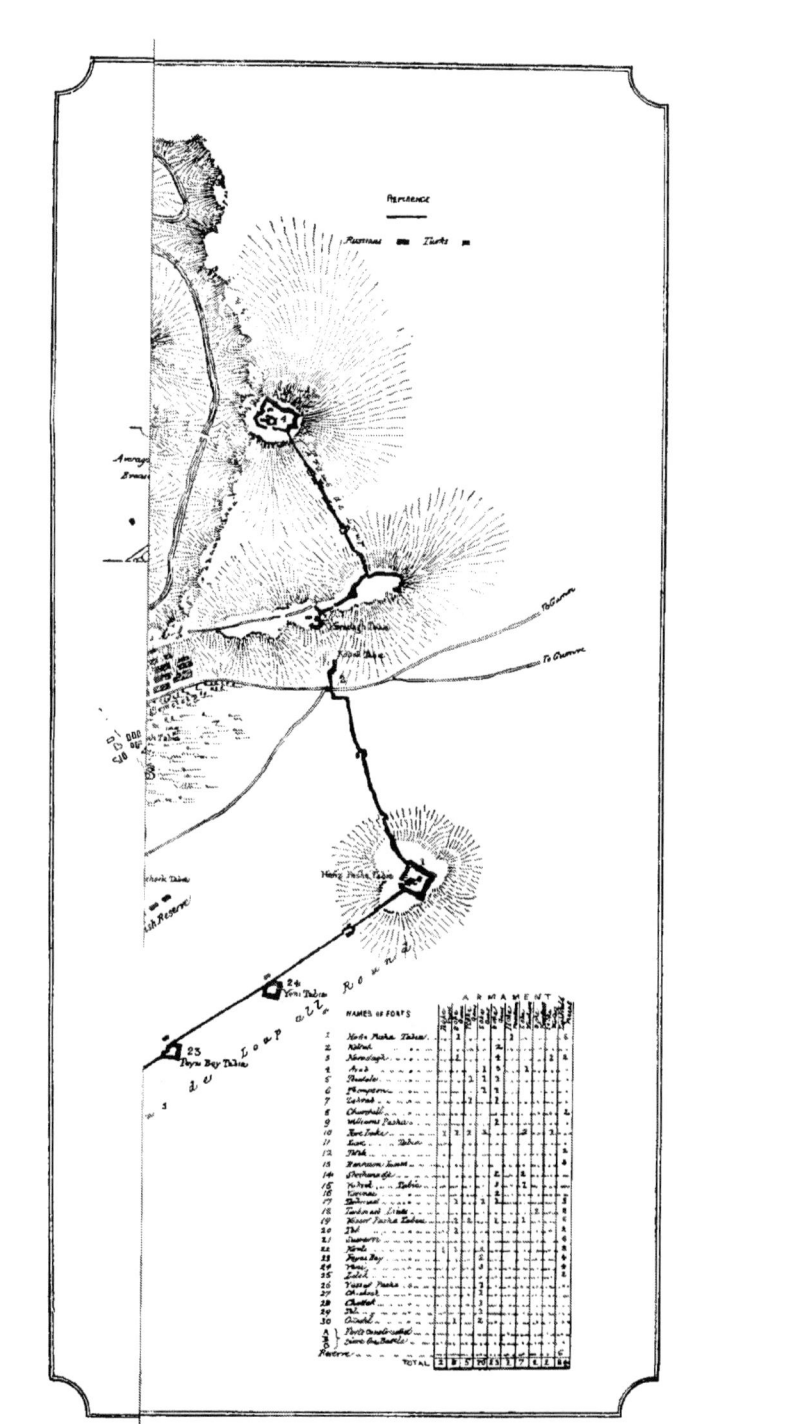

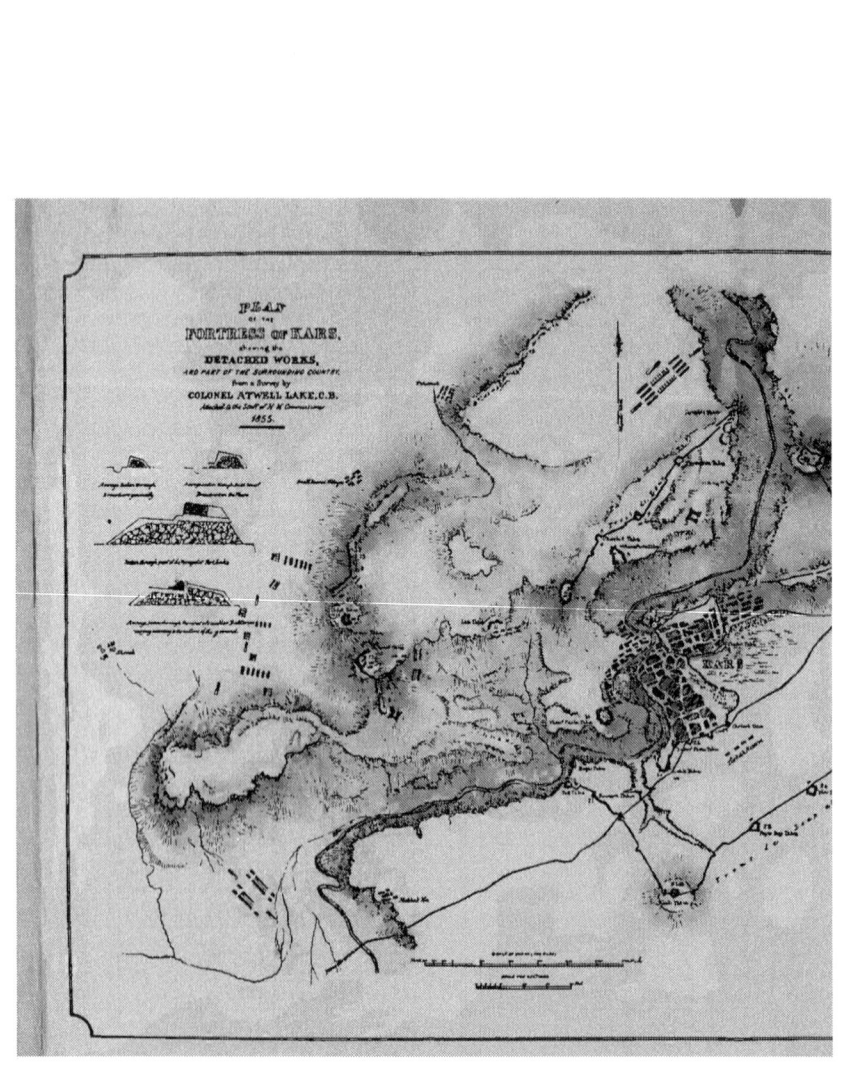

PLAN
OF THE
FORTRESS OF KARS,
showing the
DETACHED WORKS,
AND PART OF THE SURROUNDING COUNTRY,
from a Survey by
COLONEL ATWELL LAKE, C.B.
Attached to the Staff of H.M. Commissioner
1855.

gained the edge of the mountain, was to have struggled on to the road which passes over the summit to Guile and Pennek.

Linen bags, or haversacks, were made up privately under the superintendence of Lieutenant-Colonel Lake, and they were issued to the men with three days' biscuit in each, under the pretence that the troops might be called on to take the field, to meet Omar Pasha or Selim Pasha, who were supposed to be coming to their relief.

General Williams now heard from Mr. Brant, begging him not to expect any assistance from Selim Pasha.

A Council of War was then held, attended by the Mushir, H.M's Commissioner and his A.D.C., Lieutenant-Colonel Lake, all the General Officers in garrison, with the Colonels commanding regiments. General Williams gave them a plain statement of facts. After a long discussion, it was determined that a retreat was now quite out of the question, as there were no horses left, and the troops had become too enfeebled by sickness and want of proper nourishment.

No other course was open to the garrison but a conditional surrender.

Major Teesdale was accordingly despatched with a flag of truce, bearing a letter from General Williams to General Mouravieff, requesting an interview next day.

Next day General Williams went to the Russian camp; a rough draft of the terms on which the Turkish Commander was willing to give up the fortress, was then and there made out, and agreed to. This was on the 25th November.

The terms were carried into effect on 28th November. General Williams and his officers, as well as the whole of the regular troops—amounting to 8,000 men—were prisoners of war, and the irregulars, numbering 6,000, were sent home.

The following were the terms of surrender—

1st. Kars to be delivered up intact.

2nd. The garrison to march out with the honours of war,

II.   18

and become prisoners. The officers, in consideration of their gallant defence, to retain their swords.

3rd. Private property of the garrison to be respected.

4th. The Militia and Irregulars to be allowed to return to their homes.

5th. Non-combatants to return to their homes.

6th. General Williams to be allowed to make a list of certain Hungarian and other European officers, to enable them to return home.

7th. All these persons bound in honour not to serve against Russia during the present war.

8th. Inhabitants of Kars to be protected in their persons and property.

9th. Public buildings and monuments of the town to be respected.

On 22nd December, Lord Clarendon wrote to General Williams :

" H.M.'s Government have observed with the utmost admiration, the zealous and indefatigable exertions which you made for the defence of that important position under circumstances of no ordinary difficulty, as well as the judgment and energy which you displayed in overcoming the obstacles of every sort with which you had to contend, and in inspiring the Turkish soldiery with that confidence which enabled them, under your influence, signally to defeat, on all occasions, the attempts made by an enemy superior in numbers and military resources, to make themselves masters, by force of arms, of the besieged town. I have to express her Majesty's entire approval of the manner in which you acquitted yourself throughout the whole period of your recent services. I have at the same time to instruct you to signify to the officers and civilians serving under your orders at Kars—namely, to Colonel Lake, to Major Teesdale, and to Captain Thompson, to Mr. Churchill, and to Dr. Sandwith—Her Majesty's entire approval of their conduct."

It was with the greatest difficulty the Turks could be persuaded to lay down their arms ; indeed, it required no little tact to prevent a serious disturbance. The troops were in such a state of physical prostration, that it occupied nearly four hours reaching the Russian camp. They were compelled to halt every half hour to rest the men, and eighteen died on this short march. The prisoners were very well received by the Russians. The troops were regaled with bread and soup, which had been prepared for them. Some of the poor fellows ate so voraciously that even this simple fare was fatal to them, and they died of repletion in a few hours.

The officers were entertained by General Mouravieff in the most sumptuous style.

Mouravieff seemed much annoyed when Colonel Lake told him he had destroyed the plan he had made of the fortifications, under the impression that he would not be allowed to keep it. Mouravieff replied, " One of my Engineer officers is going to make one, and you shall have a copy of it." Nothing could exceed his kindness and courtesy. He thanked Teesdale and Lake for their efforts in saving the wounded Russians on the field of battle from the ferocity of the Turks.

On the night of surrender, Colonel Lake was billeted on Colonel Kauffmann, the Commandant of Sappers and Miners.

On November 30th, Colonel Lake and Captain Thompson commenced their journey to Russia, bound for Tiflis, *viâ* Gumri.

On 2nd December they stopped at Gumri for two days ; set out on the 4th for Tiflis, and drove into that town on 8th December. Every window was filled and every street crowded, so eager were the inhabitants to see the captives.

On 1st January 1856, General Williams suffering from fever, Lake, Thompson, and Teesdale paid a visit of ceremony to General Mouravieff. The Commander-in-Chief took Lake into his study, and read him a letter just received from St. Petersburg, with instructions that General Williams, his A.D.C., and

18 *

secretary, were to be sent to Riazan, 180 miles from Moscow, while Lake and Thompson were to go to Penza, 700 miles east of Moscow.

On the 9th January, Lake, Thompson, and Polivanoff (Ensign of the Erivanski Regiment, who had been directed to accompany them), started on their Trans-Caucasian tour. They travelled *viâ* Dushet and Dariel to Vladi Kaukas, which they reached on the 16th, and on the 20th were at Ekaterinograd.

On 21st night they reached Georgievsk, whence, passing through Alexandrofski, after a two days' journey, they arrived at Stavragsol at midnight.

By the 1st February they had passed the Cis-Caucasian provinces, and were in Russia itself, and in the country of the Don.

On the 10th February they reached Tamboff, and by the 20th arrived at Penza, at which place Colonel Lake and Captain Thompson were to remain while they were prisoners. At this place they were treated most hospitably; indeed, generally throughout their enforced stay in Russia, they never had the slightest cause to complain in any way of their treatment. At Penza Captain Thompson's health became impaired by what he had undergone at Kars, as well as owing to the severity of the weather during their journey.

On 30th March the Governor of Penza sent for Colonel Lake, and told him that he had just received orders to inform them that they were no longer prisoners of war.

They accordingly resolved to return *viâ* Moscow and St. Petersburg.

On 5th April they heard that they would be compelled to travel *viâ* Odessa. This was extremely unpalatable to them, and, with some little trouble, they got this order altered.

On 13th April they left, *viâ* Moscow and St. Petersburg, travelled by road to Moscow, *viâ* Saransk and Nijni-Novgorod, and thence to St. Petersburg by rail.

They left the Russian capital on 31st May, passed a day off

Cronstadt waiting for cargo, where they landed and drove all over the place, after which they proceeded direct to England, landing at Hull, where they were kindly and enthusiastically received by the warm-hearted citizens of that place.

General Williams was rewarded with a baronetcy, and became Sir Fenwick Williams of Kars. He also received a pension of £1,000 a year for life, and the rank of K.C.B. He also obtained the honorary degree of D.C.L. at Oxford, and last, but not least, the Freedom of the City of London.

Atwell Lake was, on 24th June 1856, appointed A.D.C. to the Queen, with the rank of Colonel in the army. He was also made a C.B.

In a letter from the Honourable East India Company, dated 1st October, it is stated : " Colonel H. A. Lake, C.B., A.D.C. to the Queen, has been permitted to retire from the service (to have effect from the 12th March 1856). As a recognition on the part of the East India Company of the distinguished services which that officer has rendered to this country during the memorable siege of Kars, a special personal allowance of £100 per annum has been granted to him. In communicating their decision, we have informed Colonel Lake that we deeply regret that the state of his health compels him to retire from the service of the East India Company, but that it is a source of gratification to us to have learnt that his merit and qualifications are so highly appreciated by H.M.'s Government that they have resolved to appoint him to an unattached Lieutenant-Colonelcy, and will consequently have the benefit of his marked ability, energy, and zeal."

Colonel Lake was appointed subsequently to the command of the Irish Constabulary, which he resigned only in August 1877. He was, besides, promoted to the rank of K.C.B. He died at Brighton on 17th August 1881, at the age of seventy-two.

The other British officers concerned received suitable rewards ; but one of them, Captain Thompson, who had done such excellent service at the Karadagh, died shortly after reaching England.

General Williams survives his gallant Lieutenant, having reached his eightieth year.

In 1856 he was appointed to the command of Woolwich, which he held till 1859. He was then sent to Canada, as commander of the British forces, and in 1865 he was appointed Lieutenant-Governor of Nova Scotia. In August 1870 he was sent to Gibraltar as Governor and Commander-in-Chief. He retained this command till November 1875. He was also raised to the dignity of a G.C.B.

CHAPTER VIII.

Persian War, 1856–57.—Causes of it.—British Minister strikes his flag.—War declared.—Outram appointed to command.—Battle of Khoosh-ab.—Redoubts constructed at Bushire.—Expedition to Mohumera.—Enemy defeated and flies.—Work of Sappers very heavy.—Enemy pursued three or four miles. —Army moves back to Mohumera.—Small expedition to Ahwaz.—Peace concluded at Paris on 4th March.—Services of the Sappers.—Deaths of Strover, Boyd, Moore, and Roberts of Madras Engineers.—Corps of Engineers.—Abolition of Addiscombe College.—College, &c. sold.—Establishment at Addiscombe College.—Various head-quarters of Madras Sappers, &c.

FOR some years before the outbreak of hostilities, the Persians, through the influence of Russia, seemed determined to oppose England, especially with reference to Herat. In 1851 the British Minister heard of an expedition against Herat. The fact was, however, denied by the Persians. Remonstrances were again repeatedly made in 1851 and 1852, but they were disregarded, and in the spring of 1852 the Persian expedition advanced on Herat. Herat was occupied, and the Persians persisted in annexing it. The British Minister urged the withdrawal of the Mission, and the occupation of the island of Kharrack, thirty miles from Bushire. The Minister continued to oppose the movement of Persian troops towards Herat, and after various negotiations the Shah conceded the principal points in dispute, and on the 25th January 1853 an engagement regarding Herat was signed. The Persian Government, however, was not sincere, and still continued to throw obstacles in the way of a satisfactory settlement.

On the 15th June 1854 Meerza Hashim Khan was named First Persian Secretary to the British Mission at Teheran. The Persian Government declined to receive him, on the plea that he had been in the Shah's service, and had not been formally discharged. Accordingly, Mr. Thomson appointed Meerza Fezl-oolah in his stead, but intimated that Meerza Hashim Khan would be appointed as soon as he received his formal discharge.

· On the 6th November 1855 Sadrazine (Persian Minister) informed Mr. Murray (British Minister) that if he (Meerza Hashim) set out for Shiraz, the Persian Government would cause him to be seized. The next step was the seizure of the wife of Meerza Hashim, by order of the Persian Government.

On the 17th November Mr. Murray gave official notice that if the wife was not liberated by noon, on the ensuing Monday (the 20th) friendly relations would be broken off.

Accordingly, on the 20th November Mr. Murray struck his flag. To make matters worse, the Persian Prime Minister said that the reason why Mr. Thomson first took Meerza Hashim Khan into the Mission was because he had an intrigue with his wife, and he afterwards made the same statement as regards Mr. Murray. An angry correspondence followed, but the necessary concessions were refused, and on the 5th December 1855 Mr. Murray withdrew his mission. The satisfaction demanded was, the restoration of Meerza Hashim Khan's wife to her husband, the Prime Minister to visit Mr. Murray and apologise for the offensive despatch, and to withdraw it. A high officer was to call at the Mission on the part of the Shah, and make apologies for the objectionable sentence in the Royal autograph letter. The chief Moollahs, who had been induced to affix their seals to a document tending to bring the Mission and Her Majesty's Government into contempt, were to call and express their utter

disbelief of the calumnies, and to state that they would contradict
them.

On the 2nd January 1856 the Persian Charge d'Affaires at
Constantinople had an interview with Lord Stratford, deplored
the rupture, but delivered a communication from the Persian
Minister complaining of Mr. Murray. In this memorandum all
the British ministers were censured, and the charge against Mr.
Murray, with reference to Meerza Hashim Khan's wife, was
repeated. The statement regarding Mr. Murray was a gross
falsehood from end to end.

It now became evident that the Persian Government intended
to break faith with the British Government in the matter of
Herat.

In December 1855 Prince Sultan Moorad Meerza set out with
an expedition to act against Herat.

In April 1856 the Persian Charge d'Affaires at Constantinople
applied to Lord Stratford to settle the difficulty, and expressed
the willingness of the Shah to receive Mr. Murray.

On the 15th May Lord Clarendon wrote that before Mr.
Murray could return to Teheran the Prime Minister of Persia
must write a letter to Mr. Murray apologising for the offensive
imputation, and a request to withdraw his letter, as well as others
containing the same imputation; that Mr. Murray should be
received, on approaching the capital, by persons of high rank,
to escort him into the town, and that almost immediately after
his arrival the Prime Minister should go in state to the British
Mission, and accompany Mr. Murray to the presence of the
Shah.

The fall of Kars emboldened the Persians. The expedition
went against Herat. The Heraties were defeated near Ghorian,
and Herat was besieged.

On the 15th June, Lord Clarendon wrote : " If Herat is
immediately evacuated, he would not insist on sending Meerza
Hashim Khan to Shiraz."

This did not produce the desired effect, and on the 11th July Lord Clarendon wrote to the Persian Prime Minister, that unless reparation were promptly made for breach of agreement in occupying Herat, and the Persians troops withdrawn, the British Government would adopt other measures.

Instructions were soon after sent to the Governor-General of India, to prepare a force to occupy Kharrack, and the city and district of Bushire.

On the 22nd November the British ultimatum was delivered to the Persian Ambassador at Constantinople.

On the 1st November a declaration of war was issued by the Governor-General of India against Persia, orders having been sent out for the despatch of an expedition to the Persian Gulf towards the close of September.

Major-General Sir James Outram was appointed to assume command, shortly after the fall of Bushire, which had been taken by Major-General Stalker, C.B., in command of the First Division.

Sir James Outram landed in the latter part of January.

The B Company of Madras Sappers did not arrive at Bushire till March, having embarked at Coconada on the 19th January 1857, so they were not present in the first part of the campaign.

On the 3rd February the army began its march. It marched to Charkota, twenty-six miles, and then fourteen more, when it was supposed to be eight miles from the enemy at Brasgoon, where they were said to be entrenched.

The enemy retreated, and we captured their entrenched camp on the 5th.

After a halt of two days the return march was commenced at midnight.

An attack was made on our rear-guard; the troops were halted, and formed to protect the baggage. Four of the enemy's guns opened on the column, while it was too dark to attempt to capture them.

At daybreak the Persian army was found drawn up in order of battle. By 10 o'clock they were completely defeated. This was the battle of Khoosh-Ab.

The troops bivouacked for the day on the field of battle, and at night accomplished a march of twenty miles over a country rendered almost impassable by the heavy rain which fell incessantly.

After a rest of six hours the greater part of the infantry continued their march to Bushire, which they reached before midnight, thus performing another most arduous march of forty four miles under incessant rain, besides fighting and defeating the enemy during its progress, within the short period of fifty hours.

Five strong redoubts were now constructed at Bushire, the four in front sweeping the width of the isthmus, and that in rear securing communication with the town.

On these being completed, it was arranged by General Outram that General Stalker should remain in command at Bushire, with two field-batteries, mountain train, the cavalry of the 2nd Division, three companies of H.M.'s 64th and 78th, the 4th Rifles, the 20th Native Infantry, and the Belooch Battalion.

Sir James Outram proceeded himself with the remainder, about 4,000 (the force at Bushire being 3,000) against Mohumera.

For some months past the Persians had been strengthening their position at Mohumera; batteries had been erected of great strength, of solid earth twenty feet thick and eighteen feet high, with casemated embrasures on the north and south points of the banks of the Karoon and Shat-ool-Arab, where the two rivers join.

The company of the Madras Sappers had proceeded to Mohumera on board the Indian Navy ss. *Victoria*, up the Shat-ool-Arab river, to within three miles of the south battery of Mohumera.

The officers with the Madras Sappers were Major Boileau, M.E., Lieutenants Prendergast and Gordon, M.E., Lieutenant Fox, 14th M.N.I., Assistant Surgeon T. Lowe, Subedar Seeloway, Jemadar Ali-Khan.

On the night of the 24th March, Major Boileau, and other staff officers, reconnoitred the enemy's position, especially with a view to ascertain if it was possible to establish batteries on the island of Dubbee, west of the northern battery.

In this reconnoissance "the Engineer officers approached the batteries within 300 yards in a small canoe, and a raft with two 8-pounder and two 5-pounder mortars was established behind a low swampy island in mid-stream, and fronting the enemy's north and most powerful battery."

"The cool daring of the men who placed, and the little band of artillery who remained on this raft, for several hours of darkness, in the middle of a rapid river, without means of retreat, and certain destruction staring them in the face should the enemy, within but a few hundred yards, be aroused to the fact of their presence, requires no commendation. The simple narration of the event as it occurred is sufficient."

At daybreak on the 26th, the mortars from this raft opened fire. The first shell killed and wounded (as was afterwards learnt) eleven of the enemy, who were at prayers at the moment, and in great consternation at not being able for some minutes to discover whence the missile came.

On the evening of the 25th, the B Company of the Madras Sappers had been transferred to the Bengal Marine s.s. *Hugh Lindsay*.

On the morning of the 26th the squadron ran up the river to opposite the forts, and engaged the batteries.

The carronades of the *Hugh Lindsay* were worked by H.M.'s 64th, assisted by the Sappers. For about three hours the Persians stood to their guns, but then their fire slackened, and by 11 A.M. the signal was given for our infantry to disembark.

By 2 P.M. all the infantry, with a field battery and fifty Scinde Horse, were on shore, and the General resolved to advance.

The division advanced through date-groves intersected by irrigation canals, many of which were bridged by date-trees felled by the Sappers.

The bridges by which the artillery and cavalry crossed the main irrigation channels consisted of trees felled on both sides of the channels, with a large Arab boat as a central support.

The enemy on our approach fled precipitately after exploding their largest magazine ; leaving their tents, baggage, stores, several magazines of ammunition, and sixteen guns, behind.

The want of cavalry prevented pursuit. The General could not wait for more cavalry before he attacked, owing to the rising of the tide having filled the creeks, and made the ground to be crossed by the Horse Artillery and the 14th Dragoons impassable.

The party of Scinde Horse, however, followed them up for some distance. The officer in command came up with their rearguard retiring in good order, but found that the road was strewed with property.

The loss of the Persians was 300 killed, among whom was an officer of rank, Brigadier Agha-Jan-Khan, who fell in the northern battery.

The work of the Madras Sappers at Mohumera was extremely heavy. Batteries were destroyed, roads made, landing-stages constructed, streams dammed or turned, and huts erected.

The Persians had the odds greatly in their favour, and could hardly expect to meet us on better terms, yet they disgracefully fled as soon as they were seriously attacked. Every tent was left standing. Just previous to their departure they blew up their reserve ammunition.

Every caution was observed by us in entering their lines, but no halt was made, the General moved at once on the track of the enemy.

The pursuit was continued for three or four miles without much result, and, as there was no chance of the 14th Dragoons or the Horse Artillery joining, a halt was sounded for the night.

On the 27th the army marched back to Mohumera, took possession of the town, and occupied the camp. Eighteen very handsome guns and mortars were taken, immense stores of grain, a great quantity of ammunition, arms, and accoutrements, besides the entire tentage of their army.

The Persians allowed a loss of 300 killed, but it must have been greater; we had only ten men killed and one officer and thirty men wounded.

The strength of the batteries was found to be very great, and they were skilfully placed and constructed. "Nothing but stout hearts within, then, was required to have made their capture a matter of bloody price to the victors; happily for us, these were wanting."

The 27th and 28th March were occupied in removing the guns, collecting the stores, and in landing supplies and our own tents. Our troops (with the exception of those to whom the Persian tents had fallen prize), had been living in the open air. Sir James Outram having heard that the Persian army was greatly disorganised and in full retreat, resolved to send three armed steamers up the Karoon, to Ahwaz, with 300 European infantry to make a reconnoissance, and, if possible, to destroy the magazines at that place.

The expedition left on the 29th March, and arrived at Ahwaz on 1st April. It was most completely successful, but as the Sappers, being engaged at Mohumera, did not accompany the force, no details need be given. The expedition returned to Mohumera on the 4th April.

On the same day news arrived that peace had been concluded at Paris on the 4th March. The force was shortly after broken up, and the B Company of the Madras Sappers arrived at

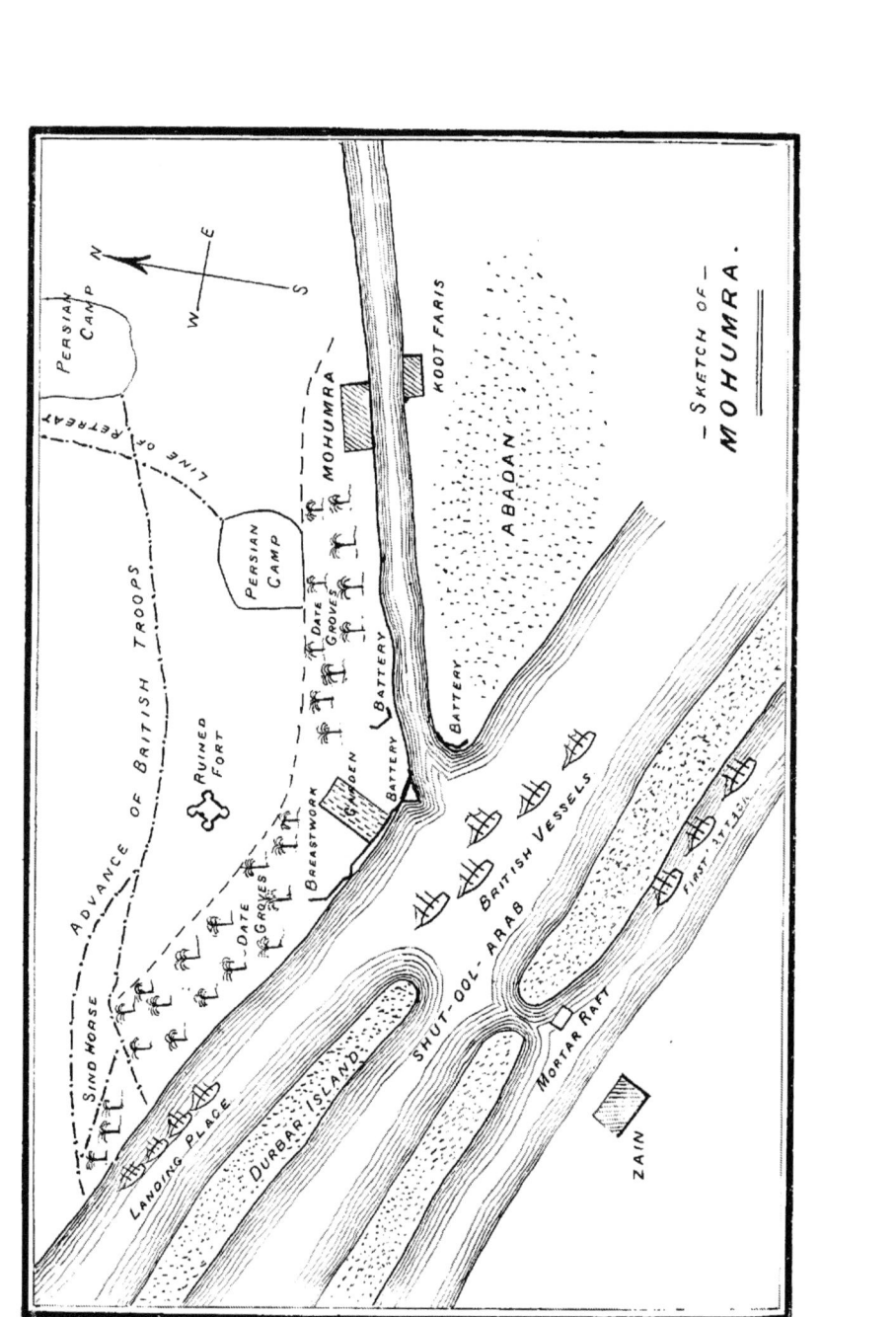

- SKETCH OF -

MOHUMRA.

Bombay on the 1st June, in time to take part in the Central
India campaign, for which service they volunteered with great
alacrity. The Chief of the Staff thus writes of the services of
the B Company:

"The conduct of the men had been exemplary since they
joined this force, and they have rendered the most efficient
service in the expedition against Mohumera, and during its
occupation. The peculiar feature of the country afforded them
ample employment, and the skill and wonderful rapidity, and
cheerful alacrity with which they constructed roads through the
extensive date-groves, bridged the canals, and formed piers for
disembarkation of troops and stores from the vessels on the
Shat-ool-Arab river, were the admiration of the whole army. I
am commanded to request you will be so good as to lay before
His Excellency, Lieutenant-General Sir Patrick Grant, this
record of Sir James Outram's appreciation of the services performed by the Sappers, and that you will permit me to convey
through you, to the officer commanding (Brevet-Major Boileau),
and to all ranks composing the Company, an expression of the
Lieutenant-General's best thanks for the very efficient service
they have rendered."

Sir James Outram himself, in his Despatch to the Governor-
General, dated the 5th July 1857, says of Major Boileau, Madras
Engineers (Commanding Engineer at Mohumera) and the
Madras Sappers:

"His and their services were conspicuous in the zeal and
activity they displayed in filling ditches, preparing bridges, &c.
to facilitate the landing and advance of the troops at Mohumera,
and subsequent incessant labours they were exposed to during
our occupation of Mohumera, and I consider that they deserve
special notice and warm commendation for the alacrity with
which they volunteered for foreign service, though they had only
very lately rejoined their families, after a separation of nearly
five years of successive absences on field service. Although sent

back to India, this devoted body of soldiers, instead of being allowed to rejoin their families in the Madras Presidency, has, I understand, been attached to the column under General Woodburn, intended for the relief of Mhow, with which they are now employed, having displayed, I am told, the utmost cheerfulness and alacrity when ordered on that duty."

As a matter of fact, the B Company volunteered for the duty mentioned, as will be clearly shown further on.

During the years 1856 to 1858 the Corps of Engineers lost the services of three young officers by accidents.

At about half-past 4 on the evening of the 3rd April 1856, Lieutenant Strover, taking his double-barrelled gun, went out alone to shoot in the jungles near Kurpoor, in the Woodiarpolium Talook of Trichinopoly. As he did not return at half-past 7, his servants and others searched for him all night. They did not succeed till 6.30 the next morning, when he was found lying dead in a thick jungle not far off his camp, with his brains blown out. It would appear, from the position in which his body was found, that he was forcing his way through the thick jungle with his left hand protecting his face, and his gun held close to his body by his right, when the trigger caught in a bush. One barrel exploded, and the ball entered his face near the left side of the eyebrow at the root of the nose, and carried the whole crown of the head away. Death must have been instantaneous.

His superior officer thus wrote of him: "The unfortunate fate of this young officer will occasion a loss to the State only to be appreciated by one who, like myself, knew the energy and zeal with which he undertook and performed all the duties of his post, and the earnest interest he felt in work under his personal superintendence."

The death of Lieutenant Boyd occurred on 31st December 1857. He was engaged in striking the centering of the ninth arch of the new bridge over the Palar. After the centering was struck, the "stuffing" clung to the intrados of the arch. Lieutenant Boyd went underneath to discover the cause of the adhesion, when a sudden disengagement took place; he was smitten to the ground, and when he was extricated, two hours after, life had long been extinct. Death was ascribed to fracture of the skull and partly to suffocation, but it is probable that the concussion on the brain proved instantaneously fatal. A maistry of the P. W. Department, who went in to dissuade him from remaining in such a dangerous place, was also killed at the same time, and six other natives were hurt, two of them seriously so.

The death of Lieutenant Moore took place on 27th November 1858. He left Tanjore and proceeded to Satiamungalum, to get into the lower part of the Paupanassum Talook. He crossed the Vennaur river by the road to Paupanassum, and then turned towards Tanjore along the left bank, for the purpose of inspecting the breaches, some of which he crossed by the aid of "coolies"; but in one case with great risk to life. He then came to a larger breach in Goodaloor, three miles and a half from Tanjore. Here the "coolies" refused to carry him across. Lieutenant Moore ordered a lascar to go in, but the man only just entered the water and then returned. Hereupon Moore took off his hat, coat, waistcoat, shoes, and stockings, entered the water, and swam two-thirds the way across, when he began to struggle, having probably been struck by some timber. The lascar was alarmed, and ran off for assistance; by the time he had returned, Moore had disappeared. His body was recovered some fifteen miles down the river, near Ammapettah.

In 1867 a very excellent officer of the Corps was drowned in the Godavery.

Lieutenant Roberts was employed on the works in the Upper Godavery. Having suffered considerably from fever during the previous seven years, he had obtained three months' sick leave. He was to leave Dumagudiem for Coconada on 16th September.

The syrang in charge of the Godavery river-steamer received orders to bring it up above the " Gorge." At the part called the " Gorge " the river is very narrow, at one part, for a distance of about three miles, being only 250 to 300 yards wide.* In this part of its course the banks of the river consist of hills rising abruptly from the river to a height of 2,000 feet above the sea. During floods the river pours its immense volume through this confined channel with great velocity, chafing against the rocks which shut it in, which form numerous whirls and eddies all over its surface.

The course of the river just above the entrance to the " Gorge" is tortuous. It describes nearly a semi-circle, with a very short radius, and just at the end of this, where the " Gorge" commences, a large rock juts out from the left or concave bank, and flings off the current, which sweeps with its greatest force along that shore. Immediately at the back of this rock there is, consequently, a whirlpool of considerable size. The little village of Kollur is situated about 300 yards above this point.

Lieutenant Roberts left Dumagudiem (150 miles from the sea), at 11 A.M., in a small open boat. He had with him three servants and five lascars. The river was high, and rising fast. Twenty-three miles below Dumagudiem he obtained a larger boat.

On the morning of the 17th he pushed on, and arrived in safety at the point where the river enters the hills. The steamer, owing to the extremely violent current, had not been able to ascend the river through the Gorge. Roberts proceeded on as far as he thought he might with safety—unhappily he went too far.

He arrived within sight of Kollur at 3 P.M., and then endeavoured to make the left bank at the village, but it was too late, the current was too strong, and the boat, missing the

* The Godavery rises in the Western Ghauts, near Nassick, in the Bombay Presidency, and drains probably 120,000 square miles.

shore, was swept down past the rock, and so into the whirl below.

Roberts saw the danger, and told the crew they would have to swim for their lives. He ordered his servants to hold on to the boat if she upset. Meantime, he pulled off his coat and prepared for the worst. He was a good swimmer. He took out his watch, and told the men it was 3 o'clock. Immediately after the boat was swept into the whirlpool, and engulfed in a moment. Two of the servants sank at once; the third, with three lascars, clung to the boat, which whirled about bottom upwards.

Roberts and the tindal (head boatman) struck out for the shore, about thirty or forty yards distant, but the whirling current ever baulked their efforts. More than once Roberts all but grasped the bank, but was finally swept round outwards towards the middle of the river. He then struck out for midstream to get clear of the eddy, but his strength failed.

Weakened as he was by innumerable attacks of fever during seven years of arduous and honourable service on the river, he failed to reach the other shore, and sank after a short struggle in mid-stream. The tindal who had followed him shared his fate. Three of the lascars and one servant, who clung to the boat, were swept some miles down the river, and then picked up in a very gallant manner by some native boatmen in a canoe.

Lieutenant Roberts' body was never found, although it was searched for as far down as Dowlaishwaram,* and even to the sea. The boat was recovered, but none of the bodies were found.

From 1829 to 1845 the Corps continued of the same strength, forty officers.

On the 10th June 1844 a letter was sent to the Court of Directors, forwarding a memorial from certain officers of Engineers regarding their unprecedented supersession by the other branches of the army.

* Dumagudiem to Kollur, 60 miles; Kollur to Dowlaishwaram, 45 miles.

The reply to this, in a military despatch dated 27th November 1844, was the addition of four First Lieutenants and two Second Lieutenants, which addition was to have effect from the 17th January 1845. The relief afforded by this was trifling, and did not meet the case in any way.

No further increase to the Corps was, however, vouchsafed till 1854.

In a letter from the Court of Directors, dated 24th May 1854, a third battalion was ordered to be added to the Corps, from 1st August 1854.

The Corps then consisted of—

> 3 Colonels.
> 3 Lieutenant-Colonels.
> 3 Majors.
> 18 Captains.
> 27 Lieutenants.
> ——
> 54

On 18th March 1858 a further increase was made of one Captain and one First Lieutenant to each battalion, bringing the total up to sixty.

Three years after this came the so-called amalgamation of the Royal and Indian armies, when the Corps of Engineers in Madras was to consist of only two battalions.

Each battalion was to have—

> 1 Colonel-Commandant,
> 2 Colonels,
> 5 Lieutenant-Colonels,
> 8 Captains,
> 8 Second Captains,
> 24 Lieutenants ;

the full strength of the Regiment being thus ninety-six.

At this time there were only eighty-four officers on the list, so that there were only thirty-six Lieutenants, with vacancies for twelve. These were not filled up, and no officers joined the Corps after 8th June 1860.

On 5th July 1872 all the First Captains were transformed into Majors, and the Second Captains into Captains. At this date (1882) the list of Madras Engineers still contains thirty-six officers.

One of the results of the extinction of the Honourable East India Company and the amalgamation of the armies, was the abolition of the Company's military college at Addiscombe.

On 30th August 1861, by direction of the Secretary of State in Council for India, Addiscombe College was sold by auction at the Auction Mart, opposite the Bank of England.

As it is probable that the particulars regarding the property will prove of interest to many who read this book, they are given below.

ADDISCOMBE COLLEGE,

A VALUABLE AND IMPORTANT

FREEHOLD ESTATE,

FOR MANY YEARS THE MILITARY COLLEGE OF THE HONOURABLE
THE EAST INDIA COMPANY.

It is

within a mile of the town of Croydon,

in the

COUNTY OF SURREY,

ON THE HIGH ROAD TO ADDINGTON, AND EXTENDS OVER
UPWARDS OF

EIGHTY-EIGHT ACRES OF LAND,

BOUNDED AND INTERSECTED BY CAPITAL ROADS.

UPON THE PROPERTY IS A NOBLE MANSION,
formerly the residence of Lord Liverpool, built in the most
substantial manner, of handsome and imposing elevation.
Approached by entrance-lodges, and in the midst of a beautifully
timbered park.

It contains—

On 2nd floor, eleven bed-rooms, &c.

On 1st floor, saloon, drawing-room, ante-room,
four bed-rooms, &c.

On ground floor, a noble entrance-hall, approached by a flight of
steps; dining-room; ante-rooms; library; four sitting-
rooms; wide oak staircase.

The ceilings and walls of staircase and saloon are supposed to
have been painted last century by Sir Wm. Thornhill.

On the basement, servants' hall, kitchens, &c.

Stable-yard, with stabling for four horses, double coach-house, &c.

A GOOD GARDEN, LAWN, AND PLEASURE
GROUNDS.

This with the beautifully-timbered park-like lands, might still
be appropriated for the residence of a nobleman or gentleman
who would like to reside within an easy distance of London.

There are also three other small residences on the estate
adapted for private occupation.

The remainder of the extensive buildings contain accommodation
for about 150 cadets, with

DORMITORIES, CLASS-ROOMS,

DINING-HALL, FORTY-THREE FEET SQUARE,

Spacious kitchens,

Rooms for non-commissioned officers and servants,

Bake-house, Dairy, Brew-house, Stores, and offices of every
description necessary for the Establishment.

The land which immediately surrounds the mansion is laid
out in park-like meadow,

Beautifully ornamented with Timber,

the whole property containing

EIGHTY-EIGHT ACRES, TWO ROODS, AND THIRTY-
EIGHT PERCHES.

The property had been originally purchased by the East India
Company in 1809 for £16,604 10s., and the sum realised by its
sale in 1861 amounted to rather more than £33,600.

The East India Company's Civil Service College of Haileybury was sold about the same time, but did not realise more

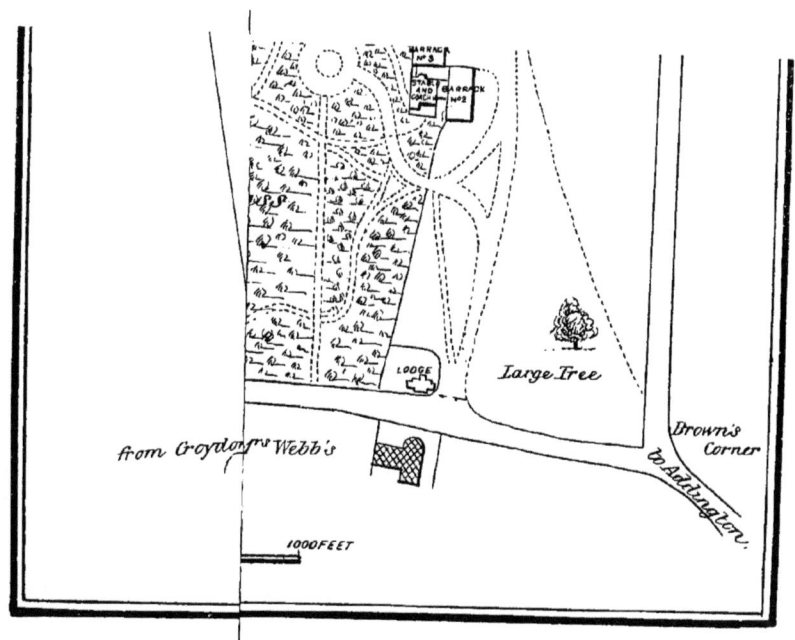

BARRACK Nº 3

STABLE AND COACH

BARRACK Nº 2

LODGE

Large Tree

From Croydon Mrs Webb's

Drown's Corner

To Addington.

1000 FEET

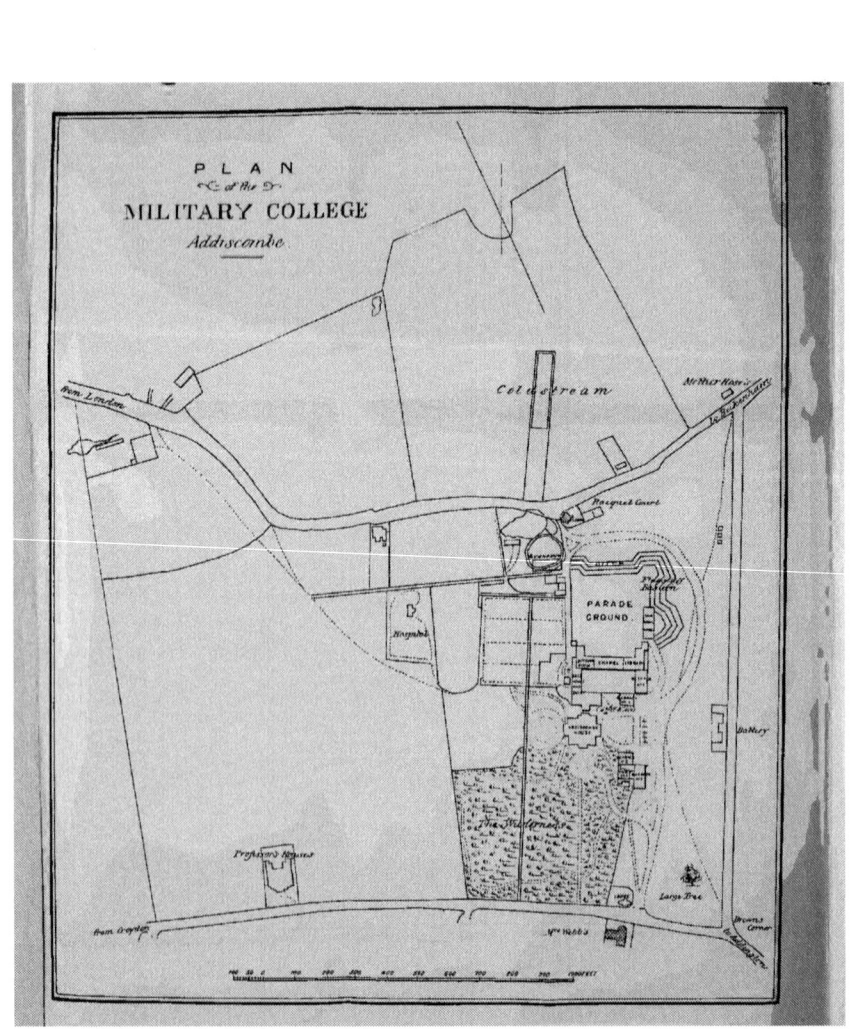

PLAN
of the
MILITARY COLLEGE
Addiscombe

than £15,200. The ground attached to Haileybury was about fifty-five acres.*

Early in the century a certain number of cadets for the Artillery and Engineers of the East India Company studied at the Royal Academy, Woolwich, and at Marlow; while others, for whom there was no room at those institutions, worked under private tuition.

Thus, in 1803 there were twenty-three at Woolwich, two at Marlow, and thirty-six at private academies.

In the early part of the year 1809, the East India Company for the first time established a "Seminary" of their own. This "Seminary" was at first only large enough to hold fifty-eight cadets, while eighteen still studied at Woolwich, and seven in private schools. Amongst those who first studied at the "Seminary," were the following cadets, who were afterwards officers of the Madras Engineers: C. C. Nattes, J. W. Nattes, Alex. Anderson, Alex. Grant, John Coventry, and Duncan Sim, while J. C. Proby was at a private establishment.

At the head of the "Seminary" was Dr. James Andrew, who was termed Professor of Mathematics and Resident Classical Master, while Lieutenant-Colonel William Mudge, R.A., was appointed Public Examiner.

In addition to these there were—

James Glennie, Esq , Professor of Fortifications.

Joseph Bordwine, Esq., Assistant Professor.

John Shakespeare, Esq., Professor of Oriental Languages, with Moonshee Meer Hussan Ali as his assistant.

In 1813 Mr. W. F. Wells was appointed Drawing Master.

Next year Mr. Glennie left and Mr. Bordwine succeeded to his post, while two assistants were allowed to Dr. Andrew.

Mr. Alexander Anderson, Mathematical Assistant.

Mr. Samuel Parlour, Classical Assistant.

Mons. Pierre Oger was appointed French Master.

* Both properties were bought by the British Land Company

In this year also a visitor in the Oriental Department was appointed for the first time in the person of Charles Wilkins, Esq., F.R.S., LL.D., and Dr. McCulloch became Chemical Lecturer.

In 1815 Mr. H. Angelo, jun., was appointed " Instructor in the new broadsword exercise."

Up to 1820 no further changes were made, but in that year Mr. Parlour became Mathematical Assistant, and Dr. Strachan was appointed Resident Classical Assistant.

Next year Colonel Sir Howard Douglas, Bart., C.B., replaced Colonel Mudge as Public Examiner, and Captain Charles Chaplin became Instructor in Military Surveying.

In 1822 the Professorship of Mathematics, &c. became vacant owing to the death or retirement of Dr. Andrew, and he was succeeded by a man well known to so many generations of cadets, the Reverend Jonathan Cape, who was appointed Head Mathematical and Classical Master and Chaplain.

About this time Richard Haughton, Esq., was made Assistant Professor of Oriental Languages, while Mr. Reeve Jones became one of the Assistants in Mathematics and Classics.

At this date, for the first time, a military man was placed at the head of the institution, and termed Resident Superintendent. This officer was Major William Carmichael Smyth, and Captain F. P. Lister was appointed his Adjutant.

In 1824 Sir Alexander Dickson, K.C.B., was appointed Public Examiner instead of Sir Howard Douglas, and Major Smyth was replaced by Lieutenant-Colonel Robert Houstoun, C.B., who next year was appointed the first Lieutenant-Governor of Addiscombe. This officer served with great distinction in India. He entered the service in 1795, having been born in 1780. He served as Brigade-Major in the Second Mahratta War, 1804. was present at the capture of the strong fort of Bhowanny in 1809. Succeeded to command of 6th Regiment of Cavalry when a Captain in 1805, and retained it till 1814. Commanded troops in South Behar in 1812-13, to protect frontier against the

Pindarries; and, in 1814, commanded on the Mirzapore frontier. Nominated a C.B. in February 1817. In 1817, after a visit to England on account of ill-health, he returned to India, and joined the Grand Army under Lord Hastings, and was nominated to the charge of the Guides and Intelligence Department. At the close of the campaign he was appointed Commandant of a cavalry depôt, which post he held till November 1819, when 2,000 men whom he had recruited and disciplined were drafted to the line, to form an additional squadron to each regiment. He was then appointed to command of the forces in Malwa (6,000 men), and this distinguished situation he held for two years, when bad health again compelled him to visit England."

In 1824 Mr. Thomas Bisset became one of the Assistant Mathematical Masters, and in 1825 Monsieur Marin de la Voye replaced Monsieur Oger as French Master.

In these years the establishment connected with military discipline was considerably increased, both in numbers and importance. The head of the establishment obtained the dignified title of Lieutenant-Governor in 1825, while three officers were placed under him—

Captain Charles O. Aveline as Adjutant, and
Lieutenant Talbot Ritherdon, ⎫
     „   David Liddell, ⎬ Orderly Officers.

In 1826 Mr. John B. Ruddock was appointed fourth Assistant Mathematical and Classical Master, and the Reverend T. Bisset became Chaplain, Cape being relieved of those duties.

It was in this year that the well-known Captain Hector Straith was appointed Assistant Professor of Fortification, while the establishment for "drawing" was increased to two by the addition of Mr. T. H. Fielding.

The whole establishment was now of considerable dimensions, and we find that in 1828 it consisted of the following :—

Sir Alexander Dickson, K.C.B., Public Examiner.

C. Wilkins, Esq. (afterwards Sir Charles, Knt.), Public Examiner, Oriental Department.

Lieut.-Colonel Robert Houstoun, C.B., Lieutenant-Governor and Resident Superintendent.

Reverend Jonathan Cape, Professor of Mathematics and Classics.

Dr. Alexander Anderson, First Assistant ditto.

Mr. Samuel Parlour, Second ditto.

Reverend Thomas Bisset (Chaplain), Third ditto.

Mr. J. B. Ruddock, Fourth ditto.

Monsieur de la Voye, French Master.

Joseph Bordwine, Esq., Professor of Fortification.

Captain Hector Straith, Assistant ditto.

Captain Charles Chaplin, Professor of Military Drawing.

Mr. E. B. Metcalfe, Assistant ditto.

John Shakespeare, Esq., Professor of Oriental Languages.

Richard Haughton, Esq., Assistant ditto.

Mr. W. F. Wells, ⎫
Mr. T. H. Fielding, ⎭ Drawing Masters.

Dr. McCulloch, Chemical and Geological Lecturer.

Lieutenant Ritherdon, Staff Officer.

Lieutenant Giles Emly, ⎫
Lieutenant E. A. Farquharson, ⎭ Orderly Officer.

Mr. H. Angelo, jun., Superintendent of Broadsword Exercise.

Mr. R. M. Leeds, Purveyor and Steward.

The establishment thus consisted of two public examiners, four officers for military discipline, fifteen professors, and one instructor.

Next year Mr. John Shakespeare retired, and was succeeded by Richard Haughton, while the well-known Charles Bowles, Esq., was appointed Assistant.

In 1834 Colonel Ephraim Stannus, C.B., Bo.N.I. (afterwards Sir Ephraim, Knt.), was appointed to succeed Colonel Houstoun as Lieutenant-Governor.

Sir Ephraim Stannus entered the service in 1800, and was posted to the Bombay European Regiment.

He served in 1803–4 in the operations * against the Cotiote Rajah under Colonel Montresor. The force was employed marching about the districts of Coonnanaad, Curtinaad, and Wynaad, sometimes enduring extreme privations, engaged with the enemy, and carrying fire and sword in every direction.

Appointed Brigade-Major to force under Colonel Lionel Smith for campaign in Kattywar, December 1811. Received the grateful thanks of Colonel Smith for his "abilities and his zealous exertions on the present service." In 1815, Military Secretary to General Lawrence, commanding Field Force on banks of the Myhie, and in November of that year Brigade-Major, and afterwards Deputy Adjutant-General to the force under Colonel East for service in Kattywar. In 1816, Deputy Adjutant-General to Field Force at Baroda, and served in the Deccan War as Deputy Adjutant-General to Sir W. Grant Keir's Division.

In 1817 he accompanied an expedition against Palhampore and Deesa, under Lieutenant-Colonel Elrington. He highly distinguished himself at the capture of Kairee, where he, with Lieutenant Marriott, were the first that entered the town through a port-hole before the scaling-ladders had arrived. In 1819 he was appointed Assistant Adjutant-General to the Guicowar's force, and directed to proceed to Cutch with Sir W. Keir. Served at the capture of Bhooj. Sir W. Keir, in his despatch, preferred a request that the General commanding the forces would be pleased to recommend Captain Stannus, Assistant Adjutant-General, and Lieutenant Remon of the Engineers (Bombay), to the Marquis of Hastings for some special mark of his lordship's favour.

* Occasioned by the surprise of an outpost, and the murder of two British officers and many sepoys, and the escape of the Pyche Rajah's nephews (accompanied by a few of our native troops) from confinement in the fort of Cannanore

Appointed Assistant Adjutant-General to the Expedition to the Persian Gulf under Sir W. Keir, in September 1819, when he was allowed temporary rank of Deputy Adjutant-General. He was again mentioned with great approval. Assistant Adjutant-General to Field Force in Cutch, May 1820, and was present at reduction of fort of Dwarka, in province of Okamundel, where the Arabs and Scindians offered a desperate resistance, fighting sword in hand. Stannus and Remon were again mentioned as having displayed great gallantry. He was thus noticed by Lord Hastings :—

"The names of Major Stannus, Captain Wilson, and Lieutenant Remon are familiar to his lordship as connected with former services, where zeal, intelligence, and gallantry combined led also to results equally creditable to their characters as British officers, and advantageous to the Government of India."

In December 1820 Stannus was appointed Assistant Adjutant-General to Expedition to coast of Arabia, under Major-General Smith. In the operations against the Beni-boo-ali tribe of Arabs he was thus noticed :—

"The services of Major Stannus, Captain Wilson, Major Mackintosh, Artillery, and Captain Dickenson, Engineers, have arrested my particular attention."

On return to Bombay he was posted to command the Bombay European Regiment in March 1821, and in January 1822 officiated as Private Secretary to the Governor, while in January 1824 he was appointed the first British Resident in the Persian Gulf. On 26th July 1823, he was made a Companion of the Order of the Bath. He resigned appointment of Resident in November 1826, and proceeded to England. He was thanked by the Bombay Government for the "zeal, decision, and judgment with which you have conducted your important duties," and for "the eminent success which has attended your exertions in preventing the revival of piracy."

In March 1834 he was appointed Lieutenant-Governor of

Addiscombe, on a salary of £800 per annum, with accommodation for himself and family.

On 7th April he assumed charge from Colonel Houstoun.

Lord Hill, Commander-in-Chief, at the request of the Court of Directors, appointed him Brevet-Colonel in H.M.'s service.

The honour of knighthood was conferred upon him on 9th May 1837. He died at Addiscombe House on 21st October 1850.

In 1836 the Court expressed approval regarding the arrangements made by Colonel Stannus, and they "fully approve of the orders issued by him with a view to the prevention of the pernicious habit of smoking, and extend the power confided to him of immediately sending to his friends any cadet who may have been guilty of any offence against the laws of the institution."

In 1836 the post of Public Examiner, Oriental Department, became vacant, and Professor Horace H. Wilson, F.R.S., Professor of Sanscrit at Oxford, succeeded to the vacancy. In this year Major Basil Jackson became Assistant Professor of Fortification, and Professor Daniell succeeded Dr. McCulloch as Lecturer on Chemistry and Geology; while in 1837 Mr. J. C. Schetky replaced Mr. Wells as Drawing Master; and in 1838 Straith became Senior Professor of Fortification, with Lieutenant T. Cook, R.N., as his Assistant. Mr. Metcalfe took the Military Drawing Department, while the Department of Military Surveying was entrusted to Major Basil Jackson.

No change now occurred till 1841, when Colonel C. W. Pasley, F.R.S., C.B., R.E. (afterwards Major-General Sir Charles, K.C.B), was appointed Public Examiner, and the Rev. Alfred Wrigley succeeded Mr. Ruddock as Junior Professor of Mathematics.

In 1843 a medical practitioner was specially appointed to the establishment in the person of Dr. Westall; while the Reverend William H Johnstone and the Reverend J. Fenwick took vacancies formed by the retirement of Dr. Anderson and Mr.

Parlour, and next year Mr. Fenwick retired, making way for the Reverend Robert Inchbald. In 1845 the chaplaincy became vacant, and Johnstone was appointed to fill the post, while the Reverend G. R. J. Tryon joined as Junior Mathematical Professor.

About this time Major Hector Straith died, when Lieutenant Cook became Senior Professor of Fortifications, with Major W. Jacob, B.A., as his Assistant.

Two lecturers were now appointed in the place of Dr. McCulloch, Mr. Ansted for Geology, and Professor Solly for Chemistry, and Monsieur Leon Contanseau succeeded Monsieur de la Voye as French Master.

From this time up to 1850 the only alterations were—Rev. A. Dusuatoy appointed to succeed Rev. G. Tryen as Junior Professor, and Captain William A. Tate as Professor of Military Drawing instead of Mr. Metcalfe.

Captain Tate entered the service in 1812 in the Bombay Engineers, and retired 5th December 1829 on account of ill-health.

In 1851 Lieutenant-Colonel F. Abbott, C.B , B.E. (afterwards Major-General Sir F. Abbott, Knt), was appointed Lieutenant-Governor (in succession to Sir Ephraim Stannus), which appointment he held till the close of the College in 1860.

"Sir F. Abbott, C.B., was educated at Addiscombe (and entered the Bengal Engineers), which has been a prolific *Alma Mater* of eminent men. When a very young officer, he secured distinction by his professional skill in the First Burmese War, 1824–26, and was wounded while leading Major Gully's column (87th Foot) near Prome on 2nd December 1825. He served as Chief Engineer of the army which, under the late Field Marshal Sir George Pollock, retrieved our laurels in Afghanistan. Captain Abbott was present at the actions of Mammoo Khel, Jugdulluck, and Tezeen, in September 1842. Again, when in 1845 war broke out with the Sikhs, he was second in

command of the Engineers, and received the thanks of Lords
Hardinge and Gough for the rapid and skilful manner in which,
after the battle of Sobraon in February 1846, he bridged the
Sutlej in a few hours with boats, over which the army with its
guns and stores marched through the Punjab to Lahore. Lord
Hardinge—*clarum et venerabile nomen*—wrote of his services
on this occasion: 'Two days before the battle of Sobraon I
consulted you and Colonel Henry Lawrence as to the best
means of overcoming some difficulties which had arisen relating
to the employment of our heavy artillery in the attack on the
Sikh entrenched camp, and I sent you to the Commander-in-
Chief confidentially to communicate with his Excellency ; the
result being a ready concurrence of Lord Gough, and the decision taken to storm the enemy's camp after the defences should
have been shaken by the fire of thirty-five pieces of heavy artillery.
The instant that great victory was achieved you returned to the
ghaut, and, without repose night or day, directed all your
energies and talents in laying down the bridge of boats by
which the army and its siege train was able in a few hours to
enter the Punjab and march to Lahore.' In September 1847
Colonel Abbott relinquished the office of Superintending Engineer, North-West Provinces, and returned to England. On the
death of Sir Ephraim Stannus, the Court of Directors conferred
the post of Lieutenant-Governor of Addiscombe on Colonel
Abbott, which he held till the abolition of that famous College
in 1860. He now found a new and congenial scope for his
talents as Member of the Council of Military Education, where
he remained until 1868. In 1859 he was nominated one of the
Commissioners for the National Defences." *

It may be mentioned here that about up to this date the
establishment at Addiscombe was designated by the strange name
of " Seminary," and it was only during the last few days of its
existence that it was dignified by the name of College.

* Extract from Mr. Low's *Memoir of Major-General A. Abbott, C.B., R.A.*

In 1851 Fielding died and Schetky became Senior Drawing Professor, while Aaron Penley was appointed to make up the establishment.

Next year Mr. Haughton retired and Mr. Charles Bowles took his place, with Major M. T. Rowlandson, M.N.I., as his assistant.

About this time Mr Angelo died and was replaced as instructor in fencing, singlesticks, &c., by Mr. Stevenson " of the Life Guards."

In 1855 Capt. John T. Hyde (late Bengal Artillery) succeeded to Jacob's post in fortification department, and next year Mr. John Callow became Junior Drawing Master in place of Schetky.

At this time Sir J. M. Frederick Smith, K.H., R.E., was appointed Public Examiner instead of Sir Charles Pasley, and retained the post till the close of the College in 1860.

In 1857 John Whitt, Esq , B.A., was appointed a fifth Assistant Mathematical Professor, but was almost immediately succeeded by the Rev G. Roberts.

In 1858 Captain John Ouchterlony, M.E., took the place of Major Basil Jackson, and next year Major F. Ditmas became Junior Fortification Professor on the death of Lieutenant Cook, R.N., while Mr. Cotton Mather took the vacancy caused by the retirement of Mr. Bowles, and E. Frankland succeeded Professor Solly as Lecturer in Chemistry, just before the close of the College.

Captain P. M. Francis became Professor of Military Drawing in lieu of Captain Tate.

It was not till 1823, when a military man for the first time was placed at the head of Addiscombe, that a staff officer was appointed. He was Captain F. P. Lister, and was styled Adjutant. Next year it was found necessary to give him an assistant, Lieutenant Talbot Ritherdon.

In 1826 this department was strengthened by the addition of a third officer ; one being termed Staff Officer, and the others

Orderly Officers. The first was held by an officer permanently, while the others held office only for eighteen months or so. The Staff officer was Lieutenant Ritherdon, and he retained the post till the year 1851, when he was succeeded by Major T. Donnelly, Bo.I., who remained at the College till its close.

The names of the officers who held the posts of Orderly Officers, are given below. Several of them afterwards attained considerable distinction :—

Captain F. P. Lister, Adjutant	.	.	1823
Lieut. Talbot Ritherdon, Assistant Adjutant	.		1824
Captain Charles O. Aveline, Adjutant	.	.	1825
Lieut. T. Ritherdon, Orderly Officer	.	.	1825
,, David Liddell, ,,	.	.	1825
,, T. Ritherdon, Staff Officer	.	.	1826
,, D. Liddell,	Orderly Officer		1826
,, Brind,	,,		1826
,, Giles Emly,	,,		1828
,, Archibald Hyslop,	,,		1828
,, Edward A. Farquharson,	,,		1828
,, Charles Whinfield,	,,		1829
,, Clements Blood,	,,		1830
,, Gother Kerr Mann,	,,		1831
,, A. F. Oakes,	,,		1832
,, John Grant,	,,		1833
,, C. W. Burdett,	,,		1833
,, Le Grand Jacob,	,,		1834
,, W. Hill,	,,		1836
,, R. C. Moore,	,,		1836
,, G. Broadfoot, M.N.I.,	,,		1837
,, Thomas Tapp, Bo.N.I.,	,,		1838
Ensign Robert Hay, B.N.I.,	,,		1838
Lieut. J. D. Scott, M.A.,	,,		1840
,, Alexander Tod, M.N.I.,	,,		1840
,, J. M. Rees,	,,		1841
Brevet Captain H. T. Tucker,	,,		1841
,, H. G. Napolett, M.N.I.,	,,		1843

Lieut. Gunthorpe, M.A.,   Orderly Officer   1844
,,   G. A. F. Hervey, B.N.I.,   ,,   1845
,,   R. Kinkead, M.A.,   ,,   1846
,,   J. P. Nixon, Bo.N.I.,   ,,   1846
,,   F. I. Goldsmid, M.N.I.,   ,,   1847
,,   W. C. Brackenbury, M.N.I.,   ,,   1848
,,   C. Taylor, M.N.I.,   ,,   1849
,,   E. J. Ferrers, M.Cav.,   ,,   1849
,,   M. Vibart, B.A.,   ,,   1850
,,   A. Pond, B.N.I.,   ,,   1851
,,   W. N. Dyett, Bo.N.I.,   ,,   1851
,,   W. Olpherts, B.A.,   ,,   1853
,,   E. H. Couchman, M.A.,   ,,   1854
,,   E. Milligan, B.A.,   ,,   1855
Brevet Captain S. Mainwaring, M.N.I ,   ,,   1856
Lieut. H. A. Maxwell, B.A.,   ,,   1856
,,   J. S. Gibb, B.A.,   ,,   1857
,,   H. M. Smith, B.A.,   ,,   1858
,,   L. Lawder, M.N.I.,   ,,   1858
,,   E. C. H. Armstrong, B.N.I.,   ,,   1859
Captain A. P. Toogood, Second Europeans   . 1859

It was in the year 1834 that the 2nd battalion of Pioneers was absorbed into the Corps of Sappers and Miners. The Corps consisted of eight companies, distributed as follows :

> Head-Quarters, Bangalore, 4 companies.
> Neilgherries, 2 companies.
> Madras, 1 company.
> Hydrabad Road, 1 company.

After the war in Coorg in this year, the head-quarters of the Sappers was removed to Mercara.

In December 1835 the Commander-in-Chief reviewed them, and "issued a highly complimentary order regarding the intelligence displayed by them in the various operations of attack and defence, which they executed during the inspection."

In February 1838 the head-quarters of the Corps was stationed again at Bangalore.

In 1855, at the suggestion of Colonel Arthur (now Sir Arthur, K.C.S.I.) Cotton, the head-quarters of the Sappers was removed to Dowlaishwaram, as it was considered they might be employed with advantage, both to the Government and to the Corps, on the works in the vicinity of the fine anicut across the Godavery, lately constructed by Arthur Cotton. They stayed at this place till the year 1865, when they returned to Bangalore, at which important station they have remained ever since. While at Dowlaishwaram in 1860, the Sappers were inspected by Sir Charles Trevelyan, then Governor of Madras, who was on an official visit to the fine irrigation works of the Godavery.

An incident is related, connected with this visit, which brings out, in an amusing manner, the great general intelligence of the Corps. After the inspection was over, Sir Charles addressed them in a very complimentary speech, couched in high-flown Bengal Hindustani; then calling out the senior subadar present (Ram Sing), he said, " I suppose the men did not understand me ? " The subadar replied, " No, sir, but I did." Sir Charles then requested him to translate what he had said into some language which the men could understand. The subadar, much to Sir Charles Trevelyan's astonishment, promptly turned to the Sappers, and repeated the Governor's speech in *English;* and Sir Charles Trevelyan left Dowlaishwaram, with a very high opinion of the intelligence of the Corps.

In February 1837, the establishment of the Corps had been revised, but consisted still of eight companies of eighty men each. In December of the same year its constitution was again altered, and was ordered to be formed into six companies; but the strength of each company was largely increased, and consisted of 120 privates, besides two native officers, six European N.C.O., twelve native N.C.O., and two buglers; total, 142.

20 *

The superior grade of Subadar was introduced for the first time; the native officers with the Corps were increased by four, while the number of naiques (native corporals) was doubled.

After the First China War, the Corps was increased to twelve companies, as it had proved of so much use in that campaign.

Early in 1862 it was again reduced to ten companies, L and M being absorbed. At this strength it has remained up to the present date.

In 1876 the Viceroy of India announced that, to commemorate the visit to India of H.R.H. the Prince [of Wales, the Queen had been graciously pleased to appoint His Royal Highness to be Honorary Colonel of several regiments in the different Presidencies. Among those selected on the Madras side was the Corps of Madras Sappers and Miners, which was now styled " Queen's Own" Sappers and Miners, and the Corps was authorised to wear on its colours and appointments, the Royal Cypher within the Garter.

Here may be fitly introduced, the complete list of honorary distinctions which the Corps has won during its career.

" QUEEN'S OWN " SAPPERS AND MINERS.

(Officered from the Corps of Engineers.)

The Royal Cypher within the Garter.

" Seringapatam "—" Java "—" Egypt " (with the Sphinx)—" Assaye "— " Mahidpore "—" Nagpore "—" Ava "—" Lucknow "—" Central India "— " Afghanistan, 1878–80."

A, B, and F Companies bear on their appointments a " Dragon," wearing an Imperial Crown with the word " China."

A	Company	" Taku Forts " and " Pekin."
C	,,	" Meeanee " and " Hydrabad, 1843."
B	,,	" Pegu " and " Persia."
A, C & E	,,	" Pegu."
G, H & K	,,	" Abyssinia."
K	,,	" Taku Forts."

Honorary Colonel.

Field Marshal, H.R.H. Albert Edward Prince of Wales and Duke of Cornwall, K.G., K.T., G.C.B , K.P., G.C.S.I., G.C.M.G.

The Corps has a Commandant, an Adjutant, a Quartermaster, and twenty Company officers, all taken from the Royal Engineers.

Shortly after the Abyssinian campaign Major (Brevet Lieutenant-Colonel) H. N. D. Prendergast, V.C., was appointed to command the Madras Sappers. This post he retained for fully eleven years (till 1st September 1880), when he was appointed Brigadier-General, Malabar and Canara. He was afterwards transferred to command the Brigade at Bellary.* Before promotion to the rank of Brigadier-General, he acted for some six months as Military Secretary to the Madras Government. He was succeeded, as commandant of the " Queen's Own " Sappers, by Major (Brevet Lieutenant-Colonel) C. A. Sim, who still retains that command.

* Brigadier-General H. N. D. Prendergast, V C., C.B., still (October 1882) commands at Bellary.

CHAPTER IX.

Indian Mutiny, 1857–59.—Report of Lieutenant J. C. Anderson on defence of Residency, Lucknow.—Services of B Company.—Relief of Asseerghur and Mhow.—Siege of Dhar.—Action at Mundisore.—Prendergast shot.—Goorariah.—Neemuch relieved.—Force returns to Indore.—Sir Hugh Rose takes command.—Marches to Ratgurh.—Siege and capture of Ratgurh.—Neville, Royal Engineers, killed. — Saugor relieved.—Sappers destroy forts.— Barodia put in state of defence.—Force marches towards Jhansi.—Crosses the Betwa.—Chandairee Fort captured by 1st Brigade.—Siege of Jhansi.— Battle of the Betwa.—Gallant conduct of Lieutenant Fox, Madras Sappers. —Jhansi stormed.—Severe casualties among Engineers.—Dick and Meiklejohn, Bombay Engineers, killed, and Bonus wounded.—Action at Koonch.— Sappers destroy Hurdooi.—Force marches towards Calpee.—Gains Golowlee on the Jamna, six miles from Calpee.—Enemy defeated and Calpee taken.—Flying column under Robertson pursues.—Orders of Sir Hugh Rose to Central India Field Force.—Rebels march on Gwallior.—Sir Hugh Rose follows them.—Defeats them at Morar and captures Gwallior. --B Company Sappers leaves Gwallior and returns to Madras.—Sir Hugh Rose highly praises B Company.—Saugor Field Force.—L Company Madras Sappers.—Column leaves trunk road at Jokehi.—Arrives at Dumoh.— Countermarching of Saugor Field Force.—Jheeghun shelled.—Battle of Banda.—Engineer officers with advanced guards.—Fort on Cane river blown up.—Advance on Kirwee.—Fort at Kirwee put in state of defence.—Whitlock marches west to Banda.—Action at Chittrakote —Punghatee Pass.— Punwarree Heights.—Relief of Kirwee.—Ludlow at Indore with Durand — Field Engineer with the Kamptee Movable Column.—Lieutenant Sankey —Entrenchments at Allahabad.—General Windham's force at Cawnpore.— Commander-in-Chief arrives from Lucknow.—Enemy defeated.—Relief of Lucknow.—C Company Madras Sappers.—Garrison of Residency withdrawn. —C Company sent to Bunnee.—Then to Alumbagh to serve under Outram. —Outram's position.—Attacked by rebels.—Second attack.—Capture of Lucknow.—Franks defeats enemy in four actions.—Gallantry of Lieutenant Innes, Bengal Engineers.—Outram crosses to left bank of Goomtee.—Enemy's

BEFORE proceeding to detail the services rendered by the Madras Engineers and Sappers and Miners in the Mutinies 1857–58, it will be as well to give a list of the officers employed, together with the general direction in which their services were made use of.

Altogether twelve officers of the Madras Engineers were engaged.

Lieutenant J. C. Anderson was engaged throughout the defence of the Residency at Lucknow, and was, towards the end of the siege, the Garrison Engineer.

Lieutenant R. H. Sankey was at Cawnpore with General Windham's force, and was afterwards employed in the capture of Lucknow by Lord Clyde in March 1858.

Brevet-Major Boileau, Lieutenants Gordon and Prendergast, were employed with Deccan and Mhow Field Force under Major-General Woodburn, with the Malwa Field Force under Brigadier-General Stuart, and with Central India Field Force under Sir Hugh Rose (now Lord Strathnairn).

Captain C. Scott and Lieutenant Burton were employed in second relief of Lucknow, defence of Alumbagh, and capture of Lucknow, &c.

Major Ludlow, Captain Hemery, and Lieutenants Howes,

Lindsay, and Wood, were employed, under General Whitlock, in Saugor, Nerbudda, and Bundelcund.

Three companies of Madras Sappers were engaged. The B Company in Deccan, Malwa, and Central India. The C Company at Lucknow, Alumbagh, capture of Lucknow, and Oude campaign; while the L Company served under General Whitlock.

The following officers of Infantry served with the Madras Sappers :—

B Company : Lieutenant Brown, 1st Eur., Lieutenant Fox, and Dr. Lowe.

C Company : Lieutenants Raynsford, 14th N.I.; Lieutenant Wynch, 31st; Lieutenant Rawlins, 7th ; and Ensign Ogilvey, 20th.

L Company : Lieutenants Campbell, 7th N.I., and Eager, 52nd N.I.

First as to the defence of the Residency at Lucknow.

The general history of this gallant defence is too well known to need to be repeated ; but it will, I think, prove interesting to insert the report of Lieutenant J. C. Anderson (who was Garrison Engineer at the close of the siege).

On the defences of the Residency—

"The outbreak at Meerut and Delhi, and reports of general disaffection among the sepoys, caused Sir Henry Lawrence to take immediate measures for the defence of the place. Some time previously he had selected the Muchee Bowan as a site for our magazine and stores, and judging it from its commanding position, and the moral effect that the occupation of it would exercise over the city, he, in the first instance, proceeded to strengthen it. The works were commenced on 17th May, and carried forward with unremitting energy by Lieutenant Innes, under the general direction of Major Anderson, Chief Engineer, until the commencement of the siege. The defence of the Residency was also commenced, though at first it received a secondary

share of attention.   It was not till after the mutiny in cantonments (30th May), and the subsequent mutinies of corps in the
districts, that it became apparent that we should have probably
to defend ourselves against a combined attack of mutineers and
rebels from the country and city.   The more clear this became,
the more clearly the inadequacy of the Muchee Bowan, as a
fortified position, became apparent.   It was also seen that if the
mutineers came on in great force we had not sufficient hands to
man both it and the Residency ; and it having been ascertained,
after full consideration, that the defects of the Muchee Bowan,
both as regards defensive measures and shelter of troops and
the large European community, were very great, Sir Henry
Lawrence made up his mind to abandon it on the investment of the city by the enemy.   On this being decided (11th
June), the defences of the Residency were prosecuted with
vigour.   Prior to this, the Chief Engineer was doubtful as to
the extent of the force he had to shelter within the works, but
now he could form a definite plan, and he lost no time in forming
a connected line of defensive works round the buildings he
thought it necessary to occupy.   The Residency compound was
first protected by a line of parapet and ditch across it, a strong
battery, since named "Redan," was constructed in a corner of
the garden, which furnished a command over the iron bridge.
A battery, called the "Cawnpore," was constructed at the opposite point, enfilading the Cawnpore road, and was then designed
chiefly as a barrier to the approach of mutineers from Cawnpore.
Two other batteries were partially constructed—one between
Gubbins' and Ommaney's compounds, the other between the
slaughter-house and sheep-pen—but neither were ready at the
commencement of the siege, and want of labour prevented their
being completed afterwards.   Heavy and light guns and mortars,
more or less protected by parapets, were placed in various positions intermediate to the above-mentioned principal batteries.
Those positions are marked in the annexed sketch, though, of

course, various changes occurred during the siege, a gun or mortar having been frequently required to silence an enemy's battery, and withdrawn when the object was accomplished. Mr. Gubbins, by means of labourers procured by his subordinates, carried on the defence of his own compound, and the general line round our positions was continued from battery to battery, and house to house, by abbatis (in lanes), and by parapets and ditches, or stockades.

" Outside our line of works, also, a great amount of labour was required. Masses of buildings extended to within a few feet of us in nearly every direction, and though some of them would act as traverses to us from the enemy's batteries, the majority were a most undoubted source of annoyance to us, and it was necessary to proceed with their removal as vigorously as our means permitted. Several mosques which occupied positions commanding us were left alone, much to our future injury; but, I believe, the reason that prevented their removal was a good one, namely, the danger of precipitating an outbreak before we were prepared for it. But, apart from this, the demolition of private buildings was far from complete.

" The affair at Chinhut brought the enemy upon us earlier, I believe, than was anticipated by any individual of our force, and our command of labour having been limited, we had to close our gates with nothing in many places separating us from the besiegers but the width of the street. The houses that remained became nests of rebels, and, besides forming secure starting-points for their mines, enabled them, from under shelter, to keep a deadly fire of musketry upon us day and night, and it is to it, and not to round shot, that we have to attribute the greater part of our casualties. The latter was mainly injurious in destroying the buildings occupied by our troops and camp-followers, and though the loss of life, considering the amount of battering they sustained, was much less than was to be expected, it was a constant source of danger and annoyance to the garrison, and the repair of damage entailed heavy labour on men who were weakened by exposure and want of rest.

"The enemy proceeded to invest the place immediately on the return of our force from Chinhut on 30th June. The Muchee Bowan was still garrisoned by troops, though the treasure and the greater portion of munitions and stores, had been previously removed to the Residency, and it now became an object of primary importance to withdraw the garrison without loss. A telegraphic message was communicated to Lieutenant Innes, the Engineer officer (Bengal), to the effect that the powder in the magazine, about 200 barrels, was to be used in blowing up the fort, and that the garrison was to leave at midnight on the 1st July. This order was carried out with perfect success, and the garrison marched into our gates without the loss of a man The Garden battery was one of the first established by the enemy. It played on the guard-house at the Cawnpore battery, the battery itself, Brigade Mess, Anderson's, and Judicial Commissioner's. The combined fire of heavy guns and musketry on the Cawnpore battery became so deadly that our guns could not be served, and eventually it was thought necessary to withdraw them, and to leave the positions to be defended by musketry, and to repair the parapets as fast as they were damaged by the enemy's round shot.

"At the beginning of the siege, the 8-inch howitzers which fell into the enemy's hands at Chinhut were placed out of sight of our guns on the opposite bank of the river, near the bridge of boats, and kept up a destructive fire on the Residency. It was by one of the shells from it that Sir Henry Lawrence was killed. Batteries were also established by the enemy on the road leading from the iron bridge, in front of Gubbins' house, the Brigade Mess, and Post Office, and at the clock tower, and all the buildings were more or less damaged by them. A portion of the Residency was battered down, and six men were buried in the ruins. Many of the buildings were reduced to such a state as to appear to be quite untenable, but the garrison continued to occupy nearly all ; and though the defences of the post have been very much weakened by the continued and heavy fire, not a single one has been abandoned ; on the contrary, several buildings (Financial Commissioners', Sago's, and Innes') have been occupied and strengthened since the commencement of the siege. When the enemy found that neither repeated attacks nor the destruction of our buildings could force us from our posts, he had recourse to mining. This had been anticipated, but the Chief Engineer, acting under the suggestion of the late Captain Fulton, B.E., would not take the initiative, as he apprehended that our enemies would at once follow our example, and that the unlimited command of labour they possessed would give us a poor chance of competing with them.

" On the 20th July the first mine was exploded by the enemy at the ' Redan.' It preceded a general attack, and, both as regards direction and distance, was a complete failure.

" This was followed by one on the 27th at the angle of the Sikh quarters, and is the only one from which any loss of life on our side has been sustained. The sound of the moving had not been heard, owing to the proximity of the cavalry horses, and the guard were completely surprised ; seven gunners were killed on this occasion.

" Two other mines at the building occupied by the Martinière boys, and at Sago's, were also exploded, on 10th August, but, beyond breaking the outer line of walls, did no damage. The enemy in no case showed any great alacrity in assaulting the breaches, and we soon formed retrenchments in rear of them.

" We had meanwhile commenced counter-mining, and on the 5th August foiled a mine of the enemy's against the guardhouse at the Cawnpore battery ; and since then, up to the arriving of the relieving force, we have been incessantly employed in mining and countermining. We have generally worked into their galleries, and after having frightened the miners away have destroyed them; or in some cases we have blown in their galleries by charging and firing our own. I need hardly add that this was a service of danger.

"Two of our mines for directly offensive objects require separate notice, the one at Sago's to the enemy's guard-room, which we blew down with a loss to them of, it is supposed, between twenty and thirty men. The second to Johannes' house, in which we destroyed above eighty of the enemy. The explosion was followed by a sortie to cover the demolition of the remainder of the house and one adjoining, which object was effectually accomplished, and relieved us from the destructive fire of many of the enemy's best marksmen. I may mention that several other sorties were made on other occasions, and with equal success.

"We had, on the arrival of the relieving force, fifteen galleries ready for countermining further operations of the enemy. Several of the enemy's galleries have since been discovered and destroyed.

"I believe I have now noted every measure of importance with reference to the defence and attack of the place, in an engineering point of view, and it remains for me to add the means at our disposal for carrying on the work.

"During the early part of the siege we had working parties of H.M.'s 32nd Regiment; on one work during the night I have had forty-two men. The soldiers, however, had their other duties to perform; they were exposed to the rain, and were very often under arms, which prevented them having a proper amount of rest. They could, therefore, have very little physical strength left to work in the trenches, and, as the siege progressed, their numerical strength became so much reduced, that it was necessary to give up European working parties almost entirely, and to depend on the sepoys. The latter came forward most willingly, and I cannot speak too highly of the way in which they worked. They have, also, been of material assistance in our mining operations, and a party of the 13th N. I., thanks to the good management of Lieutenant Aitken, have constructed a battery for an 18-pounder, worked the gun, and dug a shaft and gallery at their own post. There has been but one squad of European miners, eight men, under Sergeant Day, all of whom have worked with the most unremitting zeal throughout.

"As regards general superintendence, the late Major Anderson, R.E., Chief Engineer, designed the defences of the Muchee Bowan and Residency, and, until shortly before his death, directed the construction of the various works and repairs.

" Captain Fulton became the senior Engineer officer on the demise of Major Anderson on 11th August. He had constructed the greater portion of the defences, powder-magazines, &c., and up to the day of his death displayed the most unremitting energy, in spite of bad health, in advancing our work. In particular, he took a most active part in foiling the enemy's attempt to destroy our advanced post by mine; and the manner in which he conducted the blasting operations during our sorties, invariably excited the admiration of all who were present, officers and men.

" In the performance of the above-mentioned engineering operations generally, he received the most able and untiring support from Lieutenants Hutchinson, Innes, Tulloch, and the late Lieutenant Birch, and latterly, since Captain Fulton's death, I have received much assistance from Lieutenant Hay, Assistant Field Engineer.

" The active part I have myself taken in the superintendence of work has been small, owing to my having suffered from continued ill-health.

" Finally, I beg to bring to the notice of the Brigadier the excellent service performed by the late Mr. Casey, Head Accountant to the Chief Engineer, who had been Sergeant-

Major of Sappers, and who was recommended by Major Anderson for the rank of Assistant Field Engineer ; of the late Mr. Supervisor Barrett ; Mr. Beale, overseer ; and Sergeant Ryder, Assistant Overseer ; all of whom have left families behind them.

(Signed)   " J. C. ANDERSON, Lieutenant,

" Garrison Engineer.

"Lucknow, 5th October 1857."

On the 14th September, Captain Fulton, B.E., was killed by a round shot, which struck him on the head.

Lieutenant Anderson succeeded him as Garrison Engineer, which post he held till the second relief, about the 20th November, when the ladies, the wives and children of the soldiers, and the sick, were removed from the Residency by Lord Clyde to a place of safety, and despatched to Calcutta.

The first relief of Lucknow, by the gallant force under Havelock and Outram, occurred on the 25th September. On the arrival of the Relieving Force, a greater extent of ground was required for the accommodation of the increased force, and a large mound and musjid adjacent to Innes's post, were taken possession of and made defensible.

The great number of wounded which accompanied the force into the position, speedily increased the number of patients from 130 to 627.

During the period between the first and second reliefs, several sorties were made under the direction of Outram.

With reference to these, Brigadier J. Inglis, in his despatch dated 12th November, remarks :—

"Neither must I omit to record my appreciation of the gallant bearing of the Engineer officers, Lieutenants Anderson (Madras), Hutchinson and Innes (Bengal), who accompanied the storming parties."

To give an idea of the sorties, it will suffice to enter here the official account of the sortie on the 29th September, sent by

Lieutenant J. C. Anderson to Colonel Napier, Military Secretary :—

" Sortie on the 29th September from the left square Brigade Mess, for the object of destroying the enemy's guns left in front of Brigade Mess, in front of Cawnpore battery, and on the left of Cawnpore Road.

" This sortie proceeded simultaneously with two others ; one from the Sikh square to the right of the Brigade Mess, and another from the ' Redan' towards the iron bridge, led by Captain McCabe, H.M.'s 32nd Regiment, with a few of the men of his regiment, who had during the siege been on duty on the posts opposite to the position to be attacked.

" The whole strength of the sortying party was 200 men with a reserve of 150.

" At daylight the party issued from an opening in the Brigade Mess wall, and formed up, under cover of a wall which runs parallel to the other at the distance of a few paces. The advance was then made in file, the men having to scramble over the *debris* of a house which had been blown down on a former occasion, and a rush made direct on the enemy's gun, an 18-pounder, which lay behind a breastwork at a distance of eighty yards from the Brigade Mess.

" The gunners fired two rounds at us when we made our appearance, but before they could fire again we had scaled their battery and driven them to flight. We then proceeded to force a building immediately to the left of the gun. The lower storey was quickly occupied.

" Captain McCabe, the gallant leader of many former sorties, was mortally wounded in the operation, and some delay having in consequence occurred, a few of the enemy in the upper storey had time to kill and wound several of our men before they were attacked and bayoneted.

" After the house had been taken possession of, a picquet of twenty-five men was left to hold it, while the main body proceeded along a narrow lane, under command of Major Simmons, H.M.'s 5th Fusiliers, to occupy two large buildings about sixty or eighty yards respectively in advance of the first, with several other smaller buildings adjoining ; the loss to the enemy, in all, being probably above thirty men. On our side we had the misfortune to lose Major Simmons, who was killed by a musket-shot while leading his men into the most advanced building.

"We had now progressed to a position from which we had a view of the enemy's 18-pounder in front of the Cawnpore battery. It lay in a lane running towards the Cawnpore road, the end of which was barricaded and loop-holed ; and directly in line with it, on the opposite side of the road, the enemy occupied a house from which they kept up a hot musketry-fire on our position.

"I then went for the reserve, and desired that an officer of rank might be sent to command the whole party.

"General Sir J. Outram, having become acquainted with our progress, sent word that, unless further advance could be made without danger of considerable loss, the design of proceeding against the enemy's gun, now in our rear, should be abandoned, and that the party should retire, after destroying in succession the houses we had taken possession of.

"After consulting with Captain Evans (attached to the Artillery), who had meanwhile destroyed the enemy's gun which we left at the first house, and also a 6-pounder in its neighbourhood, I returned a reply to the General that further advance could not be made without considerable loss, and 1 proceeded to demolish the three large houses we held, commencing with the one furthest in advance, and withdrawing the party gradually to the rear.

"This operation, in which thirteen barrels of powder were expended, destroyed the principal musketry cover of the enemy against our defences between the Brigade Mess and Cawnpore battery ; and the destruction of the gun in front of the latter, together with that effected by the sortieing parties acting in conjunction with us to the right, has relieved a considerable portion of our work from serious annoyance. The party returned about 9.30 A.M.

(Signed)   "J. C. ANDERSON, Lieutenant,

"Garrison Engineer."

The casualties on this occasion were 2 officers killed, Major Simmons and Captain McCabe, 1 sergeant and 9 men killed, 1 officer wounded, Captain Lockhart, and 1 sergeant, 1 corporal, and 10 men wounded. Total casualties—25.

After the second relief of Lucknow, Lieutenant J. C. Anderson was sent down to Calcutta very ill, suffering from scurvy brought on by privations which he, in common with the rest of the garrison, endured ; and on the 30th December 1857 he obtained three years' leave on sick certificate. Eighteen months of this he was allowed to count as service, as the illness had been contracted by service in the field.

On the 24th March 1858, he obtained his brevet-majority for his services with the "illustrious garrison" of Lucknow.

We will now turn to the services of Major Boileau and the B Company Madras Sappers.

On the 1st June 1857, the B Company disembarked at Bombay on its return from service in Persia.

On the 8th Major Boileau wrote to the Adjutant-General, Bombay Army, asking that the company might be attached to the force about to be sent from Poona against the mutineers.

On the 10th Major Boileau and his Sappers received "the thanks of Government for the readiness with which they have volunteered their services."

Their services were accepted, and on the 16th June they proceeded by rail and road to Aurungabad, and joined the Deccan Field Force, under Major-General Woodburn, C.B., on the 5th July.

On the 7th there were execution parades for men of 1st

Hydrabad Contingent Cavalry who had mutinied at Aurungabad some days previously.

On the 12th the force left Aurungabad, and, having crossed the rivers Poornah, Taptee, and Nerbudda, relieved Asseerghur on 23rd July, and Mhow on 2nd August, the Sappers having had frequent employment by the way, as pioneers, in making roads passable, and in ramping banks of rivers and streams.

During the monsoon, which broke on 2nd August, it was impossible to march, and the Sappers were employed in strengthening the defensive post at Mhow.

On the 20th October the left half company marched, under command of Lieutenant Fox, with Major Keane's column for Dhar. Lieutenant Prendergast acted as Brigade-Major to the force.

The force consisted of the 86th, with half B Company Sappers, Woolcombe's battery, some troopers of Hydrabad Cavalry, and a squadron 14th Light Dragoons.

There were no roads, and, owing to the late rains, the country was almost impassable to the artillery and baggage. The first day they marched to Ochanna, and the next only five miles.

At 8 P.M. on 21st, Major Keane was directed to march on Dhar next morning; to draw up on a ridge 800 yards east of the Fort, but not to engage till arrival of Brigadier Stuart.

On the 22nd, at 3 A.M., they marched from Decklaun river, crossed by a strong stone bridge. The enemy's cavalry were seen in rear of a village two miles from Dhar. They retired, and our troops halted on the ridge about a mile from Dhar.

A reconnoissance was now made. Troops were observed in the fort, as well as in our front and left front. Shortly afterwards the great gun on north-east tower opened fire. We drew up in order of battle, 1,300 yards from the fort. Skirmishers appeared, and the enemy's cavalry extended 700 yards to the right.

Captain Orr's Hydrabad Cavalry were forced to retire by

21 *

enemy's light infantry, one native officer being killed. Skirmishers were thrown out on right by the dragoons, but the enemy's cavalry being too strong, Captain Orr was directed to drive back enemy with his irregulars. The artillery also opened fire.

Brigadier Stuart's column was now approaching. Major Keane was ordered to drive in picquets in front, and join the Brigadier to the left without exposing his men to the heavy guns of the fort. The light company of the 86th was thrown out as skirmishers to front and left.

The Madras Sappers, on right of the infantry, covered advance of artillery. One troop of dragoons remained with the guns, and Orr's cavalry skirmished with enemy's cavalry on the right.

Shortly after the guns were brought to bear, the enemy got the range, and their artillery was well served, one ball passing 86th detachment, and another burying itself in the midst of the Artillery. The guns were charged and captured, and the enemy retired to the fort.

On the 21st the other half of the B Company conducted the siege train from Mhow to Dhar. It did not reach Dhar till the 24th.

Lieutenant Christie, Bo.A., was most unremitting in his exertions on this occasion.

The camp was pitched a mile and a half from the fort on the south, in a ravine surrounded by heights broken by fissures.

Dhar is considered the strongest fort in Malwa, and presents a most formidable appearance. The walls are rubble faced with red stone, very neatly built, and varying from 50 to 70 feet high. The fort is built on an eminence rising about 40 feet above the plain, 330 yards east of the town.

A hill, forming an admirable parallel to the east front of the fort, has its summit 270 to 350 yards from the fort walls.

A reconnoissance was made, and south-west tower fixed on as point of attack.

" On 23rd night a sand-bag battery was thrown up on the

height. The sand-bags were built from the interior, as for a revetment, for five feet; a second was built in front, but soil being very hard, little of the intervening space was filled in. No. 1 battery was for one howitzer, and one mortar, to enfilade the west side of the fort, and to dismantle the heavy guns in south-west tower."

" Next day at 11 A.M., the Sappers commenced to fill sand-bags; the horsekeepers carried the bags to the battery, where they were placed in position by Sappers. The working parties were withdrawn at 5.30 P.M., when the interior wall was six feet high, and interior filled to four feet. One N.C.O. and six privates were placed in the battery to prevent the enemy placing sand-bags, &c. in embrasures to cover a heavy gun in south-west tower, which had been brought to bear on the town, and its platform raised and arranged so that the gun could be depressed. At 6 P.M. the working party of the 86th and 25th N. I. commenced work, and at 6.30 thirty-five Sappers returned; the whole were broken off at half-past 10. During the night the battery was finished, and the guns brought into position."

"25th.—At 3.45 A.M. fifty Sappers were ordered to make a road for heavy guns. At 4.15, all men not on duty, of the 86th and 25th, were posted on heights running parallel to west face of fort at 400 yards. Their fire was so accurate that the enemy in the fort were unable to man the guns. The point for attack was the curtain between the south-west tower, and the adjoining tower on the west front. The mortar and howitzer opened fire at 6 A.M. Practice was good, but little effect was produced on the walls, or from the fire of three howitzers, which were brought on the newly-occupied hill. Fire of gingalls on howitzers was so heavy that the pieces could not be worked. The Sappers were employed in dragging 18-pounders into the town, and constructing battery No. 2. There was no opposition to the construction of No. 2 battery, except musketry-fire. No. 2 battery was for one howitzer and two guns, to breach the curtain."

"*26th.*—Battery No. 1 continued firing six rounds an hour. Some buildings in the fort took fire. A few rounds were fired at the gate."

"*26th and 27th.*—Battery No. 2 was continued. Enemy attempted to burn the pettah, but were unsuccessful. On 27th the fort was completely surrounded."

"*27th and 28th.*—Battery No. 2 completed, and No. 3 commenced for two guns to dismantle gun on south-west tower, and to destroy parapet of tower, curtain, and adjacent tower. It was afterwards converted into a battery for two $5\frac{1}{2}$-inch mortars."

28th and 29th.—Battery No. 4 was commenced for two howitzers to fire on palace and gateway; but it was afterwards adapted for one mortar and one howitzer. Nos. 2 and 3 batteries were armed, and in action early on the 28th, but constant work was required at them till the end of the siege, the Sappers frequently revetting and improving the embrasures in broad daylight, and always working fifteen hours out of twenty-four."

" On the 27th, the village was fired at night by Major Woolcombe, Lieutenants Strutt and Chrystie, some men of the Bombay Artillery, Lieutenant Fenwick, and a company of the 25th N. I. In returning, Lieutenant Chrystie missed his way, and, while swimming across the tank, was fired upon by grape from one of his own guns. He cried out, ' Don't shoot me!' and luckily crossed in safety."

" On the night of the 28th–29th, battery No. 4 was erected, and the screen approach to it was made the following morning. Fire was kept up almost unremittingly from the batteries till the evening of the 31st. Corporals Hoskins and Clarke of the Sappers examined the breach in broad moonlight, at a time when there was every reason to suppose they would be fired on at every step, and almost certainly shot on the breach."

" On the 30th a white flag was hoisted on the fort, and a parley ensued without any result."

" On the 31st the breach was reported practicable, and orders were issued for storming the fort before daybreak."

" On 1st November, the storming party was to consist of—

Thirty men of the 86th, Lieutenant Henry ;

Sixty men of the 25th N. I., Captain Little ;

Fifty Madras Sappers, Captain Brown ;"

but the enemy escaped during the night. The fort was found deserted, and Dhar was occupied without any further opposition. In his despatch, Brigadier Stuart brought to notice the services of Major Boileau, and the officers and men of the Madras Engineers and Sappers, and trusted that Corporals Hoskins and Clarke would be rewarded for their gallantry.

On 8th November, the B Company marched from Dhar with the Malwa Field Force, under Brigadier-General Stuart, for Mundisore.

On the 14th, Major Orr overtook the rebels at Rawul, defeated them, and captured eight guns. He had with him the cavalry of the Field Force. Dr. Orr had a hand-to-hand encounter with a Rohilla, and speared him. The force marched to Oneil, thence to Taul, and on the 19th reached Hernia, on the banks of the Chumbul. The river was crossed by the 20th, and on the morning of the 21st the force encamped four miles south of Mundisore. Major Robertson, 25th Bo. N. I., commanded the outposts. About midday, his picquets were driven in by a determined advance of the enemy's infantry, which, however, was checked by a charge of cavalry till the main body of the Field Force, hitherto concealed from the enemy by the rising ground occupied by the outposts, had formed for action. The villages in which the outposts had been placed were speedily prepared for defence by the Sappers, who afterwards aided in the defence, and in the defeat of the enemy on the subsequent advance of the Field Force.

Second Lieutenant Prendergast, M.E., was shot through the chest while charging with the cavalry ; the ball passed through just to the left of his heart   For his gallant services on this and other occasions, he received the Victoria Cross.   At Mundisore he saved the life of Lieutenant G. Dew, 14th Light Dragoons, at the risk of his own, by attempting to cut down a Valaitee who covered Lieutenant Dew with his piece, from only a few paces to the rear.   Lieutenant Prendergast was wounded in this affair, by the discharge of the piece, and would probably have been cut down had not the rebel been killed by Major Orr.

On the following day a short flank march was made without serious opposition, to place the force on the road to Neemuch, then besieged by the rebels.

On the 23rd the force marched north; but before long they found the Shahzadah's army, which had been encamped before Neemuch, in the strong position of Goorariah, five miles north-west of Mundisore.   The Brigadier at once prepared to attack, and eventually charged the batteries in the centre of the position.   The Sappers were in echelon on the left of the 25th N. I., in the advance.   During the action a strong body of rebels marched from Mundisore with the intention of attacking in reverse the right of the British line, which was already out-flanked by the preponderating strength of the army from Neemuch.   Their attempt, however, was frustrated by prompt action on the part of the rear-guard, consisting of detachments of the 14th Light Dragoons, 1st and 4th Hydrabad Cavalry, Madras Sappers in charge of an 8-inch howitzer, and 25th Bo. N.I.

Havildars Appoo* and Gooroosammy, of the Sappers, were distinguished for their readiness in loading and firing the howitzer at a critical moment.

Next morning the village of Goorariah was shelled, and at 4 P.M. 86th and 25th N. I. and Sappers stormed and carried it. The Sappers were especially useful in knocking down walls and making approaches by which the troops could advance upon the enemy under cover.

* Afterwards Subadar Bahadoor.

Naique Vellien (afterwards Subadar Major, "Sirdar Baha-door"), distinguished himself by his cool courage.

Thus four days' fighting was brought to a close, Neemuch was relieved, and the camp again pitched at Mundisore.

A breach was effected by the Sappers in one of the walls of the Mundisore Fort, and the force prepared to march to Indore, *viá* Mahidpore.

Sir Hugh Rose arrived next day, and the force assumed the name of Central India Field Force. On visiting the hospitals, Sir Hugh Rose said that Government were highly pleased with the Madras Sappers.

On 8th January 1858 the siege-train commenced to march from Indore towards Sehore. Sir Hugh Rose's force was divided into two brigades, 1st under Brigadier-General Stuart, 2nd under Sir Hugh Rose himself. The Madras Sappers were attached to the 2nd Brigade. While at Sehore 149 rebels were shot.

The 2nd Brigade left for Ratghur on the 16th,* encamped on the 18th at Bhopal, on the 21st reached Bhilsa, on the 23rd Gwanopore, and on the 24th marched four miles from camp, when the road was found obstructed.

The Sappers were ordered to clear the way, which they did with intense labour. The heavy guns were also dragged up by the Sappers.

On the 24th bivouacked in the jungles, and arrived at Ratghur at 1 P.M. on the 25th, after driving the enemy (who sallied forth with the intention of holding the ford of the Beema) into the fort.

On the 25th a reconnoissance was made by Sir Hugh Rose and Major Boileau, and siege materials were collected.

On the 26th the pettah north of the fort was taken, from which commenced the right attack. At the same time troops moved by a circuitous road to within 300 yards of the east face of the fort, to commence the left attack.

* The 1st Brigade under Stuart marched along the trunk road to capture Çhandairee.

On this day the B Company of Sappers were throwing up a battery for the attack, when Captain Brown, commanding the company, told the Subadar Seeloovey that General Rose and the Chief Engineer, Major Boileau, wished to know if there was a ditch in front of a certain wall they intended to breach, and called for volunteers to ascertain the fact. The Subadar at once volunteered, and with him Jemadar Appavoo and Privates Chinnatumby, Appasammy, and Samathevan advanced under a heavy fire, jumped into the ditch, took all the requisite measurements, and returned safely with the report.

The river Beema washes the precipitous south and west fronts of the fort, and the fords of the river were entrusted to the Bhopal Regiment. The Sappers were employed in making the road to the left attack, and in making such protective works as were practicable for men and guns, by cutting brushwood for screens, and building stone breastworks. By unremitting labour cover for the troops had been made by the Sappers parallel to the east face, and an elevated sand-bag battery for two 18-pounders and one 8-inch howitzer, to breach a curtain between two towers, was erected by daylight on the 27th.

On the evening of the 28th the breach was inspected by Corporal Linahan and Privates Pitchamootoo and Chinnatumby (all of the Sappers), and found practicable.

Two days afterwards the Chief Engineer, wishing to know the progress made in breaching the wall, Captain Brown called for volunteers to accompany Corporal Linahan, B Company, on this service. Lance-Naique Pitchamootoo and Private Samathevan at once volunteered to accompany him (the latter had already been to the ditch on the 26th), and proceeded to the breach under cover of the Enfield rifles of 3rd Bombay Europeans and blank firing of the heavy guns. Corporal Linahan jumped bravely into the ditch, followed closely by both privates, under very sharp fire from the enemy; everything that was required was ascertained, and was reported by the Corporal in the most correct manner, as was found on the following morning. All these native sappers received the 3rd class of the "Order of Merit."

The enemy evacuated the fort during the night, crossing a ford of the Beema south-west of the fort, and passing through the Bhopal camp.

On the 30th the Sappers occupied the fort, and commenced mining and demolishing the buildings. Sir Hugh Rose received information that the rebels had taken up a position eight miles off, and went after them with Horse Artillery, 3rd Europeans, some Cavalry, and Sappers. Captain Neville, R.E., who had just joined, was killed by a round shot striking him on the head.

On 3rd February the Brigade relieved Saugor, and on the 6th a parade of all troops took place.

On the 8th, half of the B Company, with an Engineer officer, marched to Nurrowlee, fourteen miles off, and returned the same day, having blown up and ruined the towers flanking the gate.

The next day they marched to Sanoda, and destroyed the fort.

On the 10th they marched to Bussaree, close to Gurracottah, and took part that afternoon in an affair with the enemy.

On the 11th the fort was reconnoitred, and batteries were commenced at night; but during the night the fort was abandoned. Captain Hare, with Hydrabad Cavalry, pursued them for twenty-five miles. The fort was occupied, and a short front was destroyed by mines, so as to leave a practicable breach in the enceinte of Gurracottah.

Madras and Bombay Sappers were employed on this work. The B Company marched back to Saugor, and then towards Jhansi, arriving at Rajiwar on 1st March.

The little fort of Barodia was taken that afternoon, and on 2nd March half the company took possession and put it into a state of repair. Lieutenant Prendergast was in charge of Barodia, and, in addition to the Sappers, had a company of

Khoonds. He posted them as guards during the night, but when he went his rounds he invariably found them asleep, and had to rouse them up.

The General now determined to gain the table-land by a flank movement through the pass of Mudhanpore. At 2 A.M. a force moved for Malthon Pass, while the remainder left at 5 A.M. for Mudhanpore Pass. In forcing the pass a sharp fight took place; the enemy were routed. The Hydrabad Cavalry were sent in pursuit, and succeeded in killing 300 of them.

As soon as the troops had rested they marched again, and halted at Pepeena. Sir Hugh Rose said he had never been under hotter fire in his life, while it lasted.

They were now encamped in sight of the fort of Sorai; the next day the Sappers marched to destroy it.

The force next marched on Murrowna, twelve miles north, and on the 7th the British flag was hoisted on the fort. A proclamation was read, and the Rajah of Shahghur disinherited. Here the force under Major Scudamore, 14th Light Dragoons, rejoined, after having an engagement with the enemy at Malthon Pass.

On the 9th the force marched for Bandipore, and Major Boileau and the Sappers blew down the palace, and fired it.

On the 12th marched towards Tal Behut, where they arrived on the 14th, the Hydrabad contingent having preceded them.

On the 14th and 15th the B Company were engaged in surveying the fort of Tal Behut, which had been evacuated by the enemy a few days previously. The Major-General now became anxious for the 1st Brigade, and despatched Captain Hare, with Hydrabad Cavalry, to communicate with Brigadier-General Stuart.

On the 16th the Madras and Bombay Sappers, with Hydrabad contingent, marched to the left bank of the Betwa, eight miles from camp. The Chief Engineer, Major Boileau, was ordered to make a bridge. The river, however, was found ford-able.

The force crossed the Betwa on the 19th. On the same day the fort of Chandairee was captured by storm by the 1st Brigade, under Brigadier Stuart. Rebels were reported to have escaped north towards Jhansi. The Hydrabad Cavalry were sent in pursuit, and cut up a few.

At midnight on the 19th the force marched to Chuckampore (fifteen miles), eight miles from Jhansi, and on the 20th a strong detachment from the 2nd Brigade advanced by a forced march of twenty-five miles, and placed picquots on all the chief roads round Jhansi.

On the 21st a reconnoissance was made by the General, and Major Boileau, accompanied by cavalry, horse artillery, and light field-guns. Lieutenant Prendergast accompanied the General.

The General did not return till half-past 6.

Tantia Topee was reported to have left Jhansi for the purpose of bringing down a large army from Calpee (chiefly Gwalior Contingent).

On the 22nd Jhansi was invested by the cavalry.

The following extracts from Sir Hugh Rose's despatch will explain the operations which now took place :—

" The great strength of the fort, natural as well as artificial, and its extent, entitled it to a place among fortresses. It stands on an elevated rock rising out of a plain, and commands the city and surrounding country. It is built of excellent and most massive masonry. The fort is difficult to breach because composed of granite. The fort was extensive and elaborate; outworks of the same solid construction, with front and flank-ing embrasures for artillery-fire and loop-holes, of which in some places there were five tiers for musketry. Guns placed on the high towers of the fort commanded the country all round. One tower, called the White Turret, had been raised lately and armed with heavy ordnance. The fortress is surrounded by the city of Jhansi on all sides except the west, and part of the south. The steepness of the rock protects the west, the fortified city wall with bastions springing from the centre of its south face. The mound was fortified by a strong circular bastion for five guns, round part of which was drawn a ditch twelve feet deep and fifteen feet broad, of solid masonry. Quantities of men were always at work in the mound.

"The city of Jhansi is about four miles and a half in circumference, and is surrounded by a fortified and massive wall from six to twelve feet thick, and varying in height from eighteen to thirty feet, with numerous flanking bastions, armed as batteries with ordnance and loop-holes, with a banquette for infantry. Outside the walls, the city is girt with wood except some parts of east and south fronts. On the former is a picturesque lake and water-palace; to the south are the ruined cantonments and residences of the English. Temples with their gardens, one, the Jokun Bagh, the scene of the massacre of our countrymen, and two rocky ridges; the eastmost, called 'Kapoo Tekri,' both important positions facing and threatening the south face of the city wall and fort.

"I established seven flying camps of cavalry as an investing force round Jhansi.

"The attack of Jhansi offered serious difficulties. There were no means of breaching the fort except from the south, but the south was flanked by the fortified city wall and mound just described.

"The rocky ridge was excellent for a breaching battery, except that it was too far off, 640 yards, and that the fire from it would have been oblique. The mound enfiladed two walls of the city, and commanded the whole of the south quarter of it, including the palace.

"It was evident that the capture of the mound was the first most important operation, because its occupation ensured in all probability that of the south of the city, and of the palace, affording also the means of constructing by approaches an advanced breaching battery.

"The desideratum, therefore, was to concentrate a heavy fire on the mound and on the south face of the city, in order to drive the enemy out of them and facilitate their capture; to breach the wall close to the mound, and to dismantle the enemy's defences which protected the mound and opposed an attack.

"This was effected, firstly, by occupying and placing batteries on a rocky knoll (the right attack), which I had found in my reconnoissance, to the south of the lake opposite the Aorcha gate and south-east wall of the town, which took in reverse the mound and two walls running from it. Secondly, on the rocky ridge there was the left attack.

"These batteries could not be completed till the arrival of the 1st Brigade with its siege guns on the 25th.

"By the evening of the 24th, there were four batteries on the right attack.

"In the meantime, the right attack opened fire from an 8-inch howitzer and two 8-inch mortars on the rear of the mound and the south of the city, with the exception of the palace, which I wished to preserve for the use of the troops.

"A remarkable feature in the defence was, that the enemy had no posts outside the city.

"Sir Robert Hamilton estimated the number of the garrison at 10,000 Valaitees and 1,500 sepoys, of whom 400 were cavalry; and the number of guns in city and fort at thirty or forty.

"The fire of the right attack on the first day (28th) cleared the mound of the workmen and the enemy. The mortars shelled and set on fire long rows of hay-ricks in the south of the city, which created a pretty general conflagration in that quarter.

"The enemy had been firing actively from the White Turret,

the Tree Tower battery in the fort, the Wheel Tower, Saugor, and Lutchman's Gate batteries in the town about midday.

" The chief of the rebel artillery was a first-rate artilleryman. He had under him two companies of Golundawze.

" The manner in which the rebels served their guns, repaired their defences, and reopened fire from batteries and guns repeatedly shut up, was remarkable.

" From some batteries they returned shot for shot. The women were seen working in the batteries and carrying ammunition.

" The Garden battery was fought under the black flag of the Fakeers. Everything indicated a general and determined resistance. This was not surprising, as the inhabitants, from the Ranee downwards, were more or less concerned in the murder or plunder of the English.

" To silence the city wall batteries to the south, and cannonade more effectually the town, two 24-pounders were placed in a battery between an 8-inch howitzer and two 8-inch mortars, and opened fire on the 25th.

" On the 25th I caused the rocky ridge left attack to be occupied by a strong picquet with two 5½-inch mortars, which played on the mound and the houses adjoining it.

" The same day, the siege train of 1st Brigade having arrived, batteries were constructed, and opened fire from the 26th to the 29th on the rocky ridge as follows: The left attack—two 18-pounders to dismantle the defences of the fort; two 10-inch mortars to destroy the fort; two 8-inch mortars and one 8-inch howitzer to act on the mound and adjacent wall and city; one 18-pounder to breach the wall near the bastion of the mound.

" In order to prevent delay and confusion, I gave names to all the enemy's batteries in the town as well as in the fort; they were thirteen in number.

" The fire of the two 18-pounders was so efficient, that towards sunset the parapets of the White Turret, the Black Tower, and the Tree Tower, which faced our attack, were nearly destroyed. The 10-inch mortars created great havoc in the fort, and having pointed out to Lieutenant Pittman, Bombay Horse Artillery, the position of a powder magazine, he blew it up at the third shot.

"The breach was practicable on the 30th. The enemy retrenched it with a double row of palisades and earth. I ordered every description of fire, including red-hot shot, to be directed on it, and the result was a considerable portion was destroyed by fire.

"Riflemen were placed in all the batteries as well as in the temples and gardens to east and south sides of the city. The Jokun Bagh, nearly opposite the mound, was occupied by riflemen.

"Two of the enemy's defences which annoyed the left attack the most, were the Wheel Tower on the south, and the Garden battery on a rock in rear of the west wall of the city.

"A new battery, called the 'East,' was established on a ridge to the east of the rocky ridge with two 5½-inch mortars. For these were afterwards substituted two 8-inch mortars, a 9-pounder and a 24-pounder howitzer, to enfilade the wall running east from the mound.

Before the sand-bag battery could be made for the 9-pounder, an Acting Bombardier, Brenner, of Captain Ommaney's company, Royal Artillery, quite a lad, commanded and pointed the 9-pounder in the open, and silenced the enemy's gun in battery in the bastion, destroying besides the defences. I praised him for his good service, on the ground, and promoted him.

"The two 8-inch mortars, and occasionally the two 10-inch mortars of left attack, answered the Garden battery, shelling also the rear Bustee and five wells, where the sepoys had taken up their quarters on account of the good water.

"The obstinate defence of the enemy, the breach, and the extent fired on, had caused a great consumption of ammuni-

II.   22

tion, so much so, that it was evident there would not be sufficient to multiply breaches in the town wall, or to establish a main breach in the south double wall of the fort. Under these circumstances the officers commanding the Artillery and Engineers called to my notice the necessity of having recourse to escalade, to which I gave my consent, requiring, however, that the breach should form an important and principal point of attack.

"I had made arrangements on the 30th for storming, but the general action on the 1st April with the so-called Army of the Peishwa, which advanced across the Betwa to relieve it, caused the assault to be deferred.

"With the view of acquiring rapid information, I established a telegraph on a hill commanding Jhansi and the surrounding country. It was of great use, telegraphing the Ranee's flight, and the approach of the enemy from the Betwa, &c. The Sappers on Telegraph Hill discovered the near approach of Tantia Topee on evening of 31st March.

"The 1st Brigade was moved along the Calpee road to right flank of the enemy. Two 24-pounders were placed on the Oorcha road near the hill. 2nd Brigade remained under arms, and the picquets were strengthened. The force available for the battle was only 1,200, of whom 500 men were British infantry.

"The enemy reconnoitred, and, deceived by the removal of the 1st Brigade, took up a position in front of our camp. Between 4 and 5 A.M. our picquets retired, and then commenced the roaring of heavy guns and field artillery. The infantry were ordered to lie down, while the Horse Artillery fired over on left flank of the enemy. The General and Captain Prettejohn charged their right and left, and turned their position. The infantry dashed forward and put them to flight, while the cavalry and mounted officers charged through and through them.

"Second-Lieutenant Prendergast, acting as A.D.C. to the General, charged, with Captain Need's troop of 14th Light Dragoons, the mutineers' infantry and artillery posted behind works. The charge was equal to breaking a square, and the result was most successful, because the charge turned the enemy's position and decided in a great measure the fate of the day.

"The 1st Brigade had moved round the hill on the Maidan on enemy's right, encountered the enemy, and drove them before them, and the 86th, 25th N. I., and cavalry pursued.

"Their front line broken, right flank turned, and our troops moving on second line, induced Tantia Topee to retreat to the Betwa. It now became a cavalry and horse-artillery affair. While Tantia Topee crossed the river he used his guns well.

"A thousand of the enemy were killed, and we captured all their guns—one 18-pounder, two 9-pounders, and thirteen native pieces, and a brass mortar."

Sir Hugh Rose mentions Lieutenant Fox's (Madras Sappers and Miners) gallant conduct. In the course of the action Lieutenant Fox killed eight men with his own hand, and amongst the officers whom circumstances called prominently into action, and who, profiting by the opportunity, did valuable service, was Lieutenant Prendergast, M.E., "who on various occasions, under my eye, has distinguished himself by his merit and gallantry, as devoted as they were unostentatious." Despatch was dated 30th April 1858, G.O.C.C. 622 of 1859.

Lieutenant Prendergast was severely wounded on this occasion, having received several sabre-cuts on his left arm, and the thumb of his left hand was almost severed.

On 2nd April orders were given to storm on morning of the 3rd. The breach was stormed by the left attack, while the right attack escaladed. A feint was made on the west face. About 3 a.m. the storming parties advanced. Right attack (escalading party)—Madras and Bombay Sappers, 3rd Europeans, and Hydrabad Infantry. Left attack—Royal Engineers, 86th and 25th N. I.

The moon was very bright, and the escalading party had to march 200 yards through a heavy fire. The Sappers planted

22 *

the ladders in three places. Three of the ladders broke. Lieutenants Dick, Meiklejohn, and Bonus, of the Bombay Engineers,
led the way. Lieutenant Dick was bayoneted and shot dead,
Lieutenant Bonus was hurled down, Lieutenant Meiklejohn was
cut to pieces, and Lieutenant Fox, Madras Sappers, was shot
through the neck; but the British pushed on, and gained a
footing from eight ladders.

The left attack carried the breach. Street-fighting took place
in every quarter, from wall to palace. A body of the enemy
were in some stables, when the 86th and 3rd Europeans rushed
in and slew fifty; but in the *melée* twelve Europeans were cut
down. Here was found the British flag (it had been presented
to the grandfather of the Ranee by the British Government for
faithful service), which was hoisted on the top of the palace.

Street-fighting still went on; the rebels fought like tigers,
and the bayoneting went on till sunset.

The next day there was also a good deal of street-fighting.

On the 5th, Lieutenant Baigree, 3rd Europeans, went to Fort
Gate, found it open, went on from gate to gate, and found
himself in possession of the Fort of Jhansi. The Ranee had
fled in the night. Our cavalry went in pursuit, and cut up 200.
Street-fighting still continued.

On the 6th the last desperate body was disposed of in the
Lal Bagh. After four days' hard fighting, Jhansi was ours.

Havildar Chendrigherryan was the handsomest man and the
smartest havildar in the B Company. He was killed during
the street-fighting which had been so fiercely carried on after
the breach at Jhansi had been carried. He was in command of
a party of Sappers, who assisted Captain Simpson of the 23rd
Bo. N. I. (doing duty with the Artillery), to dislodge a body of
the enemy from a strong building of which they had possession.
The Sappers were on the arched roof, through which they
"jumped" holes, with the object of dropping live shell among
the enemy. While he was on the roof, one of the rebels fired up

through the hole in the roof and killed the havildar on the spot. Captain Simpson was dangerously wounded in the same way.

Killed and wounded, upwards of 300 ; of the enemy some 3,000 must have been killed. Forty guns were found in the fort.

The father of the Ranee, and the Jhansi paymaster were captured by a zemindar twelve miles to the west, and brought in on the 18th. Both were hanged next day, near the nullah where the massacre had taken place.

Sir Hugh Rose, in his despatch, says: "It will be a gratification to the relatives of Lieutenants Meiklejohn and Dick of the Bombay Engineers, to know that these two young men had gained my esteem by the intelligence and coolness which they evinced as Engineer officers during the siege. I should have recommended both for promotion, if they had not died in their country's cause, for conspicuous gallantry in leading the way up two scaling ladders."

The Sappers' mess before the battle of the Betwa had eight members ; it was now reduced to two.

Lieutenant Prendergast wounded in cavalry charge on 1st April.

Lieutenant Fox wounded in storm, by bullet in neck.

Lieutenants Meiklejohn and Dick killed.

Lieutenant Bonus wounded, and Captain Brown sick.

Lieutenants Goodfellow and Gordon escaped unhurt.

Jhansi was garrisoned, and on 22nd April Major Gall, 14th Light Dragoons, moved out to reconnoitre.

1st Brigade started for Calpee at midnight on the 25th. 2nd Brigade to follow.

On the 29th they moved on Sunrie ; country flat, wells almost dry. Arrived at Pooneh on 2nd May. Major Gall went on to a fort a few miles off, surrounded it, blew open the gate, and every man in the fort was slain. The rebels were now collected at Koonch, fourteen miles in front ; the Ranee of Jhansi, the Rajah of Rampore, the Nawab of Banda, the Rao Sahib, and Tantia Topee were with them. The 2nd Brigade joined on 5th May.

The 1st Brigade camped ten miles from Koonch, while the 2nd took route to south of it. Hydrabad Contingent to east. The General and 1st Brigade to the west. Enemy were found at Koonch. They opened a battery, which was answered by our guns. In less than an hour Koonch was in our hands. Cavalry and Horse Artillery pursued, and cut them up. Many officers and men were prostrated by the sun. The General fell three times, but struggled till victory was won. We captured eight guns, ammunition, and grain. Enemy numbered 20,000, of which 7,000 were cavalry.

On 9th May we camped at Hurdooi. The Sappers destroyed the defences of the fort. The General moved off with the column, leaving the company of Sappers to complete demolition.

On the 11th the Sappers started to rejoin the General. On arrival at Oorai, they found that the force had marched towards Calpee. The Sappers marched on at once, and reached the Brigade at 2 P.M., having marched twenty miles. The weather was now most frightfully hot, and liquor of all sorts was most scarce. Eighteen, twenty, and twenty-six rupees a dozen was given for beer.

Brigadier Stuart reported sick after Koonch, and the command devolved on Lieutenant-Colonel Campbell, of the 71st.

From the Nerbudda to the Jumna, the enemy had no longer any place if they lost Calpee. The Ranee of Jhansi and Tantia Topee were both there. Colonel Maxwell was to the north of the Jumna.

On the 15th the force gained Golowlee, six miles from Calpee to the east, and pitched camp along the bank of the Jumna. The enemy expected we should have marched direct on Calpee, and among the tombs had posted large batteries, and large bodies of infantry and cavalry; but we left the road, marched on their left flank, with ravines between us. After our arrival, the enemy's cavalry came down on the baggage, but were repulsed with loss.

The 2nd Brigade with Major Orr's force, had an encounter with the enemy on the 10th. It was a hard fight, but, as usual, the enemy were discomfited. Between our camp and Calpee there was an extraordinary labyrinth of ravines, over which cavalry and artillery could not go. They afforded good cover for the enemy's infantry. To the south of Calpee were great numbers of huge tombs, capable of affording shelter to large bodies of troops.

On the 17th the 2nd Brigade was attacked, and the attack did not cease till 8 P.M.; they then joined the 1st Brigade.

On the 20th the enemy made another attack from the ravines. The same evening two companies of the 86th, the Camel Corps, and 120 Sikhs, crossed the river from Colonel Maxwell. For the last two days the town was shelled by a mortar battery.

On the 21st, batteries from Colonel Maxwell's camp opened upon the fort and town.

Between 8 and 9 A.M. on the 22nd, large bodies of the enemy advanced from the Calpee road, and our picquets retired.

On our right we had the 86th, 3rd Europeans, and four companies of the 25th Bo. N. I., half a field battery, a troop of the 14th Dragoons, and one of the 3rd Light Cavalry. On right of centre, half a field battery, Royal Engineers, and some of the 25th N. I. In centre, siege guns, howitzers, and rockets, with Madras Sappers under Lieutenant Gordon; wing of 71st, some 3rd Europeans, squadron of the 14th Light Dragoons, one of the 3rd Light Cavalry, and Royal Artillery guns. To left of centre, Horse Artillery, and two troops of the 14th Light Dragoons; beyond these Camel Corps, field battery, and Sikhs. Extreme left, Hydrabad Contingent.

Enemy extended to our extreme left. Our shot and shell began to tell after a time, and the enemy limbered up, and began to retreat.

A dense mass of cavalry and a field battery tried to get on our left flank. Hydrabad Contingent was too quick for them, and turned them. After two hours' pounding, the General advanced with Horse Artillery, field battery, and cavalry, when the rebels fled, and our guns and cavalry routed them; volleys of musketry going on all along the ravines.

On the right, their infantry advanced close to our field-guns and mortars. H.M.'s 86th and 25th Light Infantry fought bravely, they were reinforced by Camel Corps, who trotted round, dismounted, and charged with the General at their head, with the 86th and 25th N. I., and 3rd Europeans. Our whole line now dashed forward, and the enemy fled. The 25th extended to Tehree and carried everything before them, driving the enemy into the village, through it, and over the plain towards the road. The enemy's infantry was completely broken up, and flying towards Calpee and Jaloun.

On our right, Colonel Smith, with part of the 86th and Camel Corps, cut up a body ten times their number and killed them in the ravines, or drove them into the river. Colonel Maxwell, all this time, was pouring shell into the town and fort. Thus ended a hard days' work, with a glorious victory over ten times our number.

On the morning of the 23rd the 1st Brigade moved on Calpee through ravines, and along the Jumna, and the 2nd, under Sir Hugh Rose, to the left, along the Calpee road.

Tehree was set on fire by Colonel Maxwell's shells. A halt was made in front of the town for an hour.

The General's force then came up. Advance was sounded, and we entered the town without resistance.

Enemy was pursued by Colonel Gall with cavalry and Horse Artillery, and Hydrabad Contingent under Captain Abbott, for many miles. All their guns were captured, with camels, elephants, and horses. A great number of the enemy were cut up.

We remained in town till 5 P.M., and then camped among the tombs. The baggage had great difficulty in reaching camp.

A flying column, under Lieutenant-Colonel Robertson, left camp to follow up the rebels, who were reported to have gone to Jaloun, intending to make for Sheerghaut, and to cross the Jumna into Oude. Enormous quantities of sugar, corn, and oil were found, and an astonishing amount of ammunition and military stores. In the arsenal was 60,000 lbs. of powder, and large heaps of shot and shell.

Sir Hugh Rose described the enemy's tactics of "unceasingly harassing his troops, and forcing them into the sun; large bodies of cavalry hanging on his positions, retiring when attacked, but ready to fall on escorts sent to a distance for forage, the want of which was the cause of serious losses. Out of thirty-six men of the 14th Light Dragoons forming part of one forage escort, seventeen were brought to camp on doolies, after two hours' exposure to the sun. A similar amount of sun-sickness had prostrated the 25th Bo. N. I. on the march to Muttra. The prostration of the whole force had become a matter of arithmetical calculation. So many hours' sun laid low so many men. The thermometer stood at 118° in the shade. A great proportion of officers and men were ill. The force, for months, had been making the strongest physical exertions, with broken sleep, or no sleep at all; watching the camp half the night, and marching the other half to avoid the sun; often all day without a rest, fighting, or on the rear-guard, or reconnoissance escorts under a burning sun. On the march from the west to the centre of India, country tracks and unbridged nullahs, with very few exceptions, were the communications. The consequence of this was, that one deep nullah often detained troops, baggage, guns, and rear-guard, for hours in the sun, while the Sappers were making it passable. Bad roads, and an unorganised system of transport and supply, were the causes why the rations were at times in arrears; and the troops on those occasions performed hard duties, or fought all day on insufficient nourishment. The Sappers were constantly employed in making roads passable throughout the march, and occasionally hauling heavy guns through difficulties."

The following order of Sir Hugh Rose is of great interest :—

" The Central India Field Force being about to be abolished, the Major-General cannot allow the troops to leave his immediate command without expressing to them the gratification he has invariably experienced at their good conduct and discipline, and he requests that the following general order may be read at the head of every corps and detachment of the force :—

" ' Soldiers ! you have marched more than 1,000 miles, and taken more than 100 guns ; you have forced your way through mountains, passes, and intricate jungles, and over rivers ; you have captured the strongest fort, and beaten the enemy, no matter what the odds, wherever you met him ; you have restored extensive districts to the Government, and peace and order now reign where before, for twelve months, were tyranny and rebellion ; you have done all this, and never had a check. I thank you with all sincerity for your bravery, your devotion, and your discipline. When you first marched I told you that you, as British soldiers, had more than enough of courage for the work which was before you ; but that courage without discipline was of no avail, and I exhorted you to let discipline be your watchword. You have attended to my orders. In hardships, in temptations, and in dangers you have obeyed your General, and you never left your ranks. You have fought against the strong, and you have protected the rights of the weak and defenceless, of foes as well as of friends. I have seen you in the ardour of the combat preserve and place children out of harm's way. This is the discipline of Christian soldiers, and this it is which has brought you triumphant from the shores of Western India to the waters of the Jumna, and establishes without doubt that you will find no place to equal the glory of your arms."

In his report regarding Jhansi, Sir Hugh Rose says:—

"'They had to contend against an enemy more than double their numbers, behind fortifications, who defended themselves afterwards in suburbs and very difficult ground outside the walls."

" The nature of the defence and strictness of the investment gave rise to continued and fierce combats ; for the rebels, having no hope, fought to sell their lives as dearly as they could.   But the discipline and gallant spirit of the troops enabled them to overcome difficulties and opposition of every sort, to take the fortified city of Jhansi by storm, subduing the strongest fortress in Central India, and killing 5,000 of its rebel garrison.   I beg leave to state the obligation I am under to Captain Brown, commanding company Madras Sappers."

Major Boileau, commanding Engineers, Lieutenant Fox, Madras Sappers, were also mentioned.

The rebels now marched on Gwallior, defeated Scindiah, captured his fort, guns, and treasure, and compelled him to fly to Agra.

It now became necessary for Sir Hugh Rose's force again to take the field.

On the 6th June the B Company marched with a detachment, consisting of battery of Horse Artillery and two squadrons of cavalry, towards Gwallior.

After a rapid march the General and his forces sat down before Gwallior on the 16th.   The thermometer stood at 130° in the shade.   The General determined to give battle at once, opened fire, and advanced.   The enemy were driven from cantonments at Morar with great loss.   The B Company*, reduced to forty-five men, took part in this action.   They were commanded by Lieutenant Gordon, who was mentioned in Brigadier Napier's despatch as having kept pace with the 71st Regiment, and joined in the attack on the ravines.

* Strength of B Company : one European officer, two native officers, forty-two N.C.O. and rank and file.

Sir Hugh Rose, after the capture of Morar,* made a reconnoissance of Gwallior, and came to the conclusion that if he
attacked it from Morar he would have to cross the plain between
Morar and Gwallior under the fire of the fort, and of masked
and formidable batteries established in strong houses and gardens
on the banks of the old canal, and a dry river in front of the
Phool Bagh Palace. Consequently, he moved with his force to
Kota-ke-Serai, about twenty miles, to effect a junction with
Brigadier-General Smith, who had been directed to march with
the Rajpootana Field Force from Segoree to Kota-ke-Serai,
seven miles to east of Gwallior.

A force was left in Morar, under Brigadier-General Napier, for
its protection, during the investment of Gwallior, and pursuit of
enemy when they retreated.

The march to Kota-ke-Serai was very harassing. One hundred men of the 86th were compelled to fall out by sun-sickness.
The column bivouacked on the left bank of the river Morar.
Meantime, Brigadier Smith, finding that the enemy occupied a
hill opposite Kota-ke-Serai, and were pressing on him, advanced,
and, following the road to Gwallior by the ford across the river,
had attacked and driven the enemy from the hills on his right
front, and occupied the road which led through a pass, two miles
long, through the hills, and to the left or south side of a very
deep and dry old canal, cut out of the rock, which led from the
ford close by the left of the road through the pass to the fort of
Gwallior. To the left of the road and canal in the pass, rose
from a narrow plain a succession of slopes, intersected by

* At the fight at Morar three sections of the B Company advanced in line with
four companies of H.M.'s 71st Regiment, when they came, unawares, upon a
nullah in which were concealed a number of the enemy; a hard fight ensued,
during which Naique Narrainsawmy saw a soldier of the 71st about to be killed
by three of the enemy. He fired at one of them, and wounded him, but as he still
continued to advance, he attacked and killed him with his bayonet. The other
two, on seeing him killed, ran away; and the Naique, by his great gallantry,
saved the life of the British soldier. The Naique was admitted to the 3rd Class
of the Order of Merit.

ravines. A ridge ran along the top of the slopes, on which the enemy had placed a battery of 9-pounders, and a numerous force of all arms was on the ridge, as well as a large body of cavalry in rear of it, about a mile and a half further back ; and about the same distance from the left of the road was stationed, in a gorge of the hills, a large body of infantry with guns. They guarded a road which branched off from the ford southwards through the hills to Gwallior.

It was clear that the enemy must be driven from both these positions. The impediment to this was the deep canal, impracticable for cavalry and infantry. To remove it, Sir Hugh Rose directed the company of Madras Sappers and Miners to make a bridge some way to the left rear of our position across the canal. The bridge, or dam, was to be ready by sunset. The General had arranged to cross during the night, get in southwards to Gwallior, place himself between Gwallior and the enemy's two positions, fall on them before daybreak to attack their front, and turn their left flank.

He now received an express from Sir Robert Hamilton that the enemy had agreed to attack him this day. The company of Madras Sappers and Miners, whose zeal and intelligence no hardships could abate, would have completed the bridge across the canal by sunset, and Sir Hugh Rose anticipated the best results from availing himself of it for the purpose of cutting off, during the night, the enemy's numerous force of all arms on the hills. It was, however, necessary to free the position in the narrow pass from the risk of a serious attack. Brigadier Stuart was ordered, with 86th, who were encamped between the pass and the river Morar, to move from the left rear, supported by 25th Bo. N. I., across the canal, ascend the heights, and attack the enemy on their left flank. Brigadier Smith, at the same time, was to move with the 95th from left of the right flank across the canal in skirmishing order, over the shoulder of the hill on which was the battery, against the enemy's left flank. This oblique movement, and the lay of the ground, prevented the 95th suffering seriously from the battery.

The 10th N. I. was to move up from the right of right front, across the canal, to support the 95th and to cover the right. The 3rd troop of Bo. H. A. was ordered up to the entrance of pass towards Gwallior, as well as a squadron of the 8th Hussars. The rest of the force was disposed of in support of attacking columns, and for the defence of the camp from the rear.

Brigadier Stuart, crossing the canal, ascended the heights; the enemy taken in flank, retired rapidly from the attack of our left flank towards the battery. The skirmishers pressed the rebel infantry so hard that they did not make a stand even under their guns, but retreated across the entrenchment. The skirmishers gave them no time to rally, but dashed at the parapet, crossed it, and took the guns (three 9-pounders) which defended the ridge. The 86th passed on after the enemy's cavalry and infantry, who fled, part to Gwallior, and part to the hills to the south.

Lieutenant-Colonel Raines now came up with the 95th, and turned the captured guns on the enemy's cavalry and infantry. The 10th Bo. N. I. moved on in support of the 95th, and, finding themselves exposed to a fire of artillery and infantry from the heights on enemy's extreme left, cleared the two nearest heights, and, charging gallantly, took two brass field-guns and three mortars, which were in a plain at the foot of the second height.

The troops were now in possession of the highest range of heights to the east of Gwallior.

To our right was now the handsome Palace of the Phool Bagh, with its gardens, and the old city surrounded by the fort, with a line of extensive fortifications round the high and precipitous rock of Gwallior. To the left lay the "Lushkar," or new city, with its spacious houses half hidden by trees. The slopes descended gradually towards Gwallior, the lowest one commanding the grand parade of the Lushkar which was almost out of fire of the fort.

Sir Hugh Rose now determined to make a general advance against all the positions which the enemy occupied for the defence of Gwallior, extending from beyond the Phool Bagh Palace on the right of the grand parade of the Lushkar, and then take the Lushkar by assault. The movement was completely successful.

The 1st Bo. Lancers charged into the Grand Parade, and pursued the enemy's infantry into the Lushkar. The 95th also charged down into the Grand Parade, and took two 18-pounders and two small mortars.

Sir Hugh Rose then advanced through the Lushkar, the enemy's cavalry and infantry retreating before him, and before sunset the whole of the Lushkar was in our possession. It was reported that the enemy had evacuated the old town and fort; orders were given to occupy it immediately.

Brigadier Smith captured the Phool Bagh, killing numbers of the enemy. He then pursued a large body of the enemy who were retiring round the rock of Gwallior towards the Residency (several miles to the north of the rock), covering their retreat with horse-artillery guns. After a short resistance, Brigadier Smith captured the guns, and killed numbers of the retreating army. He continued the pursuit of those escaping towards the Residency till long after night, and until his men and horses were unable to move on. On this occasion he captured more guns.

It was found that the enemy had not evacuated the fort. The fort was invested, as closely as possible, from the old city and the Lushkar, and by the officer commanding cavalry at Phool Bagh.

The next morning the enemy again fired from the fort. Lieutenant Rose (25th Bo. N. I.), Lieutenant Waller, and a party of the 25th, with some of Scindiah's police, burst open the main gateway of the fort, and surprising the other gates before the garrison, a party of fanatical Mussulmans, could shut them, reached an archway on which the rebels brought a gun to bear. Lieutenant Rose and his party got through the archway, and then engaged in a desperate hand-to-hand conflict with the rebels, who defended the narrow street leading into the fort. But the determined gallantry of Lieutenant Rose and the men of the 25th, aided by Lieutenant Waller, who climbed, with a few of his men, on the roof of a house and shot the gunner, carried all before them. They took the fort, and killed every man in it; but the gallant leader, Lieutenant Rose, fell mortally wounded, after taking Gwallior by force of arms.*

Abandoning the defence of Gwallior, whilst the troops were still fighting, Tantia Topee, with a considerable body of cavalry and infantry, attempted to retreat southwards, by the road to Punniar and Goornah; but learning that Punniar was occupied by Major Orr, he went to the Residency. The Residency was to have been occupied by Colonel Riddell; but that officer, owing to the difficulty of crossing the ford of the Chumbul at Dholpore, was unable to effect this.

Brigadier Napier pursued the enemy in the most able manner, and effected the capture of twenty-five pieces of artillery, and the total dispersion of the enemy.

Sir Hugh Rose wrote to Sir Robert Hamilton suggesting the immediate return of Scindiah, and the next morning Scindiah arrived, was received with every mark of respect, and was escorted by Sir Hugh Rose, and all his principal officers who were able to be present, to the Palace of the Lushkar, with a squadron of the 8th Hussars and another of the 14th Light Dragoons. Scindiah was greeted by the inhabitants with enthusiastic acclamations.

* Lieutenant Rose was a brother of Major Rose, the present representative of the ancient family of the Roses of Kilravock-Nairn. Lieutenant Waller received the V.C. for his gallantry, and Lieutenant Rose would also have obtained it had he survived the capture.

He wished to present the army with six months' batta; but this was not considered desirable, and he then expressed a wish to give a medal for "Gwallior."

Sir Hugh Rose recommended that this second request might be complied with, and offered to give up his claim to the decoration if it would facilitate the army obtaining it.

Sir Hugh Rose thus closes his despatch :—

"But as the Commander of the forces engaged, it is my duty to say that, although a most arduous campaign had impaired the health and strength of every man of my force, their discipline, devotion, and courage remained unvarying and unshaken, enabling them to make a very rapid march in summer heat to Gwallior, and fight and gain two actions on the road—one at Morar cantonments, the other at Kota-ke-Serai—arrive at their posts, from great distances, before Gwallior before the day appointed, 19th June, and on that same day carry by assault all the enemy's positions on strong heights and in most difficult ground, taking one battery after another, twenty-seven pieces of artillery in the action, and twenty-five in the pursuit, besides the guns in the fort, the old city, the new city, and, finally, the Rock of Gwallior—held to be one of the most important and strongest fortresses in India.

"I marched on 8th of June from Calpee, and on 19th of the same month the Gwallior States were restored to their Prince."

The B Company marched from Gwallior a few days later, and with the exception of one affair on the banks of the Jumna, when, under command of Lieutenant Gordon, it routed a detachment of the enemy, it had no more opportunity of distinguishing itself in the Central Indian campaign.

The company took the field with six European officers, two native officers, four havildars, eight naiques, and 105 privates and artificers ; and it returned to Madras forty-one strong of all ranks, commanded by the junior subaltern, Lieutenant Gordon.

II.   23

The officers of Madras Engineers and Sappers who were rewarded were—

Major Boileau, Brevet of Lieutenant-Colonel and Colonel.

Captain Brown, Madras Fusiliers, Brevet of Major.

Lieutenant H. N. D. Prendergast, M.E., Brevet of Major, and Victoria Cross.

Assistant Surgeon T. Lowe, Brevet Surgeon.

Subadar Seloway, " Bahadoor."

Jemadar Ali Khan, " Sirdar Bahadoor."

The following native officers, N.C.O., and privates, of the Sappers, were admitted to third class of the " Order of Merit " for conspicuous gallantry at Ratghur and Morar :—

Subadar Seloway.

Jemadar Appavoo.

Naique Narrainsawmy.

Lance Naique Pichamootoo.

Privates Savathean.

„ Appasawmy.

„ Chinnatumby.

The following extract of a letter from Sir Hugh Rose will show how highly he appreciated the services of the Company :—

" I have already praised the excellent conduct of the B Company, Madras Sappers and Miners, which formed part of my force ; but I now beg leave to request most respectfully His Lordship, the Commander-in-Chief in India, to have the goodness to convey to H.E. the Commander-in-Chief of the Madras Army, the high sense which I entertained of the excellent service which they performed under my orders. They lived on the very best terms with their English comrades ; no work was too dangerous or too difficult for the gallantry and devotion of this Company, which has been twenty months on foreign service.

" On account of the great length of hard service which the company had gone through, it was to return to Madras from Calpee, but on Gwallior falling into the hands of the rebels, the company again took the field with the utmost alacrity, and again earned not only my sincere approbation, but that also of the Central India Field Force, by its unvarying gallantry and zeal.

" Captain Brown deserves to be specially mentioned for having led this distinguished company at the escalade of Jhansi, and for having commanded it from 5th July 1857 (when its commander was appointed to the Staff) till the close of the operations against Jhansi, when he fell sick. Lieutenant Gordon then took the command of the company, and I beg to mention him specially for the satisfactory manner in which he performed his duty. The Subadar (Seloway) of the company has a full right to be mentioned for his admirable conduct throughout the campaign."

In accordance with the recommendation of the Commander-in-Chief—

Lieutenant H. N. D. Prendergast was allowed to count as service for retiring pension fifteen months' sick leave, which was necessary for the recovery of his health, and Lieutenant T. R. Fox, Madras Sappers, was similarly allowed to count eighteen months.

The Madras troops of the Saugor Field Division,* having assembled at Jubbulpore, advanced northwards early in 1858.

Their task was to afford assistance that might be required to the Bombay Division advancing on its left, as well as to prevent the rebel troops from breaking southwards out of the Saugor and Nerbudda territories.

At the date of leaving Jubbulpore, it was uncertain whether the Rajah of Rewah, who was wavering in his policy, might not throw in his lot with the revolted troops and chiefs of Central India, and so increase the number of the enemy in this locality.

The division, to which was attached a very large siege train

---

* Wing 12th Lancers, Colonel Oakes; 1st Regiment Hydrabad Cavalry, Macintire; A Troop, M.H.A., Mein; F Troop. H.A., Brice; 14th Battery, R.A., Palmer; Horse Battery, M.A., Gosling; 43rd Regiment, Primrose; 3rd M. E. Regiment, Apthorp; 50th M. N. I., Reece; 1st M. N. I., Gotheux; and L Company of Madras Sappers, Lieut. Campbell, 7th N. I., and Lieut. Eager, 52nd N.I.

and park of Engineers, accordingly marched, for the reasons given, in the first instance, along the grand trunk road in the Rewah direction. Matters in that territory having, however, taken a more favourable turn, General Whitlock changed his line of march westwards at Jokehi. Up to this place the progress of the division having been along a metalled road, not much difficulty had occurred with the line of carts of artillery and engineer material, which stretched to a length of some ten miles.

With the exception of a few bridges and culverts, which had been destroyed by wandering bands of rebel troops, and which were speedily made passable by the Sappers under the direction of the Engineer officers of the force, there was no obstacle to the progress of the Madras troops.

At Jokehi, however, the division entered upon a cross country track, where the services of the Engineers and Sappers were frequently required, in making approaches to streams and in improving the road as far as possible.

Arriving at Dumoh, the column halted for news of the Bombay force under Sir Hugh Rose, who had then just reached Saugor (early in February).

After a personal consultation with Sir Hugh Rose, General Whitlock gave orders for the complete demolition of Garrakotah, situated about half-way between Saugor and Dumoh.

Lieutenant Howes and Wood, M.E., were told off for this duty, and had prepared their park of material, but the demolition was countermanded, and the Madras force somewhat suddenly started in a north-easterly direction to Purnah.

The object of this move was to contain the stragglers of the enemy, who, escaping from the defeats suffered at the hands of Sir Hugh Rose during his rapid advance from Saugor, might endeavour to double southwards into the Nagpore and Jubbulpore countries.

From Purnah the Saugor Field Division turned north-west to Chickharee, thus zigzagging through the eastern Bundelcund

States, and over-awing by its presence the petty chiefs as well
as the more powerful Rajah of Rewah, whose territory, lying
between Mirzapore and Jubbulpore, might have been used by
the rebels to intercept British communications.

While, therefore, the Bombay Army was reaping a glorious
harvest of laurels in their gallant advance northwards, the
Madras Division was employed in producing a "moral effect,"
by marching through districts whose loyalty was doubtful. It
was, besides, held in reserve to afford that aid to Sir Hugh Rose,
which (as events proved) was never at any moment needed.

At the same time, their position on the flank of the Bombay
force compelled the northward retreat of the fugitives flying from
Sir Hugh Rose's master-strokes. In that direction they would
eventually be offered a warm reception by the British force on
the Jumna.

The history of the Saugor Field Division during the early
part of 1858, would suffice to show that the Madrasees were
no ordinary troops, if, as Marshal Saxe averred, "the secret of
the art of war lies in the legs." In addition to the perpetual
marching and countermarching to which they were subjected,
it must be remembered that the troops of the Saugor Field
Division underwent the severest labour, owing to the quantity
of military matériel with which they were burdened, the care of
which entailed extraordinary exposures and pains on all branches
of the force.

Getting under arms at midnight, it was the usual thing that
the rear-guard did not enter camp till after the following mid-day.

At Chickharee the dull prospect of mere usefulness to which
they had been condemned seemed to brighten for the Saugor Field
Division. Sir Hugh Rose had won the battle of the Betwa,
and the fall of Jhansi took place soon afterwards. Events
seemed, therefore, preparing for the final sweeping of the rebels
northwards, and the Madras troops were directed in a north-east
direction on Banda, their line of march being north-eastward,

and parallel to the route followed by Sir Hugh Rose from Jhansi to Calpee.

On the outset of this last advance, General Whitlock made a short detour, and destroyed Jheejhun, the ancestral village of Dess Putt, a petty Bundelcund chief, who had for some time previous been outlawed, and for whose marauding talents the outbreak of the Bengal Mutiny with its subsequent chaos of lawlessness had created a fitting stage. While on his rapid advance to Jheejhun, with a battery of Horse Artillery and two squadrons of Lancers, the General and Staff of the Madras Force encountered Dess Putt quite unexpectedly.*

* Lieutenant Wood was riding, as orderly officer, with General Whitlock at Jheejhun, while the village was being shelled by the A Troop of the old Madras Horse Artillery. Round the foot of the hill on which Jheejhun was situated was a belt of thorny jungle, from which the Bundoola matchlock-men were keeping up a sharp fire upon our party. The General moved off, just outside the skirt of this jungle to the left, in order to reach a better spot from whence the effect of the shells on the village might be observed, and Lieutenant Wood and a Lancer orderly (of 12th Lancers) followed him. Passing along the edge of the jungle at a foot's pace, Lieutenant Wood noticed that a matchlock-man was making particularly good practice, and that shot after shot whistled nearer and nearer. Just then General Whitlock halted to use his field-glass, and Wood took the opportunity of turning to the Lancer orderly, and said, "You had better go and polish that fellow off, or else he will soon be hitting one of us"; so the orderly trotted off gaily on his errand, and disappeared behind a thick patch of the jungle from whence the matchlock-man was firing.

The General continued watching with his glass the effect of the fire of the battery on Jheejhun, and Wood began to get rather uneasy as the Lancer orderly showed no signs of re-appearance, so he stole off gently after him, and having turned the corner of the thorny patch of jungle where he saw him disappear, the following scene was presented to his eyes. The Lancer had speared the Bundeola through the body, and the mortally wounded man was hanging on with both hands to the staff of the lance. Embarrassed by this, as well as by the thick thorny surrounding bushes and the boulders of rock which strowed the place, the Lancer could not get sufficient space to turn his horse and gallop away. Consequently, he was induced to keep tugging away at his lance, in order to free himself from his dying victim. He had, apparently, been engaged for some few minutes in this employment, and had lost his temper at the Bundeola's tenacity of grip; for, just as Wood came up, he dropped the lance with his right hand, leaving it suspended to his arm by the sling. Doubling his fist, he leant over the dying man, and shook it energetically in his face, with the words, "G——d d——n your eyes, if you don't let that there go I'll get off my horse and punch your b——y head!"

The Bundeela chief escaped by a mere accident, for his knowledge of the paths through the surrounding jungle alone enabled
him to avoid the different officers who spurred in hot haste after
Dess Putt, when made aware of his identity from the sudden
exclamation of their guide. Jheejhun was then shelled, and set
on fire by the artillery; while the cavalry cut up some Bundeela skirmishers who attempted to oppose the proceeding. The
whole of the Engineer officers were present, and Lieutenant
Wood attended General Whitlock as orderly officer throughout
the day.

A day or two subsequently brought the advance-guard of the
Saugor Field Division into collision with a reconnoitring party
posted at Kubrai, in advance of the rebel forces, which were
collected at Banda under the Nawab of that place. Some guns
posted behind a ridge of rocks, at a point where the road passed
between two low hills, somewhat unexpectedly opened fire at
daybreak on the Deputy Quartermaster-General and a group of
officers who were with him, in advance of the column of march.
The halt thus caused did not, however, last for any long time,
as the speedy arrival of a battery of Horse Artillery, which
opened with shrapnel on the rebels, soon cleared the way for
the advance of the cavalry attached to the Madras Division.

Owing, however, to the entire ignorance of the Staff officers
of the locality, the rebel detachment effected its retreat without
having suffered much loss in this enterprising attempt to check
the British advance.

Two days afterwards, the Saugor Field Division was engaged
in the first of the two general actions that fortune somewhat
unkindly thought to be a sufficient recompense for troops which
had undergone many months of severe and laborious, though
still inglorious, work. On this occasion, the infantry of the
force had a share of those warlike duties of the campaign which
had hitherto been monopolised by their more fortunate brothers
of the cavalry and artillery, while the Madras Sappers were also

engaged in company with the line. At Banda, as elsewhere, previously and hereafter in the history of the Saugor Field Division, the officers of Engineers were employed as orderlies on the staff of the Major-General. In fact, the utter lack of any professional duties which they might fulfil was of so much advantage to them during the campaign that it allowed of their usually being with advanced guards, and seeing all that there was to be seen of the actual fighting that fell to the lot of the Madras Force.

After the occupation of Banda, however, their more strictly professional labours commenced in earnest. Quarters were prepared for the troops, and fortified positions were constructed. The stone fort on the left bank of the river Cane, on which Banda was situated, was blown up, under the immediate direction of Lieutenant Howes, while all buildings of the town situated within short musket-shot of fortified posts were demolished by the Sappers, under the orders of the Engineers, and the debris removed. During the whole of the hot weather, therefore, both Engineers and Sappers were fully employed in most arduous duties, while the remainder of the troops were resting from their long and trying march.

Having been reinforced by his 2nd Infantry Brigade, General Whitlock, leaving a strong detachment at Banda, advanced with the bulk of his force on Kirwee, about forty miles to the east. Here, again, disappointment awaited his troops; for the rebels dispersed at the approach of the Saugor Field Division, leaving all their material, together with forty guns and an immense treasure, behind them.

As regards the last, the various Law Courts in England for many years afterwards were the scene of a costly and prolonged litigation between the various field forces who put forward their claims to share the prize of war that was made by the actual captors, the Madras troops.

At Kirwee the Engineers and Sappers were again employed as

at Banda. The small fort was put in an efficient state of defence, and garrisoned with a battery of artillery, together with a detachment of European and Native infantry. Brigadier Carpenter was left in command, with Lieutenant Wood as Garrison Engineer, and though the place did not admit of much professional skill being devoted to its improvement, it was made strong enough to enable a very reduced detachment of troops to hold their own against an enormously larger number of rebels who invested Kirwee, in December following, during several days.

With the larger portion of his division, General Whitlock marched westward to Banda, whence several flying columns were pushed in pursuit of various fugitive bodies of rebel troops, whom the decisive operations of Sir Hugh Rose at Calpee had thrown broadcast over the country south of the Jumna. With these columns Captain Hemery and Lieutenants Howes and Lindsay served.

The whole of Bundelcund soon, indeed, swarmed with such bands of rebel fugitives, and Brigadier Carpenter, finding a body of these collecting in larger numbers than he cared for, in close proximity to Kirwee, sallied out to Chittrakote and inflicted a severe defeat on them.

Lieutenant Wood on this occasion had command of a squadron of Metga Sikh Horse, a body of irregular cavalry that had been sent from Cawnpore to reinforce General Whitlock.

The Sikh Rissaldar of the squadron was, unfortunately, shot dead on this occasion while conversing with Lieutenant Wood.

Soon after the fight at Chittrakote, a Bundeela chief, Rummust Singh (who had formerly been one of the rebel chiefs of the force which had dispersed from Kirwee), found in the jungles south of this place an appropriate refuge and central point where many of the rebel fugitive bands formed a junction.

To prevent an inconvenient increase to Rummust Singh's forces, Brigadier Carpenter moved southwards in pursuit of the rebels, who retreated before him, but made a short stand at the Punghattee Pass, leading up to the jungle-covered highlands of Bundelcund. During this march of Brigadier Carpenter's troops, Lieutenant Wood was employed in command of the squadron of Irregular Sikh Cavalry before mentioned to reconnoitre the line of advance. At the Punghattee Ghaut itself, he was sent forward to prepare the road for the passage of the guns, and returned to camp in the afternoon with his troopers, after setting the native working-parties to their duties. These, after the withdrawal of the Sikh cavalry, were attacked, and handled rather roughly, by a reconnoitring party from Rummust Singh's bands, who occupied a large village called Kothee, a few miles beyond the head of the Ghaut.

Next morning Brigadier Carpenter advanced, and found the Ghaut occupied in force by the rebels. Having opened fire from his two small guns, the ascent of the Pass was speedily made with small loss, while the Sikh Horse, under Lieutenants Gompertz, 1st N. I., and Wood, of the Engineers, pursued the flying rebels beyond Kothee.

The great facilities offered to the fugitives by the thick jungles of the locality, prevented their suffering much loss at the hands of the horsemen. A few days subsequently, another jungle encounter took place between the rebels and a detachment of Brigadier Carpenter's force; but the bulk of the enemy had retreated on a second and larger mass of fugitives, who were encamped some twenty miles from Nagode. This second body of rebels were composed of many flying bands, which had been driven headlong eastwards by the incessant operations of Sir Robert Napier's flying column against the Gwallior Contingent and the forces under Tantia Topee on the western confines of Bundelcund.

Brigadier Carpenter confined himself to observing this body of rebels, who were stated to be 20,000 strong, and to increase

At the same time, General Whitlock's scattered detachments were concentrated at Banda in this conjuncture, though strong detachments were left in Calpee and Hummerpore.

The General himself marched with his head-quarters *viâ* Punnah to reinforce Brigadier Carpenter at Nagode; but left again for Banda, on a report that Rummust Singh's force, now swelled to still greater numbers, had broken up their camp, and gone hastily northwards.

Brigadier Carpenter was also directed once more on Kirwee, by the same route he had traversed in following Rummust Singh southwards. When within a few marches of Kirwee, the Brigadier found that a general action had been fought very recently on the Punwaree heights, some four miles from Kirwee, and that General Whitlock had utterly routed and broken up the considerable forces under Rummust Singh. It is necessary to explain that this enterprising chief had, in lieu of marching directly north from the neighbourhood of Nagode, turned sharply north-east.

Misled by the information of the political officers, General Whitlock was at the same moment pressing north-west in the direction of Mahoba, on reaching which place he received the unexpected and alarming information, by express, that Rummust Singh was engaged in besieging the small garrison that had been left by Brigadier Carpenter in the fortified post at Kirwee.[*] The General immediately made a forced march of ninety miles in thirty-six hours, with his horse-artillery and cavalry. On his approaching Kirwee, the troops of Rummust Singh drew off to the Punwaree heights, where they remained in observation, and where they were energetically attacked immediately upon the

---

[*] On the 21st the enemy had reached Kirwee, and at once captured the town Captain Woodland, of the 1st M. N. I., had been left to defend the post with 104 men, which included a mere handful of the 43rd. For three days the enemy made incessant attacks, but were invariably repulsed. On the third day the rebels obtained some artillery, and now the position became very perilous; but relief was at hand, and the besiegers retreated on the 25th.

arrival of the infantry brigade, which followed the flying column as speedily as possible from Mahoba and Banda. In the action of Punwaree, Captain Hemery and Lieutenants Howes and Lindsay were present. Major Ludlow had previously left the Division to take up the Duties of Chief Engineer of the Saugor and Nerbudda territories.

The detachment under Brigadier Carpenter, to which Lieutenant Wood was attached, was, as has been already stated, marching on Kirwee, and was within a short distance of it when the action took place at Punwaree, and they had no share in it, but the interception of a few fugitives who unexpectedly found Brigadier Carpenter immediately on the line of their flight.

With the action of Punwaree, the history of the Engineer officers employed with the Saugor Field Division comes to an end.

Though engaged subsequently in a few small jungle fights, their duties consisted—until the country entirely calmed down—in providing for the necessities of the troops of the Madras Force, which were cantoned in various localities, between the Nerbudda and the Jumna, east of the line of the Betwa.

The Engineer officers present with the force under General Whitlock were—

> Major Ludlow.
> Captain Hemery.
> Lieutenant Howes.
>   ,,   Lindsay.
>   ,,   Wood.

Captain Hemery joined General Whitlock's column at Jubbulpore on 12th February 1858, and was present at Banda, Jheejhun, Kubrai, and Kirwee. He left the force on the 10th November on account of illness, and obtained three months' leave.

Major Ludlow, previous to the campaign under General Whitlock, had experienced disagreeable adventures, and seen some active service. He was present with Colonel Durand at Indore in the previous year.

On the 1st July two of Holkar's regiments mutinied. Colonel Durand despatched a messenger to Mhow for the European battery, but before it could arrive, he (the Resident) was compelled to betake himself to flight. Colonel Durand, with the ladies and officers at Indore, found his way to Sehore, and thence to Hoosingabad, on the Nerbudda, a distance of 160 miles. From thence, Captain Ludlow went to Jubbulpore, as next month he was Field Engineer with the Kamptee moveable column, under Brevet-Colonel Millar, at Dumoh.

On the 1st September 1857 the force, consisting of about 800 men, marched against Balacote, fifteen miles distant; a large village with an old fort on a neighbouring hill, the residence of Rajah Surrop Singh, who had assisted in the attack on Dumoh. A skirmish took place, and the enemy were driven in; the artillery opened fire on the village, and after a few rounds the infantry entered it and found it evacuated. The village was destroyed, and the detachment returned to Dumoh.

On the 18th September, the 52nd B. N. I. mutinied at Jubbulpore, and it was then decided that the town and district of Dumoh should be abandoned, and that the moveable column should return and defend Jubbulpore.

The column left Dumoh on 21st September, and, having been delayed three days in crossing the Nowlah, reached Singrampore on 26th September. News was here received that the mutineers of the 52nd B. N. I., 500 strong, had taken up a position at Kanee west of Heran river, twelve miles below Kuthenghee.

On the 27th a party, consisting of one company of the 33rd M. N. I. and 12 troopers of the 4th Madras Light Cavalry, was sent off at 2 A.M. to secure the boats on the Heran at Kuthenghee, under Lieutenant Watson; and Major Jenkins, Assistant Quartermaster-General, accompanied. At 5 A.M. two troopers galloped in, with the news that the party had been surprised by the 52nd, that the two officers had been killed, and the party was retreating on our camp.

Our force consequently pushed on and took possession of Gohra, three miles in front of Singrampore, which commands the mouth of the Pass. The 52nd were now seen marching along the road; two guns were fired into them, when they left the road and advanced against us. We retired 200 yards, close to the village; after a brisk fire for about half an hour, the enemy were driven back. We then advanced, with skirmishers thrown out, through three or four miles of jungly country, driving the enemy before us. On reaching open country near Kuthenghee, the cavalry were sent forward, when the enemy were seen making off up the hills. The cavalry were unable to follow them, and before the infantry arrived the greater number escaped. Some were, however, killed, and a few taken prisoners and afterwards hanged.

When near Kuthenghee, Major Jenkins and Lieutenant Watson rode up to the column; they had succeeded in cutting their way through the ambuscade, and had concealed themselves on the hills. Lieutenant Watson was wounded in the cheek by a musket-ball, and Major Jenkins' charger had two bullets through him.

The body of Captain McGregor, 52nd B. N. I., was found at the entrance to the town on the road, with his throat cut, a shot in his breast, and a bayonet wound in his body. The mutineers had murdered him before they attacked us, having taken him prisoner at Jubbulpore. The 120 men of the 52nd B. N. I. who were with our force, had been disarmed when the mutiny at Jubbulpore was heard of, and Colonel Millar's movements were much hampered by having to keep a sharp eye on them during the action.

The Madras troops behaved well, and proved that they had no sympathy with Bengal mutineers. A colour-havildar of the 52nd B. N. I. was captured by a havildar and two sepoys of

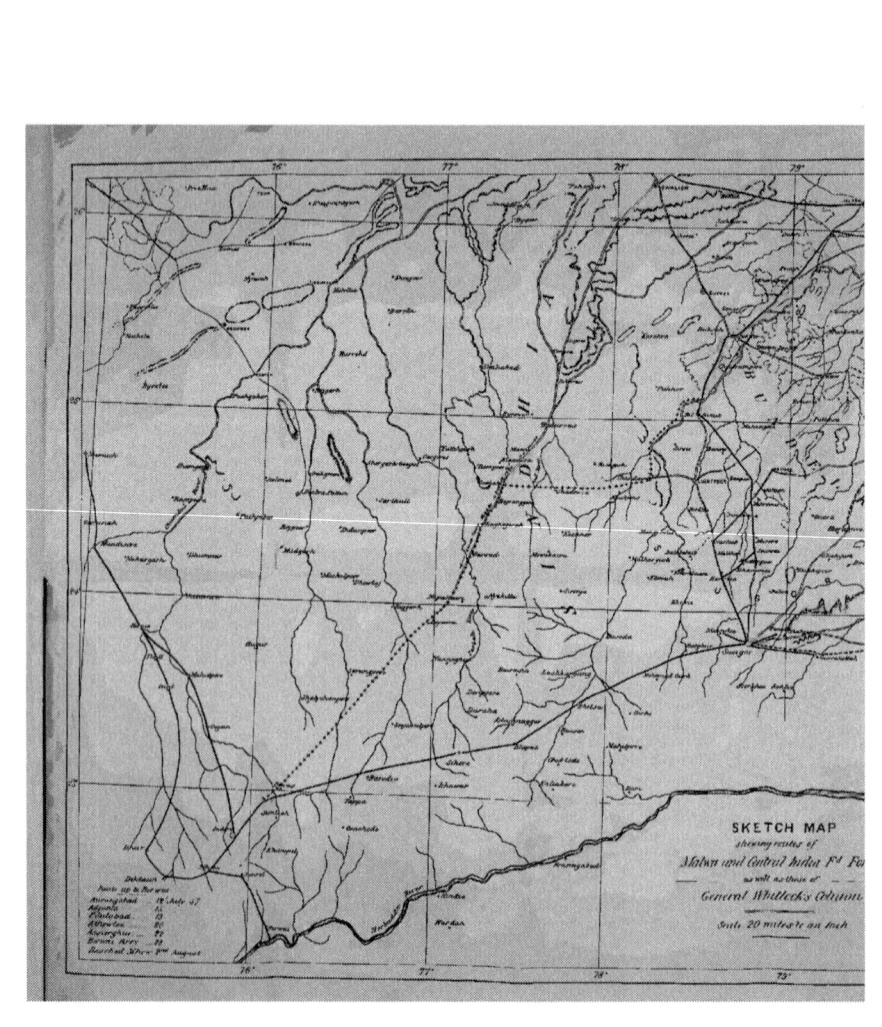

SKETCH MAP
shewing routes of
Malwa and Central India F^d Force
as well as those of
General Whitlock's Column
Scale 20 miles to an inch

the 1st Irregular Infantry ; the former was promoted to jemadar, and the others to havildars.

Colonel Millar stated in his despatch that he had received every assistance from Captain Ludlow, M.E., Captain Harrison, and Captain Pinkney.

Before narrating the services of C Company of Madras Sappers at Lucknow and elsewhere, it will be as well to state the services of Lieutenant (now Colonel) Sankey before the actions at Cawnpore in November 1857.

Lieutenant Sankey was appointed Additional Secretary to Government of India P. W. D. on 2nd June 1857, and almost immediately after his arrival at Calcutta was sent up country for service in the field.

He proceeded to Allahabad on special duty in July, and was there engaged in carrying out, under Major H. Yule, the entrenchments, which extended a considerable distance along the left bank of the Jumna, between the fort and the Kyd Gunge hospital. These earthworks gave cover to the steamer-ghaut, &c., as well as to several temporary hospitals for the reception of wounded from Havelock's force, to the number of 450. Some 5,000 or 6,000 people were engaged on this work.

As the level of the Ganges lowered, it became necessary to make arrangements for assisting the crossing of the advanced detachments of Sir Colin Campbell's force; and Lieutenant Sankey constructed 1,000 yards of causeway across the deep muddy bed, and established two boat-bridges over two branches of the river. The causeway was formed of brushwood, fascines, &c., over which rough timber frames, planking, straw, and sand, were placed for the roadway.

During most of the time Lieutenant Sankey was the only Engineer officer at Allahabad. On being relieved by Captain Impey he went to Benares, and received orders to establish temporary shelter for the detachments of European troops all along the grand trunk road. On this duty he proceeded to Cawnpore, and was present in the actions against the Gwallior Contingent by General Windham.

The force with General Windham at first was a little over 500 men. The Commander-in-Chief, Sir Colin Campbell, crossed the Ganges into Oude on 9th November 1857, to relieve Lucknow, leaving General Windham to guard Cawnpore.

The entrenchments on the right bank of the Ganges had been commenced the previous summer. They were limited in extent, and unfinished. The part on the canal side was enclosed by a stockade. It was an indifferent tête-du-pont covering the bridge of boats.

General Windham's orders were to improve the defences, watch the Gwallior Contingent force, and to make as much show as possible, if threatened; to leave a sufficient guard in entrenchments, and look well to his line of retreat; but not to move out to attack, unless compelled by circumstances.

The works were extended, and glacis partly cleared. Two thousand coolies were employed under Major McLeod, B.E.

The Gwallior Contingent was at Calpee and Jaloun, forty miles south-west of Cawnpore. About the middle of November the Gwallior troops crossed the Jumna gradually, and on the 19th were reported to be 9,200 strong, and 38 guns, with reserves, at Jaloun.

Calpee ...	...	3,000	and 20	guns.
Bogulpore	...	1,200	,, 4	,,
Akbarpore	...	2,000	,, 6	,,
Shewlie ...	...	2,000	,, 4	,,
Shirajpore	...	1,000	,, 4	,,
Total	...	9,200	and 38	guns.

About 14th November, General Windham got leave to detain detachments instead of forwarding them to Lucknow, and by the 20th he had 1,400 bayonets in the field, besides 300 left in the works. He at first determined to attack the enemy at Shewlie and Shirajpore, strike a blow rapidly, and return. The Commander-in-Chief, to whom he applied, gave no reply, being much engaged ; but a message was sent to General Windham that he would get a reply shortly. Immediately after this the roads to Lucknow were closed, and he got no answer.

General Windham, although very weak, detached some Madras N. I., with two 9-pounders, to proceed to Bunnee, to hold that post, and communicate with the Alumbagh.

On the 24th the General advanced his camp close to the bridge by which the Calpee road crossed the canal.

On the 25th the enemy's main body was reported to be at Suchowlee, and their leading division on the Pandoo Nuddee, three miles from camp. General Windham resolved to strike a blow at Pandoo Nuddee, and return.

On the 26th the General and Staff reconnoitred. Enemy were found in motion. Our force was ordered to advance with 1,200 bayonets of 34th, and parts of 82nd, 88th, and 2nd Rifle Brigade, with four 9-pounders and four 6-pounders—the latter Madras guns.

On our approaching the enemy's position they opened fire. The enemy held their ground for some time, and poured in several rounds of grape. Our troops advanced with a rush, crossed the stream, and the position was won. The enemy fled, leaving two 8-inch howitzers, one 6-pounder, and some ammunition waggons. They were followed for some distance, and their defeat completed by the artillery.

General Windham, having halted to rest his troops for some time, returned to a position in front of Cawnpore.

The main body of the enemy were observed to be not far distant, and followed up the British as they retreated.

Our loss was 1 officer and 13 men killed, 5 officers and 73 men wounded. Total, 92.

General Windham now received a letter from the Commander-in-Chief to say that all was well, and that they were coming back to Cawnpore with the Lucknow garrison.

The camp at Cawnpore was pitched on open ground outside the town, across the Calpee road, in front of brick-kilns.

On the 27th the troops were under arms before daybreak. Accurate information was not obtainable, several of our spies having been maimed during the previous days, and there was no cavalry to bring intelligence.

About 10 A.M. the enemy attacked us in front and on right flank. The heavy fighting in front fell on Rifle Brigade, commanded by Colonel Walpole, supported by 88th, four guns Royal Artillery, and two guns manned by seamen of the *Shannon*. The flank attack was met by 34th, Colonel Kelly, and Madras Battery, Lieutenant Chamier, with part of the 82nd.

General Windham conceived the attack on the right to be the more important, owing to the entrenchment being more readily got at on that side; so he went there himself. Two actions were thus being fought—at each point 600 bayonets.

The attack of the enemy in front was vigorous, and their artillery-fire rapid and well directed. The enemy was also found to be advancing on left flank. Two companies 64th were taken from the fort to meet them.

The fight had now lasted several hours. The enemy gradually advanced their artillery, but did not bring their infantry to close quarters. The British troops fell back on the brick-kilns, and about 5 P.M. were in position there.

General Windham now went to see how the fort was. He was met by a staff officer, who said that the enemy were in possession of lower part of the city, and were attacking the fort. A detachment of the Rifle Brigade had just arrived. General Windham put himself at their head and led them through the streets, and the mutineers fled.

General Dupuis, who had been left in command in front, was ordered to withdraw from the kilns. He accordingly retreated to the entrenchment without being pressed, and lost not one man in the operation.

The success of the enemy was entirely due to their enormous superiority of men and guns. Number of enemy, 25,000 with 50 guns. General Windham's force amounted to 1,700 bayonets and 10 guns. His infantry consisted of various detachments that had never acted together before; cavalry, none worth mentioning; artillery, ten pieces, manned by men of different nations, and drawn by bullocks, eight field-guns and two 24-pounders.

A night attack was now proposed, but no information could be obtained.

The next day (28th) the enemy attacked again. The great object of General Windham was to keep the enemy as far as possible from the works, and prevent their flanking the bridge.

Two separate engagements were fought—one on the left front, near the old dragoon lines; the other on the right, beyond the Baptist Chapel. The former was a complete victory for us, and two guns were captured. The enemy attacked on the right in immense force, and the ground gave them great advantages. The fighting was very severe, but the position in front of Assembly Rooms was held till nightfall. Our total loss on the third day amounted to 300 men.

During night of the 28th the enemy took complete possession of the city. The same evening chief part of force from Lucknow encamped on the other side of the Ganges.

On morning of the 29th the enemy established heavy guns to north of entrenchments, and opened fire on the bridge. They struck the boats three times, but they were held in check, and finally driven away, by a cross-fire from guns of Commander-in-Chief's force on left bank and those in the fort.

On the 29th and 30th the force from Lucknow crossed, and encamped near the old dragoon lines.

24 *

On 6th December an easy victory was gained over the Gwallior Contingent, and they were pursued to the fifteenth mile-stone on the Calpee road, leaving their camp, seventeen guns, and ammunition in our hands.

On 8th December Sir Hope Grant was sent in pursuit, and succeeded in capturing fifteen more guns. Altogether thirty-seven guns were captured—

> 3 on 26th November.
> 2 on 28th   ,,
> 17 on   6th December.
> 15 on   8th   ,,

Before detailing the services of Lieutenant Sankey before Lucknow and while serving with Jung Bahadoor's force, it will be convenient to relate as succinctly as possible the second relief of Lucknow, in which the C Company Madras Sappers were engaged, as well as the operations of Sir Colin Campbell's and Outram's forces after the relief up to the time that Jung Bahadoor's force joined the besieging army.

The C Company of Madras Sappers was engaged for a considerable time at Lucknow and in the province of Oude, during 1857–59.

In 1857 it was quartered at Dowlaishweram, where the fine anicut is placed across the river Godavery.

In August 1857, the C Company embarked for Calcutta, the officers with it being Lieutenant F. M. Raynsford, and Ensign D. S. Ogilvie, M.N.I.

At the end of August, Lieutenant W. H. Burton, M.E., joined the company.

For a short time the company was quartered at Howrah with 1-3 E Troop, M. H. A., under Lieutenants Bridge and B. Gordon.

In September they formed part of a moveable column under Brigadier FitzHardinge Berkeley, 32nd, *en route* to Lucknow.

This column consisted of C Company Madras Sappers and

Miners, 1-2 E Troop M. H. A., left wing of 53rd Infantry, Military Train (mounted on horses of disbanded 8th Madras Light Cavalry), and 27th M. N. I.

They went by rail as far as Raneguuge, marching fifteen miles a day onwards from thence up the grand trunk road.

Going through the Southal hills, they momentarily expected to be atacked by mutineers and Sonthals. However, nothing occurred.

In a month they reached Benares. They found on their way that all the villages and roadside bungalows had been burnt.

At several of the unbridged rivers the Sappers had to work to enable the force to cross.

From Benares they marched without delay to Allahabad. At this place the Commander-in-Chief (Sir Colin Campbell) broke up the brigade, and the Madras Sappers were sent into Cawnpore.

Lieutenant C. Scott, M.E., joined at Allahabad, and took command, and was also appointed Field Engineer.

They proceeded by rail to Futtehgurh, a distance of forty miles, and then by three forced marches of twenty-five, twenty-eight, and thirty, to Cawnpore.

They halted in the bridge entrenchment for a week.

From Cawnpore they marched with the 23rd Company R. E. to Bunnee bridge, eighteen miles south of Lucknow.

The bridge (which the mutineers had blown up) had consisted of a brick arch of twenty feet. The Royal Engineers and Madras Sappers encamped three or four days at Bunnee bridge with the 8th Foot, repaired the bridge with jungle timber, and then marched to within a few miles of the Alumbagh, where was collected a force of 5,000 men for the second relief of Lucknow.

The force near the Alumbagh at Buntera had been under the command of Brigadier (afterwards Sir Hope) Grant. Sir Colin Campbell joined on 9th November. He waited a few days for reinforcements.

On 14th November, all was ready, and an advance was made from camp in rear of the Alumbagh towards Dilkhusha and the Martinière.

The Madras Sappers were ordered to the front to make passages through the Dilkhusha park wall (at A in Map), when the enemy opposed us at "long bowls."

Lieutenant Burton, M.E., took up a detachment of about thirty men, with Corporal Britten; and whilst knocking a passage through the wall, Burton's horse was shot in the ribs just behind the girth.

As soon as the Sappers had done their work, the whole force passed through the park, driving the enemy before them.

Our force then encamped at the Martinière.

Burton, M.E., and Lang, B.E., were the two first on the top of the Martinière, and they planted our flag on it.

On the 15th a halt was made at the Martinière, when Colonel Goodwyn, who was commanding the Engineer Brigade, left, being sick, and Lieutenant Lennox, R.E., became Brigadier of Engineers.

On 16th November, the Secundra Bagh was attacked. This was a high-walled enclosure, 120 yards square, carefully loop-holed all round, and numerously defended. Fire was hotly maintained for an hour and a half. A small breach was made, and the position was then stormed in the most gallant manner by the 93rd Highlanders, 53rd Foot, and 4th Punjab Infantry, supported by a battalion of detachments under Major Barnston.

After this, Captain Peel, R.N., with his siege train proceeded to the front towards the Shah Nujeef. This was resolutely defended for three hours. It was then stormed by 93rd Highlanders.

On the 17th, a building called the Mess House was cannonaded by Captain Peel, and stormed by a company of the 90th, under Captain Wolseley (now Sir Garnet), and a picquet of the 53rd. The place was at once carried, and the troops lined the wall separating the Mess House from the Motee Mahal. Here a final stand was made, but after an hour's fighting, the soldiers poured through with a body of Sappers, and accomplished communications with the Residency; and shortly afterwards Sir Colin met Sir James Outram and Sir Henry Havelock, who came out to meet him.

The Commander-in-Chief sent out a detachment of Madras Sappers under Lieutenant Burton, M.E., to occupy some trenches, and drive out the enemy from them, as the rebels were annoying us from this point.

The Residency garrison was now withdrawn.

The Engineers and Sappers had made a battery at the Motee Mahal, whence to bombard the city and the Kaiser Bagh, still held by the enemy, and the troops were in hopes of fighting their way through the city and clearing it of rebels, of whom some 60,000 or 80,000 were still said to be there. However, the Chief's first object was to withdraw the garrison.

Fire was opened on the Kaiser Bagh on the 20th; and when the enemy was led to believe that an immediate assault was intended, the garrison with the women and children withdrew through the picquets at midnight on the 22nd.

The mutineers were completely deceived, and continued firing on the old positions hours after they had been evacuated.

The Chief's force thus became, as it were, the rear-guard of the now retreating British army. They thus got back to the Alumbagh, where Outram had previously left a strong detachment in a walled garden containing a large house.

Thence the C Company Madras Sappers was detached to Bunnee bridge to join the 27th N. I., under Colonel Fischer, in forming the village of Bunnee into a defensive post for the protection of the bridge against further injury.

In addition to the 27th M. N. I., there were two guns of the Madras Artillery under Lieutenant Chamier.*

* Now Colonel Chamier.

On the 27th, the Commander-in-Chief, Sir Colin Campbell, passed through Bunnee *en route* to Cawnpore with his force, and most of the Lucknow garrison, and all the women and children.

Sir James Outram was left with a force of about 4,000 men, to hold a position at the Alumbagh until the return of the Commander-in-Chief for the capture of Lucknow.

After two weeks' work at Bunnee, the C Company of Madras Sappers, after some difficulty with Colonel Fischer, got away to the front again with Sir James Outram. They were the only Sappers with his force, although there were several Engineers :

> Lieutenant G. Hutchinson, B.E., Commanding Engineer.
> Lieutenant C. N. Judge, B.E.
> Messrs. May and Taite, Civil Engineers.
> Major Oakes, B.I.
> Lieutenant Hon. J. Fraser, B.I.
> Lieutenant A. Tulloch.
> Mr. Birch, Indian Navy.
> Lieutenant C. Scott, M.E.
> Lieutenant Burton, M.E.
> Ensign Ogilvie, M.S.

Lieutenant Raynsford had gone with the Commander-in-Chief to take charge of the Engineer's park with his force.

On 22nd December a skirmish took place at Guilee between the enemy and a portion of Sir James Outram's force under Brigadier Stisted.

The numbers engaged on our side were 190 cavalry, 1,227 infantry, and six 9-pounders. With this force there were forty Madras Sappers under Lieutenant Ogilvie.

Four guns and twelve waggons filled with ammunition were captured.

The Military Train (112) under Major Robertson followed the enemy up so rapidly, that they dispersed their cavalry and drove their guns into a ravine, where they were captured.

The Military Train was far ahead of the infantry and unable to remove the guns. They were menaced in front by a large body of fresh troops from the city, and attacked on right flank by 2,000 men ; but by the bold front shown by the Train, and the gallant advance of their skirmishers, the enemy were held at bay, till the arrival of a party of 5th Fusiliers, and two 9-pounders under Major Olpherts, secured their capture and enabled a working party of the Madras Sappers, under Ogilvie, to extricate them from the ravine into which they had been driven.

Outram's position was of considerable extent. The most advanced post, that nearest to the city, was the Alumbagh itself, a walled garden a quarter of a mile square, with a mosque at the angle nearest to the city. At each of the angles was a battery for two guns. Two thousand yards to the left was the left front picquet, about 1,600 yards distant from enemy's line of works ; the mosque close to the Alumbagh not being more than 1,000 yards. Between these two posts three batteries were thrown up, two guns each, 2,000 to 2,500 yards from the enemy's works, to sweep the ground between the Alumbagh and the left front picquet. The left centre picquet was 1,500 yards in rear of the left front, and connected with it by a trench, the left rear picquet being 2,700 yards in rear again—the connection being carried on by a line of abattis. The rear picquet where two guns were posted, was on the Cawnpore road, 3,300 yards distant from Alumbagh ; and at a mosque two miles further along the road there was a cavalry picquet. In a dry tank about 1,000 yards to right of left centre picquet, two guns were placed to play on the ground in front of the left front and centre picquets. Between the left rear picquet and rear picquet on the road, was a large jheel or swamp, and to the left of left rear picquet was another smaller one.

On the right a parapet was made from south angle of Alumbagh for a distance of 500 yards, connecting the garden with another battery about half a mile to the right of the Cawnpore road (which ran right through the centre of the position). This battery was to sweep the ground to the right of Alumbagh, as well as that in advance of right front picquet, which was placed about a mile to right of the battery (the battery facing east). This picquet was strengthened by trenches, abattis, &c., and was connected with the centre of the position by a line of abattis; the centre being 2,000 yards in rear of Alumbagh. One thousand five hundred yards south-east of the right front picquet was the fort of Jellalabad, to the west of which lay the considerable village bearing the same name, strengthened by abattis, &c. Eight hundred yards south of the fort was the right rear picquet at a point where a road crosses a small stream by a bridge. The right rear picquet was three miles and a half to east of left rear picquet, which space was covered by the cavalry picquet previously mentioned as being placed at a mosque on the Cawnpore road, two miles beyond the rear picquet.

The total circumference of the ground thus held was fully twelve miles, the Cawnpore road running for a distance of four miles right through the centre of the position. Roads were formed connecting all the outposts with the centre, the roads thus made being some ten or twelve miles in length.

From November 1857 to March 1858 Outram's force occupied this position, and during this time the Madras Sappers made the several field batteries C C C, and did other works in the shape of trenches, abattis, rifle-pits, &c. A large quantity of coolies were imported from surrounding villages to assist and work under the Engineers and Sappers.

The C Company was commanded by Brevet-Captain Scott, M.E., but they were worked indiscriminately under the Engineers previously named.

On 12th January the rebels attacked the position, but were repulsed with considerable loss. As Outram had heard that the enemy intended to intercept his communications, he sent a stronger escort than usual to accompany his convoy, then on its way from Cawnpore, the escort consisting of 450 infantry, eighty cavalry, and four guns.

The rebels were encouraged by this reduction of his force to make an attack. About sunrise large masses of the enemy were seen on the left front, and they gradually spread round the whole front and flank of the position, extending from our left rear outposts to near Jellalabad on our right, a distance of six miles, and their force amounted to fully 30,000 men.

Our right brigade (713 strong), and the left (733), with 100 men of the regiment of Ferozepore, were formed in front of their lines. The enemy first advanced on the left front and flank, covered by skirmishers; on which, two regiments from the left brigade were detached to support the outposts, and extended in skirmishing order on their flanks. At the same time, Major Olpherts, with four horse-battery guns, supported by a detachment of Military Train, was directed to check the enemy on left rear, where their cavalry showed in greatest strength. The Volunteer and Native Cavalry were drawn up to protect the rear of the camp. As soon as the enemy were well within range, they were exposed to a severe fire from Alumbagh, and from the advanced batteries of the outposts on the left front and centre, and they fled without having come within musket-range, except at left centre outpost, where a considerable number entered a grove of trees, usually occupied by our outlying picquets, from which they were driven in a few minutes.

On the left rear Major Olpherts moved out his guns at a gallop, and drove off and dispersed a very large body of infantry and cavalry which was endeavouring to penetrate our rear. He did much execution by the fire of his guns in their masses at 500 yards.

At this time Outram received a report that Alumbagh and Jellalabad were threatened, and, proceeding to the right, he found that the enemy had brought three horse-artillery guns, supported by an immense mass of infantry, against the picquets which connected his right with Jellalabad, and which had been strengthened to 100 men and two guns. He moved the regiment of Ferozepore and 5th Fusiliers, with two guns of the bullock battery, from right brigade to the front, taking the enemy in flank and driving them back. They were then exposed to the fire of Maude's guns from Alumbagh, which played upon them with great effect.

About this time the enemy again advanced on the left front and flank, their cavalry being more to the front than before. Alexander's and Clarke's guns opened upon them, and drove them back in confusion. At the same time, the enemy on the right again advanced from the heavy cover of groves and villages into which they had retreated, and re-opened their guns on the Jellalabad picquet, but were finally silenced and driven off by the fire of the two guns.

Simultaneously, the enemy advanced upon Alumbagh, and established themselves in the nearest cover. About noon they also advanced into the open, but were at once dispersed and driven back by fire of Maude's guns, and the riflemen from Alumbagh. By 4 P.M. the whole of the enemy had retired to their original positions in the gardens and villages in our front, or to the city.

Our casualties were only one officer slightly wounded, and five privates wounded.

On 16th January the enemy made a similar attack on the position, except that their attack was bolder than before. In the morning they made a sudden attack on the Jellalabad picquets, but were received with a heavy fire, which drove them back, leaving their leader, a Hindoo devotee representing Hunooman, who was advancing bravely at their head, and several killed and wounded, whom they were unable to carry off. They removed many bodies, and their loss was severe. Two 9-pounders under Captain Moir, completed their expulsion from the cover in front.

On the left front and flank they advanced skirmishers, and threatened us during most of the day. After dark they assembled in great strength in front of the left advanced village outpost, and attacked it with a large body of infantry, who were allowed to approach within eighty yards of the post, when they were received with discharges of grape from three guns and a heavy fire from the rifles of the post, and were driven off. Some shells from an 8-inch mortar hastened their retreat. The Enfield rifles and Captain Maude's guns in Alumbagh had several opportunities of inflicting some loss on the enemy, which were promptly taken advantage of. A large body of cavalry showed on our left rear, and were safely left to the vigilance of Major Olpherts and his four guns, supported by a detachment of the Military Train under Captain Clarke.

Our casualties were—

   1 Artilleryman killed.
   1 ,,   wounded.
   7 European Infantry wounded.

There were several other attacks made on the Alumbagh, but always with the same result.

The Sappers were employed every day, and all day from morning to night, and sometimes all night, in case of any new or advanced battery being required.

The enemy's and our sentries frequently approached one another within 200 yards. The enemy made zigzags of approach up towards the walled Alumbagh, and built batteries, with gabions, &c., with the village coolies, whom our Sappers had taught. It was said (but the truth of it was doubted) that there were some Bengal Sappers in the mutineers' ranks.

The position at the Alumbagh was held by Outram till the 1st March 1858, when the Commander-in-Chief returned to effect the capture of Lucknow; so that Outram, with his small force, held the place for more than three months against fifteen or twenty times his numbers.

Sir James Outram's testimony to the conduct and services of the C Company of Madras Sappers and Miners is highly honourable to them.

"Their skill as workmen, their industry, their cheerful alacrity and general good conduct, commanded the respect of all who saw them at Alumbagh; and their coolness and bravery when called upon, as they were on every occasion of attack on our position, to act as soldiers, was conspicuous."

During the time that Sir James Outram was engaged in holding Alumbagh, &c., Sir Colin Campbell remained at Cawnpore making preparations for a final advance on Lucknow.

On 4th February 1858 our troops commenced to cross the Ganges at Cawnpore.

On the 28th the Commander-in-Chief transferred his headquarters to Buntera, the camp of Sir E. Lugard.

The divisions under Sir Hope Grant and Walpole joined the next day. It was decided that it would be necessary in the attack on Lucknow to operate from both sides of the river, so as to enfilade the enemy's new works.

This plan would also close an avenue of supply, which was important. The city being twenty miles in circumference, it was hopeless to attempt to invest it.

The siege-train having arrived, the Commander-in-Chief went to the Alumbagh on 1st March, and on the 2nd the Dilkhusha was seized—a gun being captured from the enemy after a skirmish.

The Dilkhusha now formed our advanced post on the right, while the Mahomed Bagh was on our left. Heavy guns were placed at both these positions.

Additional troops arrived during the two following days, and Brigadier-General Franks, C.B., joined on 5th March, having traversed a distance of 150 miles. He was in command of the

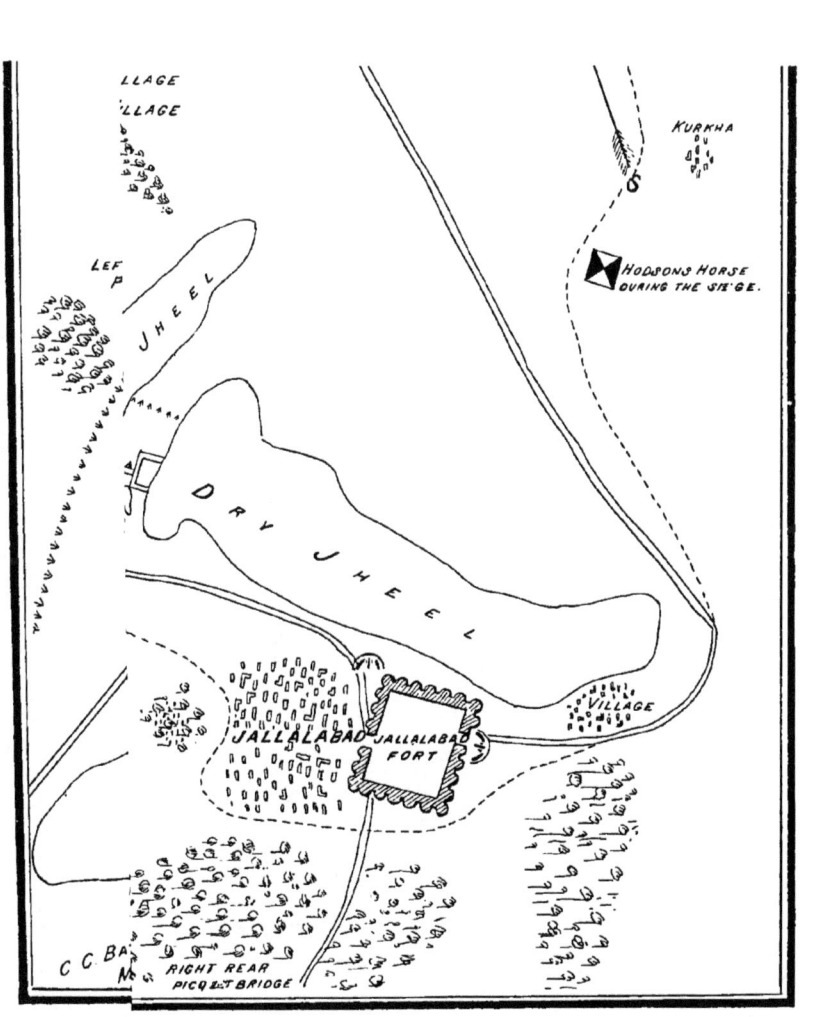

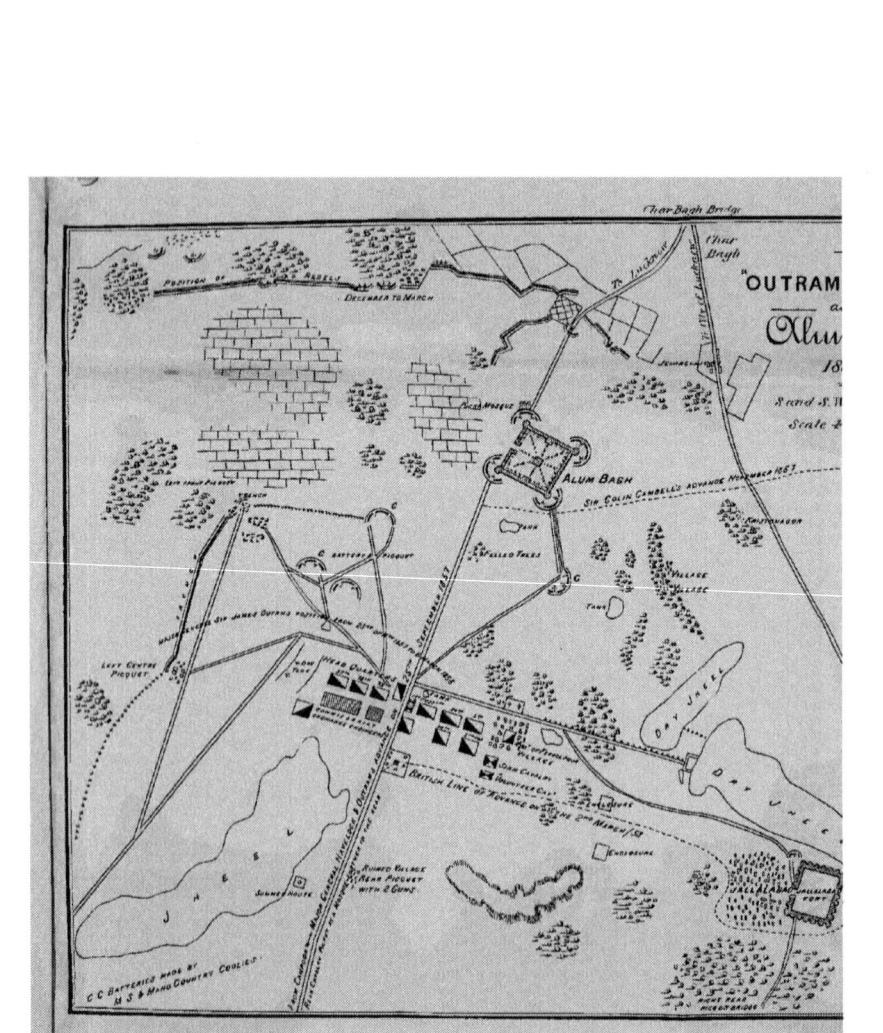

Juanpore Field Force, consisting of nearly 6,000 fighting-men; Besides Goorkhas, infantry and artillery, six battalions, he had—

> 10 European officers.
> 96 Native officers.
> 2,913 non-commissioned officers and men.
> ———
> 3,019

On Jung Bahadoor reaching Lucknow, the Goorkhas were withdrawn from General Franks', and joined H.E. Jung Bahadoor's force.

During his march General Franks defeated the enemy in four actions.

On 23rd January, at the position at Nursutpore near Secundra, three guns were taken.

On 19th February General Franks left Singramow, crossed the Oude frontier, and attacked the rebels at Chanda, drove the enemy before him, and captured six guns. When this was over, he took ground across the road to Ameereepore. Near sunset the enemy appeared, were again attacked and discomfited, and retreated in disorder towards Waree. The lateness of the hour, and rapid flight, alone saved the rebel artillery from capture. Enemy's loss estimated in these two actions at 800 men.

On the 20th Franks halted. During this time enemy remained at Waree. Franks' flank movement and the Nazim's defeat at Ameereepore having thrown him off his direct line of retreat on Lucknow, he contemplated occupying the strong jungle pass and fort of Budhungun, nine miles in our front; but Franks forestalled him. Five companies of Goorkhas were thrown into the fort, and six companies and two guns posted on the nullah which runs through it; while the main force was encamped two miles in advance.

During the 22nd Franks remained halted; and in the course of the day the Nazim reached Badshahgunge, two miles beyond

Sultanpore. The rebel force numbered 25,000 men, 5,000 being sepoys and 1,100 cavalry, with twenty-five guns.

A sketch of the position was drawn up by Lieutenant Innes (B.E.), Assistant Field Engineer, from information furnished by Lieutenant Smith, 58th N. I., and Lieutenant Tucker, 8th B. C.

The enemy were attacked and totally defeated, the result being that an army of 25,000 men was driven from a position of great strength and scattered to the winds with a loss of 1,800 killed and wounded, twenty-one guns (nine siege calibre) being left in our hands. Our loss was only eleven.

The effect of this engagement was to open the road to Lucknow for the unopposed march of this force, as well as for that of the Maharajah Jung Bahadoor.

Franks resumed his march, and arrived at Selimpore, eighteen miles from Lucknow. In this day's march a most dashing cavalry combat took place, in which Captain Aikman, commanding 3rd Sikh Cavalry, with 100 of his men, attacked a body of 500 infantry and 200 horse with two guns, three miles off the road, utterly routing them, cutting up more than 100 men, capturing the guns, and driving the remaining force into and over the Goomtee.

Franks halted at Selimpore till the 4th. On the evening of the 3rd he received a message to push on to Lucknow, and at 6 A.M. on the 4th he marched from Selimpore, and reached without opposition a mosque a mile beyond Amethie, eight miles from Lucknow. Here news was brought that a large force, with two guns, was posted in and round the fort of Dhowrara, two miles to right of road, and situated among ravines which run into the Goomtee.

Franks resolved to drive them out. About 500 originally occupied the fort, while 3,000 were collected in the vicinity. Most of these escaped down the ravines and across the river when they saw our cavalry circling round their flank, but 200 fell back and prepared to defend it.

Two H. A. guns were brought into action at 600, 400, and 200 yards, and silenced the enemy's guns, but failed to do the same with the matchlock-men. However, after a time, a few of the assailed, seeing themselves about to be surrounded, attempted to escape up a ravine ; but after a desperate resistance they were despatched by the native cavalry posted at every outlet. Companies of 20th and 97th effected an entrance into the fort and bayoneted 120.

Repeated attempts having failed to break down the door of a house in which the survivors had barricaded themselves—the shot from one of their own guns turned on it making no impression on the massive door, a fire kindled having no effect, and the only Engineer officer, Lieutenant Innes, B.E., being severely wounded while trying to burst open the entrance—General Franks determined to withdraw, having secured the two guns, which were carried off under a heavy matchlock-fire that the enemy continued from the loop-holes.

The force resumed its march, and reached the Commander-in-Chief's camp the same evening, without further interruption.

These operations have been given in some detail, as it is supposed that it will be of interest to note the gallantry of Lieutenant Innes, B.E. General Franks wrote :—

"Lieutenant T. T. McLeod Innes has been of the greatest assistance to me with his professional aid. I have already mentioned his distinguished conduct at the attack on Dhowrara. It is now his due to relate that at the action of Sultanpore, far in advance of the leading skirmishers, he was the first to secure a gun which the enemy were abandoning. Retiring from this, they rallied round another gun further back, from which the shot would in another instant have played through our advancing columns, when Lieutenant Innes rode up unsupported, shot the gunner about to apply the match, and, remaining undaunted at his post, the mark for a hundred matchlock-men sheltered in some adjoining huts, kept the artillerymen at bay until assistance reached him. For this act of gallantry, surpassed by none within my experience, it is my intention to recommend him for the honourable distinction of the V. C."

Lieutenant Innes obtained the V. C. in consequence.

To proceed with the capture of Lucknow. Bridges of casks had been prepared by the Engineer department, for crossing the Goomtee. Between our left and Jellalabad (the right of the Alumbagh position) there was an interval of two miles occupied by Hodson's Horse. Brigadier Campbell, with a strong brigade of cavalry and infantry, secured our left.

An Engineer brigade was formed under Colonel R. Napier (now Lord Napier of Magdala), and to this the C Company of the Madras Sappers was attached. The Engineers' brigade consisted of two companies of Royal Engineers, C Company of Madras Sappers and Miners, and two or three companies of Punjab Sappers and Miners, a regiment of Muzbee Sikhs, under Chalmers, and a regiment of Purbea Sikhs. All these were employed indiscriminately in breaking a way for the army through the closely-built city, over ground parallel to the road into the Kaiser Bagh.

On the 5th the Goomtee was bridged near Bibiapore, and next day Outram crossed to the left bank of the river, and pushed his advance up the left bank; the troops in the position of Dilkhusha remaining at rest till it was apparent that the first of the enemy's works was turned. The works are thus described by Sir Colin Campbell:—

"The series of courts and buildings called the Kaiser Bagh, considered as a citadel by the rebels, was shut in by three lines of defence towards the Goomtee, of which the line of the canal was the outer one; the second line circled round the large building called the Mess House, and the Motee Mahal; and the third, or interior one, was the principal rampart of the Kaiser Bagh, the rear of the enclosures of the latter being closed in by the city, through which an approach would have been dangerous to an assailant. These lines were flanked by numerous bastions, and rested at one end on the Goomtee, and at the other on the great buildings of the street called the Huzrut Gunge, all of which were strongly fortified, and flanked the street in every direction. Extraordinary care had been expended on the defences of the houses and the bastions, to enfilade the street."

Outram pitched his camp on the 6th in front of the Yellow House.

On the 7th he was attacked by the enemy, but they were driven back.

On the 9th the Yellow House was seized, and the whole of Outram's force advanced. He then occupied the Fyzabad road, and was able to plant his batteries to enfilade the works on the canal. While this attack was being made, a very heavy fire was kept up on the Martinière from Dilkhusha. At 2 P.M. the 42nd, supported by the 93rd, 53rd, and 70th Regiments, stormed the Martinière, under Sir E. Lugard, K.C.B., and Brigadier Hon. A. Hope. The 4th P. N. I., supported by the 42nd, climbed up the entrenchment abutting on the Goomtee, and swept the whole line of works till they reached Banks' house, when it became necessary to close operations for the night.

On the 10th Outram strengthened his position. At sunrise on the same day Banks' house was attacked, carried by noon, and secured as a strong military post.

The second part of the plan of attack against the Kaiser Bagh now came into operation. This was to use the great blocks of houses and palaces extending from Banks' house to the Kaiser Bagh as our approach, instead of sapping up to the front of the second line of works. Thus the Commander-in-Chief was able to turn the second line of works on the right, while Outram, in his advance, was enabled to enfilade them.

Outram had received orders to plant his guns with the view of raking the enemy's position, and to annoy the Kaiser Bagh with vertical and direct fire, as well as to attack the suburbs

25 *

near the iron and stone bridges. Outram carried all this out with marked success; but the enemy still held to his own end of the iron bridge, on the right bank.

The operations had now become those of an engineering character, and every effort was made to save the infantry from being hazarded before due preparation had been made.

Brigadier (now Lord) Napier (of Magdala) placed the batteries with a view to breaching and shelling a large block of palaces called the Begum Kotee.

At 4 A.M. on the 11th the latter was stormed by 93rd, supported by 4th Punjab Rifles and 1,000 Goorkhas under Brigadier A. Hope. This was the sternest struggle which occurred during the siege.

From thenceforward the Chief Engineer pushed his approaches with the greatest judgment through the enclosures, by the aid of the Sappers and heavy guns; the troops immediately occupying the ground as he advanced, and the mortars being moved from one position to another as ground was won on which they could be placed.

The buildings to the right and the Secundra Bagh were taken in the early morning of the 11th, without opposition.

On the 10th, Maharajah Jung Bahadoor, with a force of 9,000 men and twenty-four field-guns, drawn by men, arrived; and on the 11th took up a position on our left, in front of the village of Bhurdurwa, to the south-east of the Charbagh. He was requested to pass the canal and attack the suburbs in his front.

During the night of the 12th Outram was reinforced with a number of heavy guns, so that he might increase his fire on the Kaiser Bagh; while at the same time mortars at the Begum Kotee never ceased to play on the Emaum Barra, the next building it was necessary to storm between the Begum Kotee and the Kaiser Bagh.

On the 12th, Brigadier Franks, C.B., with the 4th Division,

relieved Sir E. Lugard with the 2nd, and on him devolved the
duty of attacking the Emaum Barra.

The Emaum Barra was carried early on the 14th; and the
Sikhs of the Ferozepore Regiment, under Major Brasyer, pressing
forward in pursuit, entered the Kaiser Bagh, the third line
of defence having been turned without a single gun being fired
from them.   Supports were quickly thrown in, and all the well-
known ground of former defence and attacks—the Mess House,
the Tara Kotee, the Mothi Mahal, and the Chutter Munzil—
were rapidly occupied by our troops; whilst the Engineers
devoted their attention to securing the positions towards the
south and west.

It is now necessary to turn to the doings of Jung Bahadoor's
force on the left of our position.

On the evening of the 12th they made an attack on the Charbagh.   The enemy were strongly entrenched on the other side
of the canal, and the attack having been commenced too late in
the day, the troops had to be withdrawn.   The Goorkhas here
showed a great deal of pluck under a heavy fire from the
entrenchments in their front.

On the 13th a battery, under Lieutenant Sankey's advice,
was established near the Hussain Gunge bridge (he was Commanding Engineer with the Goorkha force), to enfilade the
enemy's entrenchments with twelve guns from point marked D.

After two hours' heavy fire, the Goorkhas, at a given signal,
rushed over the entrenchments in their front, and carried all
before them to a point in the city marked I, three quarters of a
mile south of the Kaiser Bagh.

Lieutenant Sankey was engaged with the Goorkhas in this
attack.   While he was waiting at point I for further orders, with
Lieutenant Robertson, they heard that Generals Franks and
Napier had then carried the Kaiser Bagh; and they at once
pushed on through the city with eighty Goorkhas, while the
enemy was on the run (magazines exploding on all sides), to the

gate of the Kaiser Bagh, along the line I–H, where they reported themselves to General Franks. At night they returned round by Banks' house, and rejoined the Goorkha force.

The various buildings worked into by the Engineer Brigade, under General Robert Napier, formed a range of massive palaces and walled courts of vast extent, equalled, perhaps, but certainly not surpassed in any capital in Europe.

Every outlet had been covered by a work, and on every side were prepared barricades and loop-holed parapets. The extraordinary industry evinced by the enemy in this respect was really unexampled. Hence the absolute necessity for holding the troops in hand, till at each successive move forward the Engineers reported that all which could be effected by artillery and the Sappers had been done, before the troops were led to the assault.

The 15th March was employed in securing what had been taken, removing powder, destroying mines, and fixing mortars for the further bombardment of the positions still held by the enemy on the line of our advance up the Goomtee, and in the heart of the city.

Hope Grant was sent on with the cavalry towards Seetapore, and Brigadier Campbell to Sundeela to intercept fugitives.

On the 15th the greater part of the Goorkha force attacked the enemy (chiefly cavalry), who was threatening the Alumbagh. On seeing the advance of the Goorkhas the enemy did not show very freely, and, after some fire on both sides, they retired with little damage.

On the 16th, Outram, with 5th Brigade under Brigadier Douglas, supported by 20th and Ferozepore Regiment, crossed the Goomtee, by a bridge of casks, opposite the Secundra Bagh, and advanced through the Chutter Munzil to take the Residency.

It now became apparent that the enemy were intending to retreat across the stone bridge. Outram was accordingly ordered to press forward, and was able not only to take the iron bridge in reverse, but also to advance for more than a mile, and occupy the Muchee Bawan and the great Emaum Barra.

On the same day the Goorkhas pushed through the Charbagh, and Lieutenant Sankey made immediate arrangements for re-establishing the bridge over the canal at M, which had been destroyed by the enemy.

This bridge was reconstructed under difficult circumstances. The gap was seventy feet wide, and thirty-five or forty feet deep, while the ripped-up roofs of houses only afforded baulks of sixteen feet.

Lieutenant Sankey had frames of them lashed together, and while planting one foot of each frame against the bank, lowered them into a sloping position. Sending men on to the upper ends of the frames thus placed, other baulks were passed on, till by these and various horizontal ties, they joined the apices of the frames thus advanced from either bank. The stiffening of the frame was afterwards easily effected, and though the whole looked light and unsubstantial, all the Goorkha force, with 5,000 carts, 300 camels, besides elephants, passed over it; and the bridge was for some months afterwards used for ordinary traffic, after the capture of the city.

While the bridge was being built, the Goorkhas attacked along the line M G on 18th and 19th, and carried a good deal of the city, sustaining some loss in the operations.

It was while the Goorkhas were thus engaged, that Lieutenants McNeil and Bogle of the Artillery reached Wajid Ali's house, rescued his harem, and with it Mrs. Orr and Miss Jackson, all of whom were got away safely in palanquins.

The enemy shortly after reoccupied portions of the quarter taken by the Goorkhas, but were finally driven out.

On the 19th, Outram moved forward on the Moosa Bagh, the last position of the enemy on the line of the Goomtee.

Sir Hope Grant cannonaded the Moosa Bagh from the left

bank, while Brigadier Campbell, moving round the west side from the Alumbagh, prevented retreat in that direction.

The rout was now complete, and great loss was inflicted on the enemy by all the columns.

On the 21st, Sir E. Lugard was directed to attack a stronghold held by the Moulvie in the heart of the city.

This position was occupied after a sharp contest, and it now became possible to invite the return of inhabitants, and to secure the city from the horrors of this prolonged contest.

Brigadier Campbell attacked the enemy when retreating from the city in consequence of Lugard's advance, pursued him for six miles, and inflicted heavy loss.

The capture of Lucknow was now complete.

Before proceeding further, it will be convenient to state on what duties the officers of Madras Engineers and Sappers with the force were employed subsequently.

Lieutenant Burton, M.E., was sent to the Moosa Bagh, which, with one European sapper and such labour as he could obtain, he was required to put into a defensible state. The Moosa Bagh was a walled garden with a few houses inside. It was garrisoned by the 97th. Lieutenant Burton remained here two weeks, when, having completed the necessary works, he was sent to the Mucha Bawan, then being converted, under Lieutenant Smith, B.E., into a fortified post to guard the iron bridge and that part of the city.

After the 10th, the Goorkhas had no more fighting. They were shortly afterwards encamped at Nawabgunge, twelve miles from Lucknow; and after a brief halt, they were marched back to Nepaul.

Lieutenant Sankey, shortly after the siege, returned to Calcutta sick, and saw no further service.

On the 2nd July 1858 he was obliged to go on six months' sick leave.

After the siege was quite over, Lieutenant Burton was employed

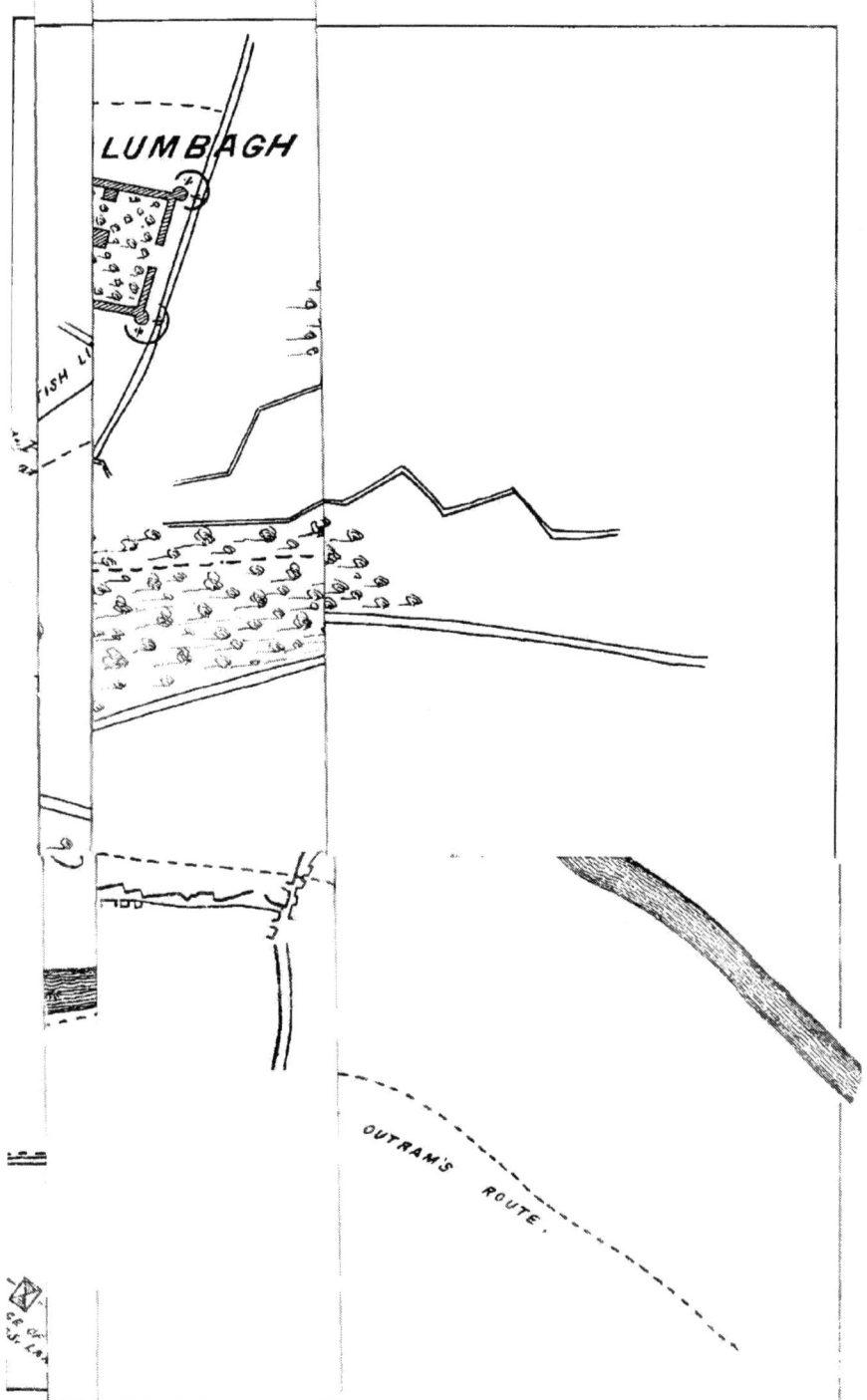

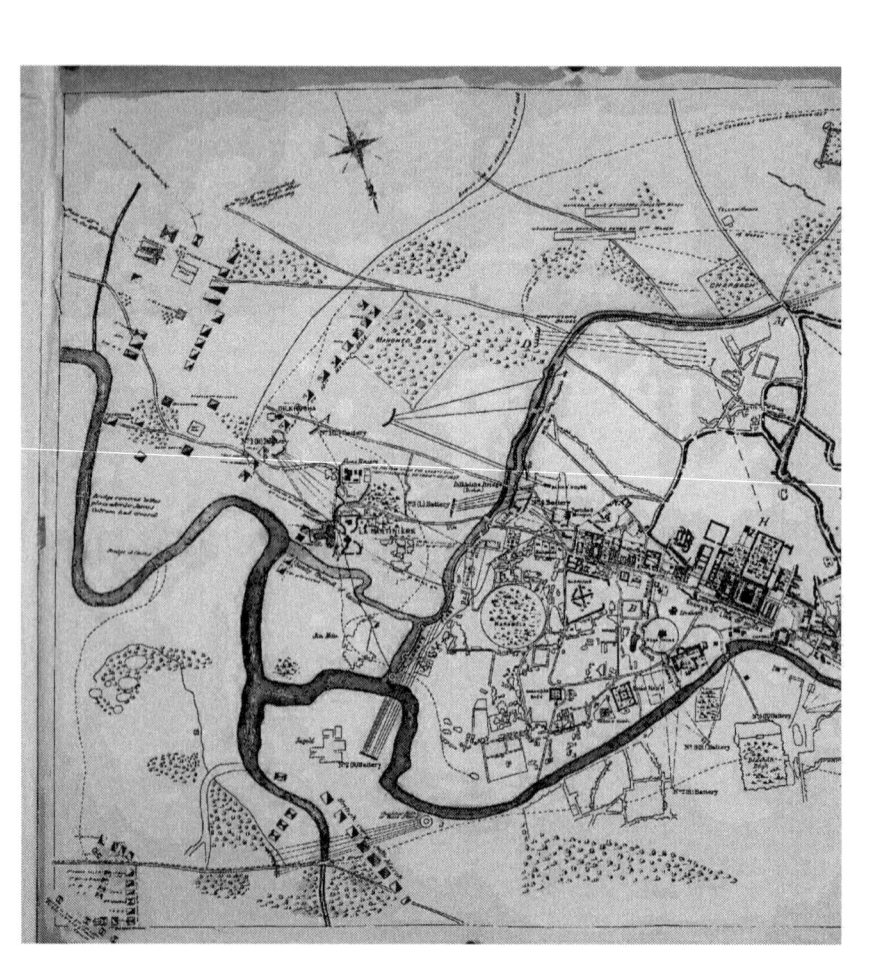

in piercing the heart of the city by three straight roads, 150 feet wide, radiating from the fort: one to Charbagh bridge, the second to Taracotta bridge, and the third to Moosa Bagh house.

The C Company of Madras Sappers, commanded by Captain Scott, marched off with one of the moveable columns under Sir Hope Grant. The other officers with it were Lieutenants Raynsford and Wynch, M.S.C.

The latter joined it at the close of the siege, *vice* Ensign Ogilvie, who was wounded near the Kaiser Bagh.

On 10th April 1858, Hope Grant was ordered to march to Barree, twenty-nine miles from Lucknow, on the Seetapore road, to clear away the rebels under the Moulvie.

He marched on the 11th with about 3,000 men. Two days after he came up with a force of 6,000 infantry and 1,000 cavalry in position on the banks of a stream, with hills on either side.

Their cavalry attacked our advanced guard, and nearly took two guns, but a squadron of 7th Hussars soon put them to flight.

The enemy now occupied a village on a hill in front of us. This village was stormed, and two colours captured. The rebels then fled.

On the 14th the force marched to Burrassie, twelve miles; on the 15th to Mamidabad; on the 16th to Belhir; and on the 19th left for Ramnugger, six miles from Bellowlie.

Orders were now received to return to Lucknow. They started on the return march on the 21st, and arrived at Mussowlie, half-way to Nawabgunge, where Jung Bahadoor's Goorkhas were stopping.

A force was sent from this place under Brigadier Horsford to destroy the fort of Rajah Ruzzul Bukhut.

After this the troops remained at Nawabgunge, and Hope Grant went to Cawnpore.

Shortly after, the force was ordered to return to Lucknow, when it crossed the Goomtee by a bridge of boats near Dilkhusha.

On the 29th they marched to Bunnee, next day to Kantha, and on 1st May to Poorwah.

The force at this time consisted of 4,800 men. They first took a small fort called Pachingaum, and then set out for Doundeakaira, a strong fort close to the Ganges, belonging to Ram Buksh; arriving on the 10th May, they found it deserted.

On the 12th they reached Nuggur, where they heard that the enemy had taken up a position at Sorsee, five miles to the east. They came up to the position at 5 P.M., and attacked at once.

By dark two guns had been taken, and the enemy were in full retreat.

Next morning our force returned to Nuggur, the following day to Poorwah, where they halted for two days, and then passed to the other side of the Goomtee, through Bunnee and Jellalabad.

On 25th May, the force marched again to Bunnee.

Sir Hope Grant left the infantry and artillery there, and proceeded to Nawabgunge on the Cawnpore road. He here waited a few days for a contingent from Raja Kuppertola.

At this time Beni Madhoo was said to be at Jessenda. Hope Grant resolved to attack him, and returned to Bunnee, but found that the enemy had vanished.

On 4th June he crossed the Sye river, and went to Poorwah.

The rebels in Oude now began to collect again at Nawabgunge on Fyzabad road, eighteen miles from Lucknow.

Their position was very strong, surrounded by a stream on three sides, while on the fourth there was jungle. The stream was crossed by a fine old stone bridge.

The object aimed at was to turn his right, and Sir Hope Grant determined to cross by a platform bridge, some two miles up the stream.

The troops marched at 11 P.M. on the 12th June, on a very

dark night. The bridge was reached half an hour before day-light, after a twelve-mile march.

It was found that two or three of the enemy's guns bore on the bridge, so some 9-pounders were brought up and silenced them.

The troops then crossed, and found themselves in the centre of the enemy, who, having been surprised, had not concentrated. Their attacks were, however, vigorous, especially that of a fine body of zemindaree men, who brought two guns into the open, and attacked us in the rear.

Sir Hope Grant says " their conduct was magnificent."

They attacked Hodson's Horse, who would not face them. The 7th Hussars were ordered up, as two guns were in danger, and four other guns opened a fire of grape. Their chief planted two green standards close to the guns, but our fire was too destructive. Two squadrons of 7th Hussars and two compa-nies of 60th came up, and forced them to retire. The 7th charged through them twice, and killed most of them.

Around the guns alone there were 125 bodies.

The fight lasted two hours. We took six guns and killed 600 men.

Our loss was sixty-seven killed and wounded. Thirty-three died of sun-stroke, and 250 men were taken into hospital.

"The victory was of the greatest possible importance, and completely broke the spirit of the rebels."

The force now remained at Nawabgunge, while Hope Grant went to Lucknow ; but shortly after he was called upon to march to the relief of Maun Singh, a raja of great importance.

He was besieged by the enemy, 2,000 strong, with twenty guns, in a large ruined fort.

On 22nd July the force left Nawabgunge, and proceeded eight miles along the Fyzabad road.

A letter was received from Maun Singh, urging speed, and Sir Hope Grant pushed on as fast as possible.

On the 29th he entered Fyzabad. Maun Singh paid him a visit; and on 2nd August Sir Hope Grant returned it at his fort, twelve miles south.

The 20,000 who had been besieging Maun Singh, had rapidly melted away as Sir Hope Grant advanced.

This relief having been effected, Hope Grant received orders to send two regiments of infantry, a battery of artillery, and 600 cavalry, to occupy Sultanpore.

On 7th August, a column marched under Horsford, and arrived on the 12th within three or four miles of the town, situated on the banks of the river Sye.

On his approach the rebels retired to the far side of the river, and Horsford awaited orders.

On the 19th, Hope Grant marched with all his available force, dragging with him four heavy guns and four 8-inch mortars.

After four days he reached Sultanpore. It was now arranged to cross the river. The great difficulty was to get boats. They had secured three small very rotten canoes hollowed out ("dug-out").

Captain Scott, M.E., and Lieutenant Raynsford, with a party of Madras Sappers, "set to work with a will," and soon converted these into a substantial raft.

Captain Reid discovered six other small boats, out of which two more rafts were made.

On the 25th the troops commenced to cross. The Madras Fusiliers and 5th Punjab Infantry got over in two hours. Two 9-pounders came next; but in embarking one of them a raft collapsed, so the guns had to be dismounted and ferried across separately.

Captain Galway, who was in command of the Fusiliers, attacked and occupied two villages in his front.

The passage of the whole force was not completed till the 27th.

On the evening of the next day the enemy attacked us, but they were repulsed.

The next morning at 3 A.M. we advanced, but found that the enemy had retreated.

A number of boats were now procured from a friendly chief, and a bridge was built by the 5th September.

The enemy was now split up into small parties, and many had joined the Amethie Rajah at his fort, twenty-five miles from Sultanpore, in direction of Pertabgurh, and eight miles distant from it.

The fort was a very large one, being seven miles in circumference. Owing to the time of the year being unhealthy, it was proposed to postpone attacking it till after the 15th October.

Sir Hope Grant now went to Allahabad to be invested with the Order of the Bath as a K.C.B., and did not return to Lucknow till the 2nd October. He received orders shortly after to march towards Tanda; left Lucknow on the 11th, and returned to Sultanpore on the 23rd.

During Sir Hope Grant's absence, Brigadier Pinckney, C.B., commanded at Pertabgurh and Sultanpore, while Brigadier Horsford was at Sultanpore.

On the 13th October Brigadier Horsford had an affair with the enemy at Shahpore, eighteen miles south-east of Sultanpore, in which the C Company of Madras Sappers was engaged.

Brigadier Horsford received intelligence that the enemy had taken up a strong position at Daodpore, eleven miles west of his camp, on the Lucknow road, with a force of 200 cavalry and 4,000 infantry, with six guns, under command of Davhie Dheen, and the rebel Nazim Mehndee Hussain. He resolved to attack them. His force consisted of—

> F Troop, B. H. A.,
> 2 6-pounder Field Battery,
> 2 9-pounder   ,,
> 101 men of Hussars,

        76 Hodson Horse,
        133 Oudh Military Police Cavalry,
        312 32nd Light Infantry,
        321 1st Madras Fusiliers,
        180 5th Punjab Rifles,
        351 Oudh Military Police Infantry,

and detachment of Madras Sappers under Lieutenant Raynsford ; his total force being 1,589.

He marched at 2 A.M. on the 20th, and arrived within three miles of the enemy's position at daylight. Two miles from Daodpore the jungle became very dense, and it was necessary to proceed with caution, as the enemy had commenced throwing up batteries to command the road. The main body of cavalry was detached to turn the enemy's right, and an advance was made by a line of skirmishers on both sides of the road. The artillery were kept on the road, supported by cavalry and infantry. The movement was successful, and the enemy were pressed rapidly through the village of Daodpore and adjoining hamlets.

It was now reported that their guns had retired towards the Kandoo Nuddee. The infantry were ordered to continue their advance, while the Brigadier started in pursuit with the artillery and part of the cavalry. After a gallop of four miles, he came up with the enemy retreating in great disorder. The enemy was soon compelled to abandon his guns, &c., which fell into our hands, several of the gunners being cut down at their guns.

The main body of the cavalry here rejoined, and continued the pursuit for two or three miles further, inflicting considerable loss on the enemy.

The Brigadier now retired four miles to some topes, where the infantry had halted, and the troops rested till 4 P.M., when the return march to Sultanpore was commenced. Sultanpore was reached at half-past 9 P.M., the infantry having marched twenty-six miles, and the cavalry and artillery fully thirty-five.

Our losses were merely nominal, consisting of two Native officers and five privates wounded, and ten horses wounded. One 24-pounder howitzer and one 9-pounder gun were captured, with ammunition-waggons, &c.

Shortly after his return to Sultanpore, Hope Grant marched to Kandoo Nuddee to drive away 4,000 rebels posted there with two batteries commanding the bridge. The enemy would not wait. The cavalry and horse artillery were sent in pursuit, and, after a thirty-mile chase, picked up two guns, one a brass 24-pounder.

On 28th October, Brigadier Horsford was sent to destroy the small fort of Mohana. It was found deserted, and was blown up, five guns being taken. The whole force now returned to Jugdespore.

Early in November the Commander-in-Chief took the field, in order to assume direction of military affairs in the Byswarra country.

On the 2nd he rode to Pertabgurh, where his camp was pitched. The column under Sir Hope Grant, which had recently been assisting the advance of Colonel Kelly from Azimghur, that under Brigadier Wetherall from Soraon, and that under Brigadier Pinckney at Pertabghur, effected combined movements for the reduction of the country and the submission of Raja Lal Madho of Amethie. Hope Grant had been ordered to move up the right bank of the Goomtee to Jugdespore, then to move south and place himself between Pursedapore and Amethie. Colonel Kelly, in communication with Brigadier Fischer, was to be responsible for the district between Tanda and Sultanpore. Wetherall was to move to Delnaigue (leaving a strong force at Soraon), thence to Bowaneegung, or Chowras; and Brigadier Pinckney to take Deolee.

On the arrival of the Commander-in-Chief at Pertabghur, Sir Hope Grant was in position six miles from Rampoor Kussia, on the Sye river. Wetherall was near Rampore Kussia, which he took on 3rd November. He was to have attacked it in concert with Hope Grant, but for some reason he disregarded this instruction. The Commander-in-Chief was much put out at this, as he considered Wetherall had incurred a heavy loss in consequence. Wetherall, however, captured the fort, with twenty-three guns, killing 300 of the enemy, with only a loss of seventy-eight killed and wounded. Sir Hope Grant made for the fort to cut off fugitives, but arrived too late.

The Commander-in-Chief now closed his forces round Amethie. The Raja tendered his submission, and the fort was occupied ; but his troops in the night, amounting to some 4,000 men, bolted. Sixteen guns were taken in this fort.

Sir Hope Grant next marched to Pursedapore, arriving on 11th November to take up a position north of Shunkerpore, a fort belonging to Beni Madho.

On the 15th the Commander-in-Chief arrived, and summoned Beni Madho. In order not to alarm him, the three brigades under Hope Grant, Pinckney, and Wetherall, were placed north, south, and east of the fort, but out of sight, although the rebel was fully aware of their presence.

On the night of the 15th Raja Beni Madho, taking advantage of the Commander-in-Chief's forbearance, evacuated the fort, and led his troops, 10,000 strong, to the west.

On the 16th Sir Hope Grant was despatched to Roy Bareilly, as the Raja was supposed to be making for that neighbourhood. Wetherall s brigade, now transferred to Colonel Taylor, was ordered to move by forced marches to Fyzabad, to commence the Trans-Gogra movements.   The Commander-in-Chief remained at Shunkerpore till the 18th, with Pinckney's brigade, now transferred to Colonel Jones, when he, also, moved to Roy Bareilly.

On the 17th Brigadier Evelegh came across part of the Raja's force, 5,000 strong, dispersed them, and took three guns. Peroo being still held, Evelegh was ordered to advance on it.   Reports were most conflicting as to the direction the Raja had taken, and Evelegh was ordered to send in his heavy guns to Roy Bareilly, move towards Doundeakaira, and to give the Raja's force no rest. The Commander-in-Chief, at the same time, moved to Buchraon, to intercept the fugitives from Beni Madho's force.

The Commander-in-Chief joined Evelegh on 23rd November, having marched sixty miles in three days, and found the enemy mustered in considerable force at Doundeakaira, under the Raja in person. The position, consisting of enclosures of jungle flanked by the fort of Doundeakaira and village of Buksar, was very strong.

He was attacked on the 24th with about 2,800 men of all arms. The enemy were completely broken and dispersed, suffering a very heavy loss, and all their guns, seven in number, were taken. Pursuit was vigorously pressed till midnight. Raja Beni Madho was now a fugitive, and was supposed to have turned to the north. The chiefs of the Byswarra country now everywhere gave in their submission.

Sir Hope Grant advanced from Roy Bareilly to Jugdespore and the Goomtee. He was then ordered to Fyzabad to take charge of the operations Trans-Gogra from that quarter, and put the brigade he had been with under Horsford, who was now moving leisurely up the right bank of the Goomtee, engaged in destroying forts and reducing that part of the country. The C Company of Madras Sappers had been engaged, under Horsford, in this work. It was in these operations that Captain Scott, of the Madras Engineers was killed.

On the 23rd November Colonel Galway marched at daybreak from Mahona with detachment F Troop R.H.A., 1 officer, 52 men, one 6-pounder and one 12-pounder howitzers; detachment Royal Artillery, 1 officer, 13 men, two 5½-inch mortars; Madras Sappers, 1 officer, 42 men; detachment 7th Hussars, 4 officers, 78 men; detachment Hodson's Horse, 1 officer,

25 men ; Madras Fusiliers, 28 officers, 566 men ; 5th Punjab
Rifles, 5 officers, 137 men—total 41 officers, 913 men ; and at
8.30 arrived before small fort of Rehora, on right bank of the
Goomtee, nine miles from Mahona.

Her Majesty's proclamation was sent into the fort, and an
answer was shortly received that the fort, and all the munitions
of war it contained, would be surrendered without opposition.
Captain Steel, with a detachment of the Punjab Rifles, entered
the fort, but found that many of the rebels were escaping with
their arms, some across the Goomtee, and some towards Koelee,
a fort about two miles higher up the river. The Punjabees
poured a fire into them, and followed the latter along the bank
of the river in the direction of Koelee, while Colonel Galway
took the Horse Artillery (supported by cavalry and infantry),
round to intercept the fugitives ; but, owing to the numerous
ravines, did not arrive in time to do more than throw a few
shells.

Colonel Galway now heard that the officer of Punjab Rifles
had suddenly come under the fire of the fort of Koelee, and that
he required support. He accordingly resumed his march, and
arrived before Koelee (which was said to be held by 200 rebels),
about half-past 12.   Our terms were offered, and rejected.

A village, between the road by which we approached and the
fort, was cleared by the fire of two mortars and two companies
of Madras Fusiliers, who had been placed on the bank of the
river to watch the ghât and prevent the rebels from doubling
back.

Colonel Galway then moved with the mortars and the remainder
of the Fusiliers round the village to the west face of the fort, of
which a view was obtained at 350 yards. While a fire was
kept up by the mortars and the supporting Fusiliers, the place
was more closely reconnoitred by Captain Scott, Field Engineer,
and Lieutenant-Colonel Galway, until they discovered the
approach to the gate, and a position from which the artillery-fire

would be more effective. To this position the mortars and two guns were brought up.

In a short time a practicable breach was opened in front of the gate; but as this only disclosed the fact that the approach was strongly flanked by defences, on which the artillery with Colonel Galway could have little effect, and as he did not think the speedy possession of such a place worth the sacrifice of life it must have entailed, he decided on suspending operations, and withdrew troops to camp about a mile from the fort.

Unfortunately, before this was decided on, Captain Scott, while more closely reconnoitring, was shot dead. Lieutenant-Colonel Galway thus writes :—

" It grieves me deeply to have to report the loss on our part of Captain Scott, Field Engineer, who was shot while endeavouring more nearly to reconnoitre the gate. I need not dilate on his value, as it was well known to the Brigadier; but must express my sorrow at being unable to return him my thanks for his zealous and active services during the day."

The first half of the Oude campaign was now finished. The advance in line from the confines of Rohilcund to Allahabad and Azimghur had compressed everything like rebellion in a large sense beyond the Gogra, except in the Seetapore district, which was about being settled by advance of Brigadier Barker, who was already beyond the Goomtee. He and Brigadier Colin Troup had executed their several instructions in a very satisfactory manner.

At Fyzabad Sir Hope Grant found a force of 4,800 men under Colonel Taylor, C.B., 79th.

Colonel Nicholson, R.E., the Commanding Engineer, having formed a bridge over the Gogra at Fyzabad, Hope Grant crossed on 27th November, and assumed command of the troops in the Goruckpore district under Brigadier Rowcroft. Grant defeated the enemy at Gonday, taking six guns and occupying the place.

Brigadier Rowcroft's force was gradually pushed across

26 *

the Raptee to Heer, driving the rebels into Toolsepore in Oude. Sir Hope Grant was now ordered to prevent the rebels passing round his right flank, to invade Tirhoot and Behar.

After the fight at Doundeakaira on the 24th, the Commander-in-Chief moved by forced marches to Lucknow.

A brigade, broken up into two movable columns, pursued Beni Madho to the banks of the Gogra. While this pursuit was going on, Brigadier Horsford intercepted Beni Madho, and drove him across the Goomtee with his cavalry and horse artillery under the officer commanding the 7th Hussars.

The Commander-in-Chief arrived at Lucknow on 28th November, but was obliged to stop there some few days to make arrangements. The brigade was, however, pushed on under Brigadier Evelegh, at once to assist in reduction of Seetapore district.

On 2nd December he occupied the fort of Oomeriah which barred the north-west road from Lucknow, remained there three days, and destroyed the fort.

By this time, Brigadier Horsford, having completed his prescribed duty on the right bank of the Goomtee, had marched through Lucknow. Another brigade at Nawabgunge, under Brigadier Purnell, C.B., was now joined to his force.

The Commander-in-Chief left Lucknow on 5th December, and reached Byramghat with Horsford's brigade on the 6th. Beni Madho's followers were still found to be lingering on the other side of the river.

Sir Hope Grant was ordered to occupy Secrore, in their rear, when they disappeared to the north.

Purnell, with his brigade, was left to collect boats, &c. to bridge the Gogra, while the Commander-in-Chief marched, at the rate of twenty miles a day, to Fyzabad, crossed the Gogra, and thence went to Secrore, followed by Colonel Christie, H.M.'s 80th, with a troop B. H. A. heavy field battery, C Company of Madras Sappers, wing of 80th, Kumaon

Battalion, 5th Punjaub Rifles, and a detachment of Hodson's Horse.

Sir Hope Grant met the Commander-in-Chief at Secrore, his troops having been pushed on towards Bulrampore on the Raptee. He was now ordered to commence his movement on Toolsepore, where Bala Rao was reported to be in considerable force.

Brigadier Rowcroft was to invade Toolsepore from north-west corner of Goruckpore, while a strong post was formed at Simree to prevent his advance being turned to the east.

The Commander-in-Chief marched to Bareitch with Brigadier Horsford, the Begum and her force retiring from Boondee, and the Nana from Bareitch as our troops moved on.

Brigadier Evelegh took post at Gonda, to form a reserve to the column marching on Toolsepore, as well as to level the fort.

Brigadier Purnell was to assist in guarding the Gogra to north-west, a small force marching up between the Chowka and Sargor to Mullapore.

Brigadier Troup, who, after the fall of Biswah, had taken post at Jehangirabad on the Chowka, was to throw 60th Rifles, with two guns and cavalry, across the Chowka, and extend the remainder of his force to his left.

The various forces on the Rohilcund frontier were put well on the alert, so as to leave no alternative to the rebels but surrender, or to take to the hills of Nepaul.

To make this pressure still more felt, Colonel Christie was detached from Bareitch with four guns B. H. A., 50 Carabineers, detachment Hodson's Horse, wing 80th, two companies 20th, 5th Punjab Rifles, detachment Oude Police Cavalry, and C Company Madras Sappers and Miners, and ordered to march up the left bank of the Sargor to Darmapore.

He left Bareitch on 21st December, having been for some days delayed by rain.

Two days after, the Commander-in-Chief left Bareitch, passed

Nonparah on the 26th, and, after marching twenty miles, attacked a body of rebels at Burgidia, who were dispersed and pursued till nightfall. Their guns were captured.

On the 27th we marched to Musjidia, which was taken after three hours' vertical fire from two mortars. The Chief Engineer was Colonel Harness, R.E.

On the 29th the troops returned to Nonparah, made a forced march on the night of the 30th to near Bankee, where the Nana had loitered. He was surprised, attacked, and driven through the jungle into and across the Raptee.

The 7th Hussars entered the river with the fugitives. Major Horne was drowned. His body was afterwards found in a deep hole. He had a firm grip of two of the enemy, and two privates were found each clutching a sowar.

In these various affairs eighteen guns fell into our hands.

Colonel Christie, with whom were the Madras Sappers, had a successful skirmish on 23rd December, and took two guns in pursuit. He then made a circuit to the north by Pudnaha, and rejoined the camp of the Commander-in-Chief on 3rd January 1859.

Meantime, Rowcroft attacked Toolsepore on 23rd December, driving Bala Rao to foot of the mountains, and taking two guns.

Sir Hope Grant, having made his right flank safe, advanced through the jungles against Bala Rao, took fifteen guns, and dispersed the rebels, Bala Rao flying into the interior as his brother, the Nana, had done before.

Thus the contest in Oude was brought to an end.

Horsford was left watching the frontier where the Raptee debouches. Similar arrangements were made in Toolsepore.

Sir Hope Grant was placed in command of the whole force on the frontier, and the Commander-in-Chief returned to Lucknow.

On the 17th January the C Company of Madras Sappers appears to have recrossed the Ganges, and shortly after returned

to the Madras Presidency, having been absent on field service
for fully eighteen months.

Before leaving the subject of the Indian Mutinies, it will be
well to add that Captain Scott, M.E.,* highly distinguished
himself in all the attacks on the Begum's palace and Kaiser Bagh
at Lucknow, and that Ensign Ogilvie's conduct at the attacks on
Emaum Barra and Kaiser Bagh at Lucknow, was most gallant.
In the taking of the latter Ogilvie accompanied the most advanced party of H.M.'s 10th Foot under Captain Norman,
assisted in the defence of their post, and went through a heavy
fire to bring up reinforcements, which he succeeded in doing,
remaining with them till severely wounded. Captain Norman
publicly thanked Ensign Ogilvie for his services on this occasion.

Captain Scott was honourably mentioned by Sir E. Lugard
as having accompanied the advanced party, on 11th March, with
powder-bags and ladders.

Lord Clyde expressed his regret at Scott's death, stating that
" he had already achieved a good reputation as an officer"; and
the Governor-General regretted his loss " as one who had earned
the approval of Government by a zealous and efficient discharge
of his duty."

Lord Clyde wrote : " The C Company Madras Sappers and
Miners were engaged and distinguished at the relief of Lucknow,
subsequently remaining with General Sir James Outram at
Alumbagh, taking a part in the siege and capture of Lucknow,
and being afterwards constantly employed in Oude during 1858."

Havildar Teroovengadum, Naique Chinnien, and Privates
Bagawaddy and Perumal, of the C Company, received the Order
of Merit for distinguished gallantry at Lucknow.   Havildar
Kistnen and some others were also favourably mentioned by
Captain Scott in his confidential recommendation rolls.

On 17th November 1857, at Lucknow, at the attack of a

---

* He obtained his Brevet Majority.

building called D Bungalow, the direct road being exposed to a heavy fire, the Sappers were ordered to open a way through the houses close to D Bungalow. It was necessary to cross a space exposed to a flank fire. The Brigadier (82nd—shortly after killed), addressing the havildar, said that some defence must be thrown up to protect his men in advancing on the D. Bungalow. He (the havildar) put three of his party of thirty to this work, to throw up the earth. He himself, to raise the cover rapidly, took up a plank and placed it so as to protect this earthwork. In the act he was shot through the left arm. All the time they were thus engaged, a heavy fire was kept up on them from the Begum Kotee.

On the 11th March 1858, Captain Scott, with his orderly, Permaul, carrying a sand-bag, and Bagawaddy carrying a powder-bag, were in advance of the assaulting column throughout the storm and capture of the Begum Kotee at Lucknow.

The latter laid the powder-bag against the inner-gate of one of the Mahals, and the former placed his sand-bag on the powder-bag. Captain Scott then fired it, and the gate was blown in under a heavy fire.

Bagawaddy was an old soldier, and had served in Coorg, Scinde, and Burmah. Permaul had been in Burmah. The coolness of both men specially attracted Captain Scott's attention.

On 14th March 1858, at Lucknow, the force was preparing to advance on the Kaiser Bagh. Captain Scott called for two privates to carry powder-bags. Chinnien and Kolundy Veloo stepped out. Captain Scott directed Kolundy Veloo to go with his powder-bag with Lieutenant Ogilvie in advance, and ordered Chinnien to accompany himself.

About thirty yards from the line of march of our troops there was a wall from which the enemy were keeping up a heavy fire. Captain Scott and Chinnien made a rush to the wall and crouched down, and Chinnien commenced with a crow-bar to dig under the wall. Chinnien placed his powder-bag, struck a light, and fired the train, and a breach was made.

The fire of the enemy on our men was so heavy, that they could only rush across the exposed space singly. When the breach in the wall was made, the enemy retreated.

We will now describe the operations of Jung Bahadoor previous to the capture of Lucknow.

In these operations Lieutenant (now Colonel, C.B.) Sankey greatly distinguished himself.

Lieutenant Sankey, shortly after the return of Sir Colin Campbell from Lucknow, received orders to join the Goorkha force under Jung Bahadoor at Goruckpoor as senior Engineer officer. He joined the head-quarters of the Goorkha force, and accompanied the leading brigade of Goorkhas to Bilwa Bagaur.

Goruckpore had been reoccupied by the Goorkha force on the 6th January 1858, the rebel Nazim Mahommed Hussain having been totally defeated by the Goorkha auxiliary force under Jung Bahadoor.

A number of British officers were attached to this force. Brigadier-General G. H. Macgregor, C.B., being Military Commissioner.

When the advanced brigade reached Bilwa Bagaur, opposite Adjoodeah, Lieutenant Sankey was detached alone to reconnoitre the Gogra near Tanda.

During his absence on this duty, Captain Plowden with a division of Goorkhas defeated and dispersed 10,000 rebels, with eight or ten guns, at Shah Gunge, on 5th February 1858.

No boats were to be had within 100 miles of Goruckpore, so arrangements had been made to cart at all speed solid jheel boats (the ordinary "dug-out" of the country) to that place.

With the help of Lieutenant Garnault, B.E., (an excellent officer), Lieutenant Sankey made up some 200 pontoons by covering the boats with tarred canvas, and placing saddles in them. These, with hastily-improvised fishermen's anchors, plenty of rope, cordage, baulks, &c., enabled them, when the advance was made to Tanda, to calculate on being able to cross the river rapidly.   These pontoons answered admirably.

It was first settled to cross the Gogra at Chupra Ghaut, but the force having been reinforced by Brigadier Rowcroft's column, consisting of the Naval Brigade and some Goorkhas convoying a large number of cargo-boats from the Ganges, it was determined to make use of the latter.

The crossing at Chupra Ghaut was thought likely to cause much delay in the upward progress of the fleet of boats, so it was determined to cross opposite Nowranee, twenty miles higher up.

On the 19th morning, the force marched twenty miles to opposite Nowranee, which place was reached in nine hours, at 5.15 P.M.

The river was crossed in boats, and about midnight the village and fort of Nowranee were seized, the fort having been evacuated.

Lieutenant Sankey accompanied the troops.

The enemy were reported to be at Phoolpore, about six miles distant on the right bank.   About 1 P.M. Brigadier Rowcroft marched with a force of 1,600 men, four 12-pounder howitzers, and six guns, and found the enemy in position in a wood on the banks of the river beyond Phoolpore.

An artillery-fire was opened by the enemy, which was briskly replied to by the Naval Brigade for about an hour.   The attack was then made, and in about an hour more the enemy gave way, and were speedily in full retreat, with the loss of three of their guns and a part of their camp equipage.

Being nearly dark when the action ceased, the success was not so great as it would otherwise have been.

"Lieutenant Sankey of the Engineers," the Brigadier stated in his despatch, "afforded me every assistance in passing orders in the field."

Lieutenant Sankey constructed a bridge of boats at Phoolpore in two days and a half, for which he received the thanks of the Brigadier General Macgregor, and subsequently those of the Government of India. This bridge was 960 feet long. Three miles of road were also made.

The next day the Goorkha army, 20,000 strong, crossed into Oude with twenty-four guns and a baggage train of 5,000 carts.

Extract from letter from Military Secretary to Commissioner :

" I am directed by the Brigadier-General to convey to you his cordial acknowledgments and best thanks for the skill and untiring energy with which you have accomplished a work of such magnitude in so short a time."

(Signed)   " MacAndrew, Lieutenant,
"Military Secretary."

From the Government of India :

" I am directed to request you will convey to Captain Sankey the thanks of Government for his great and successful exertions on that occasion " (constructing bridge of boats over Gogra).

On 26th February, while on the line of march from Mobaruk-pore to Akbarpore, as Jung Bahadoor and Brigadier-General Macgregor were proceeding along the road, they were informed that at a small fort near by, called Jumalpore, there was a small party of rebels.

As it was feared they might attack the baggage, Jung Baha-door sent some of his body-guard.

The rebels said they would submit in about two ghurries (forty minutes), the cavalry having surprised them. The Goorkhas unaccountably fell into the trap ; and on their return with a reinforcement of three companies they were fired on, and several killed and wounded.

This news reached camp, six miles distant, and Jung Baha-door sent back his brother, and subsequently went himself.

Lieutenant Sankey, at the request of the Brigadier-General, thus describes the small gurree :—

" Viewed from the outside, nothing very suspicious or formidable was discoverable about the place. It had all the appearance of an ordinary clump of bamboos at the corner of a village, which latter, like all inhabited places in this part of the country, was very well screened in foliage. Some newly-planted bamboo slips, eight to ten feet high, all round the clump above mentioned, alone marked the place as differing from others, and on another occasion would be sufficient warning to induce caution in approaching what proved to be a very hedge-hog of fortification. The fort itself was a complete wall, surrounded by a ditch more or less formidable; this, again, by a belt of high bamboos, which was succeeded by another ditch, some ten or twelve feet deep; the row of bamboo slips above mentioned being planted on the immediate lip of the counterscarp of the latter.

"The works were quite new, and were situated on the south-east corner of the village. A well, inclosed by the outer line of ditch (within a sort of demi-lune) lay on the east, and a pond, not included in the works, on the north. The only immediate entrance was on the pond side; the approach to it leading round the north-east bastion, and, curving round in a narrow thorny path, led out at the east of the well. Nothing could be more difficult of approach, every portion bristling with thorns and intercepted by ditches and banks.

" The mud ramparts of the fort were fifteen feet above the level of the ground; the upper portion for about seven feet, consisting of a thin mud-wall, was loop-holed in every direction; the lower part being from ten to twelve feet thick, and furnishing a banquette for the defenders.

"In plan the fort was some sixty-feet square, with circular bastions at the angles, the banquette on all sides ten feet wide, leaving forty feet square for the enciente, within which the defenders could retire when the fire was too hot, and where were two thatched sheds. No steps led to the banquette, a bamboo ladder being the only means of communication. When once, therefore, the defenders were driven from the upper works, they were caught in a trap."

The following is the account given by Captain J. De O. Baring, in military charge of the 2nd Brigade 1st Division Goorkha Force :—

"Instructions were received to detach a party to dislodge the insurgents. On arriving in front of the enemy's position (where I had nine companies and three guns), I was reinforced by two other regiments and two companies with seven guns, under military charge of Captain Edmonstone. The difficulty of our operations was materially increased by the enemy's position being completely surrounded by an impenetrable hedge of bamboos, which prevented our ascertaining the nature of the defences within. Under these circumstances I deemed it expedient to suggest to the General, Dere Shumsheer, that he should open with shell from the guns on the south side, sending a regiment out on each flank to prevent escape. After firing for some time, and finding we made little or no impression on the position from its natural defences, we determined on altering our tactics, and moved three guns to the east side. I now suggested the propriety of pushing the men up to the place in extended order, under cover of the guns, with the view of taking it by assault. This plan was adopted, and the troops rushed on with a cheer, and succeeded in obtaining a lodgment in the bamboo fence and trench within it. The assailing regiments here finding that they were unexpectedly opposed by a high wall and bastion, the necessity for bringing up a gun became manifest, and accordingly with great labour a 6-pounder was dragged through the outer fence of bamboos, and brought up to within a few yards of it. Five or six rounds having effected a partial breach, Lieutenant Sankey, M.E., followed by the men, carried the place by storm. Nothing could exceed the gallantry of all engaged—the Goorkhas charging with great bravery."

"Captain Edmonstone gallantly led the men of the Rifle

Regiment into the entrenchment, and also afforded me valuable assistance. I beg to bring his name prominently to the notice of the Brigadier-General, as well as that of Lieutenant Sankey, M.E., whose conspicuous bravery elicited the admiration of all."

Our losses were 8 men killed and 42 wounded. Total, 50.

Captain Edmonstone, in his report, said: "The only approach to the place was at last discovered; a gun was then forced, with great labour, into a position within ten or twelve yards of the wall; another, a 12-pounder, and a third, were placed at right angles to the first, and the cross fire thus produced was attended with the happiest results."

"Lieutenant Sankey, of the Engineers, who had been on the ground the whole day, discovered a small breach made by the first gun; it ceased firing. He enlarged the opening with his hands until it was sufficiently large to admit his head and shoulders, forced himself through it, and was the first man inside. The gallantry of this act, which, as I was standing with him close under the wall, I was an eye-witness of, I venture to bring particularly to the notice of the Brigadier-General."

"I myself immediately followed the two first Goorkhas, I believe, who penetrated into the enclosure by a ladder which was placed against the wall close to me. Our men then forced their way in through the breach by the ladder, and through a narrow opening, apparently the entrance to the place, but which only came half-way down the wall; and the enemy (thirty-one bodies were subsequently counted) were all, I believe, cut to pieces."

General Macgregor says the number of enemy killed was thirty-two.

Captain Baring, who was present, says: "Loss of enemy was between forty and fifty killed."

The Military Commissioner, in his despatch to Government, remarked: "The conspicuous gallantry of Lieutenant Sankey was the admiration of everyone. It was by his advice the gun was brought up which breached the wall, and he was the first man in the fort, followed by the Rifle Regiment with Captain Edmonstone."

For his conduct on this occasion, Lieutenant Sankey was most strongly recommended for the distinction of the Victoria Cross.

The following note was written by the Military Secretary to the Commissioner to Lieutenant Sankey :—

"The General this morning has confided to me the pleasing duty of telling you that he has recommended you for the V.C. for your conduct at capture of Jumalpore. As the Governor-General keeps your plan of it, and is much pleased with that business altogether, I should think there is very little doubt of your getting that much-coveted distinction. At any rate, the General has done what he can for you ; and there is no officer in the force, including your humble servant, who does not think you richly deserve it, and does not feel that the granting of it to you will reflect credit on our whole campaign. I offer you my most hearty congratulations, and hope you may live long to wear it. You must be the first officer of Madras army to whom it will be given."

Lieutenant Prendergast, M.E., was recommended for acts at Mundisore, 21st November 1857, Ratghur, 24th January 1858, and Betwa, 1st April 1858 ; so that the gallant acts of Sankey at Jumalpore and Prendergast on the Betwa and at Ratghur occurred within a short time of each other.

The following extract from a letter from General Macgregor to Military Secretary, India Office, will show the unfortunate way in which Lieutenant Sankey was deprived of the honour he so richly deserved :—

"In March 1858, when I was Military Commissioner with Jung Bahadoor's force in Oude, I recommended Major Sankey for the V.C. for conspicuous gallantry at capture of fort of

Jamulpore in Oude by the Goorkha force. The late Earl Canning supported the recommendation, and forwarded it to England ; but as it came direct from the Government of India, without having been previously submitted to the Commander-in-Chief, it was considered informal, and was referred back to India. Sir Hugh Rose referred the case to a committee of officers, and their report was, I believe, to the effect that, while considering the action a gallant one for which the recommendation was made, yet, from the circumstance of Major Sankey having been made a Brevet Major while a subaltern, they could not support it.

"The fact of Major Sankey having been made a Brevet-Major one month earlier than he had a right to expect,* can hardly be looked upon as weighing in the balance against a decoration which in many respects is deservedly considered the proudest honour in the gift of the Crown. No man, in my opinion, ever better earned the V.C. than did Major Sankey. In the performance of his duty he exposed himself to almost certain death, setting a brilliant example of courage to the men who were engaged with him at the fort ; and I may add, with much truth, that his services on that occasion contributed greatly to the capture of the place, and while it would be a mere act of justice on the part of Her Most Gracious Majesty to confer the V.C. on Major Sankey, it would be at the same time a delicate compliment to the memory of the lamented Earl Canning, who recommended Major Sankey for that honourable distinction."

In reply to this, a cold and somewhat curt answer was received from the Assistant Military Secretary (General Macgregor's letter having been addressed to the Secretary) :—

"I am directed by the Secretary of State to acknowledge the

---

* Lieutenant Sankey was first made a Brevet Major on 20th July 1858 ; but after some years it was discovered that, being a subaltern at the time, he had no right to it ; it was changed to 28th August 1858, the day after he attained to the rank of Captain in the Madras Engineers.

receipt of your letter of 14th July, and to acquaint you, in
reply, that applications from persons resident in this country on
behalf of officers in India for promotion or other reward cannot
be entertained. I am, however, directed to add that the claim
of Major Sankey, M.E., to the distinction of V.C. had been
decided on agreeably to the opinion expressed by the Commander in-Chief in India, and that this decision cannot be
departed from."

It will be seen from the note to General Macgregor's letter
that Lieutenant Sankey, after all, was a Captain before the date
of his Brevet Majority ; but how the date of a Brevet Majority
can affect the question of a V.C. it is utterly impossible to
understand, as he would certainly have obtained that, even had
he not been present at the capture of Jumalpore. His services
in bridging the Gogra and Goomtee, &c., would have sufficed
for that.

It should be mentioned that the Right Hon. the Governor-
General, in publishing the reports of the capture of the fort of
Jumalpore, said :—

"To Generals Runoodeep Sing and Dere Shumshere, to
Lieutenant Sankey of the Madras Engineers, Captain Edmonstone, and all the officers and men who took a part in effecting
the capture of the fort, the Governor-General offers his hearty
thanks."

From Akbarpore the force marched to Sultanpore on the
Goomtee.

Lieutenant Sankey constructed a bridge over the Goomtee at
Sultanpore, for which he received the thanks of the Government
of India.

"Lieutenant Sankey's exertions were as conspicuous as they
were successful, and they merit the best thanks of the Government."

The bridge at Sultanpore was partly constructed by the
Goorkha army in its own fashion. This consisted in their

attacking all the neighbouring trees with their "kookeries," hewing off forked limbs, using these as piles, and straight ones as baulks for the roadway. It was a singular sight to see some 13,000 men thus engaged, some up at the tops of the highest trees, and others wading up to their necks in the river fixing the piles, &c. The work was a perfect ant-swarm, from which a very effective bridge emerged.

Lieutenant Sankey's part consisted in placing boats across all the deep portions of the stream, and linking them with the piled parts.

Shortly after the Goorkha force crossed the Goomtee they were engaged with the enemy at Kandoo Nuddee.

On 5th March 1858, at this action, Lieutenant Sankey was present, and was mentioned in Brigadier-General Macgregor's despatch to the Government.

The enemy amounted to 4,000 men, under Nazim Mehndee Hussain. They had taken up a strong position on the Kandoo Nuddee, had erected a battery by the side of the bridge on the Lucknow road, and had advanced across the bridge.

The Goorkha division advanced in quarter-distance column, and on viewing the enemy were deployed into line.

The ground between the right brigade and the enemy at first appeared level cultivation; but afterwards proved to be deep ravines with brush jungle, though that in front of left brigade was a plain.

Our guns now opened. After a few rounds the advance was sounded. The right brigade advanced fifty yards, when the enemy opened a sharp fire of musketry on our right front from a jungle.

A brigade was turned on this point. The troops rushed gallantly into the jungle with a loud cheer, formed a line of skirmishers, and forced the rebels to make a rapid retreat. The Goorkhas' pursuit was so rapid that numbers of the enemy were shot and cut down. The pursuit was followed up for miles, when the "assembly" was sounded, and camp was formed on the Nuddee.

A few days after, the Goorkha force reached Lucknow (which Sir Colin Campbell was besieging), and took possession (on the left of his force) of a suburb south-east of the Charbagh.

The services of the Goorkhas, at the siege of Lucknow, under Jung Bahadoor have already been related.

CHAPTER X.

War with China, 1860.—Cause of war.—Our squadron repulsed, 25th June 1859.
—British and French Governments agree to enforce treaty.—French
assemble at Shanghae—we at Hong Kong.—Madras Sappers reach
Talien Whan Bay, June 1860 —Lieutenant Gordon drowned.—We disembark
at Pehtang.—Force leaves Pehtang.—Sinho occupied.—Engineer brigade
formed.—Tang-koo captured.—Taku forts.—All the Taku forts taken.—
Shaw Stewart with A Company ordered to Tientsin.—Battle of Chang-kia-wan.
—Battle of Pa-li-chow.—Summer Palace taken by the French.—Breaching
batteries at Pekin constructed.—An-ting Gate surrendered.—Convention
signed and ratified.—Position of breaching batteries.—Army leaves Pekin.—
Sappers sail for Hong Kong.—Weather very trying towards close of campaign.—Notices regarding Sappers.—Sir Hope Grant's despatch.—Shaw
Stewart a brevet major.—Bhotan War, 1865.—Expedition to the Little
Andamans.

THE cause of this war appears to have been the unwillingness
of the Chinese Government to ratify the Treaty of Tientsin,
which, according to the provisions of that agreement, should
have been completed on or before 26th June 1859.

On 17th June Admiral Hope, Commander-in-Chief of H.M.'s
naval forces in the Eastern seas, appeared at the mouth of the
Peiho to announce the approach of the English and French
Ministers. The Admiral was told that the passage had been
closed by the Militia without the orders of their Government.
These untrue representations were supported by false appear-
ances; the batteries of the forts were masked, no banners were
displayed, and no soldier was seen. No communication was
allowed with the shore. After promising to remove the obstacles
at the river mouth the Militia repudiated the promise.

Such was the state of affairs when the British Minister, the Hon. F. Bruce, arrived outside the bar on 20th June. Finding that the Chinese officials kept aloof, while the Militia continued to assert that the obstruction was their own unauthorized act, he called upon the Admiral to take such steps as were necessary to reach the capital by the time appointed.

This, on the 25th June, the Admiral was proceeding to effect, when the forts, which for eight days previous had appeared deserted, suddenly opened fire on the squadron. The result was that our squadron was repulsed, and that we were obliged to abandon some ships, guns, and *matériel*.

The British and French Governments now entered into a treaty to enforce the Treaty of Tientsin by force of arms, if necessary; and it was agreed that 10,000 English and 7,000 French should be sent to China.

The French army had to be despatched from France, ours chiefly came from India. The French assembled at Shanghai, we at Hong Kong.

The A and K Companies of the Madras Sappers formed part of our force. They were commanded by Captain J. H. M. S. Stewart, Madras Engineers.

A Company—
> Captain Dakeyne, Madras Infantry.
> Lieutenant Gordon, Madras Engineers.
> Lieutenant Filgate,   ,,   ,,

K Company—
> Captain Swanston, Madras Infantry.
> Lieutenant M. Foord,   ,,   ,,
> Lieutenant Trail, Madras Engineers.

Assistant-Surgeon Pearse being in medical charge.

The Sappers embarked at Madras in the transport *Statesman*, reached Singapore on 28th March 1860, and Hong Kong on 27th April. They disembarked at the latter place, and remained for about three weeks at Kowloon, on the north side of Victoria Harbour.

On 18th May they left Hong Kong, and, after a stormy passage, arrived, on 16th June, at Talien-Whan Bay, which had been fixed upon as the place of rendezvous for the English forces, the French being at Chefoo on the opposite side of the entrance to the Gulf of Petcheli.

Immediately after their arrival the Sappers were employed in digging wells for watering the fleet, building piers, making roads, &c.

Lieutenant Gordon, M.E., and Sergeant Hoskins, of the Sappers, joined at Hong Kong, having arrived from Madras on 16th May.

The English army was ready for action by the middle of June, but the French were not so forward with their arrangements, and fixed the 25th July as the earliest date on which they could assume offensive operations.

While the English army remained inactive at Talien-Whan Bay, Lieutenant Gordon, of the Engineers, was drowned on the morning of the 11th July. He went across the bay to inquire for letters, which he had heard were on board the steamer *Lightning*. He was accompanied by Captain Lumsden, D.A.Q.M.G. They put off in a boat belonging to the *Imperatriz*. The boat was manned by the third officer and two sailors. On their return from the opposite side, the wind blew strong; and at about 5 P.M., when half-way across the harbour, a sudden gust capsized the boat. For some hours they all clung to the boat, till between 8 and 9 P.M., when there seemed to be doubts of it being able to sustain them all. The shore was distant about four miles, with a strong wind blowing, and a very heavy sea. Captain Lumsden volunteered to try to reach the shore, with the view of lightening the boat and sending assistance to the sailors, neither of whom could swim. Lieutenant Gordon followed him with the same object, but he was numbed with cold, and his strength soon failing he was obliged to return to the boat.

According to the testimony of one of the crew, Gordon's strength was so far gone that he was barely able to clutch at this man's legs as they hung in the water. His strength soon failed altogether, he lost his hold and sank.

Captain Lumsden, by a most marvellous feat of strength and pluck, succeeded in reaching the shore, and the officer and men belonging to the *Imperatriz* were picked up during the night by boats which chanced to pass. Lieutenant Gordon's body could not be found, although every exertion was made to recover it.

Captain Shaw Stewart, in his report, remarks: "Lieutenant Gordon's services, though short (about four years in India), had been most brilliant and distinguished, and a very promising career lay before him. Our corps has lost in him a much-beloved brother officer, the Madras army a distinguished ornament, and the State a most zealous and able servant. He served at Mohumera in the Persian war, and was present throughout the whole of the Central India campaign under Sir Hugh Rose, having been mentioned with approval by that distinguished soldier."

The Madras Sappers remained encamped near Talien-Whan Bay till 24th July. During this time they were employed on various duties connected with the safety and well-being of the force.

On 24th July they re-embarked on the *Statesman*, and, after lying at anchor for some days in the Gulf of Petcheli, they disembarked, without opposition, on the 7th August, at Pehtang, a large village situated on a river of the same name, ten miles north of the Peiho.

On the 1st August the 2nd Brigade of 1st Division, supported by the French, had landed, experienced great difficulty in getting through the mud, and passed the night on the mud-flats.

The 2nd Division remained on board the ships.

The forts looked formidable, but no active opposition was offered to the disembarkation; the chief difficulty was the mud.

In the morning the forts and town were taken possession of. The Chinese, before withdrawing, had buried large shells with trains with spring locks, so as to cause an explosion should the latter be accidentally pressed by the foot. Warning was, however, received in time to prevent damage.

On 3rd August the troops had a skirmish with the Tartars, in which Major Greathed, R.E., was wounded.

By the 7th August all the troops had landed. The quarters allotted to the Sappers were found full of putrid matter, the Chinese having killed their animals prior to abandoning the town, and distributed parts of them over the different houses, doubtless with a view to cause a pestilence among the invaders. After making the houses habitable, the Sappers were employed in making a road through the marshes (which surrounded Pehtang, and which had been rendered very difficult by late rain), so as to facilitate the transit of the guns and heavy baggage to the main embanked road, which led to the entrenchments in front and to the Taku forts.

On the 9th Captain Wolseley reconnoitred to the right, by which the enemy's left might be turned. He ascertained that the country in that direction was practicable for all arms.

The allied force left Pehtang on 12th August, and marched in the direction of Sin-ho, a large village on the Peiho, about eight miles from its mouth, the Tartars being known to occupy a strongly-entrenched position on the line of march.

The 2nd Division, to which the Madras Sappers were attached, went in advance, by the route to the right, to take the entrenched camp in flank. The 1st Division, and the French force, moved along the causeway. On approaching the entrenchment, a large force of Tartar cavalry came out and hovered about our flank to charge, but without effecting it. Upon one occasion the brigade to which the Sappers were attached was halted, and formed into squares to receive them; but our fire kept them most effectually at a distance.

A small detachment of K Company Sappers, under Lieutenant Trail, had been sent in advance with Milward's battery of Armstrong guns, to improve the road, which was extremely heavy. The work was excessively severe, and several Sappers were obliged to fall behind from sheer fatigue. Two men who had fallen out of the line of march were taken prisoners by the Tartar cavalry, which had been hovering on our flank and rear; one of these men was returned on 17th August, but of the other no certain news was received.

Notwithstanding the work of the Sappers, the marsh was so bad that the horses stuck, the guns sank up to their axles, and it was found absolutely necessary to leave behind many of the waggons. After many hours of hard work (the start had been made at 2.30 A.M), struggling against these difficulties, the guns were dragged through about two miles of marsh, and eventually landed on hard ground about 10 A M., when the troops were halted, the enemy being known to be close in advance. After a short rest, the advance was ordered, and the Tartars were soon observed in sight. In spite of some gallant attempts at charges on their part, they had to retire and leave the Allies in possession of the entrenchment at Sinho; and the army bivouacked there for the night.

Next day the force moved to the east of Sinho, within two miles of the fortified town of Tang-koo. An Engineer Brigade was then formed under the orders of Lieutenant-Colonel Mann, commanding R. E.

The brigade consisted of 10th and 23rd companies R. E., half of the 8th Company, with A and K Companies of Madras Sappers.

On the night of the 13th a working-party, consisting of details of R. E. and Madras Sappers and a strong body from the line, were sent in the direction of Tang-koo, for the purpose of throwing up cover for the riflemen. Lieutenant Trail, on this occasion, was in command of the Sappers. After reconnoitring the fort closely, the party was set to work, and by daybreak a good line of cover had been thrown up about 400 yards from the fort.

About 6 A.M. the 1st Division advanced to the attack, the English on the right close to the Peiho, while the French attacked the gateway.

A strong body of Artillery and Engineers accompanied the force. Among the latter were parties of Madras Sappers, with scaling-ladders and powder-bags, Lieutenant Filgate being in charge of the former, and Lieutenant Swanston of the latter. The Artillery opened fire at a distance of 1,500 yards, and, gradually approaching the fort, silenced the Tartar fire after a sharp cannonade of three hours.

The pontoons and scaling-ladders were then called for; but before they reached the ditch a few riflemen had crept round the work close to the river, and found that the Tartars had fled and were crossing to the south side as fast as they could. Twenty-four guns were taken in this fort.

The capture of Tang-koo left us in a very strong position in rear of the Peiho forts.

The following days were occupied in reconnoitring, and on the 17th the Commander-in-Chief (Sir Hope Grant) determined that the fort to the north of the Peiho should be first attacked.

Its shape was nearly square, each side measuring 150 to 200 yards. In the centre was an immense tower of solid earth, on which were mounted three very large brass guns. The whole of the fort was strongly defended by smaller batteries.

The enemy had lost no time in strengthening the land defences; all their heavy guns had been turned round, the parapet had been raised and strengthened with enormous piles, and fresh embrasures and loop-holes had been cut.

But it was in what may be called its " passive " defences

that the fort especially excelled. Throughout a circuit of about a mile the country was intersected by numerous canals and deep ditches, running in every direction. The fort itself was surrounded by three wet ditches—the outer one broad and shallow, and the two inner ones varying in breadth from twenty to twenty-five feet, and four to eight feet in depth; the intervening spaces, as well as the berm, were protected by very strong abattis, and by masses of sharp-pointed stones and bamboo spikes firmly rooted in the ground.

All were agreed that few places of the kind have ever been more perfectly supplied with obstacles of this nature. Nothing seemed to have been neglected. *Trous de loup*, crows' feet, and strong iron spikes were scatterred in abundance to impede our progress, while the garrison was defended against night surprises by alarm bells, which anyone attempting to cross the abattis must inevitably sound.

The 18th and 19th August were taken up in preparing small bridges to carry the artillery over the canals and ditches.

At 5.30 P.M. on the 19th, a party started to place these bridges in position. The Sappers who were employed in this work were under the orders of Lieutenants Dakeyne and Filgate.

They returned at 8 A.M. on the 20th, having effected their purpose, besides making two dams to shut off the supply of water from the canals.

On the afternoon of the same day, Lieutenants Hime, R.E., and Trail, M.E., were directed to trace five batteries in positions which had been fixed after the reconnoissance and personal inspection of Sir Robert Napier (second in command), B.E.

This duty was carried out without much opposition from the forts.

When night closed in, all the available men of the Madras Sappers were marched out to complete the necessary works before daylight, by which time it was intended that the guns should be in position and ready to open fire.

This intention was successfully carried out, and the Tartars did not notice that the English were in position till 4.30 A.M. on the 21st, when they opened fire.

Lieutenants Swanston, Dakeyne, and Foord, each had charge of the construction of one battery.

The elevation of the enemy's guns was, fortunately for us, too great, and, as by their arrangements this could not readily be altered, their fire did comparatively little harm.

Our guns at once returned the fire of the enemy, and a very heavy cannonade was kept up for about four hours, when the Taku fort was somewhat silenced.

The 44th and 67th Regiments were pushed forward as skirmishers, followed by the Sappers, &c. with pontoons and ladders.

There was some delay in crossing the ditch, owing to the size and weight of the pontoons, and during this slight halt our troops suffered severely from the heavy cross-fire.

The Sappers accompanying the storming party were divided into four sub-divisions : the pontoon party under Lieutenant Pritchard, R.E.; the ladder party under Lieutenant Hime, R.E. ; the detachment for removing obstacles under Lieutenant Trail, M.E.; and the powder-bags with Lieutenant Clements, R.E.

Once over the ditch, the scaling party were not long in effecting a lodgment in the work, despite the fierce attempts of the Tartars to repulse them.

Lieutenant Trail was with the ladder party, and was among the first of those who entered the fort.

Lieutenant Filgate, with a party of Sappers, was highly praised for the rapidity with which, under a heavy fire, he made a causeway for heavy artillery across a canal close to the fort.

The escalade was greatly facilitated by the Chinese coolies from the south ; who, rushing into the ditch, and throwing ladders across their shoulders, formed a temporary bridge, over which the assailants passed.

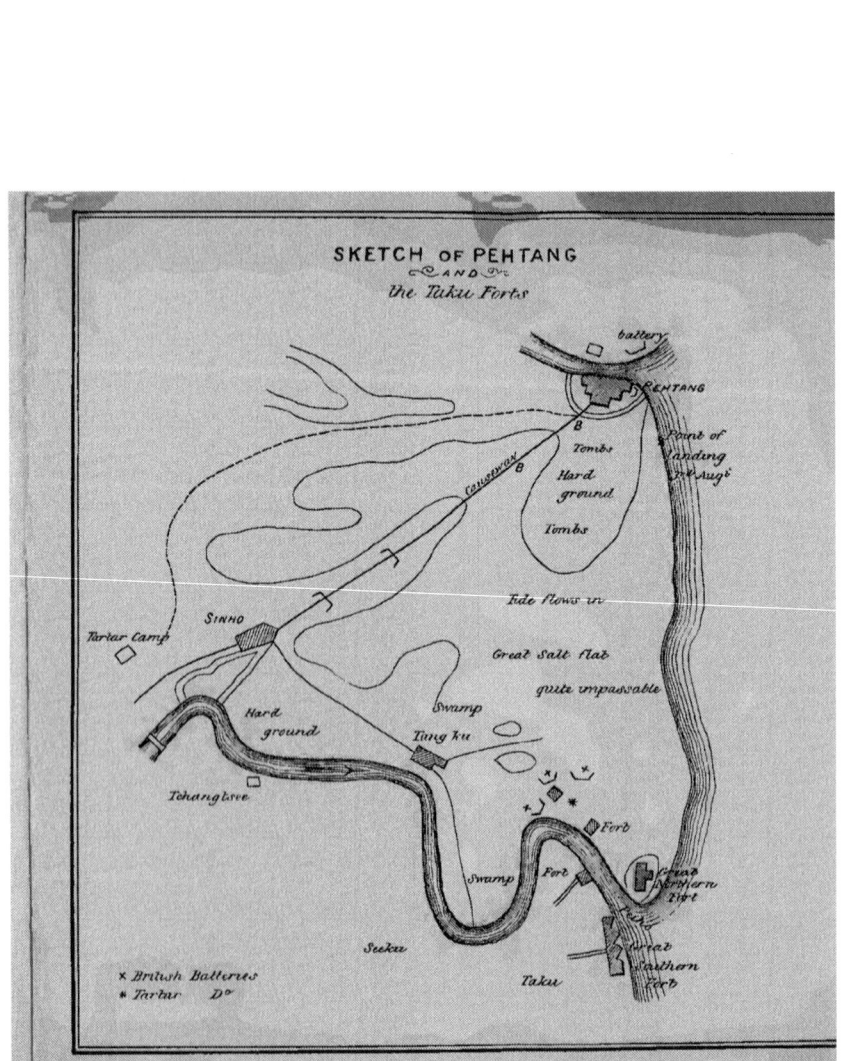

SKETCH of PEHTANG
AND
the Taku Forts

battery

PEHTANG

B
Tombs

Point of
Landing
1st Aug.

Causeway
B

Hard
ground

Tombs

Tide flows in

Tartar Camp
SINHO

Great Salt flat

quite impassable

Hard
ground

Swamp

Ting ku

Tchangtsee

Swamp

Fort

Great
Northern
Fort

Fort

× British Batteries
✳ Tartar D.o

Seekae

Taku

Great
Southern
Fort

Many of the coolies were wounded, but, instead of retiring to the rear, they took up their position behind the first mound, which offered the slightest shelter, and thence viewed the attack going on in front.

In the afternoon we moved against a second fort. We were allowed to take possession of it without opposition, and one after another the remaining forts capitulated.

This was a very fortunate circumstance, as almost immediately after heavy rain came on, which so saturated the mud, that moving the guns would have been a task of a very serious nature in the face of the enemy.

During the 22nd and 23rd, all the forts on the south side of the river were evacuated and surrendered to the Allies.

It was now thought the campaign was finished.

The 1st Division moved up to Tien-tsin on the 30th, and the 2nd followed on 1st September.

On the advance of the expedition *towards Tien-tsin, part of the K Company of Madras Sappers was left at the forts under the command of Lieutenant M. E. Foord, orders being at the same time given to Lieutenant Trail to make the necessary arrangements for the demolition of the forts on the south side of the river, while the French undertook the destruction of those on the north. Instructions were likewise issued to complete a survey of the forts before they were demolished.

In accordance with these directions, the Wasp and Artillery forts were completely destroyed, and the mining of the South fort proceeded with until stopped by the conclusion of peace at Pekin.

The forts were very formidable, and their mode of construction curious. Piles about twelve inches square having been first driven in at short intervals, straw ropes about two inches in diameter were twisted in and out. These were covered with stiff clay, rammed hard at each foot of height. The outline was irregular, being in some forts nearly a circle, in others egg-shaped—irregularly elongated. The centres of the small forts were occupied by a cavalier commanding the whole fort, as well as the ground outside. In the main fort on the south side there were three such cavaliers, dividing the space nearly into four equal parts.

Owing to the unexpected interruption of the negotiations at Tien-tsin, a large part of the force then at that place was ordered to march in the direction of Pekin.

On 10th September, Captain Shaw Stewart received orders to take the A Company of Sappers to Tien-tsin, with the view of proceeding further north.

The army marched by Pookow, Yang-tsin, and Hose-woo, which last place it reached on the 13th.

On the 14th, a mission, consisting of Messrs. Parkes, Loch, &c., started for Tung-chow.

The army moved forward on the 18th.

Although carrying a flag of truce, Messrs. Parkes, Loch, and their whole party were taken prisoners, and most shamefully treated. Many of them were cruelly tortured to death.

On the 18th was fought the battle of Chang-kia-wan, when the enemy were signally defeated and driven back with great loss on Tung-chow.

Tung-chow was occupied, and the army remained there till the 21st.

Captain Shaw Stewart was directed to proceed alone from Tien-tsin to join the army as soon as possible, leaving the A Company to follow. He joined our force at Chang-kia-whan on the evening of 20th September, in time to be present at the battle of Pa-li-chow.

From this place General Montauban, the French Commander-in-Chief, derived his title as Count Palikao.

The French attacked the bridge of Pa-li-chow on the right, while the English assaulted the enemy on the left.

It was at this bridge that Brabazon and the Abbé de Luc

were beheaded by the order of the Tartar Commander-in-Chief, San-ko-lin-sin.

The enemy were driven from one intrenched position after another with great loss, and we pursued them till within about five miles of the south-east angle of Pekin.

Their large force being principally cavalry, their loss was not so great as it otherwise would have been. Indeed, the action on our part was chiefly fought with artillery and our small body of cavalry, Barry's battery of Armstrong guns and the King's Dragoon Guards particularly distinguishing themselves.

The strength of the enemy was estimated at 70,000 men. Of their wounded nothing was known, but their killed considerably exceeded 1,000 men.

The enemy retreated to Pekin, east and north-east of the city.

It was now necessary to establish a base at Tung-chow.

By the beginning of October, complete arrangements having been made at Tung-chow, and the siege-train having arrived from Tien-tsin (escorted by the A Company of Madras Sappers, with Captain Dakeyne, Swanston, and Lieutenant Filgate), the army was ready to advance, and on 3rd October the Allies moved round the north-east angle of Pekin to gain an open plain.

All this time negotiations were in progress for the surrender of the prisoners treacherously taken on 18th September.

The negotiations having failed, on 6th October our army took up their quarters in the large suburb north of the city; the French on the same day taking possession of Yuen-ming-yuen, the Emperor's magnificent summer-palace with its stores of treasure and unrivalled collection of rare and valuable works of art.

The Emperor and the principal Mandarins having fled to Gehok, notice was sent to the highest Mandarin remaining in the city, on the 9th October, requiring the surrender of all the prisoners and the cession of the An-ting gate on 13th, failing which, Sir Hope Grant threatened to commence breaching the walls.

On the 12th, Messrs. Parkes and Loch, with a French officer and a Sikh duffadar, were released ; a few more Sikhs and French were subsequently sent in, and the Mandarins then stated that no more of the prisoners remained alive.

They afterwards sent in the bodies of all who had been murdered, with the exception of two, Captain Brabazon and the Abbé de Luc, who had, as stated before, been beheaded at the bridge of Pa-li-chow, having met the Tartar army on its retreat on 21st September.

From the 9th to 12th October the Engineer Brigade was busily employed in constructing breaching batteries near the north-east angle of the city.

On the morning of the thirteenth everything was ready, and, the gate not having been delivered up, the artillery had orders to open fire at noon, when at the last moment—11.45 A.M.— the An-ting gate was surrendered and taken possession of by H.M.'s 97th and 8th Punjab Regiments, with Desborough's battery.

The bodies of the murdered prisoners were buried on the 17th with great solemnity.

On the same day Lord Elgin wrote to Prince Kung that when Sir Hope Grant wrote, demanding possession of the An-ting gate and naming the terms on which he was willing to spare Pekin, he was ignorant of the barbarous treatment of the prisoners treacherously taken on the 18th, and that more than half of them had been murdered, in spite of the pledges which His Highness had given of their safety in many of his despatches. Under these circumstances he would be quite justified in setting aside the conditions named in the General's letter ; but from an anxiety for the safety of the people, Lord Elgin said he was ready to make peace.

His terms were that 300,000 taels should be handed over by 22nd October, to be distributed among those who had suffered * and the families of those who had been murdered.

He notified, also, that it was intended at once to utterly destroy all that remained of Yuen-ming-yuen, within the precincts of which several of the British captives had been subjected to the grossest indignities.

Before the 20th Prince Kung was to inform Lord Elgin that he was willing to sign the convention.

On the 18th October the 1st Division, under Sir John Michel, marched to Yuen-ming-yuen, and set fire to all the palaces.

On the 19th the fires were still burning, and the wind carried the smoke over our camp right into the city. By the evening the summer palaces had ceased to exist.

On the 20th Lord Elgin received Prince Kung's absolute submission.

On the 21th the convention was signed by Lord Elgin and Prince Kung (brother to the Emperor). Sir Hope Grant was present at the proceedings, while Sir Robert Napier had charge of the military arrangements connected with them.

The French convention was signed next day.

Both treaties were afterwards sent to Gehok, where they received the Emperor's signature.

The position selected for our breaching batteries is a point of interest worth record. It was about 600 yards to the east of the An-ting gate. The guns were to be placed within the high wall which surrounded the Te-tsu or Temple of the Earth.

Four 8-inch guns were to make a breach between the second and third square flanking towers east of the gate. Two Arm-

---

* Prisoners returned safe—Messrs. Parkes and Loch, Monsieur L'Escayrac de Lauture, 11 Sikh soldiers, 5 French soldiers. Total, 19.

Prisoners murdered—Lieutenant Anderson, Mr. De Normann, Phipps, K.D.G., Mr. Bowlby (*Times* Correspondent), Captain Brabazon, R.A., Abbé de Luc, 4 French officers and soldiers, 10 Sikhs. Total, 20.

strong 12-pounders were to play upon the breach, whilst two others fired down the road leading to the gate, two more to be in reserve. A battery of 9-pounders to counter-batter. Our mortars to play on the breach.

Our guns were placed on wooden platforms laid down behind the massive brick walls of the temple.

The French had no regular breaching guns, but they hoped to make their heaviest field battery serve instead. Their battery was to our left, and only 60 yards from the walls. Ours was 200 yards.

Shelter was dug in advance for our infantry, so that the Chinese gunners and the breach might be well plied with rifle-fire.

Nothing now remained for the army to do in the north, and the march to the south shortly commenced.

The Madras Sappers left Pekin on 7th November, with the 2nd Division under Sir Robert Napier. They reached Tien-tsin on the 12th. There the Sappers were embarked on board gun-boats and taken to the mouth of the Peiho. They there found their transport, the *Statesman*, Captain Marshall, ready. They weighed anchor on 17th November, and sailed for Hong Kong.

"The weather in the latter part of the campaign was extremely cold and trying to the troops, especially the natives of India. The sudden transition from heat to cold was very remarkable. On 6th October, the day we marched into the north suburb, the heat was almost unbearable. Within less than a week the north wind had set in, and the keen biting cold became intense. On the march south from Pekin the thermometer at night was often below 20° Fahrenheit, and on the day after we weighed anchor the thermometer at noon was at 35°, hail and snow having fallen several times."

The Governor in Council at Madras, in noticing Captain Shaw Stewart's reports to the Commandant of Engineers, observed " that the reports are most creditable to the detachment of the

Madras Sappers recently employed in China, where they appear to have well sustained the ancient reputation of their Corps."

Sir Hope Grant, in a letter to the Viceroy, dated 21st November 1860, thus writes :—

"The two companies of Madras Artillery under Captain Hicks, and the two companies of Madras Sappers under Captain Shaw Stewart, rendered good and useful service in the operations which preceded and led to the fall of the Taku forts. The latter Corps was most energetic in working without reliefs at the construction of the batteries, and have always shown themselves to be cheerful and willing workmen."

Captain Shaw Stewart was recommended to favourable notice for his exertions in trench duties, and promoted to a Brevet Majority from 15th February 1861.

The Bhotan Field Force had, early in 1865, been divided into two independent commands—the right brigade under Brigadier Tombs, the left under Brigadier Frazer Tytler.

Tytler commenced operations on the 15th March, recaptured Balla, and moved towards Buxa on the 23rd.

Tombs was at Gowhatty on 7th March; thence he marched forty-one miles to Koomrekatta, and made arrangements for the capture of Dewangiri.

The passes were reconnoitred, and on 1st April an advance was made by the Durungah Pass. Dewangiri was captured, after which the troops were withdrawn and the place abandoned.

The two brigades were then consolidated, and placed under the command of Brigadier-General Tytler, with head-quarters at Gowhatty.

Further operations were contemplated later in the year, and Captain Æneas Perkins, B.E.,* was appointed Chief Engineer of the force, and towards the end of September moved to Buxa.

* Now Colonel Perkins, C.B., A.D.C. to the Queen.

28 *

Lieutenant W. T. Whish, R.(M.)E., joined the force at this time.

It was intended to drive forward a road along the chain of mountains that contain the Tchin-chu river on the west. The Engineers worked up from Buxa, about 1,800 feet above sea-level, over the ridge in front (5,500 feet), by the track, which, on the summit, was called the Tchin-chu-la, and continued their line to a place called Tapee, and thence to Murichom, in all about twenty miles.

The object was to continue the line first to Chuka (two marches ahead of Murichom), where a dip would have been made to the river, which it was proposed to cross by a native canti-lever bridge of 100 feet span ; secondly, along the left bank of the river so gained, direct upon Panakha (the capital), about fifty or sixty miles from Chuka.

The work was a most laborious one, carried on, as it was, during the winter season.

The labours of the Engineers, however, proved of little account; for what was a most promising expedition, and one greatly needed to remove the stain left on our arms by the sad discomfiture the previous year at Dewangiri, was brought to an untimely and miserable termination by a peace patched up by our political officers.

The Engineers retired to Buxa, and in February 1866, when Captain Perkins left the force, Lieutenant Whish took charge of all stores, &c., and remained in charge of the Buxa garrison work.

In 1867 an expedition was despatched from Port Blair to the Little Andamans, with the view of ascertaining the fate of the captain and European crew (seven in number) of the *Assam Valley*, supposed to have fallen into the hands of the inhabitants of the island.

It consisted of 1 lieutenant (Much), 1 sergeant, 1 corporal, and 8 men of 2nd-24th; Naval Brigade, 1 petty officer and

6 seamen; Madras Sappers, 1 jemadar, 1 havildar, and 6 men. Assistant-Surgeon Douglas in medical charge; Lieutenant Glasfurd, 9th B.N.I., volunteer.

They embarked on board ss. *Arracan* on 6th May, to effect a landing on Little Andamans Island and endeavour to obtain intelligence regarding the crew who, it was supposed, had been murdered.

At 4.15 P M. they arrived at East Bay, and anchored for the night. At daybreak next day the steamer proceeded to the south coast of the island, and dropped anchor about a mile and a half from where the crew were supposed to have been captured.

At 8.30 A.M. Lieutenant Much left the steamer in the second cutter with the petty officer and six Naval Brigade men, Jemadar Mootien, and four Sappers. They made for the rock where the massacre was reported to have occurred.

The second gig followed, containing Mr. J. H. Homfray (Assistant to Superintendent in charge of Andaman Home), a havildar, and two Sappers, with some Andamanese.

The first cutter, containing one sergeant, one corporal, and eight men of 24th, followed next to act as coverers to the other parties when on shore.

About 150 yards west of the rock the surf appeared to admit of a landing. Mr. Dunn, the officer in charge of the boats, accordingly ran the boat in stern on, and, on a hint from that officer, they all jumped out, wading to shore in four feet and a half to five feet of water, rifles in hand, the ammunition being slung round their necks. Part of the ammunition was thus unavoidably wetted.

The party having landed, the second cutter moved off outside the surf.

The havildar and two Sappers in the second gig were unable to land, as Mr. Homfray did not bring his boat in close enough to give them a chance.

The first thing done on landing was to dry the ammunition.

After this, the party under Lieutenant Much moved along the shore in an easterly direction towards the rock, where they found the skull of an European; and a little further on an ankle-boot such as is worn by sailors. Beyond this, still nearer to the rock, the knees and planking of a boat that was painted white inside and lead-colour outside. Here, also, closer into the jungle, the ground had evidently been cleared for cooking. Proceeding on 100 yards past the rock, they noticed a party of aborigines, who showed themselves from time to time, as they strove apparently to have a peep from behind the bushes skirting the jungle, and who discharged their arrows at the party as it approached.

Lieutenant Much noticed that many were retiring with the probable intention of surrounding his men, so he threw back the left flank of his little party and advanced.

On arriving at the point, Lieutenant Much, finding his ammunition was running short, his own in part damaged and remainder expended, signalled to the second cutter to come in shore and take them off.

By this time the surf had greatly increased, and was running fifteen to twenty feet high. Mr. Dunn backed the cutter in, but in so doing it was upset, all hands being washed out of her. Some gained *terra firma* without assistance, others were dragged from the surf, Mr. Dunn among them, much exhausted, but Lieutenant Glasfurd, 9th B. N. I., was drowned. This occurred at about 11 A.M.

Seeing the fate of this boat, Lieutenant Much marched the party on towards East bay, in the hope of meeting with a suitable spot for disembarkation.

The first cutter, containing the men of the 24th, coasted along as the party on shore advanced, and kept up a fire on the natives who were not visible to those on shore.

Three hundred yards further on, the bodies of four men were observed, the heads of which (mere skulls in appearance) protruded from the ground, the bodies being partially covered with sand ; but to these bodies Lieutenant Much could not give more than a cursory glance, his whole attention being occupied by the critical position in which they were placed from the want of ammunition, the apparent small chance of boats ever reaching them, and the knowledge that in their state, with the enemy attacking them in any number, their case was hopeless.

Between 1 and 2 P.M., finding that the boat containing the 24th men, as also the other boats, were not following, but, on the contrary, were signalling them to return, they retraced their steps nearly to the place where they landed in the morning.

Here it was that the first cutter sent a raft ashore. By this thirty rounds of ammunition were sent, which was a great boon, as the party on shore had at this time only two rounds left in all.

Lieutenant Much, Mr. Dunn, one Naval Brigade man, and one lascar, got on to the raft. The raft remained for fully five minutes exposed to the violence of the surf, from which it was very slowly hauled out. They proceeded, holding on the best way they could, for 300 yards from the beach, when a wave larger than usual swept Mr. Dunn and Lieutenant Much off. They at once struck out again for the shore, which they all but reached utterly exhausted, but were luckily dragged out by those standing there.

A fresh attempt was made to send the raft ashore, but without success.

About an hour later in the day, Dr. Douglas, 2nd-24th, and four privates (David Bell, James Cooper, William Griffiths, and Thomas Murphy), gallantly manning the second gig with its sekunnie (helmsman), made their way through the surf almost to the shore ; but finding their boat was half filled with water, they retired.

Those on shore seeing their approach, attempted to meet them part way, but failed to do so, losing in their endeavours the greater part of their arms and spoiling what little ammunition they had left.

A second attempt made by Dr. Douglas proved successful, five of the shore party being safely passed through the surf to the boats outside.

A third and last trip got the whole of the party safe to the boats, when all proceeded on board the steamer, reaching it at half-past 5, much exhausted, and almost destitute of clothing, having had to strip to gain the boats.

With the exception of Lieutenant Glasfurd, there were no casualties.

On the 8th morning the steamer left, reaching Port Blair the same afternoon.

Lieutenant Much wrote:—

"I cannot speak too highly of the manner in which all behaved. To commence with Dr. Douglas, who, at the risk of his life, gallantly made three trips through the surf with his soldier crew. He stood on the bows of the boat and worked her in an intrepid and seamanlike manner; cool to a degree, as if what he was then doing was an ordinary act of every-day life. His four gallant volunteers were equally cool and collected. I have likewise great pleasure in reporting the excellent manner and bearing of the Naval Brigade men under Petty Officer Wilson; also of the Sappers and Miners under Jemadar Mootien, both of whom, under most trying circumstances, behaved with every degree of pluck, rendering Mr. Dunn and myself, when perfectly helpless in the surf, the greatest assistance, and helped us out to the boat when Dr. Douglas came to rescue us."

The Sappers on shore were—

Jemadar Mootien.

Private Annacolum.

,,   Ramasawmy.

,,   Lazar.

,,   Mausee.

Those in the second gig were—
> Havildar Iyanen.
> Private Poonasawmy.
>   ,,   Permaul.

The Governor of Madras brought Dr. Douglas' "disinterested and intrepid conduct to the special consideration of Her Majesty's Government through the Government of India," and the Governor-General " received with the highest satisfaction the report of the excellent conduct of all engaged, and particularly the gallant behaviour of Assistant Surgeon Douglas and the four men of the 2nd-24th."

"The conduct of Dr. Douglas and these men, as well as that of Lieutenant Much of the same regiment, who behaved so creditably, will be brought to the notice of Her Majesty's Government."

Jemadar Mootien, Madras Sappers and Miners, was admitted by the Governor-General in Council to the Order of Merit, for the excellent services rendered by him on this occasion.

Petty Officer Wilson of the Naval Brigade, and Toke, sekunnie, were also suitably rewarded for the part taken by them in this hazardous service; a silver watch with an inscription being given to the former, and a donation of two months pay to the latter.

CHAPTER XI.

It was on 13th August 1867, that the English Government
telegraphed to Bombay that Sir Robert Napier was to be Commander-in-Chief of the expedition to Abyssinia, which had been
resolved on for the purpose of rescuing Mr. Rassam, Consul
Cameron, and other prisoners, from Theodore, who had stubbornly refused to set them free.

Preparations were at once commenced, and on September 16
a reconnoitring party sailed from Bombay, to ascertain the best
point for landing.

The party consisted of Lieutenant-Colonel Merewether, C.B., as President, and Lieutenant-Colonel Phayre, Q.M.G., Lieutenant-Colonel St.-C. Wilkins, Royal Bo.E., with the senior naval and medical officers, members of a committee to decide the points.

They were accompanied by nine other officers and an escort of one company Marine Battalion, eight Sappers, and forty of the 3rd Bombay Cavalry. Captain Goodfellow and Lieutenant Jopp, of the Bombay Engineers, were with them.

Zulla, in Annesley Bay, was selected as the best landing-place for the army.

This having been arranged, the advanced party examined the passes through the mountains to the table-land, and finally Kumayli Pass was chosen.

Meantime, the advanced brigade arrived in Annesley Bay, on 21st October, and landed on 30th.

Nos. 3 and 4 Company of Bombay Sappers accompanied this force.

Early in November Colonel Merewether thoroughly surveyed the Kumayli Pass, and as soon as he returned to Zulla, despatched working parties to improve the road.

Directly the road was sufficiently good, Colonel Merewether resolved to push forward the advanced brigade to the high lands, and on 5th December Senafè was occupied.

At this time the Sind Brigade from Kurrachee reached Zulla, and at the same time Sir Charles Staveley arrived.

By order of Sir Robert Napier, he dissolved the committee of which Colonel Merewether was president, and assumed command of the forces.

For about a month Staveley remained in command, and during this time more troops arrived from England and from Bombay, including two companies of the Madras Sappers.

A pier 900 feet long, was commenced at Zulla. This was very necessary, as the bay had a very shelving shore.

Great difficulty was experienced in carrying out this work, as stone had to be brought ten miles, from a place called Dissee, and there was no timber to be got.

Arrangements were made for the supply of water by condensers, and a second pier was commenced for the Commissariat Department. Large wooden sheds were also erected.

On 2nd January 1868, Sir Robert Napier, with General Malcolm and staff, arrived at Annesley Bay. He disembarked on the 5th, but did not land in state till the 7th.

Up to the beginning of January Captain Goodfellow, Bo.E., was in charge of the works at Zulla, but early in that month he was ordered to the pass between Kumayli and Senafé, and Captain Chrystie, M.E., succeeded him at Zulla.

Kumayli is fourteen miles from Zulla. The road here entered the mountains, but for three miles further was nearly level, when the ascent began, the track following the dry bed of the stream.

As the ascent was continued, the mountains grew closer and closer together, rising more precipitously and to a greater height, till at Lower Suru, ten miles from Kumayli, there was only a fissure a few yards wide.

This narrow defile was over two miles long to the station of Upper Suru.

At this place a detachment of Beloochees and Sappers were stationed to make the road, and after six weeks of hard labour they formed a road safe for field artillery and wheeled traffic.

It was certain, however, that this road would be swept away by the first rains, and it was therefore necessary to store Senafé as far as possible with supplies.

For thirteen miles beyond Suru, the road, ascending, twined along the water-course till it reached Undul Wells. This brought us to Guinea-fowl plain, where fine vegetation commenced.

From this plain the road again ascended for eighteen miles to Rahajuddy, 6,000 feet above Zulla and 4,000 above Suru.

Eight miles further of ascent, and the table-land of Senafé was reached—7,000 feet above the sea.

A good road was now made as far as Kumayli, and the railway pushed forward.

Between Kumayli and Suru the road was widened and cleared for the passage of carts, and the Senafé Ghaut was made practicable by a fine display of engineering talent.

The Sappers and Pioneers attached to the force consisted of—

10th Company R. E., under Major Pritchard.

H, G, and K Companies Madras Sappers, under Major Prendergast, V.C., R.M.E.

2nd, 3rd, and 4th Companies Bombay Sappers, under Captain Macdonnell, R.E.

23rd Punjab Pioneers, under Major Chamberlain ;

and the Beloochees.

The K Company M. Sappers, after a short stay at Zulla, were employed on the Senafé Pass, but all this time the other two companies were retained on the coast. The H Company, indeed, was employed during the whole campaign on the works at Zulla.

In the defile, working on the road (seventy miles), between Zulla and the high lands, were the Beloochees, 10th Company R. E., Bombay Sappers, detachment Punjab Pioneers, and K Company Madras Sappers.

By the end of January the railway was half-way to Kumayli, and the telegraph reached to Suru.

Mules were purchased in Egypt, and camels from the coast of Arabia, and these were disembarked by means of barges, tugs, and native boats; but the second pier for the commissariat proceeded slowly, owing to a want of skilled labour.

Early in January mules arrived from Lahore and Rawul Pindi, and with their aid the Commander-in-Chief was enabled to occupy Goona-Goona, twelve miles beyond Senafé, on January 18th.

Preparations were now made for a general advance. The transport and baggage of every officer and man was reduced to the smallest possible dimensions, and, by the 25th, Sir Robert Napier thought he was justified in commencing an advance on Antalo, and the troops which were to complete the force were ordered to be sent on in troop-ships as rapidly as possible.

On the 25th Napier left Zulla for the front, and a brigade under Brigadier Collings was ordered to march on Antalo.

Sir Charles Staveley remained at Zulla till he should be relieved by General Russell from Aden.

The construction of the railway was placed in charge of Captain Darrah, R.E., and under his orders were Lieutenant Willans, R.E., Lieutenant Pennefather, R.E. (Madras), and Lieutenant Graham, 108th.

Lieutenant Willans had made a rough survey of the line by the time the 2nd Brigade arrived, and was told off to that work for the first half of the campaign, when he was sent to the front.

Captain Darrah, Lieutenants Willans and Pennefather, went on with it, Graham being left at Zulla to land stores, &c.

Darrah surveyed the line; Willans made all the bridges, and had charge of the work-sheds; while Pennefather had general superintendence of the line and kept the accounts.

When the line had sufficiently advanced to allow of trains being run, Lieutenant Baird, R.E., was appointed traffic manager.

As soon as the last bridge was completed, Willans was sent to the front.

An Army Works Corps of 1,000, partially organised in Bombay by Captain Ducat, R.E., was employed on the works at Zulla.

An amusing incident occurred the first day the men were paid, showing how little they knew of the terms of the agreement they had signed. The first gang was engaged a week before the second, and, of course, had an extra week's pay due to them. By some mistake the first gang received the pay of the second (a week too little for them), and went away quite happy, until they had compared notes with the second gang, who had received a week's pay in excess of their dues. The men of the second gang stoutly refused to give up their extra money, and those of the first gang as rigidly refused to do any more work till the pay was made all right. At Lieutenant Pennefather's suggestion, the first gang were paid for another fortnight, so as to put them a week ahead of the second gang, and the following month a week's pay all round was cut from them. They were perfectly contended, though they could not possibly have understood the arrangement, the more so, as there was nobody who could converse with them.

The difficulties to be met at Zulla were very great. No material of any kind was procurable from the resources of the country, even the coral for the stone pier being brought in Arab dhows from Dissee_Island, or the mainland, some eight miles distant.

The time of one Assistant Engineer was almost entirely taken up in going from ship to ship in the bay endeavouring to purchase tools (especially augurs), marine glue, cordage, spare spars, and wood of any kind. Nearly 350 feet of one of the wooden piers sent from Bombay was unavoidably cut up to supply miscellaneous requirements of wood.

The work, also, at Zulla was excessively trying.

Under a burning sun, and in a tropical climate, with an apportioned allowance of water, and with perpetual clouds of dust, lodging in every pore, physical labour was exceedingly severe; but the piers, roads, and railway had to be made, and made they were.

Sir Robert Napier arrived at Senafé on 29th January. This post formed the secondary base of operations, and was the great store-house for supplies and provisions. The camp was situated on the plateau, two miles in front of the issue from Kumayli defile, on some elevated rocky ground. On its east side rose some high sandstone cliffs, scarped and water-worn. On the west the spurs of Mount Sowayra protected the left flank.

In front was a large plain, over which stretched the road to Antalo. Beyond the sandstone cliffs a steep ascent of some 1,000 feet led into the valley of the Marab, over which, to the south, could be seen the mountain of Adowa, a magnificent view.

It was at first supposed that the country beyond Senafé would furnish abundant supplies; and when this hope was found to be delusive, it was thought that Adigerat would be the "promised land." Nothing, however, but fire-wood and meat could be got there. Antalo was then said to be the point where every difficulty of supply would vanish.

At that place grass was certainly procured. Barley, also, was purchased, but not nearly in sufficient quantities. Meat was obtained, and the wood wherewith to cook it, but vegetables, tea, sugar, and spirits had all to be carried, so that the security of the food of the army depended upon good and uninterrupted communications.

The Commander-in-Chief left Senafé on 3rd February, and marched to Goona-Goona; on the 5th he reached Adigerat.

From Senafé to Goona-Goona the road ran for eight miles over the plain in front of the camp; it then turned to the west into a valley with steep and lofty sides of sandstone. Here, for the first time, growing crops were met with.

About ten miles beyond this Focada is reached, whence to Adigerat is some twelve miles.

Six miles from Focada the track rose with a long and gentle slope to the top of a hill, down which it fell abruptly into the valley of Adigerat. This was an important strategical point, as here the roads from Adowa and Antalo unite.

Major Grant, who had been sent by Napier as envoy to Kassai, Prince of Tigre, returned on 7th February from Adowa, and joined the Commander-in-Chief at Adigerat.

The Pioneer force, consisting of 200 cavalry, two companies of infantry, and two of Pioneers, occupied Dolo, seventy miles south of Adigerat, within two marches of Antalo, on 10th February.

Antalo was occupied by Colonel Phayre five days later, with 150 cavalry.

On 11th February a column under Brigadier Collings was pushed forward to support the Pioneer force. It consisted of a wing of 33rd, Penn's battery, and 100 Sind Horse.

At this time Captain Chrystie was ordered from Zulla to Senafé, to relieve Captain Goodfellow (who had been ordered to the front), and he accordingly handed over charge of the Zulla works to Captain H. W. Wood, R.M.E. " Captain Wood completed the pile pier, and built a new head to the stone pier, greatly improving it. Captain Wood's work was distinguished by its solidity and permanent character. That the piers were not damaged by the late gales is attributable to this officer's good work at the head of the piers. Captain Wood was, unfortunately, afterwards taken ill, and had to go on board the hospital-ship, Lieutenant H. H. Lee, R.Bo.E., assuming charge."

The Commanding Engineer testified to the excellent work done by this officer also.

Captain Chrystie remained at Senafé till the 24th February, improving the ghaut by extending the zig-zags, &c. He also constructed three miles of bullock-road over a saddle of the Sedra mountain, towards Tekonda, as an alternative route for the retirement of the force via the Huddas Valley.

In the end of February Captain Chrystie was moved up to take charge of the entrenched camp at Adigerat.

Napier halted at Adigerat till the 18th February.

At this time there was great deficiency of transport, and it was proposed to put the troops on half rations, but the Commander-in-Chief declined to entertain the proposal. Troops at this time consumed 170 mule-loads of provisions daily.

The Transport Corps soon became more efficient. It was formed into two divisions, one for highlands and the other for lowlands, and as far as Adigerat. The former followed the army. This division consisted of four sections of 2,000 mules each, subdivided into troops of about 150.

All this time a party of Engineer officers were occupied in making an accurate triangular survey of the country. Every exertion was at this time made to reduce baggage, but the climate interfered. The thermometer frequently stood at freezing point, and often lower. Warm clothing and blankets were hence absolutely necessary.

While at Adigerat the Commander-in-Chief was joined by 4th King's Own, Beloochees, 10th Company R.E., and Murray's Armstrong battery. Two elephants were brought up to show to Kassai, Prince of Tigre. The Abyssinians considered this a very wonderful sight, as they had never previously supposed that these enormous animals could be tamed. The Armstrong guns proved, also, of great interest and curiosity to the people.

At this time the latest news of the captives was dated 17th January. Theodore was reported to be one day's journey from Magdala, but not expected to arrive before the end of February, unless he abandoned his baggage and guns. The prisoners were in the fortress.

Napier left Adigerat* on the 18th February, the Beloochees and one company of Sappers having been previously pushed forward to repair the road.

The force with the Commander-in-Chief consisted of a wing of 4th K. O., wing of 10th N. I., four Armstrong guns, 3rd Bombay Cavalry, and detachment R. E. The garrison left at Adigerat was composed of wing of 25th Bo. N. I., under Colonel Little, two Armstrong guns, and two companies Sappers.

These were all the troops in front of Senafé.

---

* Before leaving Adigerat the baggage of the force was greatly reduced: each officer 75 lbs., and each man 25 lbs., including bedding.

On February 24th the force was ordered to advance from Adabagi (two marches in front of Adigerat), when news of the approach of Kassai was received. A meeting was arranged to take place on the banks of the Diab, half-way between Adabagi and Hauzzain.

On the 25th Napier and Kassai met. A review of our troops took place, followed next morning by a visit to Kassai's camp. The friendship of Kassai was of the greatest consequence to us. He was chief of a country in which the route of our army lay for 150 miles, and his refusal to assist us would have involved a campaign in Tigre before we could proceed.

After a farewell visit from Kassai our force, on 26th February, began its march to Antalo.

On the 28th the banks of the Dolo were reached. A halt was here found necessary to rest the wearied troops; but on 2nd March Napier reached the neighbourhood of Antalo, half-way between Zulla and Magdala.

At the end of February the entrenched camp at Adigerat was incomplete, and Captain Chrystie, on reaching that place, proposed certain modifications at its western extremity which tended to hasten its completion, as well as improve the trace, besides omitting from the interior space some ground which was completely commanded at 200 yards both from the west and the north.

These works were carried out to completion by the working-parties furnished by the wing of the 25th Bo. N. I. Large huts were constructed, also, to give shelter to commissariat stores.

The Pioneer force, consisting of 280 cavalry and 500 infantry (two companies 33rd, two companies Beloochees, one company Punjab Pioneers, and 3rd and 4th companies Bombay Sappers), had been sent forward. By direction of Colonel Phayre, they commenced to clear a road leading to Antalo, by way of Mai Musgi Musno and the defile of Gurubdek-dek; but after they

29 *

had been employed for five days on this, a better route was discovered from Mai Musgi by Meshik.

The distribution of the Sappers and Pioneers at this time was as follows :—

Pioneer force : 3rd and 4th Companies Bombay Sappers, and two companies 23rd Punjab Pioneers.

1st Brigade, 1st Division : 10th Company R. E., and two companies Beloochees.

2nd Brigade, 1st Division : K Company Madras Sappers, seven companies Punjab Pioneers, and wing of Beloochees.

Adigerat : 2nd Company Bombay Sappers.

Kumayli : G Company Madras Sappers.

Zulla : H Company Madras Sappers, five companies 21st Punjab Pioneers.

The troops intended to compose the 1st Division, who were not already at Antalo, were now ordered up to the front.

The 3rd Dragoon Guards and 12th Bengal Cavalry were instructed to proceed forward by double marches.

By the middle of March all the troops which were to advance on Magdala were round or in front of Antalo.

On 12th March the Commander-in-Chief left Antalo, moving by route which leads by Amba Mayro and Alagi Pass (9,500 feet) to the Antalo valley.

Three days after he joined the Pioneer force, and directed its operations in person.

On the 17th Sir Charles Staveley moved with the 1st Brigade from Antalo to Belago, five miles short of Makhan, which place he reached next day. The march from Antalo to Makhan (fifteen miles) was very severe, the Belago Pass being 9,700 feet above the sea.

On March 18th Napier moved to Ashangi, while Staveley was ordered to halt at Haya.

The route from Makhan to Ashangi lay round the edge of a mountain range covered with juniper-trees, which formed a thick jungle. After crossing a deep valley, a summit of 9,100 feet was gained, whence the first view of the Lake of Ashangi was obtained. The lake was small, four miles by three, surrounded by fine hills, which enclosed a fertile valley with crops of standing corn, with numerous villages on the hill-sides. The uninhabited border of the lake consisted of swampy ground.

An advance was now made on Lat.

On 20th March Napier marched to Mesagita. It was here reported that the pass beyond, over Womberat hills to Lat, was very difficult, and two companies of Bombay Sappers and two of Pioneers were marched forward to improve it, and a wing of the 33rd was sent to assist.

Two days after, a battery of R. A. and four companies Beloochees, under Staveley, marched in one day from Ashangi, and joined Napier at Lat.

At Lat new arrangements were made for the distribution of troops and Pioneer force, while the 1st and 2nd Brigades were ordered to proceed without baggage, and it was from this place that the rapid advance on Magdala was commenced.

On the 23rd Napier advanced to Marawa (eleven miles), and next day to Dildi. The road was very mountainous, bad, and narrow. The first part was passed without great difficulty, but afterwards it was rugged, devious, and broken, and Dildi was only reached late in the evening. A halt of one day was made at Dildi, when a move was effected to Wondaj. During this march the force was exposed to a terrific thunderstorm. The distance was only seven miles, but there was a continuous rise of 3,000 feet to the head of the Wondaj Pass. From this point, 10,500 feet above the sea, a grand view of the valley of the Takkazzi was obtained.

On the 27th the advance was continued to Moga.

At this time Theodore was reported to have crossed the Beshilo, and to be advancing to defend the passage of the Takkazzi.

Napier determined to secure the passage of the river, and on the 28th moved to the banks of the Takkazzi.

Working parties of the 4th King's Own, Beloochees, and Punjabees were pushed forward at once, under Captain Good-fellow and Lieutenant Le Mesurier, to form a practicable path up the precipitous south bank, which rose 4,000 feet above the river. After no great length of time a Sapper on the summit signalled "road prepared," and the force began to climb the ascent.

Before night the ascent was complete, the passage of the Takkazzi secure, and orders were sent to Staveley to push on and concentrate on the advanced force.

The 1st and 2nd Brigades were massed at Santara, on the edge of the table-land of Wadela, 11,500 feet above the sea. The range of the thermometer was here very great; for although in the day-time it was as high as 75°, it fell at night as low as 10° or 20°.

Between the Takkazzi and the Beshilo, besides the Wadela plateau, lay Dalanta and Damt south of the Beshilo; and in the fork formed between that river and the Kulkulla lay the mass of mountains of which Magdala is the key.

On 31st March the 1st Brigade went to Gaso, next day to Abdakom, and on 2nd April to Yesendie, followed closely by the 2nd Brigade, and two days after the force crossed the ravine of the Jidda to Dalanta plateau.

At Bethor the army struck the road made by Theodore on his march from Debra Tabor to Magdala.

For some days the force was delayed on the Dalanta plateau,* owing to want of supplies; but on 9th April it was enabled to move forward five miles across the plain to the top of the descent into the Beshilo, where it encamped within sight of Fahla Selassie, Islamgi, and Magdala, around which Theodore's army could be clearly distinguished.

___
* The weather was very stormy at this time, rain and thunder being of nightly occurrence.

On 5th April, Napier made a formal demand for the surrender of the prisoners.

While on the Dalanta plateau, scaling-ladders and sand-bags were got ready. Arrangements were also made to cut off Theodore's retreat. Dejatch Masheshu was requested to occupy Amba Kuhait, and the Queen of the Gallas was asked to close the avenues to the south.

On the farther side of the Beshilo lay a rugged mass of broken ground, in the centre of which the Amba of Magdala rose to an almost equal height with the plateau of Dalanta. The rugged country, studded with a bushy vegetation, was bounded in the distance by the table-land of Tanta and of Ambala Suda. From the former the mountain mass of Magdala was separated by the ravine of the Menchouan, from the latter by the Kulkulla torrent. Both of these rivers were tributaries of the Beshilo.

The mountains of Magdala form a crescent, of which Magdala is the eastern horn, Fahla the western; midway between the two, in the centre, lies the plateau of Selassie. Magdala and Selassie are connected by the saddle of Islamgi, and Selassie with Fahla by the saddle of Fahla.

The highest of these plateaux is Magdala, 9,000 feet above the sea and 3,000 above the ravines surrounding it. Its sides are scarped and very steep, but at two points they fall on the terraces of Islamgi and Sangallat. It is at these two points alone that an entrance can be made to the Amba, by the Koket-bir and Kaffir-bir gates.

From the foot of the Fahla saddle the Worehi Waha valley runs down to the Beshilo, and between the upper part of the stream which forms the valley and one of its tributaries lies the plain of Arogi. At the foot of the ascent to Fahla, and west of the same tributary, at a higher elevation than the plain of Arogi, lies the plateau of Afficho, which dips down towards the Beshilo in the Gumbaya spur.

On 25th March Theodore had reached Islamgi, where he pitched his camp and awaited the attack of the British.

On 10th April he assembled his army, ordered a road to be prepared for the passage of his guns from Magdala to Fahla, and here he posted four large guns and four smaller ones.

On the same day the British final advance commenced, and the whole of the army was moved down to the Beshilo, twelve miles from Magdala. Napier determined to occupy the spur leading towards Fahla, called Gumbaya and Afficho; he could thence operate on either side of Fahla.

As the only supply of water between the Beshilo and Magdala was under the enemy's fire, all the water-carriers were organised for the purpose of carrying forward regular supplies of water from the river.

The 3rd Bombay Cavalry, 3rd Scinde Horse, and 12th Bombay Cavalry were posted to hold the Beshilo, and the remainder of the 1st Brigade moved across the river, the 2nd Brigade being directed to remain in the bed of the Beshilo as a support.

The infantry of the 1st Brigade was intended to occupy the Gumbaya spur, and cover a reconnoissance of Colonel Phayre in the direction of Fahla.

The 1st Brigade consisted of 1,819 men, and included—

        20 10th Company, R.E.
        575 23rd Punjab Pioneers.
        259 27th Beloochees.
        70 Madras Sappers.
        283 Bombay Sappers.

The troops toiled painfully up the rugged slopes of the Gumbaya spur, suffering severely from the great heat and want of water.

Four companies of Sappers were to make a path up the

Gumbaya spur for guns, &c.* Colonel Phayre, however, took the Sappers as his escort, and the road remained unmade.

Colonel Phayre, some time after, sent word that, having secured the head of the pass, the Sappers would be left to hold it, and that the guns and baggage might take the route by the King's road.

Napier accordingly ordered the guns, rockets, and baggage to move up by the King's road. He then proceeded himself to the front, and passing the infantry brigade, arrived on the Afficho plateau, when he found, to his astonishment, that at the point where the King's road emerged from the Werki Waha ravine, 1,200 yards from him and 700 feet below, there were no troops.

He at once ordered Staveley to send Chamberlain's Pioneers to the left, and hurried up the 1st Brigade. This was effected only just in time, for the leading mules of Penn's battery were seen to be emerging from the pass. A few moments later a round shot from Fahla whirred over the heads of the Staff, and at once the steep path and mountain sides of Fahla were covered by masses of warriors, rushing down to secure the wealthy booty.

They were led by Theodore's favourite General, while he himself remained on Fahla. The assailants were fully 5,000 in number, and among them were 500 mounted chiefs.

The Naval Brigade now hurried up and opened with their rockets on the advancing masses, who nevertheless advanced with great confidence against the head of the column on the plateau, while another party bore down to attack the artillery and the baggage.

The 4th King's Own, a wing of Beloochees, the detachment of Royal Engineers, and the Bombay Sappers rapidly descended the path which led down from the Afficho plateau. As they rose on the brow of the plateau of the Arogi plain they opened

* This, being on the reverse side of the Gumbaya spur, would be secure from the guns of Fahla.

fire. Their fire told with fearful effect, and the enemy were driven back slowly but stubbornly. They were finally driven off the plain of Arogi, down the slopes, into the ravines at the head of the Werki Waha defile.

Another party of the enemy tried to pass round the sides of the Afficho plateau to turn Staveley's right, but were checked by rockets and the exertions of the K Company Madras Sappers under Major H. N. D. Prendergast, V.C., supported by Loch with the Bombay Cavalry.

As soon as these were repulsed, the fire of the rockets was directed on Fahla, and one nearly killed Theodore, who was engaged in person with his artillery.

Meantime a sharp action had been fought at the point where the King's road issued from Werki Waha valley. A large body of Abyssinians bore down on the position occupied by Milward's guns and Chamberlain's Pioneers. Chamberlain advanced, and a close contest ensued between spears and bayonets. The Abyssinians made a gallant resistance, but were forced off into the ravines on Chamberlain's left front.

The baggage master, Lieutenant Sweeny, 4th King's Own, massed the baggage, and the baggage guard was brought forward and checked the attempt of the enemy to penetrate into the defile. Arrested by the baggage guard, closed in upon by Chamberlain's Pioneers and two companies of 4th King's Own which Staveley wheeled up against their flank, the enemy suffered very severely.

It was 4 P.M. when the engagement commenced, and 7 before the enemy were completely driven off.

There was heavy rain during the greater part of the action.

The troops bivouacked for the night on the ground which covered the issue of the Werki Waha valley.

During the night the 2nd Brigade marched up the valley from the Beshilo and occupied this position.

The Abyssinian loss was 700 killed and 1,200 wounded,

including many chiefs of note; among them was the Commander-in-Chief himself.

Our loss was trifling—only 20 wounded, of whom 2 died.

This great disparity of loss was due to the persistent attacks of the Abyssinians against a better disciplined and better-armed force, as well as to the cool courage everywhere evinced by our troops.

Theodore, after some hesitation, now sent down Lieutenant Prideaux, Bombay Army, with Mr. Flad and a chief (Theodore's son-in-law) Dejatch Alami, to the British lines, with a verbal message desiring reconciliation.

Napier, in reply, demanded all the Europeans in his hands, and further guaranteed honourable treatment to Theodore. Prideaux and Flad returned with this letter.

Theodore, having considered it, wrote a paper (he did not condescend to write a letter), with which he returned Napier's letter. This paper closed with the words, "A warrior who has dandled strong men in his arms like infants will never suffer himself to be dandled in the arms of others."

Prideaux and Flad had again to return with Napier's original letter, and an intimation that he could grant no other terms.

Theodore, it appears, after he had sent his insulting missive, spent some time in meditation and prayer, and finally, after taking counsel with his chiefs—some of whom recommended the murder of the prisoners and resistance to the last—he ordered the prisoners to be released. Immediately after giving this order he attempted to shoot himself with a pistol, but was prevented by a chief, the bullet just grazing his ear.

After this he had an interview with Mr. Rassam. The result was that Mr. Rassam and the remainder of the British captives, and several others, were sent down the hill, while Mr. Meyer was despatched in advance to announce their approach. He met Lieutenant Prideaux and Mr. Flad returning. They turned back and accompanied Mr. Meyer, and one hour after sunset Mr. Rassam and all the captives arrived free men.

Early next morning Napier received an apologetic letter from Theodore, releasing all. He also sent a present of cows and sheep as a peace offering, but these were not allowed to come within our picquets, as it would have meant that there was peace, whereas Napier intended to insist on unconditional surrender.

The Germans who had escorted Mr. Rassam's party down the evening before, returned to the mountain. They took up with them the remains of the Abyssinian leader, Fituarari Gabri, and the body was at once burned in Magdala. On finding he could not obtain peace without his personal surrender, Theodore went into the Amba and spent a restless night.

Besides Mr. Rassam, Consul Cameron, Mr. Flad, Lieutenant Prideaux, and Dr. Blanc of the Bombay Army, there were 55 other prisoners—22 men, 10 women, and 23 children.

Napier had promised to abstain from hostilities for twenty-four hours, and he waited twice the time he had agreed to ; but on Monday, when he found that the conditions he demanded had not been complied with, he prepared to attack Theodore's position.

Our troops were paraded on the plain. They consisted of—

> 750 men of 33rd.
> 450 men of 4th.
> 400 men of 45th.
> Beloochees.
> Punjabees.
> Detachment of Royal Engineers.
> Six companies of Sappers and Miners.
> Detachment of 10th N. I.
> Murray's Armstrong Battery.
> Two mountain batteries.
> Naval Rocket Brigade.
> Two 8-inch mortars.

The cavalry had previously been sent to close the issues from Magdala which were not already held by the Gallas.

Napier determined to attack Islamgi by the King's road. The Armstrong guns and mortars were placed in position, with Selassie in front and Fahla on the right, so that they could fire in long range in support of our advance.

At this time large bodies of the King's troops on Fahla had surrendered, and it was rumoured that Theodore contemplated flight from Magdala by the gate on the further side of Magdala. Napier at once sent word offering a reward of 50,000 dollars for his capture.

Theodore, if he ever really intended to fly, reconsidered the matter when he found the outlet from Magdala watched by the Gallas, and resolved to defend the place.

The Beshilo was held by cavalry, to prevent escape by the Menchana ravine.

At 7, some cavalry (50 sabres) was sent up the Fahla saddle to communicate with those of Theodore's troops which had surrendered.

Staveley was now ordered to advance on Islamgi and occupy Fahla and Selassie. The three hills—Fahla, Selassie, and Magdala—were surrounded at the top by steep and precipitous scarps. Fahla and Magdala were joined to Selassie by saddles, and were nearly at right angles to the central hill. A good but very steep road led up the north side of Fahla over the saddle of Fahla, then along the south side of Selassie and by the next saddle of Islamgi into Magdala. A pathway branched off the road at the Fahla saddle to the left, ran along the foot of the Selassie scarp for some distance, and then turned up a zigzag to the top, near the entrance to Magdala. Another path led direct up to Selassie from the Fahla saddle.

Both Fahla and Magdala had flat tops, but Selassie sloped upwards from the scarp, and its summit commanded the other

The artillery having been placed to cover the head of the ascent, the advance was ordered at half-past 8.

The division moved up the road with the 2nd Brigade in advance, headed by a ladder party of Sappers (detachment of 10th Company R. E. and K Company Madras Sappers).

There were—

                    694 men of 33rd.
                    125   „   45th.
                    271   „   10th N. I.

About mid-day the head of the column reached the Fahla saddle, when two companies of the 33rd were pushed on to the summit of Selassie, supported by artillery; but the road was so bad, that only three mountain guns could be passed up.

When Selassie was crossed, the King's troops were ordered to lay down their arms and retire to the plain below.

The first part of the order was quickly obeyed, but it took many hours for the large mass of people to pass down.

The numbers were estimated at 25,000 to 30,000, one-third being armed men.

The positions of Fahla and Selassie were immensely strong, and if defended would have caused us very severe loss.

When they were secured, the Armstrong guns and 8-inch mortars were brought up.

About noon, Theodore, with 100 followers, left the Amba and went towards the market-place of Islamgi, where his guns were posted.

At this time, a detachment of the Bombay Light Cavalry had emerged on the Islamgi Saddle, and Sir Charles Staveley pushed down a company of 33rd, with orders to keep Theodore's guns under fire.

Theodore observed these detachments, mounted his horse, and careered about in a defiant manner; while Colonel Loch made arrangements for preventing the escape of any by paths leading down from the Islamgi saddle,

For some time Theodore's attendants continued to drag their guns towards Magdala, but, one of the party being shot, they left them, retired within the Amba, and shut the gate.

A dreadful stench was now observed by our troops; this came from the dead bodies at the foot of the precipice on the right. Theodore had massacred a large body of prisoners on the 9th, and thrown them over the precipice. Many were alive when thrown over. The British soldiers were greatly incensed by the sight of this wholesale slaughter.

Napier, meantime, reconnoitred Magdala. At 1 P.M. he ordered a sharp cannonade to be directed on the gate, and Sir C. Staveley then made dispositions for the assault of the fortress by the 2nd Brigade, supported by the 1st, which had advanced by the lower road after Selassie had been occupied.

The 33rd, ten companies strong, was to advance across Islamgi, two in skirmishing order, two in support, and the remaining six, headed by a detachment R. E. and the K Company Madras Sappers, under Captain Elliot, with ladders, crowbars, &c., were to form the storming-party. Two companies of Bombay Sappers, under Captain Leslie and Lieutenant Leacock, were to follow in rear of the 33rd.

On nearing the foot of the steep ascent to the gate, the skirmishers were to halt, and, with the supports to keep up a heavy fire on the gateway. The 45th Regiment was to advance in line in rear of the 33rd. The 1st Brigade, with the exception of Punjab Pioneers, and two companies 10th N. I., left to guard the camp at Arogi, was to move in column as a reserve, two companies of 10th N. I. having been detached to Selassie to guard captured arms, &c.

The Armstrong guns and 8-inch mortars were to advance along the main road south of Selassie, as far as possible, to cover the advance, while the mountain-guns and naval rocket-batteries at foot of Selassie were to keep up a fire on the gate.

At 3 P.M. the batteries opened fire, and at 4 the advance to storm was ordered.

The 33rd soon surmounted the precipitous cliff which lay between it and the outer gate. On arrival at the gateway our progress was arrested, for the gate was closed, and the Sappers had not at hand the powder-bags.

The Sappers at once set to work with the crowbars, and the gate was soon broken down, when it was found that the gateway was completely blocked up with large stones to a height of twelve feet (afterwards found to be fifteen feet in thickness).

While the Sappers were engaged with the gate, the garrison maintained a constant fire on them, and nine men and officers at this time received wounds or contusions. Meantime, Lieutenant Le Mesurier, Bo.E., found a point where the wall was low enough to be surmounted by means of a scaling-ladder, and, with some men of the 33rd, he first entered the fortress of Magdala, and, taking the defenders in flank, drove them up a narrow path leading to another gateway, seventy yards higher up. Through this the leading men of the 33rd rushed, and, being followed by the whole regiment, the summit was quickly occupied, and the standard of England was planted on Magdala. Theodore's followers now threw down their arms, and asked for quarter.

This fortress of Magdala, so easily captured, was one of the strongest which could be found in the world.

At the outer gateway several of Theodore's chiefs were found dead. Among them Ras Engedda, who had proposed the massacre of the European prisoners. It appears that when Ras Engedda fell, Theodore divested himself of his gold-brocaded mantle and hurried farther up the fortress. As soon as the outer gateway was carried Theodore shot himself with a pistol, and fell dead.

All Theodore's guns, thirty-seven in number, were captured, and the whole (with the exception of one 56-pounder, which

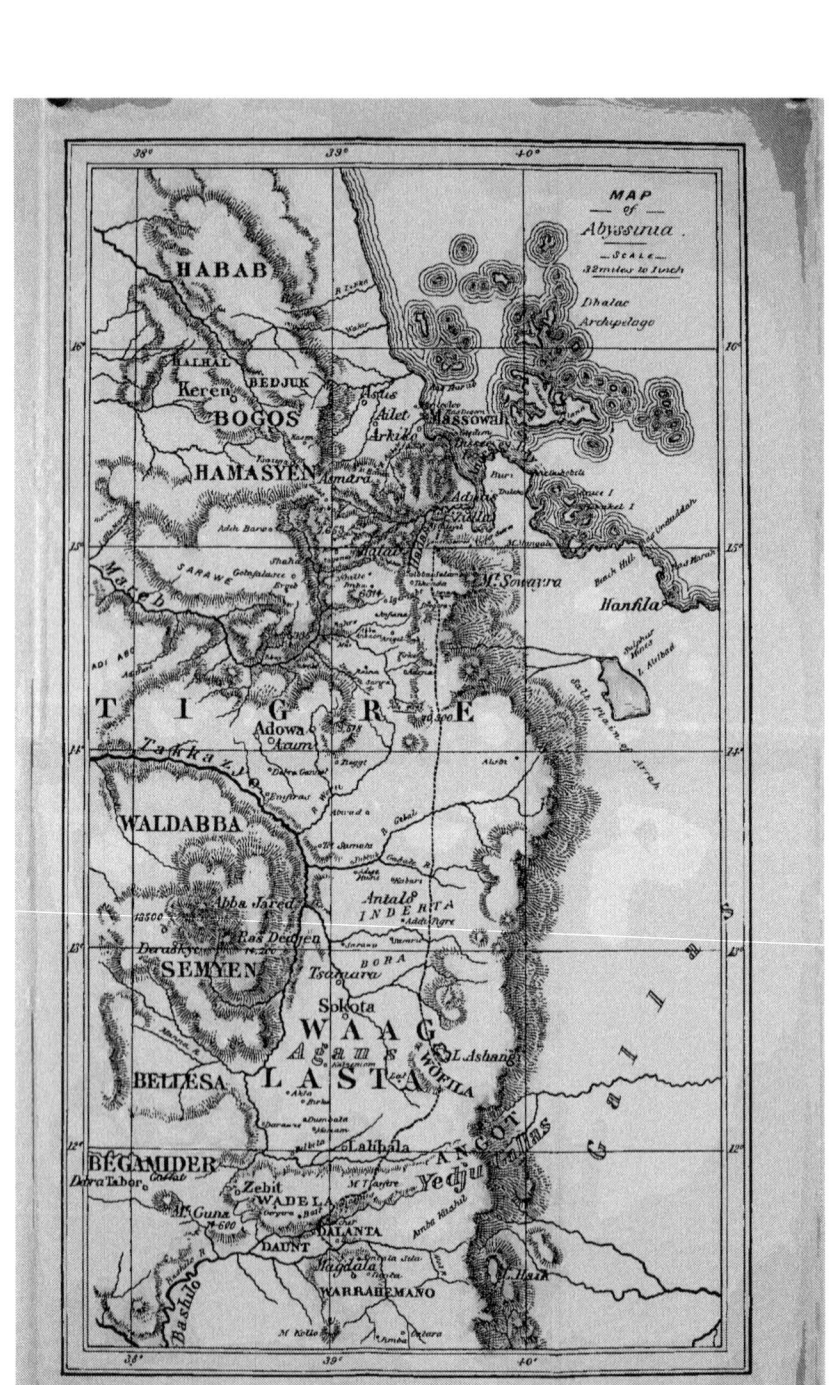

had burst on the 10th April), were found serviceable, and well supplied with ammunition.

The British casualties were trifling :—

Major Pritchard, R.E.

Corporal Hobson,

Sapper Dennis,

5 men 33rd,   }Wounded.

1 Madras Sapper,

1 of Light Cavalry,

Captain Elliott, Madras Sappers,

Cornet Dalrymple, attached to

   Madras Sappers,

Corpl. Fielding, Madras Sappers,   }Received contusions.

Sergeant Dean, R.E.

Lieutenant Morgan, R.E.

At the action of Arogi Captain Roberts and three men of 4th King's Own, and thirteen men of 23rd Punjabees were wounded.

At the time of the capture of Magdala nearly all the posts were being pressed by the Abyssinians. Senafé, Adigerat, Goona-Goona, Agula, Belago, Makhan, Ashangi, and Dildi garrisons had frequently at this time to repel casual attacks made on them. Had Napier's force been unsuccessful, and compelled to retire to the coast, the attacks would certainly have increased in frequency and importance, and would have proved most embarrassing to the withdrawal of the force.

Magdala was first offered to Wagshum Gobaze, but he refused to take possession ; it was then given to Masleeat, Queen of the Gallas.

The captured guns were all burst, the defences of the gates mined and destroyed, and fire applied to the palace and other houses.

On 18th April the British force left Magdala and crossed the Beshilo, and next day preparations were made for the return of the force to Zulla.

II.   30

On 20th April Lieutenant-General Sir Robert Napier, G.C.S.I., G.C.B., issued an address to his army, dated Camp, Dalsulo :—

"Soldiers of the Army of Abyssinia,—

"The Queen and the people of England intrusted to you a very arduous and difficult expedition—to release our country-men from a long and painful captivity and to vindicate the honour of our country, which had been outraged by Theodore, King of Abyssinia.

"I congratulate you with all my heart on the noble way in which you have fulfilled the commands of our Sovereign. You have traversed, often under a tropical sun, or amidst storms of rain and sleet, 400 miles of mountainous and difficult country. You have crossed many steep and precipitous ranges of moun-tains, more than 10,000 feet in altitude, where your supplies could not keep pace with you.

"When you arrived within reach of your enemy, though with scanty food, and some of you for many hours without either food or water, in four days you passed the formidable chasm of the Beshilo and defeated the army of Theodore, which poured down upon you from their lofty fortress in the full confidence of victory.

"A host of many thousands have laid down their arms at your feet.

"You have captured and destroyed upwards of thirty pieces of artillery, many of great weight and efficiency, with ample stores of ammunition. You have stormed the almost inaccessible fortress of Magdala, defended by Theodore, with the desperate remnant of his chiefs and followers.

"After you forced the entrance, Theodore, who never showed mercy, distrusted the offer of mercy held out to him, and died by his own hand.

"You have released not only the British captives, but those of other friendly nations.

" You have unloosed the chains of more than ninety of the principal chiefs of Abyssinia.   •

" Magdala, on which so many victims have been slaughtered, has been committed to the flames, and remains only a scorched rock.

" Our complete and rapid success is due, first, to the mercy of God, whose hand, I feel assured, has been over us in a just cause; secondly, to the high spirit with which you have been inspired.

" Indian soldiers have forgotten the prejudices of race and creed to keep pace with their European comrades.

" Never has an army entered into a war with more honourable feelings than yours. This has carried you through many fatigues and difficulties; you have been only eager for the moment when you could close with your enemy.

" The remembrance of your privations will pass away quickly, but your gallant exploit will live in history.

" The Queen and the people of England will appreciate your services.

" On my part, as your commander, I thank you for your devotion to your duty and the good discipline you have maintained. Not a single complaint has been made against a soldier of fields injured or villages wilfully molested in property or person.

" We must not forget what is due to our comrades who have been labouring for us in the sultry climate of Zoulla and the pass of Koomaylee, or in the monotony of the posts which have maintained our communications. Each and all would have given all they possessed to be with us; they deserve our gratitude.

" I shall watch over your safety to the moment of your re-embarkation, and to the end of my life remember with pride that I have commanded you.

" R. Napier,

" Lieutenant-General, Commander-in-Chief.

" Camp, Dalsulo, April 20th, 1868."

30 *

On 24th April Napier was at Abdakom, and received an audience of a large party of Abyssinians of note, who had been liberated by our operations. The principal chiefs liberated were thirty-four in number. Seven of them had been more than ten years in captivity, while four had been detained by Theodore for fourteen or fifteen years; the remainder had suffered imprisonment for terms varying from one to seven years.

On the 26th our returning force reached the Takkazze valley. It was at this time that the works in the Suru pass were damaged by a severe storm. Captain Chrystie, R.M.E., was ordered over from Adigerat to take charge of the works. He reached Upper Suru on 2nd May, and relieved and took under his orders Lieutenant Mainwaring, R.E At this time the force under Napier had reached Lat.

Captain Chrystie found that the pass had been closed to traffic for about a week, but that although the road for wheeled transport had been everywhere washed away, the only very serious obstacles were at the Devil's Staircase, a mile below Upper Suru, where about fifty yards of ramp had been destroyed, and at the defile of Lower Suru, where the ravine had resumed its original state as found by our Pioneer force.

The only men available for the work was a wing of 10th N. I. returning to Zulla, and detained by the breaking up of the road. In two days the road was again made passable for mules and camels, and the regiment resumed its march to the coast. On Captain Chrystie representing the state of affairs, the following working-parties were despatched to his assistance :—

> 2 companies Bombay Sappers.
> 2   ,,   16th P. N. I.
> 150 Bengal Cavalry Corps.
> 60 Masons.
> 200 Lahore Muleteers.

Lieutenant Mainwaring had charge of the lower part of the work, while Captain Chrystie himself directed that in the upper portion. The road was repaired in a most substantial manner at the gaps in the Devil's Staircase and at other difficult points, the work being cyclopean throughout, stones of large size being rolled down from the hill-side and dragged into position with three companies at once on the drag-ropes. Hardly had the work been well completed, when, on the afternoon of the 19th May, a terrific thunderstorm broke over the pass and the hills to the north of it. Before detailing the damage done and the steps taken to make it good, it will be as well to mention the movements of the Commander-in-Chief.

On the 10th May he was at Meshib, at which place Theodore's queen was reported to be ill.

The march had been very trying, owing to the constant storms of rain. The tribes, also, were very troublesome, and constantly made attacks on us. In some of these both Abyssinians and Gallas were killed.

This shows what difficulties would have been experienced had the force been returning unsuccessful.

At Haik Hellat the queen died ; her son Alawayo afterwards accompanied Napier to England.

On May 24th Napier reached Senafé, and a review was held by him in honour of Her Majesty's birthday. Prince Kassai was present on this occasion.

Three days after, Prince Kassai reviewed his troops, and next day Senafé was evacuated by our force, and by the close of the month the Commander-in-Chief was ready to pass down the Suru defile.

It will thus be apparent that the storm of the 19th May was a very serious matter, and had occurred at a most critical time, calling for the most strenuous exertions to repair the damage done.

The storm had been quite local, no damage being apparent two miles above Suru, and it only lasted half an hour, but during that brief space not only were the water-courses foaming torrents, but the sides of the hills themselves were sheets of white water, whilst the reverberations of the thunder hardly rose above the roar of the torrent and the din of the falling rocks and stones. In the main pass itself the flood rose with extreme rapidity and irresistible violence. Seven men of the working-parties were carried away before they could reach the hill-side, only a few yards distant; whilst at the lower part of the defile two officers riding down to Kumayli, overtaken by the water, had such a narrow escape that the horse of one was swept from under him just as he reached the rising ground, the rider being saved by his companion seizing him.

Some idea of the force of the water may be formed from the above and the two following incidents :—

At the Devil's Staircase a cart was deposited on the summit of a rock $22\frac{1}{2}$ feet above the bed of the torrent; and a little above where the hills close in at Lower Suru, a rock 6 by $4\frac{1}{2}$ by 4 was forced on to a shelf of rock in mid-valley about ten feet from the ground.

Next morning Captain Chrystie inspected the pass, as far as possible. All work was found to have been effaced. The local character of the storm and the sudden cessation of the flood had not permitted time for the holes scooped out, whilst it was at its height, being refilled by deposit, as would have been the case had it subsided gradually. The consequence was that the narrow parts of the defile were a succession of precipices and pools· The worst place was near the centre of the lower defile, where a passage with nearly vertical rocky sides, four feet wide at bottom, led for a distance of about forty feet to the edge of a perpendicular drop of eighteen feet to the surface of a pool fourteen feet in depth.

Although there was no place so bad as this, still, for fully 200 yards beyond, the same features were repeated again and again on a smaller scale.

The very morning after the storm the Antalo Brigade, under

Brigadier Collings, arrived at Suru at 7.30, after a twelve-mile march from Undee Wells, and by 9 the following working-parties started to make the pass practicable :—

> Left wing 45th Foot.
>   ,,   3rd Bo. N. I.
> Wing 10th P. N. I.
> K Company Madras Sappers.

They worked till 3 30, when the weather looked so threatening that, fearing another catastrophe, the parties were withdrawn.

They resumed work on the 21st at daylight, and at 1 P.M. the brigade, with their baggage, passed through the lower defile *en route* for Kumayli.

Thus, by the exertions of 2,000 men working for ten hours, four miles of the most difficult portions of the pass were made passable for laden animals of all kinds. The road was made almost entirely by building ramps of loose stones and covering them with sand ; and as this process had been repeated three times, all the stones easily procurable from the sole of the valley and the foot of the hills near the narrow parts of the pass had already been used, and material for the only kind of road possible had become so scarce that had another torrent of the same violence come down, and subsided with equal rapidity, the pass could not have been re-opened in the same time without a much larger number of men.

Work was continued for ten days longer, the narrow parts were blasted out, grades eased, boulders removed, &c., so that it became possible to withdraw all the wheeled carriages which still remained in the highlands ; but it did not, of course, recover the condition of a good carriage road.

On 1st June the Commander-in-Chief passed through the Suru defile, and reached Kumayli and Zulla.

The troops were despatched to England and to Bombay, and on 10th June Sir Robert Napier embarked for Suez and England.

Mr. Disraeli (afterwards Earl of Beaconsfield), in congratulating the House of Commons on the success of the expedition, made a remarkable speech on the subject.*

As the account of such a campaign as this can hardly be considered complete without the report of the Commanding Engineer, it will be as well to state that it is to be found in the official report of the expedition, under date Zulla, 30th May 1868, addressed to the Assistant Quartermaster-General, Expeditionary Force.

The report is unavoidably somewhat lengthy, but must always prove of interest, especially to Engineers. The Commanding Engineer, Lieutenant-Colonel St. Clair Wilkins, R.Bo.E., was, very much against his own inclinations, obliged to remain at the coast during the campaign, as Sir Robert Napier justly considered that the safety and welfare of his force would be entirely dependent upon the works at Zulla and the railway to Kumayli.

A curious incident may here be mentioned in connection with an Abyssinian trophy. A silver drum was among the spoils, and half of this was given to the 10th Company R. E., while the other half fell to the K Company Madras Sappers. It was decided to send this home to Elkington, with the view of having it made into a cup. It was accordingly carefully packed into a tin case, with an outer wooden one, and sent to England in the care of Mrs. Young (wife of the doctor of the Sappers). About two months after, a letter was received, stating that the case had been opened in the Custom House and found to be empty. This created a good deal of astonishment, as great care had been taken with the packing, and an officer had actually seen it packed and escorted it himself to the doctor's house. It was suggested that as the drum fitted the case very tightly, and the silver was much discoloured, it might have been overlooked and mistaken for the inside of the tin case. In point of fact, this

* On 2nd July 1868.

actually was the case, and on receipt of a letter from Bangalore Mrs. Young communicated with the Custom House authorities, who then found it. All this time the case had been in an open lumber-room of the Custom House unobserved. It was found quite safe, and, fortunately for the Corps, had not been thrown away.

Lieutenant C. A. Sim was employed in executive charge of the Kohat Division from November 1866 to May 1869, and again, when a Captain, from June 1871 to January 1873.

During the first period he was engaged in an attack on Gara, and while there for the second time he accompanied an expedition to the Dour valley.

In March 1868 the Bazotie Afreedees (a clan close to Kohat) commenced to annoy our picquets. Not quieted by their (Ooblow) pass being blockaded, they one day appeared in great force on a round knoll not far from the Mahomedraye picquet. Our force was hurried out to the village of Mahomedraye to attack them. The dread of our cavalry and artillery forced them up the Ooblow valley, but they established themselves in a " sanga" on the top of a knoll. Some mistake in the orders issued resulted in a sad disaster. The cavalry thought it possible to cut off the enemy from the main range, when a direct attack by the infantry would force them to retire from their stronghold. The knoll was found, however, to be connected with the main range by a saddle. The direct attack was a matter of alpine climbing, and resulted in the death of one commandant, with his subadar-major, and some twenty-five men (the adjutant was also wounded), and the driving back of a second regiment with its commandant badly wounded. The body of the commandant (Captain Ruxton) could not be recovered on the day of the fray, but was sent in some days after, owing to the dissensions of two clans, who both claimed it as battle spoil.

Up to the early part of 1869 the Bazotie Afreedees still continued to annoy the station outposts, and arrangements were therefore put in hand to make a demonstration against the tribe from three sides : first, by a small force advancing from Peshawur in the direction of Fort Mackeson ; second, by a column from Kohat to assault Gara (lying just within their border) and burn both it and Dana Kwoolla, if possible ; third, by a feint on the part of Saodan Kwaja Mahomed Khan and his Khuttucks against the Aleezye section of the Afreedees.

At midnight on 24th February 1869 the force moved out of Kohat, Lieutenant Sim accompanying it.

It consisted of 1st and 4th Punjab Infantry, two mountain-guns, and a strong force of mountain levies. A reserve was left to guard the mouth of the Ooblow pass, drawn up between Mahomedraye and the foot of the pass. Colonel Keyes, C.B., V.C. (now K.C.B.), with the Deputy Commissioner, Captain Cavagnari (afterwards the much-lamented Sir Louis Cavagnari), and twelve orderlies, rushed up the steep ascent, expecting to find a strong post at the summit on the water-shed, the boundary between British and Afreedee territory ; but all was silent and deserted.

At 6 A.M. on the 25th the Punjab Infantry were ordered to leave two strong companies to hold the ledge and line some hills immediately above, while the remainder advanced slowly to allow of ten headmen of Gara coming forward to tender their submission. A shot was fired by an Afreedee, a general fusilade at once commenced, and our skirmishers advanced gradually to the village. As the inhabitants left it, the fighting-men of the tribe took up a position in a natural stronghold behind and above it.

Our men occupied the outskirts of the village, and speedily set fire to the huts and stacks of corn.

Our unexpected visit had, as the Afreedees themselves said, "lifted the purdah of their stronghold," and the flames of Gara announced that Ruxton was avenged.

The steady fire now kept up by the villagers from their stronghold clearly showed that others besides the inhabitants were engaged in the fight. On all sides white puffs of smoke told of new arrivals. Dana Kwoolla, our original destination, was still six miles off, and the frontier was aroused. The Afreedees are said to number 40,000 fighting-men; sufficient mischief had been done with a loss of only two or three men on our side, and our retreat to the kotal and home by the Ooblow Towers was sure to be disputed and followed up.

As quickly as we had arrived, so the order for retiring was passed round. Hardly could our men leave individual rocks and cover before they were occupied by the Afreedees. Our whole force was quickly and successfully drawn off to Kohat, after just twelve hours' stay in Afreedee territory. It was politically reported that the sharpness of the attack astonished and cowed the Bazoties, and it is certain that no more depredations took place up to the beginning of 1873.

The Government of India thanked Colonel Keyes and the force employed for this most successful expedition.

On 6th February 1872 Brigadier-General Keyes, C.B., accompanied by Colonel Kennedy, 2nd Punjab Infantry, the Commissioner, Major Munro, his staff officer, Captain Mackenzie, and Captain C. A. Sim, R.E., left Bunnoo about the middle of the day to reconnoitre in the direction of the Tockee Post, the route for the next day's march.

About twenty of the 2nd Punjab Cavalry accompanied them, as well as a large number of frontier militia, horse and foot. They followed the bed of the Tockee Nulla for six or seven miles, until high precipitous banks closed the pass and forced them to ascend the Shinkee Kotul, where Mahomed Hayat Khan had been sent forward with 1,000 Bunnoochees and Wuzeerees to guarantee a safe passage the next day. As they rode up towards him, his undisciplined levies showed signs of falling back, rallied for a moment when they saw us, and finally bolted clean back to Tockee and Koorum.

The escort was sufficient to ensure the safety of our party back to camp, at Dregonde, where they found assembled fifty Punjab Cavalry, 900 Sikh Infantry, and 430 Punjab Infantry, besides six guns and two howitzers. Captain Sim had with him, in addition, fifty picked coolies, under one of his contractors, Jummoo Khan; and while the party was reconnoitring, Mr. Hilton, Captain Sim's assistant, had been easing slopes and removing boulders from the road along which they were to march next day.

By 9 A.M. on the 7th February the whole force had marched the seven easy miles, and were ready to ascend the kotul. The Government of India having limited the General to an expedition of twenty-four hours, the chief consideration was how quickly the guns could be dragged over the pass.

A Sikh regiment was told off to assist Captain Sim, and by half-past 2 the guns were on the opposite side ready to march into the Dour valley. An hour previous to this, the General had reconnoitred up to Haider Kheyl, where he found drawn up in front of the village, with a marsh in front of them, the fighting strength of the Dour valley.

The 1st Sikhs were now coming up in skirmishing order, the howitzers were ready, while the cavalry made a wide detour to get round the village. A hostile shot was fired, and the 1st Sikhs advanced with a rush, firing heavily. Haider Kheyl was soon in flames, and the population in full flight, only to fall into the clutches of our cavalry. One man only was wounded on our side. Had a determined stand been made in the Shinkee Kotul, there would have been some tough fighting; as it was, our guns and cavalry saved us from any loss in attacking such an open valley as the Haider Kheyl.

The Dour valley had never been visited by our troops before, and the expedition served the purpose of suppressing all sorts of raids that had been constantly occurring for a long time past. The Lieutenant-Governor of the Punjab " had much pleasure in placing on record his admiration of the brilliant manner in which Lieutenant-Colonel Campbell led his regiment to the successful attack and capture of Haider Kheyl. He also fully appreciated the difficulty experienced in dragging the guns of the Light Field-Battery over nearly twenty-five miles of boulders ; but the successful manner in which that difficulty was overcome, and the efficient fire of the battery when brought into action, reflect the greatest credit upon it and its commanding officer." His Honour " also noticed with special approval the services of the officers mentioned in the General's despatches, Captain Mackenzie, Captain Sim, Executive Engineer Kohat Division, and Mr. Hilton, Assistant Engineer."

The Dufflas, a wild tribe of the Himalayas, in February 1873 carried off a number of Assamese as prisoners ; attempts were made to get them back by negotiations, but all efforts failed.

In October 1874 an expedition was organised to punish the Dufflas and recover the prisoners. The force consisted of 900 Native Infantry, half a company of Bengal Sappers, and two mountain-guns, besides 1,200 transport coolies, under the command of Brigadier-General Stafford, C.B.

In January 1874 Lord Napier of Magdala had visited the camp of Exercise at Bangalore, and having been greatly struck with the working of the signalling-parties, and especially with the heliostat, he determined to send Captain E. Begbie, Madras Sappers, with the expedition as signalling officer. Accordingly, Captain Begbie received the following telegram : " Lord Napier specially selected you for employment Duffla Expedition."

On 9th November he sailed with signalling equipment and two men (Bugler Maple and Private Ragoo) for Calcutta.

He started with the impression that the Bengal force had its own signalling establishment, and that he had merely been selected to illustrate the working of his system of signalling and of the heliostat, so that a comparison might be made.

After a tedious journey up the Bramahpootra, they arrived at Borgain on 12th December 1874, and joined the head-quarters of the force. He then found that the General supposed he was bringing a complete party. The misunderstanding was, happily, of no great consequence, as the country was far from suitable for visual signalling, as the march was chiefly through perennial forests, in which they could generally hear a shout further than they could see. Captain Begbie, however, managed to send messages between stations twenty miles apart, and sometimes they were useful to the Q.M.G. and Commissariat Departments by signalling information in half an hour which would take more than a day by field-post.

The expedition itself was uneventful, and the enemy not the ferocious savage expected, but a mild inhabitant of the wood, fond of tobacco, rum, and illustrated papers.

The prisoners were recovered (thirteen). This involved a good deal of hard marching, all in single file; for there were, of course, only mountain-paths, and one day the march led over a mountain 7,700 feet high.

There was a little excitement one night in one of our camps. During the day there had been rumours that the advanced force a few miles distant was likely to be attacked. At midnight the sharp cracks of a few rifles was heard in the direction of the advance. The fire steadily increased till there was no doubt that a severe fight was going on. This lasted for an hour and a half, when the noise of battle gradually got less, and finally ceased.

There was naturally much excitement in the camp, and the troops were hurried into the stockade with the stores, and every preparation made. On the firing ceasing it was supposed that the enemy had been repulsed.

Early next morning messengers were sent forward for news, but returned with the disappointing intelligence that there had not been any fight; and the terrible firing, which had been taken for Sniders and mountain guns, proceeded from the bursting of bamboos in a jungle which had caught fire !

Captain Begbie was assisted by Lieutenant C. R. Roberts, of 72nd Regiment, and Sergeant McQueen, Bengal Sappers, who volunteered for the service. With this assistance he was enabled to work four signal-stations with two European officers, one European sergeant, and two Sappers—total, five. In accordance with the code there should have been fourteen ; so, considering the circumstances, the operations, though limited, were satisfactory.

By the 23rd February 1875, the operations came to an end.

The immediate cause of the campaign in the Malay Peninsula in 1875-76, was the murder of Mr. Birch, British Resident in Perak.

On 2nd November 1875, Mr. Birch ascended the river to Passir Sala, seven miles from the Residency, to fix up proclamations showing the powers of the British Resident in the government of the country.

About 9 A.M. he went into one of the small neat bath-houses on the river-bank to bathe.

Some armed Malays tore down the proclamations, stabbed Mr. Birch's interpreter, and made for the bath-house where Mr. Birch was. The Malays thrust their spears through the mat sides of the bath-house, and thus murdered the Resident.

Lieutenant Abbott, R.N , was at the time shooting on the opposite bank, and Mr. Swettenham, C.S., was at Qualla Kampa, on duty. Both reached the Residency in safety.

News of the murder arrived at Penang on 4th November, and one officer with sixty men of the 1st–10th Regiment, under Lieutenant Booth, left for the Residency, accompanied by Captain Innes, R.E., as Commissioner.

They arrived on the 6th November, and next day (Sunday) started up the river to attack the Malays. A landing was effected a little below Campong Baia stockade, and the small force marched up the bank. They were suddenly fired into from the Campong Baia stockade. They then attempted to take it by assault, but were obliged to retire.

Captain Innes, R.E., was shot through the heart, while Lieutenants Booth and Elliot, of 1st–10th, were both wounded. Besides these casualties five men were killed and seven wounded.

A retreat was unavoidably made to the Residency to await reinforcements. These reached the Residency on the 8th and 9th, consisting of a detachment of 1st–10th under Captain Whitla, one gun R.A. under Lieutenant Monckton, and eighty men of the Naval Brigade with one gun, two 12-pounder howitzers, and two 24-pounder rocket-tubes under Commander Sterling, R.N.

Boats were as soon as possible prepared for the guns, and on the 15th all was ready for an advance. The force accordingly started up the river to attack the stockades. When they got near Campong Baia the land force disembarked, and, marching up, kept pace with the boats.

The land force captured the stockade without the loss of a man, the enemy flying before them. They also captured the stockade at Passir Sala, and during the day four stockades were taken. The troops burned all the houses, destroyed as much of the stockades as possible, and returned to the Residency to await orders.

Meantime the Governor of the Straits Settlement telegraphed to Hong Kong and India for reinforcements.

General Colborne, with 300 men of 80th, left Hong Kong on 11th November 1875 ; and General Ross, with 3rd Buffs, 400 1st Goorkhas, and a battery R.A., left Calcutta towards the latter end of November.

The remainder of the battery already in Perak, left Singapore, under Major Nicolls, R.A., for the Residency.

The C Company Madras Sappers, under Lieutenant A. Howlett, was ordered, on 17th November, from Rangoon to proceed to Penang. They left Rangoon on the 22nd, and, arriving at Penang on the 29th, found head-quarters, and four companies of the Buffs, and half a battery of artillery already there.

The assembled force left the same evening for the mouth of the Larut river, forty miles south-east of Penang, landed at Telook Kartang, about six miles up the river, on 1st December, and marched to Qualla Kangsa, about thirty miles due east on the Perak river.

The general plan of operations was for General Colborne, with 200 men, to advance from the Residency, up the Perak river to Blanga, while the force from India, under General Ross, was to advance from Larut to Qualla Kangsa. The two forces were then to converge on Kinta, the chief town, and attack it on south and north.

The company of Madras Sappers was attached to General Ross's force.

General Colborne arrived at the Residency (Banda Bahru) on 24th November. His troops remained there till the 8th December, the delay arising on account of the difficulty in procuring boats for the transport of the force up the river.

On the 13th they reached Blanga. At Blanga General Colborne expected to hear from General Ross at Qualla Kangsa; but as he got no news, he pushed on to Kinta.

He had considerable difficulty in moving to Kinta, owing to the badness of the track; but on the 17th succeeded in reaching it, and having shelled and fired rockets into Kinta for some time, the chief town of Perak fell into our hands. All the houses on the right bank of the river were burnt, and our force encamped for the night.

We must now turn to the movements of General Ross's force.

Colonel Cox, 3rd Buffs, with two companies of his regiment and C Company of Madras Sappers, landed, as we have seen, up the Larut river on 1st December.

The Sappers were employed until the arrival of the main body at Gapis and Campong Royale. The former they stockaded in a few days, and did much to render the latter habitable by the troops, and to forward tents, &c.

Owing to insufficiency of transport provided by the Colonial Government, the C Company Sappers was, on 8th December, sent in advance to Qualla Kangsa to erect hutting. By the exertions of the Sappers, aided by ten Chinese, hut accommodation was provided as fast as the troops could be moved.

The Sappers, while employed on this, were at work from sunrise to sunset in all weathers; and between 8th December and end of the month no less than 10,000 square feet of hutting were erected.

Major Twigge, R.E., in his report, says:—

" Considering the climate and the difficulties which had to be contended with in the nature of the work, and the use of material to which the men were unaccustomed, I venture to submit that they were deserving of especial praise for the readiness of resource they displayed."

Besides the hutting, they enclosed the position by palisading, bridges were built, and communications to the rear improved.

General Ross landed in Larut about 8th December, and reached Qualla Kangsa on the 15th (two days after General Colborne had left Blanga).

The original plan of marching on Kinta through the jungle from Qualla Kangsa was abandoned, probably on account of its impracticability, and it was determined to move down to Blanga by boats.

A party of the Naval Brigade, under Lieutenant Wright, R.N., was sent down the river for boats. They captured several without opposition, and on the 19th Colonel Storey, 1st Goorkhas, with 50 Goorkhas, 100 of the Buffs, and 50 or 60 Naval Brigade, with one rocket-tube, left Qualla Kangsa for Blanga, where they arrived the same evening.

Lieutenant Rich, R.E., in his *Campaign in Malay Peninsula* says :—

"Considering that these troops were able to get from Qualla Kangsa to Blanga in one day, whilst it took General Colborne's force five days to get from the Residency to the same place, there seems to be no excuse for them not arriving in time to join General Colborne's force at Blanga."

There seems to be no sufficient justification for this remark. Colonel Cox only arrived at Qualla Kangsa on 12th December, whilst we have seen that General Colborne left Blanga on morning of the 13th. Colonel Cox was naturally obliged to remain at Qualla Kangsa until he received orders from the General commanding as to his movements.

General Ross did not arrive at Qualla Kangsa till the 15th. After his arrival it took four days for him to get boats; so that even if Colonel Cox had at once set to work to procure boats they could not have been obtained till the 16th or 17th, and on the latter date Kinta had been captured by General Colborne.

Moreover, at the time Colonel Cox reached Qualla Kangsa it is to be presumed that the advance on Kinta from Qualla Kangsa was fully intended to take place through the jungle, and it was hence no part of the duty of Colonel Cox to procure boats; and as he was unaccompanied by any of the Naval Brigade he would have found much difficulty in obtaining them.

General Colborne, on the contrary, had eighty men of the Naval Brigade under Captain Butler, R.N., and yet was compelled to remain at the Residency from 24th November to 8th December (fourteen days), owing to the difficulty of procuring boats.

When Colonel Storey reached Blanga he found that General Colborne was at Kinta, and so followed him there as soon as possible, leaving the Naval Brigade at Blanga.

He reached Kinta on the 21st, having marched the distance in two days.

31 *

On 17th December our troops had got possession of the whole of Perak. They commanded the rivers Perak and Kinta, and possessed all the chief towns.

Early in January 1876, General Colborne, after holding a consultation with General Ross at Kinta (Queen's Commissioner, Major McNair, also present), left it under command of Colonel Storey, and went to Penang to obtain instructions from the Governor.

The force at Qualla Kangsa had still some little work to do.

On 4th January it was determined to search the village of Kota Lama (three miles above Qualla Kangsa), which had for long been known as the haunt of all the worst characters in Perak. Part of the force skirmished up the right bank, and part up the left.

The party on the right were not opposed, and, having reached the village, placed double lines of sentries round the outskirts, and entered the village. They searched portions of the village, and took 100 spears, eighty muskets, three barrels of powder, a number of knives and other weapons, which they carried to Qualla Kangsa.

The party on the left bank were opposed. The enemy fired several times at them, but we advanced through the village, the enemy retiring into the jungle.

General Ross and Staff landed on the left bank in the centre of the village. He had with him four Goorkhas as escort, and twenty sailors joined the group.

Major McNair was explaining to a group of women that they need fear nothing, when suddenly a party of Malays fired a volley and rushed from the jungle. They were driven off after a short time, but we lost Major Hawkins (Brigade-Major), 1 marine, 1 sailor, and 1 Goorkha killed, and Dr. Townsend and 2 Goorkhas wounded.

The troops then burnt a large part of the village, and returned to Qualla Kangsa the same night.

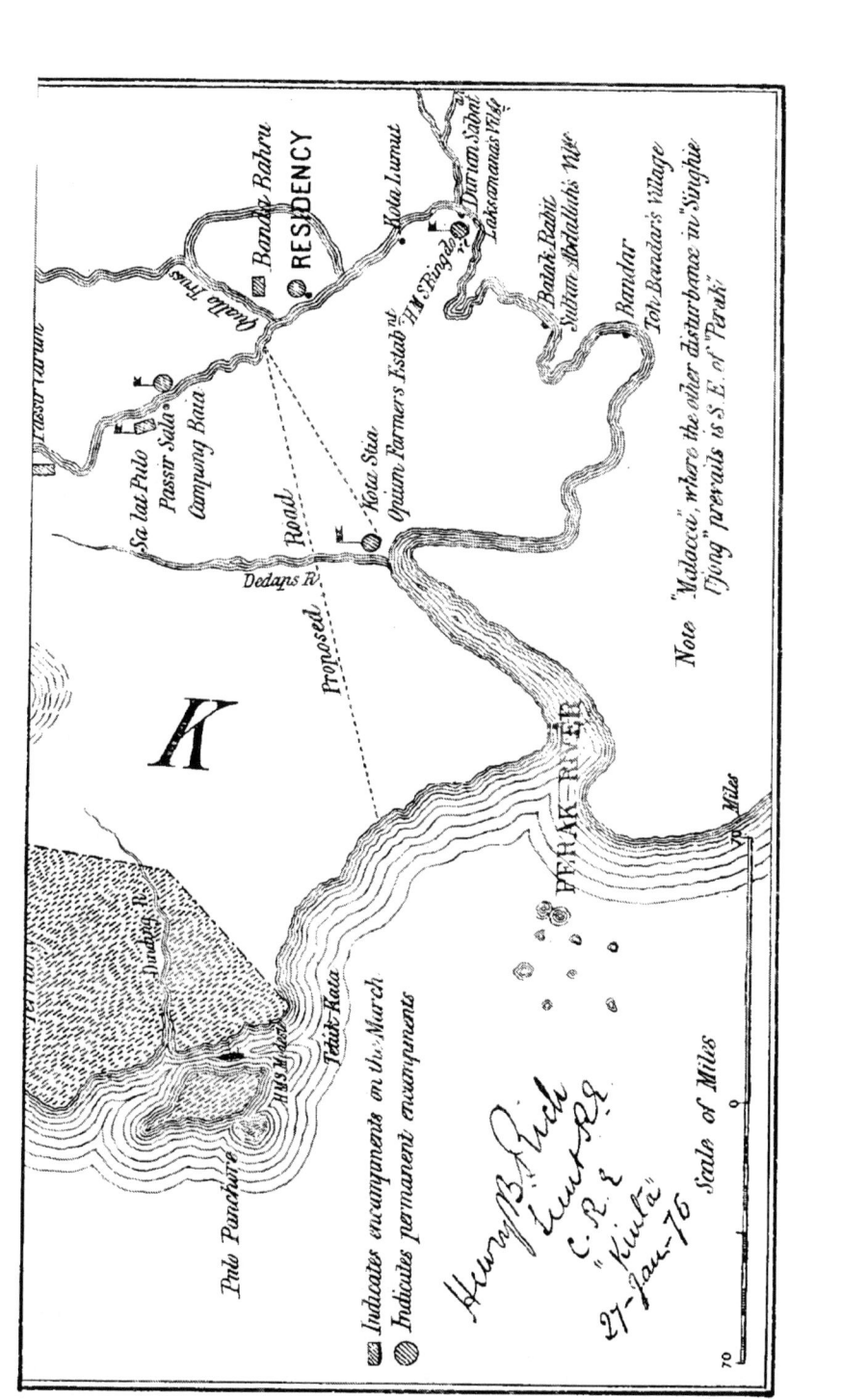

Note "Malacca," where the other disturbance in "Singhie Tjing" prevails is S.E. of "Peraki"

RESIDENCY

Bandar Bahru

Quala Tries

Passir Parune

Sa lat Prlo
Passir Sala
Campung Bata

Kota Lumut
H.M.S.Thistle
Opium Farmer's Estab.nt
Kota Stia

Durian Sabat
Laksamanas Hs.

Badak Rahit
Sultan Abdullah's Ho.

Bandar
Toh Bandar's Village

Dedaps R.

Road

Proposed

K

Dindings R.

Prlo Punchore

Tebik Raia

H.M.S.Eneid

PERAK RIVER

Miles

Indicates encampments on the March
Indicates permanent encampments

Henry B Bich
LieutRR.
C.R.8
"Kiula"
27-Jan-76   Scale of Miles
0

70

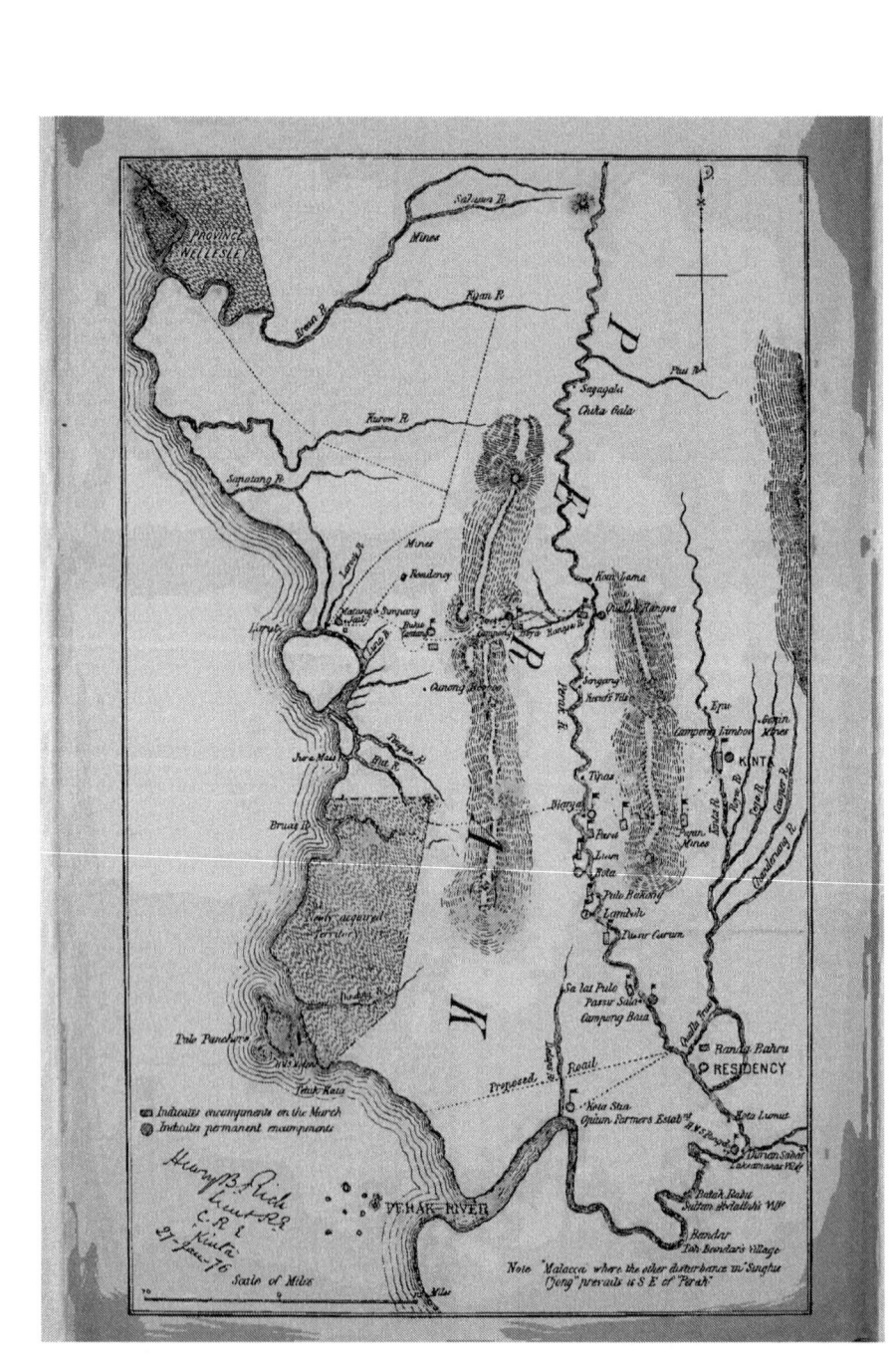

On 19th January a party of fifty Malays murdered a Malay policeman and an officer's servant who were proceeding from Qualla Kangsa to Campong Baia.

Meanwhile the C Company Madras Sappers (Lieutenant Howlett), under Lieutenant Hare's (R.E.) directions, had begun to form a road up the right bank of the Perak river to Kota Lama. The working-party was covered by fifteen of the 1st Goorkhas.

On one day a party of Malays advanced to within fifteen yards of the working-party, and wounded a havildar of Sappers and a Goorkha. The Goorkhas returned their fire, but the Malays escaped into the jungle.

Another attack was now planned on Kota Lama, from which place these Malays had come.

On 28th January it was carried out successfully. The troops burnt the remaining parts of the town and returned to Qualla Kangsa. A strong stockade was then built at Kota Lama.

The manner of skirmishing through the jungle was in the form of a hollow square; at a halt all the skirmishers faced outwards. The success of this plan was shown by a fact afterwards learnt, that a hostile rajah with an armed force was following the whole day, but failed to get an opportunity of attacking.

In the month of December a campaign was carried on in Junghie Ugong, which was most successful. Junghie Ugong is a small province north-east of Malacca.

A rising took place in beginning of December 1875. A force which had originally been intended to cross from the mouth of the Bruas to Blanga was diverted to Junghie Ugong.

The garrison of the Residency at Rassa consisted of fifty men of the 1st–10th, under Lieutenant Hinxman. He was in great danger of being surrounded, so he called up Lieutenant Peyton from Malacca with thirty more of 1st–10th, and then marched with eighty 1st–10th and forty auxiliary troops to attack Paroa on 7th December. They took the village after a hard fight, casualties being forty-one killed and wounded out of 120.

Reinforcements arrived on 17th December, consisting of 300 Goorkhas, half a battery of artillery, two 7-pounders, and two rocket-tubes, with 200 of 3rd Buffs under Colonel Clay. He advanced to Paroa, and on the 20th sent out a party of twenty-five Goorkhas under Captain Channer to reconnoitre.

Captain Channer came suddenly on a strong stockade, went up to it looked over the parapet, and found the Malays at their evening meal. He at once attacked, and took it with the loss of one killed and two wounded.

The stockade was the right flank of the enemy. Captain Channer fired into two other stockades, and, large reinforcements arriving, both were taken. Captain Channer obtained the V.C. for his gallant conduct on this occasion.

After this the force in Junghie Ugong had no difficulty. The Malays became panic-stricken and would not face us.

Our total loss in the campaign was 2 officers killed and 4 wounded, about 20 men killed and 41 wounded. Grand total, 67 killed and wounded.

Brigadier-General Ross, C.B., thus writes of the Madras Sappers to Major-General Sir T. Colborne, K.C.B.:—

"I would solicit your Excellency's commendation for the very excellent work performed by the Madras Sappers under Lieutenant A. Howlett. Working eight or nine hours a day, they were ever willing and cheerful, and proved themselves in every way to be right good and valuable soldiers."

The C Company re-embarked for Madras, *vid* Rangoon, on 22nd March 1876, having thus been four months on active field-service in Perak.

CHAPTER XII.

Expedition to Malta and Cyprus, 1878.—Sappers disembark at Malta, 27th May.
—Land at Larnaka 16th July.—Hard work of Sappers.—Sail for Bombay,
2nd November. — Arrive at Bangalore, 29th November. — Disturbances
in Rumpa, near Rajahmundry.—War in Northern Afghanistan, 1878-79.
—B. E. and K Companies sent under command of Major Sim.—Employed in the Khyber Pass. Basawul, Jellalabad, and Gundamuck.—Return
to Bangalore. July 1879.—Account of road, Peshawur to Gundamuck.
—Renewal of hostilities in September.—A. C. and I Cos. Madras Sappers
sent on service.—Arrive in Afghanistan in November and December.—
Major Ross Thompson in command.—A Company at Basawul, C at Lundi
Kotal, and I at Jellalabad.—Whole of Sappers sent to Daranta Gorge.—Attack
on Momunds near Dakka.—Expedition in Lughman Valley.—Girdikas river
road.—Thompson reconnoitres route through Adrak Badrak Pass, between
Jellalabad and Kata Sang.—Expedition to Wazeeree country.—Expedition to
Hissarak country.—Action of Maizena.—Besud affair.—Expedition against
the Momunds.—I Company with Brigadier-General Arbuthnot, C.B., in
Lughman Valley.—Preparations for return to India.—The three companies
march to Hassan Abdul, viâ Kohat—And thence to Bangalore.—Services of
Lieut.-Colonel Lindsay and Major S. C. Clarke in Afghanistan.—Railway
accident on Madras Railway to Madras Sappers, October 31st, 1879.

In April 1878 Lord Beaconsfield determined to despatch a
force from India to the Mediterranean, to show that England
was prepared, by every means in its power, to prevent Russia
from utterly crushing Turkey, and that they had resources
available in India of which free use would be made. Seven
thousand men were ordered to embark at once for active service,
the troops being selected from all three Presidencies.

From Bengal—

         13th B. N. I.
         31st P. N. I.
         2nd P. W. O. Goorkhas.

From Madras—

     25th M. N. I., under Colonel Gib.
     G and H Companies of Queen's Own Sappers.

From Bombay—

     9th Bo. N. I.
     3rd and 5th Companies of Bombay Sappers ;

besides cavalry and artillery.

The officers accompanying the Madras Sappers were :—

Col. H. N. D. Prendergast, V.C., R.M.E., commanding.
Capt. A. F. Hamilton, R.M.E., Staff officer.
Lieut. C. Wilkieson, R.E., commanding H Company.
Lieut. Ellis, R.E., commanding G Company.

Lieutenants Conner, Lindley, Attree, and Grant, all of the R. Engineers, Surgeon Lee, in medical charge ; Conductor Jones ; Subadar Anthony ; and Jemadars Caullemootoo, Rajahman, and Rajahlingum.

On 30th April the two companies arrived at Bombay, and at once embarked.

On 2nd May they sailed in the *Canara*, accompanied by Lieutenant-Colonel McLeod, R.M.A.

On the 26th they steamed into the Marsa Muschetto harbour of Malta, amidst the cheers of the British troops at Ricasoli, St. Elmo, and Mauvel.

The next day they disembarked, and occupied the Lazaretto barracks.

Two days after, the Bombay Sappers arrived, with the following officers :—

         Major J. H. Cruickshank, R.Bo.E.,
         Captain Marryat, R.Bo.E.,
         Captain Stock, Bo. Infantry,

Lieutenants Fullerton, Innes Jones, Bethell, Coles, and Bate; Surgeon Dane; two Subadars and two Jemadars.

While at Malta the Sappers were employed in handling the parks, making roads, looking after water-supply, covering-in all the hospital-huts and tents of British soldiers with bamboos, thatch, or tarpaulins. They also did various work in the way of hutting, bridging, &c.

On the 12th June the Governor of Malta (Sir Arthur Burton, K.C.B.) paraded the troops; and on the 17th all the troops in Malta were inspected by H.R.H. the Duke of Cambridge.

At noon on 10th July orders were received for the Madras Sappers to be ready to embark for Cyprus at 5 P.M. The G Company was at San Antonio, and the H at Lazaretto. Carts, &c. had to be procured for the former.

The order for the Bombay Sappers was received at 6 P.M. (Half the 5th Company Bombay Sappers was left behind at Malta in charge of the Bombay Park.)

By a little after midnight all the Sappers were on board the *Canara*, and ready to start.

Before noon next day the *Canara* sailed, under orders for Cyprus, and arrived off Larnaka on the 16th.

The orders received were of the vaguest description, so much so that it was not known whether the Sappers would have to take the island or not.

On arrival, a commencement was made to land the siege-train, which was continued till the 19th, when the last man landed.

Light landing-stages were constructed for the disembarkation of the troops expected the following week, and the Royal Navy, under H.R.H. the Duke of Edinburgh, commenced building a pier, in which the Queen's Own Sappers rendered assistance, under Colonel Prendergast.

Orders were now received to choose a camp for 10,000 men, and to make arrangements for landing, transporting, and feeding

them.   There were but five days to do this in, and, when required, the Sappers could show six piers, a road to the camp at
Chifflik, and water-supply troughs at the camp, with carriage
enough to take the regiments on as they landed.

The Sappers became very friendly with the sailors, and His
Royal Highness appeared to take a great interest in the Sappers
(both officers and men), who helped very materially in building
the Duke's pier by swimming about all day, taking out timbers
to their places.   To procure timber the Sappers had to forage
about, pull down old houses, and search the bazaars, and as every
man in Cyprus, as a general rule, lies, it was difficult to do or
get anything unless you set about it yourself.

On 22nd July Sir Garnet Wolseley arrived.

On the 24th and 25th Major Hamilton accompanied him in
his visit to Famagousta and Limasole, to select camping-grounds
for the Native Infantry, and inquire into the water-supply.
Lieutenant Wilkieson was directed to report on the road between
Larnaka and Nicosia, while Lieutenants Lindley and Attree
surveyed the country between Famagousta and Nicosia.

On the 26th the G and H Companies moved into camp outside Larnaka, leaving half a company of 5th Bombay Sappers with
the Bombay Park, which had now arrived.   A line of visual
signalling was started between Chifflik and the Sapper camp,
with heliostat, and from the Sapper camp to Marina by flag,
which was much used by the Commissariat Department.   After
the arrival of 31st Company R. E., this line was superseded by
a wire.

Mr. Archibald Forbes, the Special Correspondent of the *Daily
News*, thus wrote of the Madras Sappers :—

" Tramping back along the sun-scorched strand, running the
gauntlet of numerous donkeys, and smells more numerous than
donkeys, I found myself back again on the east flank of the
Marina, close to the jetty which the blue-jackets had been constructing.   Here I found a half-melted Engineer officer striving

to overcome the *vis inertiæ* of a very miscellaneous batch of native labourers, Turks, Greeks, and nondescripts. In marked contrast to their pottering was the honest labour at the road-making of the Madras Sappers and Miners, dark lissom fellows, stripped to the dhotie and streaming at every pore, but working steadily on at their heavy toil with the cheery contentment of willing men, to look at whom did one good, although it scarcely made him cooler."

At first Colonel Prendergast was the senior Engineer officer in Cyprus, and would in ordinary course have been Commanding Royal Engineer, but Lieutenant-Colonel Maquay was sent out from England, and, being about six months senior to Prendergast as Lieutenant-Colonel R. E. (although two years younger), became Commanding Royal Engineer. Colonel Prendergast returned to India 25th August.

It was now determined to improve the road between Larnaka and Nicosia, and on 7th August the company at Chifflik was brought to head-quarters camp to be deployed along the road. The H Company marched to Peroi (eleven miles from Nicosia), a section being left at Gosli, eight miles from Larnaka.

A half section of the G Company went with 31st R. E. to Nicosia, and the other half relieved the Bombay Sappers at Marina, while the latter took the road between Larnaka and Gosli.

By this time all the companies were a good deal impaired in strength by the almost universal fever. Lieutenant Bethell's report on a place called Mathiati, caused its selection as a site for the winter hutment. This necessitated a change in the disposition of the companies along the road; the Larnaka end was an entirely new trace for about five and a half miles out; the main road was then joined; this was improved and a small diversion made beyond Gosli.

At this point the road to Dali turns off; this was afterwards improved to one mile short of Dali, when a new road was traced (two miles) to Perokoria, thus avoiding the crossing of the Dali river. From Perokoria to Haia Varvara a cart-road was improved, and from the latter place to Mathiati the road was almost an entirely new trace, having to surmount a "col" into the Mathiati valley.

The huts for the winter encampment began to arrive on 23rd September, and the G Company was employed for twelve hours daily on the beach, superintending the disembarking and loading of these huts. The duty was very heavy, and both Captain Marryat and Lieutenant Ellis, who succeeded him, were knocked up by the work. During all this time various Engineer officers were employed in making surveys and reconnoissances.

The G and H Companies Queen's Own Sappers, and the 5th Company B. S., remained in Cyprus till the end of October, and embarked on *Simoom* on 1st November.

The 3rd Company Bo. S. arrived next day, having been marching all night. The *Simoom* sailed at noon on the 2nd, and anchored in Bombay Harbour on 20th November.

The men were landed on the 22nd, and next day the Queen's Own Sappers left by rail, arriving at Bangalore on 29th November, after an absence of just seven months.

Colonel Prendergast, in his report, stated :—

" The conduct and efficiency of the Sappers (officers and men) were remarkable even in a picked force such as the Indian Expeditionary Force ; that the Queen's Own Sappers proved themselves not inferior to the R. E. or Bombay Sappers in any respect ; that no task was imposed upon them which they could not perform right well ; that the labour of preparing press, roads, watering and slaughtering arrangements for a force of all arms, 11,000 strong, together with the landing of an R. E. park and commissariat stores in five days, was accepted cheerfully by all ranks ; and that the fatigue of landing, sorting, and setting up huts in the most inclement weather was undergone with no less alacrity and goodwill."

The following were the casualties :—

	Officers.		European N.C.O.		Native ranks.		Public followers.	
	M.	Bo.	M.	Bo.	M.	Bo.	M.	Bo.
Invalided from Malta ...	—	1	1	—	4	6	—	1
Invalided from Cyprus ...	1	3	—	1	—	—	—	—
	Dr. Lee.							
Died	—	—	2	—	2	1	1	2
Total ...	1	4	3	1	6	7	1	3

Colonel Prendergast thanked Major Hamilton for " his valuable services," and added that " the officers commanding companies, Lieutenants Wilkieson and Ellis, deserve high praise," while " Conductor T. Jones acquitted himself admirably as officer in charge of the park, a most important and onerous duty."

On 31st October the following order was published by Sir Garnet Wolseley :—

" The Madras and Bombay Sappers being about to embark for India, the Lieutenant-General cannot allow them to leave the command without placing upon record his sense of the valuable work they have done in this island " ; and in permitting Colonel Prendergast to proceed to India he desired that the Commanding Royal Engineer " will inform him of Sir G. Wolseley's appreciation of the excellent work done by himself and the officers and men under his command in this island."

Brigadier-General Macpherson, C.B., V.C., in taking leave of the troops under his command at Malta and Cyprus, " offered to all ranks his very best thanks for the admirable discipline that has been maintained throughout the expedition, under circumstances of no ordinary temptation. The highest authority in the army has represented to Her Most Gracious Majesty his high appreciation of their soldier-like bearing in terms of which every individual of the Indian Contingent must feel justly proud."

The troops thus addressed were :—

G and H companies Queen's Own Sappers and Miners.

3rd and 5th companies Bombay Sappers.

13th Bengal Native Infantry.

31st Punjab Native Infantry.

2nd P. W. O. Goorkhas.

25th Madras N. I.

Owing to .certain serious disturbances which took place, in 1879, in the hill-tracts of Rumpa and Golconda (situated to north and north-east of Rajahmundry, in the Godavery district), it was found necessary to despatch troops to those parts, and in July 1879 two companies (D and G) of the Queen's Own Sappers were ordered there with the following officers :—

Lieutenant-Colonel Howes, R.M.E., in command; Lieutenants Rawson, R.E., Hamilton, R.E., Wabab, R.E., D Company; Major Hamilton, R.M.E., Lieutenants McDonnell and Gale, R.E., G Company.

They proceeded to Dowlaishwaram by means of the Buckingham (East Coast), Kistna, and Godavery canals, and the head-quarters were located there, the camp being pitched on the site occupied by the Sappers in former years, when the head-quarters of the Corps was stationed at Dowlaishwaram, close to the splendid anicut (or dam) built across the Godavery river by Arthur Cotton (now General Sir Arthur Cotton, K.C.S.I.).

It was intended at first that the Sappers should be employed entirely on the river; but a party of sixty men, D Company, under Lieutenant Hamilton, R.E., was sent above the "gorge" of the Godavery to Wuddagudiem to guard the village and watch the banks of the river, in order to prevent rebels from crossing to the Nizam's territory.

The Sappers at head-quarters were employed as guards on board the steamers. The party at Wuddagudiem improved the camp, strengthened the village, and constructed a landing-stage.

On one occasion an attack was made on Chendriah (the rebel leader) and his followers near Vencatapollium; but he retired into the jungle and evaded pursuit.

The Sapper detachment was afterwards withdrawn and replaced by Nizam's troops.

Meanwhile, the other half of D Company was employed, under Captain Rawson, R.E., at Chodarum, in Rumpa, garrisoning the place, improving the camp, and watching the movements of the rebels. Lieutenant McDonnell had also taken a party of the G Company further up the country to construct a bridge of casks across a stream which at times was not fordable. Owing to unforeseen difficulties, however, and to the bridge not being urgently required, the project was abandoned.

In October 1879 Captain Rawson's party was withdrawn, and Lieutenant Gale took some of the G Company to Yellaishwaram,* on the borders of Golconda, to watch events. They hutted the men, improved the camp, and were occasionally employed on escort duty.

In December Lieutenant Gale was relieved by Lieutenant Hamilton.

About this time heliostats were received, and Lieutenant McDonnell opened out a station on the Kappa Konda, a large hill in Rumpa, and from thence communicated with Rajahmundry and with the party in Golconda.

About February 1880 the whole of the Sappers, with the exception of a few signallers, were withdrawn to Dowlaishwaram, as the men had suffered a great deal from fever, and there was really no work for them to do in the jungles. At Dowlaishwaram they were merely employed in quarrying and road-making.

Afterwards, the D Company improved parts of the road near Chodarum, in Rumpa.

In January 1881 the D Company returned to Bangalore, followed by the G Company in July.

* The 10th M. N. I. were in camp at this place.

During the time the Sappers were employed Lieutenant-Colonel Howes, Lieutenants Hamilton and McDonnell were invalided. Lieutenants Wahab and Gale were transferred to other duties, and Lieutenant Ellis eventually took command of the G Company.

Beyond road-making, constructing and strengthening camps, and signalling, very little work had been forthcoming for the Sappers.

In July 1878, Shere Ali, the Ameer of Afghanistan received a Russian Envoy in Cabul, having frequently in previous years refused admittance to any English one.

Lord Lytton, the Viceroy of India, considering this an intentional affront put upon England, organised a mission with Sir Neville Chamberlain, G.C.B., G.C.S.I., at its head.

This mission, as is well known, was stopped at Ali Musjid and obliged to return to Peshawur.

An apology was demanded, and it was required to be received before the 20th November; but as none was received, on the morning of the 21st our troops crossed the frontier, and the war with Afghanistan commenced.

On the 1st December the B and E Companies of the Queen's Own Sappers and Miners received orders to join at Peshawur, and accordingly left Bangalore on the 5th, followed a fortnight later by the K Company.

Major C. A. Sim, R.E. (Madras) in command.

Surgeon Charles Sibthorpe in medical charge.

B Company.—Lieutenants W. D. Conner, R.E., F. J. Attree, R.E., R. A. Wabab, R.E. ; Sergeants Price and Dove ; Corporals Roberts and Terry ; Subadar Raja Ram ; Jemadar Ramalingum.

E Company.—Captain T. H. Winterbotham, Madras Infantry ; Lieutenants W. D. Lindley, R.E., A. C. MacDonnell, R.E. ; Sergeants Balding and Fraser ; Corporals Clarke and Curtis ; Subadar Gregory ; Jemadars Mootoosammy and Annasammy.

K Company.—Lieutenants C. C. Rawson, R E., P. B. Poulter, R.E., R. E. Hamilton, R.E.; Sergeant Anderton; Corporal Sparkes; Subadar-Major Narrainsammy; Jemadar Pudmanaben.

The B and E Companies reached Jumrood on 9th January 1879, and the K Company on the 23rd.

Directly the Sappers arrived they were set to make a road from Ali Musjid to Jumrood. This was a tedious affair, as for 100 yards it had to be cut through hard rock. The road by February was wide enough for the passage of convoys of camels, and was opened for cart traffic on 17th March.

In January the Sappers were likewise employed in preparing a defensive post at Shargai, two miles from Ali Musjid.

On 25th January a force of about 900 men started from Ali Musjid for the Bazar valley, and two officers and fifty men of the Sappers accompanied it.

At Karumna ten towers were destroyed, when the force marched to Boorg and blew up three more towers. An onward march was then ordered, and on the evening of the 26th, Cheena, the entrance to the Bazar valley, was reached.

The picquets were attacked all round the camp during the night, and continuous firing was kept up till the morning.

On the 28th the Sappers accompanied a reconnoitring party to a distance of four miles; and next day another tower, three miles distant from camp, was blown up.

Nothing very eventful occurred during the stay in the Bazar valley, which was quitted on the 3rd February, and the force arrived at Ali Musjid next day.

On 26th February, Lieutenant Wahab, R.E., with Jemadar Rajalingum and two Sappers, accompanied a party to ascend the surrounding hills in search of a suitable site for an encampment for the hot weather. After visiting Rotäs they returned, on 1st March, without having succeeded in finding one.

During February work was continued on the road, and on the 27th a party of Sappers were employed in building a wall

II.   32

alongside the road from Ali Musjid fort to the river to afford cover to the road from the tops of the surrounding hills.

On 12th March a party of one officer and fifty Sappers started towards Jumrood to meet the elephant battery from Peshawur. The guns were brought up Mackeson's road by the elephants, but the store and ammunition waggons (thirty-five in number), drawn by bullocks, could not get up till hauled along by the Sappers with drag-ropes.

On 22nd March the head-quarters of the 2nd Division moved up to Lundi Kotal, and five days after, the B Company joined them there.

The Sappers were again employed in road-making, as well as in quarrying and well-sinking, while an entrenchment was also formed round the camp. Some sangas were also built.

The country between Lundi Kotal and Dakka was at this time in a very disturbed state, so it was determined to build a strong post at Torkumar, half-way between the two places.

On 29th April the company marched to Lundi Khana, when the encampment at that place was put into a thorough state of defence. The next day they commenced work at Torkumar.

On the 10th May, while the Sappers were at work, several shots were heard. Work was at once abandoned, and the company proceeded to the scene of action. They found that a body of Afreedees had driven off a large herd of cattle. Pursuit was at once given, but the marauders got clear away before the Sappers could come up with them.

The very next day, a large body of Zukka Kheyls appeared from the direction of the Bazar valley, and attacked a company of the Mhairwarra battalion, half-way between Torkumar and Dakka. The Sappers joined in the pursuit. The Zukka Kheyls took up a very strong position on the top of a precipitous hill, and remained there till a party of the 25th tried to cut them off, when they retreated precipitately. The Sappers killed two, and the 25th three of them.

On the 14th the Sappers were again interrupted; pursued the enemy as usual, but without success.

On the 22nd the work at Torkumar was completed, and three days later the company returned to Lundi Kotal, leaving a small party at the post with the 25th.

At Lundi Kotal the new cantonment was laid out, and the men were employed in boring for water, and in superintending the erection of huts.

At this time there was a bad outbreak of cholera, and on 19th May one of the British regiments was ordered back to Peshawur; and the Sappers consequently had to furnish all the picquets round their part of the camp, thirty-six men being on guard at the same time.

The company lost three men by cholera on this occasion.

The E Company remained at Jumrood, on the road towards Ali Musjid.

By the 23rd January a fair driving road had been cleared to the Sar Kaye Nulla, along two miles of sand preceding the ascent up the Khyber gorge.

The E Company with fifty men were ordered to precede the advance of the Jumrood force, and clear the road for the camels and elephants of the transport train. After leaving the Khyber, the road was but a hill track, and it took the company the whole twelve hours of each day to prevent a block.

The whole force was enabled to reach Barakas on the afternoon of the second day. On leaving Barakas the Sappers were again sent on in advance to join the detachment of the B Company in destroying the towers of Boorg. After this they marched to Cheena.

On 29th January a detachment of Sappers accompanied Colonel Thompson's force, to blow up the two towers of Halwai.

On the return of this expedition the E Company received orders to join the B Company at Ali Musjid, and the two worked

32 *

together till the middle of April, when the E Company was marched to Basawal.

The K Company reached Jumrood on 24th January, and two days after marched on to Lundi Kotal. They were employed till the 16th March on the ghaut road from Lundi Kotal to Lundi Khana.

On 10th March this company was ordered to be transferred to the 1st Division, and on the 18th it marched to Dakka with the elephant battery, and next day reached Basawal.

On the 26th the Company marched into Jellalabad, and was brigaded with the Bengal Sappers. It remained there till the end of the month, and then marched with the advanced brigade under General Gough, reaching Futtehabad on the 1st April.

They formed part of the reserve during the action of Futteh-abad against the Khugianies (where Major Battye of the Guides was killed).

Lieutenant R. E. Hamilton, R.E., gave the following account of what he had seen of the action near Lokhi :—

"About 2 p.m. a body of men became visible on the hills west of Futtehabad, about three miles off. About 3 p.m. the artillery opened fire against the enemy, who were on the heights in great numbers behind rough breastworks. The artillery-fire had little or no effect, and the enemy advanced, driving the guns back. The infantry had meanwhile come up, and advanced on the flank of the cavalry. The enemy, however, on the other side, continued to advance up the nullahs and harass the guns ; so the Guides and 10th Hussars charged, and it was at this period that Major Battye (Guides Cavalry) lost his life. The infantry had meantime advanced on the other side, and lost an officer (Lieutenant Wiseman) who attempted to capture a flag carried by one of the enemy. After the loss of this officer the infantry retired a short distance ; but being ordered on, again advanced on the breastwork, which was found deserted. The cavalry then started in pursuit, and went some five or six miles, driving the enemy into the villages.

"The British loss was 2 officers killed, 2 men killed and 30 wounded (chiefly Guides Cavalry).

"The enemy's loss was not known, but from their own account probably 150 killed and 50 wounded."

Three days after the action the Sappers blew up six towers and a gateway.

Until the 13th the companies remained at Futtehabad engaged in road-making both towards Gundamuck and Jellalabad, after which they marched to Nimlah, and on the 14th reached Gundamuck, where they remained till the close of the campaign, detaching two parties for the construction of Forts Rozabad and Battye between Jellalabad and Gundamuck.

Lieutenant Poulter, R.E., was engaged at the former fort, while Lieutenant Rawson, R.E., built Fort Battye.

On 8th May the company was on parade, when the Ameer, Yakoob Khan, came into Gundamuck; and on the 24th they were brigaded with the Bengal Sappers at the general parade of the whole of the 1st Division in honour of the Queen's birthday.

During their stay at Gundamuck the company was variously employed—road-making, hutting, constructing water-troughs, &c. &c.

A party of two naiques and twenty Sappers accompanied Lieutenant Bartram, R.E., Bengal Sappers, to the hill about five miles from Gundamuck in the direction of Cabul (where the 44th Regiment made its last stand during the former Afghan war), and were there employed in building a monument to those of the 44th who fell on that occasion.

This party rejoined the company at Dakka on 5th June, having come down the river from Jellalabad on a raft with a party of Bengal Sappers. This detachment was fired on by the Momunds during its passage down the river, and one Bengal dooly-bearer was killed.

Late in May orders were received to break up the 1st and 2nd Divisions, and for the three companies of Queen's Own Sappers to return to Bangalore.

The K Company left Gundamuck on the 31st, and joined the others *en route*. They reached Jhelum by the 4th July, and marched into Bangalore on the 29th, after a ten days' quarantine at Kistnaveram to recover from the effects of cholera.

The companies had left Bangalore with 11 European officers, 7 native officers, and 370 N.C.O. and privates, besides 184 followers; they returned with 9 European officers, 6 native officers, 343 N.C.O. and privates, with 173 followers, having lost 2 European officers, 1 native officer, 27 N.C.O. and privates and 11 followers.

The European officers were Captain Winterbotham, died at Peshawur 14th February 1879; Lieutenant Poulter, died at Peshawur 22nd June 1879.

The native officer was Jemadar Padmanaben, died at Jubbulpore 10th July 1879.

Lieutenants Rawson, Hamilton, Wahab, MacDonell, and twenty rank and file and artificers, left Kistnaneram for Rumpa without coming into Bangalore.

In the official account of the 2nd Bazar Expedition, Lieutenant-General Maude wrote:—

"The services of . . . . Major C. A. Sim, R.E., were cheerfully given when required."

Again, on the conclusion of the campaign, he wrote:—

"Major Sim, R.E., Madras Sappers and Miners, is a good, practical, hard-working officer. Both he and his two (B and E) companies did excellent services."

Lieutenant-General Sir S. Browne, K.C.S.I., C.B., commanding 1st Division P.V.F.F., reported:—

"With regard to the K Company Madras Sappers under Lieutenant Rawson, which joined the 1st Division before leaving Jellalabad, I have to record my satisfaction of their conduct."

A brief account of the road from Peshawur to Gundamuck may fitly close the record of the work of these three companies of Sappers.

"From Peshawur there was a well-made road as far as Hurric Sing Ka Boorg, a village on the old frontier, from thence to Jumrood the road was over an open very stony uncultivated plain, through which a path had been partially cleared. Jumrood is on a low-lying plain, about the same height as Peshawur, 1,500 feet above the sea. From Jumrood to the fort of Ali Musjid is nine miles. The Khyber pass is entered about two and a half miles from Jumrood; the entrance is very wild and picturesque, through a narrow gorge between high hills. Soon after entering the pass the road ascended along a well-made, though narrow and steep declivity, made by Colonel Mackeson during the previous war; Mackeson's road, near the entrance to the Khyber, was very much improved by means of diversions, bridging, &c. At the summit of this it reaches a small undulating plateau, called the Shargai heights, from which the fort of Ali Musjid first becomes visible. It was from these heights that the heavy batteries shelled Ali Musjid and the 'sangar' on the hills above it. About four miles further on the road drops to a pathway, which runs partly along the bed of the Khyber river. The road from the Shargai heights down to the Khyber was very bad, and was covered with dead camels, whose hearts had been broken by the climbing, and whose dead carcases polluted the air horribly till means were taken to bury them; but t is was the case at all the more difficult parts of the road. The bed of the river at this point is about 600 feet higher than Peshawur, and the fort of Ali Musjid is situated on a hill fully 450 feet above the river, but commanded and surrounded on every side.

"Ali Musjid was named after a mosque built by Mahomed Ali in one of his marches; the ruins still exist. It seems to have been a sacred spot for centuries. A Buddhist tope was disinterred at the entrance, which must have been built just before the Christian era.

" All this part of the pass is very wild, with scarcely any vegetation. There was only one village, surrounding which were some well-cultivated fields, and the inhabitants had spent much trouble and ingenuity in constructing rude canals for the purpose of irrigation. This village was burnt by us on account of the murders its people had committed.

" From Ali Musjid to Lundi Kotal the road passed through the narrowest gorge in the whole pass. This gorge formed a very weird piece of scenery. The path was through the bed of the river, winding among enormous boulders. A road was eventually cut, at great cost, by Colonel Limond, R.B.E., out of the sheer face of the cliff.

" About a mile beyond this, on passing Katti-Kurthi, the pass opens out, and the road passed through the centre of a valley containing several villages, and well-cultivated.

" About half-way to Lundi Kotal another Buddhist tope is passed, in excellent preservation, the hills close by being full of caves, in which the priests lived.

" Lundi Kotal is situated, as its name signifies, at the top of the pass, and is 1,000 feet higher than Ali Musjid. The camp was pitched round a ruined fort, in the midst of an elevated plain surrounded by hills. There were several villages on this plain, which was much cut up by huge deep ravines. There was great difficulty in getting water for this camp; it had to be carried a mile or more from two very prettily-situated streams, which were named Venus' and Diana's baths.

" Lundi Khana is the next station, four miles further on, and 1,000 feet lower, the decline being got over by a very narrow steep road, made by Colonel Mackeson, greatly improved by the K Company Madras Sappers, and eventually became a capital road. At the junction of the road from Peshawur and the one leading to the camp at Lundi Kotal, the Sappers put up a signboard with three arms, one pointing towards Lundi Khana, marked 'To Cabul,' the second towards camp, marked 'To Lundi Kotal,' and the third showing the road to Peshawur, marked 'To Madras,' which last-named amused passers-by not a little.

"The view from the Kotal was very fine, with all the rugged hills of this portion of the pass in the foreground, backed up by the ever-beautiful snow-covered range of the "Safed Koh" in the far distance.

"Dakka is ten miles beyond this again, and is reached by a road gradually descending towards the Cabul river. This was one of the most dangerous parts of the road, as there were direct paths from it to the 'Barah' and 'Tirah' valleys, whence the Zukka Kheyls made frequent raids.

"For a distance of seven miles the road is very narrow; after this, it enters a small plain stretching down towards the Cabul river, close to the bank of which is the large mud-walled fort built within the last few years by the late Ameer. It was erected for the purpose of over-awing the Mohmunds, and the Khan of Lalpura, whose village is on the other side of the river. The fort at Dakka is 1,200 feet above the sea.

"From Dakka to Bassawul is ten miles. The road first passes through the Khoord Khyber pass, a short but very steep ascent, which required a great deal of work before it was made practicable for carts. Having surmounted this, the road was found fairly level all the way to Bassawul. The plain on which Bassawul is situated is an extensive one, and towards the north can be seen the snow-covered peaks of the 'Safed Koh.' A great portion of this plain consists of very fertile land, but immediately around the camp, on the river-side, there is much low-lying marshy ground. Bassawul is 1,500 feet above the sea.

"From Bassawul to Buttikot, or Barrukab, a distance of ten miles, the road passes over this plain, but beyond Barrukab it proceeds through another pass into the Jellalabad valley, Jellalabad being twenty-six miles from Bassawul. There is an alternative route by the river from Bassawul to Jellalabad, passing through a village called Girdi-Ras, but the road was not complete, nor was it practicable even for camels.

" From Jellalabad to Gundamuck the distance is thirty miles, the road having a steady rise the whole way to Gundamuck.

" The distances are : to Futtehabad, seventeen miles ; to Mimlah, eight ; and to Gundamuck, five miles.

" It was only the K Company of Sappers which was moved as far as Gundamuck, a distance of 105 miles from Peshawur. The E Company went no further than Bassawul, while the B Company had to confine its operations to the line between Ali Musjid and Lundi Khana."

In accordance with the Treaty of Gundamuck, the British Mission left India in June 1879. It consisted of Sir Louis Cavagnari as Envoy, with an assistant, Mr. Jenkins, Lieutenant Hamilton, in charge of the escort, and Dr. Kelly, in medical charge. They reached Cabul on the 24th August.

On the 3rd September, as is well known, a revolt took place in Cabul, and an attack was made on the Residency. It was stormed and set on fire, and the whole of the mission, together with the escort, were slaughtered to a man. But their defence was magnificent, and though none (except a few absent at the time) escaped, the assailants suffered very heavily. Immediately on receipt of this news, the renewal of the war was imperative, and a force was at once despatched to Cabul under Sir Frederick Roberts, *viâ* the Shuturgardan pass, at the head of the Kurram valley.

Roberts fought the action of Charasiab on the 6th October ; on the 8th Sherpur was entered, and next day our whole force encamped on the Seah-Sung plateau overlooking Cabul.

On the renewal of hostilities the Madras army was ordered to furnish three regiments of Native Infantry and three companies of Sappers for service in Afghanistan, and Colonel W. A. Gib, M.S.C., was appointed Brigadier-General.

The regiments selected were the 1st, 4th, and 15th N. I., while the Sappers consisted of the A, C, and I Companies.

The A Company left Bangalore on 3rd October, followed two days after by the I Company. The former arrived at Lundi Kotal on 14th November, while the latter advanced to Jellalabad by the 19th.

The C Company was at this time in Rangoon. It left that place on 16th November, and reached Lundi Kotal on Christmas Day. On their arrival they found the A Company at Basawul, and the I Company at Jellalabad.

The whole force of Queen's Own Sappers was under the command of Major Ross Thompson, R.M.E., while the Company officers were :—

A Company.—Lieutenants C. H. Darling, R.E., W. D. Lindley, R.E., R. A. Wahab, R.E.

C Company.—Lieutenants A. R. F. Dorward, R.E., L. Langley, R.E., G. E. Shute, R.E.

I Company.—Lieutenants A. E. Dobson, R.E., C. B. Henderson, R.E., T. Digby, R.E.

Major Ross Thompson, at the time of Roberts's advance, was at Rangoon. He and Lieutenant Dobson sailed from that place on 5th October, leaving Lieutenant Dorward, with the C Company, to follow. Thompson arrived at Calcutta on 10th October, left it on the 14th, and overtook the A and I Companies at Mean Meer on the 17th, where he assumed command.

The A Company, after arrival at Lundi Kotal, was at first employed in building protective-works, and in surveys, &c. In December it was moved on to Basawul, and was engaged in completing the defences of that position.

The I Company was, in the meantime, constructing a bridge over the Cabul river, and improving the defences of Fort Sale at Jellalabad.

In December a part of this company was with a force sent out against some Afghan raiders beyond Barikot. The villages were surrounded, and the villagers surrendered without fighting.

At the commencement of the year 1880, we find the three companies posted, the A at Basawul, C at Lundi Kotal, and the I at Jellalabad.

Towards the close of this month the I Company was ordered to the Daranta gorge, on the Cabul river, to make a road over the Seah Koh range into the Lughman valley. It was shortly after joined by the A Company; and, later still, the C Company advanced to Jellalabad—left half of the company to push on with the bridge over the river, while the other half marched to the Daranta gorge to take up the work commenced by the A and I Companies.

On the 21st January the A Company took part in an expedition against Batekot, just previous to its advance; while the C Company (a detachment) had been engaged about the middle of the month in an attack, under General Doran, on a body of Momunds estimated at 5,000 strong, who had crossed the Cabul river near Dakka and threatened that post.

The plan arranged for this expedition was for the force at Dakka (650 strong) to give out that they were afraid to attack. By this means, it was hoped that the Momunds would be drawn close to Dakka. A force (1,350) was then to advance from Lundi Kotal and endeavour to get behind the Momunds. The Dakka column was to defer its attack till 1 P.M., by which time it was hoped the Lundi Kotal force would be sufficiently advanced. Unfortunately, the Dakka force commenced its attack too soon, drove the Momunds back too rapidly, and the Lundi Kotal force only arrived in time to see the Momunds crossing the river, and to shell their rear-guard. The force had left Lundi Kotal at 4 A.M., and had a long and most tiresome march of eighteen miles, over a "villainous" country. Lieutenants Dorward and Shute took part in this march, part of the

Sappers marching with the guns, and part with the baggage-guard.

Colonel Hodding, 4th M.N.I., who commanded the baggage-guard, reported very favourably on the work done by the Sappers, without whose aid the march of the baggage-animals would have been considerably delayed, if not stopped altogether.

On the next day (16th January), it being decided to pursue the Momunds across the river, preparations were made for crossing. There being no materials at hand suitable for rafts, orders were sent to Jellalabad for skins. These were floated down during the night, and formed next day into rafts by Sappers, under Afghan superintendence.

The place selected for crossing was a straight reach where the river was 120 yards wide, running in the centre with a surface velocity of five miles an hour.

Before nightfall 600 men, and the Sappers, under Colonel Boisragon, B.S.C., had crossed the river and occupied the village of Rena. Orders for the destruction of the village and its tower were issued that night; by 4 A.M. the Sappers were hard at work, mining the tower, levelling the village walls, and " ringing " the mulberry-trees, and in six hours the village was level with the ground.

Orders were then received from General Doran for the Sappers to return at once to Kam Dakka and join his force, which was returning to Lundi Kotal, and for the remainder of Colonel Boisragon's force to proceed to Dakka.

On reaching Kam Dakka about 1 P.M., the Sappers found the village deserted, and no guide left to show the way by which General Doran's force was marching. The direction in which they had started was pointed out by an Afghan, and after a rest of two hours the Sappers marched. In a very short time they lost their way among the hills, and wandered into Dakka late that night, thoroughly worn out. Next day they returned to Lundi Kotal.

Everybody was much pleased with the way the Sappers worked, and the General said the passage of the river reflected the greatest credit on all concerned. As it was the Sappers, assisted by twelve Momunds, who did all the work, the whole credit was theirs.

Three hundred of the 4th M. N. I., under Colonel Hodding, had formed our baggage-guard in this expedition, and had a very hard and uninteresting time of it. Three hundred of the 1st M. N. I. formed the rear-guard of the column. Both regiments were deservedly complimented—the 4th for getting the baggage over a very difficult country, and the 1st for its marching power.

The 1st reached Lundi Kotal after forced marches on evening of the 14th, and marched into Kam Dakka (after an eighteen-mile march over hills and stones) during night of the 15th in capital order.

Lieutenant Dorward, R.E., was specially pleased with the work done by Sergeant Reddaway and Lance-Naique Shaik Madar, of the Queen's Own Sappers.

On the C Company reaching the Daranta gorge late in January, they found that a narrow path had already been cut by the A & I Companies, over which a portion of General Bright's force had marched into the Lughman valley, the baggage crossing the river by fords below and above the pass.

The instructions given to the C Company were to widen the path to seven feet, and to reduce the steep gradients, so that it might be everywhere suitable for camel traffic.

Four hundred Hazara and 200 Afghan coolies were employed to assist the Sappers ; and in less than a fortnight a good road, three miles and a half long, nowhere less than seven feet wide, with a maximum gradient of 1 in 7, was completed and in use.

The work was very favourably noticed by General Bright in his despatches.

Extracts from orders by Major-General R. O. Bright, C.B., commanding Khyber Division, 10th March 1880 :—

"The Major-General commanding desires to place on record his appreciation of the services rendered by the officers and men concerned in the construction of the road over the Seah Koh range at Daranta for the passage of the Jellalabad Moveable Column into the Lughman valley. The line (a most difficult one to select) was chosen by Lieutenant-Colonel Limond, R.E. (Bengal), C.R.E. Khyber Division, K F.F., and the work carried out by the A, C, and I Companies Queen's Own Sappers and Miners, under the command of Major Ross Thompson, R.E., aided by working-parties from H.M.'s 12th and 25th Foot and the 27th and 31st B. N. I."

"Work was commenced on the 24th January, and on the 28th the infantry and mountain guns of the force passed safely into the Lughman valley. As the work was one of unusual diffi-culty and magnitude, the Major-General considers the rapidity and skill with which it was carried out reflect great credit on Colonel Limond and the officers and men working under his orders."

Both the A and the I Companies took part in the reconnoitring expedition along the right bank of the Alishaug river in the Lughman valley. No opposition was encountered, and the force reached the fort of Buddeabad, eight miles north-east of Torgain, where Lady MacNaghten, Lady Sale, and the English captives were imprisoned by Mahomed Akbar Khan in 1842.

While there a visit was paid to Lamach's (Noah's father) tomb.

The force now returned to Fort Asmatullah Khan, having penetrated into an entirely new country, and enabled the surveyors to map the new route to Cabul.

The I and C Companies of Sappers were ordered back to Jellalabad to make the Girdikas river road from Bassawul to Jellalabad, to avoid Barikab. Colonel Limond returned with them ; but Major Thompson, with the A Company, remained with General Bright.

Major Thompson was at once despatched to reconnoitre the route through Adrak Badrak pass, between Jellalabad and Kata Sang on way to Cabul. The escort consisted of 100 of 25th K. O. B., 300 of 30th P. N. I., and A Company Queen's Own Sappers and Miners.

They improved the road for twenty miles. The country was found to be barren and desolate, but so far, easy from an engineer's point of view.

Slight attacks were made on the escort. At this time Ross Thompson and Ramsay of 25th were on some miles ahead reconnoitring, and did not hear the firing. On retracing their steps they were surprised to meet fifty of 30th P. N. I. who had been sent out to escort them back, as they were considered in danger of being cut off.

They passed out of the Adrak Badrak country by a defile which brought them out at Jagdalak. To reach this place they had to pass through the Pari-Dara pass—a forty minutes' quick walk.

"This was a grim, weird, wild place, reminding one of Gustave Doré's illustration in Dante's *Inferno*—so narrow that two can scarcely ride abreast, cliffs on either side hundreds of feet in height, with huge vultures, great eagles with black heads, and big ravens sitting like stone birds amongst the cliffs, motionless, except when they drop slowly from their pinnacles and swoop swiftly and noiselessly down the pass close overhead. I was glad when we emerged into sunshine and open country at the end of the pass."

During the months of March and April the C and I Companies of Sappers were employed on the river road from Jellalabad to Basawul.

When the half C Company returned from the Daranta gorge in February, to Jellalabad, they found that the other half had completed the bridge over the Cabul river, and on the 20th the whole company marched to Ali Boghan. The alternative road from Jellalabad to Basawal had been decided on, in order to avoid the difficulties experienced on the established route *viâ* Banikab owing to want of water. With the exception of the six miles from Ali Boghan to Lachipur, the whole of the road was over a sandy plain, and required little labour; but for those six miles it had to be cut almost entirely out of the slopes of rocky hills.

The I Company was marched to camp at Lachipur to execute the two miles and a half nearest to that place, while the remaining three and a half were entrusted to the C Company. Fortified posts with shelter for the garrisons had to be constructed at Ali Boghan and Lachipur.

In the previous campaign a track nine feet wide had been made along the river by the Bengal Sappers. The gradients in many places were steep, unfitted for wheeled traffic; and the orders now given were to widen the road everywhere to eighteen feet, and to reduce the gradients as far as practicable. Colonel Limond, C.R.E., had promised the military authorities that the road would be open for traffic on 1st May*; and on that date the road was everywhere ten feet wide and ready for traffic.

The fortifications at Ali Boghan were nearly finished, and the buildings had been commenced.

In May the I Company was moved to Rozabad, when the whole road and the fort at Lachipur were handed over to the C Company to complete. Half the company, under Lieutenant Shute, was consequently sent to Lachipur.

The heat was now very great. In the huts at Ali Boghan the thermometer stood daily between 112 and 114; and the temperature at night, owing to the heat given out by the rocks, seldom fell below 100.

---

* Colonel Limond reported to the General that " the Madras Sappers have done splendid work "

Up to this time the Sappers had been wonderfully healthy, but now the constant work and exposure to the sun commenced to tell upon them, and at the end of May about 10 per cent. were in hospital, and fully 5 per cent. more were only fit for light work.

All this time the A Company remained with Major Thompson in the neighbourhood of Gundamuck.

On the 26th March an attack had been made on Fort Battye. As a punishment a fine of 5,000 rupees was imposed on the villages in the Wazeer country. They, however, declined to pay, and an expedition was sent into their country on the 4th April.

Our force consisted of—

> Four guns R. H. A.,
> Two guns Mountain Battery,
> Carabineers,
> Regiment Bengal Cavalry,
> Central India Horse,
> 25th K. O. B.,
> 12th Foot,
> 31st P. N. I.,
> 8th B. N. I.,
> 9th B. N. I.,
> 4th M. N. I.,
> A Company Queen's Own Madras Sappers,

taken from Jellalabad and Gundamuck.

Next day an envoy from the Wazeerees came into our camp and interviewed the Political Officer. He asked how many men we had. When told that the number was 3,000, he said, "You must have nine at least. We can't fight unless we have 12,000. Perhaps we had better pay up. Anyhow, take your army away." He was told that this was impossible, and that we were going to stay till they paid, and intended eating their grain and blowing up their towers, &c., until they did.

On the 5th our force turned out, and worked up to the forts and villages near. No resistance to speak of was met with.

As the money did not come in, Darling, with the A Company, blew down a tower. After waiting an hour two more were demolished, and the fort of the chief men engaged in attack on Fort Battye was fired. After another pause two more towers were sent into the air.

On the 6th our force cautiously approached a large square fort nearer the foot of the range of hills. This was mined by the Sappers.

A messenger from the enemy now came into camp with 3,500 rupees, and a promise of the remainder, so our force retired to camp.

"This part of the country is very fertile, and some portions are lovely beyond description. Magnificent mulberry, walnut, and plane trees, great orchards of pomegranates, groves of cherry, apricot, almond, peach, pear, and apple trees, and enormous vines with their bright green tendrils trailing from tree to tree and rock to rock. Numerous streams and little waterfalls, fed by the eternal snows of the Safed Koh. Splendid stretches of bright green fields of wheat and barley; the snow-capped range of the Safed Koh pushing its brilliant peaks far up into the deep blue sky, and jutting its dark spurs covered with deodars and other pines far out into the valley where we were, made up a picture which it will take long for us to forget. Groups of Lancers, Carabineers, and men and horses with bright steel flashing about them, made a foreground to this lovely scene which must ever live in the memories of all who had the good fortune to be there. Parts of Afghanistan may be said to be like Heaven, while others can only be characterized by the word Hell."

On 7th April the balance of the money demanded was paid. and the force returned to head-quarters—Gundamuck and Rozabad.

33 *

A few days after this an expedition was sent to Fort
Masullah Khan in the Hissarak country, to enforce a demand
for 10,000 rupees on account of the murder of Thurlow of
the 51st.

On the 11th the force moved from Gundamuck to Pezwan.
It consisted of—

> Two guns H. A. on elephants.
> Eight guns Mountain Battery.
> Carabineers.
> 4th Bengal Cavalry.
> Central India Horse.
> 51st Foot.
> 8th B. N. I.
> 1st Goorkhas.
> A Company Queen's Own Madras Sappers.
> 6th Company Bengal Sappers.

The next day we advanced six miles into the country before
the enemy was met. After reconnoitring under a heavy fire the
mountain guns began to shell the "sangas" and rocks. The
51st shortly after moved down to attack in front, while the 8th
B. N. I. and 1st Goorkhas advanced on the enemy's flanks.

The mountain-gun practice was splendid, and forced the
enemy to retire to a second position. From this they were
again driven.

Meantime, the remainder of the force moved down, crossed
the plain, and occupied the fort of Masullah Khan.

This closed the affair for the day, but the enemy kept up a
dropping fire throughout the night.

Besides Thompson, Darling, Lindley, and Henderson, of the
Sappers, were present.

Next day the village and fort were placed in a better state of
defence.

On the 14th a portion of the force went out. The A Company was told off to burn villages and houses of men concerned

in Thurlow's murder. Very little difficulty is experienced in burning their houses, as they are made of deodar, and the roofs are supported by a post in the centre.

About three miles from camp our force encountered the enemy, who at once opened fire. The Afghans held to their sangas and rocks most pluckily and with consummate skill in covering themselves. When a shell exploded in a sanga, up they jumped waving their knives and shouting "Allah-il-Allah-Allahulu"; then down they went again when they saw another shell coming.

Two men were very persistent in this attention. Darling managed to silence one, whether by shooting or frightening him to death is not known. He told off Sergeant Bassett and four good shots to get his range accurately; then by watching with binoculars, whenever Darling saw his head appearing, he gave the word, and away went a volley of five, the shots landing unpleasantly close to his head, the dose being repeated three or four times before he gave in.

The other man was not to be beaten. He "whanged" away until at last the gunners sent a shell at him which went spinning over his head, but up he popped again and again like an old Jack-in-the-box.

The whole affair was a series of loose fighting. We hustled them about a good deal, but got no decided advantage. It was now too late to follow them up into the larger range of hills, and we had no food, &c. so as to enable us to bivouac.

The enemy, as we returned to camp, followed us closely. Palmer, the Commissariat officer, was shot through the back (died next day). Hamilton, R. A., was hit in the left arm, and Nugent was struck by a spent ball.

On the way back the Sappers burnt two villages. The enemy did not cease firing at us all night.

After dinner Thompson and some other officers went up to the top of the tower of the fort for a smoke, and to watch the firing.

The Afghans saw them against the sky, although all were lying on their faces, for they had not been there many minutes before the jezail and Enfield bullets began to drive over their heads, and bits of telegraph-wire to flit by, with a noise like a flight of asthmatic bumble-bees.

Our men scarcely fired at all in reply.

Next day the enemy received a reinforcement of 600 men, so it was determined to strengthen the village, and by night any amount of traverses and shelter-trenches were got ready.

On the 16th we evacuated the fort and village, and marched back to Gundamuck. The A Company of Sappers marched with the artillery and field-park, in front. Before leaving, the Sappers blew up five towers of the fort. Stafford (Bombay Sappers), Mayne, Henderson, Darling, and Lindley lighted fuzes simultaneously, and there was a fine explosion.

The enemy still continued to fire on us, and wounded five. The 51st laid a trap for them. An officer and ten men remained behind a small ruin ; the enemy came on unsuspiciously, up jumped the 51st men and fired a volley, killing four, which effectually stopped the remainder for some time ; but they did not leave us completely till we were near Pezwan.

On the 17th April General Bright and staff returned to Gundamuck, and next day No. 1 column marched to that place, while the other remained at Pezwan, on towards Jugdulluck.

Thompson, with the Sappers, returned to Gundamuck. The A Company, and 4th Bengal Cavalry, formed the baggage-guard in front.

As it was expected that we should be attacked on our way back, the Sappers and 4th B. C. crowned the heights, and scouted as far as the Surkh-ab river (two miles). The enemy, however, did not molest us.

We did not succeed in getting the 10,000 rupees, nor did we sufficiently " slate " the enemy, but we certainly did con-siderable damage to their crops, villages, &c.

This expedition lasted a week, and during the whole time the officers were unable to take off their clothes, day or night. This was by no means pleasant, as it was now getting decidedly warm.

There was now little chance of the Madras Sappers getting to Cabul, as there were too many Bengal Sappers in front. One company of them was at Jugdulluck, and another at Lataband.

Lieutenant Dobson, R.E., at this time was much knocked up with the heat, while engaged on the river road; but went into Jellalabad for a time, got better, and returned to his company at Ellachpore.

In a letter dated 17th June, Lieutenant Dobson is mentioned as being in an "excellent state of health, and delighted at the prospect of going up to Gundamuck," where he was to proceed with the I Company.

At this time the company was at Rozabad. It is sad, however, to state that the improvement in Dobson's health was merely temporary, and that this energetic officer died at Rozabad, shortly after.

It has been mentioned before that Brigadier-General W. A. Gib* was sent up in command of the Madras N.I. Shortly after coming up to Afghanistan he was placed in command of the 1st section of the Khyber Line force, composed of various British and Bengal corps, but, with the exception of the 15th N. I., the Madras troops were not included in his command.† It will prove of interest to many to note here that Brigadier W. A. Gib (formerly commandant 25th M. N. I.) highly distinguished himself in the campaign, more especially at the successful action of Maizena, where he commanded a force, which started from Peshbolak about 11 P.M. on 18th May to surprise the Fakir Ghulam Ahmed, who had been engaged for some time in raising large bodies of men for a hostile purpose, and had murdered

* At one time this officer commanded a company of Madras Sappers.
† Major W. Coningham, M.S.C., was his Brigadier-Major

several officials of the Governor of Jellalabad and Khan of Lalpura.

On the 19th they arrived at Shershai, and bivouacked.

Early on the 20th they advanced towards Maizena, where, after a most spirited action, which lasted some three or four hours, the enemy were completely defeated with considerable loss, and compelled to fly into the Shinwari country. The Fakir, unfortunately, escaped, but several of his principal moollahs and adherents were killed and wounded.

On the 21st the force returned to Shershai, and on the 23rd to Peshbolak. The Brigadier stated that the battery of artillery (L 5) did splendid service in the action. It was commanded by Captain Domville, as the major (Brough) was so ill that his doctor forbade his going with the expedition. The Brigadier said "the guns were brought into action with great difficulty and labour, over such bad ground that but for its state of efficiency it would, perhaps, never have reached the field at all. The credit of having the battery in such good order is fairly due to Major W. R. C. Brough, who, to my great regret, was unable to accompany it owing to severe illness, though most anxious to do so." Major Brough originally belonged to the Madras Artillery.

Brigadier-General W. A. Gib was, in consequence of his distinguished services on this occasion and during the campaign, appointed a Companion of the Bath.

Before the I Company went up to Rozabad, a detachment of them, under Lieutenant Digby, were engaged in the Besud affair, not far from Jellalabad, in which Lieutenant-Colonel Dawson, 1st M. N. I., distinguished himself.

On the 3rd and 4th June sixty men of the C Company were employed, under Lieutenants Dorward and Langley, in making skin-rafts and in rowing troops across the river to the village of Kama, preparatory to an expedition against the Momunds. They had to cross the river in flood, and, as insufficient orders were given, the result was confusion.

The Central India Horse (a fine body) swam their horses over, and only lost one in the operation.

The baggage-animals were to cross the second day. No officer in charge; the result being that Dorward and Langley had to manage the business. This took the whole day, and was very wearisome, but it was effected without a single casualty. The Sappers, meantime, camped on an island that night, as Dorward had received no orders to cross.

The rafts started at A, and only reached the other shore at B. A raft, constructed with an Austrian pontoon, was worked on a rope stretched across the second branch of the river at E. The width of the first stream was 180 yards, and the second seventy-five.

At 3 A.M. Dorward received orders to cross the second branch, and join the force in Kama. Meantime, the river had risen, and the pontoon raft at E was found to be unworkable. Dorward left Langley and twenty men to get it into order, and then forded the river with the remainder of the Sappers by the line C D. An Afghan "cooly" took them across the ford. The water was three and a half feet deep, and the current some five miles an hour at the worst places.

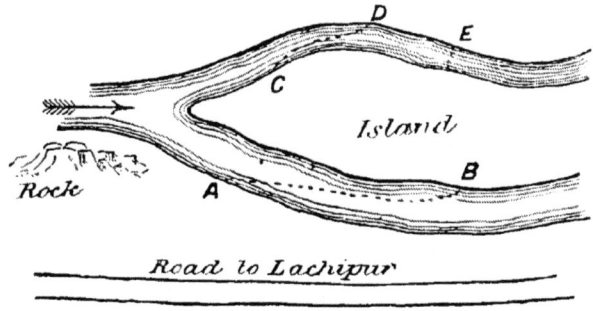

Some Sappers were nearly lost in the crossing, the picks, &c. which they carried, steadied the men, and by holding together they got across, but not without considerable difficulty. One man got out of line by sheer carelessness, and was just saved by a string of Sappers holding each other and catching him. Dorward was much relieved when he found he had succeeded in getting the party across in safety.

At Kama the force was found comfortably camped under mulberry-trees. Langley, having put the pontoon raft in order, followed with the remainder of the men, and arrived an hour or so after.

It appears that all the Sappers were required for was to blow up some towers. Had this been known to Dorward, he would not have risked the ford, but, thinking some emergent work was required of him, he at once set out.

Six towers and two gateways were blown up, and two villages burnt* by the Sappers, assisted by the 32nd P. Pioneers, under Lieutenant Wells, R.E. As soon as this was complete the force was directed to re-cross the river.

The C. I. Horse and the guns crossed on the first day, and the rest of the force on the second. As before, no orders were given, and no staff officer turned up to superintend the crossing arrangements. Four mules were drowned. Three were foolishly tied together and driven into the water; the ropes got twisted round their legs, and they went down in a heap.

The Sappers, who had all the work to do, crossed last. They had worked hard, and when the Austrian pontoons were run into a rock and smashed, everybody was pleased with the rapid and efficient way they patched them up with old " ghee " tins.

The Sappers justly received praise for their excellent work on this occasion. The C. I. Horse swam their horses across (all stallions and spirited) in a very dashing way, and did the scouting very perfectly. It is doubtful if any regiment of European Cavalry could have crossed such a stream with the loss of only one horse.

---

* They had harboured the enemy.

In May, Lieutenant George Henry, R.E., Queen's Own Sappers, was ordered from Bangalore to Afghanistan, and passed along the road *en route* to Jellalabad, as the troops were engaged in this crossing. He was stationed at Jellalabad and Rozabad till the close of the campaign.

After this expedition the C Company returned to Ali Boghan. The company was favourably mentioned in General Doran's despatches, in which he stated that " the exposure to the heat involved in this duty was most severe. Both at the river and at the demolition of the forts on the 5th June the C Company Madras Sappers wrought hard and well."

It was about this time that Lance-Corporal Narrainsammy, owing to hard work and exposure at Lachipur, died. He was buried at Jellalabad, and was the only man the C Company left behind them in Afghanistan.

On 3rd June, Major Ross Thompson, with the I Company, accompanied Brigadier-General Arbuthnot, C.B., into the Lughman valley. The force was absent twelve days, and had a very rough time of it. The heat was extreme, thermometer 110° to 122°, with hot winds, and dust-storms by night. There was only one day's shooting, on the 11th, when the force was re-crossing the Cabul river, which was 200 yards wide, with a current of five and three-quarter miles.

The passage was effected on " mussuck" rafts. When all but ten rafts had crossed, the enemy opened fire, but the attack was kept under by those who had already crossed the river. Car-thew, the D.A.Q.G., got a knock in the thigh from a spent ball, and a hole in his " puggry"; and Major Burnaby, 51st, got a hit on the nose from a splash of lead off a ricochet-bullet.

The I Company, under Lieutenants Dobson and Digby, " managed in this expedition to blow up twelve towers, and destroyed by fire about the same number of forts and villages. They found it ' mighty dhry ' in the dusty old towers."

After this, the I Company returned to Rozabad, but on the 17th June were under orders to join at Gundamuck; while the C Company, after the completion of the forts and buildings at Ali Boghan and Lachipur, were ordered to Jellalabad to assist in completing the works there.

It was about this time that Dobson died at Rozabad. During the expedition to the Lughman valley this excellent officer had been in capital health and buoyant spirits.

The state of affairs at this time on the Khyber line was very unsettled, as was manifested by telegraph-wire cutting, miscellaneous shooting into camps, &c.

Henderson, at this time, had been compelled to go to Murree for the sake of his health, and Shute had been appointed Adjutant.

Preparations now began to be made for the return of the troops to India, and the Sappers were largely employed in the construction of barrel-pier rafts, it being decided to convey sick men and stores from Jellalabad to Dakka by river.

In consequence of the Momunds coming down to the left bank and firing on the rafts, it was arranged that a position on that bank should be occupied and fortified. A company of the 1st M. N. I., another of the 9th B. N. I., and a small detachment of the C Company of Sappers, under Dorward (whole force under Major Shaw, M.S.C.), were rafted down the river to Sirdao, a village opposite Lachipur, for the purpose.

A garden surrounded by a mud wall eight feet high was selected, and in two days the men, working under Sapper supervision, had put the garden in a very excellent condition of defence. Water was let into the garden from an irrigation channel outside, and means were adopted to prevent the supply being cut off. The work was no sooner done than the whole detachment was ordered back to Jellalabad, it being considered dangerous at head-quarters to have such a small force in the enemy's country cut off from support by the river.

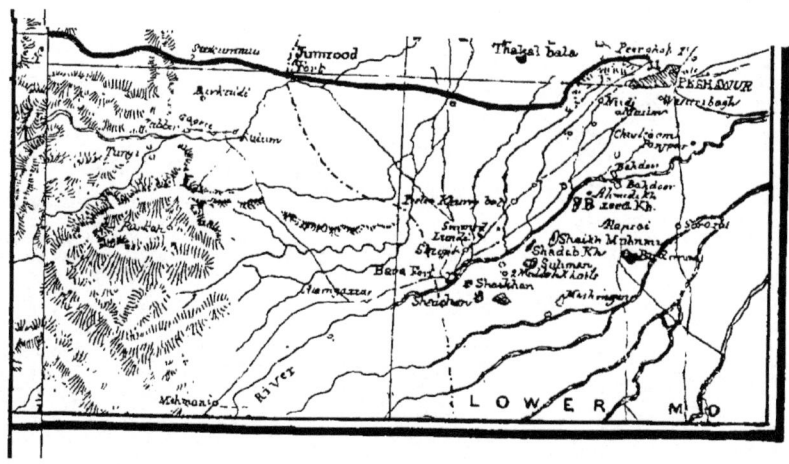

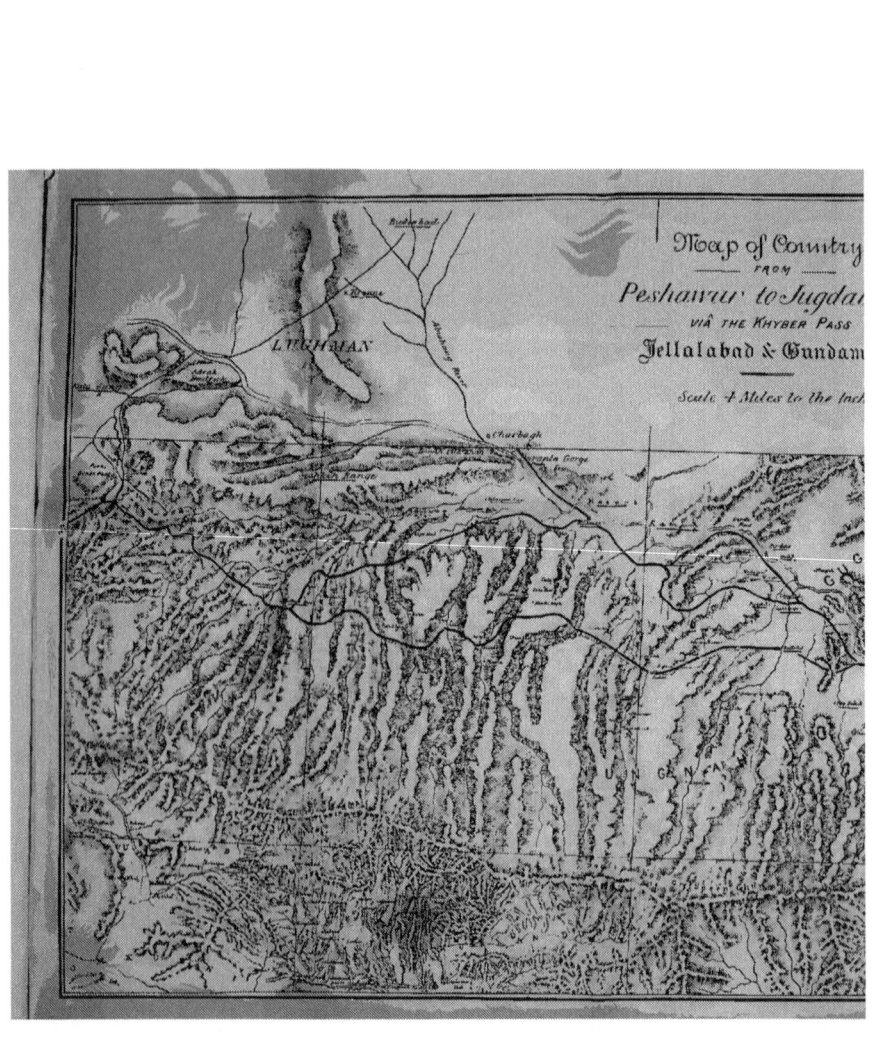

In his report Major Shaw brought prominently to notice the excellent and hard work done by the Sappers.

It was intended, shortly after this, to send an expedition against the Shinwarries, under General Bright, and the C Company was to have formed part of the force.

The Sappers were in high spirits at the idea of seeing some real fighting at last, after so many months of nothing but hard work ; but their hopes were doomed to disappointment, for the expedition never came off, and orders instead were received for the company to march to India with the 5th Fusiliers and the 9th B. N. I.

After waiting a few days at Peshawur the C Company was joined by the A and I Companies, and the three companies, with 150 of the 1st M. N. I., the whole under the command of Lieutenant Dorward, were ordered to march to Hassan Abdal, *viâ* Kohat.

This long and difficult march (twenty-three miles), through the Kohat pass, proved very trying to the men in their weakened state, and great delay was caused owing to break-downs among the baggage-animals on the steep gradients.

The C Company transport was, owing to the exertions of Sergeant Reddaway (who had charge of it during the whole campaign), always in excellent order, and to him it was mainly due that the company was always fit to march at a moment's notice.

On arrival at Hassan Abdal the Sappers were handed over to Major Ross Thompson, and under his command the three companies marched to Jhelum, and went thence by rail to Bangalore, reaching their homes in excellent condition, after having done probably harder and more continuous work than any other troops employed in the Khyber.

It may be mentioned, in conclusion, that " the health of the men of the Madras Army in Afghanistan was remarkably good.

Brigadier-General Gib, C.B., reported that the average of sick in 1st M. N. I. was 13·53, not more than it would have been in Madras Presidency. In the 15th N. I. the daily average of sick was only 4·22, and the Sappers and 4th N. I. were also exceedingly healthy. The immunity of the Madras troops from pneumonia, from which the Bengal sepoy has suffered so much in Afghanistan has been remarkable. To whatever cause this is attributable, it shows that the native soldier of Southern India is able to serve efficiently under conditions of climate not natural to him "

The C Company, when working at Ali Boghan in March 1880, were throughout particularly healthy, on an average only 2 per cent. sick; while in the Sikh company of 30th P. N. I. the daily sick amounted to nine.

Majors C. A. Sim and Ross Thompson, in consideration of the excellent services they and their Sappers had been able to render, were both appointed Brevet Lieutenant-Colonels, the former from 23rd November 1879, and the latter from 2nd March 1881.

There were three other officers of Madras Engineers employed in Afghanistan—Colonel Sankey, Lieutenant-Colonel Lindsay, and Major Clarke. The first served with Sir Donald Stewart, as C.R.E., and an account of his work will be found in the next chapter.

Lieutenant-Colonel Lindsay was appointed Chief Engineer of the Sukker and Sibi railway. He had served in the railway branch of the D.P.W. since 1862, designed and marked out the Mysore State Railway from Bangalore to Mysore, since completed; designed and constructed the Northern Bengal Railway, and was managing it when he was called away to Afghanistan and started at a few hours notice.

The railway was rapidly pushed on across the desert under his able supervision. The country traversed was quite flat and presented no engineering difficulties, but marvellous energy was displayed in its construction. It was laid at the rate of about 1⅓ miles per diem.

The difficulties successfully encountered by the Chief Engineer were very great.

The labour employed was chiefly imported from Southern India, and the Chief Engineer had to provide food, shelter, and water for the whole of them in a country singularly destitute of those necessaries.

After the rail was completed to Sibi, Lieutenant-Colonel Lindsay surveyed a line of rail from that place up to the Quetta plateau through the hills in Afghanistan to Kandahar. A portion of this line was constructed, but the country was a difficult one, and the railway perforce advanced at a slower pace.

After the Maiwand disaster it was considered necessary to vacate that line of communication, and Colonel Lindsay joined Sir R. Phayre, K.C.B., as Commanding R.E. He intrenched a position in the Khojak, commanding the pass of that name, and was subsequently favourably mentioned in despatches by Sir R. Phayre, and his name brought to the notice of the Commander-in-Chief for special services rendered.

Major Clarke was ordered to North Afghanistan with a small party of warrant and N.C.O. towards the close of 1879.

He left Peshawur in November to prospect the various proposed routes for the Peshawur-Jellalabad railway, lying between the Jumrood valley and Jellalabad.

He arrived at Jellalabad on 12th December, having reconnoitred the Khyber river route, which was selected in preference to the road line opened out by the military authorities direct from Jumrood Fort.

He completed the survey from Peshawur to the debouchment of the Khyber river, three miles west of Jumrood, in January 1880, and then started for the Kuram valley, arriving at Kohat in February.

He completed the preliminary survey from Thull to the Peiwar range and between Thull and Kohat in March and April.

During May and June he was employed in various duties in

the vicinity of Kuram and the Peiwar camp, and in July started for the Kandahar railway.

Arriving at Sibi about the close of August, he was at once employed in laying out a fort for that place, which project was, however, finally abandoned.

In October he was ordered to take charge, as Executive Engineer, of the Quetta cantonment, was afterwards sent by Sir F. Roberts to open the Bolan pass after a heavy flood had passed through it, and finally was placed in charge of the Sibi cantonment.

During December and the first three months of 1881, he completed several Government buildings there, and in April 1881 left for England on leave, having been employed in various parts of Afghanistan for fully sixteen months.

On the evening of 30th October 1879 the second half of the E Company Madras Sappers, under command of Lieutenant G. Henry, R.E., left Bangalore for Madras to embark for Burmah, the first half having preceded it under command of Lieutenant Connor, R.E.

On the following morning, at about 4.45 A.M., when the train was running at a rate of thirty miles an hour, over the thirty-eighth mile from Madras, near Chinnamapet, a fearful accident took place, which resulted in the death of Subadar Gregory, fifteen sappers, one European woman, two children, and one private follower, besides a large number wounded.

Besides the engine the train consisted of a truck with hounds, after this a truck containing a carriage followed by a brake van. Immediately behind the brake van were four second-class carriages containing the sappers, and next to these was a first-class saloon carriage containing Lieutenant Henry. Between Lieutenant Henry's carriage and the brake-van at the end of the train were two or three passenger carriages.

The embankment on which the accident occurred had been

lately constructed by famine labour in 1877, and it would appear that for a distance of five or six miles between Arconum and Chinnamapet, the line, during wet weather, had been a source of considerable anxiety to the railway engineers. Between November 1878 and February 1879 the embankment required frequent repair and ballasting. At the time of the accident it was raining hard, and had been raining so heavily in the neighbourhood for some days past that it was feared the line might suffer from floods.

It was not known, however, that the line was anywhere in a dangerous condition, although at the site of the accident the embankment proved so soft that it sank beneath the pressure of the train.

The engine ran off the rails, ploughing its way through the soft earth along the side of the line; but it soon came to a standstill, and the driver and stoker both escaped uninjured.

Both trucks which followed the tender escaped with but little damage—one conveyed the hounds, the other a carriage. The heavy brake-van came next, and its weight was sufficient to smash the rail at a joint, and the impetus of the van was suddenly stopped by the rail, which pierced through the bottom of the van and impaled it. Here the van stopped with the solidity of a barricade, the four following carriages containing the sappers were crushed one into the other, and became a confused mass of debris. These carriages, which measured nearly 100 feet in length, were compressed into a space hardly reaching twenty feet, and the result, as may be imagined, was most fearful. The first-class carriage, with Lieutenant Henry, following these, fell over on its side, but was not greatly injured, and the rear carriages escaped altogether.

Had not the brake van in front of the sappers' carriages been held by the rail, it is likely that the accident would have been of a much less fatal character. As it was, the havoc made was most fearful.

II.   34

Immediately after the accident the work of extricating the wounded was commenced by such of the survivors as were unwounded and clear (about six in all), while the guard and engine-driver took the necessary precautions for the safety of the remainder of the train, and telegraphed from Chinnamapet for assistance, returning immediately to assist Lieutenant Henry.

Another train was due in a quarter of an hour from the north-west line. Steps were taken to stop this train. In this train were Dr. Harris, the railway medical officer, as well as Dr. Leapingwell of the Madras army. These officers, aided by Major Pigott and Lieutenant Henry, and later on by Messrs. Saunders,* Robinson, Church, and Dr. Sturmer from Madras, devoted themselves to rescuing and attending to the wounded Sappers. The process of withdrawing the wounded men from the heap of debris was a most laborious and heart-rending work.

It was not till 2 P.M. that the last living man was removed from the wreck. Shortly afterwards the wounded were despatched to Madras for treatment at the General hospital, whilst Lieutenant Henry remained with his six unwounded or slightly wounded men to identify and bury the dead, and collect the arms and accoutrements of the company.

By nightfall they had collected, identified, and buried (by permission of the magistrate) fifteen sappers and one follower in four graves dug by the railway company on slightly rising ground to the south of the line. Those of one caste were buried in the same grave.

The Subadar's body was removed to Bangalore, and buried in the Roman Catholic cemetery, all the officers at the Sapper head-quarters attending the funeral. The bodies of the European woman (wife of Sergeant Terry, R.E.), her child (a girl), and a boy of Sergeant Price, R.E., were taken to Madras.

Lieutenant Henry, in his report, stated that the conduct of

* The Agent, the Chief Engineer, and the Traffic Manager of the Madras Railway.

the survivors of the half company under the trying circumstances was admirable, and he acknowledged the assistance given, not only by the medical officers and railway authorities, but also by several of the passengers, especially Major Pigott.

The wounded numbered over fifty. The majority suffered from bruises, cuts, and chest wounds. One Sapper had his arm broken in two places, and also a compound fracture of the leg. Several men were seriously wounded in the chest.

The Europeans were Sergeants Roberts, Terry, and Price, all badly wounded. The wives of the two last were in the train—Mrs. Terry was killed, while Mrs. Price with her husband had to be invalided home. The other two recovered.

Many of these Sappers who were killed and wounded in this terrible accident served with the greatest credit in the Khyber, during the late campaign in Afghanistan, from which country they had only returned some three months before, the company having suffered very severely from cholera at the close of the war. Subadar Gregory had only a week before been appointed a Bahadur.

On the 8th October the Corps of Engineers sustained a severe loss by the death of Major Herbert Wood.

"He was an officer of conspicuous ability, who had made a name for himself outside the limits of his own profession. His travels in Central Asia a few years ago, and his researches in regard to the old bed of the Oxus, caused no little sensation at the time. In 1874 he accompanied the expedition sent under the auspices of the Imperial Geographical Society of Russia to examine the Amu Darya. He passed many months in the countries round Lake Aral, an account of which is given in his book, *The Shores of Lake Aral*, published in 1876.

"He was endowed with an intellect of a high order, and was ever a diligent student of physical science. He was also well versed in ethnology, and as a man of general culture had few equals."*

* Extract from Madras *Mail.*

34 *

Major Wood was a Fellow of the Royal and of the Imperial Russian Geographical Societies, and a Corresponding Member of the Society of Geography of Geneva.

The Government of Madras wrote as follows:—

" His Grace the Governor in Council learns with much regret the death of Major Wood, R.E., by which the public service has been deprived of an officer of distinguished ability."

Major Wood served twice on active military service—first in the suppression of the Indian Mutiny in 1858, and next in the Abyssinian Expedition of 1868.

CHAPTER XIII.

War in Southern Afghanistan, 1878-79.—Colonel Sankey appointed Commanding
Royal Engineer.—Reconnoitres River Indus.—General Stewart arrives at
Mooltan, 28th October.—Leaves Mooltan, 17th November.—Reaches Dadur,
30th.—At Quetta, 8th December.—Our forces concentrated in the Peshin
Valley.—Sankey reconnoitres the Gwaja Pass, 15th December.—Gwaja Pass
made suitable for heavy artillery.—Stewart's force marches by the Gwaja
to Shah Pusand.—Cavalry combat near Ghlo Kotul.—Stewart's force con-
centrated near Deh Haggi, 6th January.—March through Kandahar, 8th
January.—1st Division starts for Kelat-i-Ghilzai, 15th January.—2nd
Division to Girishk.—Kelat-i-Ghilzai surrendered, 21st January.—Fort of
Kelat-i-Ghilzai.—Subadar Major 12th Native Infantry decorated.—Recon-
noitring party sent to Argandab Valley.—Another small force sent to Argeshan
Valley.—Head-quarters left Kelat-i-Ghilzai, 2nd February.—Reached Kan-
dahar, 11th.—Arrangements made for return to India—some by Bolan.—
General Biddulph by Tul-Chotiali route.—Sankey ordered to Madras.—
Arrangements made for the garrison.—Sankey appointed C.B., and Le
Messurier and Call obtain brevets.—Concluding remarks regarding Madras
Engineers.

EARLY in October, Colonel Sankey, R.E., Madras, was appointed
C.R.E. to the South Afghanistan Expeditionary Force, under
Lieutenant-General Sir Donald Stewart, then on his way from
England; and with his Assistant-Lieutenant E. S. E. Childers,
R.E., reached Mooltan, at that time the base of the operations,
on the 13th idem.

Some of the troops composing* Major-General Biddulph's
force had already been pushed on to Rajanpore on the right

* The 1st and 2nd Punjab Cavalry, under Colonel Kennedy, had in fact started
in advance for Quetta.

bank of the Indus, in readiness for an immediate advance to
Quetta, which from the extremely weak state of the garrison
was held as not unlikely to invite a sudden attack on the part
of Shere Ali.

At this time no hopes were entertained that, however desirable,
the road to the Bolan pass, from Sukkur through Shikarpore
and Jacobabad, would be sufficiently free from inundation to be
fit for wheeled artillery or baggage cattle, and the orders issued
by the Quartermaster-General's department were that Colonel
Sankey should at once, as the best alternative, explore the
following routes for the advance of the force, and render the one
selected practicable for wheeled artillery as far as means admitted,
i.e., with working parties of sappers and regiments when on the
march.   Labour of any effective kind from the inhabitants was
not to be expected.

The routes west of the Indus which thus had to be explored
were—(1) the northern broken mountain track, known as the
Dera-Bugti line, leading from Rajanpore by Lalgoshi, Bun-
dowali, Dera, Chigeri, and debouching into the Katchi plain
near Lehri; (2) the southern track* skirting the south of the
Dera-Bugti hills by Kashmore, Toz, Uch, Shapur, and Chatter
to the same place, Lehri.

With reference also to whichever of these routes might be
selected, it remained to decide on the point for crossing the
Indus. Both these routes were known to be open to serious
objections, the first leading through an extremely broken
country unfitted for wheeled artillery and deficient in water,
forage, and, indeed, supplies of all kinds; and the latter, if anything, worse in all respects—the ground, though mostly level

---

* This route was, a little later on, explored and reported on by Lieutenant
Barton, R.E., who, with this object, left Rajanpore under a small cavalry escort
on the 21st October. His report was most discouraging, scanty brackish water
supply and deep sand being the rule throughout the whole of this line, all in
fact, desert from Dan to Beersheba.

throughout, being so heavy with sand as to be unfitted for artillery.

So impressed were the local authorities at Rajanpore with the serious difficulties presented by both the southern routes to Quetta, that they strongly advocated the new, and in its western portion very little known track, which, passing north-west from Rajanpore through the friendly Khatran country (where supplies of grain were promised) leads by Chotiali,* Tul, and Pooi—the reputed Kafila route in Akhbar's time—to the Pishin valley and Kojak pass.

For some not easily explained reason the cavalry regiments in advance had sent back to Mooltan no sufficiently detailed information as to their experiences of the Dera-Bugti route which they had traversed; but, fortunately, the carefully-kept journal of Lieutenant Childers, made during his march in the previous year with a company of Sappers over the same ground to Quetta, had been printed and was available.

It will be readily gathered from the foregoing observations that just at this time, although the campaign had practically opened, and even some of the troops had been pushed forward, the greatest doubt existed as to the selection of the best, or more correctly the least harassing, route for the advance of the main force.

The inundation of the Indus, extending from twenty-five to thirty-five miles along its left, and for a narrower strip on the right bank, not having as yet sufficiently subsided, it became primarily essential to obtain a clear idea of the best points for crossing, and if necessary of bridging with boats the mighty stream, also of the practicable approaches to the point so selected ; all, again, having reference to whichever of the routes beyond might be chosen by the General for his advance.

* Subsequently, as will be seen. this route was fully explored by General Biddulph and a small force, in March 1879, with no favourable results.

Before, however, attempting to carry out the requisite investigations, Colonel Sankey had to put in train the collection (from such boat-bridges on other Punjab rivers as could most readily be spared) of enough boats, platforms, anchors, and all gearing as would suffice for a length of bridge of not less than a mile and a quarter, that being estimated as the minimum width of the Indus. The work was to be entrusted to Lieutenant Hoskyns, an energetic officer of Engineers, then in charge of the Mooltan division.

Arrangements had likewise to be made for the no less necessary construction of between thirty and thirty-five miles of light railway to be laid across the inundated belt, on at least the left bank of the Indus, so as to connect the South Punjab railway line with the proposed bridge of boats.

Preparations were moreover made for the collection under another able officer, Lieutenant C. F. Call, R.E., of the materials, ponies, camels, and staff required for the Engineer park to accompany the force.

These matters attended to, Colonel Sankey started on the 17th October with Lieutenant Childers for an examination of the Indus, commencing at Mittankot, a little below the junction of the Chenab, and extending as far down as Gobla ghaut, near the Sarhad railway station, where the inundation was narrowest; in all some 135 miles of river.

Any examination north or south of these points would have been quite useless for the object in view.

With the river steamer *Outram* (Indus steam flotilla, Captain Galway) at disposal, they were engaged up to the 26th October in exploring the river and the country on both banks.

Though having for reference fine topographical maps of the Baugulpore state, on a scale of an inch to the mile, executed only six years previously, they found that owing to the shiftings of the river bed which had occurred in the interval—changes in fact taking place every instant—these were comparatively useless,

and that only very few, and those distant points, could be fixed
with any certainty.

Even Mittankot, one of the most stable of the several towns
on the river bank (excepting the old high bank near Kashmore),
had been devoured by the river, and rebuilt no less than three
times in a very few years.

It would serve no purpose to give the details of the explora-
tions, but surely few have had such mud-larking on a grand
scale. Their horses, though at first objecting strongly, soon got
accustomed to jumping off and on the steamer when laid alongside the bank ; but they never quite reconciled themselves to
wading through the slime, or "gup" as it is locally called, of
the inundated ground.*

At one place near Kinpost, when some ten miles from their
steamer, it cost them a weary hour's work to force the frightened
animals into and across the grimy expanse of gup which barred
their way ; and on their return from the steamer to the Nowshera station it took them from noon on the 25th till 1 o'clock
the following morning merely to work across twenty-seven miles
of country.

At one place in this march the horses had to wade through
a sheet of "gup" over five miles across, the guide having
frequently in the darkness to dismount and feel his way by cattle
marks, and the animals often sinking to their bellies in the slime.
On such occasions they became so alarmed as to threaten
serious consequences, and it was necessary to dismount—in
fact, in two or three places it seemed as if further progress was
out of the question.

---

* The inhabitants of all the inundated tract migrate eastwards annually from
May till August, if not later. Many of them lead a precarious existence, some
living on the turtles found in the swamps, others on alligators. The turtle-
feeders, of whose repasts we found frequent leavings, are said to hold the
consumers of alligators in light esteem as creatures of low tastes, much as
Calcutta adjutants are understood to look down on the crows of that unclean
city.

Nowshera railway station reached, Lieutenant Childers had himself shampooed by an ancient camel-driver with paws like a hand-saw; but Colonel Sankey never had the courage to ask him how he appreciated the application, of which it would not be surprising to hear that he still bears the marks.

At an interview with General Biddulph and Mr. Fyers, the Commissioner at Rajanpore. before starting down stream, it was generally concluded that the best arrangements for the advance of the force would consist of—(1) a light railway from the Khanpore station to Chachar, and five miles beyond to the Mittankot ferry; (2) a bridge of boats at the latter place, not less than one mile in length; (3) the improvement, if not also the railing, of the twelve miles of road between Mittankot and Rajanpore; (4) the preparation of this last-named place as the advanced base of operations, from which troops and materials conveyed by rail and river could be pushed on, either through the Bolan or along the Tul-Chotiali line to the Pishin valley.

The examination of the river quite confirmed these conclusions, which accordingly were wired to Head-quarters, Simla, on the 27th October.

The "best laid schemes of mice and men gang aft agee," and most of the arrangements, preparations, and speculations were at this moment (luckily in this case) brought to an abrupt termination by a very simple occurrence, viz. the unexpectedly early subsidence of the Indus inundation between Sukkur and Jacobabad, thus at once opening up the easiest route to the Bolan pass.

Had this not occurred it is needless now to surmise what might have been the results of the main body of the army having to advance by any of the lines under contemplation. However, from the experiences of General Biddulph's force, which had no option but to accept with all its defects the Dera-Bugti route, there can be no question that the march would have proved most harassing to all concerned.

The 59th Foot and both the Native Infantry and Sappers of
General Biddulph's force, suffered considerable hardship, aggra-
vated, on reaching the Dasht-i-bedowlat (some 6,000 feet above
sea-level, and searched throughout by keen cold winds), by their
not having with them their warm clothing which, to lighten the
baggage, had been left behind at Mooltan.

The miseries of the unfortunate *kahars* (dhooly-bearers) and
camp-followers generally were by all accounts dreadful, and the
difficulties of the road proved so serious to the D 2 H. A.
troop that it was understood nearly half the horses (Australians)
had been placed *hors-de-combat*.

General Stewart's arrival at Mooltan on the 28th October,
quickly followed as it was by the cheerful news regarding the
probable early practicability of the Jacobabad route, gave life
as well as a new and favourable turn to all the operations.

At first came in a report from Colonel Nutall, Superintendent
of the Sind frontier, which showed that the inundation due to
the spill of the Indus along its right bank, commencing below
Kashmore, was sensibly abating, and soon afterwards a date
was named by which it was thought the force might advance to
Jacobabad, though some little difficulty was still to be anticipated in crossing twelve or thirteen miles of inundated land
in advance of that place before reaching the *putt* or Katchi
desert.

Although the unexpectedly early opening of the Jacobabad
route thus at once, and definitely, led to the abandonment of the
Dera-Bugti road * for the main body, with artillery and baggage,
of General Stewart's force, it was thought that, in order to ease
the strain in the matter of supplies, &c., the cavalry brigade under

---

* One of General Stewart's first measures on assuming command at Mooltan
was to press strongly on the attention of the Government of India the immediate commencement of the Sukkur-Jacobabad-Dadur Railway, which, had it
been undertaken at an earlier date, as urged by Sir Andrew Clarke, would have
proved of incalculable benefit in this campaign. However, the short-sighted
policy of leaving Quetta *en l'air* till the very last was persistently adhered to.

Brigadier-General Fane might make use of it, and this was accordingly done.

All energies were now directed to the preparation of the requisite material for the force, and so far as concerned the Sappers and Miners, of which two companies (No. 4, Telegraph, under Lieutenant Haslett, R.E., and No. 10, Bridge, under Lieutenant Browne) were attached to the General's force, much of the ordinary equipment had in one case to be set aside and returned to stores.

Of the equipment of No. 10 Company it was decided to take only three out of twelve pontoons and three chess carts, it being clear that in case the Helmund had to be crossed during flood, when its width is some two miles, a train which had only material for the construction of fifty yards of bridge would be of no possible use; while the numbers of bullocks required for the pontoons must at best prove a serious encumbrance. Three pontoons, with their adjuncts, might, however, be of use in getting across the narrow, and at times deep, streams in the Pishin valley, and could be used as ferries for the Helmund.

As matters turned out, the pontoons were not used in the campaign; and the bullocks drawing the wagons split their feet to such an extent over the boulders and pebbles in the Bolan that one of the pontoons had to be abandoned not far from Mach.

The whole equipment of the Telegraph Company, on the other hand, consisting of twenty-four miles of wire on carts and six on mules, was taken; but authority was sought for transferring twelve miles to camels and the remainder to mules so as to dispense with wheeled carriage.

As regards the Engineer field park, fresh scales had to be made out for an equipment more suitable to the campaign before us than that laid down. The materials had then to be brought together from different arsenals, and all distributed into four-maund loads for camels, and half that for the ponies. The adjustment of the *kajawahs* (camel crates), saddles, and harness, with the camping and exercising of the drivers and their beasts, all required much thought and constant attention. Besides the difficulties also attending the bringing together of park-sergeants,* lascars, guards, &c., it seemed at one time as if any adequate number of artificers could not be collected, although with this object feelers were thrown out as far as Allahabad and Bombay. Eventually, however, owing to the intelligence, excellent system, and unwearied attention of Lieutenant Call, the whole of the material and establishment was brought into excellent form in a surprisingly short time, considering all the circumstances.

In forming the park, attention was paid to arrangements for always having at hand a supply of entrenching tools which could at once be made available for supplementing any requirements of troops on the march whose regimental equipment might be deficient.

Materials for constructing quickly piled causeways across the deep muddy streams of the Pishin valley were prepared.

For infantry bridges of a light character, some seventy prepared buffalo hides (*sonais*) were taken, these, on inflation, affording a sufficient buoyancy for infantry in single file at four or five feet intervals. Brushwood not being procurable in Afghanistan, supplies of Jones' hoop-iron gabions were added to the equipment, and efforts were made, not, however, with much success, to secure good light material for sand-bags, the ordinary cloths being very weighty for transport. The supplies of rope were found not to be over-trustworthy, and both the

---

* No men being kept on training at the head-quarters of Sappers and Miners for this kind of work. practised in the care and lading of pack-animals. proves a serious drawback at the commencement of a campaign. It would on this account be most desirable to keep together at least a sufficient nucleus of a field park in times of peace at the head-quarters.

The Bengal Sappers have few or no artificers in their ranks ; not so. however, the Madras Corps, which is thus better able at the commencement of a campaign to assist in furnishing the establishment for a field park. Special arrangements for meeting this important requirement should, however, be made

material and make of bill-hooks and pickaxes were not satisfactory.

The park, when organised, was got under weigh with about 120 camels and 200 mules, and some extra animals for the " kit " of the establishment.

In addition to the field park, measures had also to be taken to get together the materials for a third-class siege-train park under Lieutenant Hoskyns, R.E., which, with a corresponding artillery park, was destined for possible operations against Herat, in case of this proving the ultimate destination of the force.

As with the field park, the difficulties of first deciding on the scale, and what materials should be taken or rejected for the authorised equipment, were very great. All the difficulties connected with the entertainment of the proper establishment here reappeared, and, without dwelling too much on them, it is almost certain that, were it not for the Commanding Engineer being so fortunate as to secure about this time the services of an energetic officer like Major A. Le Messurier, R.E., as Brigade-Major, and arranging for his going to the Ferozepore arsenal (en route to join), and there personally arranging for the despatch of the train, it is difficult now to see how this matter could have been pulled through satisfactorily.

Prior to the departure of the force, great attention was bestowed by General Stewart on the weeding out of physically unfit men among the dhooly-bearers, servants, and camp-followers generally, and in seeing that all were adequately provided with warm clothing.

Inspection parades of all followers were, with this object, held at Mooltan under the medical officers, and a judicious increase on the ten pounds of baggage originally allowed by regulations for each servant (i.e. one for each officer and one for each of the two horses) permitted.

At times the cold in the campaign was such that, although

turning into bed (consisting of felts sewn together as a mattress, and with two thick blankets sewn along the two sides and end like an envelope) with all clothes on, fur cap covering all but nose and mouth, and three pairs of fisherman's socks, it was scarcely possible to sleep. Some embers placed in a hole at one corner of the tent afforded a little warmth; but if one did not fall asleep at once on the strength of this, it was difficult to do so afterwards.

Regimental officers sometimes, by chumming two in a tent, and especially in having a mess to look to for supplies, cooking, &c., were enabled to rub along fairly; not so, however, Engineers and other members of the Staff, liable to detached duty, for whom at such times the aid of one servant to pitch tent, load and unload the camels, cook, fetch water under an intensity of cold, freezing the poor native to the marrow, and rendering him well nigh useless, proved insufficient, and caused a good deal of hardship.

Most of the troops composing General Stewart's force having been pushed on by rail to Sukkur and thence by road towards Jacobabad, the General with head-quarters were able to leave Mooltan finally on the 17th November.

Rohri, opposite Sukkur, was reached early next day, and the crossing of the Indus (effected by the steamer and flats of the Indus flotilla), proved a simple operation compared with the work of the Engineers in the first Afghan war, when the great river had to be bridged with boats.

From Sukkur the head-quarters reached—

Mangrani	...	19th November	...	11 miles.
Shikarpore	...	20th ,,	...	11 ,,
Hammayoon	...	21st ,,	...	12 ,,
Jacobabad	...	22nd ,,	...	13 ,,
Nusseerabad	...	23rd ,,	..	9 ,,
Halt	...	24th ,,		
Shapur	...	25th ,,	...	22½ ,

Chutter	...	26th November	...	$11\frac{1}{2}$ miles
Pulagi...	...	27th ,,	...	$9\frac{1}{3}$,,
Lehri ...	...	28th ,,	...	16 ,,
Mittri ...	...	29th ,,	...	27 ,,
Dadur ..	...	30th ,,	..	$14\frac{1}{2}$,,

The last-named place is situated in the Katchi plain a few miles from the southern entrance of the Bolan pass. As the marches between the Indus and this place were of an uneventful character, a few observations regarding them will suffice. It was necessary to make careful arrangements for the daily marches of the different corps and batteries with reference to the available supplies of food and water, and also to insure that the troops arriving by the Dera-Bugti route from the junction point at Lehri and onwards should not clash with those arriving from Jacobabad. Our able Quartermaster-General, Major Chapman, however, made excellent arrangements for this, under the General's orders.

The Indus inundations not only reach Jacobabad (forty-five miles from Sukkur,* and protected all round by a flood bank), but to Nusseerabad twelve miles beyond. Owing, however, to the rapid fall which had taken place in the level of the water, the road to the first-named place was comparatively good, and it was only during the march to Nusseerabad that inconvenience was found from the *gup* still remaining † over wide tracts of country. Beyond this, and extending up to the clay hills of Dadur, lies the wide, flat, treeless expanse of the Katchi plain locally called the " putt," traversed by streams (like the Narra),

---

* Jacobabad, which is some forty feet below the level of the spill of the Indus at Kashmore, has of late years been considered, at times, in danger. spite of these embankments and of others along the right bank of the Indus, which cost some seven lakhs of rupees to construct.

† At one place where the inundation water was two feet deep, a bridge on earthen pots was constructed for the infantry ; but the baggage animals, having to wade in the slime, came to " much grief," and there were many wet kits that night.

which, descending from the Dera Bugti hills, wander in broad shallow beds almost at will, and eventually lose themselves in the plain.

In the wet weather great portions of this vast plain—originally, no doubt, deposited by the Indus—are wholly untraversable from the deep adhesive mud ; while in the dry season the heat (rising at times to 130° and 140° in the shade), want of water and supplies, prove sufficient obstacles in themselves to the ordinary traveller, and constitute serious impediments when applied to the march of a large force.

To add to the inconveniences, the rivers in many places have in their wanderings deposited such quantities of deep loose sand as to become serious impediments to wheeled artillery, and to all baggage animals except camels.

So great were the obstacles presented by these combined causes along the ordinary route to Dadur, that, before leaving Jacobabad it was seriously contemplated to adopt the route by Burshorie, Noura, Bagh, Hajji-ka Shahir, following, in fact, the line of the Narra river along the west of the Katchi plain. The arrangements for the first-named route had, however, so far been completed as regards supplies, and the difficulties in the matter of water at Burshorie (twenty-six miles across the *putt* from Jacobabad) were such that the General decided in favour of the one originally chosen.

A little later in the season the Engineer field park, under Lieutenant Call, followed the second route, and the inconveniences encountered in its first portions have been sufficiently recounted by Major A. Le Messurier,* who accompanied him. Later still, however, under altered circumstances, this route was adopted as the main road to the Bolan by General Phayre.

Though there was no great or continuous work for the Sappers, they had, nevertheless, ample occupation, especially when it is

* Diary of Major Le Messurier, R.E., Brigade-Major R. E. with the Quetta column.

II. **35**

considered that they had to work while on the march, and
keep, at the same time, at least one day in advance of the force.

At the crossing of the Katr river, a little south of Chatter,
the 10th Company had to halt for a day to prepare the crossing
through the deep sandy sides and bed, by laying down a roadway of grass and *jhow* (a brushwood found in the inundated
tracts), cleaning out some temporary wells sunk in the bed of
the river, &c.

In advance of Pulagi a few irrigation channels had to be
ramped down for the artillery. Between Lehri and Mittri more
channels; one especially, at twenty-two miles from the former
place, being deep, required a good deal of work. The crossing
of the Narra river, however, at Mittri was found to be easy,
there being only two feet of water at the ford. When full
the stream is 250 feet wide, and then very dangerous from
quicksands.

Some work was required in the pass through the fantastic
flat-topped hills of indurated mud five miles and a half west of
Mittri, on the Dadur road, the track here being in places
narrow, tortuous, and difficult for artillery.

The marches usually commenced at 3 or 4 A.M., and, the camel
having strong objections to be loaded before daylight, trouble
was generally experienced in getting the camp fairly off.

Often the camels arrived at the next camp too late in the
afternoon to secure even an indifferent meal of the camel-thorn
or other suitable fodder; and although the deaths at this time
were inconsiderable as compared with subsequent mortality, the
condition of the animals was lowered, and was a bad preparation
for the heavy tramp before them in the Bolan, and on to
Kandahar.

For officers and men the early marching was exhilarating, as the
climate, even down so close to sea-level (Dadur is only some 400
feet above this) was very bracing, and nothing could exceed the
glorious rosy light of morning, as gradually expanding through

the upper air it tinted with pale pink every fleeting cloud, illuminated the great mountain range behind Gandava, and then broadened into day over the distant plain with a play of mirage probably not to be equalled in other regions. At half march a halt was ordinarily called for breakfast, when the inevitable dhooly was brought to the front groaning, not with the wounded or dying, but with the weight of plates and dishes, which, being distributed to the hungry warriors, were soon turned to the best account.

At times camp was pitched early in the afternoon, but sometimes later, when the camels had a bad time of it.

At Dadur, in addition to the troubles connected with the arrangements for supplies throughout the Bolan pass, a difficulty had to be overcome in regard to the camel-men which proved to be sufficiently serious. Through some misapprehension that the Khan of Kelat would supply the force with Brahuis camels at Dadur for the Bolan pass and the country beyond, a promise it is understood had been given (or possibly only hinted at) to the owners of the Scindian camels, that they should receive fifteen rupees per mensem for each animal (more than double the ordinary fare) up to this point, and then be allowed to return in peace to their Scind homes. On the other hand, it was contended that such an exorbitant rate would never have been given unless the camels were intended to proceed to Quetta. Whatever may have been the precise amount of truth in either of these contentions, it was found, on arrival at Dadur, that our most loyal ally the Khan, notwithstanding our boasted political influence, had failed to provide a single Brahuis camel, and that the expeditionary force must at once be deprived of all means for advance if the contention of the owners was allowed to be valid. Advance a step into the pass they swore they would not; and as desertions had already commenced on a sufficiently large scale, guards were put over all the baggage animals night and day.

35 *

Unluckily, similar precautions were not taken in regard to camel-drivers, no doubt under the idea that the men would hardly attempt to desert leaving their beasts behind; but on the night of the 1st December forty of them bolted, leaving the force to do as best it could without their aid. Starting from Dadur, the head-quarter marches were as follows :—

2nd December to Koondilani	...	$10\frac{3}{4}$ miles.
3rd ,, Kirta ...	...	12 ,,
4th ,, Bibinani...	...	$8\frac{1}{4}$,,
5th ,, Mach ...	...	14 ,,
6th ,, Darwaza...	...	$15\frac{1}{4}$,,
7th ,, Sir-i-Bolan	...	$16\frac{3}{4}$,,
8th ,, Quetta ...	...	6 ,,

It is not here necessary to dwell on the features of the Bolan pass, which have been frequently described, or to give details of each day's march. Suffice it to say that at this time (prior to the excellent road-work executed at a later period by General Phayre with the Bombay Sappers and Grenadiers), marching over an endless boulder-bed for some sixty miles, with only such little nourishment for the horses as could be obtained from the scanty stores of *bhoosa* * and insufficient grain, was, to put it mildly, somewhat trying.

Camels, though better fitted for such rough ground than other animals, fared very badly, as, owing to their late arrival in camp daily, and to the scant supply of rank grass, supplemented only by two seers of barley, they were unable to sustain their strength. Numbers fell out in the marches, and either died at once without making a sign, or were shot when it was found that they were unable to rise.

The bullocks engaged in drawing the second line of wagons with the Artillery Batteries fared even worse, as they split open

---

* Chopped rice-straw, the usual fodder throughout Afghanistan, to which comes next dry or semi-dry lucerne, procurable at Kandahar, and usually where there is irrigation.

their feet over the boulders and became utterly useless. Horses and ponies did better, though they, too, had a very bad time of it.

Fortunately, however, if fodder was scarce (or, as was the case at times, entirely wanting), there was, as a rule, abundance of clear, cold, limpid water throughout the pass, excepting for some eight miles and a half where the Bolan river (between Tungi and Bibinani) disappears completely under the boulder-bed. The source of the Bolan river is found at Sir-i-Bolan, about three miles and a half north-west of Mach, where a gush of crystal water over some rocks on the south bank of the defile, sufficiently marks the spot.

Ramps had to be prepared by the Sappers for crossing the various small channels led off from the Bolan river in the neighbourhood of Dadur, and after that in the crossings of the river itself near Pir, which is close to the southern entrance of the pass. All through the narrow portion of the lower defile between Koondilani and Kirta (where the line crosses the stream fourteen times), the Sappers had constant work in easing descents to the bed, and clearing a road for the artillery through broken clay deposits covered by rank grass; also in making a short ghaut in the more open part beyond, on the left of the stream.

From Kirta onwards there was occasional work of the ordinary character, but no serious or heavy undertaking calling for long halts.

After passing the Sir-i-Bolan the upper defile* is entered, and water is only to be found at times in a spring some mile and three-quarters up the Doozan ravine north; in advance of this is the great ascent to the elevated plain known as the Dasht-i-Bedowlat (6,000 feet above sea-level), and Darwaza.

* The first march with heavy guns was performed by Lieutenant Lyster in 1876, with three 24-pounders and one 8-inch howitzer. With the aid of two companies of the 32nd Pioneers he took eighteen days in getting over the sixty miles of pass, taking no less than three days in doing the upper defile above Doozan, and losing ten bullocks.

The small sharp ghaut over a rocky spur found at the head of the pass before entering on the " Chota Dasht" had been improved by the company of Sappers from Quetta, and they had also sunk a well at Darwaza 110 feet deep by 15 feet in diameter, yielding at this time (6th December) about 1,800 gallons in twenty-four hours.

Two deep katcha wells, constructed by Aludin, the Pass Sirdar, exist at one and two miles respectively from Darwaza; but the supply was trifling, and altogether inadequate. There is thus in the whole toilsome journey of nearly thirty miles between Sir-i-Bolan, over the dreary waste of the Dasht, where there is nothing but southern wood to be found, practically no fodder, and only such an insignificant supply of water as to be valueless for a large force.

At Darwaza for the first time the keen winter air was fully experienced, a slight northern wind being sufficient to make the morning march disagreeable, numbing the limbs and requiring the greatest exertion to get any feeling into the extremities. The sarwans (camel-drivers) could not be induced to load their animals till late in the morning; one man was heard to say, in reply to an order to load up sharp, "Sahib, you may shoot me now, but I won't load." Involuntarily the reflection rose to the mind, What would have been the results on our force, and, indeed, on the fortunes of the campaign, if, instead of a dry north wind, and an open winter, we had had to encounter the wet, cold, and discomfort of the ordinary winter weather in these regions, when the Katchi plain below, and the Dasht-i-Bedowlat above, are converted into a vast sea of mud, over which all movement, particularly for baggage-animals, is simply impossible.

However, to proceed. The line of march from Darwaza gradually falling to Quetta, past Sir-i-ab, was very fair, except where some ingenious individual had cut two deep ditches along his line, and carefully placed all the boulders excavated from these on the roadway, seemingly with the apparent object of prohibiting all possible movement. As neither the Sappers, nor any amount of labour, could get rid of these in time, and as, luckily, the old kafila track fairly answered our purpose, this latter was made use of instead, excepting through the irrigated land near Quetta, where the so-called " made " road fortunately improved.

The fort of Quetta consists of an arc, or citadel, placed on an artificial mound commanding the irrigated plain and town below, by about 150 feet, and surrounded by the same description of mud wall, with round towers, so common throughout India.

The outworks had been considerably improved by Lieutenant-Colonel J. Browne, R.E. (Bengal), and a couple of 8-inch howitzers, and two 24-pounders, had been placed on elevated salients, quite sufficient to warn off an Afghan attack ; but for some unexplained, and apparently unexplainable, reason the greater part of the *enceinte* was occupied by hovels tenanted by tribesmen admitted to belong to dangerous classes. The only precaution at this time deemed advisable was the search of each individual for arms as he entered or left the fort, and this, too, after the very recent murder of a Public Works officer in open day by a party of workmen in the immediate vicinity.

Extreme filth, and the neglect of every sanitary rule, appeared to be the leading characteristic of Quetta at this time ; the place was, moreover, deserted by all the Brahuis, who, in their nomad fashion, had already migrated to the Katchi plains to maintain their cattle, and raise such winter crops as they needed.

The site for the barracks of the two Native Infantry regiments in garrison had been selected (not by an Engineer officer) in the midst of irrigating channels, and had been nearly all washed away during the heavy rains of the previous July. Large sums had, in fact, been expended on these semi-permanent barracks, with, apparently, very little useful result.

Little or no wood being procurable in the country, Lieutenant-Colonel Browne had constructed double platforms, sufficient for three regiments of Native Infantry, at a convenient site, for the sepoys' "pâl" tents, pitched back to back, with a fire-stack so placed in the dividing wall, that the whole of both tents could be comfortably warmed. Screen-walls of mud at both ends added to the comfort of each small block by protecting the door ends of both tents from the wind. The winter housing of the garrison had thus received such attention as the circumstances admitted before General Stewart's arrival.

In other respects matters were by no means in a satisfactory condition, but the General's short halt of two days did not afford the time for meeting any but the most pressing requirements. These had chiefly relation to the establishment of a base hospital on a sufficiently large scale, in view of the possible contingencies of a prolonged campaign.

It was found that accommodation for 150 European and 450 Native troops could be arranged for. Subsequently, however, this provision was increased, and under the able direction of Surgeon-General Smith and the medical officers in successive charge, assisted by Lieutenant Olivier, R.E., the hospitals were made very fairly comfortable.

On the same date as that of General Stewart's arrival at Quetta, the Political Agent, Major Sandeman, and Captain Hanna, A.Q.M.G. of General Biddulph's advanced column, had ridden with a few horsemen up the Kojak defile, and found that the celebrated pass, the possession of which would at least, it was thought, be stoutly disputed, was quite unoccupied, and the country beyond apparently clear of the enemy.

It was, therefore, decided to push on the head-quarters at once, and the following are the dates and distances of the march to Killa Abdoola, at the opening of the Kojak valley :—

			Miles.
10th December,	Kuchlak	... ...	12¾
11th	,,	Syed-yaroo-karez ...	11
12th	,,	Haikalzai	9¾
13th	,,	Aramby-Karez (close to Killa Abdoola) ...	14

Here, after a pretty general concentration of the forces in the Pishin valley, including General Biddulph's, a redistribution of commands was made, with the needful arrangements for an advance on Kandahar so soon as the rest of the troops, especially the artillery (at this time labouring through the Bolan) could be brought to the front.

Had it not been for the open winter[*] with which we were so singularly favoured, the march of the artillery and baggage across the Pishin valley up to this point could only have been accomplished with difficulty, and it may even be doubted whether, in case wet weather had set in, the march through the clay soil of this valley, and the passage of the several streams, could have been undertaken by at least certain portions of the force, e.g. the 40-pounder batteries. As regards these streams, two broad, but not deep ones, are passed in the valley between Quetta and the Murgai pass, leading over a spur of the Takatu range; then between Kushlak and Haiderzai three streams, united with one from Sir-i-ab, had to be crossed twice; and a third, the Kakar Lora, between Syed-Yaroo, Karez, and Haikalzai,[†] the Surkh-ab, and further in advance small feeders with the main stream of the Lora river (the largest, in fact the main stream in the Pishin valley) are met with. It runs in a deep trough, and has rather a muddy bottom.

As it happened, the march was uneventful. Sapper work, on the whole, simple, and chiefly confined to making good ramps down to the streams, the banks of which were generally vertical, some twenty to thirty feet high, and the beds, though too deep and

* As it was, the nights had, since leaving the Dasht, been so cold as to make sleep very difficult, but at Arambi Karez the maximum and minimum thermometer usually placed outside Captain Rogers, R.E.'s tent indicated one degree below zero. Ink generally, at this time, froze on the paper so quickly after writing in the morning that it was necessary to thaw and blot the writing by holding the paper over the cooking-fire. Hands were nastily gashed and cut into by the cold, till the habit of rubbing hot mutton fat once or twice daily well into the skin became general, a plan which proved quite effectual.

† Pronounced by the inhabitants " Haikalzi."

muddy for comfortable crossing, not at this time impassable.
With a little more water we should have had to " pile " across at
least two of the above-mentioned streams; if not, indeed, all.

The 4th Company of Sappers, under Lieutenant Haslett, was
sent by the western route over the Gazaband pass to Gulistan-
Karez, this having been selected as the best road for the heavy
guns.   They ramped down the banks of the two streams crossed,
viz. the Sir-i-ab and the Pishin Lora, and cleared the pass
sufficiently.   This route to and from Quetta has since then been
in more general use than the Haikalzai route, which was the
only one apparently utilised in the first Afghan war.

An examination of the Kojak pass showed that, although easy
up the first eight miles and sufficiently open, the ascent close
under the kotul, or saddle, on the summit of the Kwaja-Amram
range (taken at 7,380 feet above sea-level), would in itself prove
a very severe trial to the artillery and baggage animals; but this,
bad as it undoubtedly was, seemed easy compared with the sharp
descent from the summit to the foot of Chaman (taken at 5,660
feet above sea-level), only three miles beyond, on the north of
the range   Here the fall in probably the first half mile was not
less than 1,000 feet, and as there was no time to make a road
suitable for wheeled artillery (one was subsequently constructed
with maximum gradients of 1 in 12, by Lieutenant Wells, R.E.,
and is now the route almost exclusively used), the C. R. E. of
General Biddulph's force, Lieutenant-Colonel W. Hichens, R.E.
(Bengal), with the 5th and 9th Companies Bengal Sappers and
Miners, made a series of slides from the top, with bollands fixed
at intervals, which, affording the requisite purchase, allowed the
guns to be let down safely, though necessarily in rather tedious
fashion.

General Stewart at once perceiving that however possible
with the lighter classes of ordnance, much risk and delay
would certainly follow the application of this plan to the guns
of the two 40-pounder batteries, with which he was especially

desirous of entering Kandahar, and as the information received led to the conclusion that another and easier route over the range (called the Gwaja* pass, and known to be employed as the kafila road) ran west from Gulistan Karez, ten miles south-west of Killa Abdoola, he directed Colonel Sankey to undertake the duty of reporting on its capabilities.

Starting on the 15th December with Lieutenant Monteith and twenty-five sowars of the 3rd Sind Horse, he was enabled to explore the pass (fearfully rough going in places), about twenty-three miles in length, and get back by evening. Lieutenant Monteith had himself reconnoitred half the length of the pass the previous day, and the General was so satisfied with the report which Colonel Sankey was enabled to make, that a reconnoissance in force, to explore the pass and search for water all along the north slopes of the range as far as Chaman, was decided on.

Making as good a breakfast as possible, for it was known they would have to bivouac out that night without tents or servants, an early start was made on the morning of the 16th December, with about 250 sabres of the 1st Punjab Cavalry and some 60 of the 3rd Sind Horse, the whole being under the command of Major Maclean of the first-named regiment.

The only inhabitant seen on this march was a goat-herd, who instantly, on discovering the party, climbed like a lizard to the top of a pinnacle some 200 feet above the roadway followed by his flock of black goats. The latter, clinging to the precipitous rock, looked exactly like a swarm of bees, and the gentleman himself was seen collecting all stones within reach for a vigorous defence of his position. With head only showing now and then over the edge he was ready for all comers, and it is doubtful if he could have been easily turned off his perch.

---

* Though ordinarily spelt on our maps and in reports Gwaja or Kwaja, such of the inhabitants as we met pronounced the word *Gwuzza* with a guttural intonation hopeless of imitation

The march, having to be regulated by the pace of the baggage ponies (these, however, only in sufficient numbers to carry barley and bhoosa for the sowars, and such few wraps for the officers as could be taken), was necessarily slow, and as evening closed in some anxiety was not unnaturally felt as to how fire-wood was to be procured in this treeless, inhospitable region.

Luckily one of the party espied some dry drift wood scattered about the boulder-bed of the valley, and in an instant all, officers and men, were out of their saddles, trudging along, each with a log (best of friends!) on his shoulders.

A scare of the enemy's cavalry being close in front caused some delay, so the encamping-ground had to be selected in almost total blackness, on ground covered by huge boulders just outside the western *débouchure* of the pass.

Nothing, however, could have been more intelligent and satisfactory than the behaviour of the sowars under Major Maclean, an officer of marked ability, and the camp was soon in good order, with vedettes thrown out all round, picquets on commanding points, &c., and the whole secure against a night attack, or chuppow, so dear to Afghan strategy.

Grand log-fires were soon ablaze, and after everyone had produced such provisions as he had with him, making a variety by indenting as much as possible on his neighbour's store, the rugs were spread, and each tried to compose himself to sleep with toes close to the fire, as best he could. But the cold was of that intense character which makes a man think of his mother, and sleep was impossible for most of them.

Up and on again at daylight, they forced the weary horses and ponies across twenty-seven miles of the northern slopes of the Gwaja Amram range forming a *talus* extending miles into the plain, every yard paved with rounded boulders varying in size from a baby's head to a dhoby's* bundle.

Throughout some portion of this stony wilderness might be

* Washerman.

traced a narrow tortuous path sufficiently wide for a single horseman, but of little use to a body such as this. The horses and ponies had a bad time of it, and the party thought themselves lucky in having to abandon only two or three baggage animals.

Only in two places were water-channels met with. The first was the Iskan-kara, a narrow crystal clear stream of water which it was fondly hoped might be traced six or eight miles into the plain, so as to be of use on the direct forward march from the Gwaja to Konchai; but this turned out a delusion, as the channel after a mile or two was subsequently found to be breached, and the supply to disappear rapidly in the bouldery soil. Another smaller stream, twenty miles from the Gwaja at the northern *débouchure* of the Rajhani pass, was even more unsatisfactory.

At two or three places the black tents of the nomads of this region (Achakzais) were met, and the inhabitants, on the party riding up, put on as lamb-like an appearance as possible. Little information could be obtained from them, though one man, who smelt *bakshish,* acted as a guide, thereby saving us some trouble.

Arriving at Chaman a little after dark, all remembrance of troubles soon vanished in enjoying the hospitality of Colonel Kennedy and the officers of the 2nd Punjab Cavalry.

The results of the reconnoissance were briefly (1) the Gwaja pass was much more capable of being adapted as a road for the heavy artillery than the Kojak; (2) no road practicable for troops or baggage could, with any means at disposal, be made along the north slopes of the Kwaja Amram range, so as to connect directly the west end of the Gwaja pass and Chaman; (3) the plain intervening between the Gwaja pass and Konchai north, on the kafila route to Kandahar, was apparently waterless.

The General having accepted Colonel Sankey's proposals to

employ a large body of troops in making the Gwaja pass suitable for heavy artillery, early arrangements were made with this object. Notwithstanding difficulties in the matter of supplies work was commenced on the 23rd December with the 32nd Pioneers (Colonel Fellowes),* the 29th Bombay N.1. Beloochees (Colonel Nicholetts), and two companies Bombay Sappers and Miners.

On the 25th idem the 25th Punjab Infantry (Colonel Hoggan), and on the 29th a detachment of the 59th Foot, were added to the work brigade under Sankey's command.

But little was required to fit the road for artillery for the first ten miles at the east, or Gulistan, end of the pass, as the line lay over an open shingle-bed at an easy gradient. After this for three miles up to the kotul, or saddle (summit taken at 6,906 feet above sea-level), a considerable amount of blasting had to be resorted to in order to widen the track, and reduce the curves sufficiently for the heavy guns.

This matter of curvature was important, as a 10-pounder gun drawn by eight pairs of bullocks occupies a total length of some 120 feet, and when all the animals are fairly in draft the versine of the curve does not much exceed ten feet. Of course the elephants attached to the battery would be always at hand to help guns round very sharp curves, but as hardly a single portion of the defile was absolutely straight the work of getting the guns along would have been exceedingly tedious, if this point had not been constantly kept in view.

The 32nd Pioneers were particularly expert in managing powder blasts, and to them was especially assigned this duty east of the kotul; but the chief work consisted in the removal by pick of semi-disintegrated shaley rock, which, though unfit

* No finer specimen of true British soldiers could have been found in the army than the two officers named; the first died, it is understood, of dysentery, in subsequently returning along the Tul-Chotiali route with General Biddulph to India, and the second of cholera later on near Kandahar

for blasting, was just hard enough to make removal extremely laborious

Immediately at the kotul and for a mile beyond towards Spinatiza,* the work, which was extremely heavy, was entrusted to the Sappers, subsequently (as the work to the eastward cleared off) assisted by the other troops.

The descent here for nearly half a mile was between perpendicular rocks, and the defile so narrow in places as just to suffice for the passage of a single laden camel.

During the first four days the Sappers had been constantly engaged in blasting away all the most prominent portions of rock here; and on the 27th, when nearly all the troops were concentrated on this small portion, the blasts ceased, and all applied themselves to wedging off large masses of the shale, shovelling stuff from the sides, &c.

Never have troops worked more with a will. The rattle of shingle shovelled in a constant shower from the mountain sides was broken by the thud of large masses of rock wedged off and flung into the gully below, which had to be filled up to a depth throughout of from eight to nine feet and widened to thirteen feet in the clear, and further kept as straight as possible, the gradient being severe.

In the afternoon of this day, Major A. Le Messurier† joined the camp; and Captain Call, after arduous work through the Katchi plain, &c., brought up his Engineer field park in most creditable condition.

In the next few days the roadway throughout was improved, and carried some two miles beyond Spinatiza, from which, for about eight miles to the end of the pass, it had only to be

---

* *Spinatiza,* or " white stone," so called from a tor-like rock streaked with white quartz veins, which stands on the south of a small open plain in the middle of the pass, with hard by a good supply of water, and a favourite halting-place for the *kafilas*. On the maps the place is given as Ispantaza, while, again, the word was pronounced Ispingi by some of the inhabitants.

† This officer has published his carefully-kept and interesting diary.

cleared in places through a boulder-bed so as to make all easy for the artillery and baggage-animals.

The scenery in the lower portion of the pass is very grand, precipices of black glistening rock rising to hundreds of feet on both sides, and gradually declining and opening as the end of the pass is reached. From this point a gradually descending plain, covered with boulders for miles, expands before the eye, and melts on the horizon into the red Seistan desert.

Such hills as lie scattered about, chiefly to the north and east, where the country rises, have all the appearance of islands in a sea of sand,* one of the nearest on the direct line to Kandahar being the Konchai hill, twenty-one miles distant. Beyond Konchai on the direct road to and visible from Kandahar is the remarkable Achak hill, while nearer north-east are the three small detached Baldak hills with Gutai and Mel Manda beyond.

The only inhabitants of the cheerless expanse are apparently a few families of Achakzais, whose black tents (*kirries*) are here and there just distinguishable at great intervals.

What with the losses of camels, chiefly in General Biddulph's force, and the tightness of supplies in the Pishin valley, which till reached had been lauded as a land of Goshen, matters about this time began to look rather serious.

---

* This waterless tract between the Kwaja-Amran range and the Dori river north, bordering the Seistan desert, has always proved troublesome in the advance of a force to Kandahar. In the first campaign the 16th Lancers, after leaving Chaman and finding no water at Gutai or Mel Manda, had to push on without halt to the Dori river (some sixty miles), into which, though the water was at the time brackish, men and horses are said to have precipitated themselves in an agony of thirst. Numbers of horses perished on this march. The following is Lieutenant Broadfoot's brief but telling account :—

" After forcing the guns over the made road (at the Kojak), and the camels over the narrow path, we found on the western slope a scarcity of water, and three long marches had to be made under the pains of thirst. At last when we reached the cultivation of Kandahar our horses were starved, our camels were failing, the men had dysentery, and the road behind was strewed with the bodies of camels and horses, and of men who had been murdered when they lagged from exhaustion."

It seemed that either an advance must be made at once on Kandahar with insufficient provisions, or that we should have to fall back on Quetta.

In the matter of water-supply, and even of the character of road beyond Konchai, the reports sent in by the advanced cavalry brigades were unsatisfactory and incomplete.

The one cheering bit of information which reached camp at the time was the discovery by Lieutenant Monteith of the small fresh-water lake (Lagoli) lying out in the plain some eleven miles from the end of the Gwaja pass, three miles off the kafila road leading to Konchai, and which promised to be of material assistance in breaking the trying march to that place.

Notwithstanding the rather gloomy outlook, our General adopted unhesitatingly the resolve to push for Kandahar without a moment's delay, General Biddulph's force to take the direct line by Gutai, Mel Manda, &c., and ours that by Konchai and Shahpusand, the whole to concentrate at Takt-i-pul.

The work brigade, which still kept its position in advance, marched on the 2nd January 1879 direct from the end of the Gwaja pass along the kafila route to Konchai—twenty-one miles—while head-quarters moved to lake Lagoli.

To add to the scanty water-supply of the two small deep wells at Konchai, the Sappers sent in advance had already cleared out some five small springs, a little way up the mountain, which proved of the utmost value.

To our good fortune, the next day's march, regarding which serious doubts had been entertained, turned out an unexpectedly easy one. From the reports received, it was understood that a tongue of the Seistan desert, of deep red sand, impassable for artillery, crossed the line in such a way as, in all probability, to compel us to diverge towards Lashkar, on the east, instead of holding on straight for Shahpusand* and the Achak hill   The

* This Shahpusand, like Takt-i-pul, Pishin, and half the names one sees figuring on our maps, is not the name of a village, but of a district: the name.

much-dreaded sand was found, however, to extend east only some three or four miles, after which an extremely easy road was found direct north to Shahpusand.

At Shahpusand, which lies close south of the Achak hill on the banks of the Dori river (where at this time there were good pools of fresh water), the work brigade, which Colonel Sankey had commanded since the 22nd ultimo, concentrated on and fell generally under the command of Brigadier-General Palliser, with the 15th Hussars, 1st P. C., some of the Sind Horse, and two field-guns.

Our advance had been so rapid, that General Biddulph's cavalry, though having the shorter line to operate on, was at this time at Lashkar; but on the morning of the 4th January the heads of both columns were fairly level, which was a matter of importance, as, by the reports brought in, the enemy's cavalry had taken up a position near Takt-i-pul.

On the morning of the 4th, Major Luck, 15th Hussars, commanding the advanced guard, with a squadron of his own regiment, and two of the 1st P. C., found some Afghan sowars in the valley between Hauz-i-Ahmed Khan and the Korkurra Kotul, over which our road lay to the Bori valley, and drove them in, killing a couple of their horses and catching one of the party, which may possibly have been 200 strong.

General Palliser coming up, it was decided to push on with the advanced guard and the two guns, so as to feel for the enemy's main body, believed to consist of 2,000 cavalry.

We had not been long in the track of the retreating sowars, when the booming of guns to the right showed that Colonel Kennedy, with his advanced cavalry brigade moving past Mel Manda, was already engaged.

moreover, often derived from some sirdar, and liable to change at his death. Hauz-i-Ahmed Khan, or " Hauz," as it is more often called, is a masonry cistern, often domed over, a sort of public charity for travellers, about four miles up the valley on the kafila road from Shahpusand, and named after its constructor The term " Hauz " is of frequent occurrence

With the hopes of taking the enemy opposed to him in rear, and catching them in the Ghlo Kotul pass, through which they must retire, a change was made to the right, in the direction of our advance, and we made straight for the kotul, some six miles to the north-east.

As the line lay across the spurs of hills on our right and over fearfully stony ground, quite impracticable for artillery, the cavalry advanced without the guns. Considering the ground, the pace was very severe, and soon the opening of the Ghlo Kotul pass was easily made out, about a mile and a half on our right front, with some Afghan sowars retiring through it.

Had we been five minutes sooner, we should probably have caught the whole body in the pass. Soon the swarm thickened, and at first, taking us for their own people, seemed unconcerned; they were, however, not long left in error, as at Luck's command, the swords flashed from the scabbards, and the three squadrons rushed straight at the ill-formed mass, aggregating at this time some 250 or 300 sowars.

Luck, ordering his men to hold their horses well in hand for the home rush—a necessary precaution, as they were a good deal blown—went himself straight for the Afghans, who by this time were trying to pull themselves together, and firing at our men. A few had turned tail, however, and were making straight down the valley in the direction of Deh Hajji and Kandahar.

Distressed as they were, the horses seemed fired with the same enthusiasm as the men, and nothing could exceed the steadiness, swiftness, and momentum of the charge.

It was no discredit to the Afghan cavalry that, in the face of such a concentrated mass of men, riding knee to knee, they at the last moment turned, not, however, before Luck had run the foremost man through, and accounted for another a little further on.

Helter-skelter down the valley went the Afghans with the Hussars and Punjabees, now without formation, close at their

36 *

heels. The bodies of some twenty-eight Afghans were counted on the ground after this charge, and it was thought at least forty in all must have been killed.

When over, one of the Afghan stragglers rode coolly across our front, and, refusing to put his horse out of a walk, was shot. The sowars killed showed great individual courage, and would no doubt have done well under proper discipline and leading. The eight prisoners captured were cool, plucky fellows, well dressed and found all round, except as regarded the carbines, of Kabul make, which were rubbish.

As the booming of one or two more guns was heard from the other side of the kotul, and as stragglers from the enemy's cavalry were still coming through the pass, General Palliser* thought it prudent to form up in readiness for any other bodies of the enemy who might yet appear on the scene.

Hardly had this been done, when some more Afghans appeared, closely followed by a large body of cavalry, whose nationality, with their backs to the sun, could not at a distance of some 500 yards, be readily distinguished.

To test the point, the regimental call of the 2nd P. C. (Colonel Kennedy's) was sounded, and, as this was not responded to, the forty or fifty hussars and sowars we had with us were ordered to dismount, and deliver a steady volley, preparatory to a charge. The command was half given, and two shots had actually been fired, when someone luckily roared out that he was certain they were our own men. Meeting a few minutes afterwards, Colonel Kennedy who (with Colonel Browne, R.E.) was at the head of our quondam enemy, he called out, "Those two fellows should be sent to punishment drill for a month for bad shooting."

After making arrangements for our own wounded (ten in all—

---

* This officer, now a K.C.B., had received a sabre-cut at Sobraon, which still prevents his drawing his sword, but here he was charging with the youngest Few have so nobly won their honours.

some slightly) as also for those of the enemy, with the prisoners and captured horses, Brigadier-General Palliser, Colonel Sankey, and Major Le Messurier, with six hussars, started to make their way in the direction of the point which it was calculated the main body of our force should have reached, and in so doing found themselves close on the enemy's picquets with the main body behind them at Takt-i-pul. In fact, after proceeding about two miles towards our supposed camp, and making a sharp turn to the left near the ruins of a village, taken to be that of Saif-ood-deen, it seemed for a moment that in the dusk they had actually got into the middle of the enemy.

Reassured, however, by seeing our guns in action a little in advance, they joined the main body of our people, who, in the absence of the Brigadier, had, after advancing with all the baggage to their present position, formed up in such a manner as to resist a possible attack from the enemy encamped across the road, not more than 1,500 yards in front.

A feint, made to draw the enemy under fire, was partially successful, and the guns made some pretty shell-practice among the Afghan sowars, as they swarmed over the brow of the hill, and down the front, about 1,200 yards from our position.

As night closed in, they appear to have thought enough had already been done in the way of resistance, and retreated hastily, not drawing rein, it was reported, till they had reached Mundhissar, where a camp had been formed outside Kandahar.

Next day, Major Maclean and Colonel Sankey, with two squadrons of the 1st P. C., and one of the 15th Hussars, pushed on past Deh Hajji and the Argeshan towards the Tarnack river, without finding any further trace of the enemy, excepting the carcases of a few horses killed by shell in front of their late encampment at Takt-i-pul.

General Stewart's entire force, comprising that under Major-General Biddulph, was now (6th January) concentrated at Abdool Ryman's village, some five miles south of Deh Hajji.

Arrangements had been made for an advance into the Kandahar plain by two routes from Deh Hajji, so as to turn any defences which the enemy might have constructed on one or other, viz. on either the direct route leading south past Kushab, or on the rather longer though better line north by Mundhissar.

Hardly had the troops commenced their march, when a deputation of Kandahar sirdars reached the General, and informed him that Mir Afzal,* Shere Ali's governor, had already retreated towards Herat with his family and treasure, and that the respectable portion of the inhabitants were most anxious for us to take immediate possession of the city, in order to prevent attempts at plundering by the disbanded soldiery and the lower orders.

On the receipt of this intelligence, orders were at once conveyed for the combined forces to march by the direct Kushab line on Kandahar, and on the evening of the 7th January, Sankey had the pleasure of seeing the city for the first time with the advanced guard from the top of the kotul, immediately beyond the village, and on the right bank of the Tarnack river.

A number of sullen-looking Afghans had squatted themselves on a slightly rising ground to the left of the kotul, and, with troops of all arms eagerly pressing on to catch a first view of the long-wished for city, formed an effective foreground group to the scene which lay in front.

About nine miles off could be just discerned the walls and towers of Kandahar, the only conspicuous objects being the mosque of Ahmed Shah, founder of the Durani kingdom, and two or three towers in the arc at the north end of the city.

---

* Mir Afzal was the father of Shere Ali's last and favourite wife. She was the mother of Abdoola Jan, the infant in whose favour the infatuated Ameer had set aside the claims of his elder sons. Yakoob and Ayoob Khan, but who shortly before this had died suddenly while the Russian embassy was at Kabul.

The Mir is believed to have had little but his family interest to recommend him as governor, and, finding himself incapable of defending Kandahar, bolted towards Furrah, after first, it is said, squeezing the city folk to the extent of two lakhs of rupees.

The plain, intersected in all directions by channels, looked at this time brown and dull. Deh Khojah and other villages, composed entirely of domed mud-huts, could be made out, surrounded by leafless gardens of fruit trees. To the south-west the trees and gardens were particularly thick, and, though now dull, promising brilliant colouring as spring advanced. A succession of jagged hills, commencing with those on the west, overlooking old Kandahar, ran round the horizon to north and north-east, including the now well-known position of General Roberts' brilliant victory, the most remarkable features being the hill known as the bullock's hump, the Babawali Kotul, Murcha pass, &c.

The sun, which was just setting, lit up for a moment the various features of this, to all of us, most interesting scene.

There was, however, not much time for sentiment, as on clearing the summit of the rocky saddle, such a cheer rang through the air as has seldom been heard, and was taken up and repeated all along the line, increasing, if anything, the repulsive looks of our sulky Afghan auditory.

The city could not, of course, be reached that evening, and camp was pitched on sloping stony ground, immediately above the highest of the irrigating channels—now dry.

To revert a little to the work brigade, it may be mentioned that although its separate existence had ceased on concentration with Brigadier Palliser's force (4th January), it had still its own specific duties to perform, though of a comparatively light character.

A short steep ghaut, covered with boulders had to be cleared and prepared for artillery in descending from the Korkurra Kotul, and the sides of several small nullas running into the Dori river had to be ramped down, up to and beyond Takt-i-pul. After this point, till reaching Deh Hajji, and the plain of the Argeshan and Tarnack rivers, little was required in the way of road-making.

Here, particularly across the irrigated ground in the neighbourhood of the rivers, the difficulty consisted in preparing
crossings of the channels (which traversed them in considerable
numbers) for the baggage animals.

The camel is not a very intellectual or observant animal. With
head proudly in the air, always engaged in slowly masticating
some intense nastiness to his own apparent satisfaction, he
slowly puts one leg forward after another in perfect ignorance as
to where it is to reach *terra firma.* If an attempt be made, by
pulling at his nose-string, to induce him to look down, the head
goes up more proudly mournful than ever, and he gazes on
infinite space.

It thus occurs that when crossing an irrigation channel, probably only three or four feet wide by two or three deep, the
descending leg suddenly fails him, and over he goes with a crash,
due to his own weight and five or six maunds of baggage. If,
more sprightly than his neighbours, he attempts to " throw a
lep," the result is at once ludicrous and serious. Flop he goes,
this time head foremost, injured, possibly, for life. As it never
occurs to these creatures to attempt to rise, once they are down,
eight or ten British soldiers, after relieving him of his load, pass
ropes under him, and, with infinite chaff, fairly drag him out
with a long and strong pull and a pull altogether. When he may
subsequently attempt to stand on his feet is a problem. After
sitting for several hours, tempted, perhaps, by handfuls of grass,
&c., he may possibly do so ; but more often he ignores all such
attentions, and should he have made up his mind to remain and
die of starvation, rather than aid in the campaign, the rear-guard
put a bullet through his head and carry off his tail, to give the
owner a chance of claiming compensation eventually. If amiable
and he allows the Britisher to load up afresh, amid groanings only
too much uttered, it is as likely as not that just before the final
knot is tied he springs suddenly to his legs, and trots gaily
across the plain in an aimless kind of way, slowly dropping every

article of baggage one by one, and followed by observations regarding himself and relations which it would be undesirable to place on record.

Several channels along both banks of the Argeshan river had to have their sides sloped down near Deh Hajji, and again at Kushab, where there was a belt of irrigated land on the left bank of the Tarnack.

Our well-meant efforts, however, to thus assist the baggage-animals was often of doubtful value, if it did not increase the difficulties, as in a very short time the whole surface of these extemporised slopes, and even the ground beyond, all of which was a stiff clay, became so slippery with a multitude of animals, each bringing up a quantity of water, as to prove absolutely dangerous, especially to the camels. These animals, in such cases, appear to have little or no command of their legs, which slide from under them, or apart, not infrequently splitting the chest-bone.

Fortunately, the wide bed of the Argandab river, and the narrower but deeper one of the Tarnack, were found to be composed of shingle, and only needed ramps on both sides.

It was decided to make a triumphal entry, and march through the city of Kandahar on the 8th January, and although the 40-pounder batteries could not take part in the display, the four field-batteries which did so, taken with the rest of the force, made up as it was of some 8,000 picked troops. European and natives, furnished a sufficiently imposing spectacle.

Unfortunately, however, credence was given to the statement of the Sirdars who formed the deputation from Kandahar, that the approaches to the city were quite fitted for wheeled artillery, and that as to the streets, they were just the finest and broadest in the world!

About 10.30 A.M. the force got fairly into the irrigated land surrounding the city, and from this time forward work was cut out for all concerned, especially for the Sappers, as the boasted main roads of approach turned out to be, in places, mere camel-paths between the fields, and it became necessary to construct temporary causeways across the irrigation channels, all deep. Water was flowing with considerable volume and velocity through these, and it was a matter of extreme difficulty to pass the guns and waggons over sharp enough before the hastily-extemporised earthen causeways, continually kept renewed, became over-topped.

At one of these, fully eight feet deep, the General commanding one of the divisions declared his horses had not sufficient rush left in them to clear the causeway in time, but the gunners proved themselves, as usual, equal to the occasion, and they have seldom had a better opportunity of showing the stuff they were made of. In fact, in this execrable march more difficulties had to be overcome than any other since leaving Mooltan, and seldom has better or bolder driving been seen.

Through the Shikarpore gate by which we entered, the Char-su, or domed centre of Kandahar, and the Bardoorani gate, by which the force left the city, nearly all the horses had to be un-hooked, and the guns hand-spiked, past the sharp right angles at each of these narrow places.

Till 8 P.M. did the weary work go on, and the tents did not come up till 9 P.M. Many of the troops had had nothing since morning, and went dinnerless and supperless to roost. Provisions for the force had, in fact, just lasted, and in some regiments were, it is understood, exhausted ; but boldness, combined with judgment, had carried the day, and, considering the time of year, the scantiness of supplies all along the march, the absence of fodder, the impossibility of procuring any baggage-animals along the whole route, the physical difficulties which had to be surmounted through the Bolan, the Khojak, and Gwaja passes and the desert beyond, &c.,—above all, the presence (in our two 40-pounder batteries) with the force of the most powerful and weighty field-artillery ever before seen in Asia,—this march of General Stewart's must rank as a most skilfully-conducted and successful military exploit. Of actual fighting there was practically nothing to speak of, but so much the more trying for the spirits of the troops.

The first duties in connection with our occupation of Kandahar were the clearance of the arc, or citadel, from the rubbish and filth, offensive to eye and nose, everywhere predominating; fitting up the buildings of the central courtyard as a general hospital; improving the defences sufficiently to obviate anything in the shape of a *coup de main*, adapting one courtyard for the artillery-park, another for the commissariat, &c.

Immediately on the flight of Mir Afzal the populace appear to have rushed into the arc and helped themselves to every remove-able article. All the window-sashes to the last scrap of wood had been wrenched out, and the powder-stores rifled in such a reckless manner that in the immediate neighbourhood of the magazines the loose material lay strewn about the ground, so very suggestive of explosions that sentries had to be instantly put on, and arrangements made for destroying all that was not required. The store here collected was enormous, all stored away in large earthen *amphoræ* (about three feet high each), packed together in small chambers under the ramparts.

A decision as to what should be done to make the arc a defensible post in any accepted engineering sense presented considerable difficulties, taking into account the manner in which it was closely hemmed in, and even commanded by, the houses of the city east and west. To clear any sufficient esplanade on these sides, and give the needful flanking defence, would not only have been a costly and very laborious operation, but, as involving the destruction of quite the best houses in the city, would, no doubt, have been looked on as a needless act of vandalism. As it was, moreover, Ahmed Shah's tomb completely commanded, at very short range, the interior of nearly all the courtyards of the arc, and to remove that historic and venerated monument was clearly impossible.

Influenced by these reasons, the General decided on merely carrying out such modified improvements as would, while rendering the place secure against a rush, meet as far as possible our immediate requirements for shelter and accommodation, as before indicated.

Captain Bissett, R E., who, under Brigadier-General Nutall, as Commandant, was put in charge of the operations, went to work energetically, and, as will be noted further on, with satisfactory results.

In the meanwhile we had sufficient proof that, however easily the great prize had fallen into our hands, it was by no means with the general assent or goodwill of the inhabitants, a large number of whom never relaxed the air of sullen suspicion and dislike, noticeable as the prevailing demeanour of the crowd which lined every available standing-point and roof on the day of our triumphant entry and march through the city.

On Friday, the 10th January, two striking examples were given of the real temper of some of the inhabitants.

One was that of Lieutenant Willis, R.A., who, while standing at a shop, was stabbed twice fatally in the chest by a Ghazi, who also succeeded in wounding three more of our men before he was cut down by Lieutenant Harvey, 1st P. C ; the other, Major St. John, R.E., who, in riding through the streets with Nawab Gholam Hussain, our lately-appointed Governor of the city, had a very narrow escape from another fanatic ruffian. The man, getting close up to Major St. John's left side unperceived, fired at his head, but somehow missed his aim. Drawing his sword, however, for a second attempt, he would probably have succeeded in his object but for the prompt action of the Nawab's escort, who secured the man. Next day, after sentence by a drum-head court-martial, the Ghazi was hung in front of the esplanade facing the gateway of the arc, full in view of his fellow-townsmen.

Rumours of a heavy fine being at once inflicted on the city, and of complete disarmament, quickly flew about, but the General deemed it sufficient to prohibit any open show of arms on the part of the inhabitants, and to issue stringent orders that officers and men in visiting the city should always be armed, and in knots of three or four for mutual help in case of attack.

There can be no doubt that a fine sufficiently heavy to make itself felt as a punitive measure must have fallen severely on all the inhabitants without exception, and with undesirable severity on the peaceful Hindu traders and others who might be well disposed, as also, again, on others whom, though not so well affected, it might be good policy to conciliate.

To carry out such a disarmament as would be effective and preclude the possibility of assassination would have been difficult, if not impossible. Great risk would here again have been run of exposing the friendly and peaceably disposed inhabitants to the attack of the ruffians, whilst it would have been next to impossible to deprive the latter of the knife, which, easily concealed in their voluminous garments, is with the Afghan the weapon almost exclusively relied on for assassination.

The great difficulties, which had all along followed the advance, of finding fodder for the large mass of baggage animals, to say nothing of the cavalry and artillery horses, though somewhat diminished on reaching Kandahar, still caused anxiety. The grazing, for the camels especially, was both poor, unsatisfying, and at too great a distance from the camps.

To these and other considerations, rendering a prolonged stay at Kandahar undesirable, was added the understood wish of the Government of India that, in case the General found himself strong enough, after getting possession of the city, to push forward in sufficient force and seize Girishk to the west and Kelat-i-Ghilzai to the north-east, this should be done.

Accordingly, after careful arrangements in regard to baggage animals and supplies, the 1st Division and head-quarters, under

General Stewart, with a total effective * of 1,993 Europeans and 2,189 Natives, officers and men, started on the 15th January 1879 for Kelat-i-Ghilzai ; Major-General Biddulph, with the 2nd Division, 886 Europeans and 2,149 Natives, having already marched, on the day previous, for Girishk.

The 4th and 9th Companies Bombay Sappers and Miners were attached to the 1st Division, as also Lieutenant Call's Engineer Field Park ; while with the 2nd Division were the 5th and 10th Companies, and its own Engineer Field Park under Captain Nicholson, R.E.

Brigadier-General Nutall was left in command at Kandahar, with 720 Europeans and 1,115 Natives, effective officers and men.

The detail of dates and distances marched were, starting from Kandahar, as follows :—

To Moman	10 miles	...	15th January.
(Road taken unnecessarily circuitous.)			
To Robat	8 miles	...	16th January.
To Ziarat-i-Akhoond .	12 ,,	...	17th ,,
To Shahr-i Saffa ...	12·4 ,,	...	18th ,,
To Tir-Andaz ...	10·5 ,,	...	19th ,,
To near Jaldak ...	14 ,,	...	20th ,,
To Pulsingi	8·4 ,,	...	21st ,,
To Kelat i-Ghilzai ...	6·5 ,,	...	22nd ,,

On the 22nd idem Kelat-i-Ghilzai was reached by head-quarters, preceded by the cavalry under Brigadier-General Fane, the fort itself having surrendered on the 21st to Lieutenant-Colonel J. Browne, R.E., Political Officer with the force. Hearing that the garrison was decamping, the last-named officer galloped forward with twelve sowars of the 19th Bengal Cavalry (just as the enemy were filing out) and secured possession.

* These numbers are taken from Major A. Le Messurier's diary.

As our march lay generally along the foot of an undulating steppe, extending for several miles from the foot of the range separating the Argandab and the Tarnack valleys, and as channels had been led from the Tarnack river, which runs parallel with the route at from half to two miles distant, so as to traverse the whole of the low-lying land skirting the right bank, the line, though ordinarily over good hard ground, had necessarily at times to cross tongues of irrigated land running up the valleys. These portions, taken with the crossings of some small streams, feeders of the Tarnack, presented obstacles for the passage of the artillery and baggage cattle.

The Sappers were thus kept fully employed. Between Moman and Robat some irrigation channels were sloped down; but notwithstanding this provision, several camels and ponies of the Engineer park fell, owing to the slippery soil and the weakened condition of the beasts.

At a mile out of Ziarat-i-Akhoond, the Sappers did good work, improving the line round a hill spur, and in the next march, at three-fourths of the distance between Shahr-i-Saffa and Tir-Andaz, heavy ramping had to be undertaken to reduce sufficiently the bank of a nullah which here crosses the line. Very careful and plucky driving was even then required by the artillery, and it was thought best to leave a working-party of the 59th Foot and Goorkhas to complete the work, under Lieutenants Olivier and Childers, R.E.

Between Tir-Andaz and Jaldak, the line, in the fourth mile, skirts the hills into the foot of which the Tarnack river has cut deeply, with high vertical clay banks, immediately above which (and dangerously near) is the roadway, practically little better than a steep camel-path. This is known as the Jalogir pass. Notwithstanding the amount of work bestowed on widening and improving this pass, special working-parties from the 59th Foot and the Goorkhas had to be employed. Orders were likewise sent to the 2nd Brigade under Brigadier Barter, which was following head-quarters at a day's march in rear, to proceed with and finish the work.

At five and a half and eight miles the services of the Sappers had, while on the march, to be put in requisition at nullah crossings; in the tenth mile, again, springs of water along the left of line produced such heavy bog that the artillery had to avoid these by passing through irrigated ground to right.

The last piece of work for the Sappers was in preparing ramps at a nullah which crossed the line just beyond Pulsingi, where there was a sheer drop of eighteen feet into the bed of the stream. Spite of careful driving two artillery waggons were here upset, owing in great measure to the reduced condition of the horses.

The cold had been very trying throughout the march, the wind increasing to almost half a gale at times, and the thermometer falling as we ascended the valley of the Tarnack. On the night of the 20th January, at Jaldak, the thermometer stood as low as 8° Fahrenheit.

This, with previous low condition, continued marching, and scanty grazing of a bad quality, necessarily told heavily on the baggage animals, and on the camels especially.

It was reported that on the second day's march out of Kandahar no less than 200 camels had died, and the loss in the Cavalry Brigade in advance was said to be fifty-five.

In fact, out of something over 3,000 camels, with which the 1st Division left Kandahar, it is believed that 1,100 died [*] on the march. Some recoupment was effected by purchases (which were made *en route*) of country-bred camels, but in insufficient numbers. These, though of smaller size than the Sindian camel, were much more serviceable, as being accustomed to the

---

[*] The deaths were no doubt numerous, but there was not wanting an apparently well-founded suspicion that a pretty free traffic was carried on between our *sarwans* and the tribesmen along the route, which would, if true, account for a goodly number of those reported missing.

climate and feeding. They all had longer hair, and some were especially handsome and "casty" looking.

Constant working parties had to be employed in digging holes for and interring the bodies outside the camps, and still the work could not be completed. For several days at Kelat-i-Ghilzai quite a large collection of dead camels lay west of the cavalry camp.

Baggage ponies and mules had, perhaps, fared a little better, but the condition even of those attached to the Engineer field park under Lieutenant Call, who spared no pains with regard to feeding and otherwise caring for the animals, was most distressing.

Pack-saddles, which had fitted well at first, galled the poor creatures as their condition fell, catching and establishing "raws" on the hips and all prominences. Mange, too, laid its grip on a large proportion.

Conceal it as we may, it must be admitted that no perfect pack animal for trans-Indus campaigns has as yet been invented. The bullock loses heart in the absence of sufficient grass, and his feet split in such a manner over shingles or bouldery ground as to render him utterly useless—except to be eaten. The mule or pony breaks down, as shown, with hard work, and, moreover, is open to the objection of requiring a disproportion-ably large number of attendants (one to every two or three beasts), each of which only carries half a camel-load, if so much. The camel, however well adapted to carry heavy loads (four to six, and even ten to twelve maunds!) over marches of thirty miles at a stretch, must have intervals about every third day, if possible, for a full feed of his beloved thorn or other padding, in addition to his grain, and for sleep followed by rumination. Marching with troops day after day unremittingly does not suit him in the least. He cannot well be laden before daylight, and is often so troublesome in the process that the beasts first loaded up have often to stand for hours before the whole are in

II.   37

readiness for the march. The pace is also so slow and stoppages so frequent, that the next camping-ground is reached and the packs removed too late in the day to allow the animals out to graze.

Without fuel the boiler fails to make steam. " Empty sack no can stand up, sar," and the empty camel, all fuel exhausted, and making no further sign, staggers out of the line, and shutting up his legs like a huge lazy tongs, calmly sits down and never rises more !

The Sindian camel needs very warm clothing in the (to him) extremely trying climate of Afghanistan, as he is very liable to fall a victim to pneumonia from cold and exposure.

As showing, on the other hand, how camels can be used for military purposes, it may here be mentioned that the Brahuis readily contracted, early in 1879, with the Commissariat for bringing up stores of grain from Dadur to Quetta. Marching at their own times and seasons, and without any guarding, they did capital work with their camels, which, under their management, seemed to suffer very little, though many of them could be seen trudging along with loads of ten and even twelve maunds !

No authentic statement has as yet been published of the total losses of camels in the campaign, but, including the Kabul operations, these can hardly have reached a less figure than double the losses in the first Afghan war, which, as stated by Hough, amounted to no less than 33,000 !

Little also has hitherto been said as to the strain which the losses of baggage animals in the campaign occasioned, not only in Sind itself, the nursery of camels, but along our whole frontier, in meeting the demands of the war, or of the requisition for ponies reaching to every part of India, even to Madras. If, however, the general impressions on this subject are substantially authenticated, it may not unfairly be concluded that the feasibility, or otherwise, of a Russian advance in force against our north-west frontier may yet turn upon the question of baggage animals. Even with the assistance of a railway up to any advanced base of operations that may be named, animals in sufficient numbers must from that point at least be found, fed, and cared for; and how this is to be accomplished for a force of sufficient magnitude, and with all the *impedimenta* of a modern army, seems with our experience not by any means easy of solution. Six months' operations in a life-and-death struggle would in all probability totally exhaust all the animal carrying power on both sides.

The fort of Kelat-i-Ghilzai which, as before shown, fell into our hands without a shot being fired, covers about fourteen acres of ground, and crowns a rather long flat-topped hill situated three-quarters of a mile north-west of the Tarnack river, detached from the steppe immediately west.

It probably owes its origin and importance, firstly, to its good strategical position on the Ghuzni-Kandahar road; secondly, to its isolated and relatively commanding position; and, thirdly, to the existence of a spring of limpid water which gushes out from below a cap of conglomerate, forming the base of the artificial mound used as a cavalier on the top of the hill.

The summit of this last-mentioned mound has no parapet, and has room only for one gun. Its top is about fifty feet above the *terre-plein* on which (to the south-east) stands the magazine. The *terre-plein*, again, commands all the surrounding ground, excepting to the north-west (where the country rises), by about 150 feet.

A well-cast bronze 12-pounder gun (the only serviceable one in the fort, and even this had its carriage disabled) was found at our entry on the top of the cavalier pointing south-west, and looking well up into the "blue" in helpless fashion.

The ramparts which now crown the hill on all sides rise nearly perpendicularly from the crest to from eighteen to thirty

37 *

feet, and have an imposing appearance, especially as viewed from the irrigated plain of the Tarnack river.

In 1839–42 it would appear that there was only a breastwork protecting the crest of the hill north and south; but of late years, particularly during the struggle for power between Shere Ali and his brothers, great additions seem to have been made to the height of the walls, which are composed of well-kneaded and sun-dried mud, with round towers at intervals, all of the familiar eastern pattern.

The main gateway on the south face is the only one now in use, that on the north-west side having been built up, as also a sally-port south-east.

Notwithstanding its relatively commanding position, and its reputation for impregnability among the Afghans, the fort is in reality but a weak place, firstly, from the want of flanking defence; secondly, from the way in which portions of the walls have been undermined at most of the drainage outlets; and, lastly, from the fact that the works can be enfiladed from hills of nearly the same height on the south-west, &c. The Afghans appear of late years to have been somewhat aware of the real weakness of the place, as on nearly all the neighbouring hills, from south-west to north-west, have been constructed *sangas* (small circular redoubts for musketry defence thirty or forty feet in diameter), each with a roughly piled up stony parapet and connecting trenches in places, the whole evidently designed with the idea of keeping an enemy at a distance and converting the entire position into an entrenched camp.

All the buildings inside the fort, with the exception of the small bazaar (immediately within the main gate), were more or less in a ruinous condition—door and window frames gone, &c.; but what we could well have dispensed with was the filth, which, unfortunately, was only too conspicuous and real.

Imagination and description would alike fail to convey even a faint idea of the accumulated nastiness, which it became the first and most imperative duty on the part of the troops to remove, in preparing the place for even temporary occupation.

Day after day had strong working parties of Europeans and natives with the Sappers to slave away at this unsavoury work with the result of eventually providing fairly comfortable and clean quarters for the sick, the commissariat, regimental officers, &c., of the brigade intended to hold the place should an advance be made to Ghuznee.

On the 24th January an interesting ceremony took place in the decoration by General Stewart of the old Subadar-Major of the 12th B. N. I., who, when pay-havildar of the regiment in the first campaign,* had helped in defending the place against apparently overwhelming odds. He was a fine old soldier, and the conference of the Order of British India, First Class, with title of Sirdar Bahadoor, on the spot where so many years before he had so distinguished himself, raised the old man at once to probably the highest and most coveted position among his fellows.

The cold at night was still very severe (the thermometer going down to fifteen degrees), and to make it more trying, a howling wind usually swept over the camp from 5 to 8 or 10 A.M. daily. This high wind, which seems to be a characteristic of the whole Tarnack valley, probably had as much to do with our losses of camels by pneumonia as bad feeding in their then weakened condition.

Supplies, also, were a constant source of difficulty, and even caused some anxiety.

Resort had to be had daily to the investigation by commissariat officers of distant villages under strong cavalry escorts. The Ghilzais, while objecting apparently as a voluntary act to

---

* This defence was made under the command of Captain John Halkett Craigie, B.N.I., with some 40 gunners and 600 Sepoys against enormous numbers of Ghilzais. Kaye says that after the repulse 100 bodies were found at the foot of the works, and that some 500 were put *hors de combat*. The old subadar however, insisted that 140 of the enemy were killed.

bring such small supplies as they had for sale to camp, exhibited no particular reluctance, when fairly unearthed under a decent show of force, not only to sell what they had, but to bleed the kafirs to the utmost. On these occasions their assumed Jewish kinship came out strong when haggling about the price to be paid for the requisitioned supplies commenced.

When they seriously meant to conceal any stores, all sorts of dodges were resorted to ; but a little practice made our sowars experts in this kind of sport.

On one occasion, the escort were tenderly entreated not to enter a certain house, as a woman had just been delivered of a child. The inquisitive sowar, however, would (*o tempora o mores*) poke his nose into the room just to make certain that there was no *ruse*. Sure enough, there was the mother and child on a pile of felts in the middle of the floor ; but as the infant struck him as looking much more like one year than one hour old, the heartless fellow walked boldly in, when the lady, jumping up with a scream, disappeared. The rugs were on examination found to cover the top of a fine large grain-pit, which was soon appraised and paid for, the owner laughing immoderately at the near success of the trick. Not the least ill-will was shown when dodges of this kind were discovered. No deception is gross, cowardly, or unfair to an Afghan if only it succeeds ; but he can also keenly relish counterplot, apparently even when he is himself the sufferer.

Still, with every vigilance as well as encouragement held out to the mallicks to help in the matter of supplies, the difficulties rather increased than diminished ; and to make matters worse, the stores of tea, sugar, and rum, which by no possibility could be replaced locally, had fallen so low, that on the 26th January all Europeans had to make the best of one-third rations of these articles. Tobacco there was none, save some queer stuff (which the British soldier dubbed " bhoosie ") obtained from the Afghans. These deficiences were mainly due to the delay of a convoy, which, though leaving Quetta on the 9th, had not as yet arrived at Kandahar.

Reports having reached the General that 4,000 maunds of the grain revenue of the district had, prior to our arrival, been carried off and secreted in the Argandab valley, it was decided to send a reconnoitring party, consisting of two mountain guns, one squadron 15th Hussars, two squadrons 8th B.C., some Goorkhas and Sappers, partly to search for the grain, and partly to ascertain as much as possible about the topography of the valley, regarding which nothing very authentic appears to have been hitherto known.

Captain Rogers, R.E., G. T. S. of India, and Lieutenant Olivier, were specially charged with the latter duty, and subsequently brought in valuable materials. Generally speaking, the valley was found to be well cultivated throughout, especially in its side valleys, but with such narrow defiles in places as to be well-nigh impassable for laden animals. Willows, poplars, and fruit trees abounded, and the scenery was considered very fine.

Another small force, under Colonel Ryley, 8th B. C., was sent east, round by Morouf towards the Argeshan valley, to explore and return to Kandahar.

This force, consisting chiefly of Goorkhas, had a trying time of it. Caught in the snow, they were for three days encamped on a high ridge on quarter rations. On their marching four miles, fifteen camels are said to have died in the first mile from camp. In fact, most of the camels perished, and had it not been for some locally obtained bullocks, which stood the cold better, and for the indomitable pluck of the little Goorkhas, which shone out in its wonted fashion, the force could hardly have extricated itself.

Arrangements were likewise made for the careful planning and sectioning of the Kelat-i-Ghilzai fort, and for constructing a topographical map of all the surrounding features, to a distance of three miles from the fort all round. These duties were assigned to Lieutenants Childers, Jerome, and Foley, of the Royal Engineers, also to Captain Sartorius of the 59th Foot.

The Sappers throughout this time had their hands full in clearing out and levelling the *terre-plein* of the fort, controlling the drainage, and preparing the place generally for the occupation of the small force under Brigadier Hughes, who, after our departure, was to garrison the fort with a wing of the 59th Foot, wing of 19th B. C., the G-4 Battery R. A., and the 9th Company Sappers and Miners, also the Engineer Field Park.

It was as well that the latter were thus allowed to have rest, as the march had told heavily on most of the ponies.

As with regard to the fortifications of Kandahar, but little was attempted in the way of adding to the defensive features of Kelat-i-Ghilzai ; our tenure of it as a fortified post, and, indeed, the ultimate objects of the campaign, being at the time insufficiently defined.

Whatever views the Government of India may have originally had in pushing on the force to Kelat-i-Ghilzai, they were now altered, and orders were received to retire on Kandahar, leaving Brigadier Hughes with his brigade in the fort. No doubt the difficulties of maintaining General Stewart's force in the neighbourhood of Kelat-i Ghilzai would have proved very serious, while, on the other hand, to advance to Ghuznee would have been well-nigh impossible in the crippled condition of the transport animals. By lightening kits to the utmost, and requisitioning from the country-side donkeys, bullocks, and every kind of transport creature, the march might possibly have been made, but not without extreme hardship to all concerned.

In the light of subsequent events, the retirement on Kandahar can hardly be regarded as a misfortune, though to a force full of spirit, confident in its leader, and burning with anxiety to get first to Ghuznee, any retrograde movement could not fail to be galling. It was, moreover, felt that the dislike and suspicion first entertained for us by the Ghilzais were gradually giving way to more friendly feelings, owing to the confidence inspired by the bearing of our General, the strict discipline maintained, and the full, even handsome, payments made for all supplies, however obtained. As a tribe, the Ghilzais, especially the southern portion, so cordially detested Shere Ali and the Duranis, under whom they had always suffered, that they had, it is said, contemplated emigrating westward ; and it was held by some who knew them well, that if encouraged by us to look for support, a man of their choosing might not only have been created Ameer, but, as being, when united, by far the most powerful sept in Afghanistan, maintained as such against all comers. This dream of a united Afghanistan in friendly relations with the British Government, apparently vanished with our withdrawal to Kandahar, and still more so with the recognition of Yakoob Khan as Ameer. But Abdur Rahman's recent victory over Ayoob, obtained in great measure by the aid of the southern Ghilzais, may yet contribute to the same result.

On the 2nd February the head-quarters left Kelat-i-Ghilzai, and reached Kandahar on the 11th idem, after a somewhat disagreeable march.

Cold strong winds prevailed all the 2nd February. In the night of the 4th, such heavy rain fell, as to convert the ground into deep mud, rendering it impossible to move the tents. The baggage-animals suffered, of course, greatly, and altogether we had a fair specimen of what a campaign during a hard winter in these regions might have been. No less than 100 camels were reported to have died in camp after this march.

On the march from Shahed Mahomed to Tir-Andaz Minar, nearly eight miles, on the 6th, 100 more camels were found to be dead or missing, and an order had to issue for the 15th Hussars to perform the following day's march on foot, the horses carrying the men's kits.

It also transpired that the last Quetta convoy, which had at length arrived, had only brought up half the number of ground-sheets needed, and new boots of sizes fit only for bugler-boys! Supplies for the natives had, moreover, run so short, that there were no rations for the camp-followers. Matters on the whole, in fact, did not wear a very cheerful aspect.

The following day a quantity of old or unnecessary stores had to be abandoned, and were eagerly appropriated by the natives of the neighbouring villages, who, vulture-like, pounced on the prey the moment the camp was cleared. From this time forward, the force moved in detachments, while head-quarters pushed on for Kandahar.

At the latter place, instead of pitching camp as before, north-east of the city, the General and Staff took possession of a garden formerly occupied by the widows of the late Ameen Mahomed, brother of Shere Ali, who had killed his son Fyz Mahomed in the battle of Kuzbaz. It appeared that the ladies had thrown in their fortune and fled with Mir Afzal immediately prior to our occupation of the 8th January.

The house, very nicely designed for both a summer and winter residence, was, perhaps, the best in the neighbourhood of Kandahar, and when the floors were covered with Persian carpets or Kandahar felts, &c., was by no means to be despised. The garden, laid out formally in squares, filled with apricot, cherries, pomegranate, and other fruit trees, and well supplied with water by one of the numerous channels drawn from the Argandab river, promised in early spring to become "a thing of beauty and a joy for ever."

With the number of fanatics known to be in the city, only about a mile distant, this garden retreat had the no small recommendation of a surrounding wall, some fifteen feet in height, which, though not a perfect protection, would at least stop an ugly rush of Ghazies.

Precautions against these gentry were by no means uncalled for, as exemplified by the occurrences in Brigadier-General

Nutall's camp, immediately prior to our return, when five fanatics, apparently sitting quite unnoticed as unconcerned spectators in the bazaar outside the camp, suddenly sprang to their feet, and dashing through the lines of the 59th Regiment, and even the quarter-guard tent, succeeded in cutting down several men, both natives and Europeans, before they were themselves despatched. Most unfortunately, in the confusion two of the 59th were shot by their own people. Of three men in the hospital on our arrival, who had been the victims of this attack, one had his nose nearly cut off, and another two fingers of both hands severed by cuts received in trying to save his head, in which, however, he was not successful, as he had also two severe scalp-wounds. The third had also four wounds, two of them on the scalp.

The Ghazi's sole object being to kill as many as he can before meeting his own certain death, he avoids, as a rule, attacking armed or prepared men, and in this case one of the men killed was stooping down cleaning his horse, with his back turned, while another was apparently taken equally unawares.

As it is sometimes stated that burning the remains of Ghazis after death has a deterrent effect, depriving, as it is supposed, the individual of the posthumous honour of saintship, it may be as well to mention that in the case alluded to, although cremation was resorted to in disposing of the remains of these Ghazis after they were cut down, no such result followed.

For precaution, General Nutall, having moved his camp a mile further from the city in a westerly direction, the friends of the burnt Ghazis collected the few charred remains,* skulls, &c., found in the deserted camp, and over these at once commenced the erection of a mound of roughly-piled stone, with a view, no doubt, to its future development into a *ziarat* (a saint or martyr shrine). Although this pile of stones on being dis-

---

* If the bodies had been placed in a mass of quicklime and the lime slaked, no trace of the bones would, it is believed, have remained

covered was so scattered, and the few bones found again burned by our people, and the dust thrown away, the friends, undeterred, renewed their attempts, whenever opportunity subsequently offered, to rebuild the demarcating mound.

Even at the distance of the new camp, the greatest vigilance night and day was found to be essential. Sentries at very close intervals were posted all round, notwithstanding which, however, every night as dark set in, shots were fired from some vantage point in the neighbourhood.

Altogether, the position was not a comfortable one, as indicating the temper of the fanatical classes, and the duties thus imposed on the troops were very harassing.

Nevertheless, with the proverbial carelessness of Englishmen, it was hard to make officers or men in visiting the city (as they did constantly) adopt the precautions ordered by the General.

The Engineers were fortunate enough to secure for their headquarters Rahmdil Khan's garden, not far from the General's. A large two-storeyed house, with the usual *tykhana* (or underground room for retreat in summer) occupied the centre, but though devoid of all glass windows, doors, &c., and dirty beyond conception, promised with a little trouble to turn into a capital mess-house, and quarters for some eight officers.

In front of the house was a formal oblong sheet of water, and the garden, surrounded by a high mud-wall (much out of repair) was filled with vine " stocks " of several varieties of grape, trained in the usual Afghan fashion. There being no spare wood in the country, the vines by this plan are planted in trenches four or five feet in depth, and the branches trained over the intervening earthen mounds. With the advance of spring, the garden promised to become a "sight for the gods."

Two companies of Sappers, with the Engineers' tents and a selection of the Engineer park, occupied the available ground close round the house, which soon acquired the designation of " Brompton Barrack."

Some other walled gardens further south were similarly available for occupation, but it was not deemed prudent to scatter the force* in this direction; and even as it was, the engineer quarter was rather more isolated than was held to be quite desirable.

Shots were occasionally fired at night by prowlers, possibly more from braggadocio than with any serious object, but no Ghazi got into the Engineers' sanctum.

While the General had been absent at Kelat-i-Ghilzai, Captain Bisset, R.E., had not only carried out generally the programme sketched for his guidance in reference to the Arc, but had effected many beneficial changes in a wonderfully short time.

In the first place, the whole of the interior had been cleansed, and all breaches and glaringly weak places in the surrounding ramparts had been dealt with as far as circumstances admitted.

In the next place, two new court-yards and the attached buildings had been added as hospitals to the central one originally selected. Altogether, the arrangements for the sick were admirable, and would have left little to be desired had

---

* The total force reassembled at Kandahar at this time, *i.e.* after the return of General Biddulph from Girishk was as follows, according to the returns of the 10th February 1879:—

	Europeans.			Natives—All Ranks.	Total European and Native Troops.	Followers.		Guns.			Draught Animals.				Baggage Animals.		
	Officers.	N.C.O. and Men.	Total.			Public.	Private.	40-pounders.	9-pounders.	7-pounders.	Horses.	Mules.	Bullocks.	Elephants.	Mules and Ponies.	Camels.	Bullocks.
Lieut.-Gen. Stewart	244	2835	3079	5187	8266	5737	1551	8	36	14	2507	175	1043	15	1179	3525	83
Major-Gen. Biddulph	93	703	796	2188	2984	1167	887	...	6	6	887	180	47	...	540	1661	25
Total	337	3538	3875	7375	11250	6904	2138	8	42	20	3394	355	1090	15	1719	5186	108

N.B.—The numbers of troops given include sick and wounded, which were at this date about 6 per cent The force was provided with 1,290 tents.

the Arc itself borne a better reputation as a healthy residence during the summer months.

The Commissariat found in the old arsenal sufficiently convenient arrangements for their immediate requirements, though a separate camel-camp had to be established outside the city to the north-west.

Good quarters had been prepared for Nawab Gholam Hussain and Major St. John, R.E., the Chief Political Officer, for the garrison staff, &c. &c. ; in fact, all that it was possible to do had been done, though it is needless to say that the radical imperfections of the place as a defensible post, in the European meaning of the term, remained, for the reasons before stated, unremedied.

In General Primrose's subsequent defence of the place, as was the case previously in General Nott's time, it was deemed essential as a preliminary measure for the defence of the Arc, to clear bodily all suspected classes out of the city, and occupy the whole with the outer ramparts, down to the Shikarpore gate, and this course would in all probability have to be invariably followed if the citadel were threatened.

It having at this time been decided that the objects of the campaign had been sufficiently attained, arrangements were commenced for the return of a considerable portion of the force to India. While some were to return by the Bolan pass, a force under General Biddulph (with Major Sandeman as Political Officer), consisting of the 15th Hussars, Goorkhas, and a mountain battery, were to explore the Tul-Chotiali route to Dehra Ghazi Khan, leaving a small garrison under Brigadier-General Nutall at Burklam in the Ketram country, where there had been a small force of Madras troops for some time, under Colonel Prendergast of Bengal Cavalry.

The Government of India also at this time directed Colonel Sankey to proceed to Madras, to take up the appointment of Secretary and Chief Engineer, Public Works Department, which had previously been offered him by His Grace the Duke of Buckingham.

All that remained for him, in the way of duty connected with the force, was to arrange with a committee appointed by the General for the proper shelter of the force which was to remain behind at Kandahar during the approaching hot weather.

The following table shows the numbers all round as forming the force for which shelter had to be provided, with the available tents :—

| Description. | Officers. | Europeans. | Natives. | Followers. | | Horses. | Tents. | | |
				Public.	Private.		Hill.	Paul.	Pole.
Artillery—									
A/B	7	125		285	46	200	6	18	1
D/2	7	144		164	27	119		17	
9/4	6	137	148	130	40	136	5	18	1
5/11	6	76		232	24	85	3	15	14
6/11	5	107							
11/11. . . .	6								
European Infantry—									
59th Foot . .	21	662		349	54			45	30
60th Rifles . .	23	666		376	75			35	39
Native Troops—									
Sappers and Miners—									
4th Company . .	2	11	110	108	16		2	12	9
10th ,, . .	2	5	82	135	22		4	8	9
Infantry—									
3rd Goorkhas . .	9			577	344	47		71	
15th Sikhs . .	7			593	395	31		65	
25th ,, . .	9			506	238	28		60	15
29th Belloochees (Bombay)	8			599	40	45	6	20	

Though incomplete in some respects, the return will sufficiently answer its purpose. Excepting a very few officers of the head-quarter staff, and the sick, all were at this time living in tents, which, though bearable enough in the cold weather, promised in the summer heats to become anything but pleasant.

For the most part the soldiers, European as well as native, lived in single fly "pâl" tents, those of the native cavalry (probably not weighing more than twenty pounds each) being only large enough to accommodate two troopers each.*

It must therefore be clear that while possibly answering well enough for sleeping purposes, men would have a fair chance of being roasted alive when the thermometer mounted in the day to 110° or even higher, as was expected.

By great good fortune the Afghans, though neglecting, had occupied, and thus in a great measure preserved, nearly all the blocks of barracks situated about a mile north-west of the city, which had been constructed for, but which, it is believed, had been but little used by, the force under General Nott in the first campaign. These consisted of a series of domed cells† fourteen to sixteen feet square, generally communicating with each other, surrounding court-yards in such a manner as to make each block compact, and, with a little flanking defence thrown out, easily defensible, the mud walls being from three to four feet thick, and impervious to field artillery.

---

* The arrangement of having one small tent with one baggage pony and a syce between every two sowars, has always been the unit of equipment for frontier service with the Punjaub Cavalry, and appears to answer well for the special duties on which they are engaged.

† Throughout Southern Afghanistan, from the absence of timber, domestic architecture consists of digging out the spaces intended for rooms to three or four feet below the ground level, and using the mud for walls and roof. For the latter 8-inch square tiles are made on the spot; and in bright weather, so suitable is the clay, that they are, with ordinary sun-drying, nearly as good as burnt tiles in about four or five days. Commencing from all four angles of the walls of the several rooms, the doming is gradually pushed on and up, the tiles being cemented together with ordinary mud, and, though radially placed, are so thrown back as to prevent chance of slipping till dry, when the whole becomes so hard and compact as to be practically indestructible, and impervious to moisture. No centering is used in construction. Every villager seems to understand thoroughly this system of construction, which is a perfect adaption of very simple means to the required end. Domes of ice-houses near Kandahar, some fifty feet in diameter, consisting of sun-dried tiles, have thus been constructed; and though some are dilapidated, enough remains to show the applicability of the system to large structures. Between the thickness of the mud walls and the sunk floor, coolness in summer and warmth in winter are alike secured.

The following is a summary of the arrangements decided on by the committee, and which, prior to Colonel Sankey's departure, received the assent of General Stewart.

The easternmost of the quadrangles forming the old cantonment buildings (with thirty-four rooms) was to be prepared for the Brigadier-General commanding and his staff, and for four surgeons.

An adjoining block was to be similarly adapted for a hospital for 100 sick, and to have day rooms built for forty more who would sleep in tents.

The two large blocks, each measuring over all 400 feet by 375 feet, were to be prepared for the reception severally of a regiment of British infantry and two batteries of artillery, the domed rooms being used for messing, &c. during the day, while the tents were to be pitched in the court-yards for sleeping in at night. Other minor blocks were to be adapted severally for officers of the Head-quarter Staff, the officers of the two native infantry regiments, main guard, &c.

A new block was to be constructed with domed rooms for the troop of horse artillery and officers of the two native cavalry regiments.

Domed shelter was also to be provided for the officers of the native infantry regiments, and for regimental hospitals, in case the plan of having all but light cases in base hospital within the arc was adopted.

To form the whole into a compact and sufficiently defensible position, with regular spaces apportioned for picquetting the artillery horses close to the barracks, and placing the followers immediately in rear, the cavalry covering the front, and a sufficient open space in the centre of the great camp as a parade and recreation ground, it was decided to acquire three small villages (Mahomed Hoossain, Jemadar Belooch, and Shukkurla Toki) situated to the north-west, and close to picquet hill.

For the native infantry and cavalry the "pâl" tents were to

be utilized in the following way. Dwarf mud walls were to be run up on the two sides and one end (two and a half or three feet high), and the poles lengthened so as to raise the flies by this amount, and long reed grass suspended over the tent ridge so as to rest on either side of the fly, and thus mitigate the effect of the sun's direct rays.

To the above were to be added all needful roads with drainage and water-supply works. The work thus cut out for the Engineers formed what may fairly be called a "large order"; but judging from the reports subsequently made on completion of the work, they and the two companies of Sappers acquitted themselves nobly of their task, the main work of which devolved on Major A. Le Messurier, Captains Bissett and Call.

Fortunately, from the first, local labour was abundant, and as all arrangements had been specially made with strict reference to this, and such materials as were procurable on the spot, no hitch, it is believed, occurred. Large numbers of the poorer classes from the city at once came on the works, and it was only necessary to take the needful precautions against fanatics secreting themselves among these people, and running *amok*.

On the 26th February, wishing good-bye to friends, Colonel Sankey with Lieutenant Childers started for Sukkur, which was reached in twenty days from Kandahar. From rain and sleet, marching was impossible on the 27th, and they found the Kojak almost blocked with snow; had it not, in fact, been for the new road opened by Lieutenant Wells, they would certainly have been detained some days.

The route followed from Takt-i-pul by the Ghlo Kotul (where earthen graves marked the resting place of the Afghan sowars who fell in the combat of the 4th January), Gutai, Chaman, Killa-Abdoola, Saigi, and over the Gazaband pass to Maitarzai and Quetta, proved short and easy at this time of the year.

At Quetta, very heavy rain having fallen, the whole valley was converted into a quagmire, and serious detention was threatened,

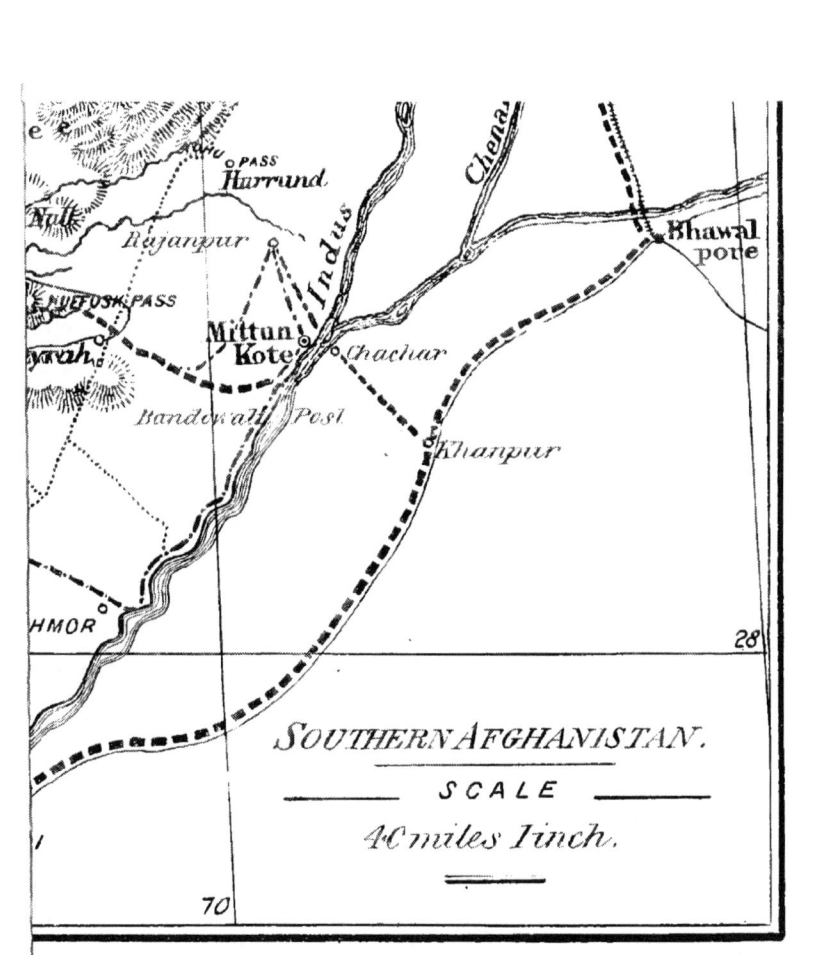

SOUTHERN AFGHANISTAN.

SCALE

40 miles 1 inch.

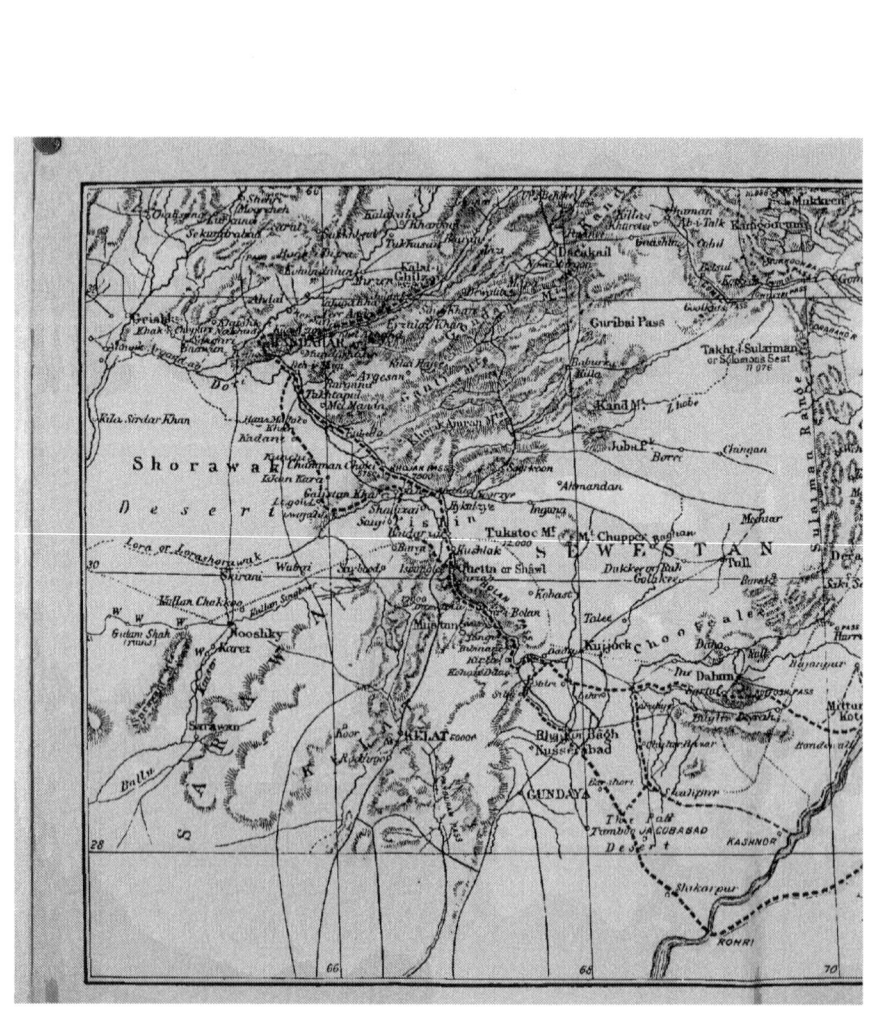

as, in addition to all other drawbacks, no camels were apparently procurable. Fortunately, however, the latter difficulty was overcome by their using some camels most obligingly lent them by Major St. John.

With the rise in temperature, the carcases of the camels which had died along the route in the winter, and which in many cases had been left unburied, became most offensive, and added not a little to the incentive to cut the journey as short as possible.

The Bolan pass on this homeward march presented a totally different aspect to its appearance during the advance. Then it was wholly deserted by all but a few kafila-men; now it was thronged almost from end to end with the Brahuis, their families and flocks, returning in a vast multitude from their winter residence (the Katchi plain) to the upper country.

The old paterfamilias of Jewish appearance, with long snaky black beard and unkempt locks, was to be seen trudging along, a huge bundle of dirty clothes, with silver-mounted matchlock on back, shield, and no end of queer little bags, and a sword, hung to him in various ways, or girt round his waist, and leading a huge bony camel, on which was crowded all his household gods.

Solemnly the camel tramps along, head erect, and bedizened all over with twisted crimson ropes, covered with tassels, cowrie-shells, and bells, which latter herald his advance with a slow measured cadence. On his back is an erection, the substratum of which consists of the family felts, tents, and carpets of every colour. Fowls, cooking-pots, with all sorts of house-hold property, are hitched on above in all directions, inter-spersed with more crimson tassels, bells, &c. On the top is placed the family *charpai*, in the centre of which sits *madame la mère*, a very Meg Merriles, with elf locks streaming from under unclean head-gear, and who, while keeping her own balance on the apex of the top-heavy swaying mass, endeavours

38 *

to preserve her family of three or four unruly urchins from rolling off and sudden death. Packed aloft with the babies are also any number of lambs, kids, &c., too young to tramp it, and fowls again.

Following this foreground group might be seen mares and their foals, young camels, sheep, goats, and other belongings of the family, with, perhaps, the rear brought up by a flock of four or five hundred lambs, in charge of a couple of wild-looking youngsters.

Taken with the mass of bare rock strewn about and the savage precipices of the upper defile, these groups, repeating themselves in endless variety, produced a series of pictures which, if faithfully delineated, would have made the fortune of any artist.

At Mach, General Phayre and the Bombay Sappers were met with, they having cleared an excellent road, almost fit for wheeled traffic in civilised countries, for a distance of forty miles from the entrance of the pass, and through the Katchi plain by Bagh and Barshori to Jacobabad.

This was a most agreeable surprise after the rough work experienced over the same ground during the advance. From this time it was all plain sailing.

We found carefully-selected camps with double pole tents, and every arrangement for comfort, at each stage. Grain was being forwarded through the pass by contract with camel owners, as before mentioned, and the animals, though often carrying double the load imposed as an average by the troops on the march, seemed well and hearty.

Beyond Dadur, and through the Katchi plain, an admirable baggage train of ponies had been organized, men and animals looking exceedingly fit. A train of carts, which promised the best results, was also being organized. To crown all, instead of having to make three or four daily marches between Jacobabad and Sukkur, we were whisked over the forty-five miles in a tonga in some six or eight hours.

The change wrought since November had, in fact, been little short of marvellous, and few who, like Colonel Sankey and his companion, had made the advance in November, could withhold their tribute of praise to General Phayre and all who worked with him.

At Jacobabad, and the hospitable Sind Horse Mess particularly, they found themselves again in civilisation, with the feeling of having formed some friendships under the best and most lasting guarantees for their permanency—a campaign.

Colonel Sankey, at the close of the campaign, thus expressed himself with reference to the officers who had served under his orders :—

"To Major Le Messurier, Lieutenants Call and Childers, and others who worked with me, I owe more than I can well express."

Colonel Sankey was appointed a Companion of the Bath, Major Le Messurier, who was his brigade-major, obtained his brevet as Lieutenant-Colonel; Captain Call also received his brevet of Major in the same Gazette.

While the foregoing account of the military services of the Engineers and Sappers was passing through the press, the rebellion of Arabi Pasha against the authority of the Khedive took place.

This was followed by the bombardment of Alexandria by the British fleet, under Sir Beauchamp Seymour, and the Egyptian expedition, under the command of Sir Garnet Wolseley, which has so happily ended in the assault of the lines of Tel-el-Kebir, and the forced marches to Zag-a-Zig and Cairo.

It was arranged that a Contingent from India, under the command of Sir Herbert Macpherson, should be sent to assist in the operations.

Two companies of the Queen's Own Sappers were directed to form part of this force.

In July 1882, in anticipation of the final orders for the despatch of the Contingent, the Indian Government was instructed to send the Seaforth Highlanders to Aden, and the I Company of the Queen's Own went with them.

The Highlanders and the Sappers arrived at Suez on the 8th August, and the Sappers were the first of the Native troops to land in Egypt. The A Company of the Sappers landed on the 23rd, fifteen days later.

Major A. F. Hamilton of the late Madras Engineers, was in command of the whole detachment, while the company officers were:—A Company—Lieutenants Darling, Andrews-Speed, and Baldwin; I Company—Lieutenants Lindley and Goodwyn, all of the Royal Engineers.

Each company consisted of—

> 2 European N.C.O.,
> 2 Native officers,
> 4 Havildars,
> 8 Naiques,
> 2 Buglers,
> 105 Sappers,

besides a Medical officer, a hospital assistant and followers; making a grand total, including officers, of 252 fighting men.

The 1 Company was at first stationed in the buildings at the lock on the freshwater canal, and formed the out-post on the right front, the road to Chalouf running past the buildings.

These buildings were put into a state of defence, and then the châlet, which was looked upon as the keep in case of attack, was made more secure by shelter-trenches, &c. This being complete, the Victoria Hospital, in which the Highlanders were accommodated, was intrenched.

On 16th August, while Lieutenant Goodwyn was surveying along the freshwater canal with some Sappers, he was attacked by a party of the enemy.

On the 20th, a section of the I Company accompanied the

Seaforth Highlanders in the advance on Chalouf, ten miles from Suez, which was shelled from the canal side by two gun-boats.

On the two following days the whole company moved to Chalouf to stop a breach made the day before by the retreating enemy in the bank of the freshwater canal.

The A Company arrived next day, and was moved up to Ismailia on 30th August.

Meantime, Lieutenant Lindley, and half of the I Company had been marching up the railway through Geneffe and Serapeum, repairing the railway and telegraph lines ; the remainder of the company being left at Chalouf.

Lieutenant Darling and part of the A Company accompanied the C. R. E. (Lieutenant-Colonel J. Browne, R.B.E.), in the trial trip of an improvised train from Suez to Ismailia.

The detachment, which was further strengthened by the arrival on 4th September of a telegraph section, was employed at Ismailia, up to the 9th September, in making a landing-stage for the Indian commissariat, and in the construction of a line of railway from the end of the freshwater canal to the railway station.

The whole of the Sappers marched on the 10th September for Tel-el-Mahuta, and next day for Kassassin.

At the latter place water-troughs were set up for the cattle of the division, a tube well was sunk, and arrangements made for watering the engines on the line.

On the 13th, the detachment marched with Sir Herbert Macpherson's division, one section being in advance, and took part in the battle of Tel-el-Kebir.

After the fight was over, the Sappers accompanied Macpherson's division in the forced march to Zag-a-Zig, which place they reached about 6 P.M., having covered about twenty-eight miles since 3 A.M.

A small party of Sappers was left behind at Tel-el-Kebir, to remove a parapet which had been erected across the railway.

On the 14th, the Sappers removed some wrecked carriages on the Benha line, and next day a bridge on the line towards Tel-el-Kebir was repaired.

On the 23rd, the whole detachment proceeded to Cairo.

So short a time has elapsed since these events took place, that it has not been possible to get a complete account of the services of the Sappers in this campaign, but this brief and bald statement of their doings will doubtless prove of some little interest.

On 5th October, the Commanding R. E. (Brigadier-General Nugent, C.B., R.E.), published the following brigade order regarding the services of the Royal Engineers and Queen's Own Sappers :—

"Cairo, 5th October 1882.

"As the British force in Egypt is about to be broken up, the Brigadier-General Commanding Royal Engineers avails himself of this opportunity to convey to the Royal Engineers and to the Queen's Own Madras Sappers under his command, his thorough satisfaction with the excellent manner in which all officers and men have done their duty. The campaign, though very short, has been far more than ordinarily trying and laborious. Nevertheless, the admirable spirit which has pervaded all ranks has enabled them to overcome every difficulty. Throughout this campaign the Corps has done good work, and has in all its branches added to its well-established reputation.

"The Brigadier-General Commanding tenders to the Corps his hearty congratulations, and thanks them for the ungrudging spirit in which they have responded to every call upon them.

"By order,

"T. FRASER, Major,

"Brigade-Major R. E. Egypt."

The Queen's Own were present at the grand review of the British troops by Sir Garnet Wolseley, at Cairo, on 30th September, when 18,000 troops, including 4,000 cavalry and artillery, with sixty guns, marched past the saluting-post.

The brigade under General Macpherson was the last, and marched past in the following order:—Mountain battery, Seaforth Highlanders, Queen's Own Sappers, 7th B. N. I., 20th P. I., and the Beloochees.

The Indian cavalry followed the British cavalry, and consisted of 2nd Bengal Cavalry, 6th Bengal Cavalry, and 13th Bengal Lancers.

The march past commenced at half-past 1, and did not conclude till 6 P.M., when it was getting dark.

On 28th October the returning troops of the Indian Contingent were publicly entertained at Bombay in brilliant style, when the whole of the city was *en fête*.

The force present, consisting of 200 European and 1,480 native troops, comprised detachments from the Seaforth Highlanders, 2nd and 6th Bengal Cavalry, 13th Bengal Lancers, and 7th B. N. I. The Queen's Own Sappers were unavoidably absent from the entertainment.

General Carnegie (commanding at Bombay), in his speech the same evening, thus referred to their absence :—

" It is a matter of great regret that some portion of the 7th Battery 1st Brigade R. A., and the Madras Sappers (Queen's Own), have no representatives here to-day, for we should have liked to have shown them how fully we appreciate the good work done by them during the late campaign. (Cheers.) But the requirements of the service prevented their detention in Bombay sufficiently long to partake in these entertainments."

On 8th November the representatives of that portion of our Indian army which was engaged in Egypt arrived at Portsmouth in the transport *Lusitania*.

They consisted of thirteen native officers, seven N.C.O., and twelve privates.

These comprised a native officer and N.C.O. of the Queen's Own Madras Sappers, and two native officers, one N.C.O., and two privates of each of the following regiments:—2nd, 6th, and 13th Bengal Cavalry, 7th B. N. I., 20th P. I., and Beloochees. Subadar Jeyram was the representative officer of the Queen's Own Sappers, and Naique Sheik Ismail, the N.C.O.

Shortly after landing at Portsmouth they left for Wimbledon, under the charge of General Sir H. Daly and Colonel Pennington. On arrival there they were taken to Sutherland House, Wimbledon Common, where they were to live during their stay in England.

The whole detachment was present at a grand review held by the Queen in St. James's Park on 18th November, when Her Majesty inspected about 8,000 of the British troops who had served in Egypt. After the review the officers and men of the Indian Contingent, under the command of Lieutenant-Colonel Pennington, 13th Bengal Lancers, went to Buckingham Palace, when Her Majesty inspected them in the East Corridor, Lieutenant General Sir H. Daly presenting and naming each individual to Her Majesty.

All the members of the Royal Family were present on the occasion.

Afterwards the officers, &c. of the Indian Contingent had the honour also of being received by the Prince and Princess of Wales at Marlborough House. Major-Generals Sir Charles Brownlow and Sir Herbert Macpherson were present.

After the review on the 18th, the following General Order was specially issued by H.R.H. the Field-Marshal Commanding-in-Chief:—

"His Royal Highness the Field-Marshal Commanding-in-Chief has received the Queen's commands to convey to General Sir Garnet J. Wolseley, G.C.B., G.C.M.G., and the officers, non-commissioned officers, and men of all the branches of the Expeditionary Force, Her Majesty's admiration of their conduct during the recent campaign, in which she has great satisfaction in feeling that her son, Major-General His Royal Highness the Duke of Connaught and Strathearn, took an active part.

"The gallantry displayed by the well-organized Contingent of her Indian Army, and by the Royal Malta Fencible Artillery, as well as by her Sailors and Marines, has not failed to attract Her Majesty's attention.

"The troops of all ranks, in the face of obstacles of no ordinary character, have shown a marked devotion to duty. For a time without shelter in the desert, under a burning sun, in a climate proverbially adverse to Europeans, their courage and discipline were nobly maintained throughout; and to this, under brave and experienced leaders, may be attributed the success which has distinguished this campaign.

"The defeat of the enemy in every engagement, including the brilliant cavalry charge of Kassassin, culminated in the action of Tel-el-Kebir, in which, after an arduous night march, his position was carried at the point of the bayonet, his guns were captured, and his whole army, notwithstanding its great numerical superiority, was completely dispersed.

"It is, therefore, with the highest gratification that His Royal Highness conveys Her Majesty's welcome to the troops whom it was her pleasure to review on the 18th inst.; and His Royal Highness, at the same time, has to express Her Majesty's thanks to the entire force, for the brave and exemplary conduct displayed by all, individually and collectively, during the campaign."

On 21st November the Queen distributed, at Windsor Castle, the medals for the Egyptian campaign to eight generals, twenty-four colonels and lieutenant-colonels belonging to the Staff, and 232 officers and men representing every branch and corps of the expeditionary force.

The town of Windsor was decorated for the occasion, and was filled with large and enthusiastic crowds of people.

The Prince and Princess of Wales, Duke and Duchess of Edinburgh, and all the other members of the Royal Family, were present.

Her Majesty made her appearance at half-past 12.

Outside the Queen's entrance a dais had been erected, carpeted with crimson cloth, and covered with Tippoo Sultan's tent.

On Her Majesty coming forward, she addressed the assembled officers and men as follows :—

"I have summoned you here to-day to confer upon you the well-earned medals commemorative of the short and brilliant, although arduous, campaign, in which all have done their duty with courageous and undaunted devotion. Tell your comrades that I thank them heartily for the gallant services they have rendered to their Queen and country, and that I am proud of my soldiers and sailors, who have added fresh glories to the victories won by their predecessors."

The distribution of medals then took place.

The ceremony terminated at half-past 1, when the band played "God save the Queen," the guard of honour and the whole of the officers and soldiers saluting.

Her Majesty and suite then retired.

The N.C.O. and men were re-formed, marched to the Riding School, and entertained. The Indian Contingent were enter-tained within the Castle, while lunch was provided for the whole of the British officers in the Waterloo Chamber.

The Medal has the Queen's head on one side and the Sphynx on the other, while the ribbon is garter blue with two stripes of white running down its length.

Colonel James Browne, C.S.I., R.B.E., who was Command-ing Engineer of the Indian Contingent, was appointed C.B., and obtained the Third Class of the Order of the Osmanieh.

Major A. F. Hamilton, R.M.E., who commanded the Queen's Own Sappers, obtained the rank of Lieutenant-Colonel by brevet; while Lieutenant C. H. Darling, R.E., commanding A Company, obtained the Fifth Class of the Medjidie, and Subadar Jeyram received a similar decoration, as well as the Second Class of the Order of British India.

Dr. Colvin Smith, Madras Medical Service, was the P. M. O. of the Contingent. He was appointed C.B., and obtained the Third Class of the Osmanieh. Thirty years ago he served with the Sappers at Prome.

Concluding Remarks.

The military history of the Corps has now been brought down to the present time, and it may with justice be said that the services performed by the Corps have been of no ordinary character.

Much arduous service and many gallant deeds have been done by the officers and men of the Madras Engineers and Sappers. The work so well done by them has all been effected in far distant countries, and has not, owing to this, received the attention which it merits; but it has, nevertheless, been excellent, and fully entitles the Corps to be placed in a high rank in our military records. Their military exploits have not, however, been the only work which they have achieved. They have distinguished themselves, perhaps, even more in their civil capacity.

Before closing this record, it will not be out of place to notice the names of a few of a Corps which, during times of peace, has greatly contributed to add to the material prosperity of our possessions in India.

There is ample material for a most interesting account of the public works of Southern India; and as the irrigation works of India are the most extensive and magnificent of their kind in the whole world, it is to be hoped that one of our many experienced officers now on the retired list, with ample leisure, will undertake to write an account of what the Corps has been enabled to do in that direction.

The services of Colin Mackenzie as a geographer, together with his researches into the history, religion, and antiquities of the country, have already been mentioned. De Havilland constructed the sea-wall at Madras, a work of no ordinary difficulty; he built churches of no mean architectural beauty; and he further, in the beginning of the century, made (for that period) a daring proposal to bridge the Cauvery by five brick arches, with very flat curves.

Again, there was J. T. Smith, whose mechanical ability was very great, and who reorganised the huits of Madras and Calcutta. Charles Orr was another man of mark, whose energy and ability led to the successful completion of the Kistna anicut, a work twenty feet in height and three-quarters of a mile long across the sandy bed of a river, draining nearly 100,000 square miles. Then there was J. C. Anderson, who distinguished himself early in the service in the north of India, was afterwards engaged in completing the works of the Kistna delta, and was the first Chief Engineer for Irrigation appointed in Madras. He afterwards became Inspector-General for Irrigation for the whole of India, but unfortunately died at the early age of 46. Ryves, again, was an equally able officer, who was engaged in similar work in the Godavery. He, likewise, died at an early age, having hardly reached his 40th year. Notwithstanding his comparative youth, he attained great distinction. He conceived the bold design of turning the waters of the Perryaur from Travancore over the watershed into the Madura district, by a huge dam across the river and a channel through the hills. For various reasons, there has been great hesitation over this work, but it may yet be carried to success. Haig, also, may be mentioned, as having constructed, in his early days, an aqueduct over a branch of the Godavery, about half a mile in length, in the brief space of three months, and who was afterwards engaged in the works devised to open up the navigation of the Godavery.

But, above all, there is Arthur Cotton, a man of high order of genius, who had the skill to conceive and the boldness to execute works from which ordinary minds shrank : witness the dam across the Godavery river at Dowlaishwaram. The bed of the river is at that point (inclusive of islands) four miles wide, and the aggregate length of the dams is fully two miles and a half.

His work on the Cauvery may, perhaps, in some respects be considered even a greater monument to his ability and genius. Here he dammed one large river and used another as a distributory channel, compensating the lands previously watered from the former river by other works. The design adopted was unlike anything previously constructed in either Europe or India, and shows a boldness which exhibits in the clearest light the great ability of the engineer.

But he was much more than a mere engineer, he may with justice be designated a great benefactor to India generally; for though his works were confined to the south of India, it was his energy and force of character which awoke the minds, not only of the Government, but of England generally, to the enormous advantages which irrigation works confer both on rulers and those ruled.

There are many others of the Corps who have also done excellent service for the State; but enough has been said to indicate that "old John Company" was far from unfortunate in the men they sent to the East from their Military College at Addiscombe, as well as previous to the establishment of that institution in 1809.

APPENDIX I.

Commandants of the Corps of Madras Pioneers and Madras Sappers and Miners (now Queen's Own) from 1792 to 1882.

Corps of Pioneers.

1792–1798, Lieutenant W. Dowse, M.I.
1799–1801, Captain W. Dowse, M.I.
1802, Lieutenant W. P. Heitland, M.I.

Battalions of Pioneers.

1st Battalion.

1803–1804, Captain W. P. Heitland, M.I.
1805–1808,   ,,   G. B. Bagshaw, M.I.
1809–1812,   ,,   R. Hughes, M.I.
1813, Captain E. W. Snow, M.I.
1814–1815, Captain A. N. Bertram, M.I.
1816–1819,   ,,   R McCraith, M.I.
1820–1824,   ,,   W. Milne, M.I.
1825, Lieutenant Wheeler, M.I.
1825, Captain Crowe, M.I.
1826,   ,,   Crowe, M I.
1826,   ,,   Wheeler, M.I.
1826,   ,,   Sinclair, M.I.
1827 to 30th June 1831, Captain William Murray, M.I.

2nd Battalion.

1803–1809, Captain J. Fitzpatrick, M.I.
1810–1819,   ,,   T. Smithwaite, M.I.
1820–1824,   ,,   E. Richardson, M.I.
1825–1826,   ,,   E. Cadogan, M.I.
1827 to 30th June 1831, Major E. Cadogan, M.I.

Corps of Pioneers.

1831, Major E. Cadogan, M.I.
1832–1833, Captain William Murray, M.I.

Corps of Sappers and Miners.

24th May 1831–1832, Captain Alexander Lawe, M.E.
5th March 1833–1838, Captain G. A. Underwood, M.E.
9th January 1838, Captain J. T. Smith, M.E.
6th July 1838, Captain T. T. Pears, M.E.
27th August 1844–1852, Captain J. W. Rundall, M.E.
1853–1856, Captain J. Carpendale. M.E.
1857, Captain J. Carpendale, M.E.
1857,   ,,   Hew L. Prendergast, M.E.
1857,   ,,   C. E. D. Hill, M.E.
1858–1860, Captain C. E. D. Hill, M.E.
1861, Captain H. T. Rogers, M.E.
1861,   ,,   G. V. Winscom, M.E.
1862,   ,,   G. V. Winscom, M.E.
1863,   ,,   C. E. Hill, M.E.
1864–1868, Lieutenant-Colonel C. E. Hill, M.E.
1869–1873,   ,,   ,,   H. N. D. Prendergast, V.C., M.E.
1874 to April 1876, Major H. L. Prendergast, M.E. (officiating).

Queen's Own Sappers and Miners.

April 1876 to September 1880, Colonel H. N. D. Prendergast. M.E., V.C., C.B.
September 1880, Lieutenant-Colonel C. A. Sim, M.E.

APPENDIX II.

DISTINGUISHED NATIVE OFFICERS, N.C.O., AND PRIVATES.

Jemadar Vencatachellum, born 1805; served with distinction in the 1st Burmese War.

Subadar-Major Coomarasammy, served at Kurnool, 1815; Nagpore, Unke-Tunke, Rajdier, Trimbuck, Malligaum, Amulnair, Asseerghur, 1817–1819; Rangoon, Kemendine, Pegu, Donabew,

Prome, Maloun, 1824–26; China War, 1840–42; Native A.D.C. to Sir Hugh Gough. Wounded in leg at Nagpore; wounded in thigh at Donabew. Recommended by Brigadier-General McDowall in 1818; General Campbell in 1825; and Sir Hugh Gough in 1840–42.

Subadar Ramsammy.

Subadar Andoo, in the 1st Burmese War 1824–26 : Jemadar Andoo, for gallant conduct, promoted to Subadar, and presented with a palankeen and an allowance of seventy rupees a month, and a pension of half-pay granted to his nearest heir after his decease.

Subadar Chokalingam, in Coorg, 1834 ; for eminent bravery in advance of the column under Colonel Foulis, presented with an honorary medal, and increase for life of one-third present pay.

Subadar Amaraputty, in Scinde and Afghanistan, 1843.

Subadar-Major Toudroyen in Scinde, 1843

Naique Mootooveerapen, in 2nd Burmese War, 1852.

Private Ramasammy,   ,,   ,,

Havildar Chendrigherryan, at Jhansi, 1858 (died in action).

   ,,   Appoo, at Goorariah (C.I.), 1858.

   ,,   Gooroosammy ,,   ,,

Subadar-Major Vellien, in Central India, 1858.

Corporal Hoskins, at Dhar.

   ,,   Clarke,   ,,

   ,,   Linahan, at Ratghur.

Subadar Seeloway,   ,,   26th January 1858.

Jemadar Appoo,   ,,   ,,   ,,

Private Chinnatomby, ,,   ,,   ,,

   ,, Savathean,   ,,   ,,   ,,

   ,, Appasammy,   ,,   ,,   ,,

Lance-Naique Pitchamootoo, at Ratghur, 28th January 1858.

Havildar Teroovengaduin, 2nd Relief Lucknow.

Private Bagawuddy, Capture of Lucknow, at Begum Kotee, 11th March 1858.

Private Permaul, Capture of Lucknow, at Begum Kotee, 11th March 1858.

Naique Chinnien, Capture of Lucknow, at Kaiser Bagh, 14th March 1858.

Havildar Kistnen and some others favourably mentioned.

Private Kolundy Velo, at Kaiser Bagh, where Lieutenant Ogilvie, M.S., was wounded.

Naique Narrainsammy, at Morar, 1858.

Jemadar Mootien, Little Andaman Island, 1867.

APPENDIX III.

Members of the Order of Merit.*

Subadar Major Toudroyen, at Meanee, 1843.
Naique Mootooveerapen, 2nd Burmese War, 1852.
Private Ramasammy.   ,,   ,,
Subadar Seeloway, Central India, 1858.
Jemadar Appoo,   ,,   ,,
Naique Narrainsammy, at Morar, 1858.
Havildar Teroovngadum, 2nd Relief Lucknow, 1858.
Lance-Naique Pitchamootoo, at Ratghur, 1858.
Private Chinnatomby.   ,,   ,,
   ,,   Appasamy,   ,,   ,,
   ,,   Suvatheau,   ,,   ,,
Naique Permaul, at the Begum Kotee, Lucknow, 11th March 1858.
Private Bagawuddy, at the Begum Kotee, Lucknow, 11th March 1858.
Private Chinnien, at Kaiser Bagh, Lucknow, 14th March 1858.
Jemadar Mootien, Little Andaman Island, 7th May 1867.

* This Order is similar to the Victoria Cross.

APPENDIX IV.

Order of British India.

First Class, or Sirdar Bahadoors.

Subadar Chokalingum, 25th May 1838.
Subadar-Major Coomarasammy, 25th May 1838, 13th August 1839.
Subadar-Major Veerasammy.
Subadar Ali Khan.
Subadar-Major Appavoo.
Subadar Veeragoo.
   ,,   Davasagayum.

39 *

Subadar-Major Appoo, 5th June 1868.
Subadar Permaul,   ,,   ,,
    ,,   Cunnean,   ,,   ,,
Subadar-Major Vellien, 1st June 1870, 16th November 1874.
Subadar Chinnien.

Second Class, or Bahadoors.

Subadar Amaraputty, 10th February 1849.
Subadar-Major Armoogun.
Subadar Mootien.
    ,,   Ram Sing.
    ,,   Veeran.
    ,,   Soobroyen, 5th June 1866.
    ,,   Lawrence, 1st June 1870.
    ,,   Narainen, 15th June 1873.
    ,,   Chelven, 1st May 1874.
    ,,   Narrainsammy.
    ,,   Jey Ram, 1882.

APPENDIX V.

Extracted from *East India Military Calendar*.

AT a meeting of the inhabitants of Singapore, held 27th
December 1823, it was resolved:—

"That on the approaching departure of Lieutenant-Colonel
Farquhar, it is our anxious wish to mark our sense of his private
worth and uniform kindness and hospitality during the period
of his residence at Singapore, by requesting his acceptance of a
piece of plate of the value of 3,000 Sicca rupees, and that
Messrs. Queiros and Parvis do wait on Lieutenant-Colonel
Farquhar to request his acceptance of the same.'

Translation of Kling merchants' address to Lieutenant-Colonel
Farquhar, 27th December 1823:—

"We, the undersigned Kling merchants of Singapore, having
received favour from God, are desirous of expressing heartfelt
pleasure and satisfaction at the late administration of Governor
Farquhar. From the day of his arrival to the period of his
departure from the settlement, as a father ever anxious to
provide for the welfare of his children, so has he evinced the
deepest interest on our behalf. He has cherished and protected
us, even to the day of embarking for Bengal and Europe."

To the Honourable Gentlemen who have charge of the State affairs in Bengal and Europe :—

" As long as Colonel Farquhar was resident at Singapore, his conduct to us was like that of a father to his children ; of a truth such was the case. We cannot, therefore, but recollect with the greatest pleasure his affectionate care and watchfulness over us, to the truth of which we all subscribe our names at the bottom of this paper. At the same time we earnestly pray for his peace and happiness, and for every blessing to descend upon him, accompanied by a long life—these we supplicate from God Almighty.

" And further we pray, that he may be sent back to Singapore, that by the same course of administration he has ever followed we may be protected and provided for as before, and may God Almighty bless him."

(Signed by 128 of principal Hindoo and Mahomedan merchants.)

Translation of an address from His Highness Areng Belawa, the Suolawatan (or Captain of the Bugis), and the Bugis inhabitants of Singapore, to Lieutenant-Colonel W. Farquhar :—

We, the undersigned, most sincerely, with spotless and transparent hearts—that is to say, we, the Bugis inhabitants, along with our chief, Areng Belawa, residing in the settlement of Singapore, with all the Bugis merchants permitted by God to enter and leave the settlement—prostrate ourselves at the feet of His Majesty the King of England and the Governor-General of Bengal. Moreover, we beg to be excused for expressing our sentiments relating to our late Governor, Colonel Farquhar. We all very much love and admire his system of government, and the great care he has taken to preserve and cherish the poor.

" If we have found favour in your sight, forgive our requesting the re-appointment of Colonel Farquhar to the Residency of Singapore.

" Written at Singapore on Thursday the 25th of December, at 1 o'clock in the afternoon, in the White People's year 1823."

(Signed by Areng Belawa, the Suolawatan, and the Bugis inhabitants of Singapore.)

The respectful address of the Chinese merchants to Lieutenant-Colonel Farquhar, presented at Singapore in the 20th year of the cycle, the 11th month, 26th day of the dynasty Taon Qwang :—

" To the most merciful and most valuable assistant of mankind, who greatly enlarged the Hon. Company's territory, and whose glory is mighty at Singapore.

"You were formerly King of Malacca more than twenty years; let your virtue be exalted to the highest degree, for you showed tender benevolence to strangers, and were the desire of the four quarters of the world; you constantly supported the black-haired people (Chinese).

"There is no individual that can be extolled before you for your acts of kindness to the country of Singapore ever since the first establishment of its Government. You daily exercised your compassionate thoughts in love to the people, and sought to promote the trade of the place both far and near.

"We, however, restrain the beating of our bowels (great sorrow), as there is nothing more noble than the celebration of your virtue, whose government may be truly said to have caused the people to rejoice.

"We most anxiously desire your happiness and preservation, and rejoice to congratulate you on the happy state of the country.

"Having just heard that you are about gloriously to raise your chariot, and return to your own country, we, the black-haired population, quickly recite to your praise the Kan Tang (Pleasant Poem).

"The whole community cannot possibly contain themselves, in consequence of their great veneration for you, so that the painfully acute feeling of their hearts cannot be expressed to the ten thousandth part. We pray Heaven to enlighten you, our King, that you may constantly enjoy ease of mind and preservation of compassion; yea, we truly pray that your preservation and happiness may be continued to the most distant period, that your prosperity may be everlasting, that your sons and grandsons may continue in one unbroken line. We pray also that the virtue of our King may be perfected, and that his illustrious thoughts may be purely chaste to the very hair's breadth.

"The whole people, in this grateful feeling, cannot possibly bless you sufficiently."

(Then follow the names of 49 seafaring men, 14 Canton merchants, and 41 Fokin merchants.)

APPENDIX VI.

Orders of "British India" and "Merit."

General Orders by the Right Honourable the Governor-General of India in Council :—Fort William, 1st May 1837.

No. 94 of 1837.—In continuation of General Orders, No. 83 of 1837, the Right Honourable the Governor-General of India in Council directs that the following Rules and Regulations be established for the "Order of British India" and "Order of Merit," the institution of which has been sanctioned for the Native portion of the Indian Army.

" *Order of British India.*"

This Order is to be conferred by the Governor-General of India in Council on Native Commissioned Officers of the Indian Army, for long, faithful, and honourable service.

The 1st Class to be composed exclusively of Subadars and the corresponding grades in the Irregular Cavalry, and limited to 100 Members, with an allowance of two Rupees a day each, in addition to their Regimental Allowances or Retiring Pensions.

> 50 for Bengal.
> 34 for Madras.
> 16 for Bombay.
> ___
> 100

The 2nd Class, of Native Commissioned Officers indiscriminately, with the same limitation as to number, and an allowance of one rupee a day each, in addition to their usual Allowances and Pensions.

> 50 for Bengal.
> 33 for Madras.
> 17 for Bombay.
> ___
> 100

The Native Officers on whom the Order of British India may be conferred in the first instance will be entitled to the extra allowance going with that distinction from this date.

The Insignia of the Order to consist of a Gold Star pendent from a sky-blue ribbon, one inch and a half broad, to be worn round the neck on the outside of the collar of the coat, on full dress parades and other occasions of particular ceremony. In the centre of the star is to be inscribed in English only, "The Order of British India."

Subadars of the 1st Class will receive the title of "Surdar Bahadoor," and Native Officers of the 2nd Class that of "Bahadoor."

A descriptive roll, specifying, in a column for remarks, the general conduct, character, and services of every Subadar and Jemadar in the armies of the three Presidencies, will be immediately forwarded (and a similar roll transmitted annually on the 1st of May), by Commanding Officers of Corps respectively, through the prescribed channel of military correspondence, to the Secretary to the Government of India in the Military Department, for the information of the Governor-General in Council.

In forwarding these rolls, His Excellency the Commander-in-Chief in India, and the Commanders-in-Chief at Fort St. George and Bombay, are respectively requested to offer such recommendations, grounded on the statements of conduct, character, and services of each Native Officer reported upon, as may facilitate the selection by the Supreme Government of the most deserving of them for a partition in the honorary rewards and solid emoluments attached to the Order. The rolls from Fort St. George and Bombay will be transmitted through the Local Governments of those Presidencies.

Native officers of Cavalry, Artillery, and Infantry of the Line, of the Sappers and Miners, and of the Irregular Cavalry of Bengal and Bombay, are eligible for admission into the Order of British India.

The number of both classes being fixed and permanent, every vacancy which may occur after the completion in the first instance of the whole promotion, will be filled up by the Supreme Government from the rolls recorded in their Secretary's Office.

Vacancies can only occur from death or removal for misconduct, and admissions into the Order will be announced in General Orders by the Government of India.

" Order of Merit."

The object of this Institution is to afford personal reward for personal bravery, without reference to any claims founded on mere length of service and general good conduct.

The Order is to consist of three classes ; the two Junior to be distinguished by a badge of Silver, and the Senior by a badge of Gold, in the shape of a Military Laurelled Star, bearing in its centre the inscription, " The reward of valour."

This badge is to be worn on the left breast, pendent from a dark-blue ribbon with red edge.

3rd Class.

Is to be obtained by any conspicuous act of individual gallantry on the part of any Native Officer or Soldier in the Field or in the attack or defence of fortified places, without distinction of rank or grade.

2nd Class.

Is to be obtained by those only who already possess the third, and for similar services.

1st Class.

Is to be obtained in like manner only by those who already possess the third and second classes.

Admission to each of these classes is to be obtained upon application to the Governor-General of India in Council, with whom alone the competency of conferring the Order rests.

The original recommendation must particularly specify the act of gallantry for which the soldier is supposed to have claims to this high distinction ; and the preparatory steps to obtaining it are to be as follows :—

After an action in which particular acts of gallantry have been performed, which may be considered as entitling a soldier to the " Order of Merit," a representation of the circumstance is to be made through the Commanding Officer of the Regiment, by the Captain or Officer commanding the troop or company, to the General Officer commanding the division, who will order a Court, composed of European and Native officers, and consisting of one Field Officer. two Captains, and two Subadars (the proceedings to be conducted by an officer of the Judge-Advocate-General's department if available), before which the individual recommended will be brought, when witnesses will be called and examined as to what they saw the soldier perform in the action referred to.

Should there be any failure of proof, the claim is not to be allowed, but, on the other hand, should the particular gallantry of the soldier recommended for the distinction appear to have been conspicuous and undoubted, the report of the Court will be forwarded—in Bengal, through His Excellency the Commander-in-Chief in India, and at each of the other Presidencies through the Commander-in-Chief and Local Government—to the Governor-General of India in Council, who has, nevertheless, the power of rejecting the claim, for reasons to be recorded at the time.

A record in each case of the particular act of gallantry for which the Star has been conferred will be kept in the Office of the Secretary to the Government of India in the Military Department, and a Certificate from that functionary, detailing the grant of the Order, and its concomitant advantages, will be given to each individual on his admission to, or advancement in it.

Admission into the Order of Merit will confer on a member an additional allowance, equal in the 3rd Class to one-third, in the 2nd to two-thirds, and in the 1st to the entire of the ordinary pay of his rank over and above that pay or the pension he may be entitled to on retirement.

The widow of a member will be entitled to receive the pension conferred by the Order upon her husband, for three years after the date of his decease; and in the case of a plurality of wives, the first married to have the preference.

No claim founded on acts of gallantry antecedent to the date of this General Order shall be considered admissible under any pretence whatsoever.

(Signed)   WM. CASEMENT, Colonel,
       Secy. to the Govt. of India Mily. Dept.

(Signed)   S. W. STEEL, Lieut.-Colonel,
       Secretary to Government.

By order of the Commander-in-Chief,

J. R. HAIG,
    Acting Adjutant-General of the Army.

APPENDIX VII.

Pioneers : Ensign MacMahon, at Pondicherry, 1760.
Engineers : Captain Leigh, at Vellore, 1761.
     ,,   Ensign Hamilton, at Modura, 1764.
     ,,   Captain McLean, at Tingricottah, 1768.
     ,,   ,,   Campbell, at Tanjore, 1773.
Adg. Engr. : Lieutenant Blackden, ,, ,,
Engineers : Major Stevens, at Pondicherry, 1778.
     ,,   Lieutenant Digby Brooke, at Mahé, 1779.
     ,,   Captain Theobald, at Permbauncum, 1780.
     ,,   Ensign Brunton, at Seringapatam, 1780.
     ,,   Captain Dugood, at Chittoor, 1781.
     ,,   Ensign Croy, at Ryacottah, 1791.
     ,,   Lieutenant-Colonel Maule, at Pondicherry, 1793.
Pioneers : Lieutenant Lalor, at Seringapatam, 1799.
     ,,   ,,   Farquhar,   ,,   ,,
     ,,   ,,   Cormick,   ,,   ,,
     ,,   Captain Grose, at Arrakerry, 1800.
     ,,   Lieutenant Shepherd, in Java, 1811.
     ,,   Ensign McLeod,   ,,   ,,
Engineers : Lieutenant Davies, at Malligaum, 1818.
     ,,   ,,   Nattes,   ,,   ,,
     ,,   Captain Scott, at Koelee, 1858.

DIED FROM DISEASE CONTRACTED ON SERVICE.

Engineers : Ensign Rowley, at Walkee, near Ahmednuggur,
                   1803.
     ,,   ,,   Jenkins, at Akowla, 1817.
     ,,   ,,   Wotherspoon, in Mahratta War, 1818.
     ,,   Captain Mackintosh, at Prince of Wales Island,
                   1825.
     ,,   ,,   Grant, at Prome, 1825.
     ,,   ,,   J. W. Rundall, in Burmah, 1852.

Lost at Sea, Drowned, and Killed by Accidents.

Engineers: Captain Bradley, lost at sea, 1809.
,, ,, E. Lake, ,, 1829.
,, Lieutenant Strover, killed by accident, 1856.
,, ,, Moore, drowned, 1857.
,, ,, Boyd, killed by accident, 1858.
,, ,, Gordon, drowned, 1860.
,, ,, Roberts, ,, 1867.

Officers Wounded.

Engineers: Lieutenant Montressor, at Colar, 1768.
,, ,, McLeod, ,, ,,
,, Lieutenant-Colonel Ross, at Tanjore, 1771.
,, Captain Campbell, ,, ,,
,, Lieutenant Geils, ,, 1773.
Adg. Engr.: ,, Bonneveaux, ,, ,,
,, ,, Barrow, ,, ,,
Engineers: Captain J. Johnstone, at Pondicherry, 1778.
,, Ensign Tyson, at Porto Praya, 1781.
,, ,, Caldwell, at Bangalore, 1791.
,, Lieutenant Hemming, at Seringapatam, 1792.
,, Ensign Caldwell, ,, ,,
,, ,, Fraser, at Malavelly, 1799.
,, Captain Caldwell (twice), at Seringapatam, 1799.
Pioneers: ,, Heitland, in Poligar War, 1801.
,, ,, ,, at Assaye (horse shot), 1803.
Engineers: Lieutenant Blakiston, at Assaye, 1803.
,, ,, Davies, at Grand Port, 1809.
,, Ensign Coventry, in naval action, 1809.
,, ,, Sim, in Java, 1811.
,, Captain Blakiston, at St Sebastian, 1813.
,, Ensign Nattes, at Nagpore, 1817.
,, Lieutenant Davies, ,, ,,
Adg. Engr.: ,, Wahab, at Sholapore, 1818.
Engineers: ,, Anderson, at Talneir, 1818.
,, Ensign Lake, at Trimbuck, 1818.
,, ,, Purton, at Malligaum, 1818.
,, ,, Underwood, ,, ,,
,, Lieutenant-Colonel Farquhar, at Singapore, 1823.
Pioneers: Captain Moncrieff, at Kykloo, 1824.
,, Lieutenant Campbell, ,, ,,

Pioneers: Captain Wheeler, at Kokien, 1824.
    ,,   Lieutenant Macartney, at Kokien, 1824.
    ,,   ,,   Campbell,   ,,   ,,
Engineers: ,,   G. Underwood, at Napadee, 1825.
Pioneers: Ensign McLeod, at Syriam, 1825.
    ,,   Lieutenant J. Smith, at Simbike, 1825.
Engineers: ,,   Ouchterlony, at Zorapore, 1839.
    ,,   ,,   J. Rundall, at Tinghae, 1841.
    ,,   ,,   J. Johnston, at Chapoo, 1841.
    ,,   Captain Rundall, at Rangoon, 1852.
Sappers: Lieutenant Ford.   ,,
    ,,   ,,   Harris, at Pegu, 1852.
    ,,   ,,   Fox, at Jhansi, 1858.
    ,,   ,,   Ogilvie, at Lucknow, 1858.
Engineers: Major Boileau, at Mundisore, 1858.
    ,,   Lieutenant Prendergast, at Mundisore and the
                      Betwa, 1858.
    ,,   ,,   Burton, at Lucknow (horse shot), 1858.
Sappers; Captain Elliot, at Magdala, 1868.
    ,,   Cornet Dalrymple, ,,   ,,

APPENDIX VIII.

ADDRESS of General Wilson, Military Member of the Council of the Viceroy of India, to the Queen's Own Sappers and Miners, after their return from Egypt on 5th December 1882.

A parade of the garrison was held at Bangalore, on the 5th inst. The troops were reviewed by General Wilson, Military Member of the Viceroy's Council. After the order had been given for the troops to march to quarters, General Wilson expressed a desire to say a few words to the Queen's Own Sappers and Miners, especially to the two companies which had recently returned from service in Egypt. The corps was marched up in front of the saluting point in close formation, and the General, riding close up to the head of the column, addressed them as follows :—

"Colonel Sim, officers. non-commissioned officers, and men of the Queen's Own Sappers and Miners,—I am glad that my short and necessarily hurried visit to this Presidency has enabled me to make the acquaintance of so distinguished a regiment as this is. You have, indeed, a proud record of war services, commencing with Seringapatam and ending with the short yet brilliant campaign from which two of your companies have but recently returned. Between the periods above-mentioned, Java, China, Scinde, Persia, Burmah, Abyssinia, Afghanistan, Egypt, each in its turn, has been witness to your useful and valuable labours on service; and you have everywhere earned for your battalion, by your discipline, valour in the field, loyalty and devotion to the Queen-Empress of India, a widespread reputation. The two companies lately in Egypt, under the able command of Major Hamilton, have well sustained your previous history—nay, by their admirable conduct they have added to your previous high character and good name. It may gratify those whom I now address if I tell them that there have been many observant witnesses of the valuable work they performed in Egypt; and a distinguished Royal Engineer officer, who recently returned to Simla from Cairo, expressed praise of their conduct in no stinted terms. But further than this a few days ago, as I passed through Bombay, the Admiral commanding the Royal Naval Squadron in the Eastern Seas, did me the honour to call upon me, and although I put no question to him on the subject, he voluntarily spoke in language of high praise of the valuable work performed by the Madras Sappers which had come under his immediate notice. I think that an observation such as this, coming from so very distinguished an officer as Admiral Sir W. Hewett, cannot be otherwise than extremely gratifying to the men of this battalion. On behalf of the Government of India I thank the men of the two companies for their services, and desire to assure them that they have fully realised the expectations formed by His Excellency the Viceroy's Government when they were selected to represent the Madras Army in a campaign in which one of Her Majesty's sons has taken a prominent part. I hope that you will shortly receive the decorations which the Queen-Empress of India has been graciously pleased to confer upon you as a reward for your services. You have won them well, and may you wear them long. Colonel Sim, I will only add that, from what the Lieutenant-General tells me of your corps, and from what I myself have seen of it this morning, it seems to me that its efficiency and appearance reflect great credit upon you and upon all under your command."

INDEX TO VOL. I.

INDEX TO VOLUME II.

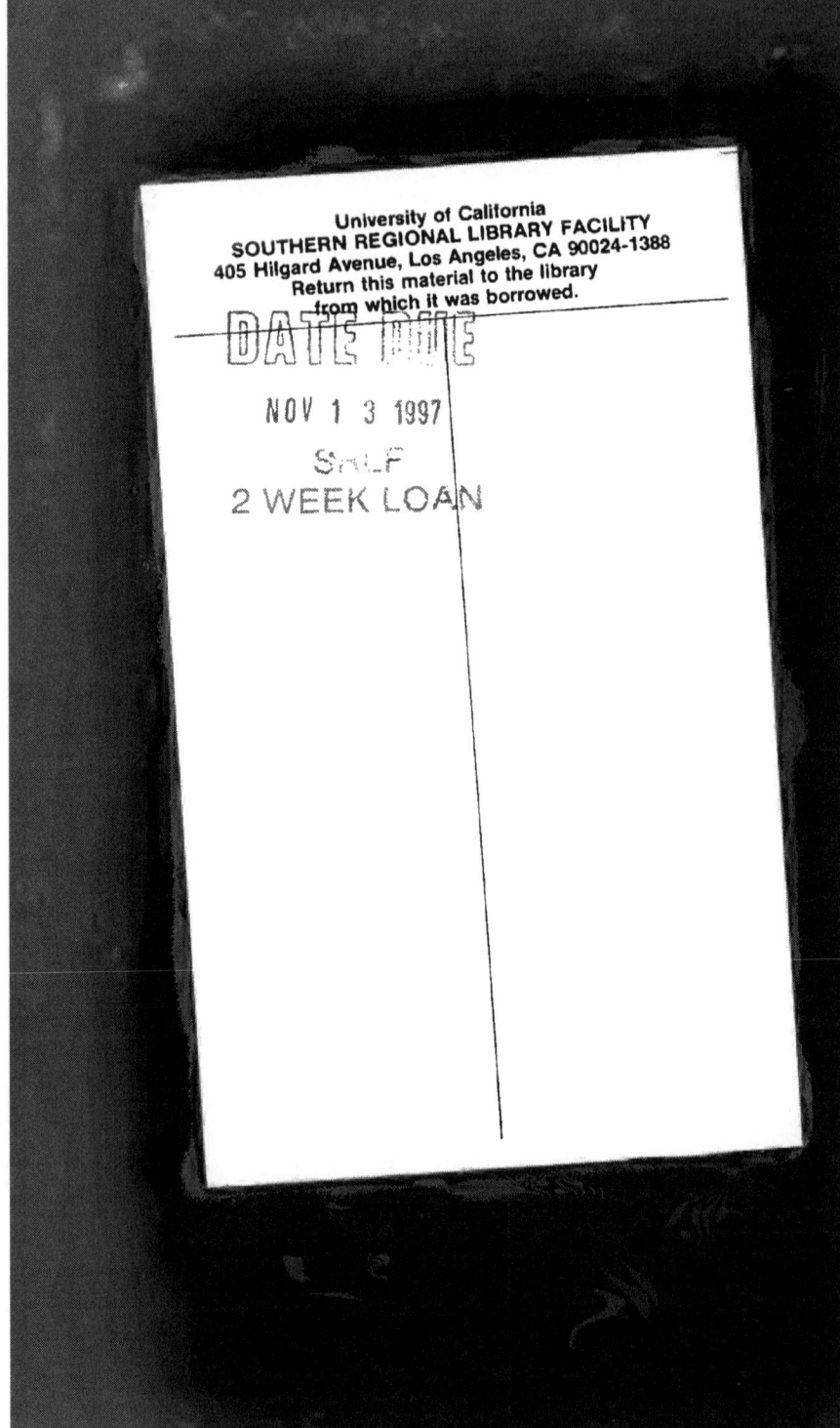

Lightning Source UK Ltd.
Milton Keynes UK
UKHW020839030120
356283UK00008B/145/P